DATABASE ANALYSIS AND DESIGN

DATABASE ANALYSIS
AND DESIGN

I. T. Hawryszkiewycz

Canberra College of Advanced Education, Australia

 ® SCIENCE RESEARCH ASSOCIATES, INC.
Chicago, Henley-on-Thames, Sydney, Toronto

A Subsidiary of IBM

To Daria, Helen, and Adrian

Acquisition Editor	Alan Lowe
Project Editor	E. Ann Wood
Compositor	Allservice Phototypesetting
Illustrator	John Foster
Text Designer	Barbara Ravizza
Cover Design	Joe DiChiarro

Library of Congress Cataloging in Publication Data

Hawryszkiewycz, I. T.
  Database analysis and design.

  Bibliography: p.
  Includes index.
  1. Data base management. 2. System design. 3. System
analysis. 4. File organization (Computer science)
I. Title.
QA76.9.D3H386 1984   001.64′2   84-1341
ISBN 0-574-21485-2

Contents

10 IMPLEMENTATION MODELS, II—DATABASE MANAGEMENT SYSTEMS   275

13 HIERARCHICAL DATABASE MANAGEMENT SYSTEMS 379

15   INITIAL DESIGN   441

Preface

Database management is now widely practiced and has become an important field of study in computing. The last few years have seen considerable evolution in database practical application and in the theoretic database foundations. This evolution has been accomplished by the development of many areas of study that together fall under the database umbrella. Some of these areas are practical while others are theoretically oriented. Examples are relational theory, data semantics, database management software, or physical file design.

To the new student it is easy to treat these areas of study as unrelated topics of interest. What, after all, is the link between relational theory and physical file design or between data semantics and database management system software. Thus one may become familiar with all these areas of study and yet not be aware of how they combine together.

One goal of this text is to unite areas of database study into a coherent field within the context of database design. One may, of course, ask why use database design for this purpose? To answer we can postulate that database design is to some extent the peak of application of the database field. Ultimately our goal is to design and use databases. If a field of database study is to be ultimately useful then it must somehow fit into the design cycle.

Apart from serving as a framework for unifying fields of database study, database design also provides the criteria to judge good databases. Again the elements of database study must provide designers with the ability to evaluate databases against these criteria. Design criteria met in practice include

- all user relevant relationships can be easily deduced from the chosen database structure
- the database can evolve to meet changes to user requirements without requiring extensive changes to the database structure and programs
- user access requests are met within reasonable performance criteria.

The fields of database study must contribute towards these criteria. It should be noted that database design itself is still not a very structured process. Early designers had few techniques or tools to assist them. In general, early designers used file design techniques for database design; many of these techniques concentrated on physical design criteria and emphasized performance rather than data structure or flexibility.

The last few years, however, have seen the development of many new approaches to database design. The trend has been to methodologies that commence with a formal analysis of the user data structure and then reduce such requirements to a physical design through a sequence of structured steps. Thus we must first study the data that we are to store and then choose its computer representation. Much of this work commenced after the development of relational theory, which provided a formal basis for choosing data structures and can be readily translated into practical terms.

Since then a variety of database analysis and design techniques has developed. Some use the relational model as their basis; others are guided by data abstractions such as entities and relationships, role or generalization, and aggregation to structure databases.

The system design cycle thus provides a basis for integrating the various database fields. Relational theory and semantic models are useful for analyzing and structuring data. The structures developed are then converted to a logical model based on some data model, which in turn is implemented by commercial database software. Hence the relationship between semantic models and commercial software. Finally the implementation may be adjusted, taking into account access requirements and physical structures available to the designer. Hence a relationship evolves from logical structure to physical design. This book follows this design cycle, outlining the database fields of study and the theory behind them as it proceeds. The book itself evolved from the author's experiences during his Doctoral dissertation at the Massachusetts Institute of Technology, where he was first introduced to relational theory by Professor Jack Dennis. Subsequently the author has drawn on his practical experiences in database design and in developing and teaching database courses to college students and in database research, both in Australia and the United States, where he spent time with Professor Edgar Sibley at the University of Maryland. It has also benefited from update courses taught by the author to database practitioners, which over the years has led to many interesting examples with practical orientations. These examples are included throughout the book.

The book has also benefited from the many constructive comments from its reviewers and in this context the author would like to acknowledge the contributions of Marilyn Bohl of IBM, Caroline M. Eastman of Southern Methodist University, and Kenneth M. Hunter of San Francisco State University, and Nancy D. Griffeth of Georgia Institute of Technology. Finally, the book would not have been possible without the constant help of SRA staff, in particular the patient guidance of Alan Lowe through its initial stages and the support provided by E. Ann Wood and the SRA editorial staff in the final production stages.

chapter one
Introduction

Databases are essential to an organization's information system. The information system supports the organization's functions, maintaining the data for these functions and assisting users to interpret the data in decision making. The database takes a central role in this process: it is the repository of the data in the information system.

Users who make decisions obtain data by accessing the database and then recording their decision in it. The database location and the facilities to access it have a large bearing on the effectiveness of the information system. Easy access to a variety of data from a number of locations enables the information system to quickly respond to the needs of decision makers within the organization, whereas poor access can of course hinder rapid response. If the data are not readily available, decisions may be either delayed unnecessarily or made with incomplete data, leading to possible system malfunction later on.

Database structures must be flexible to meet changing organizational needs. As new functions arise in an organization, new decisions follow in their wake. Since the database will need to store new data and accommodate new relationships to support the new decisions, it must include facilities to allow such changes to be easily made.

This text covers the design of databases to meet information system requirements. In doing this, it discusses such important issues as data models, the structure of data records in the database, and the effect of alternate physical database organizations on system performance.

COMPUTERS AND DATABASES

Obviously, data must be stored on physical devices; in addition, physical means to transfer these data between the database and its users are needed.

Designers of information systems must choose such physical devices. File drawers, pieces of paper, card catalogues, and personal files have long served as storage devices. But computers are now increasingly used both to store the database and to assist users in much of the data interpretation. This is not to say that all data used in an organization will be maintained on a computer. Some are not amenable to computer storage, given the current economics, and some may take time to convert to a computer system.

Apart from data storage, computer systems provide the facilities to access data and make them available at various locations. Access languages enable users to retrieve or store data. Terminals transfer data by accessing computers from distant sites and through computer-communications networks. These facilities thus meet the requirements of information systems, whose goal is to make data readily available to their users.

THE EVOLUTION OF DATABASE DESIGN PROCEDURES

The growing use of computer databases has led to greater emphasis on database design procedures. And these procedures have changed as databases have found new uses. Early databases usually supported one organizational function. Thus there may have been one database for the accounting system, another for the inventory system, and so on. Most were batch systems providing regular status reports. Many contemporary database systems differ from these early systems in numerous respects. There is now greater integration of user functions, and many databases now support more than one organizational function. Further, databases are now much more closely integrated with the user environment. Rather than providing regular standard reports, they allow on-line access to users for both standard and *ad hoc* reports.

The evolution of database systems has created a need for design procedures to cope with the problems raised by greater database complexity and by the database integration with user functions. Such design procedures can differ significantly from earlier ones. Many early processes emphasized physical implementation and placed considerable importance on access to data records. Designers often had to consider one or at most a few files for one system function. They then chose the appropriate indexing techniques to realize satisfactory performance for this one function. Today there are many more criteria. It is necessary to

- reduce data redundancy
- provide stable data structures that can be readily changed with changing user requirements
- allow users to make *ad hoc* requests for data
- maintain complex relationships between data elements
- support a large variety of decision needs

Database design in this environment can be quite a complex task. To carry this task out effectively requires proper techniques; it also calls for procedures that apply these techniques in an orderly manner.

A distinction is purposely made between techniques and procedures. The techniques are the tools used by database designers. They include various computations, documentation methods, diagrammatic representation of the user enterprise, various conversion rules, database definition methods, and programming techniques. Procedures, on the other hand, determine the sequence in which these techniques are applied. Thus a given procedure may require a designer to first develop a diagrammatic representation of user data and then use conversion rules to propose a database structure. The next step may be to optimize the structure by using specific computations. Once this is done, the database is defined and programs written.

Design techniques generally fall into two classes:

- data analysis techniques for analyzing the semantics of user data
- technical design techniques for converting the analysis results to a technical database implementation

These two classes of techniques deal with two specific problems. The first problem concerns the need to properly structure data. This problem is solved by techniques that remove data redundancy, provide database stability, and structure the data so that they can be readily accessed to support a variety of user needs. The second problem is to ensure that implementation uses resources efficiently. Technical design techniques take care of this problem by ensuring satisfactory storage use and efficient access.

WHAT ARE THE DESIGN PROCEDURES?

The two distinct classes of problems in database design tend to inhibit a one-step design procedure of the type shown in Figure 1.1. One-step design is usu-

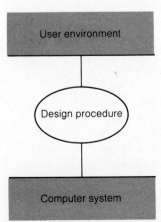

Figure 1.1   A one-step design procedure

ally informal. A user requirement is perceived in the user environment. This requirement is then converted to a database, using some *ad hoc* design procedure.

One-step procedures were used effectively early in computing, when the designers' environment was bounded. Many systems were designed to meet one user function and were implemented on a machine with a small range of data structures. The problems in this environment were usually bounded and emphasized the choice of physical parameters, given an available file structure. Such choices included the physical block-sizes or file index structures. Successful designs were reported in many instances. Today methods of this kind are still effective in bounded environments, such as specialized retrieval systems.

Most contemporary systems, however, no longer exist in such bounded environments. These newer systems differ from earlier ones in many respects. Now, for example, we have the following situations:

• There are a variety of users, each using different subsets of data and each using different data relationships.
• Various physical structures are available to realize such systems; this diversity results mainly from the availability of database management systems.
• The user system requirements are less stable and more likely to change than was true earlier.

One-step design procedures can be quite ineffective here because a greater number of design trade-offs must be made. The computational and intellectual capacity to manage all these trade-offs concurrently is usually not feasible. The results, more often than not, are such frequently mentioned problems as unmet deadlines, unmet user requirements, and cost overruns. Hence the tendency now is to use staged design processes in which each trade-off is considered at different stages and the stages are integrated to yield a satisfactory design.

WHAT ARE THE DESIGN STAGES?

The staged approach to database design has as its foundation the advantages generally cited for top-down design. It recognizes that design must consider different problems at different levels of detail. Further, it recognizes that each problem class has a different natural universe of discourse. Hence the proper discourse, along with its associated techniques, must be chosen for each stage. For example, the design semantics for analyzing user data will be completely different from those used when choosing physical data structures. Staged design recognizes such differences. It resolves them by first defining design stages so that each stage solves some part of the total design problem. It also provides the tools and techniques to enable that problem to be solved in its natural terms.

Apart from removing the complexity inherent in one-step design, the staged

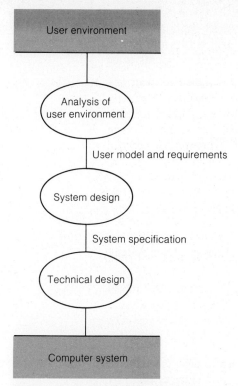

User environment

Analysis of
user environment

User model and requirements

System design

System specification

Technical design

Computer system

Figure 1.2 Staged design procedure

design has one further advantage. It formalizes the design process by introducing formal design tools rather than relying on *ad hoc* design methods. It then combines these stages so that the combined sequence is a progressive elaboration of the user system requirement through a number of stages to a final implementation by computer devices. This sequence of stages, together with the design tools used at each stage, is often called a *design methodology*.

The general trend in design methodologies is to first separate the user requirement decisions from technical design decisions, as shown in Figure 1.2. Each of these major stages is then often broken down into more detailed steps.

The first stage in Figure 1.2 is to analyze the current user environment. This analysis includes data and data flows. The output from this stage is a model of the user environment and requirements.

Once the model of user data and requirements is produced, the designer must propose a new system to meet the requirements. In doing so, the designer may examine current structures and procedures and identify any existing problems. New structures and procedures may then be proposed. If users agree with these proposals, the proposals are included in the *system specification,* which is the formal specification of the proposed operation of the new system. The specification includes sufficient detail to commence technical design.

Many people view this specification as one of the most important design documents. It is seen as the main communications document between users and computer professionals, and it must effectively convey the requirements to be met by the new system. To do this the document must

- be unambiguous, clear, and precise
- be a correct representation of the user requirements
- use documentation techniques that are clearly understood by both users and computer technical staff

TOOLS FOR ANALYSIS AND DESIGN

Many tools have been proposed for systems analysis and design. User systems are usually described in three parts:

- the data flows in information systems
- the kind of processes used in data interpretations
- the structure of the data themselves

There are many design methodologies currently in use to describe systems. One popular class of methodologies is known as *structured systems analysis*. This analysis commences by using graphical techniques to express information flows between processes. Figure 1.3 shows a system description that is expressed by using the techniques of structured systems analysis. Here circles represent system processes (or functions), and lines joining the circles represent information flows between the processes. To express the processes, various formal techniques are used, such as decision tables, tight English, or structured English.

Processes can also access data stores to store and retrieve data. Structured systems analysis uses formal techniques to define the data structures that are part of the information flows and data stores. Most methods of structured systems analysis use hierarchical descriptions of data. Usually these data descriptions are stored in a data dictionary. Later they are reduced to a data model or a semantic model (both will be described later in this chapter).

Other design methodologies concentrate on the data. These are sometimes called *databased methodologies*. They commence by defining the data elements and structures in the user system. The user functions are then defined. An important element in this description is to define the data elements and structures that each function uses. This relationship between data and function is usually expressed graphically. Data in databased methodologies are usually described by a data model or a semantic model. The model is chosen to capture the essential features of the organization's data and to express them in terms that are readily converted to a computer structure. This data description is often documented in a data dictionary.

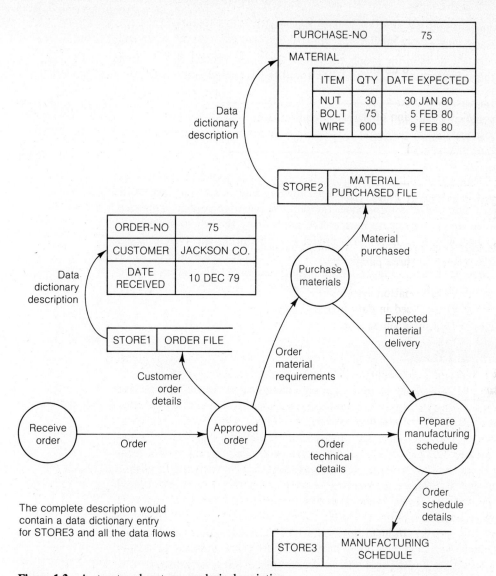

Figure 1.3 A structured systems analysis description

Thus in both classes of methodology the final system description contains the same three parts. The main difference is the techniques used to obtain the system description. In structured systems analysis there is early emphasis on defining the functions and information flows, which are then used to produce the data descriptions and a data model or a semantic model. The databased methodologies first define the data structures and the data or semantic model. Then system functions are defined.

In either case the same techniques are often used to document both the current user system and the system specification. Thus the graphical techniques that are used to define the information flows in the current system can be also used to define the flows in the proposed system. Similarly, process specifications can take the same form in both the current and the proposed systems.

REQUIREMENTS OF DATABASE SPECIFICATION AND DESIGN

Database design can also be divided into stages that correspond to the stages in Figure 1.2. The database design stages are shown in Figure 1.4. The goal of the first stage in this figure is to analyze the data in the user system. This step, usually called *data analysis,* is part of the analysis of the whole system and produces a user model of data. This model is used during the system design stage to produce a *database specification.* This specification is made up of the three components shown in Figure 1.4: the enterprise model, the access requirements, and the quantitative data. The information in these three components includes the following:

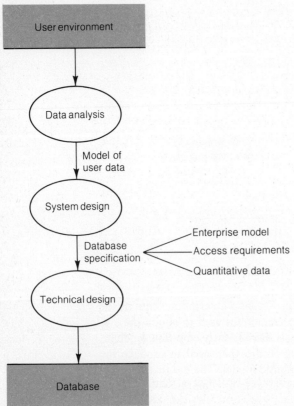

Figure 1.4   Staged database design

1. The enterprise model:
   - data items in the enterprise
   - data relationships in the enterprise

2. The access requirements:
   - the way that the data are to be stored and accessed
   - access to be on-line or batch

3. The quantitative data:
   - frequency with which the data are accessed
   - time and place at which the data must be available
   - volume of the data
   - location at which the data are captured

All three of these components are needed to implement a database. It is essential to know the data items and relationships to ensure that the required data are stored in the database. Access requirements are used to structure the data in a way that makes them easily accessible to all interested users. The quantitative data are necessary to ensure that the chosen systems have sufficient capacity to store all the data.

TECHNICAL DESIGN OF THE DATABASE

The next major stage of database design is technical design. The designer is given the database specification and an implementation model. This model defines the data structures available at the designer's computer installation. The designer must then use the model to construct the database. To do this, it is necessary to choose

- methods to store all the required data on hardware devices
- the software used to maintain and access the data
- the database structure that will enable the data to be accessed by users in the required way
- methods to distribute the data to a variety of locations

During technical design, designers must ensure that the physical implementation of the database meets the following criteria, which are identified in the first step (data analysis):

1. *Data availability.* The required data and relationships are stored in the database.
2. *Data reliability.* The data will not be lost or corrupted.
3. *Data currency.* The data value is the latest value of the data item.
4. *Data consistency.* The same data values will be obtained for the same item in different queries at the same time.

5. *Data flexibility.* Extensions can readily be made to meet new requirements.
6. *Data efficiency.* The data are stored and retrieved at minimum cost.

TECHNIQUES IN DATABASE DESIGN

Different techniques are used at each of the design stages shown in Figure 1.4. In data analysis the designer is concerned primarily with defining the data in the organization, for this definition becomes the enterprise model. This model must include all the important data relationships; further, it must use terms that are understood by both users and computer professionals. If the definition is satisfactory, the model can become a specification, which users can approve and which is useful to technical designers at the second stage.

Technical design implements the database specification on the machine. The separation of analysis and implementation is made quite consciously. Its goal is to delay the consideration of implementation issues as long as possible. Implementation imposes such technical constraints as choice of file access key or program access commands. If these limitations are considered too early, unnecessary restrictions may be placed on users. The result is that the user specification may not be ideal, and therefore either the system will not be fully utilized or early changes will be requested. Hence the goal is to ignore such issues initially and define the ideal user requirement without considering constraints imposed by machines. Once the ideal is known, implementation issues are brought in. Each implementation choice can be judged by its effect on the ideal structure; a designer can then evaluate whether the benefit achieved by a particular choice justifies any loss of the properties defined in the ideal structure. If implementation issues are brought in too early, all the ideal characteristics may not be defined. Choices are then made without all the facts being known. The upshot is a design that may not be as good as it could be.

What Are the Design Techniques?

Various techniques are available for database design. Database designers can select certain techniques and combine them into a design methodology. A large number of techniques can be combined into a variety of design methodologies; some methodologies may be better than others in certain circumstances. Some writers have in fact developed methodologies made up of selected techniques and proposed them as ideal tools for database design. The goal of this text is not to propose yet another ideal design methodology. Rather, it is to describe the various techniques available for design and the methods for combining them into methodologies. The advantages of alternate choices are also discussed. However, the text leaves it up to designers to make their own decisions on which of these techniques are most appropriate for their environment and problem.

THE BROAD STRUCTURE OF THE TEXT

The general environment of database design sets the theme for the structure of this text. The text follows the broad philosophy of staged design and the distinction between techniques and methodology. The majority of the text covers techniques, and it is only later that alternate combinations of techniques into methodologies are considered. The techniques are described in a sequence that broadly follows the staged design procedure of Figure 1.4. The first chapters deal with the development of the enterprise model and the database specification; the later chapters cover technical design. The final chapter deals with the integration of the design techniques into design methodologies.

Data Analysis

One reason for separating the specification of data requirements from technical design is to define the ideal structure of data before implementation commences. Thus the data analysis techniques must ensure the following:

- All the details of data and of the use of these data are captured in the formal enterprise model.
- This model is an ideal representation of these data.

What are ideal data characteristics? Here are some commonly suggested characteristics:

1. Each fact is stored once, improving update consistency and eliminating redundancy.
2. The data structure is resilient to change and allows
   - new methods of access to be easily added, and
   - new data to be added without affecting existing programs.
3. The terms used in the model can be understood both by the users and by technical designers.
4. The model is independent of physical structure.

Chapters 2 through to 7 describe alternative methods of modeling data. They commence with the relational model. This model has been widely accepted by the data processing community as a model of data. It was introduced in 1970 by

E. F. Codd, who stressed its independence of physical structure. Codd also introduced the notion of normal form, which is a nonredundant representation of data. These early ideas about the relational model are described in Chapter 2. Later other writers developed relational ideas further and introduced formal relational design procedures, which are described in Chapter 3.

The last few years have seen further developments in data modeling. Since the introduction of the entity-relationship model by Chen in 1976, a new class of modeling techniques has been used. These techniques, here called *semantic modeling,* emphasize the object level rather than the data element level of information and as such have found popularity in the initial analysis stages. Chapters 4 through to 7 describe semantic modeling techniques. They also discuss the relationship between the semantic model and the relational model—and do so for a specific purpose. Many writers have found an advantage in combining the ideas of relational theory with semantic models. Semantic models present a meaningful high-level interface to the user; relational theory, through its normal forms, is then used as a guideline that ensures that the enterprise model does not include unnecessary redundancy.

On completing the discussion of semantic modeling, the text turns to the possible forms of data specification. Chapter 8 describes how the enterprise model combines with the access requirements and quantitative data to produce a database specification.

Implementation Models

Before describing technical design, the text covers a number of implementation models. The general structure of these models is discussed in Chapters 9 and 10. Chapter 9 describes the access methods supported by many systems. It covers file structures supported by these access methods and the commands used to access data in such files. Chapter 10 continues the discussion by describing the structure of database management systems and the data models that they support. Then Chapter 11 describes relational database management systems, Chapter 12 covers systems that support the network data model, and Chapter 13 covers those that support the hierarchical data model.

The text is then ready to delve into alternate technical design strategies. These are discussed in Chapter 14. The major philosophical difference between design strategies is the method used to integrate the access requirements to the data structure. Two distinct approaches can be identified. In one approach early emphasis is on data structure to produce the ideal logical data structure; later, access requirements are considered and the structure is amended to satisfy the access needs. The other approach places early emphasis on access requirements to ensure that the data structure is specifically oriented to access needs.

In any case, design proceeds through a number of iterations. Usually an initial feasible design is proposed. This design is evaluated and further refinements are made to the design. Chapter 15 describes the method used to derive initial feasible designs. It discusses the limitations imposed on designers by the various implementation models and the effect of these limitations on the chosen method. Chapter 16 then describes the method used to evaluate proposed designs. Finally, Chapter 17 covers the choice of design methodologies.

Problems

A large number of problems are included in the text. The problems in the initial chapters concentrate on techniques used in data analysis. As we proceed toward technical design, the scope of the problems becomes larger. It is difficult to set bounded problems in a design context because it is the complexity of the problem itself that poses interesting design issues. Hence problems in technical design are less bounded than those in data analysis. Technical design problems are offered in the appendix and in four design projects at the end of the text. The appendix contains a database specification that is used to illustrate the technical design techniques described in the text. The design projects are included in a special section at the end of the text. They include database specifications that you can use as inputs to technical design.

chapter two
Relational Model

INTRODUCTION

In Chapter 1 we explained why decisions about user requirements are separated from technical decisions in database design, and we proposed a staged design. In a staged design each stage deals with well-defined design decisions involving techniques and terms natural to the stage.

The first design stage is the analysis of user data requirements. Here techniques must be based on a formal model that meets the following objectives:

1. It can be used to identify user requirements and present them in a way that is easily understood both by users and by computer professionals.
2. It can be easily converted to a technical implementation.
3. It provides rules and criteria for efficient logical data representation.

The relational model was among the first models to address these three objectives. One of its main contributions was the use of formal criteria for logical representation, criteria known as *normal relational forms*. The formal rigor of these criteria, together with their practical interpretation, has established the relational model as an important foundation of database design. Many of the other models that were later proposed for data analysis also use relational criteria to choose logical structures.

This chapter describes the basic structure of the relational model and introduces the criteria for developing normal relational forms. The next chapter will delve further into these criteria and describe relational design procedures. Later chapters will discuss application of relational theory to other models.

THE RELATIONAL MODEL—
A HISTORIC PERSPECTIVE

The relational model was introduced to the database community by E. F. Codd (1970). This innovation stressed the independence of the relational representation from physical computer implementation such as ordering on physical devices, indexing, and using physical access paths. The model thus formalized the separation of the user view of data from its eventual implementation; it was the first model to do so. In addition, Codd proposed criteria for logically structuring relational databases and an implementation-independent language to operate on these databases.

Since the introduction of the relational model, there have been many further developments in its theory and application. The early ideas of normal form have been extended to include additional criteria, particularly fourth normal form, which was introduced by R. Fagin (1977).

Relational design procedures have also received considerable attention in the last few years. P. A. Bernstein (1976) had proposed synthesizing relations from functional dependencies, and Fagin's work in 1977 then drew attention to the decomposition approach to design.

RELATIONAL MODEL—THE BASIC STRUCTURE

We can gauge the usefulness of the relational model in data analysis by considering the three objectives outlined earlier. To meet the first objective—identify user requirements—the model must serve as a communication medium between the users and the computer personnel, giving them an interface that they can clearly and unambiguously understand. The independence of this interface from computer implementation is of the utmost importance. Such independence eliminates early consideration of constraints imposed by physical devices, thus ensuring that emphasis is placed on producing user specifications that emphasizes user logical needs.

The relational model uses tables to provide this interface. The enterprise model of data is specified as a set of tables, or relations. Figure 2.1 illustrates one such relation, named PERSONS. The PERSONS relation contains information on people in an organization; it stores each person's NAME, ADDRESS and DATE-OF-BIRTH. A complete specification of enterprises usually consists of a large number of relations.

The tabular presentation of relations satisfies the first objective of data anal-

RELATION: PERSONS

NAME	ADDRESS	DATE-OF-BIRTH
JACK	NATICK	010363
JOHN	NEWTON	030465
JIM	CONCORD	070961

Figure 2.1   A relation

ysis. It is readily understood by users as well as computer professionals. It is also complete in the sense that it can be used to specify the data within any organization.

The second objective, the conversion to physical implementation, is also satisfied by the relational model. One obvious approach is to directly implement the relational model on a machine. To do this a database management system that supports the relational model must be available on a computer system. A particular set of relations can then be directly declared by using the definitional language provided by this system. Such direct conversion was not feasible when the relational model was first proposed by Codd in 1971, but the acceptance of the relational model for describing systems has led to the development of database management systems that support this model on the machine. As a result, direct conversion from a relational specification to physical implementation is becoming increasingly possible.

It is, of course, not essential to have a relational database management system before using the relational model to specify user requirements. A relational specification can also be converted to other physical structures. For example, suppose a conventional file system is to be used in the implementation. In this case each relation (or table) can be converted to a file, each column to a field, and each row to a record. Hence the second objective is satisfied.

The third objective deals with the following criteria for good logical data structures:

1. Each fact should be stored once in the database.
2. The database should be consistent following database operations.
3. The database should be resilient to change.

As for the first criterion, storing each fact once at most not only removes storage redundancy but also improves database consistency. If the same fact (for example, a person's address) is stored twice, there will perhaps be times when only one copy of this fact is updated during the execution of some complex operation. The database then becomes inconsistent. In an inconsistent database it is possible to obtain different database outputs about the same fact from different places, raising doubts about the reliability of information in the database. The first and second criteria are therefore related. The second criterion requires the database to be consistent at all times. Storing each fact once only improves database consistency by ensuring that consistent information be obtained from the database after any database operations. The third criterion deals with a different aspect. It is a consequence of the environment in which databases exist. This environment is usually in a state of constant change; consequently, the database must also be continually redesigned to meet continually changing user requirements.

These criteria, of course, did not originate with the relational model; they had already been informally accepted by designers.

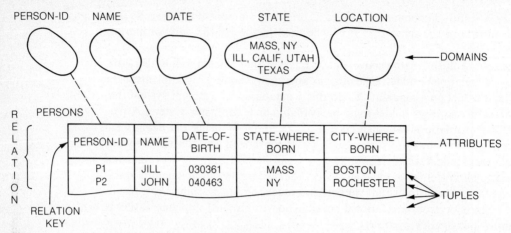

Figure 2.2   Terminology for the Relational Model

Terminology

A well-founded terminology is associated with the relational model (Figure 2.2). Informally, a database is made up of any number of relations. Each relation is given a name; the relation in Figure 2.2 is named PERSONS. As mentioned earlier, the relation can be viewed as a table that is made up of a number of rows and columns. Each column is called an *attribute* and given a name. Thus the names of columns in Figure 2.2 are PERSON-ID, NAME, DATE-OF-BIRTH, STATE-WHERE-BORN, and CITY-WHERE-BORN. The rows of the relation are called *tuples* and contain the data. Thus the first row in Figure 2.2 contains data about a person identified by PERSON-ID = P1. This person has the name "JILL" and was born on March 3, 1961, in BOSTON in MASS. The values in each column of each row come from a *domain* of values. One such domain is associated with each attribute and defines the range of allowed values for that attribute. For example, the range of values of STATE-WHERE-BORN is defined as MASS, NY, and so on. NAME, on the other hand, may be any alphanumeric value. Finally, the *instance* of a relation is the content of the relation at a particular instant of time.

Attributes and Domains

At this stage you may be wondering why we bother to make a distinction between domain and attribute. In Figure 2.2, for example, why not use the same name for both domains and attributes? The reason for this separation is that a domain is a *set* of values; as such it may appear in more than one relation or

RELATION: MANUFACTURE

PARTS	PARTS	INTEGER	Domains
ASSEMBLY	COMPONENT	QTY	Attribute
AUTO	ENGINE	1	
AUTO	WHEEL	4	
AUTO	CHASSIS	1	
WHEEL	TIRE	1	
WHEEL	NUTS	6	
ENGINE	CYLINDER	4	

Figure 2.3 Relation MANUFACTURE

sometimes more than once in the same relation. Consider the domain PARTS in Figure 2.3. This domain contains the names of all the parts of interest to an organization. Relation MANUFACTURE stores the components that make up each part. Thus an AUTO is made up of 1 ENGINE, 4 WHEELS and 1 CHASSIS. A WHEEL in turn is composed of 1 TIRE and 6 NUTS; and an ENGINE has 4 CYLINDERS. In relation MANUFACTURE the domain PARTS appears twice. Therefore we need to distinguish between the first and the second set of the same domain in the one relation. We can do so by using attributes. Both the attributes ASSEMBLY and COMPONENT map to the same domain, PARTS. But the values in each column, although they come from the same domain, have different meanings. Thus WHEEL in column ASSEMBLY means that WHEEL is the major part or assembly made up of some other parts; WHEEL in the column COMPONENT means that WHEEL is the component of some major part or assembly.

It is common to choose domain names to signify value sets; for example, INTEGER, ALPHANUMERIC, and so on are domain names. Attribute names, on the other hand, are chosen to be meaningful within the context of the enterprise. For example, consider relation WORK in Figure 2.4. The attribute names here are chosen to identify as closely as possible the meaning of values in their columns. The values in the column headed by that attribute name will be from the set of values of the domain that the attribute maps onto. For WORK,

RELATION: WORK

PERSON-ON-PROJECT	PROJECT-WORKED-ON	HRS-WORKED-ON-PROJECT
RYAN	P#1	5
SMITH	P#2	3
BROWN	P#1	2

Figure 2.4 Relation WORK

RELATION: A

X	Y	Z
RYAN	P#1	5
SMITH	P#2	3
BROWN	P#3	2

Figure 2.5   Relation A

the attribute PERSON-ON-PROJECT maps onto the domain ALPHANU-MERIC because the values are alphanumeric, being the set of names of all the people in the organization. Similarly, the attribute PROJECT-WORKED-ON maps onto the domain PROJECT-NUMBERS; and the attribute HRS-WORKED-ON-PROJECT maps onto the domain INTEGER.

The use of such meaningful names adds to the clarity of the relational representation. For example, compare Figures 2.4 and 2.5. Both contain the same rows but have different attribute names. Obviously, additional information must be associated with Figure 2.5 to explain what the columns are. This additional information is not required for Figure 2.4 because the attribute names are self-explanatory.

It should be noted that an attribute may also consist of more than one domain. For example, in Figure 2.6 the attribute NAME may map onto two domains: FIRST-NAME and LAST-NAME.

It is also possible to have relations where the attribute values are themselves relations. The attribute domains are instances of that relation. For example, Figure 2.7 illustrates the relation LIVED-IN, which identifies the places of residence of people. Here the domain of attribute RESIDENCE is a relation. The relation attributes are CITY and DATE-MOVED-IN. The values of these attributes state the city in which a PERSON resided, together with the date on which that person first took up residence in that city.

Properties of Relations

Each relation possesses the following properties:

1. There is one column in the relation for each attribute of the relation. Each such column is given a name that is unique in the relation.
2. The entries in the column come from the same domain.
3. The order of the columns or attributes in the relation has no significance.
4. The order of the rows is not significant.
5. There are no duplicate rows.

RELATION: NAMES

| PERSON-ID | NAME | |
	FIRST-NAME	LAST-NAME
S7530	JACK	LONDON
S7601	JILL	INGLES
S7903	JOHN	EVERETT
S8017	JOCK	STEWART

Figure 2.6 Relation NAMES

Keys of Relations

Now we can consider what is perhaps the most important term of all: the *relation key*. This key is the attribute or set of attributes that uniquely identifies tuples in a relation. A relation key is formally defined as a set of one or more relation attributes concatenated so that the following three properties hold for all time and for any instance of the relation:

1. *Uniqueness:* The set of attributes takes on a unique value in the relation for each tuple.
2. *Nonredundancy:* If an attribute is removed from the set of attributes, the remaining attributes do not possess the uniqueness property.
3. *Validity:* No attribute value in the key may be null.

It is possible for relations to have more than one relation key; each key is made up of a different set of attributes. For example, the relation key of rela-

RELATION: LIVED-IN

PERSON	RESIDENCE	
JACK	CITY	DATE-MOVED-IN
	NEW YORK	030371
	BOSTON	070780
	WASHINGTON	080881
MARTHA	CITY	DATE-MOVED-IN
	BOSTON	040573
	PHILADELPHIA	070675
	CHICAGO	080877

Figure 2.7 Relation LIVED-IN

tion PERSONS in Figure 2.2 is PERSON-ID, as there is one tuple for each person. The relation WORK in Figure 2.4, on the other hand, has a relation key made up of the two attributes, PERSON-ON-PROJECT and PROJECT-WORKED-ON; values in these two columns together uniquely identify tuples in WORK. PERSON-ON-PROJECT cannot be a relation key by itself because there can be more than one tuple with the same value of PERSON-ON-PROJECT. That is, one person can work on more than one project. Similarly, PROJECT-WORKED-ON cannot be a relation key on its own because more than one person can work on the same project. An example of a relation with more than one relation is described later (Figure 2.17).

The relation key is often called the *candidate key*. If a key is the only key of the relation, it is generally referred to as the *primary key*. In this text we use the general term relation key in lieu of candidate key and primary key.

Two other expressions round out the terminology. A *prime attribute* is an attribute that is part of at least one relation key. A *nonprime attribute* is not part of any relation key. For example, in relation PERSONS in Figure 2.2, PERSON-ID is a prime attribute; NAME, DATE-OF-BIRTH, STATE-WHERE-BORN and CITY-WHERE-BORN are all nonprime attributes. In relation WORK in Figure 2.4, PERSON-ON-PROJECT and PROJECT-WORKED-ON are both prime attributes; HRS-WORKED-ON-PROJECT is the only nonprime attribute in this relation.

Consistency

Now that you have some grasp of the terms used in describing relations, we can turn to the criteria that distinguish between good and bad relational design. Our goal is to choose relations that preserve consistency following database operations and that store each fact at most once in the database. Relations that do this are said to be in normal form.

In nonnormal relations anomalies can arise after database tuple operations. Before defining the criteria for normal relations, we will describe here the database tuple operations and the anomalies that can crop up when a relation is badly designed.

Tuple Operations

The three tuple database operations are as follows:

1. *Add tuple* (relation name, ⟨attribute values⟩). This operation adds a new tuple to a relation. The attribute values of the tuple are given as part of the operation. For example,

add tuple (PERSONS, ⟨BILL, CAMBRIDGE, 060969⟩)

would add a new row to the relation in Figure 2.1. An add-tuple operation will not be allowed if it duplicates a relation key.

2. *Delete tuple* (relation name, ⟨attribute values⟩). This operation deletes a tuple from a relation. For example,

delete tuple (PERSONS, ⟨JACK, NATICK, 010363⟩)

would delete the first row from the relation in Figure 2.1.

3. *Update tuple* (relation name, ⟨old attribute values⟩, ⟨new attribute values⟩). This operation changes the tuple in a relation. For example,

update tuple (PERSONS, ⟨JIM, CONCORD, 070961⟩,
⟨JIM, CAMBRIDGE, 070961⟩)

would change JIM's address in the relation in Figure 2.1. An update will not be allowed if it duplicates a relation key.

In a normal relational structure no anomalies arise after the application of any one of the three preceding operations with any set of attribute values. Various anomalies are possible if relations are not in normal form.

Anomalies

Anomalies can be illustrated by considering the relation ASSIGN of Figure 2.8. This relation describes the time spent by persons on projects, together with the project budget.

It is seen here that the project budget is unnecessarily repeated. Thus the fact that project P1 has a budget of 32 appears twice. Similarly, to store the budget of a project that has no person assigned to it requires dummy or null values to be used in the columns PERSON-ID and TIME-SPENT-BY-PERSON-ON-

RELATION: ASSIGN

PERSON-ID	PROJECT-BUDGET	PROJECT	TIME-SPENT-BY-PERSON-ON-PROJECT
S75	32	P1	7
S75	40	P2	3
S79	32	P1	4
S79	27	P3	1
S80	40	P2	5
–	17	P4	–

Figure 2.8 Relation ASSIGN

PROJECT—for example, project P4. The existence of null values in a relation is regarded as an anomaly.

Now consider some tuple operations. Suppose the operation

add tuple (ASSIGN, ⟨S85, 35, P1, 9⟩)

is executed to add the fact that person S85 has worked on project P1. This operation creates an anomaly because now there will be two tuples in ASSIGN with conflicting PROJECT-BUDGET values for the same project (P1).

Similarly, consider deleting the fact that S79 worked on project P3:

delete tuple (ASSIGN, ⟨S79, 27, P3, 11⟩)

This operation inadvertently also deletes the project budget of P3, thus creating a delete anomaly.

Finally, let's say that to change P1's budget, we use the operation

update tuple (ASSIGN, ⟨S75, 32, P1, 7⟩, ⟨S75, 35, P1, 7⟩)

Again we have an anomaly, because now there are two tuples with different values for P1's budget.

These undesirable properties can be removed by decomposing ASSIGN into the two relations in Figure 2.9. The results:

1. No anomalies arise if a project budget is changed by the operation

   update tuple (PROJECTS, ⟨P1, 32⟩, ⟨P1, 35⟩)

2. No dummy values are necessary to store projects budget values for projects that have no persons assigned to them.

3. Deletion anomalies do not arise if a person's contribution is deleted. For example,

   delete tuple (ASSIGNMENTS, ⟨S79, P3, 11⟩)

   does not also delete the budget of project P3.

RELATION: PROJECTS

PROJECT	PROJECT-BUDGET
P1	32
P2	40
P3	27
P4	17

RELATION: ASSIGNMENTS

PERSON-ID	PROJECT	TIME-SPENT-BY-PERSON-ON-PROJECT
S75	P1	7
S75	P2	3
S79	P1	4
S79	P3	11
S80	P2	5

Figure 2.9   Decomposition of relation ASSIGN

4. No anomaly can be created if a person's contribution is added to ASSIGN-MENTS. For example,

   add tuple (ASSIGNMENTS, ⟨S85, P1, 9⟩)

cannot inadvertently create an anomaly.

So one design goal must be to represent user information by relations that do not create anomalies following tuple add, delete, or update operations. For this purpose the relations must be in *normal form*. At this point we need the concept of functional dependency to define these normal form relations.

FUNCTIONAL DEPENDENCY

Functional dependency (FD) is a term derived from mathematical theory; it concerns the dependence of values of one attribute or set of attributes on those of another attribute or set of attributes. Formally, a set of attributes X is functionally dependent on a set of attributes Y if a given set of values for each attribute in Y determines a unique value for the set of attributes in X. The notation $Y \rightarrow X$ is often used to denote that X is functionally dependent on Y. The attributes in Y are sometimes known as the *determinant* of the FD $Y \rightarrow X$.

In the simplest case, both X and Y are made up of one attribute. To return to the example in Figure 2.8, PROJECT-BUDGET is functionally dependent on PROJECT because each project has one given budget value. Thus once a PROJECT name is known, a unique value of PROJECT-BUDGET is immediately determined. Hence we have the FD PROJECT $\rightarrow$ PROJECT-BUDGET.

Such FDs show up clearly in a diagram. In Figure 2.10, for example, the arrow indicates that each value of PROJECT uniquely determines a value of PROJECT-BUDGET.

Similarly, in relations ASSIGN or ASSIGNMENTS (Figure 2.9), once values for PERSON-ID and PROJECT are known, a unique value of TIME-SPENT by that person in that project is determined. Formally, this FD is defined as

PERSON-ID, PROJECT $\rightarrow$ TIME-SPENT

Figure 2.11 is a diagram of this FD.

Figure 2.10   Functional dependency diagram

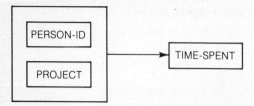

Figure 2.11 Another functional dependency diagram

It is also possible to have two attributes that are functionally dependent on each other. In this case both $X \rightarrow Y$ and $Y \rightarrow X$ hold. The notation $X \leftrightarrow Y$ is commonly used to denote such mutual FD.

It is important to realize that functional dependency is a property of the information that is represented by the relations. That is, functional dependency is not determined by the use of attributes in relations or by the current contents of a relation. For example, in Figure 2.12 we show a set of tuples at a certain time in relation $R4$. In this particular instance it appears that each person can work on only one project. Hence we could falsely assume that PERSON-ID $\rightarrow$ PROJECT. But the nature of the information represented in $R4$ is such that a person can work on more than one project. It just so happens that by some chance at a particular time each person works on only one project.

Full Functional Dependency

Given a functional dependency $Y \rightarrow X$ (where X and Y are both sets of attributes), a unique value for each attribute in X is determined once the values for Y attributes are known. However, it is sometimes possible that values of X can be uniquely determined by only a subset of the attributes of Y. Thus in relation ASSIGN it is true that

PERSON-ID, PROJECT, PROJECT-BUDGET $\rightarrow$

TIME-SPENT-BY-PERSON-ON-PROJECT

RELATION: $R4$

PERSON-ID	PROJECT	TIME-SPENT
S20	P1	7
S23	P2	3
S17	P3	7

Figure 2.12 Relation $R4$

Hence the values of PERSON-ID, PROJECT, and PROJECT-BUDGET determine a unique value of TIME-SPENT-BY-PERSON-ON-PROJECT. However, it is enough to only know the value of a subset of {PERSON-ID, PROJECT, PROJECT-BUDGET}—namely, {PERSON-ID, PROJECT}—to determine TIME-SPENT-BY-PERSON-ON-PROJECT.

The term *full functional dependency* is used to indicate the minimum set of attributes in a determinant of an FD. Formally a set of attributes X are fully functionally dependent on a set of attributes Y if

1. X is functionally dependent on Y.
2. X is not functionally dependent on any subset of Y.

Thus

PERSON-ID, PROJECT, PROJECT-BUDGET $\rightarrow$
$\qquad\qquad\qquad$ TIME-SPENT-BY-PERSON-ON-PROJECT

is not a full FD. Rather, the full FD is

PERSON-ID, PROJECT $\rightarrow$ TIME-SPENT-BY-PERSON-ON-PROJECT

because neither PERSON-ID $\rightarrow$ TIME-SPENT-BY-PERSON-ON-PROJECT nor PROJECT $\rightarrow$ TIME-SPENT-BY-PERSON-ON-PROJECT holds true.

Like functional dependency, full functional dependency is a property of the information that is represented by the relation; it is not an indication of the way that attributes are formed into relations or the current contents of relations.

NORMAL FORMS

When determining whether a particular relation is in normal form, we must examine the FDs between the attributes in the relation (not the current contents of the relation). Accordingly, a notation can be adopted to emphasize these relational characteristics. In the notation first proposed by C. Beeri, and co-workers (1978), the relation is defined as made up of two components: the attributes and the FDs between them. It takes the form

$R1 = (\{X, Y, Z\}, \{X \rightarrow Y, X \rightarrow Z\})$

The first component of the relation is the attributes, and the second component is the FDs. For example, in Figure 2.8 the first component of relation ASSIGN is

{PERSON-ID, PROJECT, PROJECT-BUDGET,
TIME-SPENT-BY-PERSON-ON-PROJECT}

The second component is therefore

{PERSON-ID, PROJECT →
            TIME-SPENT-BY-PERSON-ON-PROJECT, PROJECT →
                                    PROJECT-BUDGET}

The FDs between attributes in a relation are obviously important when determining the relation's key. A relation key uniquely identifies a row; hence the key or prime attributes uniquely determine the values of the nonkey or nonprime attributes; and therefore a full FD exists from the prime to the nonprime attributes. It is when there are full FDs whose determinants are not keys of a relation that problems arise.

For example, again consider relation ASSIGN in Figure 2.8. In this relation the key is {PERSON-ID, PROJECT}. However, PROJECT-BUDGET depends on only part of the key; alternatively, the determinant of the FD PROJECT → PROJECT-BUDGET is not the key of the relation. This undesirable property causes the anomalies discussed earlier. Conversion to normal forms requires a choice of relations that do not contain such undesirable dependencies.

There are a number of normal forms. The three best known are the first, second, and third normal forms, often referred to as 1NF, 2NF, and 3NF. Relations are in *first normal form* if all domains are simple. In a simple domain all elements are atomic. Most of the relations that we have discussed so far are in first normal form. The only relation not in 1NF is LIVED-IN in Figure 2.7, where the domain RESIDENCE is not simple. Relations that have nonsimple domains are not in first normal form; they are called unnormalized relations.

A relation is normalized by replacing the nonsimple domains with simple domains. The normalized form of relation LIVED-IN is shown in Figure 2.13.

A relation R is in *second normal form* if every nonprime attribute of R is fully functionally dependent on each relation key. The relation ASSIGN in Figure 2.8 is not in second normal form because the nonprime attribute PROJECT-BUDGET is not fully dependent on the relation key PERSON-ID and PROJECT. Here PROJECT-BUDGET is, in fact, fully functionally dependent on PROJECT, which is a subset of the relation key. In Figure 2.9 relation

RELATION: LIVED-IN

PERSON	CITY	DATE-MOVED-IN
JACK	NEW YORK	030371
JACK	BOSTON	070780
JACK	WASHINGTON	080881
MARTHA	BOSTON	040573
MARTHA	PHILADELPHIA	070675
MARTHA	CHICAGO	080877

Figure 2.13   Relation LIVED-IN normalized

ASSIGN was decomposed into two relations, PROJECTS and ASSIGN-MENTS. Both these relations are in 2NF.

A relation *R* is in *third normal form* if it has the following properties:

1. The relation *R* is in second normal form.
2. The nonprime attributes are mutually independent; that is, no nonprime attribute is functionally dependent on another nonprime attribute.

Example

An example of a relation that is in 2NF but not in 3NF is shown in Figure 2.14. The FDs for the attributes in relation SUPPLIERS are diagrammed in Figure 2.15. In this diagram, DISTANCE is the attribute whose value is the distance of a city from, say, the main office of an organization. There is only one relation key: SUPPLIER. Both CITY and DISTANCE are nonprime attributes that are fully functionally dependent on SUPPLIER, and so the relation is in 2NF. However, relation SUPPLIERS (Figure 2.14) has one undesirable property: the distance of a city from the main office is stored more than once. This situation occurs because a dependency exists between the nonprime attributes. Since DISTANCE is functionally dependent on CITY, the nonprime attributes are dependent.

The information in SUPPLIERS can be represented by 3NF relations by decomposing SUPPLIERS. The result of the decomposition are the two relations SUPPLIERS and DISTANCES in Figure 2.16. Both these relations are in 3NF. Distances of cities from the main office are now stored once only.

Boyce–Codd Normal Form

In our definition of third normal form we have assumed that the relation has only one relation key. Problems arise with the definition when it is used with

RELATION: SUPPLIERS

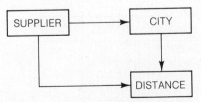

SUPPLIER	CITY	DISTANCE
S1	BOSTON	200
S2	BOSTON	200
S3	CHICAGO	1800
S4	CHICAGO	1800

Figure 2.14 Relation in 2NF but not in 3NF

Figure 2.15 Functional dependencies between SUPPLIERS attributes

RELATION: SUPPLIERS   RELATION: DISTANCE

SUPPLIER	CITY
S1	BOSTON
S2	BOSTON
S3	CHICAGO
S4	CHICAGO

CITY	DISTANCE
BOSTON	200
CHICAGO	1800

Figure 2.16   Decomposition of SUPPLIERS

relations that have more than one relation key. For example, consider the relation GRADES (Figure 2.17) and the FDs between the attributes of relation GRADES (Figure 2.18). Relation GRADES stores the results of students in courses as well as the students' phone numbers. Each student had one unique nonshared PHONE-NO. Each student takes any number of courses and obtains a grade for each course.

Both {STUDENT-ID, COURSE} and {PHONE-NO, COURSE} are relation keys of relation GRADES. They are overlapping keys because COURSE appears in both keys. The relation satisfies 3NF conditions. The nonprimary attribute GRADE depends fully on each relation key; there is only one nonprime attribute, GRADE, and so there is no dependence between nonprime attributes. But the relation GRADES has some undesirable properties:

1. The phone number of each student is stored more than once; hence there is unnecessary redundancy.
2. A student's phone number cannot be stored until that student takes at least one course.
3. A student's grade in a course cannot be entered unless the student's phone number is known.
4. If a student withdraws from all courses, all tuples that include this student are deleted, a procedure that also inadvertently deletes that student's phone number.
5. If the student's phone number changes, more than one tuple must be changed.

RELATION: GRADES

STUDENT-ID	PHONE-NO	COURSE	GRADE
760137	112233	CP1	A
770593	899899	CP1	F
770593	899899	IS1	B
790379	544077	IS1	B
790379	544077	IS2	C

Figure 2.17   Relation GRADES

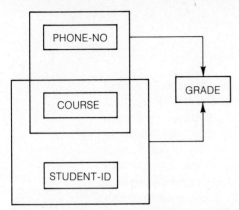

Figure 2.18 Functional dependencies in relation GRADES

These problems arise because there are dependencies between key attributes; STUDENT-ID and PHONE-NO are functionally dependent on each other. To remove these problems, Boyce proposed a normal form generally known as the *Boyce–Codd Normal Form* (BCNF).

A relation R is in BCNF if every determinant in the relation is a relation key. For example, suppose

$$R = (\{A, B, C, D\}, \{A \rightarrow BCD, D \rightarrow A\})$$

Here relation R will be in BCNF if both A and D are keys of R.

In Figure 2.17 relation GRADES does not satisfy this condition. The relation contains the FDs STUDENT-ID $\rightarrow$ PHONE-NO and PHONE-NO $\rightarrow$ STUDENT-ID, but neither STUDENT-ID nor PHONE-NO is a key of GRADES.

To remove the undesirable properties, we decompose relation GRADES into the two relations STUDENTS and RESULTS. Then, by decomposition, we get

STUDENTS = ({STUDENT-ID, PHONE-NO},
   {STUDENT-ID $\rightarrow$ PHONE-NO})

and

RESULTS = ({STUDENT-ID, COURSE, GRADE},
   {STUDENT-ID, COURSE $\rightarrow$ GRADE})

Both these relations are BCNF: STUDENT-ID is a key of STUDENTS, and {STUDENT-ID, COURSE} is a key of RESULTS.

FUNCTIONAL DEPENDENCIES
AND RELATIONAL DESIGN

So far in this chapter we have considered conditions that characterize normal form relations. We have not presented a formal method to derive such relations, although we have suggested that normal relations can be obtained by decomposing nonnormal relations. The next chapter will describe algorithms, or formal procedures, used to construct normal relations: namely, decomposition methods for decomposing nonnormal relations to normal forms, and synthesis procedures for constructing relations from FDs.

As a preliminary to these algorithms, we will, in the next section of this chapter, describe FDs in more detail and outline those FD properties that are used in design algorithms.

Properties of Functional Dependencies

The definition of functional dependency allows new FDs to be derived from known FDs. For example, if it is known that $X \rightarrow Y$ and $Y \rightarrow Z$, then it is also true that $X \rightarrow Z$. To some extent, this derivation is obvious. If a given value of X determines a unique value of Y, and this value of Y in turn determines a unique value of Z, then the value of X also determines this value of Z.

Conversely, it is possible for a set of FDs to contain some redundant FDs. An FD in the set is *redundant* if it can be derived from the other FDs in the set. Many design algorithms must commence with a nonredundant set of FDs. This situation applies particularly to synthesis algorithms. The basic function of synthesis algorithms is to construct relations from FDs. All FDs with the same determinant become one relation. Thus if an FD $XY \rightarrow Z$ exists in the information, a relation $R = (\{X, Y, Z\}, \{XY \rightarrow Z\})$ is created. This design method, however, is not effective if it commences with a nonredundant set of FDs.

For example, suppose the following FDs are identified:

$$X \rightarrow Y \quad Y \rightarrow Z \quad X \rightarrow Z$$

These FDs suggest the following relations to represent them:

$$R1 = (\{X, Y, Z\}, \{X \rightarrow Y, X \rightarrow Z\})$$
$$R2 = (\{Y, Z\}, \{Y \rightarrow Z\})$$

One relation, $R1$, in this set is not in BCNF; there is dependency between the nonprime attributes Z and Y. Relation $R1$ is not in BCNF because a redundant FD, $X \rightarrow Z$, was used to construct it. If only nonredundant FDs are used, the two synthesized relations become

$$R1 = (\{X, Y\}, \{X \rightarrow Y\})$$
$$R2 = (\{Y, Z\}, \{Y \rightarrow Z\})$$

Both these FDs are in BCNF.

Thus design algorithms require designers to commence with a nonredundant set of FDs. To be able to detect redundant FDs it is necessary to have a set of rules that can be used to derive one FD from other FDs. A simple way to detect a redundant FD is as follows:

1. Commence with a set **S** of FDs.
2. Remove an FD, f, and create a set of FDs $\mathbf{S}' = \mathbf{S} - f$.
3. Test whether f can be derived from the FDs in $\mathbf{S}'$ by using the set of rules.
4. If f can be so derived, it is redundant and hence $S = S'$. Otherwise replace f into $\mathbf{S}'$ so that now $\mathbf{S} = \mathbf{S}' + f$.
5. Repeat steps 2 to 4 for all the FDs in **S**.

Now the question is, What are the set of rules? As you can see, a minimum set of rules is required to avoid unnecessary looping in step 3. This set of rules has been found (Armstrong, 1974 and Beeri, 1978) to be as follows:

- If $Y \subseteq X$, then $X \rightarrow Y$ (reflexivity).
- If $Z \subseteq W$ and $X \rightarrow Y$, then $XW \rightarrow YZ$ (augmentation).
- If $X \rightarrow Y$ and $Y \rightarrow Z$, then $X \rightarrow Z$ (transitivity).
- If $X \rightarrow Y$ and $YW \rightarrow Z$, then $XW \rightarrow Z$ (pseudotransitivity).
- If $X \rightarrow Z$ and $X \rightarrow Y$, then $X \rightarrow YZ$ (union).
- If $X \rightarrow YZ$, then $X \rightarrow Y$ and $X \rightarrow Z$ (decomposition).

For example, suppose an algorithm commences with the following set of FDs:

$$Z \rightarrow A \qquad B \rightarrow X \qquad AX \rightarrow Y \qquad ZB \rightarrow Y$$

Here $ZB \rightarrow Y$ can be shown to be redundant because it can be derived from the other FDs in the set as follows:

1. $Z \rightarrow A$ by augmentation yields $ZB \rightarrow AB$.
2. $B \rightarrow X$ and $AX \rightarrow Y$ by pseudotransitivity yield $AB \rightarrow Y$.
3. $ZB \rightarrow AB$ and $AB \rightarrow Y$ by transitivity yield $ZB \rightarrow Y$.

The existence of such inference rules leads to three other terms: closure, covering, and nonredundant covering. A *closure,* $\mathbf{F}+$, of a set $\mathbf{F}$ of FDs is defined as all the FDs that can be derived from $\mathbf{F}$ by using the FD rules. Thus if

$$\mathbf{F} = \{X \rightarrow Y, Y \rightarrow Z, X \rightarrow YZ\}$$

then the closure of $\mathbf{F}$ would include the following FDs:

$$X \rightarrow Z, X \rightarrow X, Y \rightarrow Z, Z \rightarrow Z, X \rightarrow YZ, X \rightarrow Y, Y \rightarrow Z, Y \rightarrow Y$$

The definition of *covering* is useful when we wish to substitute one set of FDs for another. Two sets of FDs are said to cover each other if they have the same closure. More formally, the set of FDs **C** is a covering of the set of FDs **F** if $C^+ = F^+$. A set of FDs **C** is a *nonredundant covering* of a set of FDs **F** if **C** is a covering of **F** but no subset of **C** is a covering of **F**.

In the preceding example,

$$C1 = \{X \rightarrow Y, Y \rightarrow Z, X \rightarrow Z\}$$

is a covering of **F**; it is not, however, a nonredundant covering because $X \rightarrow Z$ can be derived from the other two FDs. On the other hand, $C2 = \{X \rightarrow Y, Y \rightarrow Z\}$ is a nonredundant covering of **F**.

The Membership Algorithm

The membership algorithm that has been proposed for detecting redundant FDs takes each FD in a given set and determines if it can be derived from the remaining FDs. To determine whether an FD, $f(A \rightarrow B)$, can be derived from a set of FDs, **S**, we go through the following steps:

1. Initialize $T = A$ (here T is a variable that contains a set of attributes; A is the determinant of f, the FD).
2. Look at FDs other than $A \rightarrow B$ to see if an FD $X \rightarrow Y$ can be found with its determinant in T (i.e., $X \subseteq T$). If any such FD ($X \rightarrow Y$) is found, then add the attributes in Y to the set of attributes in T (union and transitivity rule).
3. Repeat step 2 every time T is changed until no more attributes can be added to T.
4. If at the conclusion of steps 2 and 3, B is in T, then $A \rightarrow B$ can be derived from the other FDs in **S** (decomposition rule).

Step 2 should be repeated every time any new attributes are added to T at step 3. All remaining FDs are examined at each such repetition. A sequential algorithm for this process is illustrated in Figure 2.19. This algorithm is n^2 order and can be quite lengthy if a large number of FDs are involved. Linear algorithms have also been proposed for this problem.

Let's apply the membership algorithm to the following set of FDs:

$$Z \rightarrow A \quad B \rightarrow X \quad AX \rightarrow Y \quad ZB \rightarrow Y$$

First, consider $Z \rightarrow A$:

- *Step 1:* $T = Z$.
- *Step 2:* No additions are made to T as there is no other FD $X \rightarrow Y$ where $X \subseteq T$.

Hence $Z \rightarrow A$ is not redundant. The FDs $B \rightarrow X$ and $AY \rightarrow Y$ can be shown to be nonredundant in a similar way.

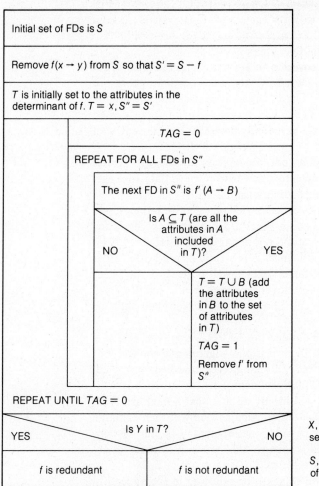

| Initial set of FDs is *S* |
| Remove *f*(*x* → *y*) from *S* so that *S'* = *S* − *f* |
| *T* is initially set to the attributes in the determinant of *f*. *T* = *x*, *S"* = *S'* |

TAG = 0

REPEAT FOR ALL FDs in *S"*

The next FD in *S"* is *f'* (*A* → *B*)

Is *A* ⊆ *T* (are all the attributes in *A* included in *T*)?

NO   YES

T = *T* ∪ *B* (add the attributes in *B* to the set of attributes in *T*)

TAG = 1

Remove *f'* from *S"*

REPEAT UNTIL TAG = 0

Is *Y* in *T*?

YES   NO

f is redundant   *f* is not redundant

X, *Y*, *A*, *B*, and *T* are sets of attributes

S, *S'*, *S"* are sets of FDs

Figure 2.19 Membership algorithm

Now consider $ZB \rightarrow Y$:

- *Step 1:* $T = ZB$.
- *Step 2:* $T = ZB + A = ZBA$ because $Z \rightarrow A$ is in the remaining set of FDs and $Z \subseteq T$.
  $T = ZBA + X = ZBAX$ because $B \rightarrow X$ is in the remaining set of FDs and $B \subseteq T$.
  $T = ZBAX + Y = ZBAXY$ because $AX \rightarrow Y$ is in the remaining set of FDs and $AX \subseteq T$.

Now Y is in T. So $ZB \rightarrow Y$ is redundant.

RELATIONAL LANGUAGES

The relational model must provide languages to access relations. A number of relational languages have been proposed. Developments in relational language are particularly sensitive to human factors. The strongpoint of the relational model has always been its natural interface. The tabular structure of relations can be readily explained to computer users. It is equally important that users can easily understand relational languages.

Another important measure of a relational language is its selective power. Relational languages should have the selective power to retrieve data that satisfy any condition covering any number of relations.

Historically, early relational languages concentrated on selective power. Codd defined the relational model in 1970 and in short order defined the basis for relational languages as relational algebra and relational calculus (Codd, 1971). Relational calculus is of particular significance. It is a form of predicate calculus specially tailored for the relational model and is used to measure the selective power of relational languages. A relational language is *relationally complete* if it can derive any data that can be obtained from a relational calculus expression.

Codd defined relational calculus and devised the ALPHA language, which is based on relational calculus. He also defined relational algebra and showed that it is relationally complete. Since that time other languages have been proposed. These have adhered to the principle of relational completeness but have continually improved the user interface. We will briefly discuss next a modified form of relational calculus known as tuple relational calculus. We will then examine some of the later languages and describe relational algebra. Chapter 11 contains a further description of relational languages that are implemented in existing relational database management systems.

Examples in the following description refer to the relations in the appendix.

Relational Calculus

Relational calculus expressions are formally defined by using *well-formed formulas* (WFFs). These definitions use *tuple variables* to represent tuples. Tuple variable names are the same as relation names. If a tuple variable R represents a tuple r at some point, then $R.A.$ represents the A-component of r, where A is an attribute of R. A *term* is then defined as

⟨variable component⟩   ⟨condition⟩ ┬ ⟨variable component⟩ ┬
                                    └ ⟨constant⟩ ─────────────┘

where ⟨variable component⟩: = ⟨tuple variable⟩.⟨attribute name⟩, and condition includes binary operations such as =, NEQ, >, ≥, <, ≤. Thus valid terms are

STORES.LOCATED-IN-CITY = BOSTON   or   ITEMS.WEIGHT > 30

All tuple variables in a term are defined to be *free*.

In defining a WFF, we use symbols commonly found in predicate calculus. These symbols are negation ($\lnot$), the existential quantifier ($\exists$), and the universal quantifier ($\forall$).

Codd defines a WFF as follows:

1. Any term is a WFF.
2. If x is a WFF, so is (x) and $\lnot x$. All free tuple variables in x remain free in (x) and $\lnot x$, and all bound tuple variables in x remain bound in (x) and $\lnot x$.
3. If x, y are WFFs, then so are $x \land y$ and $x \lor y$. All free tuple variables in x and y remain free in $x \land y$ and $x \lor y$, and all bound tuple variables in x and y remain bound in $x \land y$ and $x \lor y$.
4. If x is a WFF containing a free tuple variable T, then $\exists T(x)$ and $\forall T(x)$ are WFFs. T now becomes a bound tuple variable, but any other free tuple variables remain free. All bound terms in x remain bound in $\exists T(x)$ and $\forall T(x)$.
5. No other formulas are WFFs.

Examples of WFFs are

HOLD.ITEM-ID = ITEMS.ITEM-ID $\land$ ITEMS.WEIGHT > 30

$\exists$ ITEMS (ITEMS.SIZE = 'SMALL' $\land$ ITEMS.ITEM-ID
$\qquad$ = HOLD.ITEM-ID)

HOLD and ITEMS are free variables in the first WFF. In the second WFF only HOLD is free, whereas ITEMS is bound. Bound and free variables are important in formulating calculus expressions. A calculus expression takes the form

RETRIEVE ⎯⎯⎯ ⟨tuple variable⟩.⟨attribute name⟩ ⎯⎯⎯ WHERE ⟨WFF⟩

so that all tuple variables preceding WHERE are free in the WFF.

Examples of calculus expressions are

1. RETRIEVE STORES.STORE-ID WHERE

    STORES.LOCATED-IN-CITY = 'BOSTON'

Here the STORE-IDs of all stores in BOSTON are retrieved.

2. RETRIEVE HOLD.STORE-ID WHERE

∃ ITEMS (ITEMS.SIZE = 'SMALL' AND ITEMS.ITEM-ID
= HOLD.ITEM-ID)

Here all STORE-IDs of stores that hold small items are retrieved.

3. RETRIEVE STORES.STORE-ID WHERE

∀ ITEMS (∃ HOLD (ITEMS.ITEM-ID = HOLD.ITEM-ID
∧ HOLD.STORE-ID = STORES.STORE-ID))

Here the STORE-IDs of all stores that hold all the items are retrieved.

QUEL

The closest implementation of relational calculus is the language QUEL. This language is supported by the INGRES relational database management system.

In QUEL all tuple variables are first defined by RANGE statements. Thus all BOSTON stores are retrieved by the statement

RANGE OF X IS STORES
RETRIEVE X.STORE-ID WHERE X.LOCATED-IN-CITY
= 'BOSTON'

The existential and universal quantifiers are not used in QUEL. Instead, all tuple variables appearing in the WFF but not in the target list are assumed to be existentially qualified. Thus stores that hold small items are retrieved by

RANGE OF X IS ITEMS
RANGE OF Y IS HOLD
RETRIEVE Y.STORE-ID WHERE X.STORE-ID = Y.STORE-ID
AND X.SIZE = 'SMALL'

Here X is assumed to be existentially qualified because it does not appear in the target list.

SQL

SQL (*S*tructured *Q*uery *L*anguage) is a relationally complete language. It was devised for and is currently implemented by the System R database management system.

The basic construct of SQL is a mapping, whose syntax takes the form

```
SELECT   ⟨attribute⟩
FROM     ⟨relation⟩
WHERE    ⟨condition clause⟩
```

The simplest condition clause appears as

⟨attribute⟩   ⟨binary operator⟩   ⟨value⟩

The binary operators include $=$, NEQ, $\geq$, $\leq$, $>$, $<$.

The output from a mapping is a set of values. The values are chosen by selecting each relation row that satisfies the condition clause. The value of the attribute of each such selected row becomes part of the output.

The simplest use of this mapping is to retrieve all the values of a relation attribute. Thus

```
SELECT   STORE-ID
FROM     STORES
```

will output the STORE-ID of all tuples in relation STORES of the appendix. It is possible to output more than one attribute by including all the needed attributes after SELECT. Thus

```
SELECT   STORE-ID, PHONE
FROM     STORES
```

would output the STORE-ID together with its PHONE number. If all the store details are required, we can use

```
SELECT   *
FROM     STORES
```

This procedure will output all the attribute values of all stores. If only stores that satisfy some condition are needed, the mapping is extended to include a condition clause.

Thus, in reference to the relations in the appendix,

```
SELECT   STORE-ID
FROM     STORES
WHERE    LOCATED-IN-CITY = 'BOSTON';
```

would result in the output {ST-B, ST-C}.

As another example,

```
SELECT   ITEM-ID
FROM     ITEMS
WHERE    SIZE NEQ 'SMALL'
```

would result in the output {I2, I3}.

It is possible to specify compound conditions in SQL using AND and OR logic. Thus

```
SELECT   ITEM-ID
FROM     ITEMS
WHERE    SIZE = 'SMALL'
AND      WEIGHT > 10;
```

results in the output {I4}. There can be any number of such conditions separated by AND or OR in a mapping.

Optional features are available in SQL to order the output values and to allow or suppress the duplicate appearance of the same value. For example,

```
SELECT   STORE-ID
FROM     HOLD
WHERE    ITEM-ID = 'I4'
ORDER BY STORE-ID ASCENDING
```

would output all the STORE-IDs of stores that hold I4 in ascending sequence.

To suppress the duplicate appearance of a value, the word UNIQUE is included in the SELECT clause. For example,

```
SELECT   UNIQUE  ITEM-ID
FROM     HOLD
WHERE    QTY-HELD > 250
```

would ensure that each ITEM-ID that satisfies this condition appears only once in the output. If UNIQUE were not included, then I3 would appear twice in the output because its holding in stores ST-A and ST-B exceeds 250.

Nested Mappings in SQL

Nested mappings allow queries to span a number of relations. For example,

```
SELECT   ITEM-ID
FROM     HOLD
WHERE    STORE-ID IN SELECT STORE-ID
                     FROM    STORES
                     WHERE   LOCATED-IN-CITY
                                             = 'BOSTON';
```

results in the output {I1, I2, I3}—these are the parts held by BOSTON stores. The semantics of nesting can be explained by defining the output of each mapping as a set of values. If this is done, the preceding nested expression is the same as

```
SELECT   ITEM-ID
FROM     HOLD
WHERE    STORE-ID IN {the set of BOSTON stores}
```

where the set in brackets is found by the mapping

```
SELECT   STORE-ID
FROM     STORES
WHERE    LOCATED-IN-CITY = 'BOSTON';
```

The output from the lower-level mapping is {ST-B, ST-C}. When this output is used as input to the higher-level mapping, it results in the output of the set {I1, I2, I3} of ITEM-IDs. These are the ITEM-IDs held by Boston stores.

Experience with using SQL has led to the development of various alternatives for stating queries that span more than one relation. We will consider here three such alternatives, one involving the expression of relational joins, and the other two using the terms EXISTS or ANY.

Expressing Relational Joins   The relations to be joined are specified in the FROM clause, whereas the join condition is in the WHERE clause. Thus the previous query becomes

```
SELECT   ITEM-ID
FROM     HOLD, STORES
WHERE    HOLD.STORE-ID = STORES.STORE-ID
AND      STORES.LOCATED-IN-CITY = 'BOSTON'
```

Now attributes from more than one relation can appear in the WHERE clause. Relation names can precede the attribute names in the WHERE clause to resolve any naming ambiguities.

Retrievals Using EXISTS   The verb EXISTS in an SQL statement can represent the existential quantifier. The previous query now becomes

```
SELECT   ITEM-ID
FROM     HOLD
WHERE    EXISTS
         (SELECT  *
         FROM     STORES
         WHERE    STORE-ID = HOLD.STORE-ID
         AND      LOCATED-IN-CITY = 'BOSTON')
```

The expression in parentheses evaluates to true for a given HOLD tuple if there exists a STORES tuple that has a STORE-ID value equaling the value STORE-ID in the HOLD tuple and also has a LOCATED-IN-CITY value of 'BOSTON.' If the expression in brackets evaluates to true for a given HOLD tuple, the ITEM-ID value of that HOLD tuple is output.

Retrieval Using ANY   Now the previous query is expressed as

```
SELECT   ITEM-ID
FROM     HOLD
WHERE    STORE-ID = ANY (SELECT STORE-ID
                         FROM    STORES
                         WHERE   LOCATED-IN-CITY
                                              = 'BOSTON')
```

Here a HOLD tuple is selected if its STORE-ID value is ANY of the values output defined by the mapping in parentheses. The term = ANY is equivalent to IN in a nested mapping.

The term ANY can be used together with the binary or operators, $<$, $>$, NOT $>$, NOT $<$, $=$ $>$, or $=$ $<$. For example,

```
SELECT   ORDER-NO
FROM     ITEMS-ORDERED
WHERE    ITEM-ID = 'I2'
AND      QTY-ORDERED < ANY (SELECT   QTY-HELD
                           FROM     HOLD
                           WHERE    ITEM-ID = 'I2')
```

Here ORDER-NOs that contain item I2 are examined. The ORDER-NO is output if the QTY-ORDERED is less than some QTY-HELD of the holdings of the item in one store. The order can then be satisfied by withdrawals from one store.

Set Exclusion   It is also possible to specify nested conditions that include set exclusion. For example,

```
SELECT   ITEM-ID
FROM     HOLD
WHERE    STORE-ID NOT IN SELECT   STORE-ID
                         FROM     STORES
                         WHERE    LOCATED-IN-CITY
                                              = 'BOSTON';
```

Here items carried by stores not in BOSTON are output.

Compound Conditions   Nesting and compound conditions can be combined in query statements. To combine them it may be necessary to use brackets. For example,

```
SELECT   ITEM-ID
FROM     HOLD
WHERE    STORE-ID IN (SELECT   STORE-ID
                      FROM     STORES
                      WHERE    LOCATED-IN-CITY
                                           = 'BOSTON');
AND      QTY-HELD > 20;
```

Here AND QTY-HELD > 20 is not within the brackets. It is therefore considered to be in the mapping that includes HOLD. If the brackets were not included, this AND clause would be considered to be in the mapping that includes STORES; a diagnostic would be output because QTY-HELD is not an attribute of STORES.

Functions

Functions allow the user to specify AVG, MAX, MIN, and COUNT of a selected set of attributes. Thus

```
SELECT   AVG (QTY-HELD)
FROM     HOLD
WHERE    STORE-ID = 'ST-A'
```

output the average amount of each part held by store ST-A.

Grouping and Partitioning

A relation may be partitioned into groups according to the values of some attribute and then a function applied to each group. For example,

```
SELECT       STORE-ID
FROM         HOLD
GROUP BY     STORE-ID
HAVING SUM (QTY-HELD) > 500
```

will output {ST-A, ST-B}. Here all rows are grouped by STORE-ID, and the attribute columns QTY-HELD are summed for each group. Thus for ST-A the SUM is 1050; for ST-B, 700; for ST-C, 400; and for ST-D, 250. Only ST-A and ST-B satisfy the conditions.

Set Comparison

The syntax to allow set comparison is more complex than that for partitioning and uses set operators, $\supseteq$, $\subseteq$, $=$, or CONTAINS. For example, suppose all stores that hold all the small items are to be output. The set of small items is found by

```
SELECT   ITEM-ID
FROM     ITEMS
WHERE    SIZE = 'SMALL'
```

To find stores that carry all these items, the syntax is

```
SELECT      STORE-ID
FROM        HOLD
GROUP BY    STORE-ID
HAVING SET (ITEM-ID) CONTAINS SELECT   ITEM-ID
                              FROM     ITEMS
                              WHERE    SIZE = 'SMALL';
```

The GROUP BY clause is here used to group rows by STORE-ID and then apply the set operation CONTAINS on the values in each group. The output will be the set {ST-A} because store ST-A is the only store that carries both I1 and I4 (these being the small items).

Relational Algebra

The *relational algebra* consists of a set of relational algebra operators. Each operator has one or more relations as its input and produces a relation as its output. The four basic relational algebra operations are SELECTION, PROJECTION, JOINING, and DIVISION.

Selection

The SELECT operator selects all tuples from some relation, $R1$, such that some attributes in each tuple satisfies some condition. A new relation, which contains the selected tuples, is then created.

As an example, suppose we have the relation STORES in Figure 2.20. The operation

$R1$ = SELECT STORES WHERE LOCATED-IN-CITY = 'BOSTON'

will select all tuples for stores that are located in 'BOSTON,' and create the new relation $R1$ shown in Figure 2.20.

We can impose conditions on more than one attribute. For example,

$R2$ = SELECT STORES WHERE LOCATED-IN-CITY = 'BOSTON' AND NO-BINS > 100

This operation would select only one tuple from the relation STORES, namely, the one where STORE-ID is 'ST-B'.

Projection

The projection operator constructs a new relation from some existing relation by selecting only specified attributes of the existing relation and eliminating duplicate tuples in the newly formed relation. For example,

RELATION: STORES

STORE-ID	PHONE	LOCATED-IN-CITY	NO-BINS
ST-A	667932	ALBANY	200
ST-B	725172	BOSTON	310
ST-C	636182	BOSTON	75
ST-D	679305	CHICAGO	105

RELATION: *R1*

STORE-ID	PHONE	LOCATED-IN-CITY	NO-BINS
ST-B	725172	BOSTON	310
ST-C	636182	BOSTON	75

Figure 2.20   The SELECT operation

$R3 = $ PROJECT   STORES   OVER   STORE-ID, LOCATED-IN-CITY

results in the relation $R3$ shown in Figure 2.21. The operation

$R4 = $ PROJECT   STORES   OVER   LOCATED-IN-CITY

results in the relation $R4$ shown in Figure 2.21. We have eliminated one duplicate line here.

Joining

Joining is a method of combining two or more relations into a single relation. At the outset it requires the choice of attributes to match tuples in the relations. Tuples in different relations, but with the same value of matching attributes, are combined into a single tuple in the output relation. Suppose in addition to the relation STORES, we also have the relation ITEMS, shown in Figure 2.22.

RELATION: *R3*

STORE-ID	LOCATED-IN-CITY
ST-A	ALBANY
ST-B	BOSTON
ST-C	BOSTON
ST-D	CHICAGO

RELATION: *R4*

LOCATED-IN-CITY
ALBANY
BOSTON
CHICAGO

Figure 2.21   The PROJECT operation

RELATION: ITEMS

STORE-ID	ITEM-NO	QTY
ST-A	I1	50
ST-A	I2	17
ST-B	I3	20
ST-C	I1	30
ST-C	I4	11
ST-C	I3	56

RELATION: R5

STORE-ID	PHONE	LOCATED-IN-CITY	NO-BINS	ITEM-NO	QTY
ST-A	667932	ALBANY	200	I1	50
ST-A	667932	ALBANY	200	I2	17
ST-B	725172	BOSTON	310	I3	20
ST-C	636182	BOSTON	75	I1	30
ST-C	636182	BOSTON	75	I4	11
ST-C	636182	BOSTON	75	I3	56

Figure 2.22   The JOIN operation

Relation ITEMS contains the number of items held by each store. We can now join the two relations, ITEMS and STORES (Figure 2.20), using the common attribute, STORE-ID, by the operation

> $R5$ = JOIN ITEMS, STORES OVER STORE-ID

The result is the relation R5 shown in Figure 2.22.

The attribute STORE-ID has been chosen as the matching attribute in both relations. The condition of the join is that tuples that have the same value of matching attributes in relations ITEMS and STORES are combined into a single tuple in the new relation, $R5$. Conditions of join may be other than equality, and we may, for example, define a "greater-than" or "less-than" join.

In an equi-join, two tuples are combined if their values of the two nominated attributes are the same. In a greater-than join, two tuples would be combined if the value of one nominated attribute is greater than the value of another nominated attribute. Consider, for instance, the relations in the appendix and the join operation

> $R8$ = JOIN ITEMS-ORDERED, HOLD OVER ITEM-ID, AND
>   QTY-ORDERED < QTY-HELD/10

RELATION: *R9*   RELATION: *R6*   RELATION: *R7*

COMPANY	LOCATION
C1	BOSTON
C2	CHICAGO
C1	WASHINGTON
C3	BOSTON
C2	NEW YORK
C3	NEW YORK
C3	CHICAGO

LOCATION
BOSTON
NEW YORK

COMPANY
C3

Figure 2.23 The DIVISION operation

The relation *R8* would contain tuples that are combinations of tuples with the same ITEM-NO in both ITEMS-ORDERED and HOLD but where QTY-HELD in the HOLD tuple is greater than 10 times the value of QTY-ORDERED in the ITEMS-ORDERED tuple.

Division

In its simplest form this operation has a binary relation $R(X, Y)$ as the dividend and a divisor that includes Y. The output is a set, S, of values of X such that $x \in S$ if there is a row (x, y) in R for each y value in the divisor.

Suppose we have the two relations R9 and R6 shown in Figure 2.23. If *R9* is the dividend and *R6* the divisor, then $R7 = R9/R6$. In the figure, C3 is the only company for which there is a row with Boston and New York (i.e., ⟨C3, Boston⟩ and ⟨C3, New York⟩) in *R9*. The other companies, C1 and C2, do not satisfy this condition.

SUMMARY

The relational model has become important in database design for three reasons:

1. Its tabular interface can be easily understood by both database users and computer professionals and hence serves as a communication tool between them.
2. It can be readily converted to computer system implementations.
3. It provides formal criteria for a good data representation.

The goal of relational design is to structure the database as a set of normal relations. Definitions of normal form use the notion of functional dependency. A set of attributes X is functionally dependent on another set of attributes Y if a given set of values for each attribute of Y determines a unique value for each of the attributes in X. The notation $Y \rightarrow X$ is used to denote that X is functionally dependent on Y.

Of the number of levels of normal form relations, a high level is the Boyce–Codd normal form (BCNF). A relation is in BCNF if every determinant in the relation is a relation key.

It is important to start designs with a minimum set of FDs. A membership algorithm can be used to find redundant FDs, given a set of FDs.

A language that can be used to access data in a relational database is characterized by its syntactic interface and its selective power. The selective power of relational languages is based on relational completeness, which stems from relational calculus expressions. A language is relationally complete if it can derive any data that can be obtained from a relational calculus expression. Among the chapter's examples of relational languages is the language SQL, which can be used to retrieve sets of attribute values of tuples that satisfy selection conditions. SQL is oriented towards on-line database access. Another language is relational algebra, which is more appropriate than SQL for batch operations. Relational algebra creates new relations from existing relations by using a set of relational algebra operations.

PROBLEMS

Problem 1

The contents (or instances) of a relation must be consistent with the FDs between attributes of the relation. Figure 2.24 shows three instances of relation $R1$. Consider the following three sets of FDs. Which of the instances in Figure 2.24 are consistent with these three sets of FDs?

- *Set 1*   NAME $\rightarrow$ ADDRESS, DATE-MOVED-IN
          ADDRESS $\rightarrow$ NO-ROOMS
- *Set 2*   NAME, ADDRESS $\rightarrow$ DATE-MOVED-IN
          ADDRESS $\rightarrow$ NO-ROOMS
- *Set 3*   NAME, ADDRESS $\rightarrow$ DATE-MOVED-IN, NO-ROOMS
          NAME, DATE-MOVED-IN $\rightarrow$ ADDRESS

RELATION: *R*1

NAME	ADDRESS	DATE-MOVED-IN	NO-ROOMS
JOE	ADD1	010179	7
JILL	ADD2	030380	9
JIM	ADD3	040481	20

INSTANCE 1

RELATION: *R*1

NAME	ADDRESS	DATE-MOVED-IN	NO-ROOMS
JOE	ADD1	010179	7
JOE	ADD4	010179	20
JILL	ADD2	030380	9
JIM	ADD3	040481	20
JOHN	ADD4	040481	20

INSTANCE 2

RELATION: *R*1

NAME	ADDRESS	DATE-MOVED-IN	NO-ROOMS
JOE	ADD1	010179	7
JOE	ADD4	020279	16
JILL	ADD2	030380	9
JIM	ADD3	040481	20
JOHN	ADD4	040481	17

INSTANCE 3

Figure 2.24 Instances of relation for Problem 1

Problem 2

The relation instance must be consistent with the FDs between its items for all time, and any new added tuples must conform with these FDs.

Consider INSTANCE 1 and CASE 2 in Problem 1. Would the following operations be valid?

add (JOE, ADD4, 050581, 17):
add (JIM, ADD5, 040481, 30);
add (JILL, ADD1, 070781, 9);

Problem 3

Sometimes the current contents of a relation seem to suggest FDs that do not actually exist in the information. For example, consider the relation WORK in Figure 2.25. The contents seem to suggest that OPERATOR → MACHINE. However, you must remember that the FDs are determined by the nature of the information rather than by the instantaneous contents of the relation. Suppose the new tuple ⟨MACH1, MAY, SHIRT, 101081⟩ is added to WORK. Obviously, OPERATOR → MACHINE no longer holds. What other FDs appear to hold in WORK, and what do they imply in the organization? (Assume for this last question that the instance of WORK is as shown in Figure 2.25 and does not include the new tuple.)

RELATION: WORK

MACHINE	OPERATOR	TYPE-OF-ITEM-MADE	DATE
MACH1	ANDRE	FROCK	070781
MACH1	ANDRE	BLOUSE	080881
MACH2	JILLIAN	HAT	080881
MACH2	MAY	SKIRT	090981

Figure 2.25 Relation WORK

How would you formulate the following conditions in the organization as FDs?

(a) An operator can work on only one machine on the same day.
(b) The condition in (a) applies, and each machine has only one operator on the same day.
(c) Each TYPE-OF-ITEM-MADE (e.g., SKIRT, HAT) must be made on the same machine.

Problem 4

Consider the following FDs:

    PROJECT-NO → START-DATE, PLANNED-END-DATE
    PROJECT-NO, ITEM-NO → QTY-USED
    ITEM-NO → COST

and the relation PROJECT-USE in Figure 2.26.

RELATION: PROJECT-USE

PROJECT-NO	ITEM-NO	QTY-USED	START-DATE	PLANNED-END-DATE	COST
PROJ1	X7	9	JAN 80	MARCH 81	10.11
PROJ1	X9	11	JAN 80	MARCH 81	22.30
PROJ1	X10	20	JAN 80	MARCH 81	5.50
PROJ2	X9	17	JUNE 80	JULY 81	22.30
PROJ2	X6	12	JUNE 80	JULY 81	6.70

Figure 2.26 Relation PROJECT-USE

Remember that to avoid anomalies, the use of additions, deletions, or updates of single *n*-tuples should not result in inconsistencies in the relation or remove unintended information.

Do the following result in any anomalies?

(a) Add the fact that PROJ2 has used part X7:

   add (PROJ2, X7, 17, JUN80, AUG81, 10.11)

(b) Change the planned end date of PROJ1:

   update (PROJ1, X7, 9, JAN80, MARCH81, 10.11) to
   (PROJ1, X7, 9, JAN80, MAY81, 10.11)

(c) Change the price of X9:

   update (PROJ1, X9, 11, JAN80, MARCH81, 22.30) to
   (PROJ1, X9, 11, JAN80, MARCH81, 24.10)

(d) Delete the fact that PROJ2 has used X6.

   delete (PROJ2, X6, 12, JUNE80, JULY81, 6.70)

(e) Add the new part X20 and its cost $6.60.

Is the relation PROJECT-USE in 3NF? If not, how would you decompose PROJECT-USE to normal relations? Once decomposition is done, is it possible to avoid any of the earlier anomalies?

Problem 5

Draw FD diagrams for the following:

(a) There can be any number of PERSON employed in a DEPT, but each PERSON is assigned to one department only.

(b) The PRICE-OF-ITEM is determined by the ITEM-NAME and the STORE in which the item is sold.

(c) A PERSON occupies a POSITION in an organization. The PERSON starts in a POSITION at a given START-TIME and relinquishes it at a given END-TIME. At most one POSITION can be occupied by one person at a given time.

(d) A TASK is defined within a PROJECT; TASK is a unique name within the project. TASK-START is the start time of the TASK, and TASK-COST is its cost.

Problem 6

(a) Explain why $R1$ is in 1NF but not 2NF.

$$R1 = (\{A, B, C, D\}, \{B \rightarrow D, \ AB \rightarrow C\})$$

(b) Explain why $R2$ is in 2NF but not 3NF.

$$R2 = (\{A, B, C, D, E\}, \{AB \rightarrow CE, \ E \rightarrow AB, \ C \rightarrow D\})$$

(c) Explain why $R3$ is in 3NF but not BCNF.

$$R3 = (\{A, B, C, D\}, \{B \leftrightarrow D, \ AB \rightarrow C\})$$

(d) What is the highest normal form of each of the following relations?

$$R1 = (\{A, B, C\}, \{A \leftrightarrow B, \ A \rightarrow C\})$$
$$R2 = (\{A, B, C\}, \{A \leftrightarrow B, \ C \rightarrow A\})$$
$$R3 = (\{A, B, C, D\}, \{A \rightarrow C, \ D \rightarrow B\})$$
$$R4 = (\{A, B, C, D\}, \{A \rightarrow C, \ CD \rightarrow B\})$$

Problem 7

Consider the FD diagram in Figure 2.27. Are the following relations in 1NF, 2NF, or 3NF form, or are they not in any of these normal forms? What are the keys of the relation in each case?

(a) (SALE-NO, ITEM-IN-SALE, QTY-SOLD)

(b) (SALE-NO, ITEM-IN-SALE, ITEM-PRICE, QTY-SOLD)

(c) (SALE-NO, ITEM-IN-SALE, QTY-SOLD, REGION)

(d) (SALE-NO, QTY-SOLD)

(e) (SELLER, ITEM-IN-SALE, QTY-SOLD)

(f) (SALE-NO, SELLER, REGION)

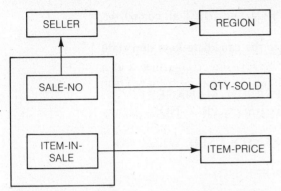

Figure 2.27 Functional dependencies for Problem 7

Problem 8

Following are a number of relations, together with the FDs between the items in each relation. For each relation, state

(a) all the candidate keys in the relation
(b) the highest normal form of the relation

$$R1 = (\{W, X, Y, Z\}, \{XY \rightarrow Z, Y \rightarrow W\})$$
$$R2 = (\{A, B, C, D\}, \{A \rightarrow BC, C \rightarrow D\})$$
$$R3 = (\{K, L, M, N\}, \{KL \rightarrow N, K \rightarrow M\})$$
$$R4 = (\{P, Q, R, S\}, \{P \rightarrow Q, Q \rightarrow R, R \rightarrow S\})$$
$$R5 = (\{T, U, V\}, \{T \rightarrow U, U \rightarrow T, T \rightarrow V\})$$
$$R6 = (\{W, X, Y, Z\}, \{WY \rightarrow XZ, Z \rightarrow W, YZ \rightarrow W\})$$
$$R7 = (\{A, B, C, D\}, \{AB \rightarrow D, AC \rightarrow D\})$$
$$R8 = (\{K, L, M, N\}, \{KL \rightarrow N, KM \rightarrow NL, L \rightarrow M\})$$

Problem 9

Consider the following FDs:

PERSON-NO → NAME, DEPT-OF-PERSON
PROJ-NO → BUDGET, START-DATE, DEPT-OF-PROJ
PERSON-NO, PROJ-NO, WEEK-NO → TIME-SPENT
ITEM-NO → COST
PROJ-NO, ITEM-NO → QTY-USED
DEPT → MANAGER

(Note that DEPT-OF-PERSON, DEPT-OF-PROJ, and DEPT all come from the same domain.)

For each of the following relations, nominate the candidate keys and state whether the relation is BCNF.

R1 = (PERSON-NO, NAME, DEPT-OF-PERSON, MANAGER)
R2 = (PERSON-NO, NAME, DEPT-OF-PERSON, PROJ-NO,
        WEEK-NO, TIME-SPENT)
R3 = (PROJ-NO, ITEM-NO, PERSON-NO, QTY-USED, WEEK-NO,
        TIME-SPENT)
R4 = (PROJ-NO, ITEM, PERSON-NO, WEEK-NO)

Problem 10

Consider the following FDs:

PROJ-NO → PROJ-NAME
PROJ-NO → START-DATE
PROJ-NO, MACHINE-NO → TIME-USED-ON-PROJECT
MACHINE-NO, PERSON-NO → TIME-USED-BY-PERSON

Are the following relations in BCNF?

R1 = (PROJ-NO, MACHINE-NO, PROJ-NAME,
        TIME-USED-ON-PROJECT)
R2 = (PROJ-NO, PERSON-NO, MACHINE-NO,
        TIME-USED-ON-PROJECT)
R3 = (PROJ-NO, PERSON-NO, MACHINE-NO)

Problem 11

Consider Figure 2.28. For each case, if column A is true, is column B also true?

COLUMN A COLUMN B

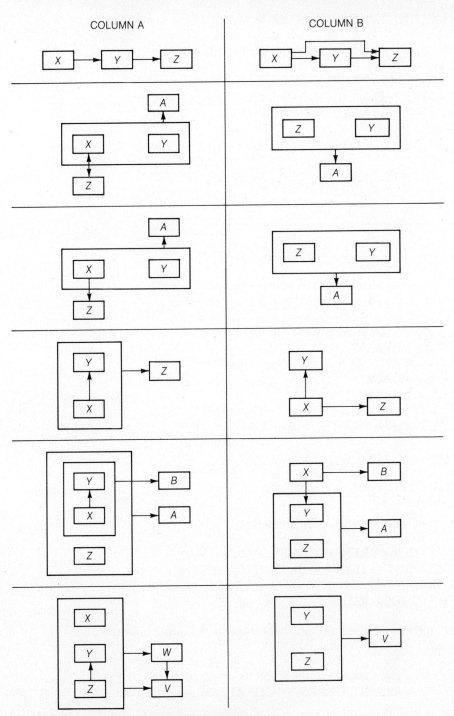

Figure 2.28 Functional dependencies for Problem 11

Problem 12

Remove any redundant FDs from the following sets of FDs.

Set 1	Set 2	Set 3
$A \rightarrow B$	$XY \rightarrow V$	$PQ \rightarrow R$
$B \rightarrow C$	$ZW \rightarrow V$	$PS \rightarrow Q$
$AD \rightarrow C$	$VX \rightarrow Y$	$QS \rightarrow P$
	$W \rightarrow Y$	$PR \rightarrow Q$
	$Z \rightarrow X$	$S \rightarrow R$

Problem 13

Following are a number of sets of FDs. Examine each set for nonredundancy, identifying any redundant FDs and proposing a minimal covering.

Set 1	Set 2	Set 3
$A \rightarrow BC$	$P \rightarrow RST$	$KM \rightarrow N$
$AC \rightarrow Z$	$VRT \rightarrow SQP$	$K \rightarrow LM$
$Z \rightarrow B$	$PS \rightarrow T$	$LN \rightarrow K$
$AB \rightarrow Z$	$Q \rightarrow TR$	$MP \rightarrow K$
	$QS \rightarrow P$	$P \rightarrow N$
	$SR \rightarrow V$	

Problem 14

Suppose we have the following relations in a database:

STUDENT (NAME, ADDRESS, COURSE, *STUDENT-ID*)
UNIT-ENROLLMENT (*STUDENT-ID, UNIT,* SEMESTER)
UNIT-LECTURER (*UNIT, LECTURER-IN-CHARGE,* SEMESTER)
UNIT-OFFER (SCHOOL, *UNIT*)

Use relational algebra to derive relations that enable the following information to be obtained.

(a) All units taken by a given student in the student's course of study
(b) All lecturers that were LECTURERS-IN-CHARGE at some time for a given student

(c) The courses of students enrolled in a particular unit in a given semester
(d) The schools in which a particular student took any unit at some time
(e) Were two students (x and y) ever enrolled in the same unit in the same semester

---

Problem 15

Suppose you are given the relational database shown in the appendix. How would you retrieve the following information by using SQL and relational algebra?

(a) The STORE-ID of stores located in BOSTON
(b) The ITEM-NO of the small items whose weight exceeds 10
(c) The ORDER-DATE of orders made by VICKI
(d) The location of stores that hold items with DESCR 'WINDOW'
(e) The stores that hold items in orders made by JILL
(f) The stores that hold all the small items
(g) The stores that hold all the items in order ORD1
(h) The total QTY of items held by each store
(i) The ITEM-ID of items that are included in orders made by VICKI and held by BOSTON stores

chapter three
Relational Design

INTRODUCTION

The relational model is attractive in database design because it provides formal criteria for logical structure, namely, normal form relations. The problem, then, is to choose a design procedure to produce normal form relations. Two different approaches have been proposed:

1. Decomposition procedures. These commence with a set of one or more relations and decompose nonnormal relations in this set into normal forms.
2. Synthesis procedures. These commence with a set of functional dependencies and use them to construct normal form relations.

Synthesis procedures appear to be more attractive than decomposition procedures in practical situations. Most designs commence with an information-gathering phase in which a set of data elements and the FDs between them are identified. The information is then used to produce normal relations. On the other hand, one could conceive of a procedure where all the data attributes are considered to form one relation, which is then decomposed in subsequent design steps. But this is not a likely procedure in a practical situation. Irrespective of their class, all design methods must satisfy the same design criteria.

THE UNIVERSAL RELATION ASSUMPTION

Before we go into relational design procedures, you should be aware of an assumption that underlies not only most such procedures but also the functional dependence theory described in Chapter 2. The *universal relation* is a term used to describe a single relation that is made up of all the attributes known to the enterprise. The universal relation also contains all the enterprise data.

Formally, the existence of a universal relation assumes that we can start with a set of relations, S, and construct a single relation, U, such that

1. U contains all the columns of the relations, S.
2. Each relation in S is a projection of its columns on U.

Perhaps the most obvious consequence of a universal relation assumption is that column names in relations must have a global rather than a local meaning. For example, it would be meaningless to have the three relations

$R1 = (\{$PERSON-ID, DATE$\}, \{$PERSON-ID $\rightarrow$ DATE$\})$
$R2 = (\{$ITEM, QTY, DATE$\}, \{$ITEM, DATE $\rightarrow$ QTY$\})$
$R3 = (\{$ITEM, PERSON-ID, QTY$\}, \{$ITEM, PERSON-ID $\rightarrow$ QTY$\})$

where DATE in $R1$ is the date of birth of a person, whereas DATE in $R2$ is the date on which a given QTY of an ITEM was delivered. Relation $R3$ describes the quantity of an ITEM used by each person. Pseudotransitivity can now be applied to the two FDs in $R1$ and $R2$ to yield

ITEM, PERSON-ID $\rightarrow$ QTY

which is an obviously meaningless derivation because it assumes that DATE has the same meaning in $R1$ as in $R2$. What is worse, this derivation suggests that relation $R3$ is redundant. This problem does not occur if global names are used for attributes. In this case the relations would become

$R1 = (\{$PERSON-ID, DATE-BORN-ON$\},$
    $\{$PERSON-ID $\rightarrow$ DATE-BORN-ON$\})$
$R2 = (\{$ITEM, QTY-DELIVERED, DATE-DELIVERED$\},$
    $\{$ITEM, DATE-DELIVERED $\rightarrow$ QTY-DELIVERED$\})$
$R3 = (\{$ITEM, PERSON-ID, QTY-USED$\},$
    $\{$ITEM, PERSON-ID $\rightarrow$ QTY-USED$\})$

Now the pseudotransitivity reduction could not be applied, as the dates have different names in both relations.

The consequence of using global names is that designers must invent column or attribute names to ensure their global uniqueness, an often cumbersome process. Usually the names are concatenations of attribute domains and their roles in a relation. For example,

DATE-DELIVERED
DATE-DELIVERED-BY-SUPPLIER
DATE-USED-BY-PROJECT
QTY-USED-BY-DEPT
QTY-USED-BY-DEPT-ON-PROJECT

and so on.

Like designers, many workers in the field question the usefulness of a universal relation. In particular, they claim that in many cases the universal relation is ill-defined and not suitable for practical applications. Frequently the form of the universal relation itself is not unique. In many cases the universal relation also has obvious undesirable properties. For example, consider the data in relations PERSONS and PROJECTS in Figure 3.1. Given these two relations, it is clear that the universal relation that represents them must contain all their attributes. However, it is not clear how the actual data are to be stored in the universal relation. The data in PERSONS and PROJECTS are unrelated, and it is not clear whether data from different relations should appear in the same tuples (as in UR2) or in different tuples (as in UR1). Irrespective of the choice, both UR1 and UR2 have one undesirable property: some values are null. It is also possible to populate the universal relation with a cross-product of the data in relations PERSONS and PROJECTS. The outcome is relation UR3. Now there are no null values in UR3, but UR3 contains duplicate data; for example, the fact that JOHN is assigned to DEP1 is stored three times. This situation can lead to the kind of anomalies described in Chapter 2. Yet each of the three universal relations in Figure 3.1 yields PERSONS and PROJECTS by projection. Thus

PERSONS = PROJECT ⟨universal relation⟩ OVER PERSON, DEPT
PROJECTS = PROJECTS ⟨universal relation⟩ OVER PROJECT,
ITEM, QTY-USED

are the same for each of the universal relations, UR1, UR2, and UR3.

The example in Figure 3.1 only shows one problem resulting from the universal relation assumption. W. Kent (1981) describes a multitude of others.

You should keep these facts in mind for the rest of this chapter. Many of the results presented in this chapter, especially those stemming from multivalued dependency, are based on the universal relation assumption. Reference will be made to this assumption whenever necessary to note its effect on the design process.

RELATIONAL DESIGN CRITERIA

Beeri and co-workers (1978) have identified three relational design criteria:

1. *Representation:* The final structure must correctly represent the original specifications.
2. *Separation:* The original specifications are separated into relations that satisfy certain conditions.
3. *Redundancy:* The final structure must not contain any redundant information.

We discussed the separation criterion in Chapter 2, where it was pointed out that the database must be separated into a number of normal form relations. The other two criteria are relatively general. In specific terms each can be ap-

PERSONS

NAME	DEPT
JOHN	DEP1
JANE	DEP2
MARY	DEP1

PROJECTS

PROJECT	ITEM	QTY-USED
PROJ1	ITEM1	5
PROJ1	ITEM2	9
PROJ2	ITEM2	11
PROJ2	ITEM3	7

UR1

NAME	DEPT	PROJECT	ITEM	QTY-USED
JOHN	DEP1	–	–	–
JANE	DEP2	–	–	–
MARY	DEP1	–	–	–
–	–	PROJ1	ITEM1	5
–	–	PROJ1	ITEM2	9
–	–	PROJ2	ITEM2	11
–	–	PROJ2	ITEM3	7

UR2

NAME	DEPT	PROJECT	ITEM	QTY-USED
JOHN	DEP1	PROJ1	ITEM1	5
JANE	DEP2	PROJ1	ITEM2	9
MARY	DEP1	PROJ2	ITEM2	11
–	–	PROJ2	ITEM3	7

UR3

NAME	DEPT	PROJECT	ITEM	QTY-USED
JOHN	DEP1	PROJ1	ITEM1	5
JOHN	DEP1	PROJ1	ITEM2	9
JOHN	DEP1	PROJ2	ITEM2	11
JOHN	DEP1	PROJ2	ITEM3	7
JANE	DEP2	PROJ1	ITEM1	5
JANE	DEP2	PROJ1	ITEM2	9
JANE	DEP2	PROJ1	ITEM2	11
JANE	DEP2	PROJ2	ITEM3	7
MARY	DEP1	PROJ1	ITEM1	5
MARY	DEP1	PROJ1	ITEM2	9
MARY	DEP1	PROJ2	ITEM2	11
MARY	DEP1	PROJ2	ITEM3	7

Figure 3.1 Constructing a universal relation

plied to attributes, FDs, or data. To define the criteria more specifically, we need a notation for relations and for the input and output of a design process.

The notation for relations was introduced in Chapter 2. You will recall that a relation is defined as made up of two components, the *attributes* and the *FDs between the attributes*. The definition takes the form

$$R = (\{A, B, C\}, \{A \rightarrow B, A \rightarrow C\})$$

Here R comprises three attributes, A, B, and C. The FDs between these attributes are $A \rightarrow B$ and $A \rightarrow C$. The notation used to describe the input and output of the design process is S_{in} and S_{out}. Both S_{in} and S_{out} are sets of relations. Here S_{in} is the input to the design process and S_{out} is the output. Most theoretical work is based on the universal relation assumption and assumes that S_{in} is one relation, the universal relation, which is defined by a set of attributes and FDs, using the preceding notation, and that S_{out} is a set of normal relations, each of which is made up of a set of attributes and a set of FDs.

Satisfying Representation Criteria

One goal of any design process is to produce an output design, S_{out}, to accurately represent S_{in}. Further, all the relations in S_{out} must satisfy the conditions for normal form. C. Beeri and co-workers (1978) have defined three representation criteria for the representation of S_{in} by S_{out}:

- REP1: The relations S_{out} contain the same attributes as S_{in}.
- REP2: The relations S_{out} contain the same attributes and the same FDs as S_{in}.
- REP3: The relations in S_{out} contain the same attributes and the same data as S_{in}.

The first of these, REP1, is trivial. It requires all the attributes in S_{in} to also appear in the relations in S_{out}. But it does not consider any dependencies between the attributes.

In regard to REP2, recall that S_{in} is defined as a set of attributes and FDs and that each relation in S_{out} will also contain a set of attributes and a set of FDs. Representation REP2 requires that each FD in S_{in} be either

- contained as an FD in one of the relations in S_{out} or
- derived from the FDs in the relations in S_{out}, using the FD inference rules.

For example, in Figure 3.2,

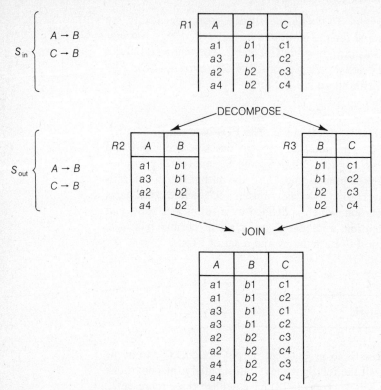

Figure 3.2   Decomposition

$$S_{in} = (\{A, B, C\}, \{A \rightarrow B, C \rightarrow B\})$$

and

$$S_{out} = (R2, R3)$$

where $R2 = (\{A, B\}, \{A \rightarrow B\})$ and $R3 = (\{B, C\}, \{C \rightarrow B\})$. Thus $R2$ and $R3$ constitute the decomposition by projection of S_{in}. Each of the FDs in S_{in} is contained in S_{out}; hence S_{out} is a REP2 representation of S_{in}.

Figure 3.3 shows a decomposition that is not a REP2 representation of S_{in}. Here

$$S_{in} = (\{X, Y, Z\}, \{YZ \rightarrow X, X \rightarrow Y, X \rightarrow Z\})$$

and

$$S_{out} = (Y1, Y2)$$

where $Y1 = (\{X, Y\}, \{X \rightarrow Y\})$ and $Y2 = (\{X, Z\}, \{X \rightarrow Z\})$. The FD $YZ \rightarrow X$ is not in any relation in S_{out}, nor can it be derived from the FDs in S_{out} by applying FD rules.

Representation REP3 also requires some explanation. Figure 3.2 includes a

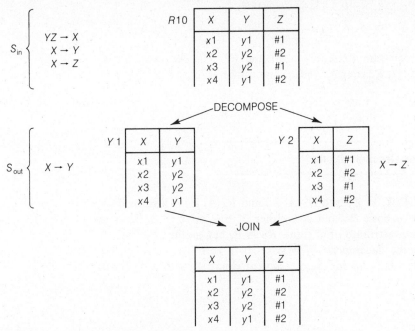

Figure 3.3 Another decomposition

relation $R1$ that is decomposed by projection into two relations, $R2$ and $R3$ in S_{out}. Note that $R2$ and $R3$ do not contain the same information as S_{in} as different responses are obtained to the same question applied to S_{in} and S_{out}. Say we ask: To what C is $a1$ related? In S_{in} the answer is $\{c1\}$ because there is only one tuple with value $a1$ in $R1$ and this tuple has the value $c1$ in column C of $R1$. In S_{out} the answer to the same question is $\{c1, c2\}$, because $a1$ appears in a tuple with the value $b1$ in $R2$. The value $b1$ appears in two tuples with $c1$ and $c2$ in $R3$. Hence S_{out} is not an REP3 representation of S_{in}. The information stored in S_{out} is the join of $R2$ and $R3$. This join, shown in Figure 3.2, contains additional tuples to those of S_{in} and is sometimes known as a *lossy join*. Hence S_{out} in Figure 3.2 is not an REP3 representation of S_{in}. Note that in Figure 3.3 the two relations $Y1$ and $Y2$ in S_{in} are an REP3 representation of S_{in} because their join contains exactly the same tuple as the original relation, $R10$.

Lossless Decompositions

Formally, a *lossless decomposition* can be described as follows. The decomposition of a relation $R(X, Y, Z)$ into relations $R1$ and $R2$ is defined by two projections:

- $R1$ = projection of R over X, Y
- $R2$ = projection of R over X, Z

where X is the set of common attributes in $R1$ and $R2$. The decomposition is *lossless* if R = join of $R1$, $R2$ over X. The decomposition is *lossy* if $R \subset$ join of $R1$, $R2$ over X.

Conditions for Lossless Decompositions

The decomposition of $R(X, Y, Z)$ into $R1(X, Y)$ and $R2(X, Z)$ is lossless if for attribute X, common to both $R1$ and $R2$, either $X \rightarrow Y$ or $X \rightarrow Z$. Thus in Figure 3.2 the common attribute of $R2$ and $R3$ is B, but neither $B \rightarrow A$ nor $B \rightarrow C$ is true, hence the decomposition is lossy. In Figure 3.3, however, the decomposition is lossless because for the common attribute X, both $X \rightarrow Y$ and $X \rightarrow Z$.

Redundancy Criteria

Redundancy criteria can be defined in various ways. One set of redundancy criteria is as follows:

- RED1: A relation in S_{out} is redundant if its attributes are contained in the other relations in S_{out}.
- RED2: A relation in S_{out} is redundant if its FDs are the same or can be derived from the FDs in the other relations in S_{out}.
- RED3: A relation in S_{out} is redundant if its content can be derived from the contents of other relations in S_{out}.

Obviously, RED1 is not a very useful criterion, because during separation it is often necessary to create separate relations that represent FDs between attributes, which may appear in other relations. On the other hand, RED2 and RED3 can be quite useful criteria. Any design algorithms should in particular avoid RED3 because it would keep the same data in more than one relation. Such relations could all be in normal form and no anomalies would occur in relations. However, interrelational anomalies would arise if some fact were updated in one relation but not the other. Designs that include RED2 would cause the same problem.

RELATIONAL DESIGN PROCEDURES

It is interesting to note that in Figure 3.2 the design S_{out} is an REP2 but not an REP3 representation of S_{in}, whereas in Figure 3.3 the design S_{out} is an REP3 but not an REP2 representation of S_{in}. This situation creates one of the thorny problems of relational theory research: namely, to find a design procedure that yields an S_{out} that is both an REP2 and an REP3 representation of S_{in}. Many available procedures yield designs that are only REP2 or only REP3 representations of S_{in}.

Similarly, design procedures should aim to reduce redundancy, but here again different design procedures can result in either RED2 or RED3 representations of S_{in}.

We will now consider some possible algorithms. They fall into two classes: decomposition and synthesis. Decomposition algorithms commence with one relation and successively decompose it into normal form relations. The concepts of 3NF and BCNF are not sufficient for decomposition algorithms, so the ideas of multivalued dependency and a fourth normal form have to be introduced. Synthesis algorithms, on the other hand, commence with a set of FDs and synthesize them into normal form relations.

Many algorithms have been proposed for relational design and each algorithm produces relations that satisfy some subset of the relational design criteria. It is not possible to describe all these algorithms here. The intention here is to describe a sample of algorithms and problems in devising them and then to show how some algorithms can overcome these problems.

DECOMPOSITION

In the decomposition of nonnormal relations into normal relations, we use an algorithm that removes functional dependency from nonnormal relations to create new relations.

Simple Decomposition Algorithm

Formally, the *decomposition algorithm* can be defined as follows:

1. Initialize S_{out} with one relation R where $R = S_{in}$.
2. Find an FD $X \rightarrow Y$ in $R(X, Y, Z, \ldots)$ where R is not in normal form and R is in S_{out}.

3. Decompose R by projection into $R1(X, Y)$, $R2(X, Z, \ldots)$; remove R from S_{out} and add $R1$ and $R2$ to S_{out}.
4. Repeat 1 and 2 on every relation in S_{out} until every relation is in normal form.

This algorithm can produce several versions of S_{out} from the same S_{in}. The design of S_{out} depends on which FD in R is removed first in step 1, as illustrated by the decomposition tree in Figure 3.4. The root of the tree is S_{in}. Each branch from the root is labeled by the FD that is removed from S_{in}. The branch terminates on a node that contains the decomposed relations. These relations at some node can in time be decomposed further. Again the branches emanating from the node are labeled by the FDs that are being removed and terminate on the newly decomposed relations. Figure 3.4 illustrates that the decomposition and the final solution depend on the sequence in which FDs are separated from the relations. One of the solutions, S_{out} (4), contains all the FDs in S_{in}. Hence S_{out} (4) is the only REP2 representation of S_{in}.

Note these two other properties of the reduction:

- It is an REP3 representation of S_{in}. The determinant of each removed relation is by definition the key of the relation, thus satisfying the conditions for lossless joins.
- S_{out} is in some cases redundant because it includes unnecessary relations.

Limitations of the Simple Decomposition Algorithm

One of the problems with the simple decomposition algorithm is that several attempts may be necessary before an REP2 nonredundant representation is found. This may not be a serious problem if the designer starts with a set of relations that are "close to normal" and each relation contains only a few FDs.

There are, however, more fundamental problems with this algorithm. To be universal, the algorithm must be applicable to any initial S_{in}. The algorithm tests relations to see if they are in BCNF and terminates when all relations are in BCNF. Some relations, however, that are in BCNF may still contain undesirable properties. Additional normal forms are then necessary to discover such relations and decompose them.

Consider Figure 3.5. Relation PROJECTS contains data about people assigned to projects and about parts used in a project. The key of relation PROJECTS is {PART, PROJECT, PERSON}. Relation PROJECTS is not in BCNF, because HRS-SPENT is functionally dependent on the subset {PERSON, PROJECT} of the key, and QTY-USED is functionally dependent on the subset {PROJECT, PART} of the key. If the simple decomposition algorithm is applied to PROJECTS, two decomposition sequences are possible, each of which results in

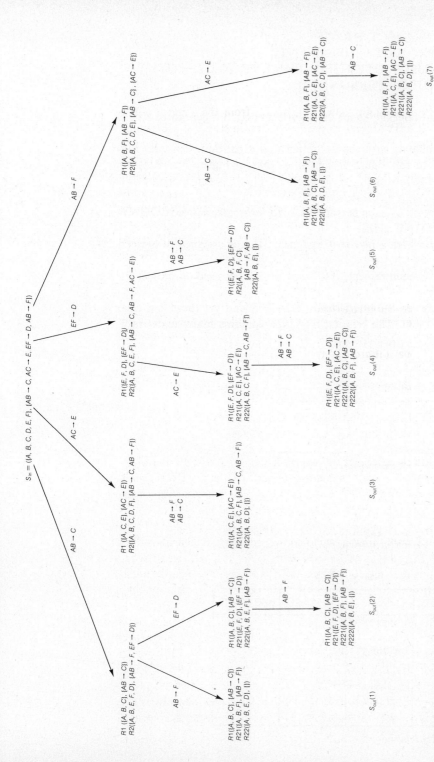

Figure 3.4 A decomposition tree

$R1 = (\{PERSON, PROJECT, HRS\text{-}SPENT\},$
   $\{PERSON, PROJECT \rightarrow HRS\text{-}SPENT\})$
$R2 = (\{PART, PROJECT, QTY\text{-}USED\}, \{PART, PROJECT \rightarrow QTY\})$
$R3 = (\{PART, PROJECT, PERSON\}, \{\ \})$

Here $R3$ is a redundant relation; hence the algorithm does not guarantee RED3 representation.

There are other problems with the decomposition algorithm. Consider Figure 3.6. The relation in this figure is similar to that in Figure 3.5. Relation STATUS contains the following:

1. The SKILLS possessed by each person; JILL, for example, has ACCOUNTING and COMPUTING skills.
2. The PROJECTs to which a person is assigned; JILL is assigned to projects P1 and P2.
3. The PARTS used on each project; NUT and BOLT are used on project P1.

There are no FDs between the attributes of STATUS and yet there is a clear relationship between them. The relation STATUS contains many undesirable

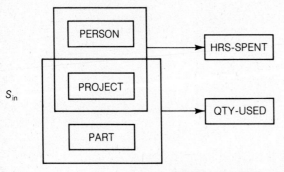

PERSON, PROJECT → HRS-SPENT
PART, PROJECT → QTY-USED

PROJECTS

PERSON	PROJECT	PART	QTY-USED	HRS-SPENT
JILL	P1	NUT	11	7
EDNA	P1	BOLT	7	17
JILL	P1	BOLT	7	7
EDNA	P1	NUT	11	17
JILL	P2	BOLT	7	32
JIM	P2	SCREW	9	45
JILL	P2	SCREW	9	32
JIM	P2	BOLT	7	45

Figure 3.5 PROJECTS relation

PERSON   SKILL

S_{in} PROJECT

PART

STATUS

PERSON	PROJECT	PART	SKILL
JILL	P1	NUT	ACCOUNTING
JILL	P1	BOLT	ACCOUNTING
JILL	P1	NUT	COMPUTING
JILL	P1	BOLT	COMPUTING
EDNA	P1	NUT	LAW
EDNA	P1	BOLT	LAW
EDNA	P1	NUT	COMMERCE
EDNA	P1	BOLT	COMMERCE
JILL	P2	BOLT	ACCOUNTING
JILL	P2	SCREW	ACCOUNTING
JILL	P2	BOLT	COMPUTING
JILL	P2	SCREW	COMPUTING
JIM	P2	BOLT	ECONOMICS
JIM	P2	SCREW	ECONOMICS
JIM	P2	BOLT	STATISTICS
JIM	P2	SCREW	STATISTICS
JIM	P2	BOLT	FRENCH
JIM	P2	SCREW	FRENCH

Figure 3.6   Relation STATUS

characteristics. For example, the fact that JILL has both ACCOUNTING and
COMPUTING skills is stored a number of times, as is the fact that P1 uses
NUTs and BOLTs. So we would like to decompose the relation. But it is not
possible to apply the simple decomposition algorithm to it because there are no
FDs between the relation attributes.

To deal with this situation, Fagin (1977) introduced the idea of multivalued
dependency and the fourth normal form.

Multivalued Dependency

Fourth normal form is based on the concept of *multivalued dependency* (MVD).
The notation $X \twoheadrightarrow Y$ is used to indicate that a set of attributes Y shows a multivalued dependency on a set of attributes of X.

Contrary to FDs, MVDs are not properties of the information represented by relations. Rather, as we will see, they depend on the way attributes are structured into relations.

Informally, MVDs arise whenever a relation with more than one nonsimple domain is normalized. In most of our earlier examples we dealt only with relations that at most had one nonsimple domain. Relation PROJECTS in Figure 3.5, on the other hand, can be seen as a normalization of a relation with two nonsimple domains. These domains are shown in Figure 3.7. One is PART within PROJECT and the other PERSON within PROJECT.

Similarly, the relation STATUS in Figure 3.6 is made up of the nonsimple domains shown in Figure 3.7. The difference between PROJECTS and STATUS is that there are still some FDs in PROJECTS, but there are no FDs in STATUS. Hence the simple decomposition algorithm can still be partly applied to PROJECTS but not to STATUS.

The objective of MVD is to identify relations that contain repeating groups at the same level and to remove such repeating groups during the decomposition process.

Formally, MVD is defined as follows: In relation $R(X, Y, Z)$, $X \twoheadrightarrow Y$ if each X value is associated with a set of Y values in a way that does not depend on the Z values. Thus, in Figure 3.6, suppose X is PERSON and Y is SKILL; then Z becomes {PROJECT, PART}. And suppose a particular value, JILL, is selected for PERSON. Consider now all tuples that have some value of Z; for example, PROJECT = P1 and PART = NUT. The values of Y in these tuples are (⟨ACCOUNTING⟩, ⟨COMPUTING⟩). Consider now all tuples with the same value of PERSON but with some other value of Z, say, PROJECT = P2 and PART = SCREW. The values of Y in these tuples are again (⟨ACCOUNTING⟩, ⟨COMPUTING⟩). This same set of values of Y is obtained for PERSON = JILL irrespective of the values chosen for PROJECT and PART; hence PERSON $\twoheadrightarrow$ SKILL. You might like to verify that in STATUS the result is

PROJECT $\twoheadrightarrow$ PERSON, SKILL
PROJECT $\twoheadrightarrow$ PART
PERSON $\twoheadrightarrow$ PROJECT, PART

Similarly, in Figure 3.5, suppose that X is PROJECTS and that Y is PART and QTY-USED (Z then becomes {PERSON, HRS-SPENT}). Suppose now a particular value is selected for PROJECT, say, P1. Now if we take any value of Z, say, PERSON = JILL and HRS-SPENT = 7, and then take all the tuples in PROJECTS that contain these values of Z and P1, the values of Y in these tuples are (⟨NUT, 11⟩, ⟨BOLT, 7⟩). These values of Y are obtained for PROJECT = P1 irrespective of the values of Z. Hence

PROJECT $\twoheadrightarrow$ PART, QTY-USED

You might like to verify that in relation PROJECTS the result is

PROJECTS

PROJECT	WORKERS		USE	
	PERSON	HRS-SPENT	PART	QTY-USED
P1	JILL EDNA	7 17	NUT BOLT	11 7
P2	JILL JIM	32 45	BOLT SCREW	7 9

STATUS

PERSON	PROJECTS		SKILL
	PROJECT	PARTS	
JILL	P1 P2	NUT BOLT BOLT SCREW	ACCOUNTING COMPUTING
EDNA	P1	NUT BOLT	LAW COMMERCE
JIM	P2	BOLT SCREW	STATISTICS ECONOMICS FRENCH

Figure 3.7 Nonnormal form of PROJECTS and STATUS

PROJECT $\twoheadrightarrow$ PERSON, HRS-SPENT

Formally, $Y_{X,Z}$ is defined as the set of Y values, given a set of X and a set of Z values. Thus suppose in relation STATUS, X is PERSON, Y is SKILL, and Z is PROJECT and PART. Then in STATUS we get

$$\text{SKILL}_{\text{JILL,P1,NUT}} = (\langle\text{ACCOUNTING}\rangle, \langle\text{COMPUTING}\rangle)$$
$$\text{SKILL}_{\text{JILL,P2,SCREW}} = (\langle\text{ACCOUNTING}\rangle, \langle\text{COMPUTING}\rangle)$$

Now to turn to the formal definition of MVD. What we need to say is that the values of attribute Y depend only on attributes X but are independent of the attributes Z. So given a value of X, the value of Y will be the same for any two values, Z_1 or Z_2, of Z.

Now the value of Y_1, given a set of values X and Z_1 is Y_{x,z_1}; and the value Y_2, given a set of values X and Z_2, is Y_{x,z_2}. MVD requires that $Y_1 = Y_2$, so $X \twoheadrightarrow Y$ in relation $R(X, Y, Z)$ if $Y_{x,z_1} = Y_{x,z_2}$ for any values Z_1, Z_2.

Another example: In relation PROJECTS, suppose Y is PART, QTY-USED; X is PROJECT; and Z the remaining attributes PERSON and HRS-SPENT. Then

$$(\text{PART, QTY-USED})_{\text{P1,JILL,7}} = (\langle \text{NUT, 11} \rangle, \langle \text{BOLT, 7} \rangle)$$

and

$$(\text{PART, QTY-USED})_{\text{P1,EDNA,17}} = (\langle \text{NUT, 11} \rangle, \langle \text{BOLT, 7} \rangle)$$

Again $Y_{X,Z_1} = Y_{X,Z_2}$ because PROJECT $\twoheadrightarrow$ PART, QTY-USED.

By now you may have noticed another property of MVDs: they always come in pairs. Thus if $X \twoheadrightarrow Y$ in relation $R(X, Y, Z)$, it is also true that $X \twoheadrightarrow Z$.

Context Dependence of MVDs

As mentioned earlier, MVDs are not a property of the information but arise from the manner in which attributes are combined into relations. Consider Figure 3.8. Here relation OFFERINGS contains information about COURSEs offered for study. Each COURSE is offered in any number of sections, and each section consists of meetings on number of days in a given room. The same TEXTs are used for the same COURSE in all sections. There is only one FD here, namely, COURSE, SECTION, DAY $\rightarrow$ ROOM. You might like to verify that

COURSE $\twoheadrightarrow$ TEXT
COURSE $\twoheadrightarrow$ SECTION, DAY, ROOM
COURSE, SECTION $\twoheadrightarrow$ DAY, ROOM
COURSE, SECTION $\twoheadrightarrow$ TEXT

Now suppose ROOM is projected out of relation OFFERINGS, leaving a new relation, $R(\text{COURSE, SECTION, DAY, TEXT})$. This new relation now contains COURSE, SECTION $\twoheadrightarrow$ DAY (which is not an MVD in Figure 3.8). Hence this last MVD depends not only on the nature of the information but also on whether ROOM is or is not an attribute of the relation OFFERINGS.

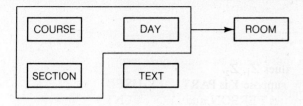

OFFERINGS

COURSE	SECTION	DAY	ROOM	TEXT
SA2	1	MON	2B4	DESIGN
SA2	1	TUES	2C5	DESIGN
SA2	1	THURS	2C5	DESIGN
SA2	1	MON	2B4	ANALYSIS
SA2	1	TUES	2C5	ANALYSIS
SA2	1	THURS	2C5	ANALYSIS
SA2	2	MON	2B9	DESIGN
SA2	2	THURS	2C6	DESIGN
SA2	2	MON	2B9	ANALYSIS
SA2	2	THURS	2C6	ANALYSIS
SA1	1	FRI	2B4	DATA STRUCTURE
SA1	1	MON	2B2	DATA STRUCTURE
SA1	1	FRI	2B4	DATABASE
SA1	1	MON	2B2	DATABASE

OFFERINGS

COURSE	SECTION	LOCATION		TEXT
		DAY	ROOM	
SA2	1	MON TUES THURS	2B4 2C5 2C5	DESIGN ANALYSIS
	2	MON THURS	2B9 2C6	
SA1	1	FRI MON	2B4 2B2	DATA STRUCTURE DATABASE

Figure 3.8 Relation OFFERINGS

Fourth Normal Form

To describe *fourth normal form* (4NF), we must define two additional terms: superkey and *trivial* MVD.

A *superkey* of relation R is a set of attributes X such that $X \to Y$ where Y is any attribute of R. It is of course possible that a subset X' of attributes of X may also be a superkey. Incidentally, the relationship between a superkey and a relation key is that the relation key is a superkey, but no subset of attributes of the relation key is a superkey.

There are two kinds of trivial MVDs:

1. $X \twoheadrightarrow \varnothing$, where $\varnothing$ is an empty set of attributes.
2. $X \twoheadrightarrow A - X$ where A comprises all the attributes in a relation.

By the definition of MVD, both these types hold for any set of attributes of R and therefore can serve no purpose as a design criterion.

A relation R is in 4NF if for every nontrivial MVD $(X \twoheadrightarrow Y)$ in R, X is a superkey of R. For example, in relation PROJECTS in Figure 3.5, the MVD PROJECT $\twoheadrightarrow$ PART, QTY-USED is a nontrivial MVD. The attribute PROJECT, however, is not a superkey of PROJECTS, and so PROJECTS is not in 4NF.

The decomposition algorithm can now be extended to include decomposition of relations that are not in 4NF. One possible algorithm is decomposition algorithm 2.

Decomposition Algorithm 2

We define *decomposition algorithm 2* as follows:

1. Initialize S_{out} with one relation R where $R = S_{in}$.
2. Find a nontrivial MVD, $X \twoheadrightarrow Y$, in $R(X, Y, Z, \ldots)$, where R is not in 4NF and R is in S_{out}.
3. Decompose R by projection into $R1(X, Y)$, $R2(X, Z, \ldots)$; remove R from S_{out} and add $R1$ and $R2$ to S_{out}.
4. Repeat 1 and 2 on every relation in S_{out} until all relations are in normal form.

Suppose this algorithm is applied to relation STATUS, which is not in 4NF. As a first step, the MVD PERSON $\twoheadrightarrow$ SKILL is projected from STATUS. The result is

SKILLS(PERSON, SKILL)
R1(PERSON, PROJECT, PARTS)

Relation $R1$ is not in 4NF because PROJECT $\twoheadrightarrow$ PARTS is a nontrivial MVD. If this MVD is projected from $R1$, we get

R11(PROJECT, PARTS)
R12(PERSON, PROJECT)

Applying this algorithm to relation PROJECTS in Figure 3.5 results in

R1(PROJECT, PERSON, HRS-SPENT)
   from PROJECT $\twoheadrightarrow$ PERSON, HRS-SPENT
R2(PROJECT, PART, QTY-USED)
   from PROJECT $\twoheadrightarrow$ PART, QTY-USED

These two relations are now in 4NF since each MVD in each relation is trivial.

MVDs and FDs

You may have noticed that in decomposition algorithm 2, FDs are no longer used. The reason is that any undesirable properties detected earlier through functional dependence now appear as nontrivial MVDs in relations. For instance, consider some of the relations in Chapter 2 that are reproduced in Figure 3.9. Relation $R2$ is not in 3NF because COLOR is not fully functionally dependent on the key (PART, PROJECT). Relation $R2$ was decomposed by the simple decomposition algorithms into

R3({PART, COLOR}, {PART $\rightarrow$ COLOR})
R4({PART, PROJECT, NO-USED}, {PART, PROJECT $\rightarrow$ NO-USED})

However, in $R2$, PART $\twoheadrightarrow$ COLOR and PART does not constitute a superkey of $R2$. Hence $R2$ is not in 4NF and would be decomposed into the same two relations by decomposition algorithm 2. Similarly, in relation SUPPLIERS,

CITY $\twoheadrightarrow$ DISTANCE

and in relation GRADES,

STUDENT-ID $\twoheadrightarrow$ PHONE-NO

The use of decomposition algorithm 2 to decompose SUPPLIERS or GRADES would produce the same result as the use of the simple decomposition algorithm. The results are identical because of a general property that FDs and MVDs share: in any R where $X \rightarrow Y$, it is also true that $X \twoheadrightarrow Y$.

Obviously, there are other properties that FDs and MVDs have in common;

R2

PART	COLOR	PROJECT	NO-USED
a	BLUE	P1	7
a	BLUE	·P2	3
b	RED	P1	4
b	RED	P3	11
c	GREEN	P2	5
d	PURPLE	—	—

SUPPLIERS

SUPPLIER	CITY	DISTANCE
S1	CHICAGO	900
S2	CHICAGO	900
S3	BOSTON	300
S4	BOSTON	300

GRADES

STUDENT-ID	PHONE-NO	UNIT	GRADE
760137	112233	CP1	A
770593	899899	CP1	F
770593	899890	IS1	B
790372	544077	IS1	B
790372	544077	IS2	C

Figure 3.9   A set of relations

these have been formally investigated by a number of writers. For the purpose of this text it is sufficient to note that the FDs between attributes that are natural to the information can result in nontrivial MVDs between attributes in relations. Whether such nontrivial MVDs occur will depend on the way that attributes are formed into relations. The goal of design is to choose structures that eliminate nontrivial MVDs.

Some Complexities of Decomposition Algorithms

The decomposition algorithms discussed so far have been simplified to some extent and do not guarantee nonredundant representation of S_{in}. It is clear from earlier discussion that the outputs of decomposition algorithm will depend not only on the kind of algorithm but also on the sequence of decompositions. Thus any algorithm must also include a set of heuristics; these indicate the sequence in which decompositions are to be applied. One such possible heuristic deals with the precedence of MVD to FD. Designers can either

- apply FD decomposition over MVD decomposition or
- apply MVD decomposition over FD decomposition

Figure 3.10 shows that neither version is an effective heuristic when decompositions are applied to two problems, PROBLEM 1 and PROBLEM 2. One decomposition gives priority to FDs, and the other gives priority to MVDs. It is seen that giving priority to FDs is more effective in PROBLEM 2, whereas giving priority to MVDs is more effective in PROBLEM 1. In PROBLEM 1, priority to FD decompositions yields a redundant relation, $R22$. On the other

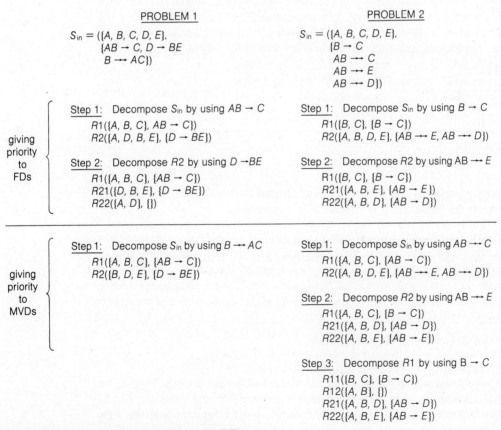

Figure 3.10 Priorities between FDs and MVDs

hand, in PROBLEM 2, priority to MVD decompositions produces a redundant relation, $R12$.

Some methods use FDs between determinants in FDs and MVDs to choose decomposition sequences. Others require designers to choose minimal coverings that satisfy certain conditions before commencing decomposition. (Refer to the literature in regard to such algorithms, which are not treated in this text.)

The importance of the universal relation assumption to decomposition algorithms should also be stressed here. Context dependence of the MVDs implies that there may be MVDs in the universal relation that will not appear in all the projections of this relation. On the other hand, the joining of all the relations into the universal relation can mean that some of the MVDs in the projections do not appear in the universal relation. Some authors describe these relations as latent MVDs. Considerable research is now under way to produce decomposition algorithms that recognize this effect. The work of C. Zaniolo and M. A. Melkanoff (1981) is perhaps one of the best examples of such research.

In practical environments designers usually start design with a number of relations that are "close to normal" rather than with a single relation that contains all the data. This set of "close to normal" relations is chosen on the basis of semantic considerations, which we will discuss later. The simple decomposition algorithms, together with some knowledge of MVD, is sufficient to decompose relations that are already "close to normal."

Alternatively, designers can use synthesis algorithms.

SYNTHESIS

Synthesis algorithms use FDs to produce normal form relations. For these algorithms to be successful it is necessary to ensure that

- FDs in S_{in} correctly represent user semantics
- algorithms can be devised to produce relations in S_{out} that correctly and nonredundantly represent S_{in}

Semantics of Functional Dependencies

So far in this text we have considered FDs only in a syntactic sense. That is, we have been concerned only with the syntactic structure of attributes when constructing relations. Care, however, must be exercised to ensure that the FDs and relations also correctly represent the semantics of user information. Consider, for instance, the following FDs:

$f1$:   PROCESS → ITEM
$f2$:   ITEM, PROCESS → QTY

Here $f1$ defines the item that is produced (i.e., the output) by a given process (assuming, of course, that each process produces only one item). The FD $f2$, on the other hand, defines the number of items used (i.e., the input) to a process. Applying the FD rules yields PROCESS → QTY because ITEM is a redundant attribute in $f2$. Obviously, this result is not semantically correct. Again the universal relation assumption becomes important here. The problem is that ITEM has a different meaning in each FD. Hence an erroneous inference is made when FD rules are applied to the two FDs. The universal relation assumption requires designers to globally distinguish between attributes with different meanings by proper choice of attribute names. For example, $f1$ and $f2$ could be replaced by

$f1$:   PROCESS → ITEM-PRODUCED
$f2$:   ITEM-USED, PROCESS → QTY

In this case incorrect semantic inferences do not arise.

An erroneous inference is often made when the attribute DATE is used. For example, consider

$f3$:   PERSON → DATE
$f4$:   DATE, PERSON → PROJECT

Here $f3$ defines the date on which a person started in an organization, and $f4$ defines the date on which a person was assigned to a project. Note that a person may be assigned to more than one project, but not on the same date. This situation leads to the incorrect semantic inference PERSON → PROJECT, which obviously is not a valid FD in the user information. Again this can be solved by the following change:

$f3$:   PERSON → DATE-HIRED
$f4$:   DATE-ASSIGNED-TO-PROJECT, PERSON → PROJECT

Another semantic problem is known as nonfunctional relationships. If you look back at Figure 3.6, you will note there are no FDs between attributes PERSON, PROJECT, PART, and SKILL. Yet obviously these attributes are related. The person has skills and is assigned to projects; each project uses parts. No FDs exist between them because combinations of attribute values do not define unique values of other attributes. The situation could change if new attributes that directly depend on the relationships were introduced. For example, the attribute DATE-SKILL-ACQUIRED would lead to the FD

PERSON, SKILL → DATE-SKILL-ACQUIRED

Similarly, the attribute NO-USED and DATE-ASSIGNED would lead to

PROJECT, PART → NO-USED
PERSON, PROJECT → DATE-ASSIGNED

Nevertheless, if synthesis algorithms are to be effective, their input must describe those nonfunctional relationships that cannot be expressed as FDs between attributes. So we introduce a nonexistent attribute for each nonfunctional relationship. For example, the nonfunctional relationship between PERSON and SKILL would be expressed as

PERSON, SKILL → ∅

To allow more than one nonfunctional relationship to be specified, additional nonexistent attributes are defined. One such attribute is defined for each nonfunctional relationship. Thus the information in Figure 3.6 would be specified as

$f1$:   PERSON, SKILL → $\emptyset_1$
$f2$:   PERSON, PROJECT → $\emptyset_2$
$f3$:   PROJECT, PART → $\emptyset_3$

Inputs to synthesis algorithms include nonfunctional relationships. The inputs must also use attribute names, which are semantically meaningful and do not lead to erroneous semantic inferences.

Synthesis Algorithms

Perhaps the best-known synthesis algorithm is the one devised by Bernstein. It is premised on grouping all FDs with the same determinant and constructing a relation for each such group. The final form of Bernstein's algorithm is given in Figure 3.12. However, to develop it we must go through some simpler versions. The first of these is here called *basic synthesis algorithm 1* and is formally defined as follows:

- *Step 1:* Divide the FDs into groups, with each group having the same determinant.
- *Step 2:* Replace each group of FDs from step 1 by one relation.

These two steps correspond to steps 3 and 6C in the final version in Figure 3.12.
   For example, basic synthesis algorithm 1 would replace the FDs

$f1$: $A, X \rightarrow B$
$f2$: $Y \rightarrow Z$
$f3$: $Y \rightarrow P$

by the two relations

$R1(\underline{A, X}, B)$ from $f1$
$R1(\underline{Y}, P, Z)$ from $f2$ and $f3$

The keys of $R1$ and $R2$ are underlined; the relations are in 3NF.

The basic synthesis algorithm 1, however, does not always result in 3NF relations. It can also produce redundant relations. For example, consider the five cases in Figure 3.11. For each case, the relations synthesized by using the basic synthesis algorithm 1 are shown, and the keys of the synthesized relations are underlined.

In case 1, $R1$ is not in 2NF since the key of the relation is AB, and F is functionally dependent on part of the key. This situation occurs because F is an extraneous attribute in the determinant of $f1$. Since $f2 = A \rightarrow F$, we can replace $f1$ by $AB \rightarrow G$. The synthesized relations now become

$R1(\underline{A, B}, G)$

$R2(\underline{A}, F)$

These relations are in 3NF.

In case 2, $R1$ is in 2NF but not 3NF because there is an FD between the nonprime attributes. This situation occurs because $f2$ is a redundant FD; it can

CASE 1

| | FDs | $f1$: | $ABF \rightarrow G$ | | $R1(\underline{A, B}, F, G)$ | $R1$ not in 2NF |
| | | $f2$: | $A \rightarrow F$ | | $R2(\underline{A}, F)$ | |

Extraneous attribute in $f1$.

CASE 2

	FDs	$f1$:	$X \rightarrow Y$		$R1(\underline{X}, Y, Z)$	$R1$ in 2NF but not 3NF
		$f2$:	$X \rightarrow Z$		$R2(\underline{Y}, Z)$	
		$f3$:	$Y \rightarrow Z$			

Redundant FD; $f2$ can be derived from $f1$ and $f3$.

CASE 3

	FDs	$f1$:	$X \rightarrow A$		$R1(\underline{X}, A, Y)$	Too many relations
		$f2$:	$Y \rightarrow B$		$R2(\underline{Y}, B, \underline{X})$	
		$f3$:	$X \longleftrightarrow Y$			

Relations $R1$ and $R2$ can be combined, and the result is in 3NF.

CASE 3A

	FDs	$f1$:	$X \rightarrow A$		$R1(\underline{X}, \underline{A})$	
		$f2$:	$A \rightarrow Y$		$R2(\underline{A}, \underline{Y})$	Too many relations
		$f3$:	$Y \rightarrow X$		$R3(\underline{Y}, \underline{X})$	

CASE 4

	FDs	$f1$:	$AB \rightarrow DP$		$R1(\underline{A, B}, C, D, P)$	$R1$ not in 2 NF
		$f2$:	$CD \rightarrow AB$			
		$f3$:	$PB \rightarrow I$		$R2(\underline{P, B}, I)$	
		$f4$:	$IA \rightarrow C$		$R3(\underline{I, A}, C)$	
		$f5$:	$C \rightarrow P$		$R4(\underline{C}, P)$	

Figure 3.11 Problems in synthesizing relations when using the basic synthesis algorithm

be derived from $f1$ and $f3$ by using FD inference rules $(X \rightarrow Y \rightarrow Z)$. If $f2$ is removed from the FDs, the synthesized relations become

$R1(\underline{X}, Y)$

$R2(\underline{Y}, Z)$

Both these relations are in 3NF.

To eliminate these two problems, we can add two steps to the basic algorithm to create basic synthesis algorithm 2. Basic synthesis algorithm 2 is made up of the following four steps:

- Step 1: Eliminate extraneous attributes from the determinants of FDs.
- Step 2: Remove any redundant FDs and find a nonredundant covering of the input FDs.
- Step 3: Divide the FDs into groups, with each group having the same determinant.
- Step 4: Replace each group of FDs from step 3 by one relation.

These four steps correspond to steps 1, 2, 3, and 6C of the final algorithm in Figure 3.12. Applying basic synthesis algorithm 2 to case 1 in Figure 3.11 yields the two relations

$R1(\underline{A}, B, G)$ and $(R2(\underline{A}, F)$

both of which are in 3NF.

Applying basic synthesis algorithm 2 to case 2 in Figure 3.11 first removes $f2$ (it is redundant) and then yields the two relations

INPUT TO ALGORITHM IS A SET OF ATTRIBUTES, A,
AND A SET OF FUNCTIONAL DEPENDENCIES, F

Steps in algorithm:

1. Eliminate extraneous attributes in each FD of F, producing a new set of FDs, F1.
2. Remove redundant FDs from F1. To do this, find a minimal covering F2 of F1.
3. Partition F2 into groups, where each group has an identical determinant.
4. Find all equivalent keys in F2 by using FD rules.
5a. For each pair of equivalent keys $X \rightarrow Y$, $Y \rightarrow X$, remove $X \rightarrow Y$ or $Y \rightarrow X$ or both from F2 if they exist in F2, and add $X \rightarrow Y$ and $Y \rightarrow X$ to H. The new set of FDs, F3, now is the same as F2, with all FDs between equivalent keys removed; H contains the FDs between equivalent keys.
5b. Find a minimal covering, F4, of (F3 + H). F4 must include all FDs in H (i.e., all equivalent keys), together with the required FDs in F3 (which may be a subset of F3), to make a minimal covering of F3 + H. Thus F4 = F3′ + H where F3′ ⊆ F3. The important point here is that F4 must explicitly contain all FDs between equivalent keys.
6a. Partition F4 into groups, where each group has an identical determinant.
6b. Merge groups with determinants that are equivalent keys.
6c. Construct a relation for each group in 6b.

Figure 3.12 Bernstein's synthesis algorithm

$$R1(\underline{X}, Y) \quad \text{and} \quad R2(\underline{Y}, Z)$$

both of which are in 3NF.

The inclusion, however, of the two new steps to basic synthesis algorithm 1 still does not eliminate the problem in cases 3 and 3A in Figure 3.11. Here there are too many relations, a situation that occurs whenever there are one-to-one dependencies of the form $A \leftrightarrow Y$ either in the FDs of S_{in} or in their covering. In case 3 the one-to-one dependency is explicitly given in $f3$. When step 3 of the basic synthesis algorithm 2 is applied, two groups are formed:

- group 1: $f1$ and $f3$ with X as a common determinant
- group 2: $f2$ with Y as a common determinant

Relations $R1$ and $R2$ are formed from these two groups. The relations, however, are redundant since they both contain $X \leftrightarrow Y$. The sets of attributes X, Y in $X \leftrightarrow Y$ are often called *equivalent keys*.

To overcome this redundancy, we could add step 3A to basic synthesis algorithm 2 to combine FD groups with equivalent keys. If this is done in case 3, all FDs are placed in one group, which yields the relation

$$R(\underline{X}, \underline{Y}, A, B)$$

This relation is in 3NF and is not redundant.

The same problem can occur even if the FDs that define the equivalent keys do not explicitly appear in S_{in}. For example, in case 3A, $X \rightarrow Y$ does not appear in the set of FDs. However, it is possible to derive $X \rightarrow Y$ from $f1$ and $f2$ ($X \rightarrow A \rightarrow Y$). Therefore $X \rightarrow Y$ and X and Y are equivalent keys. It is now possible to show that $A \rightarrow X$ because $A \rightarrow Y \rightarrow X$; hence $A \leftrightarrow X$. Similarly, $Y \rightarrow A$ because $Y \rightarrow X \rightarrow A$; hence $A \leftrightarrow Y$. So A, X, and Y are equivalent keys. All FDs in case 3A can now be grouped, yielding the relation

$$R(\underline{X}, \underline{Y}, \underline{A})$$

which is both in 3NF and nonredundant.

Finally, there is still one more problem, which is illustrated in case 4 of Figure 3.11. When FDs between equivalent keys are added to S_{in}, as was done in case 3A, the addition of a new FD may make one of the existent FDs in S_{in} redundant. In case 4 it is possible to show that AB and CD are equivalent keys as follows:

1. $AB \rightarrow P$ in $f1$, and $PB \rightarrow I$ in $f3$ infers $AB \rightarrow I$.
2. $AB \rightarrow I$, and $IA \rightarrow C$ in $f4$ infers $AB \rightarrow C$.
3. Now $AB \rightarrow C$, and $AB \rightarrow D$ in $f1$ infers $AB \rightarrow CD$.

Hence $f1$ and $f2$ can now be placed in the same group for constructing relations. The result is $R1$, which is not in 2NF since P, derived from $f5$, is functionally dependent on a subset of the key CD.

The reason for this result is that after introducing $AB \to C$ to S_{in}, the FD $AB \to P$ becomes redundant since $AB \to C \to P$. ($AB \to C$ has been derived and $C \to P$ comes from $f5$.) If the redundant dependency $AB \to P$ is removed from $f1$, then $R1$ will become $R1(\underline{A}, \underline{B}, \underline{C}, \underline{D})$, which is in 3NF.

To overcome this problem, we add further steps to basic synthesis algorithm 2 to eliminate derived dependencies between equivalent keys. These steps are added between steps 2 and 3 of basic synthesis algorithm 2. When they are added we get the final form of Bernstein's algorithm shown in Figure 3.12. Here one-to-one dependencies are found in step 4. Any newly found one-to-one dependencies are then added to the set of FDs in step 5(a); other FDs, which now become redundant, are eliminated in step 5(b). The effect of steps 5(a) and 5(b) is to force FDs between equivalent keys into the minimal covering. Bernstein (1976) has shown that this algorithm yields a minimal set of 3NF relations.

It should also be noted that the synthesis algorithm (as compared to the decomposition algorithm) does not always produce relations that have the lossless join property. An extension that produces a minimal set of relations with the lossless join property has been discussed by J. Biskup and co-workers (1979). It requires the final set of relations to include a relation whose relation key is also the relation key of the universal relation, U. The universal relation U in this case contains all the attributes contained in the FDs that are input to the synthesis algorithm.

RECENT DEVELOPMENTS IN RELATIONAL THEORY

Relational theory is a continually developing field, and more results can be expected in the future as new insights are gained into the structure of data or into algorithms to develop well-formed data structures.

One recent development is the fifth normal form. It arises from work by Aho and coworkers in 1979, who discovered relations that cannot be nonlosslessly decomposed into two relations but can be losslessly decomposed into three or more relations. Relations of this kind are usually "all key" and have no FDs or nontrivial MVDs between their attributes.

A relation that exhibits this property is shown in Figure 3.13. It is named PERSON-USING-SKILLS-ON-JOBS as it stores information about people applying all their skills to jobs to which they are assigned (but only if the job needs that skill). Thus person P1 who possesses skills COMP and MECH applies them to job AUTO1 as job AUTO1 needs both these skills. The same

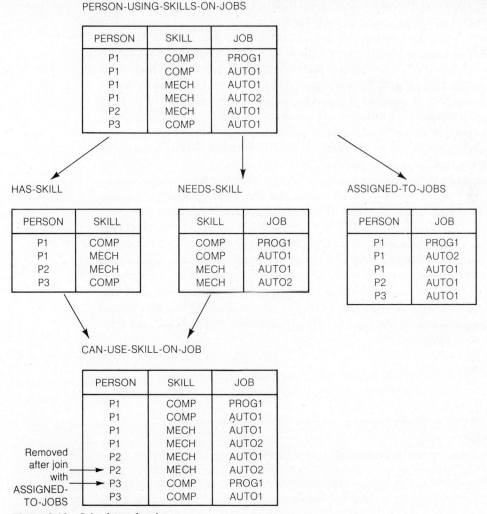

Figure 3.13 Join dependencies

person P1 only applies skill COMP to job PROG1 as job PROG1 only needs skill COMP but not skill MECH. Relation PERSON-USING-SKILLS-ON-JOBS can be decomposed into three relations, HAS-SKILL, NEEDS-SKILL, and ASSIGNED-TO-JOBS. You will note that no two of these relations realize a join that has the same data as PERSON-USING-SKILLS-ON-JOBS but a join of all three of these relations will yield a relation that has the same data as relation PERSON-USING-SKILLS-ON-JOBS. Thus each relation acts as a constraint on the join of the other two relations.

The reasons for this phenomenon are semantic. If we join HAS-SKILL and NEEDS-SKILL (as is illustrated in Figure 3.13) then we get relation CAN-USE-SKILL-ON-JOB. This relation stores data about people who have skills applicable to particular jobs. But each person that has a skill required for a particular job need not be assigned to that job. The actual assignments are given by relation ASSIGNED-TO-JOBS which when joined with CAN-USE-SKILL-ON-JOB removes tuples that describe possible assignments that did not eventuate. Similarly if we joined ASSIGNED-TO-JOBS with HAS-SKILL we would get a relation that contains all possible skills that can be applied to each job (as persons assigned to that job possess those skills). However, some of the jobs do not need all the skills and redundant tuples that show unnecessary SKILL and JOB combinations would be removed by joining with NEEDS-SKILL.

Relation PERSON-USING-SKILLS-ON-JOBS is in BCNF and 4NF but can lead to anomalies because of the dependencies between the joins. For example if we delete ⟨P1,MECH,AUTO1⟩ then we must also delete ⟨P1,COMP, AUTO1⟩. Because of relations with such join dependencies, there is an emerging trend to define a fifth normal form (see Fagin 1979). One can postulate that eventually (once there is a wide acceptance of the definition of the fifth normal form) design algorithms that lead to 5NF relations will evolve. Watch the literature for such developments.

SUMMARY

In designing relational databases, the primary goal is to ensure that relations represent the original data specifications correctly and without redundancy. Two alternate kinds of design methods are decomposition methods and synthesis methods.

Decomposition methods start with one relation and decompose it in a sequence of steps. To provide sufficient decomposition criteria, we use the fourth normal form (4NF), which is based on the concept of multivalued dependency. An algorithm is used to reduce a relation to a set of 4NF relations.

Synthesis algorithms differ from decomposition algorithms because they commence with a set of FDs and use them to construct relations. Effective synthesis algorithms must commence with a minimal set of FDs to ensure that a minimal set of relations are produced by the design algorithm. An algorithm, conceived by P. A. Bernstein, meets this requirement.

PROBLEMS

Problem 1

Consider the following FDs:

PERSON-ID, QUALIFICATION → DATE-ACQUIRED
PERSON-ID, CURRENT-POSITION-NO →
                                    DATE-OF-APPOINTMENT
CURRENT POSITION-NO → SECTION-NO, DATE-ESTABLISHED

and the relation PEOPLE shown in Figure 3.14.

PEOPLE

PERSON-ID	QUALIFICATION	CURRENT-POSITION-NO	DATE-ACQUIRED	DATE-OF-APPOINTMENT	SECTION-NO	DATE-ESTABLISHED
U101	BE	P66	1972	030375	S1	FEB 71
U101	ME	P66	1975	030375	S1	FEB 71
U101	BE	P97	1972	060678	S2	OCT 71
U101	ME	P97	1975	060678	S2	OCT 71
U203	BA	P88	1974	040476	S1	NOV 73
U203	BA	P88	1974	040476	S1	NOV 73

Figure 3.14 Relation PEOPLE

Can you make the following changes to the database by adding, deleting, or updating one tuple only?

(a) U203 receives an M.A. in 1978.
(b) U101 is appointed to a new CURRENT-POSITION-NO, P123, on 060677.
(c) A new position, P90, is established in section S2 on JULY 80.
(d) Position P97 is moved from S2 to S1.

How would you restructure the database to allow the preceding changes to be effected by one tuple only?

Problem 2

Suppose the relation

SUPPLIES (SUPPLIER, PART, BUYER, QTY)
 BUYER → PART
 PART → SUPPLIER
 SUPPLIER, BUYER → QTY

is decomposed into SUPPLIERS (SUPPLIER, PART, QTY), BUYERS
(BUYER, PART). Has any information been lost in this decomposition?

Suppose now the decomposition becomes SUPPLIERS (BUYER, PART,
QTY), BUYERS (BUYER, SUPPLIER). Has any information been lost in
this decomposition?

Problem 3

Consider the following relation:

OCCUPANCY (GARAGE, BUILDING, APT, TENANT, PET)
 GARAGE → BUILDING
 BUILDING, APT → TENANT
 TENANT → BUILDING, APT
 TENANT, PET → ∅

(a) What other nontrivial FDs can you derive from the given FDs?
(b) Decompose OCCUPANCY into 3NF relations by taking out the FDs. Try
   different sequences of FD removal and compare answers.

Problem 4

Using the simple decomposition algorithm, decompose

R1(PERSON, SKILL, DATE-SKILL-ACQUIRED, MARRIED-TO,
   DATE-OF-MARRIAGE)
 PERSON, SKILL → DATE-SKILL-ACQUIRED
 PERSON, MARRIED-TO → DATE-OF-MARRIAGE

Comment on the result.

Problem 5

Construct a minimal set of relations for the FDs in Figure 3.15.

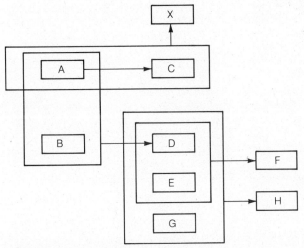

Figure 3.15   A set of FDs for Problem 5

Problem 6

(a) Suppose you are given the following FDs:

$$A \rightarrow D \quad B \rightarrow A$$
$$B \rightarrow C \quad C \rightarrow D$$
$$A \rightarrow B$$

Apply steps 3 and 6 of Bernstein's synthesis algorithm (Figure 3.12).
What are keys of the synthesized relations? Are the relations in 3NF?
Remove any redundant FDs and try again. Merge equivalent keys and try again.

(b) Apply the synthesis algorithm to the FDs in Problem 3. Do the resulting relations represent all the information in OCCUPANCY?

Problem 7

Are there any redundant FDs in the following set?

$$X, R1 \rightarrow C \qquad R1 \rightarrow A \qquad B \rightarrow R1 \qquad A \rightarrow X$$
$$Y, R2 \rightarrow B \qquad R2 \rightarrow A \qquad C \rightarrow B \qquad R1, A \rightarrow B$$
$$R2, B \rightarrow C \qquad A, B \rightarrow C \qquad Y \rightarrow B$$

Synthesize a set of 3NF relations from these FDs.

chapter four
Syntactic and Semantic
Design Issues
in Data Analysis

INTRODUCTION

So far we have described the relational model and the algorithms that can be used to construct normal form relations. The database designer finds these relational normal forms attractive particularly because they allow the nonredundant representation of data and they help avoid anomalies following database operations.

To be useful in database design, however, the relational model and its associated design algorithms must be integrated within the system development cycle. To do this the relational model must meet the following additional requirements:

1. It should provide a useful interface to users and designers during early analysis phases.
2. It should readily convert to a computer implementation in the technical design phases.

Conversions to a computer implementation depend on the kind of database management system available to the designer. A number of database management systems now directly support the relational model. If such a database management system is available, the outcome of relational designs can be directly implemented on this system. In this case designers create data definitions in explicit relational terms, and these definitions are then accepted as direct inputs to the database management system. If a relational database management system is not available to the designer, the results of relational design must be converted to the data structures supported by the available database management system. These data structures are called the *implementation model* in this chapter. The conversion method depends on the implementation model.

Let's say the implementation model is a set of COBOL files. A possible conversion method is to convert each relation to a file, each tuple to a record, and each attribute to a field. Conversions to implementation models other than COBOL files are usually more complex. They require links to be set up between different files or record types and therefore need additional conversion rules. One such rule, for example, can be to establish links between records that represent relations having common attributes in their keys.

In general, though, the recordlike structure of relations provides a sufficient basis for conversion to record-based implementation models. A conversion that preserves this record structure will ensure that the properties of normal form relations are carried through to the implementation.

There are, however, some drawbacks in using relational design during the early stages of system development.

THE RELATIONAL MODEL IN SYSTEMS ANALYSIS

The goal of systems analysis is to produce a user requirements specification that includes a model of user data. This model must be easily understood by both users and computer professionals. There is little argument that in this respect the tabular form of the relational model is acceptable. However, the fact that the relational model is a useful tool as a final presentation of the results of systems analysis does not imply that it can be used throughout the analysis process. In fact, it does create two problems peculiar to systems analysis:

- It is too detailed to use at the initial design stages.
- It lacks the semantic structure to make unambiguous choices in modeling enterprises.

These problems are to some extent related to the staged elaboration of user problems in the system life cycle. Generally, the life cycle commences with a broad set of user requirements. These requirements are elaborated into more detail as design proceeds. Relational analysis does not fit easily into this scheme of things. It emphasizes FDs as the only means for defining the semantic nature of data. After first identifying all data elements in the enterprise, the designer must then determine all the FDs between these data elements. This process is detailed and time-consuming. Most designs in their early stages are usually explorative and deal with structures at a higher level than the data element. Their goal is first to model the enterprise at a high level and then to make decisions on which part of the enterprise to implement on the database. Once this is done, detailed evaluation begins. The relational model does not fit easily into this process because it cannot be easily used at the higher levels; it can be effectively used only when detailed design commences. Consequently, some means must be provided to integrate relational design with other techniques in the system development process.

The integration method used will depend on the other techniques used in system development. One notable procedure is discussed by C. Gane and T. Sarson (1979). Their method is to employ the graphical techniques generally associated with structured system analysis. Here the first step is to identify the major data flows. Then the data elements in these flows are determined and stored in hierarchical form in a data dictionary.

Gane and Sarson propose that relational analysis commence once this data dictionary, which includes all the data elements of interest to the designer, is completed and suggest a series of analysis steps (Figure 4.1). The first step is a local reduction to eliminate repeating groups in the hierarchical data structures, a step that corresponds to the normalization of first normal form. Subsequently, structures with common key elements are put together. For example, all structures with the key ACCOUNT-NO are combined into the structure ACCOUNT. Similarly, all structures with the composite key ACCOUNT-NO, CUSTOMER-NO are combined. The combined relations are now examined to determine if they satisfy BCNF conditions. Relations that do not satisfy these conditions are decomposed. For example, the functional dependency CUSTOMER-NO → ADDRESS is removed from CUSTOMER-IN-ACCOUNT and RECEIPT into a separate relation.

Semantic Problems in Relational Modeling

The relational model has been criticized for its semantic modeling problems. For example, consider the FDs in modeling an enterprise where persons are assigned to departments, each department has one manager, and each manager only manages one department. In this case the FDs are

PERSON → DEPT
MANAGER ↔ DEPT
PERSON → MANAGER

There are two minimal coverings here:

Covering 1	*Covering 2*
MANAGER ↔ DEPT	MANAGER ↔ DEPT
PERSON → MANAGER	PERSON → DEPT

An unbiased synthesis algorithm can therefore produce one of two designs:

DESIGN 1: ASSIGN (PERSON, DEPT)
            MANAGERS (DEPT, MANAGER)

or

DESIGN 2: ASSIGN (PERSON, MANAGER)
            MANAGERS (DEPT, MANAGER)

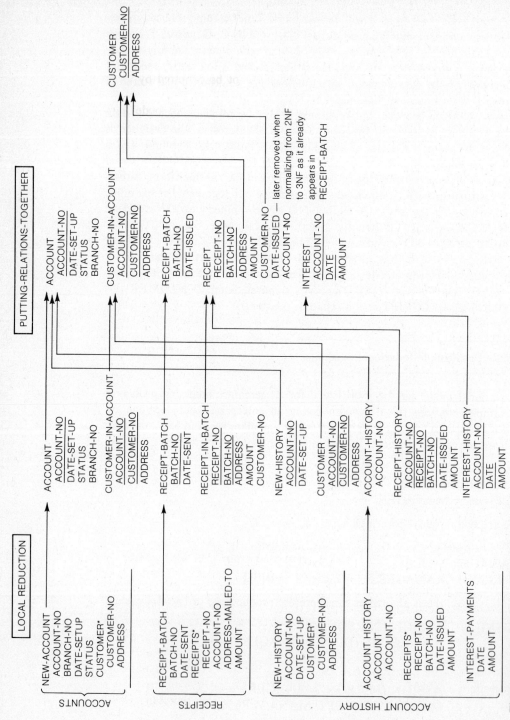

Figure 4.1 Reduction of data flow structures

Although both these designs are nonredundant and contain the same data as the original specification, they express different semantics of assignment. DESIGN 1 is preferable if PERSONs are assigned to DEPTs, whereas DESIGN 2 is preferable if PERSONs are assigned to MANAGERs (as may occur in a project team situation). This semantic property cannot be captured by using FDs but must be expressed in some other way.

Another semantic problem with relations is that it is difficult to model constraints between relations, although such constraints may exist in the user information. Suppose a SUPPLIER-PART relation contains a tuple for each part that a supplier supplies. A SUPPLIER relation contains information about suppliers—address, status, and so on. It is possible to add a tuple to SUPPLIER-PART that contains a supplier who does not appear in SUPPLIER. These relations are all in 2NF but have the anomaly that a supplier who has not yet been defined can supply a part.

A further problem is that in the relational model all domains are of the same importance. In an enterprise, however, it is semantically convenient to distinguish between different "kinds" of domains. Some domains may identify specific objects in an enterprise, whereas others may describe properties of these objects. Thus a domain whose set of values identifies persons is to some extent more important than a domain that has as its value set the age of the person; the latter depends on the existence of the former.

Given these arguments, it is valid to consider alternatives to purely relational design. Some general alternatives:

- Use a record oriented data model in data analysis.
- Enrich the relational model.
- Use another abstract data model in data analysis, or
- Use either a record or abstract model during analysis and then convert the results to a relational model for design.

RECORD-BASED DATA MODELS

Two record-based data models have been popular in the past, the *hierarchical* and the *network* models. These models are directly supported by a number of contemporary database management systems. In the hierarchical model, user entities are structured into hierarchies, which are then directly converted to a hierarchical data definition. Similarly, user entities in the network model are structured into networks, which are then directly converted to a network data definition.

These models have the advantage that they are also a natural representation of many enterprises. For example, take the specification of an organization's structure. Here SECTIONs are supervised by DEPARTMENTs, which are in turn supervised by DIVISIONs. This problem can be simply represented by a hierarchy and converted directly to a database management system. Conversion to a relational model would be seen here as an unnecessary intermediate step.

The most telling arguments against record-based models is that they usually assume certain physical access paths early in design; these in turn influence logical design. For example, let's say we are using a hierarchical model to model the use of PARTs in PROJECTs. Then either PARTs can be the parent of PROJECTs or PROJECTs can be the parent of PARTs. Our choice depends on physical use rather than logical structure. In the relational model both PARTs and PROJECTs would appear as attributes of equal significance in logical design. We would delay our choice of access path until we had considered access requirements.

Further, record-based data models possess few, if any, formal guidelines for choosing nonredundant logical structures; relational theory includes normal forms to serve this purpose. For this reason the relational model has become popular for data analysis. It is, however, feasible to either extend the relational model or associate it with other semantic models. Semantic models are particularly useful as initial guidelines to the choice of "close to normal" relations in the initial stages of design.

ENRICHING THE RELATIONAL MODEL

Considerable work is being done to enrich existing data models. A well-known example is the work of H. A. Schmid and J. R. Swenson (1975), who have strengthened the semantics of the relational model. Their aim is primarily to remove the intrarelational anomalies that were discussed earlier. Schmid and Swenson have proposed an information model that includes object types, characteristics, and associations between object types as additional constructs.

For example, SUPPLIER and PART would become object types; SUPPLIER-ADDRESS and PART-COLOR would become characteristic object types. Relationships between object types and characteristic object types are called *characteristics*. Relationships between object types are called *associations*. Characteristics of the object type of the same kind are represented by a characteristic relation.

Similarly, associations can be represented by association relations. Semantics (i.e., operations and structure) are then defined in a way that prevents intrarelational anomalies from occurring.

Other extensions to the relational model have been discussed by Codd (1979).

SEMANTIC MODELS

Semantic models are yet another alternative for data analysis. They consist of a model structure made up of a number of abstractions that are used to capture the essential semantic features of the enterprise. These abstractions are then combined consistently with the rules of semantic model structure to form the enterprise model. Semantic model abstractions are of a higher level order than data elements; they usually allow modeling at an object level and the formation of object classes and associations between such classes. Data elements can be added to the model once the essential semantic structure is agreed upon. Semantic models, however, do not usually possess criteria that can be used to prevent anomalies and eliminate redundancies. Since these criteria characterize relational normal forms, it is suggested that an ideal design process integrate the semantic model in the early design stage with the relational model in later stages. In this process the semantic model would be used to capture the essential enterprise semantics. The relational model would then provide the syntactic criteria that characterize satisfactory logical structures.

The relational model can be combined with semantic models in the three ways shown in Figure 4.2. For completeness this figure includes all the other methods discussed so far. Each method's goal is to convert the user requirement to an implementation model, which is usually a record-based model supported by COBOL or a database management system. One of the methods in Figure 4.2 is the *ad hoc* classical approach used in the past. Another is that in which

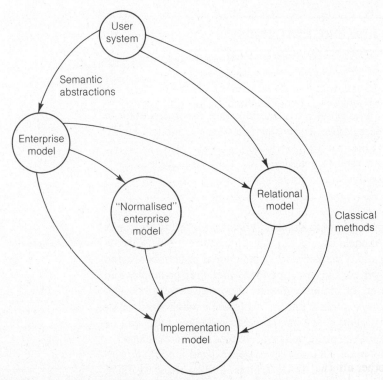

Figure 4.2   Alternative design methods

the user system is reduced to relations, as discussed in earlier chapters. These relations are then converted to the implementation model.

The availability of abstract semantic models suggests three additional methods. The first step in all these methods is to develop an enterprise model of the user system in terms of the semantic model abstractions. Three possibilities then arise:

- Convert the enterprise model directly to the implementation model.
- "Normalize" the enterprise model, using relational criteria, and then convert to an implementation.
- Convert the enterprise model to relations and then convert the relations to an implementation.

The last two of these choices give the designers three advantages:

1. It is possible early in design to use the semantic abstractions at a higher design level and then convert to a data element level at later design stages.
2. A user problem can be modeled by semantic concepts specially chosen to capture their essential features.
3. Relational theory can be used to provide the criteria for structuring data.

HOW SEMANTIC MODELS MODEL ENTERPRISES

Semantic Abstractions

The goal of semantic models is to provide abstractions that naturally adapt to the way that users describe enterprises. To do this the semantic models must

- support the mental processes used in analysis
- use the natural terms for analysis
- provide the model structure

It could be argued that since we would expect all mental modeling processes to be the same, all semantic models should use the same abstractions. This argument could, of course, be valid if we knew what the mental processes are and how they are defined. This is yet not the case, and many modeling principles and abstractions have been proposed for semantic models. Nevertheless, even though such mental processes are not yet clearly known, there are enough similarities between semantic models to suggest that some common modeling basis can be proposed and that a generalized set of modeling principles can be developed.

Much early work on developing a common set of generalized modeling principles rested with set-theoretic concepts. D. L. Childs' (1968) work on these concepts was one of the earliest examples of this method of modeling; it is seen by some as the forerunner of the relational model. You may recall that the relational model itself is founded on set-theoretic notions and that its contribution is to relate the set concepts in relations to the more pragmatic world of tables, files, and records. Another set of mathematical models has used graphical abstractions.

Recent semantic models have been pragmatically oriented and do not need excessive mathematical notation. The idea behind them is to allow designers to specify their broad requirements by a user-oriented structure with minimal mathematical notation. These semantic models provide the user with a number of abstractions to represent the user enterprise. The question then is, What abstractions are the most suitable for modeling enterprises?

Early work on set-theoretic concepts suggests that one modeling generalization is the construction of set collections of objects and of associations between these objects. Usually objects with similar properties are grouped into sets, as are associations between objects from the same object sets. These objects and associations can then be represented by sets of tuples. This procedure is further elaborated by G. M. Nijssen (1976), who suggests a general abstraction for the analysis of information. Nijssen recommends that the analysis process include the major steps of

- naming the perceived objects within an enterprise
- selecting the objects of interest to be included in the model
- classifying these objects into sets

Semantic models provide a variety of abstractions for defining, naming, and classifying object sets and associations. Most models allow designers to define different *object set types* and *association types*. These types can be viewed as concrete representations of modeling abstractions and are analogous to variable types in programming languages. Thus, analogously to *real* or *integer* types, a semantic model provides, say, the *entity* set type, the *relationship* set type, and so on.

This analogy can be extended to the definition and population of enterprise models. To do this it is necessary to consider semantic modeling at three levels:

1. The semantic model level, which defines the abstractions and rules for classification of object sets
2. The enterprise level, which defines an enterprise consistently with the semantic model rules
3. The object level, which creates objects within the enterprise level consistently with the semantic model rules

Analogously to programming languages, the semantic model level can be viewed as a programming language. The enterprise level corresponds to the declarations in a programming language. That is, an enterprise model is analogous to a declaration in a programming language. The model can be made up of any number of declarations of instances (or variables) of allowed types. For example, just as any number of integers or real variables can be defined in a program, so it is possible to declare any number of variables of a given set type or association type. All such declarations must, however, be consistent with the abstraction rules. Such rules also exist in programming languages. For example, some languages restrict operations to particular types—for example, an integer variable can be associated only with another integer variable in addition. Similarly, in an enterprise model only certain object types can appear in given association types.

Finally, the third level concerns values of the variables. Just as integer or real variables assume values in a program, so do object set variables and association variables in an enterprise. But there is one important difference between programming language and semantic models at this level. Values of set or association types are sets of objects or sets of associations rather than the elementary integer or real numbers that are common in programming languages.

The notions of naming and classification provide an acceptable basis for defining semantic models. A semantic model provides a user with abstractions to classify objects in the enterprise. Many such abstractions are available and include abilities to specify distinct object classes, interactions between object classes, subclass object associations, and dependency and other categories of object sets. The semantic model also includes rules that must be satisfied by objects within object and association sets.

Because of the variety of object classes and associations, and the different ways of structuring them, a large variety of semantic models can also be defined. Among the better-known of these are

- the entity-relationship (E-R) model, which encompasses the entity and relationship semantic concepts
- the recently proposed role model, which has the role semantic concept as an integral component
- semantic models based on the aggregation and generalization abstractions

These models are not mutually exclusive: they may use the same abstractions but use different terms to name them and different model structures. So the same user enterprise can be described by each of the models although in different ways. In the next three chapters we will compare semantic models and illustrate the different ways in which they model the same enterprise.

Representing Semantic Models

Semantic structures are illustrated in this text by semantic nets. The *semantic net* (Figure 4.3) is a graph made up of

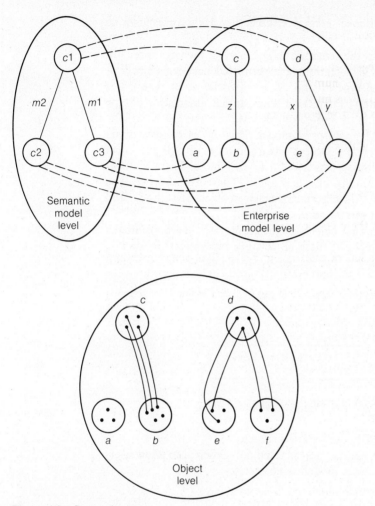

Figure 4.3 Semantic nets

- a set of points or nodes, which describe semantic objects
- a set of links to represent the associations between these objects

A semantic net can be used to describe a semantic structure at any level. If it models a structure at the semantic model level, the points represent semantic abstractions, and the links the allowed associations between such abstractions. If the semantic net models an enterprise model, the points represent object sets, and the links the association between these sets. Such associations must be consistent with the associations in the semantic model level. If the semantic net models an object level, the points represent actual enterprise objects. The objects can be associated consistently with the associations in the semantic model. Obviously, the levels are generic and the enterprise model is generated from the semantic model; the classification of enterprise objects in turn corresponds to the enterprise model.

In Figure 4.3 the first level is the semantic model level. It includes three object set types, $c1$, $c2$, and $c3$. Associations are permitted between objects of types $c1$ and $c3$ and objects of type $c1$ and $c2$. An association of type $m1$ is allowed between objects in $c1$ and $c3$ object set types, and an association of type $m2$ is allowed between objects in $c1$ and $c2$ object sets.

The second level illustrates an enterprise model. This model consists of six object sets, named a, b, c, d, e, and f. Object sets c and d are of type $c1$, object sets e and f are of type $c2$, and object sets a and b are of type $c3$. There is a type $m1$ association named z between object sets b and c. There are also two type $m2$ associations named x and y. Association x is between object sets e and d and association y is between object sets f and d.

The third level models the actual objects in the enterprise. There are now a number of objects in each object set; these objects are represented by dots in the semantic net. Associations are represented by lines joining the associated objects.

Semantic nets will be used extensively in the next three chapters to describe semantic models.

SUMMARY

The relational model suffers from two main drawbacks:

1. It cannot be effectively used in early design stages.
2. Its semantic structure (FDs and MVDs) is often not sufficient to allow users to make unambiguous choices in modeling enterprises.

There are, however, advantages in using the relational model in database design. Its normal forms provide designers with very effective guidelines for deriving data structures that avoid duplication and maintain consistency during database operations. The question is how to make use of these relational properties within a design methodology.

Semantic models are a major alternative to relational design. They can capture the essential semantic features of an enterprise in initial design stages by using abstractions that closely reflect the users' mental modeling processes. Semantic models, however, do not as a rule possess the detailed criteria of data structure that characterize normal relational forms.

It is possible to combine semantic models with the relational model in database design. A semantic model could be used to identify the essential enterprise constructs. It could then be modified by applying relational criteria to the enterprise model constructs. The goal of the modification is to ensure that the attributes of each semantic model construct correspond to a normal relation.

Semantic modeling can be considered at three levels: the semantic model level, the enterprise level, and the object level. The three levels can be seen to correspond to a programming language, the definition of variables, and variable values. Semantic nets can be used to describe semantic models.

PROBLEMS

1. Describe the advantages and disadvantages of the relational model in database design. What stages of the design cycle best suit the relational model?
2. What is the difference between a semantic abstraction and a semantic model?
3. Describe the three levels of semantic modeling and their relationships to programming systems.

chapter five
Semantic Modeling, I–
Entities and Relationships

INTRODUCTION

One abstraction that is commonly used and generally understood is the *entity*. An entity serves as an abstraction for objects that are well established and have a distinctive purpose in an enterprise. So it is not surprising that this abstraction is commonly used in semantic modeling. The two best-known semantic models based on entities are the entity-relationship model and the entity model. As we will see, they differ in the way that they model interactions between entities.

THE ENTITY-RELATIONSHIP MODEL

The *entity-relationship (E-R) model* was introduced by P. P. Chen (1976) and has found wide acceptance in database design. It provides the analyst with three main semantic concepts: entities, relationships, and attributes. Designers who use the E-R model in data analysis must describe the enterprise in terms of

- *entities*, which are distinct objects within a user enterprise;
- *relationships*, which are meaningful interactions between the objects;
- *attributes*, which describe the entities and relationships. Each such attribute is associated with a *value set* (domain) and can take a value from this value set.

In E-R modeling it is important to consider the entities as abstract but meaningful "things" that exist in the user enterprise. Such "things" may be described by attributes; they may also interact with one another in any number of relationships. We can use a semantic net as one way of describing an E-R model made up of a number of entities. The semantic net in Figure 5.1 describes an E-R model of an enterprise made up of four entities; two persons (*e*1 and *e*2) and two projects (*p*1 and *p*2). The symbol · represents entities, whereas the symbol ◇ represents relationships in the semantic net. There are four attributes

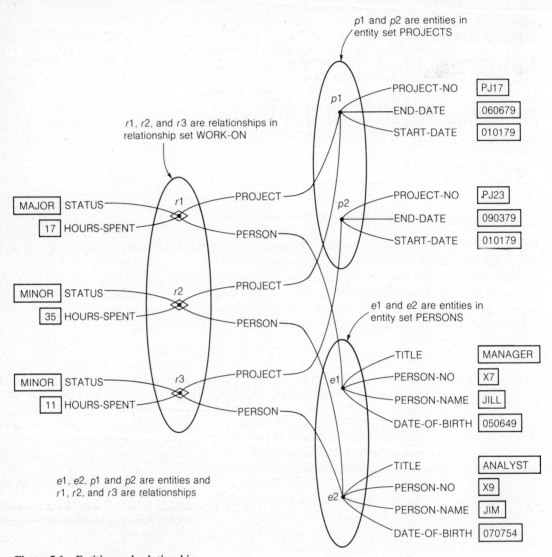

Figure 5.1 Entities and relationships

associated with each person: TITLE, PERSON-NO, PERSON-NAME, and
DATE-OF-BIRTH. Each attribute takes a value from its associated value set.
Thus the value of attribute PERSON-NO for entity e2 is X9. Similarly, proj-
ect entities have three attributes: PROJECT-NO, END-DATE, and START-
DATE.

Relationships are also treated as abstract objects. There are three relationships in Figure 5.1: r1, r2, and r3. Each relationship describes an interaction
between a PERSON and a PROJECT. The relationship is joined by lines to the
entities that participate in the relationship. The lines are labeled by names that

are unique when compared to the names of other lines emanating from the relationship. Thus relationship $r1$ is an interaction between PROJECT $p1$ and PERSON $e1$. It has two attributes, STATUS, HOURS-SPENT, and two links, PERSON and PROJECT, to its interacting entities. Attribute values of a relationship describe the effects or method of interaction between entities. Thus HOURS-SPENT describes the time that a PERSON spent on a PROJECT; STATUS describes the status of a person on a project.

Entity and Relationship Sets

Entities are grouped into entity sets, and relationships are grouped into relationship sets. Entities with the same attributes fall into one entity set. Likewise, relationships with the same attributes fall into one relationship set. In Figure 5.1 there are two entity sets and one relationship set.

Each entity set and each relationship set in an E-R model is given a unique name. In Figure 5.1 the entity set that includes $e1$ and $e2$ is named PERSONS. The entity set that includes $p1$ and $p2$ is named PROJECTS. Similarly, the one relationship set in Figure 5.1 includes the relationships $r1$, $r2$, and $r3$ and has the name WORK-ON.

A Diagrammatic Representation

Entities and relationships can be represented diagrammatically by an entity-relationship (E-R) diagram. In this diagram each entity set is represented by a rectangular box, and each relationship set by a diamond-shaped box. The diamond-shaped boxes (relationship sets) are joined to the rectangular boxes (entity sets of entities that participate in the relationship).

Figure 5.2 is an E-R diagram that depicts the entity and relationship sets in Figure 5.1. Here the two entity sets PERSONS and PROJECTS are represented by two rectangular boxes, and the relationship between them by a diamond-shaped box. The entity and relationship attributes are often listed next to the corresponding entity and relationship boxes. The values N and M indicate that the relationship between person and project in $N{:}M$. N persons can work on one project and a person can be assigned to M projects. It is also possible to have 1:1, 1:N, and N:1 relationships.

Figure 5.3 illustrates 1:N and N:1 relationships. The relationship between DEPT and PERSON is 1:N; that is, there can be N PERSONs in a DEPARTMENT, but a PERSON can only be in one DEPARTMENT. The relationship between PROJECT and PERSON is N:1; in this case a PERSON can manage any number of PROJECTs, but each PROJECT has only one PERSON as manager.

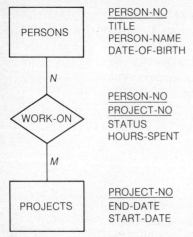

Figure 5.2   An entity relationship diagram

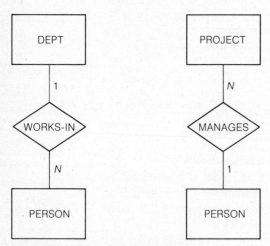

Figure 5.3   1:*N* and *N*:1 relationships

Multivalued Attributes

Although so far we have assumed that each attribute takes one value, it is possible for attributes to take more than one value. For example, suppose a person has the attribute SKILL; this attribute can take more than one value if the person has more than one skill. This situation can be represented semantically in the two ways shown in Figure 5.4. In case 1, each person is modeled as

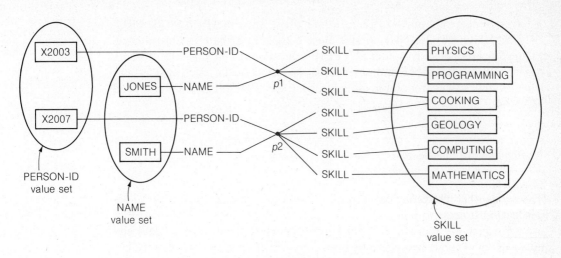

CASE 1
MULTIATTRIBUTE

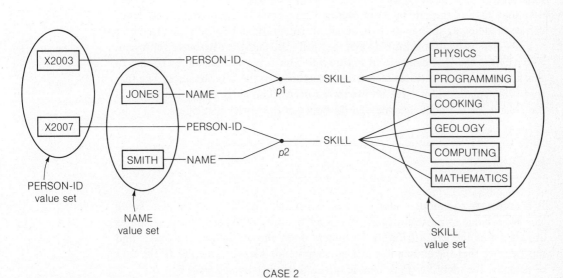

CASE 2
MULTIVALUE

Figure 5.4   The semantic representation of a multivalued attribute

possessing a number of SKILL attributes. Thus the person whose PERSON-ID is X2003 has three SKILL attributes, whose values are PHYSICS, PROGRAMMING, and COOKING. Case 2 shows an alternate semantic model of this enterprise. Now each person has only one SKILL attribute, but this attribute can take more than one value. Thus the person whose PERSON-ID is

X2003 now has only one SKILL attribute whose value is (PHYSICS, PRO-GRAMMING, COOKING). A still more complex attribute is illustrated in Figure 5.5. Here there is a set of SUPPLIER entities (*s*1 and *s*2), each of whom has a SUPPLIER-NAME and any number of CONTACTs. Each contact now is made up of values from three different value sets: PHONE, ADDRESS, and MANAGER.

Nonfunctional Dependencies

There is another interesting comparison between E-R models and functional dependencies. It deals with nonfunctional relationships. Consider the FDs in Figure 5.6, which are reproduced from Figure 3.6. Here there are four data elements. Each of these data elements is an identifier of entities in entity sets, but there are no FDs between the identifiers. You may recall that nonexistent attributes were introduced to model the interaction between the entity identifiers by FDs. But an E-R model does not require such nonexistent attributes. You may note that each of the attributes in Figure 3.6 represents an entity set and hence can be modeled as such in an E-R diagram. Interactions between the attributes are modeled as relationships between the entity set that the attributes represent. The result is the E-R diagram in Figure 5.6. The only relationship attributes in this figure are the identifiers of entities interacting in the relationships. The fact that these relationships have no attributes other than their entity identifiers is the reason for the nonexistence of FDs between the entity identifiers.

Identifiers

It is necessary to uniquely identify each entity in a particular entity set. To do this, we use one or more entity attributes as an entity identifier; these attributes are known as the *key attributes*. Designers must choose the key attributes and must ensure that the chosen key attributes uniquely identify entities. In the case of persons, the identifier may be one of the following data elements:

1. Person id number
2. Person name

The person id number is generally preferable because it uniquely identifies one person. Person name may not be a suitable identifier since there may be two or more persons with exactly the same name.

Similarly, identifiers of relationships in relationship sets are attributes that uniquely identify relationships in a particular set. Relationships are usually identified by more than one attribute. Most often the identifier attributes of a

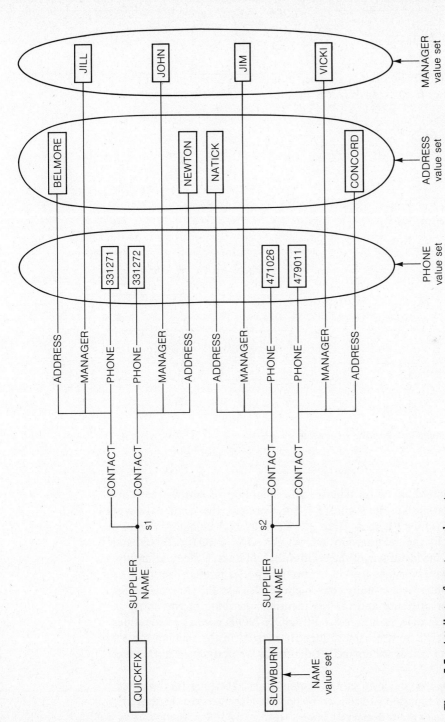

Figure 5.5 Attributes from two value sets

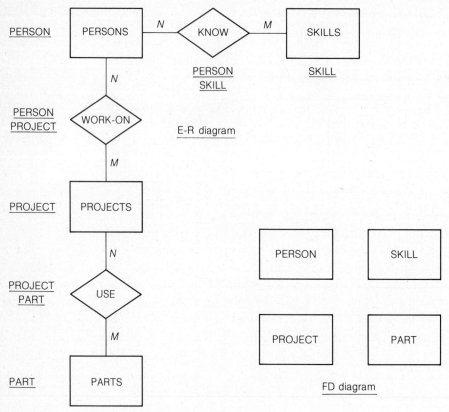

Figure 5.6 Nonfunctional relationships from Figure 3.6

relationship are those data values that are also identifiers of entities that participate in the relationship. In Figure 5.1, for example, the combination of a value of PROJECT-NO with a value of PERSON-NO uniquely identifies each relationship in the relationship set WORK-ON. PROJECT-NO and PERSON-NO are the identifiers of the entities that interact in the relationship.

If the same domain of values is used to identify entities in their own right as well as in relationships, it is usually convenient to also use the same name for the entity identifier attribute and for the identifier attribute of the entity in relationships. For example, in Figure 5.1 PERSON-NO is used as an identifier in PERSON entities; it is also used to identify persons in the relationship set WORK-ON. Object set identifiers in E-R diagrams are underlined in this text from now on.

Identifiers can be also modeled on the semantic net. The lines that emanate from an entity or relationship and that correspond to identifiers can be specially marked, although they are not marked in this text.

Modeling with the E-R Model

A designer who wishes to use the E-R model in system analysis would probably proceed by first identifying the entity sets, then the relationship sets, and then the attributes of each of these sets. Although this sounds fairly straightforward, it does involve a certain amount of personal perception of the importance of various objects in the enterprise. The result is that the design process is not deterministic: different designers can produce different enterprise models of the same enterprise.

The differences in user perception depend on the importance the designers place on objects in the enterprise and consequently on what objects they model as entities or attributes. Take, for example, PART and COLOR. Most designers would consider PART as the more important of the two and therefore model COLOR as an attribute of PART entities, as shown in Figure 5.7a. However, someone who is interested in paint production may consider COLORs as distinct and important objects in the enterprise. In this case it is quite valid to model COLOR as an entity. Now the COLOR of a PART will be represented by relationships, like the relationships $r1$ and $r2$ in Figure 5.7b. Thus Figure 5.7 illustrates two possible E-R representations of the same enterprise by the E-R model.

There are many such examples. Another is the location of companies in cities, as illustrated in Figure 5.8. Companies COMPA, COMPB and COMPC are located in Chicago, and companies COMPD and COMPE are located in Boston. Companies are usually considered to be distinct objects in any infor-

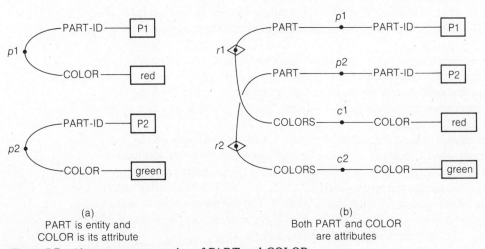

(a)
PART is entity and
COLOR is its attribute

(b)
Both PART and COLOR
are attributes

Figure 5.7   Alternate representation of PART and COLOR

COMPANY-NAME	LOCATION
COMPA	CHICAGO
COMPB	CHICAGO
COMPC	CHICAGO
COMPD	BOSTON
COMPE	BOSTON

Figure 5.8   Location of companies

mation system; hence companies can be modeled as an entity set with COM-PANY-NAME and LOCATION as attributes of this entity set. But here again, it is reasonable to question whether LOCATION should instead be an entity in its own right rather than an attribute of companies. And it is reasonable to argue that cities are well-established and distinct objects and should be modeled as entities. How can we resolve this problem? Some designers argue that the following *existence rule* be used in making any decision on what is to be an attribute and what is to be an entity.

Suppose we have two attributes AA or AB in an entity or relationship set R. Attribute AA can take any value of the value set $a1, a2, \ldots, an$, and attribute AB can take any value of the value set $b1, b2, \ldots, bn$. Now suppose all relationships that involve some value of AB, say, bi, are removed from R. In this case bi no longer exists in our information structure. If bi now also ceases to be of interest in the enterprise, AB is simply a property. However, if bi still has a meaning in the enterprise, AB is an entity identifier.

For instance, again consider Figure 5.8. Suppose COMPD and COMPE are deleted. No relationship that contains the value BOSTON for the attribute location now exists. However, if BOSTON is still of interest in the enterprise as a possible location of suppliers, then LOCATION should be modeled as an entity set.

Similarly, returning to parts and colors, suppose all parts that have the same color are removed from the relations. Is the color still of interest to the enterprise? If so, it should be considered as an entity and not an attribute. For example, if an enterprise manufactures its own dyes, a color is important even if not currently used on a part.

Another case of this type is shown in Figure 5.4. Here a value of SKILL may be of interest even though it may not be currently possessed by any person within an enterprise. However, this case differs from the preceding one in that a person may possess more than one SKILL, whereas in the manufacturing enterprise each PART possessed only one COLOR. The difference now is that if SKILL becomes an entity, the SKILL, PERSON relationship becomes $N:M$ rather than $1:N$, as is the case with COLOR and PART.

ENTITIES, RELATIONSHIPS, AND RELATIONS

A number of writers have discussed conversion from the E-R model to relations. The suggestion is that each entity set and each relationship set is converted to a relation. The question then is whether each such relation is in normal form. The answer depends on the original choice of entities, relationships, and attributes. For example, consider Figure 5.9. This figure shows the data attributes in the enterprise modeled by Figures 5.1 and 5.2 and the FDs between these attributes. The identifiers and properties of entities in the same entity set are enclosed. So are identifiers and attributes of relationship sets. Each entity set and each relationship set is represented by a separate relation. The attributes of entities in the entity set become the attributes of the relation, which represents that entity set. The entity identifier becomes the key of the relation. Each entity is represented by a tuple in the relation. Similarly, the attributes of relationships in each relationship set become the attributes of the relation, which represents the relationship set. The relationship identifiers become the key of the relation. Each relationship is represented by a tuple in that relation.

Thus the E-R model in Figures 5.1 and 5.2 are converted to three relations:

PROJECTS (<u>PROJECT-NO</u>, END-DATE, START-DATE)
  from entity set PROJECTS

PERSONS (<u>PERSON-NO</u>, TITLE, PERSON-NAME, DATE-OF-
  BIRTH) from entity set PERSONS

WORK-ON (<u>PROJECT-NO, PERSON-NO</u>, STATUS, HOURS-SPENT)
  from relationship set WORK-ON

These relations are all in BCNF. But such a simple conversion does not always produce normal form relations. Whether it does or not often depends on the modeling choices made by the analyst. In Figure 5.1 the analyst chose entities with attributes that are functionally dependent on the entity identifier. Moreover, the relationships are binary; that is, at most two entities interact on each relationship. The nonkey attributes of the corresponding relation are therefore functionally dependent on the relationship key.

A conversion, however, is not always so straightforward. Suppose the analyst chose to model persons as the only entity in the enterprise, with project as its attribute. The project attribute of each such entity can now take more than one value for the same entity. The corresponding relation would no longer be in normal form. For this reason some writers call entities that have attributes that take more than one value nondeterministic. The relation that corresponds to a nondeterministic entity set would no longer be normal.

This problem particularly arises with multivalued attributes, such as those shown in Figure 5.4. Now, in case 1, the conversion shown in Figure 5.9 results in

SKILLS (PERSON-ID, NAME, SKILL, SKILL. . . . . , SKILL)

which does not meet relational requirements as an attribute is repeated. In case 2, the conversion yields

SKILLS (PERSON-ID, NAME, SKILL)

which is not in normal form because SKILL is not a simple domain.

CHOICE OF ENTITIES AND RELATIONSHIPS

We could now argue that analysts should consider the correspondence between entity and relationship sets to normal relations when choosing entities and relationships; and that they should amend their E-R model by changing attributes to entities to ensure that the entity and relationship sets in their final model are deterministic and correspond to normal relations. So in the case where projects were chosen to be an attribute of person, the analyst on discovering this relation to be not normal would make projects an entity.

We could also argue, however, that this approach can sometimes yield an E-R model with entities created solely for the sake of normal relational considerations rather than because it is a well-defined enterprise object. Take, for example, a person who has more than one qualification—B.Sc., M.Sc., and Ph.D. If qualification is an attribute of person, then relation

PERSONS (PERSON-ID, QUAL DATE-OF-BIRTH)

will not be in BCNF. Should QUAL then be considered an entity in order to force BCNF correspondence? And what about a SUPPLIER with multiple ADDRESSes or a PERSON with several PHONE-NOs or several SKILLs, as in Figure 5.4? Should ADDRESS, SKILL, and PHONE-NO also be considered as entities in these enterprises? Such a choice, however, violates the existence rule. If a SUPPLIER is deleted, the supplier's ADDRESS is no longer of interest and therefore, by the existence rule, need not be maintained in the database. Hence by the existence rule ADDRESS should be an attribute and not an entity. Thus, making ADDRESS an entity is inconsistent with the existence rule. On the other hand, the choice of SKILL as an entity is consistent with the existence rule because particular SKILLs may be of interest even if they are not currently possessed by persons within the enterprise. There are two ways to deal with this conflict. Either allow attributes to have multiple values and ignore correspondence to normal relations or use the idea of dependence between entities.

WORK

PROJECT-NO	PERSON-NO	STATUS	HOURS
PJ17	X7	MAJOR	17
PJ23	X9	MINOR	11
PJ17	X9	MINOR	35

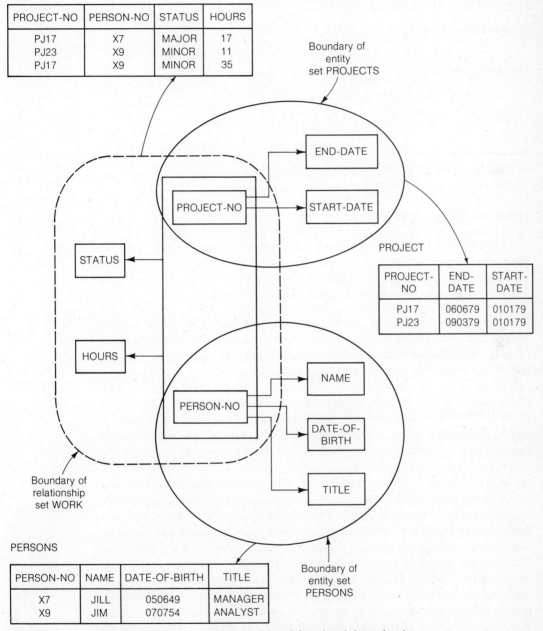

PROJECT

PROJECT-NO	END-DATE	START-DATE
PJ17	060679	010179
PJ23	090379	010179

PERSONS

PERSON-NO	NAME	DATE-OF-BIRTH	TITLE
X7	JILL	050649	MANAGER
X9	JIM	070754	ANALYST

Figure 5.9 Correspondence between the E-R model and functional dependencies

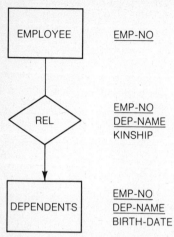

Figure 5.10   Employees' dependents

DEPENDENCE BETWEEN ENTITIES

There are many enterprises in which interest exists in one set of entities because of their dependence on another set of entities. A good example is the dependents of an EMPLOYEE. The dependents are only of interest while the employee is part of the enterprise; once the employee leaves the enterprise, the dependents also cease to be of interest. The term *owner entity* is used to refer to an entity on which another entity depends for its existence. The EMPLOYEE is the owner entity of DEPENDENTS. Both the employees and their dependents are considered as entities and can be modeled by an E-R diagram. In Figure 5.10 kinship indicates the relationship of the dependent to the employee. It may take the value "son," "daughter," and so on. An arrow terminating on a rectangular box in the E-R diagram indicates that the box represents a dependent entity. The source of the arrow indicates the entity on which the dependent entity depends.

Dependent entities are often identified by composite keys. These are keys made up of more than one attribute. Usually composite key identifiers of dependent entities include two attributes. These two attributes are the identifier of the owner entity and an attribute that uniquely identifies the dependent within its owner. For example, in Figure 5.10 dependents are identified by a composite key made up of the EMP-NO and a DEP-NAME. The attribute DEP-NAME may be some name, perhaps first name, that uniquely identifies the dependent with the employee. Note that the relationship also has the same identifier as the dependent entity. Hence when modeling dependent entities the relationship between the owner and dependent entities is often not included on the E-R diagram.

As another example, consider an enterprise that cannot place orders with a supplier unless some contract has been negotiated with that supplier. Both the order and the contract are well-defined distinct objects in the user enterprise. However, the existence of an order depends on the existence of a contract. This situation is illustrated by the semantic net in Figure 5.11. Here $o1$, $o2$, $o3$, $o4$, and $o5$ are order entities. These order entities depend on the contract entities, $c1$, $c2$, and $c3$; hence the order and contract entities are linked directly and not through any relationship. On the other hand, contract entities appear in relationships with supplier entities; and project entities appear in relationships with order entities.

A composite key is also used to identify orders in contracts in Figure 5.11. Each order is identified by its CONTRACT-NO together with an attribute ORDER-IN-CONTRACT; an order within a contract has a unique value of ORDER-IN-CONTRACT.

Problems with the Use of Composite Keys

One problem with identifiers of dependent entities occurs when the dependent entity has more than one owner. Take Figure 5.10, for example. The dependent entity set DEPENDENTS and the relationship set REL are represented by the two relations

DEPENDENTS (<u>EMP-NO, DEP-NAME,</u> BIRTH-DATE)
REL (<u>EMP-NO, DEP-NAME,</u> KINSHIP)

If now there are two EMPLOYEEs with the same dependent, that dependent appears twice in the relation DEPENDENTS. What is worse is that each occurrence of this dependent has a different identifier. For example, if a dependent son, JIM, has a mother, ID = 2251, and a father, ID = 3920, then that dependent son will appear as two tuples in relation DEPENDENTS. In one tuple he will be identified as (2251, JIM) and in the other as (3920, JIM). The BIRTH-DATE for that dependent is now stored twice in the database. This problem also occurs if, to minimize the number of relations, DEPENDENTS and REL are joined to yield

NEW-RELATION (<u>EMP-NO, DEP-NAME,</u> KINSHIP, BIRTH-DATE)

The BIRTH-DATE of a dependent JIM will also appear twice in NEW-RELATION.

The only way to prevent multiple occurrences of a dependent is to give the dependent its own unique identifier. Each dependent will then be stored once, and the dependence on its owner will appear only in a relationship and not as part of its key.

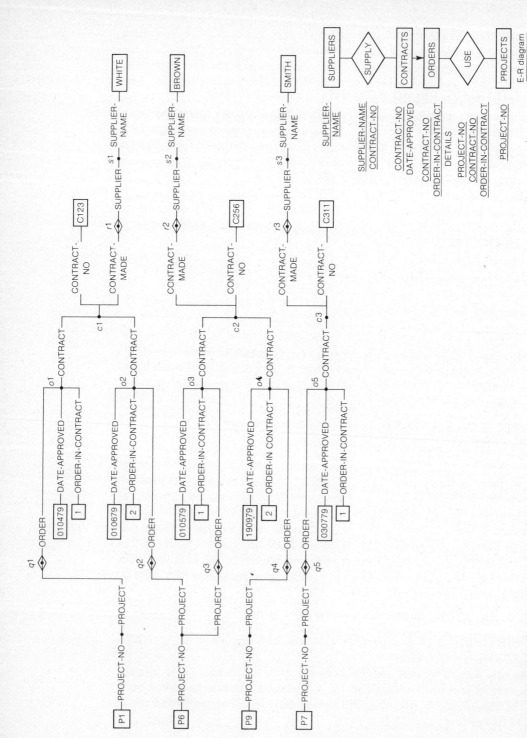

Figure 5.11 Modeling the dependence of order on contract

Thus in the preceding example we could introduce the dependent identifier DEP-ID. The relations DEPENDENTS and REL would now become

DEPENDENTS (<u>DEP-ID</u>, DEP-NAME, BIRTH-DATE)
REL (<u>EMP-NO, DEP-ID,</u> KINSHIP)

There would now be only one tuple for each dependent in DEPENDENTS. So if in our example JIM were given the unique identifier JIM-NO, there would be one tuple (JIM-NO, Jim, Jim's birthday) in DEPENDENTS. There would still, however, be two tuples about JIM in REL to show Jim's kinship to the two employees in the enterprise. Note that DEPENDENTS and REL can no longer be combined into the one relation NEW-RELATION, for they no longer have the same key.

Improper Use of Composite Keys

Improper use of composite keys can also lead to non-BCNF relations. A particular problem occurs when a composite key of a dependent entity includes an identifier of an entity on which it does not directly depend. For example, suppose (SUPPLIER-NAME, ORDER-IN-SUPPLIER) is chosen to be the identifier of the dependent entity ORDER in Figure 5.11. This will replace (CONTRACT-NO, ORDER-IN-CONTRACT) as the ORDERS identifiers. (Note that CONTRACT-NO still remains as an attribute of ORDERS to indicate the contract under which an order is made.) Now suppose a relation that represents orders is created and takes the form

ORDERS (SUPPLIER-NAME, ORDER-IN-SUPPLIER,
   CONTRACT-NO, DETAILS)

Since CONTRACT-NO → SUPPLIER-NAME, relation ORDERS has two keys (SUPPLIER-NAME, ORDER-IN-SUPPLIER) and (CONTRACT-NO, ORDER-IN-SUPPLIER); therefore SUPPLIER-NAME is dependent on only part of the second key. Relation ORDERS is then not in BCNF.

To avoid these problems composite keys of dependent entities must include only the identifier of the entity on which it directly depends. In our example orders depend directly on the contract and not on the supplier, so we now make the composite key (CONTRACT-NO, ORDER-IN-CONTRACT). Then we replace relation ORDERS by ORDERS (CONTRACT-NO, ORDER-IN-CONTRACT, DETAILS). Relation ORDERS is now in BCNF.

MULTIPLE RELATIONSHIPS

Earlier, relationships were defined to be meaningful interactions between entities. Relationships with the same properties were classified into relationship sets. Relationships in the same set included entities from the same entity sets. Each relationship in Figure 5.1, for example, includes one entity from entity set PERSON and one entity from entity set PROJECT. Moreover, there is at most one relationship between two distinct entities. Thus $p1$ and $e1$ appear together once only in a relationship, because this is sufficient to store all the information about their interaction, namely, the total hours spent by a person on a project.

There are, however, many occasions when it becomes necessary to model relationship sets that include more than one interaction between the same two entities. Usually this situation comes up when the interaction between the entities occurs at a number of instances over time. For example, suppose Figure 5.1 is extended to model the time spent by persons on projects each week of the year. A person may have worked on the same project for more than one week. There may then be more than one interaction that includes the same person and the same project. One such interaction will appear for each week that person worked on that project.

Models of multiple interactions must distinguish between the individual interactions of the same entities. This distinction can be made in one of the three ways shown in Figure 5.12. The options are as follows:

- *Option 1: Extend the relationship identifier.* The relationship identifier contains attributes in addition to the identifiers of the interacting entities. Thus the identifier of WORK relationships contains WEEK-NO as well as the entity identifiers PERSON-NO and PROJECT-NO.

  The FD for relationship work becomes

  PERSON-NO, PROJECT-NO, WEEK-NO → TIME-SPENT

  which in turn reduces to the relation

  WORK (<u>PERSON-NO, PROJECT-NO, WEEK-NO,</u> TIME-SPENT)

- *Option 2: Create a history dependent entity.* A history entity set is created for one or more entities in the multiple relationship. Each history entity is a dependent entity because its existence is conditional on the existence of the entity whose history is modeled.

  The FDs for this option become

  HISTORY-ID → PERSON-ID, WEEK-NO
  HISTORY-ID, PROJECT-NO → TIME-SPENT

  which in turn reduces to the relations

  HISTORY (<u>PERSON-ID, WEEK-NO,</u> HISTORY-ID)
  WORK (<u>HISTORY-ID, PROJECT-NO,</u> TIME-SPENT)

HISTORY-ID can be an attribute on its own. Alternatively, it can be the composite identifier (PERSON-ID, WEEK-NO). Figure 5.12 uses the composite identifier form for HISTORY-ID. In this case HISTORY and WORK reduce to

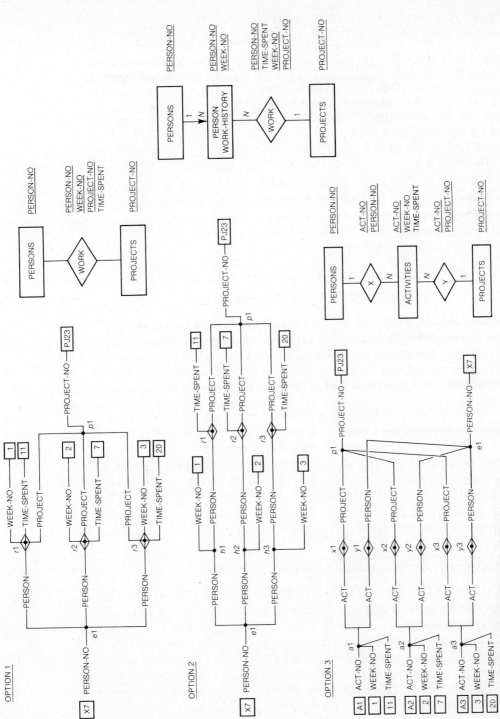

Figure 5.12 Modeling multiple relationships

HISTORY (<u>PERSON-ID, WEEK-NO</u>)
WORK (<u>PERSON-ID, WEEK-NO</u>, PROJECT-NO, TIME-SPENT)

Note that in this case HISTORY could include attributes that describe a person's status for the week irrespective of the projects on which the person worked.

• *Option 3: Use an interaction identifier.* Each interaction between a project and a person now becomes an entity in its own right called ACTIVITY in Figure 5.12; its identifier is ACT-NO and its attributes are WEEK-NO and TIME-SPENT. Each activity appears in only one X relationship with a project and only one Y relationship with a person.

The FDs that describe this model are

ACT-NO → PERSON
ACT-NO → PROJECT
ACT-NO → TIME-SPENT, WEEK-NO

These FDs are combined to form the relation

WORK (<u>ACT-NO</u>, PERSON, PROJECT, TIME-SPENT, WEEK-NO)

You will note that in the last two options each entity from one set appears in at most one relationship with the same entity from another set. Thus in option 2 there is at most one interaction between the same project and the same person-history entity. In option 3 there is at most one interaction between the same project and the same activity as well as the same person and the same activity.

Multiple Relationships and Composite Keys

Multiple relationships can also use composite identifiers, which in turn can result in non-BCNF relations. For example, suppose we choose the identifier of ACTIVITIES in option 3 of Figure 5.12 to be (DEPT-NO, ACTIVITY-IN-DEPT) instead of ACT-NO. Suppose also that we allocate each project to one department, so that PROJECT-NO → DEPT-NO. The relation Y in option 3 now becomes

Y(DEPT-NO, ACTIVITY-IN-DEPT, PROJECT-NO)

Again (DEPT-NO, ACTIVITY-IN-DEPT) and (PROJECT-NO, ACTIV-ITY-IN-DEPT) are keys of Y, but DEPT-NO is dependent on a subset of the second key. As always, care must be taken in the construction of composite keys. A composite key for a dependent entity should include only identifiers of entities directly related to the dependent entity. In this case the activity is not a dependent of only one project, or only one department, or only one person, but a combination of them. Hence a composite identifier including only identifiers of one of these entities should not be constructed.

If care is exercised, then multiple relationships, which are represented by relations with more than one relation key, are usually in BCNF. One example of such a BCNF relation is ASSIGN, which represents a multiple relationship between persons and positions; this relationship is defined by the relation

ASSIGN (PERSON-NO, POSITION-NO, DATE-ASSIGNED, STARTING-SALARY)

It is assumed here that a person can be at most assigned to one position on the same date, and one position has only one person assigned to it on the same date. Now both (PERSON-NO, DATE-ASSIGNED) and (POSITION-NO, DATE-ASSIGNED) are relation keys. The relation is in BCNF.

BINARY AND *n*-ARY RELATIONSHIPS

Multiple relationships can be extended to relationships that include more than two entities. For example, suppose the QTY of PARTS delivered to each STORE by each SUPPLIER is of interest in the enterprise. A supplier in this enterprise can deliver more than one kind of PART to any number of stores. The E-R model for this relationship is illustrated in Figure 5.13, and the semantic net is shown in Figure 5.14. One interaction in Figure 5.14 shows that S1 delivered 30 parts (where PART-NO is PX302) to store STORE1.

The *n*-ary relationships have a number of undesirable features. One is that it is no longer meaningful to label the E-R diagram with 1:*N*, *N*:*M*, or *N*:1 relationships. If the SUPPLIERS to STORES relationship is *N*:1 and the SUPPLI-

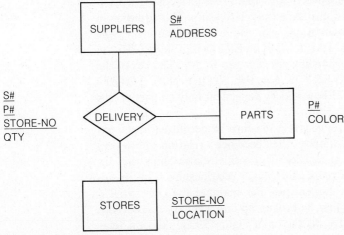

Figure 5.13 An *n*-ary relationship

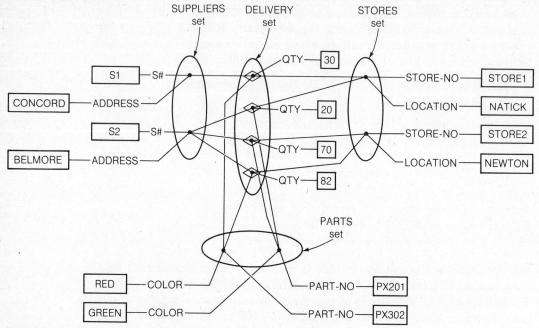

Figure 5.14   The semantic net for the *n*-ary relationship in Figure 5.13

ERS to PARTS relationship is 1:*N*, the label between SUPPLIERS and DE-LIVERY would have to contain both 1 and *N*.

Another undesirable feature is that *n*-ary relationships can become clumsy, especially if a very large number of entities interact in a relationship. With many entities interacting, the possibility of nonnormal relational equivalence increases, because designers may inadvertently create relationships with attributes that depend on a subset of the entities in the relationship. This situation in turn can lead to non-BCNF representations. For example, in Figure 5.13 the inclusion of the attribute TOTAL-PARTS-DELIVERED-BY-SUPPLIER in DELIVERY would make the corresponding relation non-BCNF. The key of the relation that corresponds to DELIVERY is (S#, P#, STORE-NO); TOTAL-PARTS-DELIVERED by SUPPLIER would be dependent only on part of this key, namely (S#, P#).

Some authors propose that only binary relationships be permitted in the enterprise model. Each binary relationship set then becomes a relation whose keys are the identifiers of the interacting entities. To do this relationships that include more than one entity must be reduced to binary relationships. This reduction leads to the concept of relationship entities. For example, the DELIVERY relationships in Figure 5.13 would first be broken up into a binary relationship between SUPPLIERS and STORES. As shown in Figure 5.15a, this new relationship becomes an entity in the entity set SUP-STORE. Each entity in this

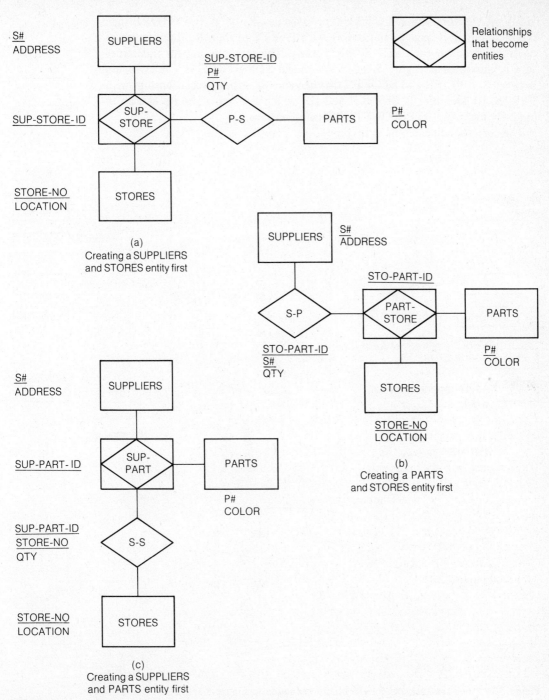

Figure 5.15 Alternative conversions to binary relationships

entity set is a store–supplier combination. This new entity in SUP-STORE then interacts in a P-S binary relationship with PARTS to indicate the number of parts delivered for each SUP-STORE entity. The semantic net for this structure is illustrated in Figure 5.16. In this model SUP-STORE is a relationship between SUPPLIER and STORES that becomes an entity in relationships with PARTS. Its identifier is SUP-STORE-ID, which is a set of values chosen to uniquely identify SUPPLIER-STORE combinations.

The corresponding relations become

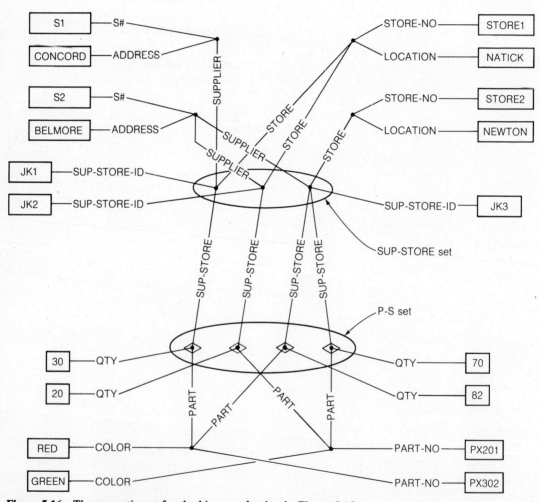

Figure 5.16   The semantic net for the binary reduction in Figure 5.15a

SUPPLIERS (S#, ADDRESS)
STORES (STORE-NO, LOCATION)
SUP-STORE (S#, STORE-NO, SUP-STORE-ID)
PARTS (P#, COLOR)
P-S (SUP-STORE-ID, P#, QTY)

It is possible to recreate the original DELIVERY relation by joining relation SUP-STORE and P-S over SUP-STORE-ID and projecting SUP-STORE-ID out of the relation.

It is of course possible to break up the 3-ary relationship of Figure 5.13 in two other ways; these are shown in Figure 5.15b and c. In Figure 5.15b the relationship between PARTS and STORES becomes an entity that interacts with SUPPLIERS. In Figure 5.15c the relationship between SUPPLIERS and PARTS becomes an entity that interacts with STORES.

Any of the three alternatives are equally valid. Again it is the analyst who must choose the alternative that seems to be the correct representation of the enterprise.

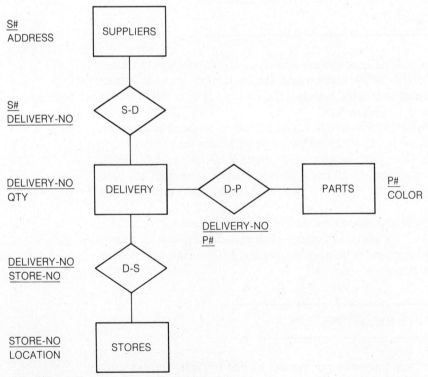

Figure 5.17 A symmetrical conversion

One way to overcome the arbitrariness of this choice is to make the *n*-ary relationships themselves into entities. Each new entity then appears in a binary relationship with each of the *n* entities that appeared in the *n*-ary relationship. This reduction is illustrated in Figure 5.17. Now DELIVERY becomes an entity that interacts with PARTS, SUPPLIERS, and STORES. The resultant relations become

DELIVERY (DELIVERY-NO, QTY);
SUPPLIERS (S#, ADDRESS)
PARTS (P#, COLOR)
STORES (STORE-NO, LOCATION)
DELIVERY-PARTS (DELIVERY-NO, P#)
DELIVERY-SUPPLIERS (DELIVERY-NO, S#)
DELIVERY-STORES (DELIVERY-NO, STORE-NO)

Each relation now represents either an entity or a binary relationship. A new identifier has been introduced to identify DELIVERY entities.

THE ENTITY MODEL

The ideas of binary relationships and the conversion of relationships to entities lead to the entity model. In the entity model the interactions between entities are themselves modeled as entities. For example, the enterprise model of Figure 5.1 would be modeled by Figure 5.18.

Now the relationship WORK-ON in Figure 5.2 can be modeled as an entity. Two new relationships, *R*1 and *R*2, are added to model the interaction of the new entity, WORK-ON, with the existing entities PERSON and PROJECT. These two new relationships are all key. The entity model ignores all key relationships since they simply duplicate the data stored in the newly created entity (WORK-ON).

The entity model that corresponds to the E-R model of Figure 5.2 (or 5.18) is shown in Figure 5.19. This model no longer includes relationship sets. Designers do not have to make distinctions between entities and relationships anymore, so the semantics of modeling are simplified.

UNREPRESENTABLE RELATIONSHIPS

Sometimes relationships cannot be represented by one relation. For example, suppose a relationship describes various things borrowed by persons. Each of these things uses different identifier attributes. Some may be books, identified

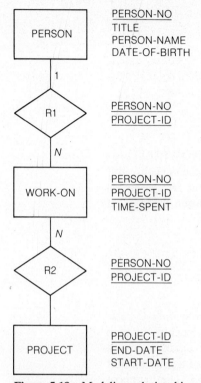

PERSON
PERSON-NO
TITLE
PERSON-NAME
DATE-OF-BIRTH

1

R1
PERSON-NO
PROJECT-ID

N

WORK-ON
PERSON-NO
PROJECT-ID
TIME-SPENT

N

R2
PERSON-NO
PROJECT-ID

PROJECT
PROJECT-ID
END-DATE
START-DATE

Figure 5.18   Modeling relationships
as entities

by a book number; others may be pieces of equipment, identified by an equipment number; and still others may be records, identified by recording studio and number. A relation that describes this relationship would take the form

BORROWING (PERSON-ID, BORROWED-ITEM-ID,
    DATE-BORROWED)

Individual tuples for this relation are shown in Figure 5.20.

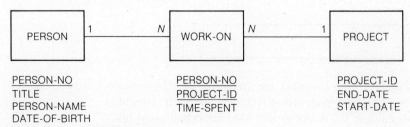

PERSON-NO
TITLE
PERSON-NAME
DATE-OF-BIRTH

PERSON-NO
PROJECT-ID
TIME-SPENT

PROJECT-ID
END-DATE
START-DATE

Figure 5.19   An entity model

PERSON-ID	BORROWED-ITEM-ID			DATE-BORROWED
PER-1	5932005			020379
PER-2	PROJ	35mm	35	040379
PER-3	DECCA	SKLP4075		040474

Figure 5.20   Relation BORROWING

Relation **BORROWING** is invalid because values of **BORROWED-ITEM-ID** take values from any of three domains, some of which are composite. But the same attribute cannot take values from different domains in a relation. Consequently, the relationship cannot be represented by a relation. In the next chapter a solution to this problem, using roles, is outlined.

MINIMALITY OF RELATIONS

Another question of E-R modeling concerns the conversion procedure to relations. Does a procedure that converts each entity and relationship set to a relation produce the least number of relations? The answer again is no. To understand why, consider 1:N relationships. The primary key of a relation that represents a 1:N relationship may have extraneous attributes. Thus suppose that in the example in Figure 5.2 a person can at most work on one project. If this new E-R model is converted to relations using the method in Figure 5.9, there will be only one tuple for one person in relation WORK-ON. PERSON-NO is then the key of relation WORK-ON. There will now be too many relations following the conversion because relation PERSONS and WORK-ON have the same primary key; they can be combined to form one relation.

The decision to combine the relations rests with the designer. The designer may wish to keep the two relations separate, for they represent separate concepts. Later, PERSONS may become a PERSONNEL file and WORK-ON an ACTIVITY file. There may be design reasons other than minimum redundancy to warrant such separation.

SUMMARY

Two major abstractions used in data modeling are the entity and the relationship. The structures of two semantic models that include these abstractions are the entity-relationship model and the entity model. One important point often raised in the chapter is the nondeterminism of semantic modeling. Semantic models, as described in earlier chapters, are designed to capture the essential features of an enterprise. The problem is that different designers may perceive different features as being essential. Hence different enterprise models can be developed for the same enterprise by different designers. Some features cannot be easily captured by the entity and relationship abstractions. The next chapter introduces two new abstractions to provide the designer with additional modeling abilities.

PROBLEMS

For each of the following problems develop an E-R diagram. Ensure that each set corresponds to a BCNF relation. Specify what that BCNF relation is.

Problem 1

Identify the entities and relationships for each of the following enterprises and draw an E-R diagram for them.

Enterprise 1

A person, identified by a PERSON-ID, can own any number of vehicles. Each vehicle is of a given MAKE. It is registered in any one of a number of states identified by STATE-NAME. A registration number (REG-NO) and registration TERMINATION DATE are of interest, and so is the address of a registration office (REG-OFFICE-ADDRESS) in each state.

Enterprise 2

An organization purchases items from a number of suppliers. It keeps track of the number of each item type purchased from each supplier. It also keeps a record of suppliers' addresses at which item types can be collected. An item type can be collected at any address. There may be more than one such address for each supplier. The price charged by each supplier for each item type is also stored.

Enterprise 3

A person keeps a record of documents of interest to her. The time and source of each document are stored along with its location. Documents may be books, identified by author and title; journal articles, identified by journal volume and number, author, and title; or private correspondence, identified by sender and date.

Problem 2

A person (identified by PERSON-ID) can originate an order (identified by ORDER-ID) in the enterprise. Each order is originated by one person, but one person can originate more than one order. Each order is associated with one SUPPLIER.

Each order is made up of any number of ITEM kinds (identified by ITEM-ID). An ITEM kind can appear in any number of orders; ITEM-QTY is the quantity of an ITEM in a particular order.

A quantity of any item in an order can be allocated to a PROJECT (identified by PROJECT-NO) in the enterprise. A project can use the same ITEM kind from different orders; one ITEM kind in an order can be used in a number of projects. ITEM-USED-IN-PROJECT is the total amount of some item kind in a project; ITEM-IN-ORDER-USED-IN-PROJECT is the amount of item kind within an order used by a project. Note that more than one project can use the same item kind from the one order.

Problem 3

Drivers (identified by DRIVER-NO, with each driver having a NAME, one HOME-ADDRESS, and a DATE-OF-BIRTH) take out vehicles to make deliveries. A vehicle (identified by VEHICLE-NO, with each vehicle being of a particular MAKE and YEAR-OF-MANUFACTURE) may be taken out of a depot whenever available and kept out for any length of time (ranging from one or two hours to a number of days). It is possible for a vehicle to be taken out more than once on a given day. Any vehicle can be taken out by any driver any number of times each day. There is only one depot.

Each time a driver takes out a vehicle, he or she takes out a load made up of any QTY of any of a number of item types (identified by an ITEM-NO and having a COLOR, WEIGHT, and DESCRIPTION). Every time a vehicle is taken out, the driver can incur expenses of allowed types (e.g., fuel cost). Each expense type has a CODE-NO. The AMOUNT and CODE-NO are recorded each time an expense is incurred. There may be one or more expenses of the same type incurred during the same trip. Any number of stops can be made during the trip. An ADDRESS of the stop is recorded for each stop, together with the QTY-LEFT of each item type left at the stop. A driver will stop at an ADDRESS only once during one trip. However, it is possible for stops to be made at the same address on different trips.

Problem 4

A university needs a database to hold current information on its students. An initial analysis of these requirements produced the following facts:

- Each of the faculties in the university is identified by a unique name; a faculty head is responsible for each faculty.
- There are a large number of majors in the university; some majors are managed by one faculty, whereas others are managed jointly by two or more faculties.
- Teaching is organized into courses. There are any number of tutorials organized for each course.
- Each major has a number of required courses.
- Each course is supervised by one faculty.
- Each major has a unique name.
- To take certain courses, a student must first pass the prerequisite courses.
- Each course is at a given level and has a credit-point value.
- Each course has one lecturer in charge of the course. The university keeps a record of the lecturer's name and address.
- Each course can have a number of tutors.
- Any number of students can be enrolled in each of the majors. Each student can be enrolled in only one major, and the university keeps a record of that student's name and address and of an emergency contact.
- Any number of students can be enrolled in a course; each student in a course can be enrolled in only one tutorial for that course.
- Each tutorial has one tutor assigned to it.
- A tutor can tutor in more than one tutorial for one or more courses.
- Each tutorial is given in an assigned room at a given time on a given day.
- Each tutor not only supervises tutorials but is also in charge of some course.

Problem 5

Extend Problem 4 to include historical data. Now it is necessary to keep the information on course and major enrollments for each semester. The following facts have been established:

- There may be a different lecturer-in-charge of a course each semester.
- There may be different tutors for each course each semester.
- The grade obtained by a student in a course at the end of a given semester is to be stored.
- A student who has not passed a course may enroll in the same course for more than one semester until the course is passed.

Problem 6

After you have completed your E-R diagram in Problems 4 and 5, the following information comes to light:

- Some tutors are part-time and some are full-time staff members. Some tutors (particularly part-time tutors but also some full-time staff) are not in charge of any units.
- Some students are enrolled in majors, whereas others are enrolled in single courses only.

How would you change your E-R diagrams in light of this new information?

chapter six
Semantic Modeling, II–
Roles and Types

INTRODUCTION

In the previous chapter we introduced entities and relationships and the ways they can be used to model enterprises. We suggested that semantic modeling is not deterministic. A designer can model the same enterprise in different ways even when using the same semantic model. The chosen method depends on the relative importance the designer places on the enterprise objects. Analysts who use the E-R model, for example, can choose the objects to be modeled as entities; they can decide to restrict the model to binary relationships and select different ways to model multiple relationships.

In the last chapter we also outlined some problems of using E-R models to model the same relationships but with one identifier attribute coming from different domains. The question that arises, then, is whether other abstractions can offer analysts further guidance in making modeling choices. Further, can other abstractions be used to model relationships that cannot be represented simply by the E-R model? The E-R model has now been widely used, and it is clear that it can model most enterprises. However, other abstractions are available to capture semantic features that cannot be explicitly modeled by entities and relationships. So it is useful for analysts to be aware of such abstractions both as supplements to the E-R model and as modeling tools in their own right. Two such abstractions—roles and types—are covered in this chapter.

C. W. Bachman (1977) first proposed roles as a modeling abstraction in the context of the role model, although Codd (1970) had used them earlier in the relational model. Codd defined roles taken by domains in relations. Codd's use of the term *role* is best illustrated by referring to relation MANUFACTURE (first shown in Figure 2.3 and again in Figure 6.1a). Here a domain that is a part identifier appears in two columns in a parts explosion relation (Figure 6.1a). In this relation a different role name is used on each PART column to indicate whether that column represents an ASSEMBLY or a COMPONENT. Codd's initial use of the word *role* in this context (Codd, 1970) eventually gave way to the term *attribute*. In the E-R model the parts explosion is modeled as an object set that participates in the same relationship in two ways (Figure

6.1b). The kind of participation is shown by a label on the semantic links between the entity and relationship sets (ASSEMBLY and COMPONENT in Figure 6.1b). This type of relationship, which we will discuss in the next section, is known as *recursive*. Bachman's concept of role can be shown as an extension to the E-R model (Figure 6.1c). Now two role object sets, ASSEMBLY-ROLE and COMPONENT-ROLE, are added. The objects in these two sets are subsets of the object set PART. Only the roles now participate in the relationship. Bachman's role model extends the concept of role to model all relationships, recursive and nonrecursive. In the role model entities take part in relationships only if they assume certain roles. Only roles take part in relationships. The type abstraction is similar to that of roles. It flows from the general need to model the frequently occurring phenomenon of entity classification. Now type sets of an object set are created. The type object sets are also subsets of an entity set and each subset contains the entities in one classification.

PART	PART	INTEGER
ASSEMBLY	COMPONENT	QTY
AUTO	ENGINE	1
AUTO	WHEEL	4
AUTO	CHASSIS	1
WHEEL	TIRE	1
WHEEL	NUTS	6
ENGINE	CYLINDER	4

(a) Using relational model

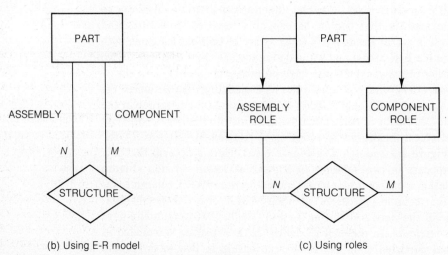

(b) Using E-R model   (c) Using roles

Figure 6.1   Representing recursive relationships

RECURSIVE RELATIONSHIPS

Recursive relationships differ from the examples in Chapter 5 in one significant way. In the examples in Chapter 5 the relationships were between entities from different entity sets. But it is also possible to model relationships between entities from the same set. When this occurs, the relationship is called recursive. A semantic net that illustrates a recursive relationship is shown in Figure 6.2. This figure illustrates recursive relationships between persons: one person in each

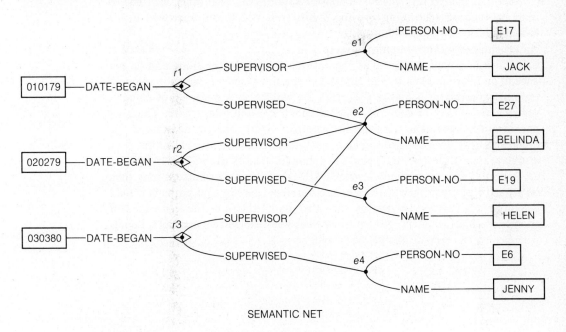

SEMANTIC NET

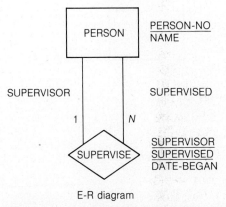

E-R diagram

Figure 6.2 Entities of the same kind in a relationship

relationship is a SUPERVISOR; the other person is SUPERVISED. Thus in relationship $r1$ JACK supervises BELINDA; this supervision began on 010179. The E-R diagram for this case also differs from the E-R diagram in Figure 5.2. Now there are two links from one entity box to the same relationship box. These links are labeled to show the way that an entity participates in a relationship; the kind of participation, or role, in Figure 6.2 can either be SUPERVISED or SUPERVISOR. Further, there is a 1:N relationship between SUPERVISOR and SUPERVISED roles. The supervisor may supervise many persons, but each person can at most be supervised by one other person.

There are many examples of recursive relationships. Two other well-known ones are the task scheduling and the family tree, which are illustrated in the E-R diagrams in Figure 6.3a and b.

One similarity (and simplifying factor) in all these three cases (Figures 6.1, 6.2, and 6.3) is that attributes of the entities are always the same and do not depend on the role taken by the entity. But the situation is different in the next example, illustrated in Figure 6.4. Here the enterprise is made up of persons, some of whom may be doctors, others patients, and still others both. They can participate in treatment relationships, one participant being a doctor and the other a patient. Doctors and patients have many common attributes, but they also have some different attributes. For example, doctors have SPECIALTY as an attribute, whereas patients have SYMPTOMS as an attribute. It may then be argued that since their attributes are different, doctors and patients should belong to different entity sets; on the other hand, they are the same kind of enterprise object, namely, person. How does one resolve this conflict? This is where roles can become useful.

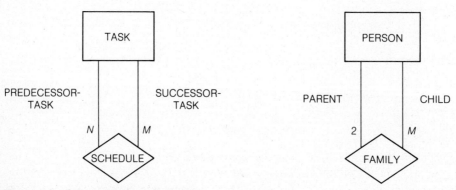

Figure 6.3   Other recursive relationships

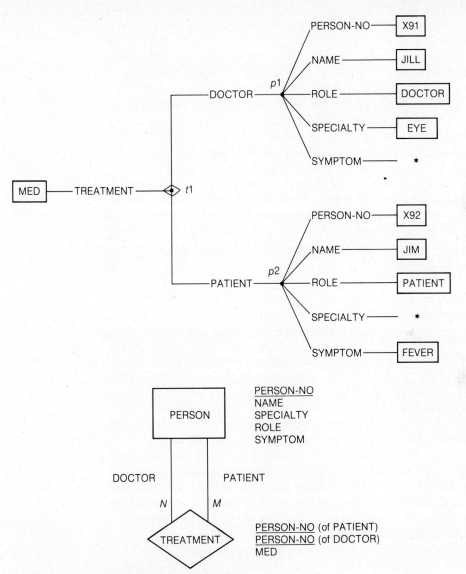

Figure 6.4 A PERSON-DOCTOR relationship

EXTENSION TO ROLES

Roles allow designers to treat entities from the same object set in different ways. That is, an object set can be divided into subsets, and objects in each subset can be treated differently. Thus we can begin to model the enterprise in

Figure 6.4 by constructing doctors and patients as subsets of the entity set PERSON. These subsets are called *role sets*. The objects in the role set are known as roles that entities take. The semantic model that includes such roles is shown by the semantic net of Figure 6.5. Role entities are represented by ⊙ on the semantic net. Here $d1$ and $d2$ are doctor role entities and $s1$ and $s2$ are patient role entities. The role entities are linked directly to the person entities. This direct link between role and role player is used to illustrate the strong dependence that exists between an entity and its role. Note how the E-R diagram in Figure 6.5 differs from that of Figure 6.4. Now there is a separate box to represent each role. Again the role boxes are linked directly to the entity box, and an arrow is used to model the dependence of role on entity. Also note that in Figure 6.5 person $p1$ appears only in the DOCTOR subset, and person $p2$ only in the PATIENT subset, whereas person $p3$ appears in both subsets. Also note that SPECIALTY is now only an attribute of DOCTOR and not PERSON, as only doctors have a specialty. Similarly SYMPTOM is an attribute of PATIENTS and not PERSONS.

Modeling Properties of Roles

Roles are useful not only for modeling recursive relationships, but for solving other modeling problems. For example, let us return to relation BORROWING in Figure 5.20. The problem here was that one of the relationship identifier attributes corresponds to entities that come from the different entity sets. These entity sets have identifiers from different domains, and so there is no common entity attribute that can be included as an identifier in the relationship. Roles can be used to resolve this problem by introducing a new role set, called BORROWED-ITEM. As shown in Figure 6.6, this role set participates with PERSONS in relationship BORROW. Roles in role set BORROWED-ITEMS can be taken by entities from different entity sets. Role sets that include entities from different entity sets are called nonuniform in this text. Their structure is discussed in more detail later in this chapter.

Another modeling property of roles is illustrated in Figure 6.7, in which role entities are used to express the same kinds of relationships between different kinds of entities. Here there are four kinds of organizational unit entities: DIVISION, DEPT, BRANCH, and SECTION. Organizational units can directly supervise other organizational units. Thus DIV1 directly supervises BRANCH1 and DEPT1 but not BRANCH2; BRANCH2 is directly supervised by DEPT1. BRANCH2 is indirectly supervised by DIV1. Certain kinds of organizational unit can directly supervise only certain other kinds of organizational unit; this direct supervision can be described by relationships. Thus in Figure 6.7a, DIVISIONs can directly supervise DEPTs (relationship $R1$),

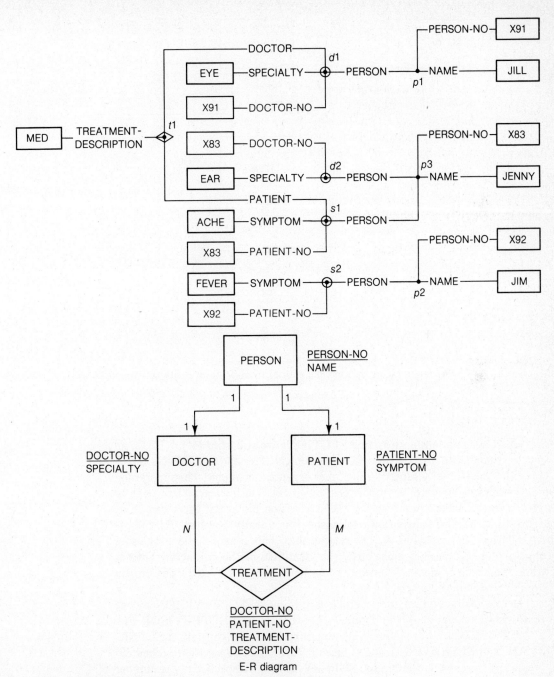

Figure 6.5 PERSON-DOCTOR relationship introducing roles

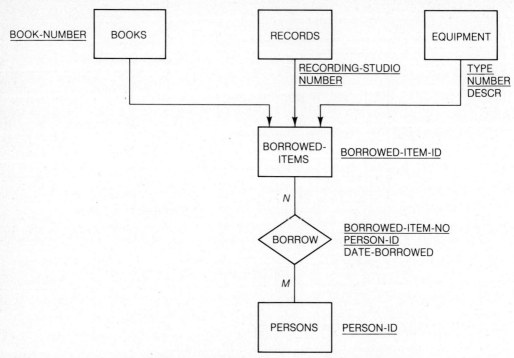

Figure 6.6 Modeling relationships that include entities from different entity sets

BRANCHes (relationship $R5$), and SECTIONs (relationship $R4$); DEPTs, on the other hand, can directly supervise only BRANCHes and SECTIONs. SECTIONs cannot directly supervise any other organizational unit. The supervision relationships in Figure 6.7a are modeled by six relationship sets, $R1$ through to $R6$. In fact, if there are n levels in the supervision hierarchy, there can be as many as $n(n-1)/2$ supervision relationship sets. Ideally, however, SUPERVISION should be treated as the one relationship. This cannot be done by using entities and relationships alone since the identifiers of the interacting entities come from many domains. Hence the relationship SUPERVISION is broken up into six relationship sets.

The role abstraction can, however, be used to model SUPERVISION by one relationship set. As shown in Figure 6.7, two role sets, SUPERVISOR and SUPERVISED, are introduced. Each organizational unit can take a SUPERVISOR and SUPERVISED role (Figure 6.7b). Direct supervision is then expressed by the one relationship set, SUPERVISION, irrespective of the number of organizational levels. Hence only one relationship set is used to model SUPERVISION. The price is that new identifier sets must be introduced to model the SUPERVISOR and SUPERVISION roles.

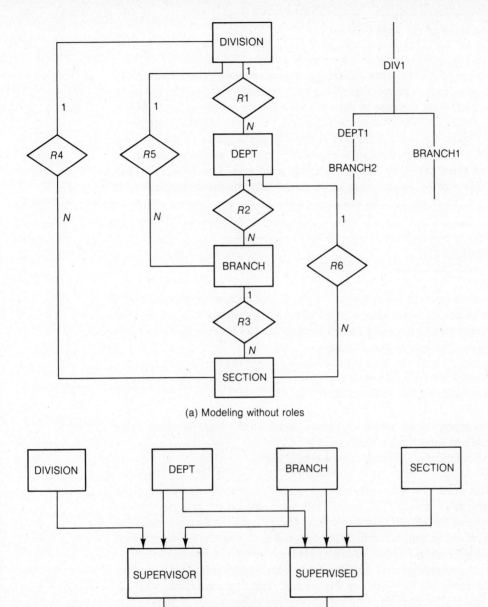

(a) Modeling without roles

(b) Modeling with roles

Figure 6.7 Using roles to express the same relationship kind between different entity kinds

Another Advantage of the Role Concept

The role concept offers one other advantage in data analysis: greater uniformity within each object set. Thus in Figure 6.5 each PERSON entity has the same attributes, which is not the case in Figure 6.4. In Figure 6.4 the value of ROLE determines whether an entity takes a SPECIALTY or SYMPTOM attribute. Further, in Figure 6.5 the attribute ROLE no longer appears as an attribute of PERSON entities; each PERSON entity now has only attributes particular to it and not those taken by it when playing some role. The DOCTOR and PATIENT role entities, on the other hand, model only the attributes particular to a role. As a result, nonhomogeneity is avoided.

NONHOMOGENEITY

Nonhomogeneity exists in an object set if there is an attribute that some objects in the same object set never take a value of (Kent, 1979). In relational terms nonhomogeneity results in a relation in which some rows never take a value in a column that corresponds to that attribute.

Before going on with the treatment of nonhomogeneity we should be clear about null values that characterize nonhomogeneity. It is important to distinguish between two kinds of null values:

- null values appearing as temporary values because the actual attribute value is not known at a particular time
- null values where the attribute cannot take a value

The first case arises, for example, when an entity is created and some of its attributes are not known at the time. Thus we could create a person record without knowing the person's date-of-birth. The date-of-birth could be added later to the record. A null value like this does not create nonhomogeneity. It is when the second reason for null values exists that we have nonhomogeneity.

To illustrate nonhomogeneity and its effects, consider the relational representation of the entity set PERSON in Figure 6.4. This representation, which is shown in Figure 6.8a, is derived by the conversion rules shown in Figure 5.9. Here each entity set becomes a relation and each entity becomes a tuple of the relation. The relation that represents entity set PERSONs after this conversion is shown in Figure 6.8a. You will now note that this representation has one undesirable property: some attributes have null values for all time. Thus the attribute SYMPTOM takes no value for a doctor, and SPECIALTY takes no value for a PATIENT. For example, SPECIALTY for X92 would never take a

PERSONS	PERSON-NO	NAME	ROLE	SPECIALTY	SYMPTOM
	X91	JILL	DOCTOR	EYE	—
	X92	JIM	PATIENT	—	FEVER

(a) Using dummy attribute values

PERSONS	PERSON-NO	NAME	ROLE	PROP
	X91	JILL	DOCTOR	EYE
	X92	JIM	PATIENT	FEVER

(b) Using meaningless attribute names

PERSONS	PERSON-NO	NAME
	X91	JILL
	X92	JIM

DOCTORS	PERSON-NO	SPECIALTY
	X91	EYE

PATIENTS	PERSON-NO	SYMPTOM
	X92	FEVER

(c) Eliminating nonhomogeneity

Figure 6.8   Tabular representations of the DOCTOR-PATIENT enterprise
(a) Using dummy attribute values
(b) Using meaningless attribute names
(c) Eliminating nonhomogeneity

value because X92 is not a DOCTOR. Such empty (or null) values can eventually lead to implementations, with the following consequences:

1. There may be excessive unused space in some implementations if there are a large number of roles, each with a different set of attributes.
2. Access programs must include provisions for handling null values.

One way to overcome the first problem is to use a meaningless attribute name to serve for both SYMPTOM and SPECIALTY. For example, consider Figure 6.8b. Here the value of PROP is a symptom if the entity is a PATIENT; the value is a SPECIALTY if the entity is a DOCTOR. The use of meaningless attributes can be considered only if the attribute values come from the same domain. The problem of unused space is minimized but not entirely avoided with meaningless attribute names. There are still two disadvantages:

- An entity that takes more than one role must be stored more than once.
- If the roles have an unequal number of attributes, null values still appear in some roles.

The use of meaningless names does not solve both of the previous problems. When meaningless names are used, access programs need not include provision for handling null values. What they now need are provisions to interpret the meaning of PROP. The only way to solve both problems is to separate the entities from roles. If this is done, the relational structure shown in Figure 6.8c results. Now each role set is represented by a separate relation. This representation has the following properties:

1. Each entity appears once and each role appears once.
2. No dummy values are necessary.
3. No attributes are used for a dual purpose.
4. No role-type attributes appear in an entity relation.

Nonhomogeneity and Functional Dependency

There is no general agreement on a formal way to treat nonhomogeneity. The treatment in this text is to apply the idea of partial functions to FDs. In this context a functional dependency $X \rightarrow Y$ becomes a partial function of X if Y is null for all time for a given value of X. If such a partial function is used to construct a relation, whose primary key is X, then such a relation will have columns with null values for all time, and so there is nonhomogeneity. One way to avoid nonhomogeneity is not to use FDs that are partial functions to construct relations. When taking this approach, analysts should ensure that each FD $X \rightarrow Y$ is such that the null value is not in the range of any attribute in X or Y, so that $X \rightarrow Y$ is a total function. This approach is used in the remainder of this text.

ROLE-MODELING STRUCTURES

Roles and entities have a number of structural properties. These properties determine the identifiers chosen for roles and the conversion of roles to relations. In the first instance role structures can be *direct* or *extended*.

Direct roles are roles that are directly dependent on (or are subsets of) an entity set. Thus both PATIENT and DOCTOR in Figure 6.5 are direct role structures. It is also possible for roles to be subsets of other roles. For example, a person who is a PATIENT may be either an OUTPATIENT or an INPATIENT. Different kinds of information may be maintained for each of these patients. Thus in Figure 6.9 an INPATIENT appears in a relationship with WARDs; this relationship stores the date on which an INPATIENT was assigned to a particular WARD. Here INPATIENT and OUTPATIENT are not the direct roles of PERSON but are roles that can be taken only if that person is already a PATIENT. Hence they are subsets of the PATIENT role set. The general term *source* is used to indicate the set of objects that can appear in the role set. Thus in Figure 6.9 the entity set PERSON is the source of role sets DOCTOR and PATIENT; the role set PATIENT is the source of OUTPATIENTS and INPATIENTS roles.

Following are further distinct kinds of role structures as well as distinct kinds of entity and source structures, some of which are illustrated in Figure 6.10.

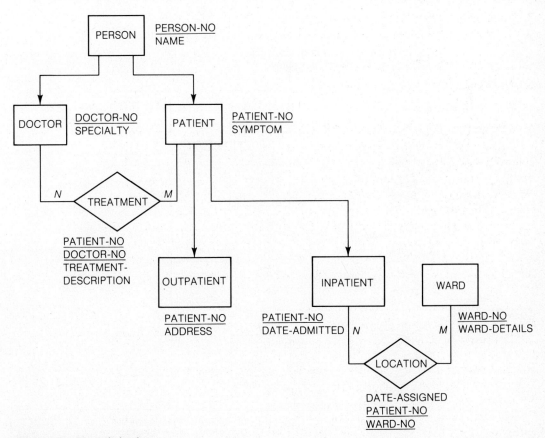

Figure 6.9 Extended roles

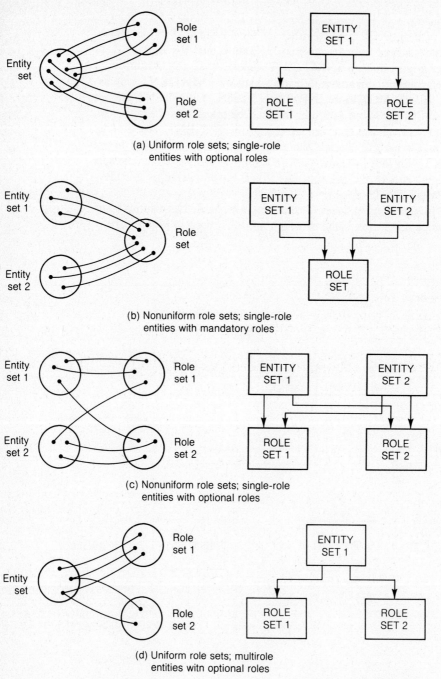

(a) Uniform role sets; single-role
entities with optional roles

(b) Nonuniform role sets; single-role
entities with mandatory roles

(c) Nonuniform role sets; single-role
entities with optional roles

(d) Uniform role sets; multirole
entities witn optional roles

Note: In all cases each role can be
taken by atmost one entity.

Figure 6.10   Role structures

1. Role structures

    (a) *Uniform role set.* In a uniform role set all roles come from only one source set. Thus PATIENT and DOCTOR in Figure 6.5 are both uniform role sets.

    (b) *Nonuniform role set.* In a nonuniform role set the roles come from more than one source set. Thus both SUPERVISOR and SUPERVISED in Figure 6.7 are nonuniform role sets. The role SUPERVISOR can be taken by entities from three entity sets: DIVISION, DEPT, and BRANCH. As another example, in Figure 6.11 some roles in the role set USER are taken by projects, and others are taken by departments. There are six such users: U1, U2, U3, U4, U5, and U6. User U1 is a role taken by project $p1$, and user U6 is a role taken by department $d3$. The users use parts; relationships between parts and users do not distinguish between projects and departments.

2. Source, or entity, structures

    (a) *Multirole source.* A multirole source is an object that can take more than one role at the same time. Thus entities in entity set PERSON in Figure 6.5 can take two roles, DOCTOR and PATIENT; most of the organizational units in Figure 6.7 can also take the roles SUPERVISOR and SUPERVISED. The term multirole entity is also used in this context.

    (b) *Single-role source.* A single-role source is an object that takes only one role at the same time. Both PROJECTS and DEPARTMENTS in Figure 6.11 are single-role entity sets. The term *single-role entity* is also used in this context.

Analysts associate role sets with their source sets. If a role set is associated with a source set, then objects in the source set can take roles in their associated role set. As seen in Figure 6.10, there are two distinct kinds of association:

- *Mandatory roles:* Each object in the source set *must* take a role in its associated role set (Figure 6.10b). The USER roles in Figure 6.11 are mandatory roles for PROJECTS and DEPARTMENTS.
- *Optional roles:* Each object in the source set may or may not take a role in its associated role set (Figure 6.10a, c, and d). The DOCTOR and PATIENT role in Figure 6.4 are optional roles of PERSON; a person may be either a doctor or a patient.

Role Identifiers and Role Structure

The choice of role identifier depends on the role structure. For example, there is no reason why a role in a uniform role set cannot use the same identifiers (that

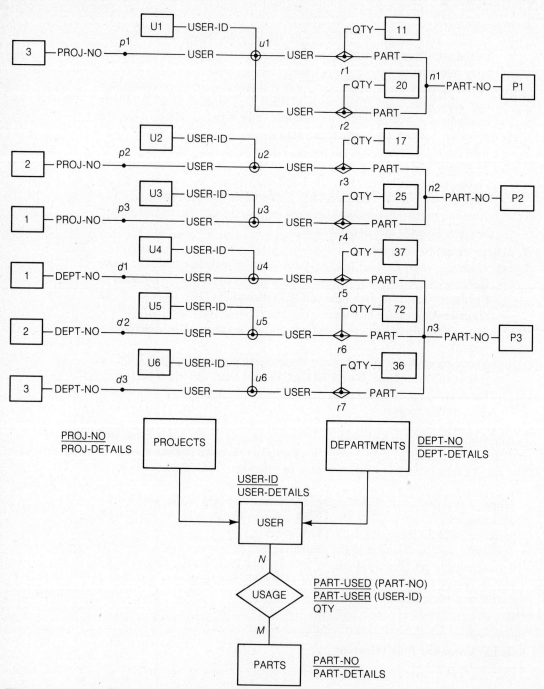

Figure 6.11   Nonuniform role set with single-role sources

is, the same domain) as its entity identifiers. In Figure 6.5, for example, the set of values that make up the person identifier can be used to identify a person, a doctor, or a patient. But how, you might ask, do we know whether a given value, say X91, identifies a person, a doctor, or a patient? The answer depends on the context in which the value is used. Thus in Figure 6.8c, the value X91 in PERSONS identifies a person, whereas in DOCTORS it identifies a doctor. It is of course possible to use one set of identifier values to identify doctors and another to identify patients. But the use of three such sets of identifier values to identify the same object may cause confusion in an organization. So whenever possible, it is more convenient to use the same set of identifier values for entities and their roles—in this case the entities persons, doctors, and patients.

A role in a nonuniform role set, on the other hand, cannot always use the same set of identifiers as the entity that plays the role. For example, consider Figure 6.11. Here the role USER is taken by both projects and departments. The users use parts; relationships between parts and users do not distinguish between projects and departments. But the identifier values of projects and departments come from the same domain of values, the set of integers. Therefore the set of values that identifies projects or department cannot be used to identify USER roles. If such a set were used, both U1 and U6 would have the same identifier (namely, 3), as would U2 and U5 as well as U3 and U4. So we must develop an identifier for the user role. We can do so in one of two ways:

- Generate a unique set of values to identify users, as is done with USER-ID in Figure 6.11.
- Use a composite identifier for each user.

The first alternative has been chosen in Figure 6.11; users are given unique identifiers—U1 through U6. In the second alternative, in which a composite identifier is used for roles, the composite identifier is made up of

- a number, USER-NO
- a type, USER-TYPE, whose domain in this case is ("DEPT," "PROJ")

If the user is a project, then USER-NO in the composite identifier takes the same value as PROJ-NO, and USER-TYPE = "PROJ"; for department users, USER-NO is the same as DEPT-NO, and USER-TYPE = "DEPT."

ROLES, SOURCES, AND RELATIONS

A relational representation of role structures includes relations to represent the following:

- Each role set as well as each entity and relationship set.
- The correspondence between role and entity identifiers. This correspondence is used to find the role, given a source, or to find the source, given a role.

Role Structures and Functional Dependencies

The way that the correspondence between identifiers is represented depends on the FDs between the role and source identifiers. If these are total functions, the correspondence is often represented by the same relations that represent the role, entity, or relationship sets. If the FDs between identifiers are partial functions, special relations are created to store the correspondence between identifiers. The actual method used depends on the FDs between identifiers, and these in turn depend on the role structure.

Uniform Role Set

In a uniform role set the role identifier uniquely determines its source (or entity) identifier. For example, in Figure 6.5, DOCTOR-NO $\rightarrow$ PERSON-NO is a total function because each doctor is a person. However, the functional dependency PERSON-NO $\rightarrow$ DOCTOR-NO is not a total function since some persons may not be doctors. So this FD should not be used to construct relations.

In Figure 6.5 two FDs that represent the correspondence between role and entity identifiers and that are total functions are

DOCTOR-NO $\rightarrow$ PERSON-NO
PATIENT-NO $\rightarrow$ PERSON-NO

Other FDs in the enterprise in Figure 6.5 are between the entity, relationship, and role properties and their identifiers. These FDs are

PERSON-NO $\rightarrow$ NAME
DOCTOR-NO $\rightarrow$ SPECIALTY
PATIENT-NO $\rightarrow$ SYMPTOM
DOCTOR-NO, PATIENT-NO $\rightarrow$ TREATMENT-DESCRIPTION

These six FDs are used to construct the relations

PERSONS (<u>PERSON-NO</u>, NAME)
DOCTORS (<u>DOCTOR-NO</u>, SPECIALTY, <u>PERSON-NO</u>)
PATIENTS (<u>PATIENT-NO</u>, SYMPTOM, <u>PERSON-NO</u>)
TREATMENTS (<u>DOCTOR-NO, PATIENT-NO,</u>
   TREATMENT DESCRIPTION)

We construct these relations by grouping FDs with the same determinant to form one relation. The relations can be further simplified if the same domains are used for the source and role identifiers, because we can remove PERSON-NO from relations DOCTORs and PATIENTs.

Nonuniform Role Set

For a nonuniform role set the FD role-identifier $\rightarrow$ source-identifier is not a total function (as was the case with uniform roles) because a role may be taken by sources from different source sets. The question then is whether source-identifier $\rightarrow$ role-identifier is a total function. The answer depends on whether the roles are mandatory or optional roles of the source. If the role set is mandatory, the FD source-identifier $\rightarrow$ role-identifier is a total function because each source must take a role. But if the roles are optional, source-identifier $\rightarrow$ role-identifier is a partial function and should not be used to construct relations if nonhomogeneity is to be avoided.

Mandatory Roles In the particular example in Figure 6.11, users are mandatory roles of projects and departments; therefore the FDs

DEPT-NO $\rightarrow$ USER-ID
PROJ-NO $\rightarrow$ USER-ID

are total functions. These FDs are combined with FDs for the role, entity, and relationship sets to construct the relations

PROJECTS (<u>PROJ-NO,</u> USER-ID, PROJ-DETAILS)
DEPARTMENTS (<u>DEPT-NO,</u> USER-ID, DEPT-DETAILS)
USERS (<u>USER-ID,</u> USER-DETAILS)
USAGE (<u>USER-ID,</u> PART-NO, QTY)
PARTS (<u>PART-NO,</u> PART-DETAILS)

These four relations, called SET1 relations, describe the enterprise in Figure 6.11.

Optional Roles Suppose now the enterprise in Figure 6.11 is changed to the one in Figure 6.12. Here a SUPPLIER role is introduced and projects can be either users or suppliers. Now USER becomes an optional role of projects because a project can be either a user or a supplier of parts or both. Nonhomogeneity is created in relation PROJECTS, for there may be some projects that are not users, and so their USER-ID value would be null.

The result now is that neither PROJ-NO $\rightarrow$ USER-ID nor USER-ID $\rightarrow$ PROJ-NO is a total function. To create FDs that are total functions, it is necessary to construct new role sets, as shown in Figure 6.13. The two newly constructed role sets are PROJECT-SUPPLIER-ROLE, which is the set of supplier projects with identifier PROJECT-SUPPLIER-ROLE-ID, and PROJECT-

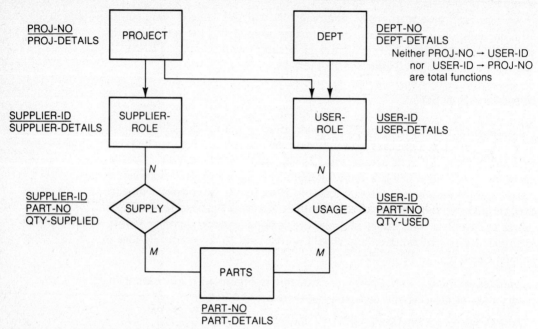

Figure 6.12   Inherent nonhomogeneity

USER-ROLE, which is the set of user projects with identifier **PROJECT-USER-ROLE-ID**.

The source of both of these new role sets is PROJECT; so the roles are uniform. Therefore the two FDs

> PROJECT-SUPPLIER-ROLE-ID → PROJ-NO
> PROJECT-USER-ROLE-ID → PROJ-NO

are total functions.

Further, USER-ROLE is a mandatory role of PROJECT-USER-ROLE, and SUPPLIER-ROLE is a mandatory role of PROJECT-SUPPLIER-ROLE. So the FDs

> PROJECT-SUPPLIER-ROLE-ID → SUPPLIER-ID
> PROJECT-USER-ROLE-ID → USER-ID

are also total functions. In addition, since SUPPLIER-ROLE is a uniform role set, SUPPLIER-ID → PROJECT-SUPPLIER-ROLE-ID.

The FDs that include identifiers of newly created roles result in the two relations

> PROJECT-SUPPLIERS (<u>PROJECT-SUPPLIER-ROLE-ID</u>,
>   SUPPLIER-ID, PROJ-NO)
> PROJECT-USERS (<u>PROJECT-USER-ROLE-ID</u>, USER-ID, PROJ-NO)

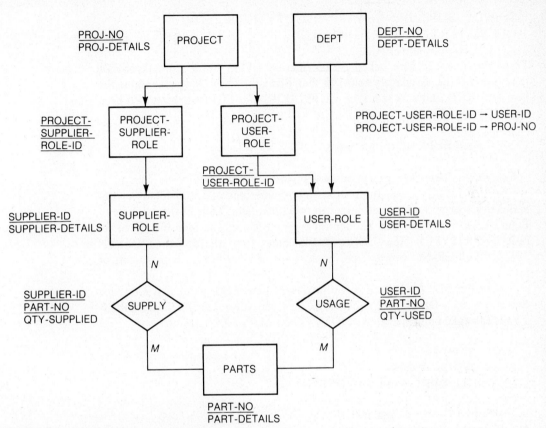

Figure 6.13 Removing nonhomogeneity

As both **PROJECT-SUPPLIER-ROLE** and **PROJECT-USER-ROLE** are uniform role sets, **PROJECT-SUPPLIER-ROLE-ID** and **PROJECT-USER-ROLE-ID** use the same domain as **PROJ-NO**; hence they can be eliminated from the last two relations, which now become

PROJECT-SUPPLIERS (SUPPLIER-ID, PROJ-NO)
PROJECT-USERS (USER-ID, PROJ-NO)

These two relations are called *correspondence relations* because they show the correspondence between the source and role identifiers.

In addition to these two relations, the relational representation of Figure 6.13 will also include

PROJECTS (PROJ-NO, PROJ-DETAILS)
DEPARTMENTS (DEPT-NO, USER-ID, DEPT-DETAILS)
USERS (USER-ID, USER-DETAILS)
USAGE (USER-ID, PART-NO, QTY-USED)
SUPPLIERS (SUPPLIER-ID, SUPPLIER-DETAILS)

SUPPLY (<u>SUPPLIER-ID</u>, PART-NO, QTY-SUPPLIED)
PARTS (<u>PART-NO</u>, PART-DETAILS)

These relations are here called SET2 relations. They differ from the SET1 relations (for the mandatory roles) in that PROJECTS no longer contains the field USER-ID and new relations. SUPPLIERS and SUPPLY have also been added for the new role.

Using Composite Identifiers for Roles

Composite Identifiers and Mandatory Roles   When composite identifiers are used to identify roles, the FDs map combinations of entity identifier domains together with entity set names to role identifiers. Thus in the example of Figure 6.11, user roles can be identified by the composite identifier (USER-NO, USER-TYPE). Here USER-TYPE comes from the domain ("DEPT," "PROJ"); USER-NO comes from the domains of identifiers of departments or projects.

To develop FDs for this case, we introduce new single-value attributes for each type; thus DEPT-TYPE can take only the value "DEPT," and PROJ-TYPE can take only the value "PROJ." The resulting FDs are now

DEPT-TYPE → USER-TYPE
PROJ-TYPE → USER-TYPE
USER-NO, DEPT-TYPE ↪ DEPT-NO
USER-NO, PROJ-TYPE ↪ PROJ-NO

The resultant relations for Figure 6.11 now become

USERS (<u>USER-NO, USER-TYPE</u>, USER-DETAILS)
USAGE (<u>USER-NO, USER-TYPE</u>, PART-NO, QTY)
PROJECTS (<u>PROJ-NO,</u> USER-NO, USER-TYPE,
  PROJ-DETAILS)
DEPARTMENTS (<u>DEPT-NO,</u> USER-NO, USER-TYPE, DEPT-
  DETAILS)
PARTS (<u>PART-NO,</u> PART-DETAILS)

The USER-TYPE attribute always takes the value "PROJ" in relation PROJECTS. Furthermore, the values of USER-NO and PROJ-NO in PROJECTS are also always the same in the same tuple. Hence both USER-NO and USER-TYPE may be omitted from relation PROJECTS. Similarly, USER-NO and USER-TYPE may be omitted from relation DEPARTMENTS.
The final set of relations that represent the enterprise in Figure 6.11, using composite role identifiers, are

USERS (<u>USER-NO, USER-TYPE</u>, USER-DETAILS)
USAGE (<u>USER-NO, USER-TYPE, PART-NO,</u> QTY)
PROJECTS (<u>PROJ-NO,</u> PROJ-DETAILS)
DEPARTMENTS (<u>DEPT-NO,</u> DEPT-DETAILS)
PARTS (<u>PART-NO,</u> PART-DETAILS)

This set differs from SET1 in that now a USER-ID field is not necessary in PROJECTS and DEPARTMENTS. PROJ-NO and DEPT-NO are part of the role key and hence serve this purpose in these two relations. Relations USERS and USAGE now use the composite identifier (USER-NO, USER-TYPE) rather than USER-ID. USER-NO is from the same domains as PROJ-NO and DEPT-NO (namely, the domain INTEGER), whereas USER-TYPE indicates whether USER-NO in a particular tuple comes from PROJ-NO or DEPT-NO.

Composite Identifiers and Optional Rules   One interesting extension of composite identifiers is in relations that represent the correspondence between optional roles and their sources. For Figure 6.13 there would be two such correspondence relations:

PROJECT-SUPPLIERS (<u>PROJ-NO,</u> SUPPLIER-TYPE,
    <u>SUPPLIER-NO</u>)
PROJECT-USERS (<u>PROJ-NO,</u> USER-TYPE, <u>USER-NO</u>)

Each of these correspondence relations is constructed by pairing an entity set identifier with an optional role identifier. Thus in the first of these relations the project identifier (PROJ-NO) is paired with a composite supplier identifier (SUPPLIER-NO, SUPPLIER-TYPE). Now in each correspondence tuple, SUPPLIER-NO and PROJ-NO will be the same because the entity identifier is part of the composite role identifier. The value of SUPPLIER-TYPE in relation PROJECT-SUPPLIERS will always be "PROJ" because each role player is a project. Hence the relation PROJECT-SUPPLIERS reduces to the unary relation

PROJECT-SUPPLIERS (PROJ-NO)

Similarly, the other correspondence relation becomes

PROJECT-USERS (PROJ-NO)

These relations in this case are lists of entities taking particular roles. They could, however, contain other attributes if some special data is stored about project users or project suppliers. The other relations for the enterprise in Figure 6.13, using composite identifiers, are

PROJECTS (<u>PROJ-NO</u>, PROJ-DETAILS)
DEPARTMENTS (<u>DEPT-NO</u>, DEPT-DETAILS)
USERS (<u>USER-NO, USER-TYPE,</u> USER-DETAILS)
USAGE (<u>USER-NO, USER-TYPE, PART-NO</u>, QTY)
SUPPLIERS (<u>SUPPLIER-NO, SUPPLIER-TYPE,</u>
   SUPPLIER-DETAILS)
SUPPLY (<u>SUPPLIER-NO, SUPPLIER-TYPE, PART-NO,</u>
   QTY-SUPPLIED)
PARTS (<u>PART-NO,</u> PART-DETAILS)

This set differs from SET2 in that the role identifier is now a composite identifier in both the role relations (USERS and SUPPLIERS) and the relations that correspond to relationships (USAGE and SUPPLY) in which the roles participate.

Short Cuts

You may have noticed that with optional roles a set of specially constructed identifiers was first constructed and then removed because these identifiers were the same as those of their source entities. This procedure was done to illustrate the formal set of steps used to produce a set of normal relations that avoid nonhomogeneity. It is not suggested that these steps be strictly followed in a practical environment. Given the existence of a semantic structure made up of roles and their sources, the designer should be able to directly construct relations that specify the correspondence between the source identifiers and role identifiers. A simple set of rules, illustrated in Figure 6.14, is as follows:

1. If a role set is uniform and its identifiers differ from the source identifier, include the source identifier in the role relation (Figure 6.14a).
2. If a role set is nonuniform and mandatory, include the role identifier in the source relation (Figure 6.14b and c).
3. If a role set is nonuniform and optional, construct a special correspondence relation (Figure 6.14d).

Where the role identifiers are composite identifiers, any attributes with the same domain in a relation can be eliminated.

TYPES OF ENTITIES

The type abstraction is used when entities of one set have both some common attributes and some different attributes. For example, it is possible to have a

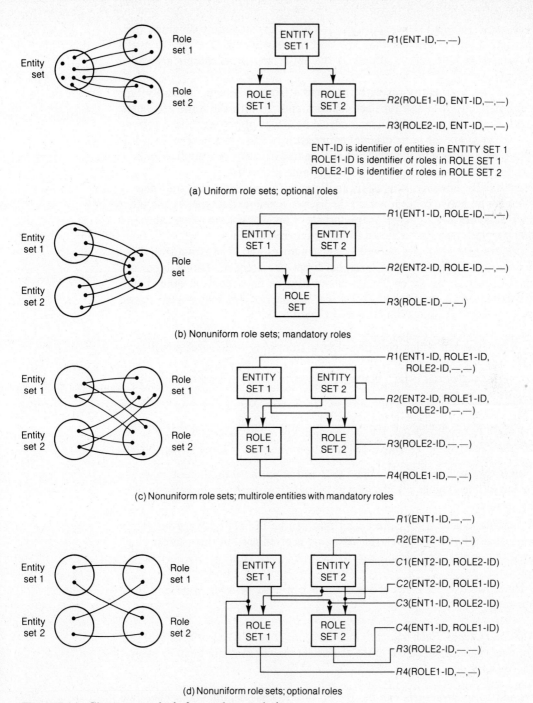

(a) Uniform role sets; optional roles

(b) Nonuniform role sets; mandatory roles

(c) Nonuniform role sets; multirole entities with mandatory roles

(d) Nonuniform role sets; optional roles

Figure 6.14 **Short-cut methods from roles to relations**

vehicle entity set. The vehicle entities, however, can have some different attributes, depending on whether they are land or air vehicles. One way to model this abstraction is to create subsets of the entity set; these subsets are called *type sets.*

All entities in an entity set with the same attributes become an entity type set; alternatively, an entity type set contains entities with the same attributes. All entities of one type can then be modeled by a type object set. Like a role, an entity will then appear in its original entity set as well as in any type set if it is of that type. In this way the concepts of type and role are very similar: roles in the same role set are also entities with the same properties.

Semantically, however, it is useful to distinguish between types and roles. A role implies an active concept within the user environment; a type, on the other hand, is semantically a passive characteristic of an entity. Like roles, entities of particular types may be restricted to particular relationships.

There are also analogies between role structures and type structures. Type structures, like role structures, may be direct or extended. Direct types are directly dependent on an entity; types can also be dependent on other types, thus resulting in an extended classification. Similarly, types may appear in two kinds of type structure, as illustrated in Figure 6.15:

- *Uniform type set,* which contains objects from only one source set (Figure 6.15a and b).
- *Nonuniform type set,* which contains objects from more than one source set (Figure 6.15c and d).

A *type source* is analogous to a role source. It comprises objects that fall into type sets and is categorized as follows:

- *A multitype source set* is an object that can be in more than one type set at the same time (Figure 6.15d). The term *multitype entity set* is often used in this context.
- *A single-type source set* is an object that can be in only one type set at the same time. The term *single-type entity set* is often used in this context (Figure 6.15a and c).

Further, two distinct kinds of associations can exist between types and their source sets:

- *Mandatory types.* Each object in the source *must* be in its associated type set.
- *Optional types.* Each object in the source set may or may not be in its associated type set.

Types and entity structures can be formed into various combinations. The two most common of these, shown in Figure 6.15, are as follows:

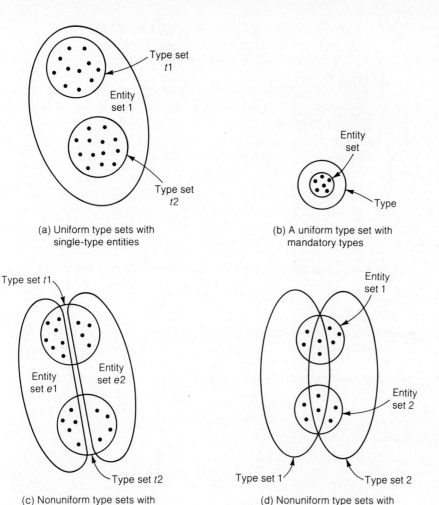

(a) Uniform type sets with single-type entities

(b) A uniform type set with mandatory types

(c) Nonuniform type sets with single-type entities

(d) Nonuniform type sets with multitype entities

Figure 6.15 Type structures

- *Uniform type sets* contain entities from one entity set. In the two cases shown, types are optional in one (Figure 6.15a) and mandatory in the other (Figure 6.15b).

- *Nonuniform type sets of optional types* contain entities from more than one entity set; each entity may optionally appear in the type sets. In the two cases illustrated, the entities are single-type in one (Figure 6.15c) and multitype in the other (Figure 6.15d).

Figure 6.16 is an example of uniform type set with optional types. Here the types are modeled by using the E-R diagram. This diagram contains one entity set, EXPENDITURES. Each expenditure is identified by an EXPENDITURE-NO; it has one attribute, DATE-INCURRED. Each expenditure may either be a CAPITAL-EXPENDITURES type or a MAINTENANCE-EXPENDITURES type. The types are optional since a particular EXPENDITURE need not be of each type. Further, both CAPITAL-EXPENDITURES and MAINTENANCE-EXPENDITURES are uniform type sets because each includes only entities from the EXPENDITURES entity set. Capital expenditures have one attribute, PROJECT-NO; maintenance expenditures also have one attribute, DEPT-NO. Note the close correspondence of this structure to the structure with optional uniform-role sets in Figure 6.5.

Modeling Entity Types

Type modeling is based on exactly the same principles as role modeling; that is,

- avoiding nonhomogeneity
- selecting identifiers for each type
- establishing correspondence between identifiers

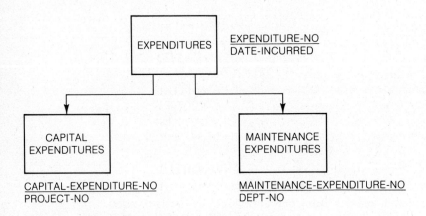

FD1:   EXPENDITURE-NO → DATE-INCURRED
FD2:   CAPITAL-EXPENDITURE-NO → PROJECT-NO
FD3:   CAPITAL-EXPENDITURE-NO → EXPENDITURE-NO
FD4:   MAINTENANCE-EXPENDITURE-NO → DEPT-NO
FD5:   MAINTENANCE-EXPENDITURE-NO → EXPENDITURE-NO

EXPENDITURES (EXPENDITURE-NO, DATE-INCURRED) from FD1
CAPITAL-EXPENSES (EXPENDITURE-NO, PROJECT-NO) from FD2, FD3
MAINTENANCE-EXPENSES (EXPENDITURE-NO, DEPT-NO) from FD4, FD5
(assuming that all identifiers come from the same domain)

Figure 6.16   A multitype entity

To illustrate such modeling, we return to Figure 6.16, where two type identifiers, CAPITAL-EXPENDITURE-NO and MAINTENANCE-EXPENDITURE-NO, are introduced. Attributes of particular expenditure types then become functionally dependent on type identifiers, as shown by FD2 and FD4. Since the type sets are uniform, each type identifier uniquely identifies an expenditure identifier, as defined by FD3 and FD5. If the same domains are used for CAPITAL-EXPENDITURE-NO, MAINTENANCE-EXPENDITURE-NO, and EXPENDITURE-NO, the FDs reduce to the relations EXPENDITURES, CAPITAL-EXPENSES, and MAINTENANCE-EXPENSES. Had different identifier domains been used for capital and maintenance expenditures, the correspondence between the entity identifier and its type identifier would appear in relations CAPITAL-EXPENSES and MAINTENANCE-EXPENSES. These would become

CAPITAL-EXPENSES (<u>EXPENDITURE-NO,</u> PROJECT-NO,
    CAPITAL-EXPENDITURE-NO)
MAINTENANCE-EXPENSES (<u>EXPENDITURE-NO,</u> DEPT-NO,
    MAINTENANCE-EXPENDITURE-NO)

Relations and Nonuniform Type Sets

Figure 6.17 is an example of nonuniform type sets. Here material and labor expenditure type sets are added to Figure 6.16. They are identified by MATERIAL-EXPENSE-NO and LABOR-EXPENSE-NO. Thus a CAPITAL-EXPENDITURE may either be a LABOR-EXPENDITURE or a MATERIAL-EXPENDITURE. Similarly, a MAINTENANCE-EXPENDITURE may be either a LABOR-EXPENDITURE or a MATERIAL-EXPENDITURE. Hence the material and labor expenditures are optional types of capital or maintenance expenditures; they are also nonuniform since either a LABOR-EXPENDITURES or a MATERIAL-EXPENDITURES set can contain both CAPITAL-EXPENDITURES and MAINTENANCE-EXPENDITURES. So far the structure in Figure 6.17 is similar to the nonuniform optional role sets in Figure 6.12.

MATERIAL-EXPENDITURES are associated with the material items used; LABOR-EXPENDITURES are associated with persons who incurred the expenditures. The association with items or persons does not depend on whether the expenditures are of a capital or maintenance nature.

As LABOR-EXPENDITURES are nonuniform optional types of CAPITAL-EXPENDITURES and MAINTENANCE-EXPENDITURES entities, no FDs can be established between material and capital or maintenance expenditures nor between labor and capital or maintenance expenditures. Any such FD would be a partial function. For example, a capital expenditure can be either a material or a labor expense; hence the FDs

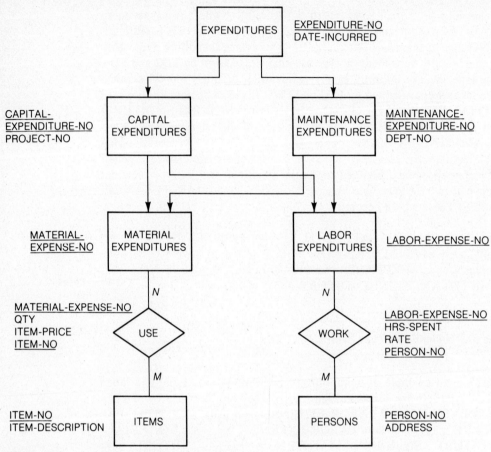

Figure 6.17 Modeling types by an E-R diagram

MATERIAL-EXPENSE-NO → CAPITAL-EXPENDITURE-NO
CAPITAL-EXPENDITURE-NO → MATERIAL-EXPENSE-NO

are not total functions. As in Figure 6.13, new types can be constructed to establish FDs between the type identifiers. CAPITAL-EXPENDITURES and MAINTENANCE-EXPENDITURES are broken up into two type sets, as shown in Figure 6.18.

CAPITAL-EXPENDITURES are now classified into two uniform type sets:

- CAPITAL-MATERIAL-EXPENDITURES, identified by CAPITAL-MATERIAL-NO
- CAPITAL-LABOR-EXPENDITURES, identified by CAPITAL-LABOR-NO

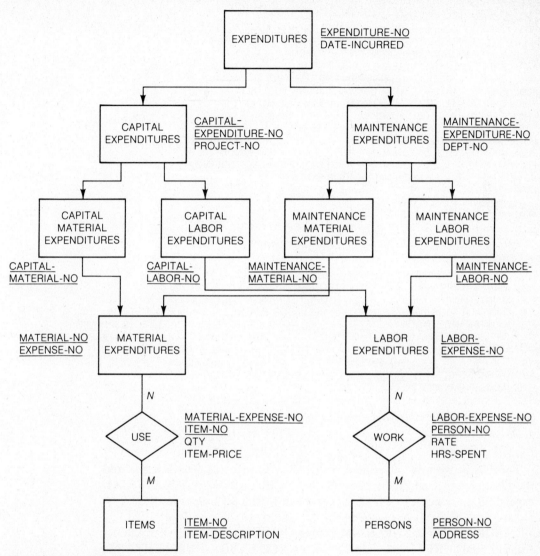

Figure 6.18   Introducing new types

Similarly, MAINTENANCE-EXPENDITURES are classified into two uniform type sets:

- **MAINTENANCE-MATERIAL-EXPENDITURES**, identified by **MAINTENANCE-MATERIAL-NO**
- **MAINTENANCE-LABOR-EXPENDITURES**, identified by **MAINTENANCE-LABOR-NO**

FUNCTIONAL DEPENDENCIES

FD1:   EXPENDITURE-NO → DATE-INCURRED
FD2:   MAINTENANCE-EXPENDITURE-NO → DEPT-NO
FD3:   MAINTENANCE-EXPENDITURE-NO → EXPENDITURE-NO
FD4:   CAPITAL-EXPENDITURE-NO → PROJECT-NO
FD5:   CAPITAL-EXPENDITURE-NO → EXPENDITURE-NO
FD6:   CAPITAL-MATERIAL-NO → CAPITAL-EXPENDITURE-NO
FD7:   CAPITAL-MATERIAL-NO → MATERIAL-EXPENSE-NO
FD8:   CAPITAL-LABOR-NO → CAPITAL EXPENDITURE-NO
FD9:   CAPITAL-LABOR-NO → LABOR-EXPENSE-NO
FD10: MAINTENANCE-MATERIAL-NO → MAINTENANCE-EXPENDITURE-NO
FD11: MAINTENANCE-MATERIAL-NO → MATERIAL-EXPENSE-NO
FD12: MAINTENANCE-LABOR-NO → MAINTENANCE-EXPENDITURE-NO
FD13: MAINTENANCE-LABOR-NO → LABOR-EXPENSE-NO
FD14: ITEM-NO → ITEM-DESCRIPTION
FD15: PERSON-NO → ADDRESS
FD16: MATERIAL-EXPENSE-NO, ITEM-NO → QTY, ITEM-PRICE
FD17: LABOR-EXPENSE-NO, PERSON-NO → HRS-SPENT, RATE

FDs between identifiers (FD6–FD13)

RELATIONS

R1:   EXPENDITURES (<u>EXPENDITURE-NO</u>, DATE-INCURRED) from FD1
R2:   CAPITAL-EXPENSES (<u>EXPENDITURE-NO</u>, PROJECT-NO) from FD4, FD5
R3:   MAINTENANCE-EXPENSES (<u>EXPENDITURE-NO</u>, DEPT-NO) from FD2, FD3
R4:   CAPITAL-LABOR-USE (<u>EXPENDITURE-NO</u>, LABOR-EXPENSE-NO) from FD9, FD8, FD5
R5:   MAINTENANCE-LABOR-USE (<u>EXPENDITURE-NO</u>, LABOR-EXPENSE-NO) from FD13, FD12, FD3
R6:   CAPITAL-MATERIAL-USE (<u>EXPENDITURE-NO</u>, MATERIAL-EXPENSE-NO) from FD7, FD6, FD5
R7:   MAINTENANCE-MATERIAL-USE (<u>EXPENDITURE-NO</u>, MATERIAL-EXPENSE-NO) from FD11, FD10, FD3
R8:   USE (<u>ITEM-NO</u>, <u>MATERIAL-EXPENSE-NO</u>, QTY, ITEM-PRICE) from FD16
R9:   WORK (<u>PERSON-NO</u>, <u>LABOR-EXPENSE-NO</u>, HRS-SPENT, RATE) from FD17
R10: ITEMS (<u>ITEM-NO</u>, ITEM-DESCRIPTION) from FD14
R11: PERSONS (<u>PERSON-NO</u>, ADDRESS) from FD15

Figure 6.19   Nonuniform type sets with optional types

The FDs between the identifiers of the newly constructed classifications and the identifiers of CAPITAL, MAINTENANCE, LABOR, and MATERIAL expenditures are given by FDs 6 though 13 in Figure 6.19. Specifically:

- LABOR-EXPENDITURES are mandatory types of CAPITAL-LABOR-EXPENDITURE and MAINTENANCE-LABOR-EXPENDITURE; hence FD9 and FD13.

- MATERIAL-EXPENDITURES are mandatory types of CAPITAL-MATERIAL-EXPENDITURE and MAINTENANCE-MATERIAL-EXPENDITURE; hence FD7 and FD11.

- The newly constructed role sets are all uniform; hence FD6, FD8, FD10, and FD12.

Now suppose the domains of CAPITAL-EXPENDITURE-NO, MAINTENANCE-EXPENDITURE-NO, CAPITAL-MATERIAL-NO, CAPITAL-

LABOR-NO, MAINTENANCE-MATERIAL-NO, and MAINTENANCE-LABOR-NO are assumed to be the same as EXPENDITURE-NO. Suppose further that separate sets of identifiers continue to be used for material and labor expenses; these are MATERIAL-EXPENSE-NO and LABOR-EXPENSE-NO. As a consequence, the FDs between identifiers are reduced to the correspondence relations $R4$ through $R7$. Note that there is one such relation for each combination of expenditure and expense (or for each newly constructed dedicated classification).

A further reduction is also possible if MATERIAL-EXPENSE-NO and LABOR-EXPENSE-NO are chosen to have the same domain as EXPENDITURE-NO; relations $R4$ through $R7$ can then be removed; MATERIAL-EXPENSE-NO and LABOR-EXPENSE-NO are replaced by EXPENDITURE-NO.

Short Cuts

The short-cut methods used for role modeling can also be applied to types. The rules now are as follows:

1. If a type set is uniform and its identifiers differ from the source identifier, include the source identifier in the type relation.
2. If a type set is nonuniform and mandatory, include the type identifier in the source relation.
3. If a type set is nonuniform and optional, construct a special correspondence relation.

The four correspondence relations $R4$ through $R7$ in Figure 6.19 would result if these rules are applied.

Aggregate Objects

An *aggregate object* describes the common properties of a collection of entities. Thus a part kind may be an aggregate object; it can describe the common properties of any number of individual parts of that kind. Up to now in this text we have made no distinction between aggregate objects and individual objects. For example, in Figure 5.6 the object set PARTS is an aggregate object. Objects in PARTS are aggregate objects because each object can represent many individual parts. However, each object in PROJECTS is not an aggregate object since it represents just one project. But we have treated the aggregate object PARTS in the figure in the same way as projects, which are individual objects.

Aggregate objects are sometimes treated as a separate modeling abstraction to represent properties common to a set of entities. Entity objects will then represent only properties of individual entities.

Aggregate objects often form classifications. The classification structures have properties similar to those of role and type structures. Aggregate object sets can be classified into aggregate-object type sets. It is then possible to have uniform and nonuniform aggregate-object type sets as well as multiple and single sources of aggregate-object sets.

Different types of aggregate objects may have different attributes, and they may also be restricted to selected relationships. Modeling problems with such classifications can be resolved by sticking to the principles discussed earlier; that is,

- avoiding nonhomogeneity
- selecting identifiers for aggregate-object classes
- establishing correspondences between identifiers

Figure 6.20 represents a classification of aggregate objects. Here a classification is developed for PART-KINDS. The model describes particular types of parts but not the individual parts. Hence PART-KINDS is a set of aggregate objects, where each object describes the properties of a class of parts. Thus each aggregate object in the set PART-KINDS describes the common properties of all individual objects of that part kind.

It is also possible that the properties of the PART-KINDS themselves depend on what type of PART-KINDS is involved. If this is the case, the aggregate objects in PART-KINDS may be classified into aggregate-object type sets. Thus in Figure 6.20 the aggregate-object set PART-KINDS falls into two classes: AUTO-PART-KINDS and TRUCK-PART-KINDS. The aggregate objects in AUTO-PART-KINDS describe those properties of PART-KINDS that are relevant to auto parts. Similarly, the aggregate objects in TRUCK-PART-KINDS describe properties of truck parts. These two classes themselves break down into WHEEL-KINDS and ENGINE-KINDS, which have different attributes.

Note the correspondence between the structure in Figure 6.20 and the nonuniform optional entities in Figures 6.13 and 6.18. You can see that in Figure 6.20 PART-KINDS is an aggregate object, whereas AUTO-PART-KINDS and TRUCK-PART-KINDS are uniform aggregate-object types because they contain only PART-KINDS; WHEEL-KINDS and ENGINE-KINDS, on the other hand, are nonuniform optional aggregate-object types of AUTO-PART-KINDS and TRUCK-PART-KINDS. Hence FDs between AUTO-PART-KINDS and WHEEL-KINDS or ENGINE-KINDS will not be total functions. Similarly, FDs between TRUCK-PART-KINDS and WHEEL-KINDS or ENGINE-KINDS will not be total functions.

We could introduce new type sets in Figure 6.20 much as we did in Figures 6.13 and 6.18 and then develop a set of FDs between newly constructed and

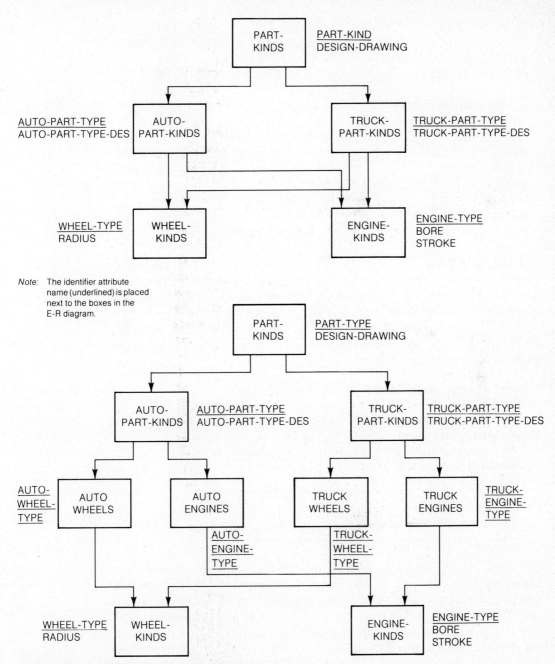

Figure 6.20 Classification of generic objects

existing type sets. But it is quicker to use the short-cut methods developed for types to describe correspondence between identifiers. We then have the following four relations to describe identifier correspondence:

TRUCK-WHEEL-KINDS (TRUCK-PART-TYPE, WHEEL-TYPE)
TRUCK-ENGINE-KINDS (TRUCK-PART-TYPE, ENGINE-TYPE)
AUTO-WHEEL-KINDS (AUTO-PART-TYPE, WHEEL-TYPE)
AUTO-ENGINE-KINDS (AUTO-PART-TYPE, ENGINE-TYPE)

The other relations describe the various types:

PART-KINDS (PART-TYPE, DESIGN-DRAWING)
AUTO-PART-KINDS (AUTO-PART-TYPE, AUTO-PART-TYPE-DES,
    PART-TYPE)
TRUCK-PART-KINDS (TRUCK-PART-TYPE,
    TRUCK-PART-TYPE-DES, PART-TYPE)
WHEEL-KINDS (WHEEL-TYPE, RADIUS)
ENGINE-KINDS (ENGINE-TYPE, BORE, STROKE)

If similar domains are used for TRUCK-PART-TYPE, AUTO-PART-TYPE, and PART-TYPE, some further reduction is possible. In particular, AUTO-PART-TYPE and TRUCK-PART-TYPE need no longer be included in relations AUTO-PART-KINDS and TRUCK-PART-KINDS.

Further, if the domains of PART-TYPE, ENGINE-TYPE, and WHEEL-TYPE are the same, the four correspondence relations will no longer be required. The result is the relations

PART-KINDS (PART-TYPE, DESIGN-DRAWING)
AUTO-PART-KINDS (PART-TYPE, AUTO-PART-TYPE-DES)
TRUCK-PART-KINDS (PART-TYPE, TRUCK-PART-TYPE-DES)
WHEEL-KINDS (PART-TYPE, RADIUS)
ENGINE-KINDS (PART-TYPE, BORE, STROKE)

COMBINING ENTITY TYPES AND AGGREGATE OBJECTS

Sometimes it is necessary to combine individual-entity type structures with aggregate-object structures. In this model the aggregate objects describe general properties of part types, whereas the individual entities describe properties of individual objects of that type. The classification of aggregate objects modeled in Figure 6.20 is reproduced in Figure 6.21, together with a corresponding classification of individual entities. PARTS is a set of parts objects, which are classified into AUTO PARTS and TRUCK PARTS. These are further classified into WHEELS and ENGINES. Here ENGINE-KINDS describe the particular properties, BORE and STROKE, of engine types. The TIME-MANUFACTURED and the FACTORY may differ for individual engines of

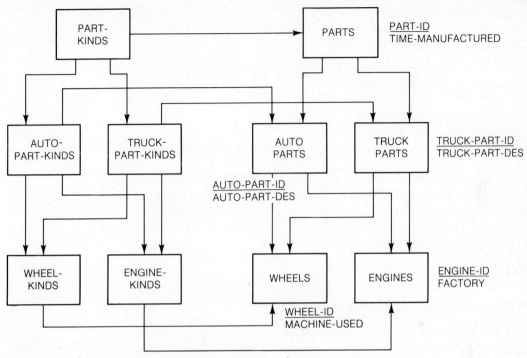

Figure 6.21   Dependence between aggregate objects and types

each type. The individual objects may themselves form a classification structure of several levels.

There is a relationship between the classification structures of the aggregate and individual objects. The aggregate structure describes the common properties of individual objects, whereas the individual-type structure describes the properties relevant to individual objects. So the aggregate object can be viewed as an attribute of an individual object.

This association can be modeled both by FDs and by E-R diagrams. In the E-R model illustrated in Figure 6.21 each individual-entity type is associated with its aggregate object. The FDs between the aggregate-object-ids and entity-type-ids will depend on the stucture and on whether the aggregate objects

• are uniform and contain one entity type only
• are mandatory for each entity type

In Figure 6.21 it is assumed that all aggregate objects are uniform and mandatory, and therefore the following FDs are total functions:

PART-ID → PART-TYPE
AUTO-PART-ID → AUTO-PART-TYPE

TRUCK-PART-ID → TRUCK-PART-TYPE
WHEEL-ID → WHEEL-TYPE
ENGINE-ID → ENGINE-TYPE

The relational representation of Figure 6.21 is a combination of three kinds of relations. These relations describe

- the aggregate-object structure
- the individual-object structure
- the relationships between the aggregate- and individual-object structures

The relations that describe the aggregate-object structure of Figure 6.20 were given earlier. If AUTO-PART-ID and TRUCK-PART-ID have the same domain as PART-ID, the other two sets of relations are as follows:

1. Identifier correspondence relations:

WHEELS (PART-ID, WHEEL-ID)
ENGINES (PART-ID, ENGINE-ID)

2. Relationships that describe the object sets:

PARTS (PART-ID, TIME-MANUFACTURED, PART-TYPE)
AUTO PARTS (PART-ID, AUTO-PART-DES, PART-TYPE)
TRUCK PARTS (PART-ID, TRUCK-PART-DES, PART-TYPE)
WHEELS (WHEEL-ID, MACHINE-USED, WHEEL-TYPE)
ENGINES (ENGINE-ID, FACTORY, ENGINE-TYPE)

Again, the correspondence relations can be removed if WHEEL-ID and ENGINE-ID are the same as PART-ID.

SUMMARY

Two abstractions can be used to extend the modeling power of the E-R model: roles and types. They can allow designers to treat entities from the same object set in different ways. An object set can be divided into role or type subsets, and objects in each subset can be treated in a different way. These abstractions are particularly useful for avoiding nonhomogeneity, modeling recursive relationships, and modeling relationships where one identifier corresponds to objects from different object sets.

Both role and type structures can be modeled by relations. An important factor in conversion to relations is the choice of identifiers for roles and types. The choice depends not only on the role or type structure but also on whether

- the role or type sets are uniform
- the roles or types are mandatory or optional
- composite or unique role or type identifiers are used

Conversion to relations proceeds as follows:

1. If the role (or type) set is uniform and its identifiers differ from the source identifier, include the source identifier in the role (or type) relation.
2. If the role (or type) set is nonuniform and mandatory, include the role (or type) identifier in the source relation.
3. If the role (or type) set is nonuniform and optional, construct a special correspondence relation.
4. If the role (or type) identifiers are composite identifiers, remove any redundant attributes. An attribute is redundant if it has a constant value for all relation tuples or has the same domain and values for all tuples as does another attribute.

A third abstraction, called aggregate entities, can be used to model the common properties of a collection of entities. Modeling techniques can in this case combine aggregate entity object sets with entity sets that model individual entities.

PROBLEMS

For each of the following problems, develop an E-R diagram (modified with role and class sets as necessary). Ensure that each set corresponds to a BCNF relation and specify what that relation is.

Problem 1 (Library Borrowings)

Library BORROWERS may be STAFF, STUDENT, or EXTERNAL. Attributes associated with these borrowers depend on who they are. STAFF have STAFF-DETAILS, STUDENTS have STUDENT-DETAILS, and EXTERNAL have EXTERNAL-DETAILS. In addition, the following different borrowing authorities are maintained for the borrowers:

- STAFF-AUTHORITY for STAFF
- STUDENT-AUTHORITY for STUDENTS
- EXTERNAL-AUTHORITY for EXTERNAL borrowers

Details of borrowings include the BOOK-NO, BORROWED-DATE, and DUE-DATE of books lent to each borrower. Only current borrowings are to be modeled.

Problem 2 (Employee Status)

A person is employed in a CASUAL, TEMPORARY, or PERMANENT capacity. Common information about each person contains an identifier PERSON-ID, together with PERSON-DETAILS. The following additional information stored about persons is relevant to their manner of employment:

- CASUAL-DATA is stored for CASUAL employees.
- TEMPORARY-DATA is stored for TEMPORARY employees.
- PERMANENT-DATA is stored for PERMANENT employees.

Each PERMANENT and each TEMPORARY employee is associated with a position, which is identified by a POSITION-NO.

Problem 3 (Data on Birds and Insects)

A scientist is interested in LIVING-THINGS of kinds BIRD and INSECT. LIVING-THINGS data are to be associated with LIVING-THINGS and include an identifier LIVING-THING-NO. In addition, BIRD-DATA is associated with birds, and INSECT-DATA with insects. Both birds and insects are classified into FLYING-THINGS and NONFLYING-THINGS. FLYING-DATA is associated with FLYING-THINGS, and NONFLYING-DATA is associated with NONFLYING-THINGS.

Problem 4 (Order Information)

(a) Tasks are assigned unique TASK-NOs within the organization. Each such task is part of one PROJECT; each task is assigned to one DEPT.

(b) Requisitions are made for items. Each requisition is assigned a REQUISITION-NO. A requisition includes the requesting department and the PROJECT for which the request is made.

(c) Each requisition is for items for one project. The requisition is made on a given REQUISITION-DATE and is allocated to only one SUPPLIER.

(d) Item kinds are identified by ITEM-NO; more than one item kind can appear in the same requisition.

(e) Any number of any item kinds may be requested in one requisition; QTY is the number of a particular item kind in a requisition.

(f) The PRICE on an ITEM-NO depends on the supplier; this price may vary over time.

(g) Prices of items are notified through a PRICE-ADVICE. The PRICE-ADVICE defines the new price for an ITEM-NO for a SUPPLIER, together with the EFFECTIVE-DATE on which this price is to become effective.

(h) Items are classified as being either of ITEM-CLASS "MATERIAL" or ITEM-CLASS "EQUIPMENT." Items of class "MATERIAL" are allocated a MATERIAL-CODE; items of class "EQUIPMENT" are allocated an EQUIPMENT-CODE.

(i) Each MATERIAL-CODE is described by a MATERIAL-DESCRIPTION, WEIGHT, and CONTAINER. Each EQUIPMENT-CODE is described by an EQUIPMENT-DESCRIPTION only.

As an example, ITEM-NO = 77 is of class "MATERIAL" and is given a MATERIAL-CODE = 93, which in turn describes the item to be CEMENT, 200 lbs, PAPER-BAG.

Problem 5 (Task Assignment)

(a) Jobs are undertaken by an organization on request from customers. Each job is given a unique JOB-NO and is for one customer, although there may be more than one job undertaken for the same customer. The CUSTOMER-NAME and CUSTOMER-ADDRESS are to be stored, and each customer has only one address and a unique CUSTOMER-NAME. Customers are identified by CUSTOMER-NO.

(b) Each job is completed as a number of tasks. Each task is assigned a unique TASK-NO in the organization. Each task is allocated to one job and one DEPT.

(c) Any number of persons can be involved in a task. Each person is given a PERSON-ID, and the PERSON-NAME and DATE-OF-BIRTH are also to be stored in the database.

(d) A docket with a unique DOCKET-NO is created every time a person works on a task. The docket also includes the TASK-NO, PERSON-ID, PERSON-START-TIME, and PERSON-END-TIME; the latter two define the times at which the person started and ended work on the task.

(e) The work performed by a person on a task is classified according to a work type. Each DOCKET-NO describes work of one type only. Two kinds of work type are possible: MACHINING and ASSEMBLY. The MACHINE-NO and SHAPE are the attributes of machining work; NO-OF-PARTS and ASSEMBLY-DRAWING-NO are attributes of assembly work.

(f) Persons can issue material authorities for tasks. Each material authority includes the PERSON-ID, MAT-AUTHORITY-NO, TASK-NO, and MAT-REQUEST-DATE. Each material authority is for one task only and is issued by one person.

(g) A material authority can include any number of ITEM-KINDs; the ITEM-QTY of each ITEM-KIND requested by each material authority is to be stored in the database.

Problem 6 (Faults-Data Database)

An enterprise includes information on faults occurring in equipment and on persons repairing these faults.

The enterprise has the following properties:

(a) Each fault (identified by FAULT-ID) is characterized by a FAULT-CODE and a FAULT-TYPE. The FAULT-CODE is a six-digit alphanumeric code; FAULT-TYPE can be either ELECTRICAL or MECHANICAL. There is a FAULT-DESCRIPTION (20 characters [chrs]) for each FAULT-CODE. There is an ELECTRICAL-DESCRIPTION (20 chrs) for each electrical fault type and a MECHANICAL-DESCRIPTION (20 chrs) for each mechanical fault type. There are 100 fault-codes, of which 50 are electrical and 50 mechanical fault types.

(b) Items of equipment (identified by EQUIPMENT-ID) are identified by a 10-chr alphanumeric code. There are 8000 equipment items in the database. The LOCATION of each item of equipment is maintained in the database; its FUNCTION is also STORED in the database; 15 chrs are to be provided to store the function.

(c) Both electrical and mechanical faults can occur in the same equipment item. Faults are evenly distributed between equipment items.

(d) In the database 20,000 mechanical fault occurrences and 20,000 electrical fault occurrences are to be represented. The TIME-REPAIRED (10 chrs) and TIME-OCCURRED (10 chrs) are to be stored for each fault occurrence.

(e) There are 150 PERSONS employed to repair faults; of these, 100 are ELECTRICIANS and 100 are MECHANICS (note that a person can be both an electrician and a mechanic). The person's NAME and LOCA-TION are stored in the database. The PERSON is identified by an eight-digit alphanumeric character. A 20-chr alphanumeric field ELEC-QUAL is to be provided to store an electrician's qualifications; one 20-chr alphanumeric field, MEC-QUAL, is to be provided to store a mechanic's qualifications.

(f) Only electricians can repair electrical faults; only mechanics can repair mechanical faults. An average of two electricians work on each electrical fault, and an average of two mechanics work on each mechanical fault. The TIME-SPENT (6 chrs) by each person on a fault is to be stored in the database.

(g) The size of the NAME and LOCATION data elements is 20 alphanumeric characters.

(h) If required, unique identifiers of 10 chrs can be developed for electricians and mechanics. Unique identifiers can also be developed for mechanical and electrical fault occurrences; these will require 10 chrs. Unique identifiers for electrical and mechanical fault types will require 6 chrs.

Problem 7 (Course Arrangements)

The training section of the enterprise organizes courses for personnel within the enterprise. Each course is given a unique COURSE-NO and is assigned a COURSE-COORDINATOR. A course has a STARTING-DATE and a FINISHING-DATE, along with a BUDGET, which includes all fees plus incidental expenses. The training course may be organized in any of the following three ways:

- By presenting it internally. The course is given by a lecturer within the enterprise itself or by a lecturer hired especially for the internal course, or both.

- By sending out the organization's personnel to an external advertised course. The COURSE-NAME, LOCATION, and ORGANIZATION-NAME of the organization presenting the course are stored together with the COST-ATTENDEE.

- By arranging an external organization to present the course on the premises of the enterprise. The COURSE-FEE is stored, together with the ORGANIZATION-NAME of the organization presenting the course.

The QUALIFICATIONS of any lecturer presenting any of these courses is also stored, along with any AMOUNT of fee directly payable to the lecturer (not through any organization) if the lecturer is external. Fees are directly payable to an external lecturer only if that lecturer is specially hired for an internal course (but not for an external course). The DAYS-SPENT by the lecturer on a course is also stored for internal lecturers. Data stored concerning the persons attending each course consist of their internal PERSON-ID, DEPT-NAME, JOB-DESCRIPTION, and JOB-CODE.

To assist you in the analysis, here are some examples:

- *Example 1:* A course on DATA-ANALYSIS is allocated a budget of $5000 and designated COURSE-NO 207. The organization decides that the most appropriate way to do this course is to send five people to a four-day DATABASE ANALYSIS course offered by ULTRA-DESIGN company in San Francisco. The COST-ATTENDEE will be $600. The lecturer is J. ENTITON, well known in this field.

- *Example 2:* A course on DB-STANDARDS is allocated a budget of $3000 and designated COURSE-NO 306. The enterprise decides that this course is best done internally. J. BLACKTON will take two days of the course to explain the organization's own standards. In addition, B. STANDARTON, hired externally for a fee of $800, will make a one-day presentation of external developments in standards.

- *Example 3:* Because of the good reports received from course No. 207, the enterprise decides to specially hire ULTRA-DESIGN to present a course on DATA-ANALYSIS to the organization personnel only. The course is given the number 407 and allocated a BUDGET of $4000. Out of this budget, $3000 is payable to ULTRA-DESIGN, which will use two external lecturers, J. ENTITON and K. RELATON. No special payments are made to these two lecturers, because they are paid through ULTRA-DESIGN.

(*Note:* It is possible that the same course will be presented more than once. Each such presentation will have a unique COURSE-NO. Thus two different presentations of ULTRA-DESIGN's DATA-ANALYSIS course would have different COURSE-NOs.)

Problem 8 (Parcel Distribution)

An enterprise mails out both documents parcels and good parcels. Information of interest includes the contents of each parcel. For goods parcels these data include the ITEM-TYPE and QTY of each ITEM-TYPE in the package and the WGT of the whole package. For documents parcels the AUTHOR and TITLE of each document in the parcel and the DOC-QUANTITY are of interest.

Document parcels are always dispatched by AIR, whereas goods parcels may be sent by AIR or SURFACE. Further, air or surface dispatches may be either OVERSEAS or LOCAL. Overseas dispatches are always made to agents, and the AGENT-NAME, ADDRESS, and COUNTRY are recorded, together with the AGENT's LOCAL-BRANCH-ADDRESS. Local dispatches can be made to any customer, the CUSTOMER-NAME and ADDRESS being recorded. For an air dispatch, the AIRLINE-NAME, FLIGHT-NO, DEPARTURE-DATE, and COST are recorded. Only COST is recorded against surface dispatches.

Problem 9 (Personnel Information)

(a) An organization is composed of a number of independent departments; each department has a unique name (DEPT-NAME) within the organization.

(b) Each department can be made up of any number of sections; each section has a unique name (SECTION-NAME) within its department. A section can be in *one* department only.

(c) The creation date for each department (DEPT-CREATE-DATE) and the creation date for each section (SEC-CREATE-DATE) are stored.

(d) Each person employed in the organization is assigned a unique PERSON-ID. The NAME and ADDRESS of the person is maintained in the organization; only the current address is maintained.

(e) A person is one of the following:
  • a department head
  • a section head
  • other
A person who is "other" is assigned to one section.

(f) The date on which a person started as a department head (DEPT-HEAD-START) or section head (SECT-HEAD-START) is maintained. An assignment number is created whenever this kind of assignment is made.

(g) Each person is employed at a certain level. There is a SALARY-RANGE for each level (a MAXIMUM and a MINIMUM salary are maintained).

(h) The LEVEL-START-DATE, the date on which each person started at a given level, is stored (it is assumed that only promotions are possible).

(i) Salaries can vary over time, and a salary history for each level is maintained. The history contains the RANGE-START-DATE for each new salary range.

Problem 10 (Diet Database)

A database on diets is to be maintained. This database can store any number of diets. Each diet is given a unique DIETNAME (10 chrs). The CREATION-DATA (6 chrs) and DIET-DESIGNER (20 chrs) are stored for each diet. Each diet may be made up of any number of servings, each of which is given a unique SERVING-NAME (15 chrs). A TIME-OF-SERVING (4 chrs) is given for each serving within a diet. A SERVING-DESCRIPTION (60 chrs) is stored for each serving.

Each serving is made up of any amount of any number of food elements. Thus SERVING1 may be made up of 10 grams (g) of beef, 20 g of potatoes, 5 g of tomato, and 3 g of peas. A FOOD-ID (6 chrs) is used for each element, and a field FOOD-DESCRIPTION (40 chrs) is stored for each food element.

To allow the nutritional value of each diet to be computed, nutrient values are associated with each food element as follows:

- A set of nutrients (VITA, VITB, etc.) is stored together with their UNIT-OF-MEASURE (10 chrs) (e.g., IU [international units] for VITA, mg [milligrams] for VITB). A NUTRIENT-ID (6 chrs), together with a NUTRIENT-DESCRIPTION, is also stored.
- The NUTRIENT-CONTENT (6 chrs) for each nutrient that applies to a particular food element is stored for a STANDARD-AMOUNT of that food element.

A patient is assigned a diet on each day of the patient's stay. Only one diet applies to one patient on the one day, but a patient may have different diets on different days. A PATIENT-ID (10 chrs), together with PATIENT-DETAILS (40 chrs), is stored for each patient.

Problem 11 (Changes in Diet Database)

Phase 1: Direct Servings

(a) Allow SERVING to be served directly to a patient. (Store NO-OF-TIMES that a SERVING is served in the day.)
(b) Allow FOOD-ELEMENT to be served directly to a patient. (Store NO-OF-STANDARD-AMOUNTS served in the day.)

Phase 2: Explosion of Dietary Units

(a) Allow each dietary unit to be made up of more than one kind of other dietary unit.
- A DIET may be made up of SERVINGs, FOOD ELEMENTs, and NU-TRIENTs (not only SERVINGs).
- A SERVING may be made up of NUTRIENTs and FOOD-ELE-MENTs (not only FOOD-ELEMENTs).

(b) Quantities are measured as the number of standard amounts of food elements or as the amounts of nutrients.

Phase 3: Introduction of Nonhomogeneity

(a) Attributes of allocation of different dietary units to patients are now different.

(b) Attributes of combinations of different kinds of dietary units are also different.

chapter seven
Further Generalizations
and Problems
in Semantic Modeling

INTRODUCTION

You may well question the need for all the abstractions defined in the last two chapters. Obviously, there is a great deal of similarity between the abstractions. For example, types and roles are virtually interchangeable; DOCTOR could easily be regarded a type of person rather than a role that the person takes. DOCTOR could equally well be considered a dependent entity of PERSON within the framework of the entity-relationship model.

On the other hand, there is considerable advantage in using a variety of abstractions, for they provide terms familiar to designers. For example, Figure 6.5 could well be extended to contain both type and role concepts. As shown in Figure 7.1, DIVISION, DEPT, BRANCH, and SECTION now become types of organizational units. The organizational units themselves can take SUPERVISOR and SUPERVISED roles, as was the case in Chapter 6. These roles can then be used to model the organization hierarchy.

Thus a trade-off exists. On the one hand, the use of many abstractions makes modeling easier. But conversion to file structures becomes more difficult because different mappings exist for each abstraction. On the other hand, fewer abstractions can mean easier conversion in later stages. Of course, in using fewer abstractions, we assume that *generalized abstractions,* with the same modeling power as those discussed in the last two chapters, are feasible. Three such abstractions have been proposed. One approach, introduced by J. M. Smith and D. C. P. Smith (1977), uses two generalized abstractions known as *aggregation* and *generalization.* In the second approach we regard the binary relationship as the generalized abstraction for modeling. The third approach is the functional model. These three models are described in this chapter.

187

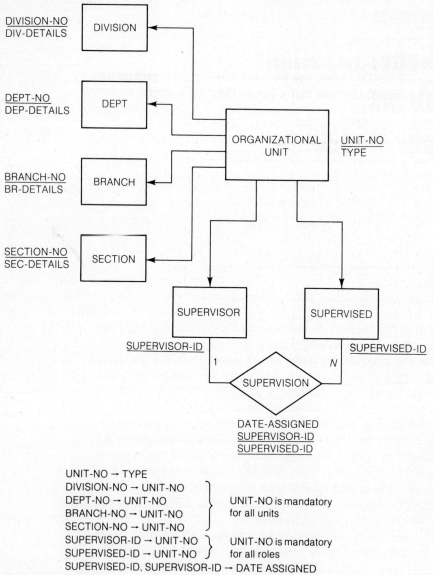

UNIT-NO → TYPE
DIVISION-NO → UNIT-NO
DEPT-NO → UNIT-NO   } UNIT-NO is mandatory
BRANCH-NO → UNIT-NO   for all units
SECTION-NO → UNIT-NO
SUPERVISOR-ID → UNIT-NO   } UNIT-NO is mandatory
SUPERVISED-ID → UNIT-NO   for all roles
SUPERVISED-ID, SUPERVISOR-ID → DATE ASSIGNED

Figure 7.1   Modeling hierarchies of different entities with types and roles

AGGREGATION AND GENERALIZATION

In Chapter 4 we pointed out that the detail of a user's perception of objects
varies with the level and type of analysis. At some levels it may well be appropriate to talk about persons, without considering their characteristics, whereas

in others it is necessary to view a person's details, such as name or date of birth. It is of course possible to combine the higher-level objects into yet a higher-level object. For example, a PERSON object and a PROJECT object can be combined into a higher-level object called, say, ACTIVITY. An ACTIVITY object would comprise one PERSON object, one PROJECT object, and perhaps another object, TIME-SPENT, the time that a person spent on a project as part of the activity.

The *aggregation abstraction* provides designers with the ability either to gradually decompose objects into their detailed components or to aggregate them into higher-level objects. When the aggregation abstraction is diagrammed, objects are represented by rectangular boxes. The decomposition of one object into its components is shown by lines directed from the object to its components. For example, in Figure 7.2 the ACTIVITY is decomposed into PERSON, PROJECT, and TIME-SPENT. PERSON and PROJECT are then decomposed into their components. The term *aggregation plane* is often used to describe the aggregation. The aggregation plane is in the plane of the paper. The upward direction of this plane implies aggregation, whereas the downward direction implies decomposition.

In the generalization and aggregation model the aggregation abstraction is complemented by the *generalization abstraction*. The generalization abstraction covers abstractions such as roles or types. It allows objects to be broken up into some specialized objects. For example, PERSONs can be specialized into subsets such as DOCTORs or PATIENTs. Inversely, DOCTORs and PATIENTs can be generalized to be PERSONs. Diagrammatically, specialization and generalization are represented in the generalization plane, which is normal

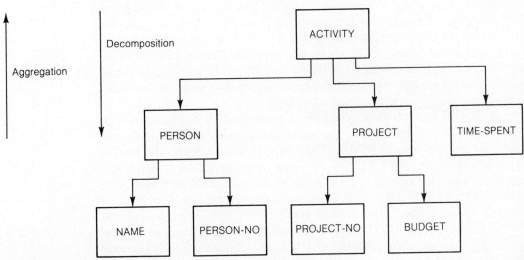

Figure 7.2 Aggregation plane

to the paper. The perpendicular direction into the paper implies specialization, whereas the direction out of the paper implies generalization.

The aggregation and generalization abstraction can be applied to many examples in the earlier chapters. For example, in Figure 6.4, PERSON can be considered to be a generalized object that models the common properties of DOCTOR and PATIENT. That is, PERSON is the generalization of DOCTOR and PATIENT. Inversely, DOCTOR and PATIENT are specializations of PERSON. The generalization PERSON can refer to DOCTORs and PATIENTs without considering DOCTOR and PATIENT details. Similarly, in Figure 6.17 EXPENDITURES is a generalization of CAPITAL EXPENDITURES and MAINTENANCE EXPENDITURES; and in Figure 6.20 PART-KINDS is a generalization of AUTO-PART-KINDS and TRUCK-PART-KINDS.

Data analysis, which uses the generalization and aggregation abstractions, proceeds by taking enterprise objects and decomposing them into their aggregation or generalization planes. For example, in the PERSON-DOCTOR enterprise of Figure 6.4, suppose we begin the analysis with the object PERSON. As shown in Figure 7.3, the object PERSON decomposes in its generalization plane into the objects DOCTOR and PATIENT. The object PERSON and each of the new objects, DOCTOR and PATIENT, are now decomposed in the aggregation plane into their attributes. Thus PERSON decomposes to NAME and PERSON-NO. DOCTOR decomposes into DOCTOR-NO and SPECIALTY. PATIENT decomposes into SYMPTOM and PATIENT-NO. We now introduce the object TREATMENT, which decomposes in its aggregation plane into DOCTOR, PATIENT, and TREATMENT-DESCRIPTION.

The aggregation and generalization model allows decomposition in any plane to any depth. This decomposition corresponds to the extended role and type structures discussed in Chapter 6. For example, Figure 7.4 models the same enterprise as Figure 6.21. The object PART-KINDs (an aggregate object in the terminology of Chapter 6) is decomposed in its generalization plane into AUTO-PART-KINDS and TRUCK-PART-KINDS; these in turn are further decomposed in the generalization planes into WHEEL-KINDs and ENGINE-KINDs. PART-KINDs, WHEEL-KINDs, and ENGINE-KINDs are subsequently decomposed into their attributes in the aggregation plane. A similar decomposition takes place with individual PARTS.

Each PARTS object is decomposed in the generalization plane into AUTO-PARTS or TRUCK-PARTS. In the aggregation plane, PARTS is decomposed into its attributes PART-ID, TIME-MANUFACTURED, and PART-KINDS. The object PART-KINDS obviously describes the kind of the part and is therefore an aggregate component of the part. Following suit, both AUTO-PARTS and TRUCK-PARTS have their particular type description in their aggregation plane. AUTO-PARTS and TRUCK-PARTS are decomposed into WHEELS and ENGINES in the generalization plane; these in turn include their type description, WHEEL-KINDS and ENGINE-KINDS in their aggregation plane.

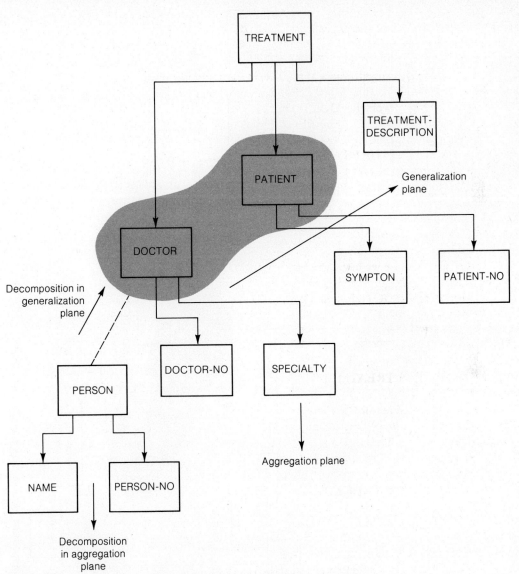

Figure 7.3 Decomposition in the generalization and aggregation planes

Clusters

The aggregation and generalization model can be extended to include the idea of cluster. *Clusters* allow objects to be decomposed in a number of directions in the generalization plane. Thus Figure 7.5 is a model of the same enterprise shown in Figure 7.1. It uses aggregation and generalization to model the orga-

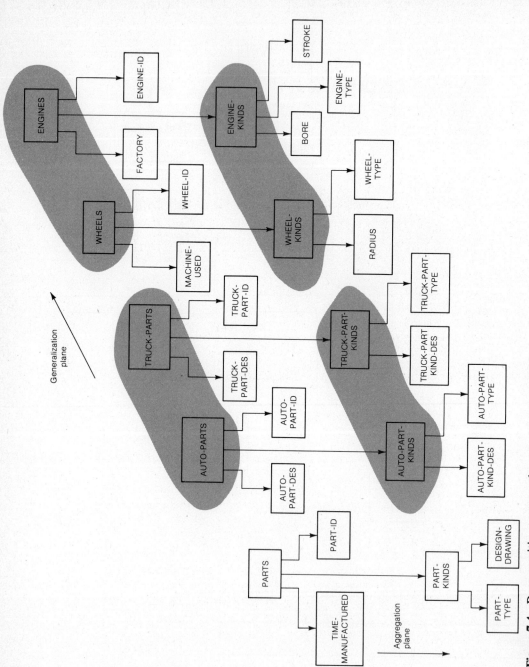

Figure 7.4 Decomposition at more than one aggregate level

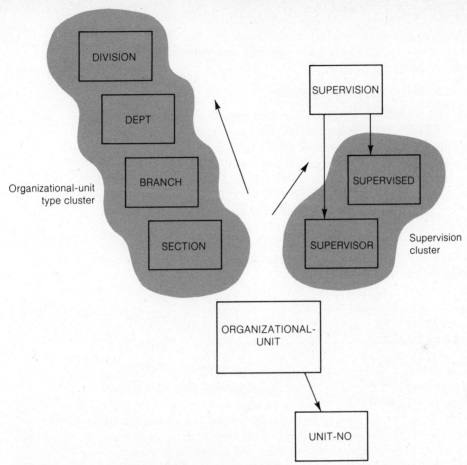

Figure 7.5 Decomposition into more than one cluster

nization's structure. Now ORGANIZATIONAL-UNIT is decomposed into two clusters in the generalization plane. One cluster contains the different types of unit; the other contains the SUPERVISOR and SUPERVISION roles. We then introduce the object SUPERVISION which is an aggregation of the SUPERVISOR and SUPERVISED roles.

One property often associated with clusters is that an object is constrained to fall into only one of the specialized objects in any cluster in the generalization plane. For example, in Figure 7.3 this constraint would require PERSON to be either a DOCTOR or a PATIENT but not both. Likewise, in Figure 7.5 an ORGANIZATIONAL-UNIT could be only *one* of the four objects: DIVISION, DEPT, BRANCH, or SECTION. Moreover, it could be either SUPERVISED or SUPERVISOR but not both.

This cluster property is sometimes useful because it leads to a special conversion to relations. The relation that corresponds to a particular object set contains one attribute for each object in its aggregation plane. It also contains one attribute for each cluster in its generalization plane. The value of its aggregation attributes is an elementary one. The value of its generalization attributes is its specialization name in the cluster. For example, the object PERSON in Figure 7.3 will convert to the relation

PERSON (PERSON-NO, NAME, TYPE)

PERSON-NO and NAME are attributes that correspond to objects in the aggregation plane. TYPE is an attribute that corresponds to the one cluster in the generalization plane and takes the value "DOCTOR" or "PATIENT." Obviously, in this case a person can be only a DOCTOR or PATIENT but not both, as TYPE can take only the value "DOCTOR" or "PATIENT" but not both. If both were allowed, DOCTOR and PATIENT would have to be modeled as separate clusters. The PERSON relation would now have a DOCTOR attribute and a PATIENT attribute, and these would take the values "YES" or "NO," depending on whether a person assumed a particular role. The cluster property then appears to be useful only if an object takes one (and only one) mandatory specialization in each cluster at the same time.

BINARY MODELING

The semantic models described in earlier chapters often left it up to the analyst to choose an abstraction to represent an enterprise object. Thus for the E-R model one designer may choose to represent an object as an attribute, while another may represent the same object as an entity. The enterprise model then depends on the importance the designer places on the objects in the enterprise. So it can be argued that the model will represent the enterprise as seen by a particular designer. Ideally, however, an enterprise model should be designer-independent. A semantic model should therefore not give designers the ability to choose alternative abstractions to model an enterprise object. And here is where binary modeling comes in. In a binary model each object becomes an entity, and each association between objects becomes a fact. There are no abstractions other than entity and fact. Thus the designer now need not distinguish between entities and attributes. They all become entities with associations between them.

When a binary model is shown pictorially, each entity set is represented by a circle and each fact by a line joining two circles. Figure 7.6, which shows a simple binary model, includes the semantic net at the enterprise model level and its object level. There are two entity sets, named PERSON-ID and DATE-OF-BIRTH, represented by circles. One fact is BORN-ON, the date on which a particular person was born. This fact is represented by associating two entities in the different entity sets. For example, the object-level semantic set shows that P105 is associated with 020261. This association represents the fact that P105 was born on 020261. The other fact is the exact opposite, namely, persons born on a particular date; thus P101 and P105 are persons born on 020261.

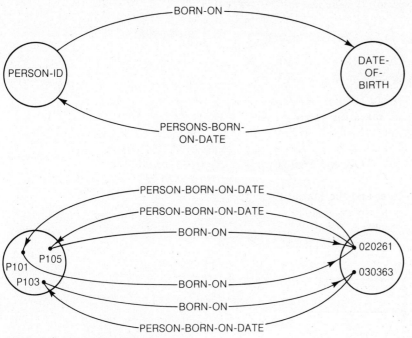

Figure 7.6   Binary modeling

This fact is shown by the association that starts on entity 020261 in the DATE-OF-BIRTH entity set.

In a convention often adopted, a fact name is chosen to be the same as an entity set name. Thus in Figure 7.7 the fact name DATE-OF-BIRTH associated with entity set PERSON-ID can lead from the entity set PERSON-ID to the entity set DATE-OF-BIRTH to determine the person's birthdate. If this convention is used, no name need appear on the lines joining the entity sets, as this line will always be labeled with the entity sets themselves. This convention is used for the remainder of this chapter. It should, however, be pointed out that a label on the line will be required if there are two facts about a pair of entities. In this case two lines, with appropriate labels, should join the entity sets.

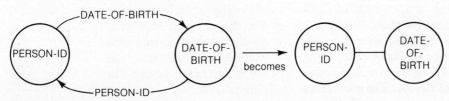

Figure 7.7   Naming convention

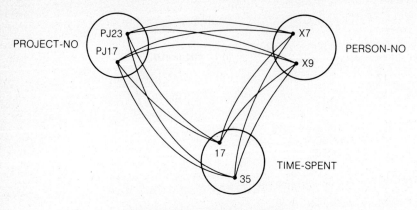

(a) Person-project interactions without
a relationship entity

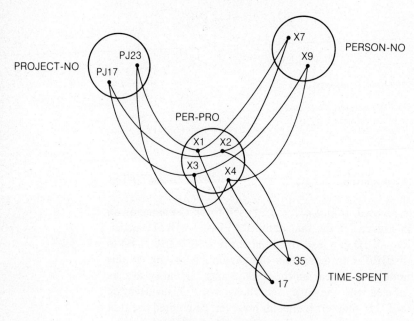

(b) Introducing an entity to
represent relationships

Figure 7.8 Modeling relationships by the binary model

One disadvantage of a binary model is that it requires special entity sets to be created to model relationships. For example, consider the standard problem of TIME-SPENT by persons on a project. Suppose this problem is modeled by the binary model shown in Figure 7.8a. We cannot unambiguously tell from this model how much time a particular person spent on a particular project. For example, either of the two instances in Figure 7.9 are possible.

PERSON	PROJECT	TIME-SPENT		PERSON	PROJECT	TIME-SPENT
X7	PJ17	17		X7	PJ17	35
X7	PJ23	35		X7	PJ23	17
X9	PJ17	35		X9	PJ17	17
X9	PJ23	17		X9	PJ23	35

Figure 7.9   Possible instances in Figure 7.8a

To remove this ambiguity, we introduce the entity set **PER-PRO** in Figure 7.8b. There is one entity in **PER-PRO** for each interaction between project and person. As you can see, the entity instances correspond to the second alternative in Figure 7.9.

Binary models have the advantage that they do not differentiate between entities, attributes, and so on. Every object set or value set is assumed to have the same semantic significance and hence becomes an entity set. For instance, Figure 7.10 is a model of the same enterprise as the one in Figure 5.1. Now, however, entities, relationships, and attributes are all represented as an entity set. Figure 7.11 shows a binary model that includes roles and the relationships between them; it involves the same enterprise as the one in Figure 6.4. Again roles, entities, and attributes are modeled here by the same abstraction.

FUNCTIONAL MODEL

The functional model is a later development that uses many ideas from earlier models. Like the binary model, it makes no distinction between the types of objects in systems. All objects can be considered as values in value sets. Any re-

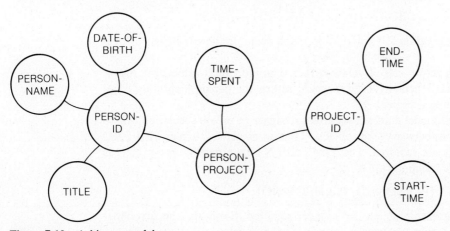

Figure 7.10   A binary model

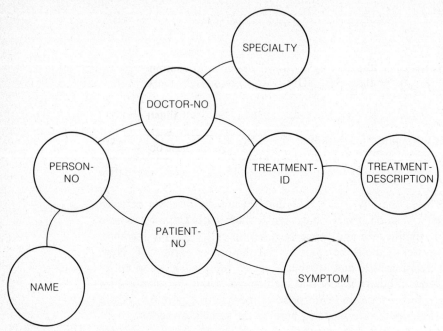

Figure 7.11 Modeling roles by a binary model

lationship between objects in object sets is expressed as a function. For example, the DATE-OF-BIRTH is a function of persons. If the function is named BORN-ON, then BORN-ON applied to a person's identifier, PERSON-ID, results in the person's DATE-OF-BIRTH. Thus BORN-ON (P101) is the DATE-OF-BIRTH of a person with PERSON-ID = P101.

The inverse of a function can also be found by a construct such as

PERSON-ID where BORN-ON (PERSON-ID) = 020261

This will yield the values P101 and P105 if the example shown in Figure 7.6 is used.

Functions can return sets of values rather than individual values. For example, PERSON-ID (PROJECT-NO) would return the person identifiers of all persons working on a project.

The functional model does not require a designer to create special objects to model interactions between other objects. Thus an object set such as PER-PRO in Figure 7.8b is not required. The TIME-SPENT by a person on a project is expressed by the function

TIME-SPENT (PERSON-ID, PROJECT-NO)

The special relationship object is no longer required. Similarly, the functional model does not require analysts to introduce specific relationship object sets as is necessary in the E-R model.

The more sophisticated form of function TIME-SPENT is

TIME-SPENT [PERSON-ID (PROJECT-NO), PROJECT-NO]

This form of TIME-SPENT implies that a value exists only for combinations of PROJECT-NO and only for those PERSON-IDs of persons who work on that PROJECT-NO.

The feasibility of using the functional data model has been illustrated by D. W. Shipman (1981). Shipman has defined a language known as DAPLEX. This language allows a user to define entities and functions on these object sets. For example, the function BORN-ON would be declared as

DECLARE PERSON-ID (   ) → **ENTITY**
DECLARE DATE-OF-BIRTH (   ) → **ENTITY**
DECLARE BORN-ON (PERSON-ID) → DATE-OF-BIRTH

Here PERSON-ID and DATE-OF-BIRTH are first declared to be ENTITY. In DAPLEX, zero argument functions define entity types. The function BORN-ON is defined to include PERSON-ID as its argument. Designers can then define various views of the data. The view of persons born on a given date is defined as

DEFINE persons-born-on-date (DATE-OF-BIRTH)
INVERSE OF BORN-ON (PERSON-ID)

Statements of this kind can be embedded in a programming language to give this language a database capability.

SUMMARY

Owing to the nondeterminism in semantic models—that is, the possibility of different designers choosing different abstractions to model the same enterprise construct—it is suggested that semantic model abstractions be sufficiently generalized and that the choice of abstraction for a particular construct is always clear-cut. Three models that have this goal are the model made up of aggregation and generalization abstractions, the binary model, and the functional model. Perhaps what distinguishes these models from those discussed in Chapters 5 and 6 is that they have fewer abstractions. In fact, each of the three preceding models has two main abstractions. The first provides the aggregation and generalization abstractions; the second, the entity and fact; the third, entities and functions.

One problem with such generalized models is that of implementing any enterprise model that uses the generalized abstractions. Designers often have several options for implementing the same abstractions on a record-based implementation model. Hence the variety of choices has been switched from data analysis to database design. So there is considerable advantage in developing an implementation that directly supports the generalized abstractions, for designers can then directly convert their enterprise model to an implementation. The language DAPLEX is used to implement the functional model. There has also been an implementation of the binary model (Senko, 1973).

PROBLEMS

Problem 1

Develop an enterprise model for the following problems by using the aggregation and generalization abstractions.

(a) Problem 1 in Chapter 6
(b) Problem 6 in Chapter 6
(c) Problem 9 in Chapter 6
(d) Problem 10 in Chapter 6

Problem 2

Develop an enterprise model for the following problems by using binary modeling.

(a) Problem 1 in Chapter 5
(b) Problem 2 in Chapter 5
(c) Problem 3 in Chapter 5
(d) Problem 1 in Chapter 6
(e) Problem 2 in Chapter 6

chapter eight
Database Specifications

INTRODUCTION

As we discussed in Chapter 1, database specification consolidates the user requirements into a form that is useful in technical design. Since the database specification becomes the input to technical design, to be useful it must

- be complete and contain all the needed technical design information
- present this information in a structured form
- be readily converted to an implementation model

The specification is made up of three parts:

1. The enterprise model, which includes the data items in the user environment, together with the relationships between them
2. The quantitative data specifications such as the size and volumes of data items and object sets
3. The access requirements, which specify the use of the database

So far this text has emphasized the enterprise model. Chapter 4 described alternate methods of representing the enterprise model, the three main methods involving, respectively,

- a set of relations
- a semantic model
- a "normalized" semantic model

We examined the relational model in Chapter 2 and the various semantic models and abstractions in Chapters 5, 6, and 7. Along the way we often discussed the normalization of the semantic models. The goal in this normalization is to ensure that object sets in a semantic model correspond to normal form relations. Designers can then use the higher-level semantic concepts early in design to identify the essential enterprise features. The semantic model can later be

modified by using normal form criteria to ensure that any subsequent implementations possess the properties inherent in normal form relations.

After the enterprise model is defined, the next steps, as shown in Figure 8.1,
are as follows:

1. Develop a database specification by adding access specifications and quantitative data to the enterprise model.
2. Convert this specification to an implementation model.

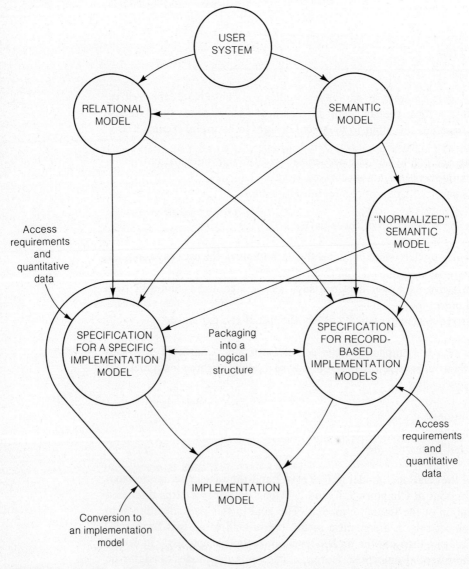

Figure 8.1   Possible conversions from the user system to implementation model

Both the access specifications and the quantitative data refer to the enterprise model. The access specifications define the object sets used by each access requirement; the quantitative data define the size of the items and the number of occurrences of objects in object sets. The quantitative data also include the frequency of database access requests.

Database designers often use the term *packaging* to denote the combination of the three specification components into one design document. This chapter will describe the access specifications and the quantitative data specifications. It will also outline some of the methods for packaging them into one design document.

CONVERSION METHODS

One requirement of the database specification is that it should be easily converted to the implementation model. To satisfy this requirement, specifications are often tailored to the implementation model. Hence the method used to package the specification will depend on both the enterprise model and the implementation model. Figure 8.1 illustrates two major packaging methods. One is to develop a specialized specification that is intended for a specific implementation model. The other is to develop a generalized specification that is applicable to a class of implementation models.

Two general classes of implementation model that are readily identified are the relational model and the record-based implementation model. Packaging from a relational or "normalized" enterprise model to the relational implementation model is straightforward because each object set or relation in the enterprise model becomes a relation in the specification. Packaging to the record-based implementation model, on the other hand, is more difficult because a conversion from the enterprise model to the general structure of record-based implementations is necessary. Designs developed for record-based implementation models group items into records and store the records as individual entities on physical devices. Many record-based implementation models also maintain links between the records. Thus to realize a record-based implementation model a conversion must

- package the enterprise model to a set of logical records, each of which preserves the normal properties of the enterprise model
- convert any links between object sets to links between logical records that represent the object sets

This chapter concentrates on packaging specifications for record-based implementation models. It describes such packaging for two cases. In one the enterprise model uses normalized semantic models, and in the other the enterprise model uses the relational model. As a preliminary, we will first briefly examine the semantic normalization process.

"NORMALIZING" THE SEMANTIC MODEL

Normalization of a semantic model is the practical embodiment of relational theory within the design process. Designers most often commence with high-level semantic models that may include considerable redundancy. These models are often derived directly from enterprise objects, functions, or activities. Since their object sets frequently do not correspond to normal form relations, the goal of normalizing the semantic model is to develop object sets that do. Such normalization does not directly correspond to either the decomposition or the synthesis approach but can at best be termed a local decomposition combined with some semblance of global synthesis. The usual practical approach is to examine each object set in turn for correspondence to a normal relation. If this correspondence does not exist, local decomposition takes place. Locally decomposed object sets are then compared globally to determine any redundancy. The redundancy is removed by combining these object sets. The normalization uses the correspondence rules between semantic models and relations (as described in Chapters 5, 6, and 7).

Figure 8.2 illustrates a typical set of steps used to reduce an invoice to a normalized semantic structure. As a first step the invoice is modeled as a single entity with a structured attribute representing invoice lines. In the second step the structured attribute is removed and made into a dependent entity of invoice. The second step corresponds to converting a nonnormal relation to a normal relation. But the object set INVOICE-LINES does not correspond to a BCNF relation because ITEM-DESCR depends on part of the key, ITEM-NO. So, as the third and final step, INVOICE-LINES is decomposed into a new entity, ITEMS, and a relationship is established between ITEMS and INVOICE-LINES. The object sets now correspond to BCNF relations.

Figure 8.3 illustrates the nonnormal entities that arise if a single entity is used to model both an entity and the relationships in which the entity participates. The first step here is to model all information about a JOB in the JOBS object set. This object set includes the JOBS attributes as well as an activity that concurrently assigns each JOB to one person and allocates each JOB to one project. All parts used in a job are also initially included in the JOBS object set. The set is nonnormal because it includes a structured attribute. There is also dependence between the attributes TIME-ALLOCATION and TIME-SPENT on PROJECT-ID and PERSON-ID, respectively. Normalization proceeds in two steps. In step 2 the structured attribute is removed. It is replaced by a relationship USE between JOBS and PARTS. In step 3 the relationships in JOBS are replaced by relationship sets of JOBS with PERSONS and PROJECTS.

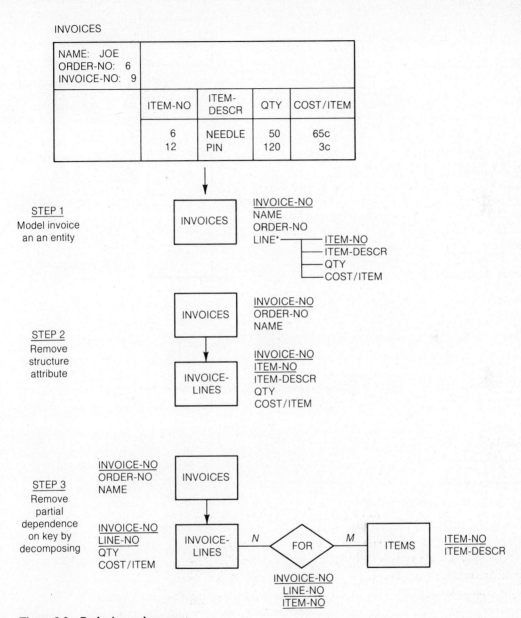

Figure 8.2 Reducing a document

Figures 8.2 and 8.3 are only two examples of the semantic normalization that occurs in top-down design. Semantic normalization is also necessary when properties are used to identify entities in relationships and, as discussed in Chapter 6, to reduce roles and types to normal structures.

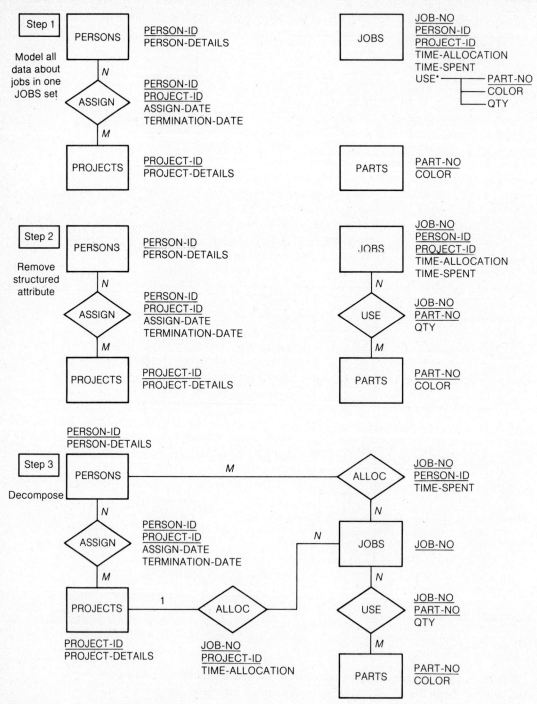

Figure 8.3 Decomposing an activity

FROM "NORMALIZED" SEMANTIC MODELS
TO RECORD SPECIFICATIONS

The most obvious way to convert a "normalized" semantic model to a record structure is as follows:

- First convert each object set to a logical record, in which each object set attribute becomes a field.
- Then link records that contain common identifier attributes.

A simple example is given in Figure 8.4. Here an $N:M$ relationship is converted to a logical record structure. Each object set in the enterprise model becomes a logical record type in the logical record structure; the data fields in the logical record types are the same as the attributes of the corresponding object sets.

You will also note that to distinguish the logical record structure from the E-R model we

- place the field names inside the rectangular boxes that represent logical record types
- place the logical record names outside the rectangular boxes.

There are links between the logical record types. Two logical record types X and Y are linked if they have a common field or fields, A, and either of the following hold:

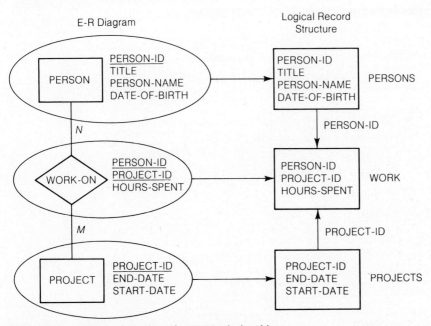

Figure 8.4 Logical conversion of a $N:M$ relationship

- For each value of A there is one record in X with that value and a number of records of Y with that value; in this case the link is from X to Y.
- For each value of A there is one record in X with that value and one record in Y with that value; in this case either the link becomes bidirectional or the records are combined.

In either case the link is labeled with the name of the common fields. Thus in Figure 8.4 there is one PERSONS record with a given value of PERSON-ID, and many WORK records with the same value of PERSON-ID. So a link labeled PERSON-ID commences on PERSONS and terminates on WORK. For a similar reason there is a link labeled PROJECT-ID originating from the PROJECTS logical record and terminating on logical record WORK.

On examining Figure 8.4 we could argue that there is no difference between the enterprise model and the logical structure. This may be true in the simple case in Figure 8.4; there is, however, scope for a greater conversion flexibility in more complex enterprises.

To illustrate this greater flexibility, we must consider one other conversion criterion: minimization of the number of logical records in the database specification. For example, consider Figure 8.5, where the enterprise model is now a 1:N relationship. To minimize the number of logical records, we combine the PERSONS and WORK-IN object sets into one logical record type while preserving normal properties. This combination is possible because for a given value of PERSON-ID there is only one record with that value in object set PERSON and one record with that value in object set WORK-IN. Moreover, combining the two records does not introduce nonhomogeneity.

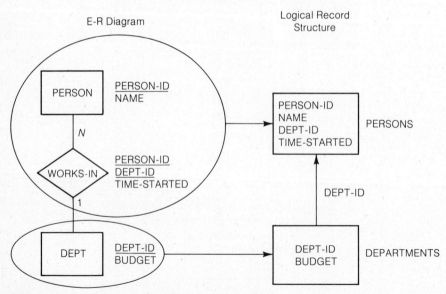

Figure 8.5 Logical conversion of a 1:N relationship

As we will see next, more possibilities arise when the enterprise includes roles and types.

Logical Structures for Uniform Roles

Figure 8.6 illustrates four options for converting the PATIENT-DOCTOR enterprise. This enterprise was described in Chapter 6. The conversion options are as follows:

- *Option 1:* There is a separate logical record for each object set. Links are established between logical records that correspond to role sets and their entity sets. The links are bidirectional (Figure 8.6a).
- *Option 2:* The entity is combined with its role (Figure 8.6b). This procedure reduces the number of logical records but can lead to duplication if an entity can take many roles. If the entity takes one role only, this option is feasible.
- *Option 3:* The roles are combined with the entity (Figure 8.6c). Hence there are no logical records for roles, but nonhomogeneity is introduced into the entity record. If the entity takes most of its roles, this option may be a viable alternative.
- *Option 4:* All the roles are combined into one logical record (Figure 8.6d). This option is similar to option 3 with the exception that a separate logical record is maintained to represent the entity itself.

Nonuniform Mandatory Roles

The range of options for uniform roles is also available for nonuniform role or type sets. The options for nonuniform mandatory roles (Figure 8.7) differ from those for uniform roles in the following ways:

- *Option 1:* A constraint is added to restrict each role to be associated with one object in the source set (Figure 8.7a).
- *Option 2:* Records representing different entity sets are now combined into a role record. Thus in Figure 8.7b, both PROJ-DETAILS and DEPT-DETAILS appear in the USERS record type. However, only one of these takes a value in a record occurrence because a role can be taken only by a department or a project but not both. Hence we have nonhomogeneity. Apart from introducing non-

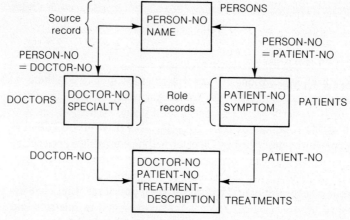

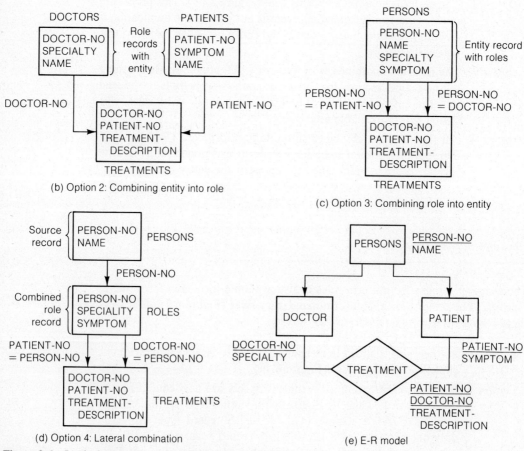

(a) Option 1: Direct conversion

(b) Option 2: Combining entity into role

(c) Option 3: Combining role into entity

(d) Option 4: Lateral combination

(e) E-R model

Figure 8.6   Logical conversion of uniform role structures

homogeneity, this option allows access to source details through a source identifier only if the implementation model includes the ability to access records by using more than one key. Therefore this option is not used frequently in practice.

- *Option 3:* This is a preferred option. Because the roles are mandatory there is no nonhomogeneity and special logical records are not required for roles. One property of this option is that data about the roles are spread across a number of record types; however, there is no duplication because each user role appears in only one source set (Figure 8.7c). There is also a constraint associated with records that correspond to relationships: these records can be associated only with one source set.

Nonuniform Optional Roles

In the case of nonuniform optional roles (Figure 8.8) it is difficult to avoid nonhomogeneity for options other than option 1 for the following reasons:

- *Option 2:* There is nonhomogeneity in the role records because each role applies to only one source (Figure 8.8a). Thus if a given SUPPLIER-ID is a project, DEPT-NO and DEPT-DETAILS are null. If it is a department, PROJ-NO and PROJ-DETAILS are null.
- *Option 3:* There is nonhomogeneity in the source records because the roles in each source are optional (Figure 8.8b). Hence if a given project is not a user, then USER-ID and USER-DETAILS are null. Role data are again spread across a number of record types, although no duplication occurs. Records that contain the roles are also constrained to be associated with only one of the role target sets.

Some General Comments on Role and Type Conversion

Role and type conversions allow many options and trade-offs for designers. For example, there are trade-offs between nonhomogeneity and the number of logical records. If each role is represented by a logical record, large numbers of roles imply many logical records but nonhomogeneity is avoided. By choosing option 3, we combine these role records with their sources. Now there are few logical records but nonhomogeneity results if the roles are optional. A designer may also wish to partition the entity sets by their roles; option 2 can be used to

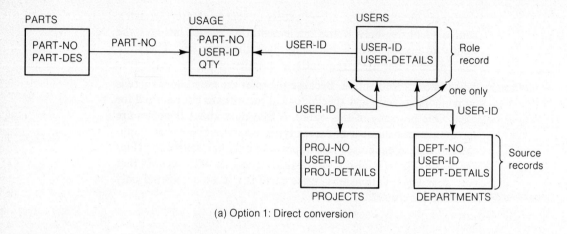

(a) Option 1: Direct conversion

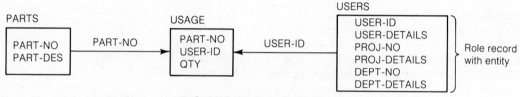

(b) Option 2: Combining entity into role

Figure 8.7 Logical conversion of nonuniform mandatory role structures

do this. Thus option 2 in Figure 8.6 is quite viable if there is some advantage in separating DOCTORS and PATIENTS into different files. Such partitioning could also be made for nonuniform role structures. Thus the SUPPLIERS and USERS logical records for option 2 in both Figures 8.7 and 8.8 could be further partitioned, as could the PROJECTS and DEPARTMENTS logical records in option 3 for Figure 8.8. The result of this partitioning is a separate logical record for each source/role pair. An example is given in Figure 8.9, which illustrates partitioning of option 3 of Figure 8.8. Option 2 of Figure 8.8 could also be partitioned into the structure shown in Figure 8.9. A consequence of partitioning is that there are many logical records, but nonhomogeneity is avoided. The final choice is the designer's, and it is often influenced by the implementation model.

FROM RELATIONAL MODEL TO LOGICAL STRUCTURE

In this section we will first define the structure criteria for the relational model and then suggest conversions to logical structure.

The general requirements for the relational model are as follows:

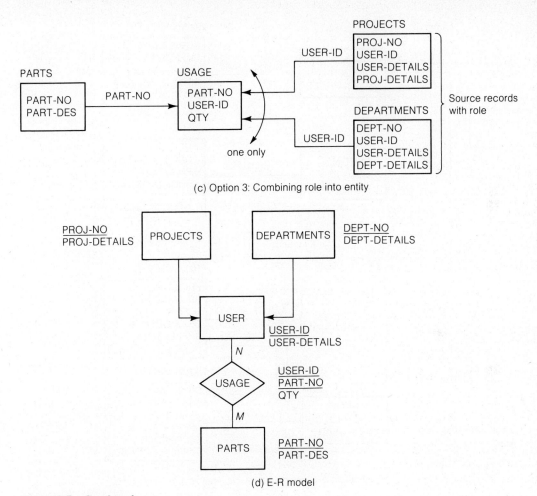

(c) Option 3: Combining role into entity

(d) E-R model

Figure 8.7 Continued

- $R1$: The determinant of each FD must be stored once only.
- $R2$: The dependent of each FD must be stored once only.

There is an alternate criterion:

- $R3$: Each row of each relation in a normalized relational database is stored once only (although its attributes need not necessarily be in contiguous physical locations).

Linking is more difficult to define for the relational model than for the semantic model. The relational model does not contain specific links between relations, whereas the semantic model includes links between object sets. Defini-

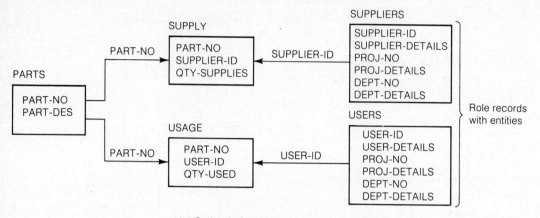

(a) Option 2: Combining entities into roles

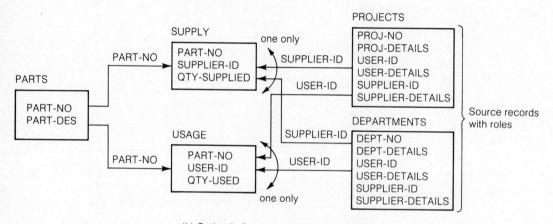

(b) Option 3: Combining roles into entities

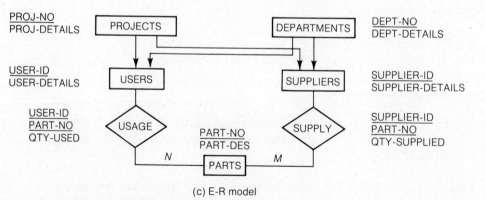

(c) E-R model

Figure 8.8 Logical conversion of nonuniform optional role structures

tions of link criteria in the relational model use the notion of the *foreign key*. An attribute (or set of attributes), A, in a relation, R, is a foreign key if

- A is not a relation key of R
- A is a relation key of some other relation

Consider, for instance, the relations

PERSONS (<u>PERSON-ID</u>, PERSON-DETAILS)
PROJECTS (<u>PROJECT-ID</u>, PROJECT-DETAILS)
WORK (<u>PERSON-ID, PROJECT-ID</u>, TIME-SPENT)

PERSON-ID is a foreign key of relation WORK because it is a relation key of PERSONS but not a relation key of WORK. Similarly, PROJECT-ID is a foreign key of WORK. The foreign key value assumes the existence of tuples in other relations. Thus a value of PERSON-ID in WORK assumes that a person with that value of PERSON-ID exists in relation PERSONS.

The most obvious conversion method is as follows:

- Convert each relation to a logical record.
- Establish links from relation $R1$ to relation $R2$ if the relation key of $R1$ is a foreign key in $R2$. Label the link with the attributes in the foreign key.

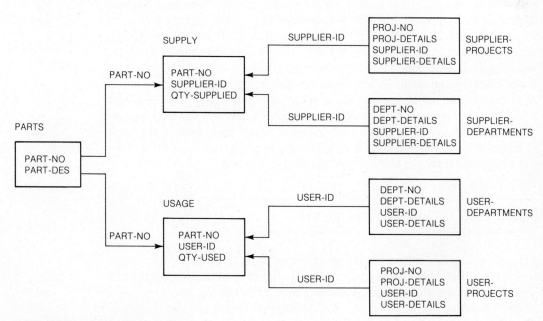

Figure 8.9 A partitioned structure

Assuming that data analysis yields a minimal set of normal relations, this conversion will yield the same logical structure as is obtained from a normalized semantic model. For example, consider Figure 8.5. The minimal set of normal relations that describe this enterprise are

PERSON (PERSON-ID, NAME, DEPT-ID, TIME-STARTED)
DEPT (DEPT-ID, BUDGET)

If these relations are converted to a logical record structure, the result is the same logical structure as the one shown in Figure 8.5. DEPT-ID is a key of DEPT but a foreign key in PERSON. Hence there will be a logical link from DEPT to PERSON.

When conversions of the relational model to logical record structures are applied to role structures, they always result in option 1 of Figures 8.6, 8.7, and 8.8. The links between source and role or type logical structure are bidirectional for two reasons: the role identifier is a foreign key in the source relation, and the source-identifier is a foreign key in the role or type relation.

MINIMAL LOGICAL RECORD STRUCTURE (MLRS)

One further minimization step is possible in logical record structures. It minimizes the number of items in each logical record, the result being a *minimal logical record structure* (MLRS). For instance, the logical record structure in Figure 8.4 has some redundancy. The fields PERSON-ID and PROJECT-ID are redundant in the logical record WORK. It is obvious from the labels on the incoming links that both PERSON-ID and PROJECT-ID are WORK attributes. Such redundant fields are removed from a logical record structure to form the MLRS. An example of the MLRS for Figure 8.4 is given in Figure 8.10a. All the logical record structures in Figures 8.5 to 8.9 can also be converted to an MLRS by removing from a logical record those fields that appear as labels on incoming logical links (see, for instance, Figure 8.10b). In the special case where links are bidirectional, no field is removed.

SPECIFYING ACCESS REQUIREMENTS

Access requirements define the proposed use of data. They may take several forms. First of all there is the completely informal method. In this method the requirement uses natural language. For example, "Find all the stores that hold an item identified by ITEM-ID = "I2." Although informal specifications may be satisfactory for relatively simple requirements, they have not been found suitable for specifying access requirements of some complexity. For this reason

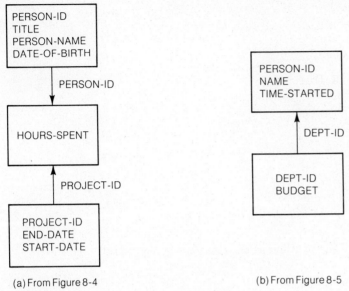

(a) From Figure 8-4   (b) From Figure 8-5

Figure 8.10 Minimal logical record structure

more formal techniques are used. The goal of these techniques is to precisely specify the fields and logical records needed to satisfy each requirement. The techniques also include the sequence in which these logical records are accessed and the frequency of access. Any one of the following procedures is used in applying these techniques:

- access paths, or graphical methods
- tabular specifications
- pseudocode

Access Paths

Access paths (or *usage paths* as they are often called) are used to specify the object sets, logical records, or implementation model record types dictated by an access requirement. They also specify the sequence used to refer to these structures and the activity at each structure. Such activity may be a retrieve, store, or insert.

The exact notation used by an access path depends on the level at which the access path is used. Notations differ among object sets, logical record structures, and particular implementation models. In this chapter only those access paths that refer to logical record structures are described.

A typical notation that can be used for access paths for logical record struc-

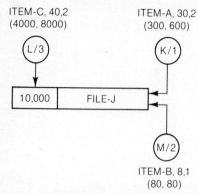

Figure 8.11 Access requirements at a record type

tures is illustrated in Figure 8.11. The notation at each access step consists of four parts:

1. An access step label made up of
   (a) a letter or name to identify the access requirement
   (b) a number to identify the position of the step in the access path sequence
   The access step label is usually enclosed in a circle, with an arrow from the circle to the logical record.
2. The names of fields whose values are known at the time the access step is executed.
3. The number of times that an access step is executed for each access occurrence; this number is followed by the number of records accessed by each such step. We can then put in parentheses the total number of access steps executed during a period of interest and the total number of logical records retrieved in that period.
4. An informal description of the activity at each step.

Figure 8.11 illustrates this notation for three access steps, each from a different access requirement at FILE-J. Here access step L/3, for example, occurs 40 times each time that access L is executed. Two logical records are needed by each access step, and the value of ITEM-C is known at the time that the access step occurs. It is estimated that access L occurs 100 times in a period of interest (which may be a month, week, day, hour, or some other time interval). The figures in parentheses (4000, 8000) are an estimate of the following:

- The total number of times that the access step is executed (in this case 40 × 100 = 4000) in the period of interest.
- The total number of logical records retrieved. This number is computed as 40 × 2 to show the number of records retrieved for each access step. This

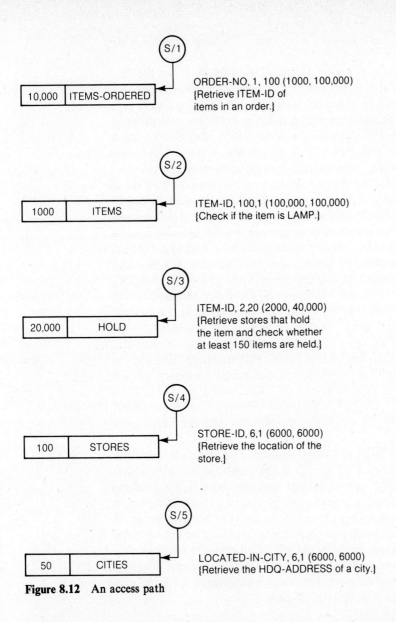

Figure 8.12 An access path

amount is then multiplied by the number of access occurrences (100) to give 8000.

Figure 8.11 shows a further extension to the logical structure. It specifies the number of logical records of each kind stored in the database. Thus there are 10,000 records in FILE-J.

A more elaborate access path is illustrated in Figure 8.12. It refers to requirement S in the database in the appendix, namely, the need to find the

HDQ-ADDRESS of all stores that hold more than 150 items named LAMP contained in ORDER1.

The access path commences at record ITEMS-ORDERED, where the ORDER-NO is known. Access step S/1 is executed once for each occurrence of the access requirement. It is estimated that 100 logical records are retrieved at each such access step because on an average the order is made for 100 different items. Consequently, there are 100 occurrences of access step S/2 to check whether the item is LAMP. It is then estimated that only 2 of the 100 checks result in the item being LAMP. Access step S/3 is therefore executed twice for each S occurrence. It finds the stores that hold each LAMP item. Twenty stores on an average hold each item. (This is the number of HOLD records divided by the number of ITEMS records.) It is then estimated that a total of 6 stores will hold quantities over 150 of all the items in an average order. The value 6 is less than $40(20 \times 2)$, which would be expected if each item were held by a different store and QTY-HELD exceeded 150 in each case. It is, however, assumed that some stores hold more than one item and that many holdings are less than 150. Hence only 6 stores satisfy the conditions. Steps S/4 and S/5 are used to find the location and then the HDQ-ADDRESS of each such store. It is estimated that access requirement S will occur 1000 times in a period of interest, so the figures in parentheses are the product of 1000 in accordance with this estimate.

There can, of course, be variations on the access path notations. Some of the quantitative data may be omitted. Alternatively, the quantitative data and activity description can appear in a separate table. One such variation is illustrated in Figures 8.13 and 8.14. Now the graphical representation (Figure 8.13) contains the access path only; the details and quantitative data are found in the table in Figure 8.14.

Access diagrams may get bulky if a large number of requests are drawn on the same diagram. Designers may often wish to use tabular specifications, dispensing with the diagrammatic representations of access requests. But it is important that designers avoid using different access diagrams for different user requests. One goal of an access diagram or access list is to bring together all user requests that access the one file; design decisions on file structure can then be made in light of all accesses made to the file. If all requests are drawn or listed on separate documents, possible design oversights can occur. That is, owing to the problems of handling a large number of documents, some requests to a file may be overlooked at the time of file design.

Using Pseudocode

Programmers or designers accustomed to a formal control structure often find the informal structure of the logical level specification (Figures 8.12, 8.13, and 8.14) difficult to use. One way to overcome this informality is to use *pseudo-*

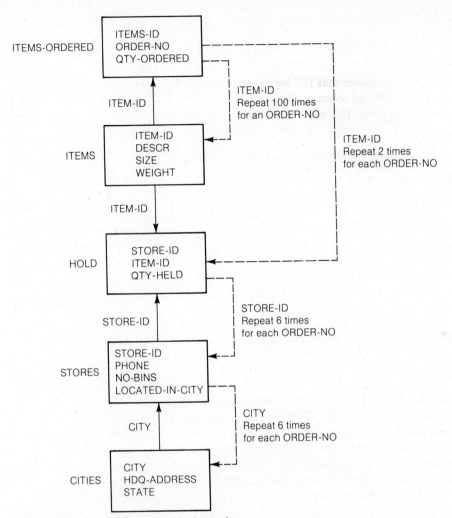

Figure 8.13 An alternate graphical notation

code to specify access requirements. Pseudocode will include both "computer-like" flow of control statements and use access commands appropriate to the implementation model. Figure 8.15 is the pseudocode for the access requirement S, which is

"FIND the HDQ-ADDRESS of STORES that hold more than 150 ITEMS named LAMP and ordered in ORDER named ORD1."

The pseudocode commences with opening of the required files. Then paragraph PAR0 is executed. Paragraph PAR0 in Figure 8.15 includes a loop to

ACCESS: S
FREQUENCY: 1000/week

ACCESS STEP	LOGICAL RECORD	INPUT	OUTPUT	ACTION	FREQUENCY FOR ONE ACCESS
S/1	ITEMS-ORDERED	ORDER-NO	ITEM-ID	Retrieves items in an order	Executed once per access S. 100 retrieved for an order
S/2	ITEMS	ITEM-ID	True or false	Check if an item is a LAMP	Executed once for each ITEM-ID found in step S/1; an average of two of five items are LAMP
S/3	HOLD	ITEM-ID	STORE-ID	Retrieves stores that hold an item	Executed once for each of the two records retrieved in S/2; each item is stored in twenty stores; because some stores are common to parts and some holdings less than 150, a total of six stores hold all the parts for one ITEM-ID
S/4	STORES	STORE-ID	CITY	Retrieves city location of a store	Executed once for each ITEM-ID retrieved in S/3
S/5	CITIES	CITY	HDQ-ADDRESS	Retrieves a city distance	Executed once for each CITY in step S/4

Figure 8.14 Tabular specification of quantitative data and activity of each step associated with the access path

read all records in ITEMS-ORDERED with a given value of ORDER-NO; it includes the commands START and READ NEXT to search files. The value of ITEM-ID in each record found during a search is used as a key value to read an ITEMS record. The value of ITEM-ID is first set; the READ statement reads the ITEMS record with that key value. PAR1 is then executed if the part is a LAMP. PAR1 is similar to PAR0; it searches file HOLD for a given value of ITEM-ID. PAR2 is initiated for each store that holds 150 of the given item. PAR2 makes two direct reads to find the HDQ-ADDRESS of the store. Pseudocode can also be used with database implementation models. In this case commands specific to a database management system are part of the pseudocode.

The pseudocode syntax depends on a particular installation. It uses control statements associated with block structured languages but often includes input-output statements used in the final implementation. Pseudocode can also be used to construct logical access paths for later analysis. Those pseudocode statements that transfer data from peripherals to memory are identified with access step labels. The designer can then enter the steps on the access path diagram and use them later in performance analysis. The designer can choose to include short-code in the access diagram or to use the pseudocode in later analysis.

```
INITIALIZE
      OPEN ITEMS-ORDERED, ITEMS, HOLD, STORES, CITIES
PAR0.
      START ITEMS-ORDERED AT ORDER-NO = 'ORD1'
      REPEAT UNTIL ORDER-NO NOT 'ORD1'
          BEGIN
          S1. READ NEXT ITEMS-ORDERED RECORD --------------------------------- step S1.
              IF ORDER-NO IN ITEMS-ORDERED = 'ORD1'
                  THEN BEGIN
                      ITEM-ID IN ITEMS = ITEM-ID IN ITEMS-ORDERED
          S2. READ ITEMS RECORD FOR ITEM-ID IN ITEMS---------------------------- step S2.
              IF DESCR IN ITEMS = 'LAMP'
                  THEN DO PAR1.
              END.
          END.
PAR1.
      START HOLD AT ITEM-ID IN HOLD = ITEM-ID IN ITEMS ORDERED
      REPEAT UNTIL ITEM-ID IN HOLD NOT ITEM-ID IN ITEMS-ORDERED
          BEGIN
          S3. READ NEXT HOLD RECORDS ----------------------------------------- step S3.
              IF ITEM-ID IN HOLD = ITEM-ID IN ITEMS-ORDERED
                  THEN BEGIN
                      IF QTY-HELD IN HOLD > 150
                          THEN DO PAR2.
                      END.
          END.
PAR2.
      STORE-ID IN STORE = STORE-ID IN HOLD
S4.   READ STORES RECORD WITH STORE-ID IN STORE ----------------------------- step S4.
      CITY IN CITIES = LOCATED-IN-CITY IN STORES
S5.   READ CITIES RECORD WITH CITY IN CITIES--------------------------------- step S5.
      PRINT HDQ-ADDRESS
```

Figure 8.15 A pseudocode specification

In principle, pseudocode appears attractive, but it lacks the continuity of the life cycle. It is often necessary to know the file structure before pseudocode is written, but the file structure cannot be finalized until the access requirements (and hence the pseudocode) are defined. The life cycle therefore becomes circular. For practical purposes, this problem can be solved only by an evolutionary approach. Both the pseudocode and data structure will have to be developed and modified together in successive design iterations.

So the designer must make the choice: either use the less formal graphical technique during database design and develop the pseudocode once the database design is finalized; or use the pseudocode throughout the design and go through the extra effort of modifying it during database design iterations.

QUANTITATIVE DATA SPECIFICATIONS

Quantitative data specifications become important in technical design. The quantitative data specification indicates

- the size and volume of the enterprise model components
- data about relationships between object sets, in particular the average values of N and M in $N:M$ relationships
- frequency of access requests

These data are used in technical design to estimate transaction performance and storage requirements.

Quantitative data can be presented in a number of ways, some of which have already been discussed. For example, Figures 8.11 and 8.12 show the number of occurrences of objects in each object set; and Figure 8.14 includes the frequency of an access request and the number of records retrieved by this access step.

We could envisage a similar extension to the logical record specification or the MLRS. An extension similar to that in Figure 8.11 could be made to each logical record to show the number of occurrences of that record. Similarly, an extension to each field could indicate its size and type. An example is given in Figure 8.16. Note that the values here imply the N and M values in the $N:M$ relationship. As there are 400 WORK records and 200 PERSONS, each person works on an average of two projects. Similarly, each project has 20 persons working on it.

A more common method, however, is to use data dictionaries to document descriptions of fields and record types. Figure 8.17 shows a RECORD FIELD

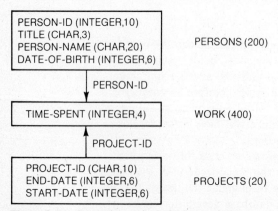

Figure 8.16   Extension to include size and volume

RECORD FIELD LIST

ITEM-NAME	SIZE	TYPE	VALUE RANGE	COMMENTS	USED-IN
DATE-OF-BIRTH	6	INTEGER	Year, month, day		PERSONS
END-DATE	6	INTEGER	Year, month, day		PROJECTS
PERSON-NAME	20	CHAR	Any value		PERSONS
PERSON-ID	10	INTEGER	Any value		PERSONS
PROJECT-ID	10	CHAR	PR followed by 8 digits		PROJECTS
START-DATE	6	INTEGER	Year, month, day		PROJECTS
TIME-SPENT	4	INTEGER	Any value		WORK
TITLE	3	CHAR	MR, MRS, MS, DR		PERSONS

Figure 8.17   Data dictionary entries

LIST in a dictionary. The fields are arranged in alphabetical order, with the details of field value and their use given in the table. A table could also be constructed for the logical record types. This table would include a list not only of all record types in alphabetical order but also of the fields that appear in each record type. More examples of quantitative data specifications are given in the appendix and in the database design projects at the end of the text.

SUMMARY

The database specification consists of three parts:

1. the enterprise model
2. the quantitative data
3. the access requirements

The enterprise model is produced during the data analysis stage. This model can be a set of relations, a semantic model, or a "normalized" semantic model. The quantitative data and access requirements are collected during the analysis of user requirements and combined with the enterprise model when the database specification is developed.

Various methods can be used to package the three parts into an integrated database specification, but the use of logical record structures is proposed as most suitable because most implementation models are record-based. In conversions from the enterprise model to the logical record structure, links between object sets must be converted to links between logical records that represent the object sets.

Three methods of defining access requirements are

1. access paths, or graphical methods
2. tabular specifications
3. pseudocode

Each method has advantages and disadvantages.

The quantitative data specifications pertinent to technical design are

- the size and volume of the enterprise model components
- frequency of relationship between objects in an object set
- frequency of access requests

Two major ways of documenting these specifications are to extend the logical record specifications and to use data dictionaries.

PROBLEMS

A number of database specifications are included in the database design projects at the end of the text. It is recommended that you select some subset of these projects and design the databases that will satisfy its specifications.

You can design the databases in several ways. Design can commence after you have thoroughly studied this chapter and then continue as subsequent chapters are completed. Once you have finished this chapter, it would be a good idea to develop a specification for a logical record structure for Design Projects A and B at least. The specification should show all the logical links between logical record structures. Time permitting, the other design projects can also be attempted.

chapter nine
Implementation Models,
I-File Structures

INTRODUCTION

Earlier chapters described the enterprise model of user data and the way that it leads to a database specification. This specification becomes the input to the technical database design stage. During technical design the database specification is implemented as a database on a computer system. Technical design will be emphasized in the remainder of the text.

Technical design differs from data analysis in one important respect. Whereas data analysis is independent of a particular computer system, technical design is not. Technical design must consider an actual computer system and the file systems or database management systems (DBMSs) supported on that computer system. So far, we have used the general term *implementation model* to describe the file or DBMSs available to implement the database. Now it is necessary to describe these systems in more detail.

The descriptions of implementation models emphasize aspects of interest to database designers and not to the builders of implementation model software. In some cases, however, detailed descriptions of implementation software are included. If you are interested in the use of the software rather than in its construction, you may wish to ignore such software details. Attention is drawn to this kind of detail at various points in the chapter.

The major components of the implementation model and their relationship to the database specification are shown in Figure 9.1 and are defined as follows:

- A set of file structures or a data model structure. The enterprise model of the database specification is converted to these structures.
- The data definition languages provided by the implementation model to define the database as logical file or data model structures. The logical structures are subsequently implemented as a physical database structure.
- The commands used to access the database structure. Access specifications are converted to programs that use these commands. The commands refer to the logical database structure but are converted (by a compiler) to instructions that access the physical database.

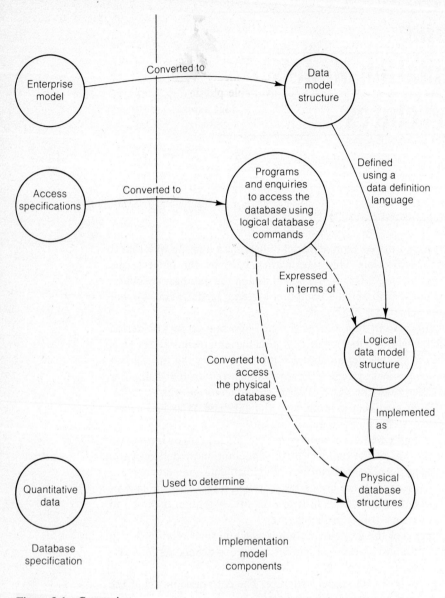

Figure 9.1 Conversion

• The physical structures used to store the database on physical devices. The quantitative data are often used to choose the physical structures for a particular database.

The database specification is converted to these components in a sequence of design steps. A typical sequence is shown in Figure 9.2. It commences with logical design to convert the enterprise model to a file or data model structure.

Logical design uses knowledge about the implementation model structures to choose the most satisfactory data model representation of the enterprise model.

The next step is physical design. Physical design techniques are used to choose the most satisfactory physical structure for the data model structure. These techniques depend on the characteristics of the available physical devices and the access methods. The quantitative data are an important aspect of physical database design. The chosen logical and physical structures are defined by using database definition languages.

Finally, software is developed to access the database. In most systems databases are accessed either by database on-line query languages or by input/output commands embedded in a programming language.

The design activities in Figure 9.2 incorporate the data structures and languages of the implementation model. We will describe such structures and lan-

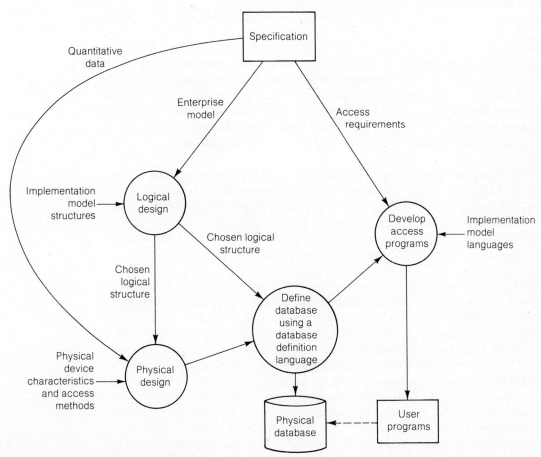

Figure 9.2 Database design techniques

guages in this chapter, which deals with some elementary file structures, and in Chapters 10, 11, 12, and 13, which cover specific DBMSs.

Elementary file structures are a combination of data structure and commands to access the data structure. In this chapter we will discuss both the data structure and the input/output commands used to access it. In this discussion we will assume that the input/output commands are embedded in the Pascal language. We can, of course, make only an assumption, because Pascal is limited in its input/output capabilities. Its algorithmic structure, however, serves as an excellent base to illustrate how program logic can use input/output commands to access files.

The chapter concludes by illustrating the kinds of input/output commands available in practice. In this case the input/output facilities available in the commercial language COBOL are described.

IMPLEMENTATION MODELS

Implementation model components are realized by software and hardware, which are often viewed as a series of levels with interfaces between them. User commands are converted through these levels to operations on stored data. The number of levels and the instructions at each interface depend on a particular implementation model. One such set of levels is illustrated in Figure 9.3, which shows the major implementation model components and their relationship to the software levels and interfaces. The interfaces are as follows:

- The *user interface* allows users to define and access databases by using database or file definition languages and access commands.
- The *logical record interface* is used to transfer single logical records between an access method and the user interface.
- The *physical record interface* controls physical storage devices and transfers single physical records between memory and storage devices.

There are two levels of software. One level directly supports the user interface. It converts the user interface commands to instructions at the logical record interface. The other level is the access method. Often part of the operating system, the access method converts the logical level operations to transfers between memory and storage devices at the physical record interface.

Database designers must consider both levels of software and the facilities offered by them. The access methods are particularly important when choosing physical structures. They usually determine the performance achieved by a given design. The user interface software, on the other hand, determines the ease of use of the database.

A clear distinction arises here between file support systems and DBMSs. Developed early in computing, file support systems provide the ability to define

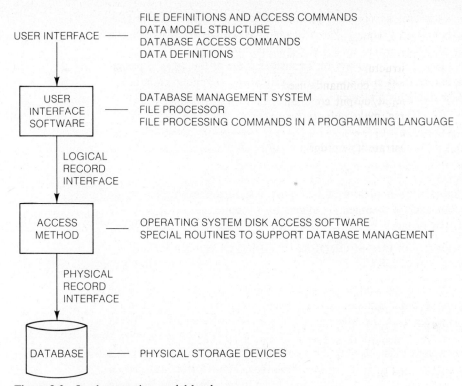

USER INTERFACE ———— FILE DEFINITIONS AND ACCESS COMMANDS
DATA MODEL STRUCTURE
DATABASE ACCESS COMMANDS
DATA DEFINITIONS

USER INTERFACE SOFTWARE ———— DATABASE MANAGEMENT SYSTEM
FILE PROCESSOR
FILE PROCESSING COMMANDS IN A PROGRAMMING LANGUAGE

LOGICAL RECORD INTERFACE

ACCESS METHOD ———— OPERATING SYSTEM DISK ACCESS SOFTWARE
SPECIAL ROUTINES TO SUPPORT DATABASE MANAGEMENT

PHYSICAL RECORD INTERFACE

DATABASE ———— PHYSICAL STORAGE DEVICES

Figure 9.3   Implementation model levels

and access data through one high-level programming language such as COBOL or FORTRAN. In most cases the user interface is embedded in the programming language as logical record interface commands. These commands are invoked whenever the program needs to refer to data.

DBMSs were a later development. They provide a higher level of user interface support, as can be seen from the following features:

- Independence from a programming language. The database is defined by a special database definition language and can be accessed by a number of programming languages.
- The provision of powerful data model structures at the user interface to naturally model user enterprises. These structures are usually converted by database software to the more elementary access method structures.
- The ability to adapt to change by allowing database amendments to be made with minimum impact on existing systems.

These facilities are provided through properly chosen software architectures that are predominantly based on the three-level framework shown in Figure 9.3.

This chapter describes the common access methods and the facilities they provide in programming languages. The next chapter extends the discussion to the general capabilities provided by DBMS architectures.

Before delving into access methods, let's consider some of the general principles used in implementation model software, particularly the integration of the three levels into a single architecture.

Level Integration

Software level integration is illustrated in Figure 9.4. In this example a single relational user interface is assumed. It allows SQL commands with only one level of nesting. For instance,

SELECT ORDER-NO FROM ORDERS WHERE CUST-NAME =
'VICKI'

This command refers to the sample problem in the appendix and requests the system to output the order numbers of all orders made by 'VICKI.' The response to this command at the user interface will be order numbers ORD3 and ORD4.

The database system must convert the relational commands to instructions on the stored relational forms. It is assumed here that each relation is stored on disk. Relations are mapped to their disk-stored form in two steps. The first step reduces relations to logical files at the logical level interface. Each relation is mapped to one logical file, and each row in the relation becomes the logical file record. In the next step, the logical file records are mapped to physical records, which are transferred between memory and physical devices, usually disks.

The mappings between levels are described in tables at two levels. Tables RELMAP and ATTMAP define the correspondence between the relations and logical files. Table RELMAP shows that relation ORDERS becomes logical file 3. Table ATTMAP shows the position of attribute values in each logical file record. Values ORDER-NO start in position 0, ORDER-DATE in position 6, and CUST-NAME in position 12.

Table FILEMAP shows the location of the logical file on disk. In this simple case it stores the physical device addresses of the first and last logical file record. Usually these tables also hold other information, such as record sizes or the positions of the file records in physical records.

Conversion Between Levels

This section provides some details (especially the system routines in Figure 9.5) that are used to convert commands between the levels shown in Figure 9.3. These details can be passed over without losing continuity in the remainder of the chapter. Also you will note that we have allowed the underline (_) character

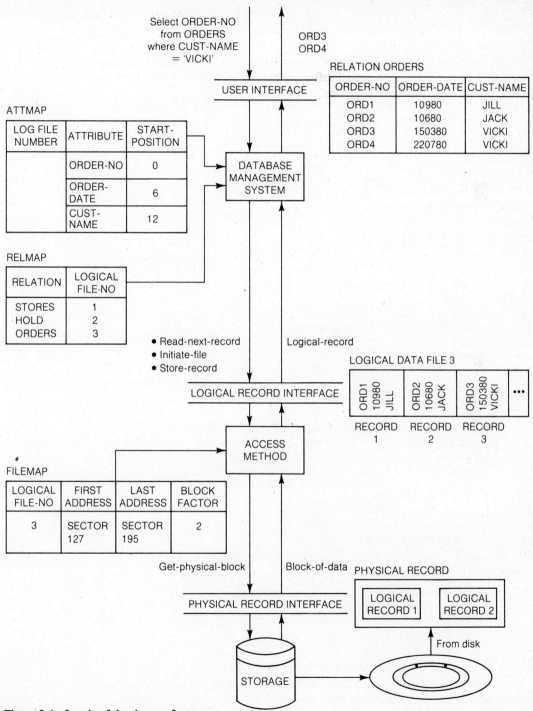

Figure 9.4 Levels of database software

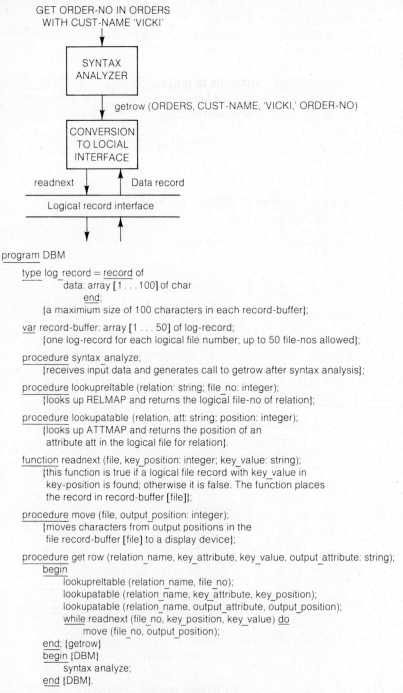

```
GET ORDER-NO IN ORDERS
WITH CUST-NAME 'VICKI'

        ┌──────────────┐
        │   SYNTAX     │
        │  ANALYZER    │
        └──────────────┘
              │   getrow (ORDERS, CUST-NAME, 'VICKI,' ORDER-NO)
              ▼
        ┌──────────────┐
        │  CONVERSION  │
        │  TO LOCIAL   │
        │  INTERFACE   │
        └──────────────┘
  readnext  │   ▲  Data record
            ▼   │
  ───────────────────────────
      Logical record interface
  ───────────────────────────
            │   ▲
            ▼   │
```

```
program DBM

    type log_record = record of
            data: array [1 . . . 100] of char
                end;
        {a maximium size of 100 characters in each record-buffer};

    var record-buffer: array [1 . . . 50] of log-record;
        {one log-record for each logical file number; up to 50 file-nos allowed};

    procedure syntax_analyze;
        {receives input data and generates call to getrow after syntax analysis};

    procedure lookupreltable (relation: string; file_no: integer);
        {looks up RELMAP and returns the logical file-no of relation};

    procedure lookupatable (relation, att: string; position: integer);
        {looks up ATTMAP and returns the position of an
        attribute att in the logical file for relation}.

    function readnext (file, key_position: integer; key_value: string);
        {this function is true if a logical file record with key_value in
        key-position is found; otherwise it is false. The function places
        the record in record-buffer [file]};

    procedure move (file, output_position: integer);
        {moves characters from output positions in the
        file record-buffer [file] to a display device};

    procedure get row (relation_name, key_attribute, key_value, output_attribute: string);
        begin
            lookupreltable (relation_name, file_no);
            lookupatable (relation_name, key_attribute, key_position);
            lookupatable (relation_name, output_attribute, output_position);
            while readnext (file_no, key_position, key_value) do
                move (file_no, output_position);
        end; {getrow}
        begin {DBM}
            syntax analyze;
        end {DBM}.
```

Figure 9.5 Database management system routines

to be included in Pascal variables. It permits hyphenated names to be used thus making programs more readable. This character is not allowed in the standard Pascal but is included in some implementations, for example, UCSD-Pascal.

User commands must be converted through the two levels shown in Figure 9.3. The first step is to convert the relational commands to instructions at the logical record interface. These instructions will access the logical records needed by the relational command. A typical software system used to convert relational commands to logical record instructions is shown in Figure 9.5. It uses a syntax analyzer to convert the user commands to procedure calls. These procedures in turn include instructions for logical record access. In Figure 9.5 the syntax analyzer converts the user command to the procedure call

   getrow (relation_name, key_attribute, key_value, output_attribute);

This command requests all the rows in a relation with a given key value. In the particular example, the parameter values at time of call would be

    relation_name = ORDERS
    key_attribute = CUST-NAME
    key_value = 'VICKI'
    output_attribute = ORDER-NO

Procedure *getrow,* which is part of the DBMS software, implements this request as a sequence of *readnext* procedure calls at the logical record interface. Each successive execution of procedure *readnext* returns successive records that satisfy a key condition. The record is returned in the record buffer. Records are returned until no more records satisfying the key condition are found. Procedure *move* is called every time that a record is returned in the record buffer by procedure *getrow.* Procedure *move* selects data items from the record in the record buffer and outputs the selected data items to a display device. The system in Figure 9.5 allows 50 buffers, each having 100 characters. Each buffer is used by a different logical file.

Procedure *getrow* looks up the correspondence tables of Figure 9.4 to determine the data file numbers and attribute positions in data records.

The *readnext* instructions are passed across the logical record interface to the access method. The access method consists of a number of modules. The simplest breakup is illustrated in Figure 9.6. One module selects the physical device address of the required record. A subsequent module makes a transfer to retrieve the record from secondary storage. The procedures used to find the record position and transfer the record to memory depend on the access method. The access method may, for example, compute the position from the key value, use an index, or simply search through the file until it finds the required record. Access methods will be discussed in detail later.

The instructions generated at the physical record interface control the mechanical operation of storage devices. They depend on the specific storage device.

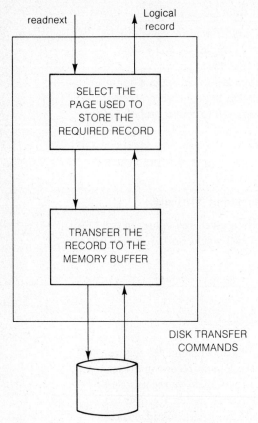

readnext | Logical record

SELECT THE
PAGE USED TO
STORE THE
REQUIRED RECORD

TRANSFER THE
RECORD TO THE
MEMORY BUFFER

DISK TRANSFER
COMMANDS

Figure 9.6 The access method structure

Generating Mapping Levels

To complete the picture, it is necessary to illustrate the construction of the correspondence tables in Figure 9.4. Such tables are constructed when database definitions are being made. Thus a user interface definition such as

DEFINE RELATION PROJECTS [ORDER-NO: INTEGER (6);
ORDER-DATE: INTEGER (6);
CUST-NAME: STRING (12)];

results in an entry RELMAP and ATTMAP. The entry in FILEMAP is often made automatically by the access method. It computes the sizes of the data file logical record and both chooses the appropriate block factor and allocates storage or disk for the file. Some systems, however, include commands that allow the user to assume control over the parameters in table FILEMAP.

Using the Framework

The structure illustrated in Figure 9.3 is important for two reasons:

- It illustrates the software philosophy used to implement DBMSs.
- It provides a useful design framework for designers.

Using the Framework in Design

The interfaces provide designers with the framework to make performance estimates. The number of records passing each interface for a given user interface command can be estimated by using knowledge of the software and hardware characteristics. One design goal will then be to minimize the number of such transfers for each access request.

Using the Framework as a Software Philosophy

The software philosophy in Figure 9.3, although simple, illustrates the basic software principles. Usually the software is distributed between the operating system and the DBMS or file system. Generally, the operating system provides the access methods. The access methods can be used by the DBMS or by a variety of compilers. The DBMS uses the operating system access method to provide higher-level database capabilities.

Of course, most systems provide a larger variety of capabilities at their interfaces than that shown in Figure 9.3. We will describe next some of these capabilities at the physical and logical record interfaces.

THE PHYSICAL RECORD INTERFACE

The physical record interface will obviously depend on the physical device. Disk storage packs have been the most common devices used to store data.

As shown in Figure 9.7, a disk storage pack consists of a number of disks, usually 10, each with two surfaces. The disks are continually rotating, and data are recorded on the disk surfaces as the disk rotates. The data are recorded in concentric circles, commonly known as *tracks*. All tracks in the same position (i.e., equidistant from the center) are sometimes called a *cylinder*. Data are recorded or read from a track by positioning a read/write head over the track. A set of such read/write heads is part of the disk pack.

A distinction is made between disk packs with movable heads and those with fixed heads. Movable heads can move across the disk surface, whereas fixed heads are fixed to particular tracks. Thus a movable head system has one head

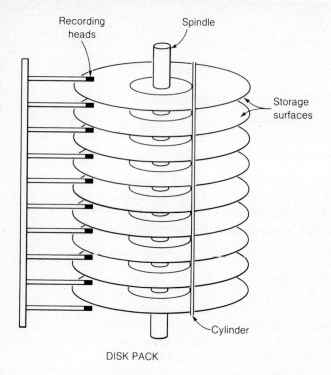

DISK PACK

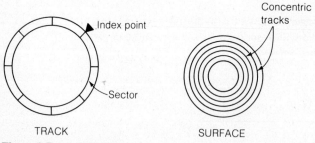

TRACK   SURFACE

Figure 9.7 A disk pack

per surface; a fixed head system has one head per track on each surface. Usually all movable heads are moved together, so that at any given time all heads will be positioned on the same cylinder. Read/write times are longer with movable head disks than with fixed head disks (which are more expensive) because some time is necessary to move the read/write head over the required track.

The tracks themselves are usually subdivided into several sectors. Each track has a marked index (or start) point, and sectors are uniquely addressable relative to that index point. An access method transfers data across the physical record interface by positioning the head over a particular track and then selecting one sector on the track. The simplest instructions required at the physical record interface to do this are

fetch (track-no, sector-on-track)
store (track-no, sector-on-track)

Each such instruction would cause the head to move to a particular track and access a sector on that track.

In practice more commands are available on particular devices. Manufacturers provide a variety of disk drives, and each drive has its own set of interface instructions (e.g., move a head, read a whole track, disable a surface). Disk drives possess other characteristics, which may differ among manufacturers and include

- the number of disk surfaces
- the time taken to move a head to a track
- the number of tracks or sectors
- the format for each track
- the number of characters that can be stored on each track

Typical systems include 10–40 surfaces and about 200–500 tracks per surface. One such system is the IBM 3330. It has 14 surfaces, and 404 tracks per surface, and it can hold 13,165 bytes per track. Head movements from track to track take 10–55 milliseconds.

Access Method Software for Disk Transfer

This section (especially Figure 9.9) contains details of DBMS routines and can be skipped if you prefer.

As shown in Figure 9.6, access method software contains routines to select the required sector and then to transfer data between this sector and memory. The selection of a particular sector depends on the logical interface supported by the access method. Usually systems support a variety of access methods. Although such methods use various techniques to select record positions on a disk, they have the same data transfer routines between disk and memory. One important routine blocks logical records into physical records. Blocking caters to the situation in which the logical record size and the physical record size are different. In this case more than one logical file record will be transferred in one physical record. The access method will then collect logical file records sent across the logical interface into blocks. The number of logical records in a block is called a *blocking factor*.

A blocking factor greater than 1 means that the number of physical records transferred over the physical interface is usually less than the number of logical records transferred across the logical interface. For example, Figure 9.8 shows logical data records passing across the logical record interface. As each record enters the access method, it is placed in a physical record buffer. This buffer is

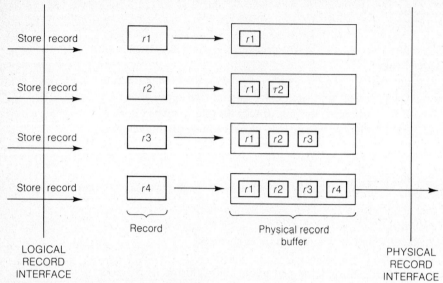

Figure 9.8 Constructing physical records

an area of memory allocated to a particular physical device. The buffer contains the data to be transferred to or from that device. As the next record arrives, it is stored in the next position in the buffer. This process continues until the buffer is filled, at which time it is written to the physical device. The process then repeats.

The access method routine to accomplish this transfer is relatively straightforward, as illustrated in Figure 9.9. Here there is one *filestore* record in *filemap* for each logical file (the system in this case supports 50 logical files). The record contains the blocking factor, the physical record size, and the first and last disk sectors used to store this file. The block factor and the current sector (which is the last sector accessed) are also stored in *filemap*. The access method also provides 50 buffers, one for each logical file. Although the buffers are all 500 characters (this being a Pascal requirement to declare fixed array sizes), most access methods can maintain variable length records. The access method in Figure 9.9 also illustrates three routines:

- *start-file* (*i*), which resets the file as to its initial position
- *write-file* (*i*), which moves the input record of file *i* to the physical device buffers for file *i* and transfers the buffer to disk once it is filled with *block-factor* (*i*) records
- *end-file* (*i*), which writes an incompletely filled buffer to storage

These routines assume that the logical file *i* record to be transferred is in *inputrecord* (*i*). The program that activates write-file must set appropriate values into *inputrecord* (*i*) before it activates *write-file*.

```
type    device_buffer = record of
              data: array [1 ... 500] of char
                          end;
        filestore = record of
        physical_record_size: integer;
        file_no: integer;
        first_sector: integer;
        last_sector: integer;
        block_factor: integer;
        current_sector: integer
                          end;
var
        blockcount: array [1 ... 50] of integer;
        filemap: array [1 ... 50] of filestore;
        buffer: array [1 ... 50] of device-buffer;
        inputrecord: array [1 ... 50] of char;
procedure move_input_record (pos: integer; buffer_no: integer);
        {this procedure moves inputrecord into position pos in
        buffer number buffer_no}
procedure start_file (file_no: integer);
        begin
              filemap [file_no] . current_sector: = filemap [file_no]   first_sector;
              blockcount [file_no]: = 0
        end {of start_file};
function allocate: integer;
        {allocate takes the value of the next available sector};
procedure write (sector_no: integer; record: device_buffer)
        {the procedure writes record to sector position sector_no};
procedure write_file (file_no: integer);
        begin
              blockcount [file_no]: = blockcount [file_no] + 1;
              move_input_record (blockcount [file_no], file-no);
              if blockcount [file_no] = filemap [file_no]. block_factor
                    then begin
                          write (filemap [file_no]. current_sector, buffer [file_no]);
                          blockcount [file_no]: = 0;
                          filemap [file_no]. current_sector: = allocate
                          end
        end {of write_file};
procedure end_file (file_no: integer);
        begin
              write (filemap [file_no]. current_sector, buffer [file_no]);
              filemap [file_no]. last_sector: = filemap [file_no]. current_sector
        end {of end_file};
```

Figure 9.9 Blocking routines

Other Physical Interface Variations

There are of course many variations in the capabilities provided by access methods. So far, for example, we have assumed that each physical record is stored in one disk sector. But some systems write and read entire tracks; others use a physical record that is a multiple of the sector size; and still others do not use fixed sector sizes but allow the system itself to choose a block size and record data, with gaps separating blocks on the track.

Other important variations are support for variable-length logical records and maintenance of multiple buffers for each storage device.

Pages

The page is in some ways the same as the physical record. The term *page* is favored in many systems to describe the unit of physical transfer between disk and memory. A page need not equal the sector size. Access methods often choose their own page sizes. Further, page numbers are not related to device addresses but are physical collections of items. Pages may be moved from place to place on secondary storage. The access method, however, must keep track of the location of each page. A page is usually transferred between memory and secondary device as one physical record. Hence the terms *page* and *physical record* are sometimes used interchangeably.

Variable Record Size

The discussion so far has assumed that each logical record in one file is the same size, so that each physical record or page contains the same number of logical records for this logical file. But there are also access methods that support variable-length logical records. In this case the page includes information on the number of logical records in it and the length of each (Figure 9.10).

The system must now search for a logical record by successively examining each logical record in the page. Once the length of the first logical record is found, the system determines the position of the next logical record, and so on. This process is more complex than it would be if each logical record had been allocated a fixed size slot in the sector.

Some systems simplify page management by allocating a fixed size slot for each logical record even where the logical records are of variable size. The user specifies the size of the longest logical record, and this amount of space is allocated to each record in the page. A considerable amount of space can be wasted in each page where there is a large variation of logical record lengths. For example, we can have the situation illustrated in Figure 9.11. Here there are four

N	C	l_1	L_1	$\cdots$	l_i	L_i	$\cdots$

N = number of logical records in the page
C = number of unused characters in the page
l_i = length of the ith logical record
L_i = ith logical record

Figure 9.10   Arrangement of variable-length records in a page

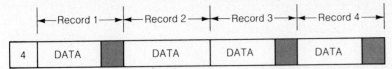

Figure 9.11 Allowing a fixed amount of store for each logical record

logical records in the sector. Only record 2 is of the maximum size, whereas all other records are smaller. Hence the shaded area represents unused space in the sector.

Other systems use the offset method shown in Figure 9.12. Here the last few page characters contain an index to the position of a record relative to the beginning of the page. The address of a record is the concatenation of (page-number + offset-number). The access method would first retrieve the page and then look up the index value in the given offset position to find the address of the record in the page.

Variable Physical Record Sizes

Some systems provide disk system hardware that supports variable-length records. A special recording format is used on the track to indicate the start and length of each record on disk. For example, take Figure 9.13. Here each record is recorded in two parts: a count part, which contains the record length, and a data part, which contains the data. The disk drive hardware reads the count and uses it to read the ensuing data records. Hence different-sized physical records are transferred between disk and memory. More elaborate systems also include

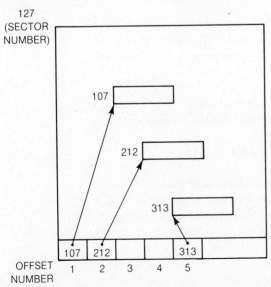

Figure 9.12 Locating records by offset value in the sector

△ START

G = gap

Figure 9.13   Hardware support for variable-length records

a key value between the data part and the count part. This inclusion allows the hardware to search the track for a record with a given key value.

Such hardware facilities can be used in various ways. One way is to store each logical record as a separate physical record on disk. The method will be effective only if the logical record size is large; otherwise the proportion of recorded data to gap will be small, resulting in waste of disk recording surface. Another method is to allow an access method to use variable page sizes with a variable number of logical records in each page.

Multiple Buffers

Some access methods can maintain multiple buffers for a file, thereby achieving some parallelism. While one buffer is being transferred between memory and secondary storage device, another can be used by a user program. There is, however, a price: more memory must be made because each additional buffer requires additional memory space.

The Physical Interface—Implications for Designers

The physical record interface has a number of implications for designers. One design goal is to improve on-line transaction performance. To do this, time spent transferring data between memory and secondary storage must be minimized. Factors that influence these times are

- the device characteristics, including head movement time
- higher blocking factors, particularly if contiguously stored records are to be accessed by the same transactions
- maintenance of more than one buffer to allow some parallelism

Blocking and multiple buffering do not come without their associated costs. Buffers require memory space. As block-factors become larger, so do buffer sizes and hence memory requirements. A compromise must be reached to ensure that any gains achieved by large buffers are not offset by losses caused by less memory available for program storage. Less program memory may lead to increased disk activity in swapping needed program parts in and out of memory.

Similarly, transaction performance can be improved if fixed head disks are used; again performance is improved only at a price.

LOGICAL RECORD ACCESS

Access methods are provided to enable user programs to access data. User programs refer to data in specific ways. Some access records in particular sequences; others access one record at a time; and still others access selected groups of records. To satisfy these needs, access methods must

- provide logical access commands to enable programs to refer to data in the manner appropriate to the programs; and
- translate the logical access commands into physical record transfers.

Further, to optimize performance, the access method must ensure that each logical access command is satisfied by the minimum number of physical record transfers.

Access methods are not sufficiently generalized so that one access method can cater to any kind of user processing while maintaining satisfactory performance for all these kinds of processing. A set of access methods is usually needed to satisfy various types of logical processing. Appropriate methods must be chosen for each kind of user processing.

We will next define some logical processing methods and then describe the access methods and discuss the suitability of each for a particular kind of logical processing.

Kinds of Logical Processing

Generalizing, we can say that, in logical processing, transactions are processed against database files. Each transaction arises because of some event in the enterprise. The effect of this event is recorded in the database. Transactions may be inquiry, update, or insert transactions. An inquiry transaction requests some data in the database; update transactions change some database values; and insert transactions create new data records in the database. Some typical transactions:

- "Find the balance of an account"—an inquiry transaction.
- "Change a person's address"—an update transaction.
- "Add a new project"—an insert transaction.

Each transaction refers to some small subset of records in the database. A distinction is then made between on-line transaction processing and batched transaction processing. In on-line transaction processing, users expect immediate response to their transactions. Hence access methods that support on-line transaction processing must provide good response times. Batched transaction processing, on the other hand, does not require immediate response; that is, transactions can be processed some time after they are received. Usually such transactions are collected over time into a transaction file. The transaction file is then processed against existing data files. In batch processing, transactions are usually sorted into the same sequence as the data file. Each file is then read in that sequence, and amendments are made in sequence order.

In another kind of processing, often called *report generation,* a report is generated about all the data in a given file or set of files. Report generation is usually carried out in batch mode.

Now let's consider some access methods and see how they differ in supporting logical processing.

SEQUENTIAL ACCESS

The simplest access method is the *sequential access method.* Here records are presented at the logical record interface in a given sequence. Records are stored on the physical storage device in that sequence. Usually records are stored in a sequence that is determined by the value of a nominated key item. Successive reads presented at the interface will retrieve records in the stored sequence. A typical set of logical record interface commands is

- *read* (f, r): read the next record r from file f
- *write* (f, r): write a record r to the next position in file f
- *reset* (f): reset file f to its initial position
- *eof* (f): set to true if the last record has been read from file f

These commands initiate access method routines to transfer data to disk. To be useful, the logical record interface commands must be embedded in a programming language. So, for the purpose of illustration, it is assumed that these commands can be used in Pascal.

The sequential access method can be effective if the entire file must be processed. It takes advantage of blocking factors to reduce the number of physical transfers across the physical record interface. Fewer physical transfers reduce input/output time. Some procedures that use sequential processing are shown in Figure 9.14. Here the file contains data about projects. The project start date and manager are stored for each project. Procedure *createfile* generates a new file, whereas procedure *printfile* reads and outputs a file.

Sequential processing, however, is not effective for on-line transaction processing. In transaction processing it is necessary to update or retrieve one particular record. Sequential processing requires the whole file to be searched or copied to do this. Procedure *findproj* in Figure 9.14 finds the manager of a selected project; *project-key* has the value of the project identifier at the time of procedure call. The file is therefore searched sequentially until the record with

```
program sequential_operations;
type     projrec = record of
                proj_id: string;
                project_start_date: integer;
                manager: string
                     end
var      project: projrec;
         projects_file, new_projects_file: file of projrec;

function next-record; boolean;
            {this function requests the next project record from some input device;
             the project details are stored in project and true is returned;
             if there are no more projects, next-record returns false}

procedure createfile;
    begin
        while next_record do                            ⎫  Create a
            write (projects_file, project)              ⎬  file
    end {of createfile}                                 ⎭

procedure printfile;
    begin
        reset (projects_file);
        while not eof (projects_file) do                ⎫  Output a
            begin                                       ⎬  file
                read (projects_file, project);          ⎪
                output (project)                        ⎪
            end                                         ⎪
    end {of printfile};                                 ⎭

procedure findproj (project_key: string);              ⎫
    var                                                 ⎪
        projfound: boolean;                             ⎪
    begin                                               ⎪
        projfound: = false;                             ⎪
        while (not (eof (projects_file))) and (not projfound) do   ⎪
            begin                                       ⎬  Find a
                read (projects_file, project);          ⎪  particular
                if project.proj_id = project_key        ⎪  record
                    then                                ⎪
                        begin                           ⎪
                            output (project.manager);   ⎪
                            projfound: = true           ⎪
                        end                             ⎪
            end                                         ⎪
    end {of findproj};                                  ⎭

procedure update_manager (project_key: string; new_manager: string);   ⎫
    begin                                               ⎪
        while not (eof (projects_file)) do              ⎪
            begin                                       ⎪
                read (projects_file, project);          ⎬  Update a
                if project.proj_id = project_key        ⎪  record
                    then project.manager = new_manager; ⎪
                write (new_projects_file, project)      ⎪
            end                                         ⎪
    end {of update_manager};                            ⎭
```

Figure 9.14   Sequential processing

the required *proj-id* is found. Hence although only one record is required, a large number of records may be transferred across the interface.

Updates raise a further problem. Sequential access does not allow one record to overwrite another in the middle of a file. So a new file must be created with one changed record. The procedure *update-manager* illustrates the change of project manager. Again more than the required number of records are transferred between memory and disk.

Sequential access methods can, however, sometimes satisfy batched transaction processing. In this case the transactions are first sorted, using the same key item as the sequential file. All the transactions are then processed in one scan of the sequential file.

DIRECT ACCESS

Obviously, sequential access will not satisfy on-line transaction processing, because only one file record or a small subset of file records is needed by each transaction. To get this one record, sequential processing would need to access most of the other records, thus resulting in unsatisfactory performance. Other methods, called *direct access methods,* must be provided to satisfy on-line transaction processing requirements. They allow a particular record to be accessed without at the same time accessing other records. One method of direct access is to use the logical record address. For example, suppose the following instructions for logical record interface are made available:

- *writed* (*f*, *r*, pos): write record *r* into logical record address pos of file *f*
- *readd* (*f*, *r*, pos): read record *r* from logical record address pos in file *f*

These instructions can be used to directly access records and are quite effective where the record has an integer field. This field is used as the logical record address to access records. For example, suppose the field PROJ-ID in Figure 9.14 is now an integer (rather than a string), and projects are allocated numbers in numeric sequence. The manager of a project can be found simply by

```
program findmanager
    begin
        readln (keyproject);
        readd (projects-file, project, keyproject);
        writeln (project.manager);
    end;
```

One possible implementation of such access is shown in Figure 9.15. Here the algorithm, given position *k*, computes the required sector position as the *k*th

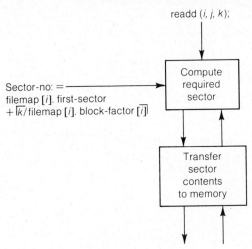

readd (*i, j, k*);

Sector-no: =
filemap [*i*]. first-sector
+ $\lceil k /$ filemap [*i*]. block-factor [*i*]$\rceil$

Compute
required
sector

Transfer
sector
contents
to memory

Figure 9.15 A direct access method

position in the logical file. It then uses the block-factor to find the required physical record, assuming that logical records are stored contiguously in key sequence on physical storage.

There are two problems with direct access by record position:

1. Sometimes it is necessary to use fields other than integer to select records.
2. Even if an integer field is used, it is common to have gaps in the key values, and so there will be unused space in the file.

For these reasons it is preferable not to restrict most direct methods to integer key fields but to allow any record field to be used as a key. These key fields are defined by the user and then used to access records. Suppose, for example, that we are able to extend the Pascal language to define keys for files. Now, as shown in Figure 9.16, an extra key clause is added to a file declaration. This clause defines the file key, *proj-id*. Records can then be directly accessed by the command

> *readkey* (*f, r*): read a record *r* in file *f* whose key field has been set to a
> given value

Thus in Figure 9.16 the value of the required project is first moved in *project.proj-id* (as part of the readln statement). The statement readkey then uses this key value to retrieve the remaining record fields.

Access methods implementations use two alternative techniques to determine a record position from its key value. These techniques employ a hashing algorithm or an index file.

```
program findproj;
type      projrec = record of
          proj-id: string;
          project-start-date: integer;
          manager: string
                end;
var       project: projrec;
          project_file: file of projrec [key: proj-id];
begin
     readln (project.proj-id);
     readkey (project_file, project)
end {of findproj}.
```

Figure 9.16   Using direct access

Hash Access Methods

A *hash access method* is implemented in the same way as shown in Figure 9.15. However, now it can no longer be assumed that the key value is the same as the logical record address. Instead the logical record address must first be computed from the key value; once this address is known, its physical location can be found. The algorithm used to compute the address is such that the address is randomly distributed with respect to the key—hence the term *hash algorithm*.

Two possibilities arise when computing an address from its key value:

1. A unique logical file address is generated for each key value.
2. More than one key value converts to the same logical file address (Figure 9.17).

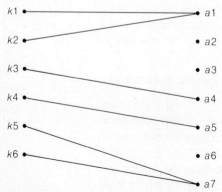

Figure 9.17   Mapping key values to logical record address

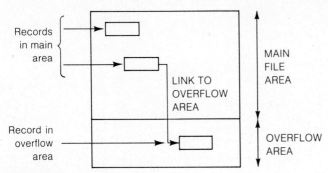

Figure 9.18   Overflow area

Problems arise if two records in the file have key values that map to the same address, a situation often referred to as *collision*. Thus in Figure 9.17, records with key values $k1$ and $k2$ would collide at $a1$. Obviously, more than one record cannot be stored in the same location, and some means must be provided to handle collisions. One method is to provide overflow areas. The file (or each page in the file) is now divided into two parts, as shown in Figure 9.18: a main file area and an overflow area. If two records hash to the same address, only one is stored in the main area and the other is placed in the overflow area. A link is maintained from the main area to the record in the overflow area. A record in the main area can usually be retrieved in one physical transfer. Records in an overflow area require more physical transfers. One transfer is made to the main area to find the link to the record in the overflow area. One or more transfers are then needed to retrieve the record from the overflow area. The goal of hash access methods is to reduce the number of records in the overflow area. Hash algorithms must be chosen so that the distribution of a given key value results in a minimum of collisions. The number of records in the overflow area is then reduced.

Index Implementations

Index file implementations take the form shown in Figure 9.19. The position of the required record is found through an index. As shown in the figure, the access method maintains two files: an index file and a data file. The index file is also stored on disk and indicates the position of records with required key values in the data file. The access method therefore first searches the index file and then uses the record position found in the index to retrieve the data record. The goal here is to choose an indexing technique that minimizes the number of index records transferred in the index search.

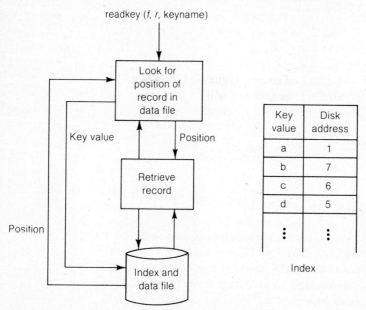

Figure 9.19 A direct access method using an index

Indexing Techniques

Index files are organized in various ways. A general feature of many index files is that they consist of record entries made up of the two fields shown in Figure 9.20. Each entry shows the address of records with a given key value. The address may be a physical address. The physical address may be surface track-number, sector number, or some concatenation of these with the disk pack number or surface number. The address may also be a logical record address such as page number + offset; in this case the access method determines the physical address for the page from the logical record address.

Index files are used as follows. The access method receives commands at the logical record interface. The commands include key values of required records. The first action of the access method is to search the index file for the index entry with the key value for a particular record. The address in that index entry is then used to locate the record.

The simplest index file structure is sequential. The index entries are ordered by ascending key values. Each index entry contains a key value and the address of records with that key value. Here it is assumed that the address is a page

KEY VALUE	ADDRESS OF RECORD WITH KEY VALUE

Figure 9.20 An index file entry

number and that each page is transferred as one physical record between secondary storage and memory. The access method makes a sequential search of the index file to find the entry with the required key value. Then it reads the data file page whose address is stored in that index entry. That data file page will contain the required record. We could, of course, argue that little is gained by this approach. The number of index entries accessed will be the same as the number of records accessed in a sequential file search. However, the advantage is that the index entries can be much smaller than the data record size. Hence the block-factor of an index file will be much larger, and fewer physical transfers will be made to find the key value in the index file.

Example 1   Assume a file of 100,000 records, each 200 characters long, and a physical block size of 3000 characters. The number of pages needed to store the file is 100,000 divided by the block-factor where the block-factor is calculated as 3000/200 = 15. Hence the number of physical records or pages in the file = 100,000/15 = 6667.

A sequential search for one record will on an average access 6667/2 = 3334 physical records (because on an average half the file is reached). Now assume that the key of the record is 10 characters and the page number size is 5 characters. Each index entry will then be 15 characters. The block-factor for the index file will be 3000/(10 + 5) = 200. Hence pages needed to store the index = 100,000/200 = 500. A sequential search of the index will on an average use 500/2 = 250 physical record transfers. Hence a record will now be retrieved in (250 + 1) = 251 physical record transfers: 250 for the index and 1 to read the record.

Thus a sequential index can save search time if the key is only a small part of the entire record. It is, however, not very effective for files with many records because considerable time can be spent searching the index. Hence alternate index structures are often used.

Figure 9.21 illustrates one such alternate structure. It can be used only where file records are stored in index key order. In this case it is not necessary to store one index file entry for each record. It is sufficient to simply make an index entry for each page. This entry is the highest key value for the page.

The procedure used to retrieve a record is similar to that used earlier:

> *begin*
>   read index file until the index key entry ⩾ key value of record
>   look up page address in that entry
>   read the page
>   search page for record (internal memory operation)
> *end*

The search, however, is now shorter because there are fewer index records. Let's again consider Example 1.

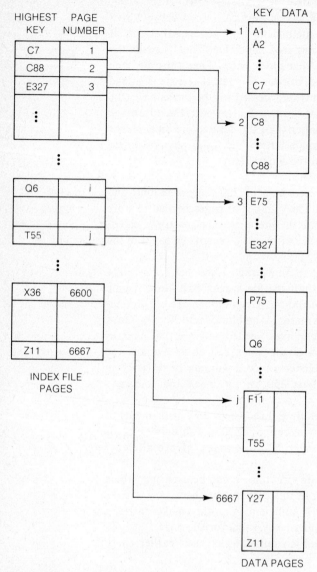

Figure 9.21 A single-level index

Example 1A Now the index will only have 6667 entries, because there are 6667 data pages. The size of index file will be 6667/block-factor = 6667/200 = 34.

The search will now on an average require 34/2 = 17 physical page reads. An additional read of the data file means that (17 + 1) = 18 pages are transferred to find a data record with a given value.

We can get still more improvement, however, by using a multilevel index.

Multilevel Indexing

A simple example of a *multilevel index* is shown in Figure 9.22. This index is made up of two levels. The first level is an index to index pages at the next level. Each entry in the first-level index block contains two items:

1. A key value, *a*.
2. The page number of a second-level index block. This second-level page holds index key entries between the key value *a* and the key value in the previous first-level index entry.

A search for a record with a given key value now takes the following form:

> *begin*
>   read first-level index page
>   find the first entry in first-level index block ⩾ key value
>   look up address of second-level index block in this entry
>   read second-level index page at that address
>   find the first entry in second-level index page ⩾ key value
>   look up page in this entry
>   read page and search the page for the required record
> *end*

Three physical transfers are necessary to find the record: one to read the first-level index page, another to read one second-level index page, and a third to read the data page.

It is, of course, not always possible to fit all numbers of second-level index pages into one first-level page. In that case two alternatives exist:

- The first index level consists of more than one page. The first-level records must then be sequentially searched.
- There are more than two index levels with only one index page at the first level. Only one page is read at each level.

Examples of either approach can be found in practice.

Dense and Nondense Indices

The index methods in Figures 9.21 and 9.22 take advantage of the fact that records are stored in index key value sequence. If this were not the case, it would not be true that the key values of all records in a block are less than the key value in the index entry for the block. An index that takes advantage of key orders is sometimes called a *nondense index*. Nondense means that it is not necessary to have an index entry for each file record. A *dense index,* on the

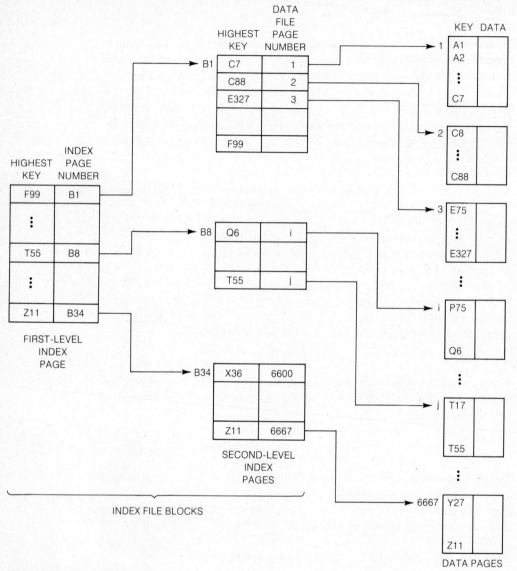

Figure 9.22 A two-level index

other hand, requires one index entry for each file record. A dense index is needed if the file records are not stored in index key sequence.

A multilevel dense index does not differ significantly from a multilevel nondense index. The dense index will contain one additional level, which contains an entry for each file record. Hence usually one extra disk transfer will be required to retrieve a record.

Maintaining Indices

Access methods must be able to add, delete, and update data records. Data record insertions and deletions require changes to be made to any data file indices, causing particular problems to occur. Suppose a new record that is inserted in a file needs to be stored in a given page to maintain key sequence. If there is no room in this page for one more record, the page has to be split into two pages. The index must now be changed to add a new entry for the new page. The index page in turn may have to be split into two pages. Sometimes this splitting leads to new index levels and an unbalanced index. If this occurs, some searches must refer to more levels than others.

Thus suppose that in Figure 9.22 all data pages and index file blocks are full. Now a new record with key value A11 is to be inserted between records A1 and A2. Data page 1 is then split into two data pages, and so an entry to the new page must be added to index page B1. As this index page is already full, it is also split into two pages. The top-level index page must now accommodate a new entry to the new index page. But since the top-level index page is also full, an entry to a new second-level index block cannot be accommodated. Hence the usual solution is to add another level of index blocks, as shown in Figure 9.23. Now records in data pages 1 and 6668 (the new data page) are accessed by referring through three index levels, whereas other blocks are accessed through two index levels. The index is now unbalanced.

Considerable work has been done to choose index structures that minimize the amount of activity following insertions or deletions. Now becoming popular is an indexing method commonly known as a *B-tree*, in which more than one key value is stored in an index entry.

B-Trees

A B-tree structure is shown in Figure 9.24. It is made up of several levels. Each index entry takes the form shown in Figure 9.25, which contains a number of key values and addresses. The addresses are locations of either a B-tree entry at the next level or a data file page. The addresses are as follows:

- P1 is the address of a page or B-tree entry that contains values less than keyvalue(1).
- P2 is the address of a page or B-tree entry that contains values between keyvalue(1) and keyvalue(2).
- P_i is the address of a page or B-tree entry that contains values between keyvalue($i - 1$) and keyvalue(i).
- P_L is the address of a page or B-tree entry that contains values greater than the last key value.

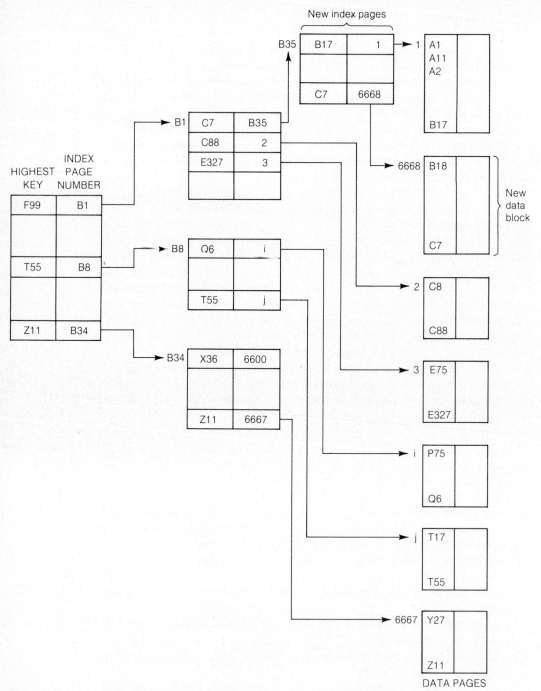

Figure 9.23 An unbalanced tree (after insertion of new record into Figure 9.22)

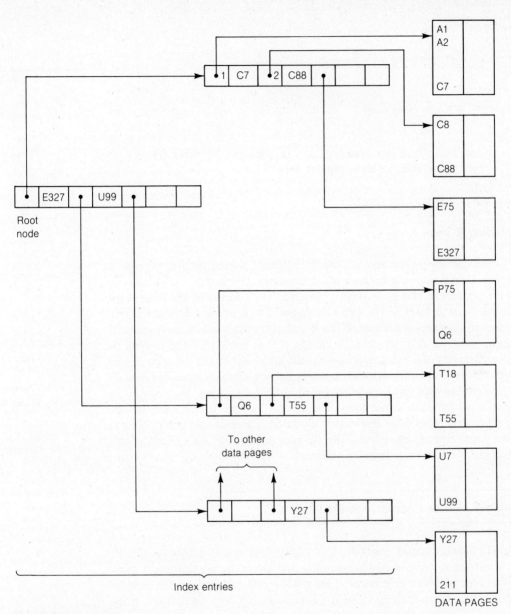

Figure 9.24 A B-tree

Initially, each B-tree entry has some spare positions. They are used later in updates. The retrieval algorithm to find a record with its key equal to key value is

read the root B-tree node
repeat until a data page is found

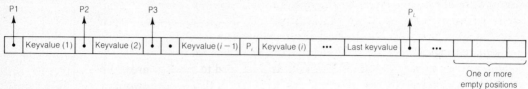

Figure 9.25   A B-tree index entry

> *begin*
>> find $P(i)$ where keyvalue $(i - 1)$ < keyvalue ≤ keyvalue (i)
>> read index entry or data page at $P(i)$
> *end*
> search the data page for record

Maintaining B-Trees

The B-tree has one advantage: it remains balanced during its life. Suppose a data page is split into two because of an insertion. The B-tree entry that contains the address of this page is also changed. The address of the page is replaced by the addresses of the two new pages. The spare space in the B-tree entry is used for the new address. If the B-tree entry itself has no more space, it is split up into two B-tree entries. A change is then made to a higher-level B-tree entry because this must now contain the addresses of the two new B-tree entries. This process continues until a B-tree entry with spare space is found. If no B-tree entries with spare space are found at the lower levels, the process can continue until the root B-tree entry is reached. The root B-tree entry is then split into two and a new root node entry is created. This new root entry points to the two pages created by splitting the old root node entry. As a result of this process, the B-tree always remains balanced.

Comparison of Direct Access Methods

The goal of direct access methods is to allow programs to access records by using a minimum number of disk transfers and hence, by implication, a minimum number of index references. This goal is best satisfied by the *relative access method*. Here the key value is the same as the record's position in the file. Hence no index accesses are necessary, and each record is accessed in one disk transfer.

Relative access is usually impractical for two reasons. First, it requires records to be identified by numeric key value. Second, to reduce waste space, records lying within a continuous key range must exist at all times. Such situations do not frequently arise.

The alternative to relative access is hash access. The record address is computed by the hash algorithm, and so no index accesses are necessary. Hash methods are effective in direct access only if collisions are minimized. If there are no collisions, a record can be retrieved in one disk transfer. It is only when collisions occur that more than one physical record transfer is needed to retrieve one required logical record. Another problem with hash methods is excessive volatility. In many access methods new records are added to overflow areas, necessitating additional physical record transfers to access them. Excessive volatility means that over time most records will be in the overflow area.

Index techniques are an alternative to hash access but have the disadvantage that extra physical transfers are needed to read the index. Insertions can also be expensive owing to the new index entries made when a new data record is added.

Index techniques are, however, the only alternative if different programs or inquiries use different keys to access the data files. Hash methods cannot be used, because it is unlikely that different hash algorithms applied to different data items in a record would hash to the same address. An index would need to be maintained for each key item.

MULTI-INDEX ACCESS

A *multi-index access method* differs from earlier methods in that it has, as its name implies, more than one index. Each such index is implemented by applying the techniques used in files with a single index. The user interface must now, however, include

- definition commands to define the file structure and indexing methods
- access commands that use the defined structures and indices

File definitions must give each key a keyname and define the data items that make up the key. Access commands then state the key to be used to access data. A possible Pascal extension to illustrate these commands is shown in Figure 9.26. The program in this figure refers to the HOLD file in the appendix. It includes an extension to the file definitions in Figure 9.16. Now file *holdfile* is defined to have three keys:

- *store-key:* can be used to access records with a particular store-id value.
- *part-key:* can be used to access records with a particular part-id value.
- *qty-held:* a key made up of two fields. The key is used to access the record with a particular store-id, part-id value.

The logical record interface commands now include

- *readkey* (*f*, *r*, keyname): reads a record *r* in file *f*. The key value of *r* is given in the field positions of the keyname of *r*. Returns are true if a record is found.
- *start* (*f*, *r*, keyname): locates a record *r* in keyname sequence. The key value

```
type holdrec = record of
            store_id: string;
            part_id: string;
            qty: integer
                end;
var   holding: holdrec;
            holdfile: file of holdrec (key store_key: (store_id));
                                      (key part_key:(part_id));
                                      (key qty_held: (store_id, part_id));
procedure get_store_holding;
    begin
            readln (holding.store_id);
            if start (holdfile, holding, store_key);
                then
                    begin
                        while readseq (holdfile, holding, store_key) do
                            writeln (holding.part_id, holding.qty)
                        end
    end {of get_store_holding};
procedure parts_held_in_store;
    begin
            readln (holding.store_id, holding.part_id);
            readkey (holdfile, holding, qty_held);
            writeln (holding.qty)
    end {of parts_held_in_store};
```

Figure 9.26   Indexed sequential access

of r is given in the field position of the keyname of r. Returns are true if a record is found and false if it is not found.

- *readseq* (f, r, keyname): reads the next record r. The key value of r is given in the field position of the keyname of r. The first record in this sequence has been located by the start command. Returns are true if a record with the given key value is found and false if it is not found.

The use of these commands is illustrated by the procedures in Figure 9.26. Procedure *get-store-holding* retrieves the quantities of all parts held in a store. It first reads the STORE-ID and then positions the file to the first record with STORE-ID, using the start command. Then all records for that STORE-ID are read. Procedure *parts-held-in-store* retrieves the quantity of a particular part held in a particular store.

INDEXED SEQUENTIAL ACCESS METHODS

Access methods that allow both direct and sequential accesses are often called *indexed sequential access methods*. They are commonly found in practice, but there are variants in the access commands supported by various manufacturers. There are also variations in the compilers that make use of the access method commands. For example, few Pascal implementations support indexed sequential access, but it is common in COBOL.

A frequent restriction in indexed sequential access results from a distinction between primary and secondary keys. The primary key index is usually nondense, whereas secondary key indices are dense. Records are stored on a physical device in primary key sequence. The readseq command can be used only with the primary key and not the secondary keys. The sequential reads in this case do not need to use an index but simply read successive file blocks.

Indexed sequential implementations use a variety of indexing techniques, among which the B-tree method is becoming increasingly popular.

LINKING FILES

It is also possible to extend access methods to include links between files. Such links can be established and maintained either by the access method or by database management software. They can also be maintained by user programs at the access method level.

One important concept in linking files is the *pointer*. The pointer is stored in one file record. The pointer value can be used to directly access a record in another file. Thus, in Figure 9.27, record *i* would be read. Its pointer value would be used to directly retrieve record *j* in file *Y*. Pointers can take one of three forms:

• actual device addresses
• symbolic pointers
• logical record addresses

Actual device address links are usually maintained only by the access methods themselves and are not made available to the DBMS or user program. As a result, access methods can move pages to different secondary storage positions without affecting user programs.

As we will see next, symbolic pointers are most often used in programming languages, whereas logical record addresses are usually used by DBMSs.

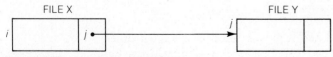

Figure 9.27 A pointer structure

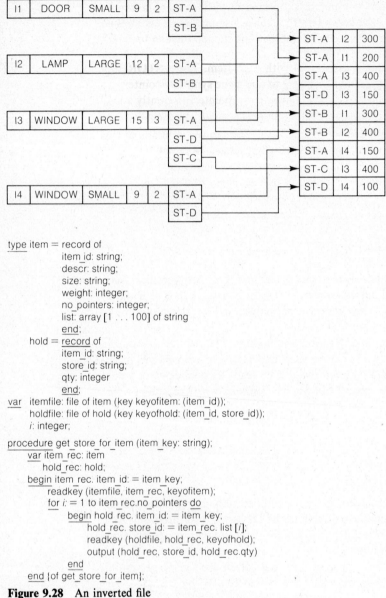

```
type item = record of
            item_id: string;
            descr: string;
            size: string;
            weight: integer;
            no_pointers: integer;
            list: array [1 . . . 100] of string
            end;
      hold = record of
            item_id: string;
            store_id: string;
            qty: integer
            end;
var   itemfile: file of item (key keyofitem: (item_id));
      holdfile: file of hold (key keyofhold: (item_id, store_id));
      i: integer;

procedure get_store_for_item (item_key: string);
      var item_rec: item
          hold_rec: hold;
      begin item_rec. item_id: = item_key;
            readkey (itemfile, item_rec, keyofitem);
            for i: = 1 to item_rec.no_pointers do
                begin hold_rec. item_id: = item_key;
                      hold_rec. store_id: = item_rec. list [i];
                      readkey (holdfile, hold_rec, keyofhold);
                      output (hold_rec, store_id, hold_rec.qty)
                end
      end {of get_store_for_item};
```

Figure 9.28   An inverted file

Symbolic Pointers

User programs use symbolic pointers to maintain links between files at the logical level interface. There are two major techniques used to maintain links:

inverted files and lists. Figure 9.28 illustrates an inverted file implemented by symbolic links. These links are from ITEMS file records to HOLD file records. There is a link from each ITEMS record to all those HOLD records that contain that item.

A set of STORE-ID values is associated with each item. These STORE-ID values are combined with the value ITEM-ID to make the symbolic pointer to a HOLD record. The no-pointers value is the number of pointers currently stored in the array. A procedure to find the quantities of a given item held by all stores is also illustrated in Figure 9.28. Here each pointer in the list is used together with the item identifier to directly retrieve HOLD records and obtain quantities of the item supplied.

Symbolic pointers can also link records into chains. As shown in Figure 9.29, there is only one symbolic pointer in each ITEMS record, and it points to the first HOLD record with that item. Each HOLD record has a pointer to the next HOLD record with the same item. The chain terminates with zero value in the pointer. Now, to retrieve all the quantities of a given item, it is necessary to follow this list. A procedure that does this is included in Figure 9.29.

Logical Record Pointers

Many DBMSs use logical record addresses as pointers. In Figure 9.12, for example, the logical record address is the concatenation of (page-no + offset-no). The DBMS would first request the access method to store a record. After storing the record, the access method would return the record's logical record address to the DBMS. The DBMS would then place this address in an appropriate link position.

The structure maintained by the DBMS would now differ from that shown in Figures 9.28 and 9.29 because the symbolic STORE-ID pointers would be replaced by logical record addresses.

AVAILABLE ACCESS METHODS

Earlier in this chapter we concentrated on the structures used to store data and on the methods used to access these structures. For illustrative purposes the structures, and particularly access methods, assumed extensions to the Pascal language. Pascal does not include a comprehensive set of input/output commands for data access. Rather, Pascal emphasizes the algorithmic process and the constructs to specify it.

A comprehensive set of input/output commands is included in the COBOL language. COBOL is primarily used for data processing. COBOL programs usually process large amounts of data and need a comprehensive set of input/

output commands to do this. The CODASYL (Conference on Data Systems Languages) committee, which is responsible for the development of a standard COBOL, has been developing such a set of commands (the committee's latest proposal appeared in the *COBOL Journal of Development* in 1978). These commands support sequential, indexed sequential, and direct processing.

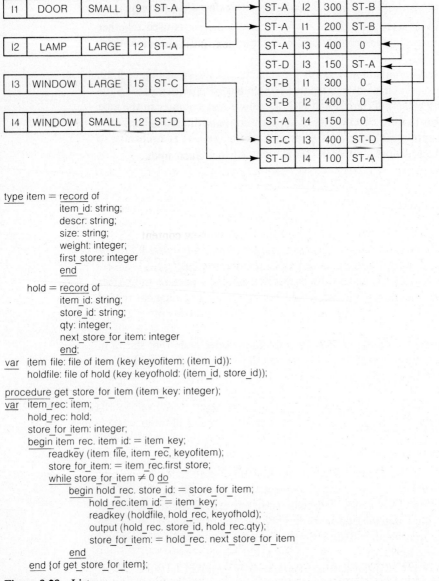

```
type item = record of
            item_id: string;
            descr: string;
            size: string;
            weight: integer;
            first_store: integer
            end

     hold = record of
            item_id: string;
            store_id: string;
            qty: integer;
            next_store_for_item: integer
            end;
var  item file: file of item (key keyofitem: (item_id));
     holdfile: file of hold (key keyofhold: (item_id, store_id));

procedure get_store_for_item (item_key: integer);
var  item_rec: item;
     hold_rec: hold;
     store_for_item: integer;
     begin item rec. item id: = item_key;
           readkey (item file, item_rec, keyofitem);
           store_for_item: = item_rec.first_store;
           while store_for_item ≠ 0 do
                 begin hold_rec. store_id: = store_for_item;
                       hold_rec.item_id: = item_key;
                       readkey (holdfile, hold_rec, keyofhold);
                       output (hold_rec. store_id, hold_rec.qty);
                       store_for_item: = hold_rec. next_store_for_item
                 end
     end {of get_store_for_item};
```

Figure 9.29 Lists

COBOL Input/Output

The COBOL sequential access commands are as follows:

1. READ file name RECORD; AT END statement-1.
The next record in the file is transferred into the user's working storage. If there are no more records in the file, control is transferred to statement-1.

2. WRITE record-name.
The record in working storage is written into the next position in the file.

New sequential files must be created following insertions, deletions, or updates. Reasons for creating the new files were discussed earlier. However, some disk sequential file implementations permit insertions, deletions, or updates to be made without creating new files. Each record in such implementations is allocated some well-defined location, such as a sector or disk. If the record is changed, only that location of the file must be rewritten. Such updates or rewrites are sometimes called *in-situ* updates. The command used for in-situ update is

REWRITE record-name

This command will overwrite the current record with the new contents.

Similarly, a file need not be recreated to make deletions. Records can be deleted by setting a tag in the file record. When the tag is set to 1, the record is considered to be logically deleted although still physically present in the file. Again, it is not necessary to copy the whole file if the file is on disk.

Indexed Sequential File Organization

Indexed sequential file organization differs from the sequential file organization in one significant way. It allows both sequential and direct access to the file by maintaining an index to the file. The index contains the key value of the first logical record in the sector or track. Most indexed sequential file implementations also maintain overflow areas to permit record insertions. Records that cannot be physically inserted into primary key sequence on the file are stored in an overflow area. Links are then maintained between records in the main file and the overflow file.

CODASYL recommends that COBOL Indexed Sequential File Organization include one primary key and one alternate key. The primary key is used to sequence the records on the physical device. Records can be accessed directly either by the primary key or by the alternate key. Sequential access, however, can use only the primary key. An ALTERNATE KEY clause is recommended by CODASYL to define the alternate key. This clause follows the file definition

```
FILE CONTROL.
      SELECT FILE—X ASSIGN TO IMP—NAME
            ORGANIZATION IS INDEXED
            ACCESS MODE IS DYNAMIC
            RECORD KEY IS FILE-KEY
            ALTERNATE RECORD KEY IS PROJECT-ID WITH DUPLICATES
DATA DIVISION
FILE SECTION
FD FILE-X
      RECORD CONTAINS 24 CHARACTERS.
01 FILE-X-RECORD.
            02 FILE-KEY.
                  03 PERSONS-ID PIC X(6).
                  03 PROJ-SEQ PIC 9(6).
            02 PROJECTS-ID PIC X(6)
            02 TIME-SPENT PIC 9(6).
```
Figure 9.30   A COBOL indexed sequential file definition

in the DATA DIVISION. Figure 9.30 illustrates the definition of a COBOL indexed sequential file.

The file key is made up of two fields: PERSON-ID and PROJ-SEQ. The PROJ-SEQ field is added to PERSON-ID to make the file key unique. The alternate key, PROJECT-ID, need not be unique; records with the same alternate key value can exist in the file.

Three kinds of access are recommended by CODASYL for indexed sequential files: *sequential* access, *random* access, or *dynamic* access. In dynamic access both sequential and random access may be used in the same program.

In the following explanation of commands for the random access mode, MYKEY is a record field that has been defined to be the key of the accessed record. MYKEY value is set to the required record key value before command execution. The commands for random access are as follows:

- **WRITE** record-name; INVALID KEY statement-1.
  Writes a record to the file. A write takes place only if a record with MYKEY value does not already exist in the file. If such a record does exist, control transfer to statement-1.

- **READ** file-name; INVALID KEY statement-2.
  Directly reads a record from the file. A read takes place only if there is a record with MYKEY value in the file. Otherwise control transfers to statement-2.

- **DELETE** file-name RECORD; INVALID KEY statement-3.
  Deletes a record from the file. Deletion takes place only if there is a record in the file with MYKEY value. Otherwise control is transferred to statement-3.

- **REWRITE** record-name; INVALID KEY statement-4.
  Replaces the record in the file. A REWRITE takes place only if a record with MYKEY value exists in the file. Otherwise control transfers to statement-4.

With dynamic access the following additional statements become available:

- **READ** file-name NEXT RECORD; AT END statement-5.
  Same as random access READ, although NEXT indicates sequential rather than direct processing. Control transfers to statement-5 when the end of file is reached.
- **START** file-name ⟨key condition⟩; INVALID KEY statement-6.
  Here the file is positioned according to some key condition. Sequential access then commences from that position. The condition can specify either

  - a particular key value or
  - the first record with a key value greater than or less than some specified value.

  If no such record is found, control is transferred to statement-6.

This text uses the term *selective sequential read* to describe access that begins with a START and follows with a number of sequential READs. Selective sequential read is particularly useful in finding all values related to the major item of a particular key value. Figure 9.31 is an example. Here PERSON-ID is the major item of the file key, and there can be more than one record with the same value of PERSON-ID. Each record in the file stores the time spent by a person on a project. The following sequence of commands can be used to read all the projects on which a particular person spent some time:

> START FILE-X KEY IS NOT LESS THAN MYKEY.
> REPEAT FOR ALL RECORDS WITH PERSON-ID = 'ID77'
>   READ FILE-X NEXT RECORD.

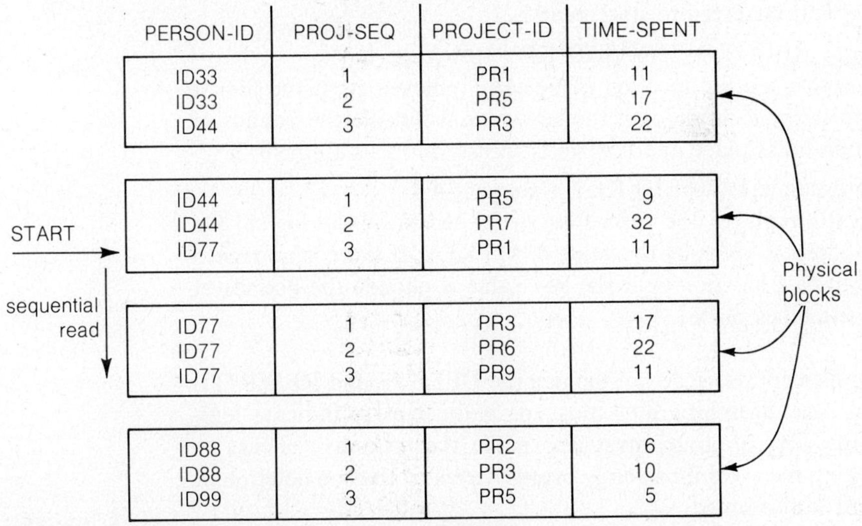

Figure 9.31 Selective sequential read on FILE-X

The first command positions the file to the record that precedes the first record with the given PERSON-ID value. The commands in the loop will then read the records sequentially until a record with a value of PERSON-ID other than 'ID77' is read. Advantage can be taken of blocking in this case because records with the same value of PERSON-ID will be stored contiguously.

Sequential access on a COBOL indexed sequential file uses the DELETE, WRITE, REWRITE, READNEXT, and START commands. If a record is to be replaced, it must first be read by READNEXT command. Once the record has been read, the REWRITE command is executed. Indexed sequential file implementations that allow direct access with an access key other than the master key provide an ALTERNATE KEY clause to define such access keys. The system establishes an index for each alternate key.

Relative File Organization

Relative file organization allows direct access by using a numeric key; the key value determines the position of the record in the file. Thus MYKEY value determines the selected file location in relative access commands. Typical commands available for direct access are as follows:

- **WRITE** record-name; INVALID KEY statement-1.
  A record is written into the selected file location. Should the location be already occupied or the key value be outside the bounds of the file, no write takes place and control is transferred to statement-1.

- **READ** file-name RECORD; INVALID KEY statement-2.
  A record is read from the selected file location. If there is no record in that location or if the key value is outside the bounds of the file, no read takes place and control is transferred to statement-2.

- **DELETE** file-name RECORD; INVALID KEY statement-3.
  The record in the selected file location is logically removed from the file. If there is no record in the location or if the key value is outside the bounds of the file, no deletion takes place and control is transferred to statement-3.

- **REWRITE** record-name; INVALID KEY statement-4.
  The record logically replaces the record currently stored at the logical file location whose address is given by the value of MYKEY. If there is no record currently stored in that location or if the key value is outside the bounds of the file, one rewrite takes place.

Many relative implementations do not include the DELETE and REWRITE commands. In that case, user programs must maintain flags to indicate logically deleted records. The program must also make the necessary checks to ensure that no existing record is incorrectly overwritten and that no deletion of a nonexistent record is attempted.

SUMMARY

A large variety of implementation models are available to database designers. It is common to distinguish between implementation models that are elementary files and those that are database management systems (DBMSs). Elementary files provide access methods that allow programs using one particular language (such as COBOL or PL/1) to access records one at a time. DBMSs, on the other hand, provide much more powerful interfaces that allow database access independently of a programming language and have the ability to refer to many records in one command.

Access methods used by elementary files allow data to be accessed in different ways. Sequential access methods are used to access records in the same sequence as they appear in the file. The whole file must be searched to get at one record. Direct access methods, on the other hand, allow programs to access particular records (using some record item as key) without examining other records in the file. Direct access in most cases is implemented by indices, and B-trees are becoming popular as index structures. Indexed sequential access methods are also available to allow both sequential and direct access to the same file.

Some access methods support more than one index to the same file and hence allow direct access, using different items as key. It is also possible to extend methods to link more than one file. The links are made between related records in different files and can be established at the user level or at the access method level. At the user level, the links are maintained by user programs, whereas at the access method level they are maintained by the access method or DBMS software. Different kinds of pointers are used in each case. Symbolic pointers are used by user programs, whereas logical record addresses are used by access methods or DBMSs. The most common way to link records in different files is by inverted files or links.

PROBLEMS

Problem 1

Figure 9.32 illustrates data about persons. Define a sequential file for these data by using the method shown in Figure 9.14. Then write procedures to

(a) create a new file
(b) find JOHN's address
(c) add a new record for MARY, who lives in BOSTON and is assigned to the ACCOUNTS department

PERSONS

NAME	ADDRESS	DEPT
ADRIAN	BOSTON	SALES
ANDREW	NEW YORK	ACCOUNTS
ANNE	BOSTON	PLANNING
CATHY	CHICAGO	SALES
DEAN	LOS ANGELES	PLANNING
HELEN	BOSTON	ACCOUNTS
IAN	ATLANTA	PRODUCTION
JEREMY	NEW YORK	SALES
JOHN	LOS ANGELES	PRODUCTION
KATHY	CHICAGO	ACCOUNTS
LARRY	ATLANTA	PRODUCTION
MARTHA	LOS ANGELES	SALES
PETER	CHICAGO	PLANNING
ROBERT	ATLANTA	ACCOUNTS
SALLY	NEW YORK	PRODUCTION
THOMAS	BOSTON	SALES

Figure 9.32   Data about persons

Problem 2

Repeat Problem 1 but this time define the file to be direct, using NAME as the file key.

Problem 3

Suppose the hash algorithm used in direct access takes the equivalent numeric value (N) of the first character ($A = 1$, $B = 2$, etc.) and assigns the record to page $\lceil N/4 \rceil$. Thus all records with names starting with A, B, C, and D will be stored in page 1, those starting with E, F, G, and H in page 2, and so on. The page organization is as follows. The first A record will be stored in the page 1 position, the first B record in the page 2 position, and so on. The remaining records are chained in the page using the offset number as pointer. Show the pages to which the records in Figure 9.32 will be allocated and the way that they are stored in a page.

Once a page is full, the records are stored in an overflow page with a link from records in the main-area page to records in an overflow page. Suppose the data pages hold at most four records (that is one for A, one for B, and so on) and the remainder must go into overflow. Show how the data in Figure 9.32 are arranged into the overflow areas.

Problem 4

The data in Figure 9.32 are stored in a file in ascending order of NAME. A single-level index is established for the file, using NAME as the index key.

(a) Draw a diagram (similar to that shown in Figure 9.21) to illustrate this index, assuming four entities in each index block.
(b) Repeat (a) but assume a two-level index of the form shown in Figure 9.22.

Problem 5

Figure 9.33 shows some additional data about the persons in Figure 9.32. Now the skills of the persons are included in the data.

SKILLS

SKILL	FIRST-APPROVED
COMPUTING	1973
ACCOUNTING	1970
PHYSICS	1969
ELECTRICAL	1971
MECHANICAL	1971
FRENCH	1968

PERSON-SKILL

PERSON	SKILL	YEAR-ACQUIRED
ADRIAN	COMPUTING	1975
ADRIAN	ELECTRICAL	1977
ANDREW	MECHANICAL	1977
BETTY	COMPUTING	1978
CATHY	ACCOUNTING	1977
CATHY	FRENCH	1979
CATHY	COMPUTING	1980
DEAN	COMPUTING	1975
HELEN	PHYSICS	1973
HELEN	FRENCH	1975
IAN	COMPUTING	1973
IAN	FRENCH	1975
IAN	ACCOUNTING	1970
JEREMY	ACCOUNTING	1971
JOHN	ELECTRICAL	1973
KATHY	ACCOUNTING	1974
LARRY	COMPUTING	1975
LARRY	FRENCH	1972
MARTHA	PHYSICS	1970
PETER	COMPUTING	1979
PETER	ELECTRICAL	1975
ROBERT	ELECTRICAL	1977
ROBERT	ELECTRICAL	1973
SALLY	COMPUTING	1975
SALLY	FRENCH	1973
SALLY	PHYSICS	1978
THOMAS	MECHANICAL	1973

Figure 9.33 Additional data about persons

(a) Define PERSON-SKILL as an inverted file, using the method shown in Figure 9.28. The file is to be inverted on PERSON and on SKILL. Write procedures to
- retrieve all the persons with a given skill
- retrieve all the skills of a given person

(b) Repeat (a) but now establish links through PERSON-SKILL. Write procedures for the two requirements in (a).

Problem 6

Repeat Problem 5 but now assume a COBOL indexed sequential implementation of file PERSON-SKILL. Choose the file key to allow all persons with a given skill to be retrieved.

Problem 7

Now extend the definition in Problem 6 to include a list through the PERSON-SKILL file linking all the records with the same person. The list will commence at PERSON records (also defined as a COBOL indexed sequential file). The PERSON-SKILL COBOL file structure is designed to retrieve all the skills of a given person. Write COBOL code to retrieve these skills, given the NAME of a person.

chapter ten
Implementation Models, II –
Database Management Systems

INTRODUCTION

The previous chapter introduced the software structure of database management systems, a structure made up of two major parts:

1. The access method, which is the general input/output software often provided by operating systems. It can be used by database management software or by programming language compilers.
2. The user interface software, which provides a natural user interface and translates commands at that interface to access method commands.

We described various access methods in the last chapter. In this chapter and the next three we will describe DBMSs, which differ from file systems in that they provide a much more powerful set of user functions and interfaces. To qualify as a DBMS, a system must possess four fundamental capabilities. These capabilities have been more clearly defined over the last few years and are now generally recognized as a requirement that distinguishes a DBMS from a file system. The fundamental capabilities are as follows:

1. The DBMS must provide a natural interface of user data.
2. The interface must be independent of any physical storage structures.
3. Different users should be able to access the same database, using different views of the database.
4. Changes to the database can be made without affecting programs that make no use of the change.

Apart from these capabilities, DBMSs must also provide the facilities to support the database in an operational multi-user on-line environment. Such operational facilities include

• control of multi-user access to the database
• provision of remote terminal access capabilities

- ability to restrict users to access parts of the database only
- ability to recover from system faults
- ability to distribute the database over a number of locations

This chapter will first describe the fundamental capabilities in detail. It will next cover the DBMS architectures used to realize these capabilities and conclude with the operational environment and database facilities for supporting a multi-user environment.

NATURAL USER INTERFACE

The term *natural interface* can in the extreme imply the use of terms natural to a problem. Thus the DBMS would provide accounting terms and structures for an accounting system, appropriate physical terms and structures for a physical system, and so on. Obviously, one single DBMS cannot be so versatile as to provide a separate set of terms and structures for each of the large variety of potential problems. What is required is a sufficiently generalized interface that can be adapted to model a variety of problems—hence the term *generalized DBMS*.

Data model is now the accepted term to define the data structures provided at the user interface by a DBMS. Data models are chosen to provide constructs that can model a variety of user problems. As shown in Figure 10.1, it should be possible to directly map distinct objects in various user systems to distinct constructs in the data model; each relationship between such user objects would also be directly modeled by the data model. Hence the data model directly represents the user system.

This kind of natural mapping gives DBMS three main advantages over conventional file systems:

1. Conversion to the computer system is easier because there is a direct correspondence between user objects and data model objects.
2. The system is easier to change. A change to some of the user system objects can be restricted to only those database constructs that directly model these objects. Database constructs, which model unaffected objects, remain unchanged; so do programs that access them.
3. The database is easier to access because distinct user objects can be readily identified in the data model.

Data Models

Most (if not all) commercial DBMSs support a single data model. However, the data models supported by different DBMSs differ, and it is common to classify these models into three classes:

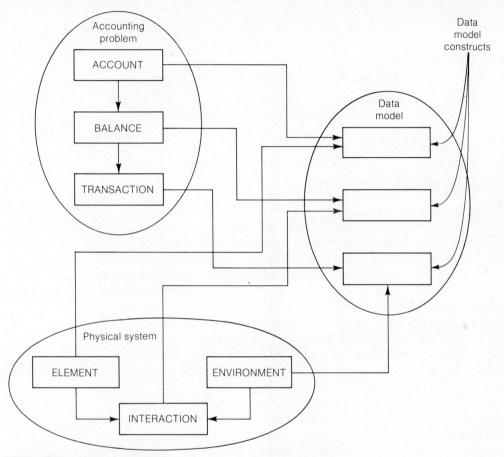

Figure 10.1 Natural mappings

1. the relational model
2. the network model
3. the hierarchical model

The relational model has been covered earlier. It provides a tabular interface to the user. The argument in its favor is that since many people are familiar with tables and use them as part of their everyday work, they do not find it difficult to use tabular structures to model their enterprises.

The other two well-known data models, the hierarchical and network models, are record-based. In both these models the user enterprise model is converted to linked record types. The links model a parent-child or an owner-member relationship between record types. The difference between the two data models is illustrated in Figure 10.2. Record types in a hierarchical structure can have at most one parent, whereas record types in a network structure can have more than one parent.

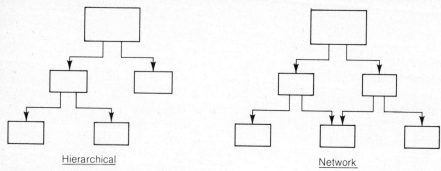

Figure 10.2   Network and hierarchical models

The hierarchical and network data models can model a large class of problems. Thus there are many problems in which entities can be classified hierarchically. Organizational structures are one example. Organizational units such as sections may report to departments; departments in turn report to divisions. Similarly, nations may be divided into states; states are then divided into counties, and so on. A network structure allows even more flexibility: entities are also modeled by record types, and relationships between entities can be modeled by links between the corresponding record types. In contrast to the hierarchical model, the network model does not restrict such relationships to hierarchical structures. The network model and the hierarchical model will be covered at length in Chapters 12 and 13.

USER VIEWS

The provision of a natural interface has one important connotation in environments where more than one user can access the database. Each user may have a different natural view of the same enterprise. Different users may see different object sets as more important and place more emphasis on different relationships. For example, if parts have different colors, those users that manufacture dyes see color as the most important enterprise entity; those that use parts consider part availability as the primary aspect. Thus each user may wish the interface to emphasize different natural aspects of the database. The term *user view* is now commonly employed to refer to the natural interface provided to a particular user. A DBMS must be capable of providing different user views of the same database to different users.

The ability to maintain such natural interfaces and different user views requires the DBMS software to maintain independence between different user views and between each user view and the physical constructs used to store the database. The term *data independence* is used to refer to this property.

DATA INDEPENDENCE

To provide natural mappings, the data model must be independent of computer-dependent structures such as indices, orderings, and physical access paths. Such computer features are not natural to user problems. They may distract designers, who may inadvertently make mappings that satisfy some computer aspect but do not naturally represent the enterprise. The result may be systems that are difficult to use and maintain. The goal of any DBMS is to present to the user an interface that emphasizes the logical structure of a user problem and is independent of computer physical structure.

Independence between the logical and the physical structure is often called *physical data independence.* It provides one important property: the ability to change the physical structure without any effect on the logical structure. Such physical changes may be made if usage patterns change. For example, new indices may be added if it is found that an item is used frequently as an access key. Since programs refer to the logical structure, they will be unaffected by any physical changes. Programs then become independent of physical structure and are easier to maintain.

Physical data independence has one important effect on the database design process: it separates design into two steps, logical and physical design, as shown in Figure 10.3. In the first step, logical design, the enterprise model is converted to a logical database structure. This conversion does not consider the detailed nature of eventual physical data structures. In the second step, the physical de-

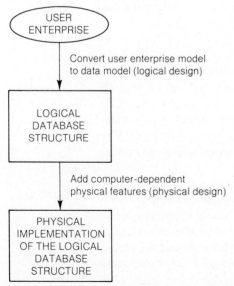

Figure 10.3 Separation of physical and logical design

sign, the physical data structures are chosen and added to the logical database structure selected during logical design.

DBMSs that support multiple user views are also said to support logical data independence. Logical data independence implies that user views are independent of one another. A change in one user view leaves other views unaffected. Data independence is particularly important in database restructuring.

Database Restructuring

Many user requirements change during the life of the database. For instance, new entities or relationships may be added or existing relationships may change. Databases must change to meet such altered requirements. DBMSs must provide various utilities to restructure existing databases. Ideally, such changes should be accomplished with minimal disruption to the existing system. In particular, programs that do not make use of any of the changes should not be affected.

A database change is usually effected through the steps shown in Figure 10.4. In step 1, new user requirements are defined. Thus in Figure 10.4 the requirement is to add to the database information about the usage of parts by projects and to add the attribute ADDRESS to object set PERSONS. In step 2 the existing data model structure is changed to accommodate the new user requirement. In this case new record types are to implement the new entities and relationships. A new field is added to record type PERSON. The data model change is then implemented.

The implementation shown as step 3 in Figure 10.4 is in two parts. First, the existing database definition is changed to include the newly added record types and data items. Then the second part of step 3 is to change the existing physical database. The change here is to the physical records that implement PERSONS and PROJECTS. Space must be provided in PERSONS to accommodate the new field ADDRESS; space must also be provided in PROJECTS to create links to the new USE records. Most DBMSs provide utilities to change the physical structure.

After the physical database is changed, one activity remains. This step (shown as step 4 in Figure 10.4) is to change existing programs to use the restructured database. Ideally, the minimal change is to recompile the programs. Such recompilation is necessary to create a new object code that refers to the changed physical records. In the ideal system, recompilation is all that should be necessary for existing programs. Program logic should not be changed unless it refers to the newly added structures.

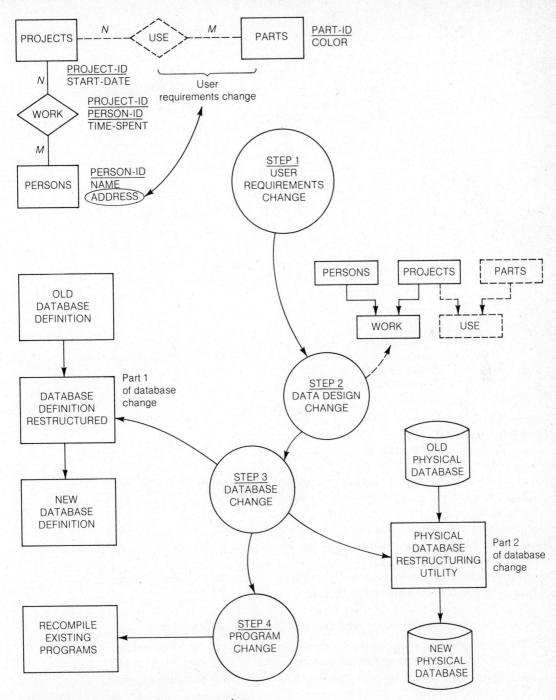

Figure 10.4 Steps in database restructuring

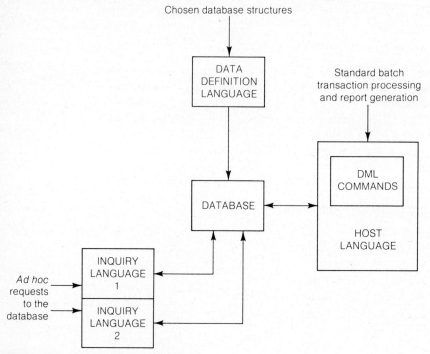

Figure 10.5 User interface software

DBMS SOFTWARE

The major software DBMS components are shown in Figure 10.5. The two central components are software to define a database and software to access the defined database.

DBMSs provide special languages to define databases. Once a database is designed, the chosen database structures are defined using the data definition language (DDL).

Software to access databases includes languages to cater to a variety of users. These users are usually classified as follows:

1. The professional programmer, who develops programs for other users.
2. The nonprogrammer, who accesses a database in the course of normal every-day activities. The nonprogrammer may be either
   (a) a parametric user (one who deals with specific and predetermined elements of data) or

(b) a generalized user (one who interacts with the database in unanticipated ways).

3. The casual user, who infrequently needs some information from the database.

Most contemporary DBMSs provide different classes of language to satisfy these users. One class embeds database access commands in a programming language. The collection of these commands is often known as the *Data Manipulation Language* (DML). These commands are then used to access databases through programs written in a high-level language such as COBOL or PL/1. They are mostly used by professional programmers to develop programs for report generation or for batch processing. They can also be used to prepare programs for on-line transaction processing. These programs are then used by parametric users.

Most systems provide query languages for the nonprogrammer user. They allow such users to access the database by user-oriented access commands rather than through procedural programs.

Few systems yet cater to the casual user, who normally requires an interface that is based on natural language processing.

Details of database access languages will be covered in Chapters 11, 12, and 13.

Using the DBMS Software

The DBMS software is used during the design and subsequent manipulation of databases. As shown in Figure 10.6, the designer must first identify the essential features of the enterprise. Then the designer must model these features by distinct enterprise model objects. The semantic abstractions defined in the earlier chapters can be used to identify such features and express them by enterprise model abstractions. Once this is done, the enterprise model is converted to the data model. The conversion method depends on both the enterprise model and the data model. If both are relational (see alternative 1 in Figure 10.6), each enterprise model relation becomes a data model relation. If the data model is hierarchical or network (see alternative 2 in Figure 10.6), the correspondence is not direct. Conversion rules must be used to convert the enterprise model to the data model. These rules will depend on the details of the data model structure, and we will discuss them and the various types of conversions in Chapter 15.

Once a data model structure is chosen for the users database, it is defined by the database definition language. The database can then be manipulated either by the query language or by DML commands or programming languages.

In this chapter and the next three, which describe data models and their im-

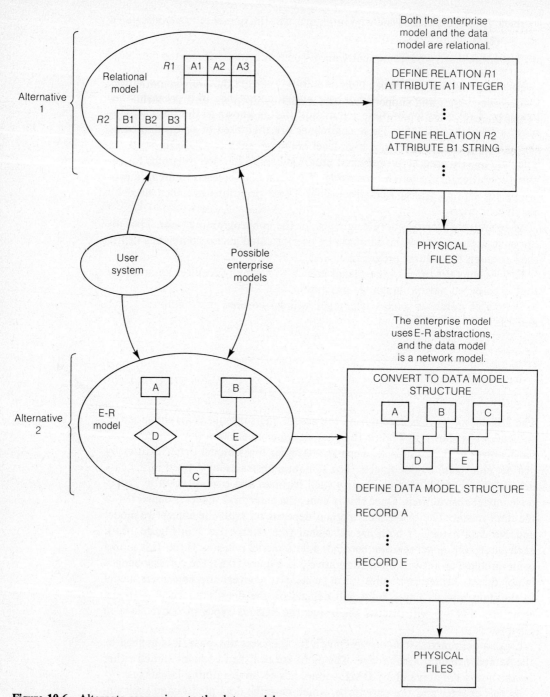

Figure 10.6   Alternate conversions to the data model

plementation, you will note that there is a subtle difference between data models and their implementation. Data models are a modeling abstraction. Implementations, on the other hand, are a software realization of the data model abstraction. Such implementations can differ between vendors. They can impose constraints on the data model structure, provide different definition and access languages, and support the data model by different physical structures. Thus there may be a number of alternate implementations of the same data model. For example, there are a variety of hierarchical, network, and relational DBMSs; each is implemented by different software structures. These software structures are often called *DBMS architectures*.

DBMS ARCHITECTURES

The primary goals of a DBMS are to provide facilities to

- define the chosen database logical structures
- define the chosen physical structure
- define user views
- access the defined database
- define the storage structures to be used to store the data

Software components must be provided for each of these functions. The combination of such software components is often called a *database architecture*.

Three-Level Architectures

A commonly accepted architectural framework is known as the *three-level architecture*. This architecture was initially proposed by ANSI/SPARC, which was established by the Standards Planning and Requirements Committee (SPARC) and the American National Standards Institute (ANSI). In 1975 this group proposed a standard architecture comprising the following three levels:

1. a conceptual level to represent a community view of the enterprise
2. an external level to represent any number of user views
3. an internal level to represent the stored form of the database

DBMSs based on the three-level architecture must provide languages to

- define the conceptual database
- define the external views
- define the storage representation of the database

Further, the DBMS software must be able to convert commands at the external-user views into commands at the conceptual level or at the storage level.

An important aspect of three-level DBMSs is the model provided to define databases at the conceptual level. Like other data models, this model should allow users to model enterprises in a natural way. And again, in the interest of generality, the data model provided at the conceptual level should support constructs and terms that can be used to model a variety of user enterprises. To do this, the conceptual level supports one data model. The user enterprise model must then be converted to the conceptual data model. However, three-level DBMS architectures do not restrict the external level to the same data model as the one used to define the conceptual schema. In such architectures it should be possible, for example, to define the enterprise by using one data model, say, the relational. It should then be possible to provide external schema by using other data models.

For example, consider Figure 10.7. Here the user enterprise is defined at the conceptual level, using a relational model. The enterprise model in this figure contains two relations, PERSONS and WORK. It describes persons working on projects. The time spent by a person on each project is stored, as well as the major skill of each person. A user view may then be a subset of the conceptual-level definition or it may be derived from the conceptual level. Further, the user views can use data models other than the conceptual-level data model.

Two user views are shown in Figure 10.7. User view 1, which uses a relational model, is derived from the conceptual level by a join operation, and shows the major skills of persons associated with projects. User view 2 uses a hierarchical model wherein persons own projects on which they work.

The internal levels of Figure 10.7 are the record structures used to store the conceptual-level objects. These levels also include indices, lists, or other physical paths that are used to access the record structures.

Generalized three-level architectures that support a variety of data models at the external interface are usually not commercially available. The lack of a general solution for the conversion of commands between any arbitrary data models at the conceptual and external levels limits the range of external views that can be supported by a given conceptual schema. Hence there are restrictions on the range of views that can be provided at an external interface. Most commercial DBMSs support external views in the following cases:

- The external view uses the same data model as the conceptual schema.
- The external view is a subset of the conceptual schema.
- Some records in the external view may contain items that are computationally derived from more than one record in the conceptual schema.

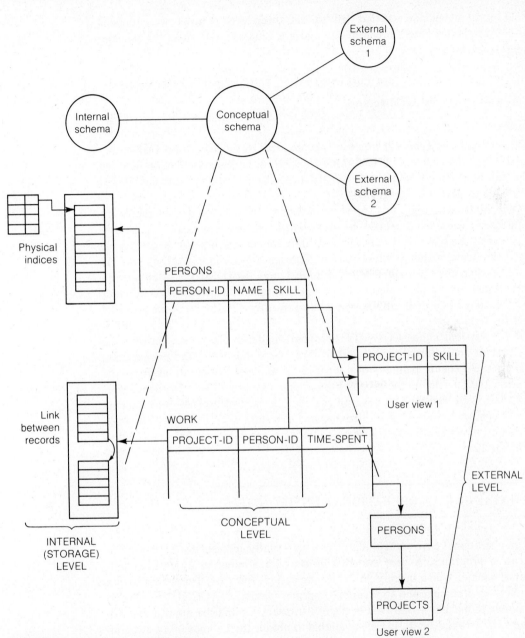

Figure 10.7   Three-level architectures

It should be noted that evolution to the three-level concept of three-level DBMS architectures has been gradual and to some extent defines an ideal. Few, if any, systems based on this ideal exist.

Practical developments that led to the three-level concept were defined earlier by the CODASYL committee and are generally known as the schema-subschema architecture.

Schema-Subschema Architectures

The *schema-subschema architecture* was proposed by the Data Base Task Group (DBTG) of the CODASYL Committee in 1971. It makes a distinction between the database definition and the definition of the part of the database made available to particular programs.

The database definition is called the *schema*. The schema defines the entire database: a *subschema* defines the user view. Since the subschema is generally a subset of the schema, it uses the same data model. Each program must have one subschema, although more than one program can share a subschema. As noted earlier, the term *Data Manipulation Language* (DML) is often used to refer to the commands available to access the database. These DML commands are embedded in a program and are used to transfer data between the program and the database.

Early versions of the CODASYL proposal made no distinction between the conceptual and internal views, and so these were defined in the one schema. Later developments pointed to a separation of physical definitions from the schema and have led to the proposal to develop a separate *Data Storage Definition Language* (DSDL) to separately define storage structures. The schema would contain only the logical definition of user data.

Some implementations of schema-subschema architectures are described in Chapter 12.

MAINTAINING AN OPERATIONAL ENVIRONMENT

In an operational environment, databases are usually accessed through user application programs. A user system consists of a number of application programs, each of which usually performs one system function. For example, in a banking environment one application program, UPDATE-ACCOUNT, may be available to make a withdrawal or deposit transaction; another application program, GET-BALANCE, is then available to obtain the balance of an account. A user who wishes to perform one of these functions must call the corresponding application program. Thus a user (or teller) who wishes to obtain a balance of an account must gain access to the GET-BALANCE application program and then run it to obtain this balance. The application program will in turn call the DBMS, which will then access the database and return the required data.

The application programs and the DBMS are managed by the operating system. The DBMS (or its routines) can thus be viewed as a program (or programs) running under the control of the operating system.

Usually on system start-up, the application programs and the DBMS are not active. As soon as a user transaction arrives at the system, the operating system activates the application program needed by the user transaction. The application program then executes under operating system control. When the application program calls any DBMS routines, the operating system activates these routines. The DBMS then accesses the database to meet the database needs of the application program.

Operating systems offer different kinds of controls for program execution. Differences exist in the number of programs that can be concurrently activated, the number of users that can run the same activated program, and the interactions of the application program with other computer system components. The kinds of program controls provided by the operating system are here called the *processing mode*. The processing mode needed for particular applications will depend on the user operational environment.

Types of Operational Environment

We can clearly distinguish two operational environments:

1. A database is set up for specialized use of one or a few individuals.
2. A database is an integral part of a business operation and must be accessible to a large number of users who may be distributed among many locations.

The operating system software capabilities needed to support such environments will obviously differ. In the first environment there is usually one user accessing the database. This user has one need that must be satisfied at one particular time. The activation of only one program is sufficient to do the job. This of course does not mean that the system can satisfy only a single need. The system may itself be complex. It may, for example, be a set of programs that supports a small business and may include various accounting, inventory, and marketing programs. However, at any one time only one of these will be needed, because there is only one user and that user can perform only one function at a time.

In the second kind of environment, a large number of users are concurrently accessing the system. It may, for example, be a banking system with many terminals at different locations. Users at some terminals may be updating accounts while users at other terminals are obtaining account balances. A number of different programs may be executing concurrently, with each program satisfying a different user need.

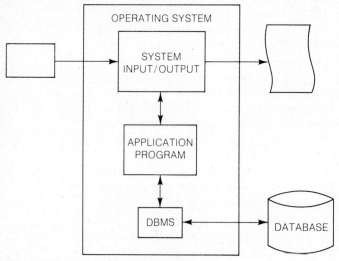

Figure 10.8   Batch use of the database

The operating system and the DBMS must together satisfy the needs of the user environment. To do this, they must support a processing mode that is appropriate for a particular user environment.

Processing Modes

Perhaps the simplest kind of processing mode is *batch processing*. It is shown in Figure 10.8. Here the DBMS is viewed as a program activated by the operating system. One user application program is also activated. During execution the application program calls the DBMS whenever it needs to interact with the database. The application program also uses the operating system input/output software to obtain input and deliver output.

On-Line Processing

The batch processing mode can be extended to allow on-line processing by providing a terminal controller. This extension is shown in Figure 10.9. Here the input and output is through a terminal, rather than cards and printer. The terminal controller is provided by the operating system. Messages received by the terminal controller are passed to the application program, which in turns calls the DBMS to access data from the database. Responses are then returned to the terminal user through the terminal controller.

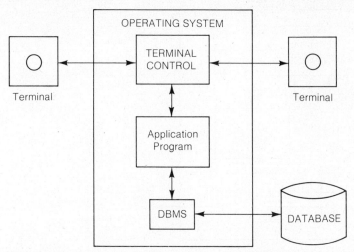

Figure 10.9 Terminal control to a dedicated program

A characteristic of the on-line operation in Figure 10.9 is that only one program is activated at one time. Hence only one program is accessing the database at the same time. This kind of environment is generally sufficient in specialized database environments or for personal systems. Here there is usually only one user accessing the database. That user is running one application program to satisfy some specialized need at a given time. The DBMS software in this environment need concentrate only on access methods and the user interface.

The processing mode in Figure 10.9, however, does not satisfy the second class of user environment, where more than one user requires concurrent database access. The figure has a system limitation that restricts execution to one program at the same time and hence permits only one user function to be performed at one time. In this processing mode, users who wish to perform other functions would need to wait until the currently activated program completes. This program would then have to be deactivated and the program for the new function activated. This changeover could take some time and hence increase response time to the user. Further, users who wish to perform the function whose program is currently activated would also need to wait until the current user's transaction is completed.

Therefore systems where a number of users can access the database concurrently must support more sophisticated processing modes. The most obvious extension to the processing mode of Figure 10.9 is that shown in Figure 10.10. Now more than one program can be activated at any instant, and each activated program can access the database. Each program performs a different function and may be communicating with different users through TERMINAL CONTROL. One program, for example, may be UPDATE-ACCOUNT, whereas the other may be GET-BALANCE. These programs may be continu-

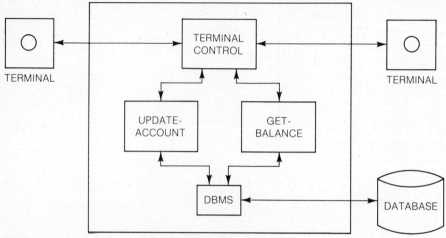

Figure 10.10   Multiple program access to a database

ously activated (or running), thus providing a continuous service to users. Two distinct methods of operation can be identified in Figure 10.10. These are sometimes called single-thread and multithread on-line processing.

Single-Thread On-Line Processing   In *single-thread processing* at most one program can be interacting with the database at the same time. So although in Figure 10.10 both application programs are activated, the DBMS will be servicing only one of them at any one time. For example, at some point the DBMS may be retrieving data for program GET-BALANCE, whereas program UPDATE-ACCOUNT may be getting some input through the terminal controller. After getting the input, program UPDATE-ACCOUNT may wish to access the database. It cannot do so until program GET-BALANCE obtains its data. Once this occurs, the DBMS begins to service the request from program UPDATE-ACCOUNT.

Multithread On-Line Processing   In *multithread processing* the database can service more than one program concurrently. Now when program UPDATE-ACCOUNT receives its input, it immediately calls the database, and the database can process program UPDATE-ACCOUNT's request concurrently with program GET-BALANCE's request, without waiting for GET-BALANCE to complete its DBMS use. However, when multithread processing is allowed, the capabilities of the DBMS must be extended. Now the DBMS must ensure that concurrent database accesses do not corrupt the database. Hence concurrency controls must be included in DBMS software.

There is still one problem with Figure 10.10. Suppose two tellers wish to use program GET-BALANCE. In the figure this cannot be done because there is

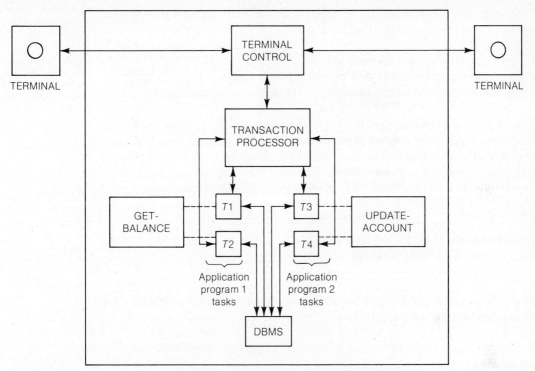

Figure 10.11   Multiple activation of the same program accessing the database

only one activation of the one program. Thus teller 2 would have to wait until GET-BALANCE finishes teller 1's request. Again response time will increase because of this wait. This problem is solved in Figure 10.11, where multiple activations (tasks of the same application program) are allowed. For example, if more than one inquiry is made about customers' account balances at the same time, there would be more than one task of program GET-BALANCE set up. A separate GET-BALANCE task would be set up for each teller, and each task would be multithreaded through the database. Thus task T1 in Figure 10.11 would be servicing one inquiry and task T2 another. Now a user's request does not have to wait for either the needed application program nor for the DBMS to finish servicing some other request.

Transaction Processor   In many systems, multiple-program activation is usually controlled by software called a *transaction processor*. The transaction processor itself runs under the control of the operating system. The user messages are directed to the transaction processor, which examines the message type and determines the program needed to process the message. The transaction processor then creates a program task and passes the message to that program task for processing.

The transaction processor thus controls the flow of user messages through the system. To do this it maintains tables about

- the program to be used for each user message type
- the terminals authorized to find various message types
- any sign-on procedures and passwords to be used at each terminal

Specific fields in each message are used to indicate the message type. The transaction processor looks at these fields to determine the message type and then checks whether that type can be sent from the sending terminal. If so, the transaction processor looks up its table to determine the program to process that message. It then sets up a task of that program to process the message.

DATABASE FACILITIES TO SUPPORT A MULTI-USER ENVIRONMENT

Multithreading and operational use place new requirements on a DBMS. The three main requirements are as follows:

1. Concurrency controls that preserve database integrity, given concurrent user operation.
2. Database access controls that restrict users to only those parts of the database needed to accomplish the user's task.
3. Recovery systems that restore the database to a correct state following a system failure.

Database Integrity

Data integrity takes on a special meaning in a multi-user environment. It is possible for integrity to be lost if more than one program operates on the same data item concurrently. For example, consider Figure 10.12. Here records in the database contain QTY-STORED of various ITEM-KINDS. Thus there is a record that shows 100 radios in store. Two programs, WITHDRAW and ADD, are available to the user. Program WITHDRAW is used to withdraw items from store. Two parameters, ITEM-KINDS and QTY-TAKEN, are used as inputs to program WITHDRAW. The value of ITEM-KINDS is the items withdrawn, and QTY-TAKEN is the quantity withdrawn. On execution, QTY-TAKEN is subtracted from QTY-STORED of ITEM-KINDS. Similarly, program ADD adds a value (QTY-ADDED) to QTY-STORED of ITEM-KINDS.

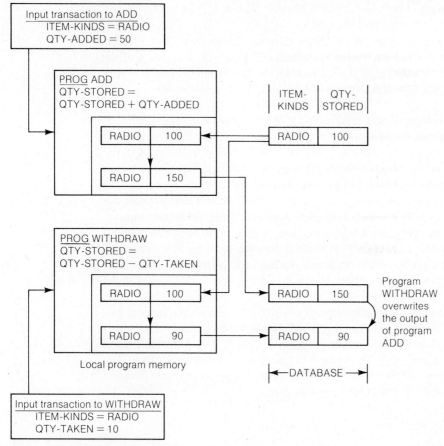

Figure 10.12 Loss of integrity

Now suppose one user activates program WITHDRAW to withdraw 10 radios. Another user concurrently activates program ADD to add 50 radios. Clearly, at the conclusion of these two programs QTY-STORED for RADIO should be 140.

However, now consider what may happen during concurrent execution. It is possible for both program activations to access the RADIO record and transfer it to their local memory. The records are first updated in the local memory of each activation and then written back to the database. The final database state will show either 150 or 90 radios, depending on which program completes last; Figure 10.12 assumes program WITHDRAW to be the last to write the record to the database. Clearly, irrespective of which program completes last, the database no longer represents the true user state, and hence integrity is lost or the database becomes incorrect.

Concurrency Control

Concurrency control is necessary to ensure database correctness. In a concurrent environment, correctness is usually defined as follows: the final state of the database must be the same as if the programs executed serially. Thus in Figure 10.12, QTY-STORED or RADIOs would be 140 if either

- program ADD executed and then program WITHDRAW executed, or
- program WITHDRAW executed and then program ADD executed.

The most common method of concurrency control is to use locks. One lock is maintained for each database component. A program obtains all such locks before making any updates. Concurrency control must ensure that at most one program gets the lock for one database part. Hence if a program wishes to move a locked item to the program working storage, it must wait until the previous program releases the lock. How this is done depends on the implementation. In many implementations, user programs include commands to lock the required records before updating them. Hence it is a program responsibility to get the lock.

Locks can introduce the problem commonly known as *deadlock*. Suppose two programs wish to access items A and B in the database concurrently. Program 1 locks A first and then tries to lock B. Program 2 locks B first and then tries to lock A. Both programs are then waiting for each other to release a lock. The usual step here is to roll back one of the programs. The rolled-back program releases all its locks and the other program is allowed to continue.

Recovery

Another important requirement of operational systems is recovery following system failure. It is recognized that in an operational environment both software and hardware errors can occur. If such errors occur during a database interaction, the database can be left in an inconsistent state. Recovery software is used to restore the database to some previous consistent state.

There are a variety of recovery algorithms. The simplest is to keep a back-up copy of a database. This copy is created at regular intervals, perhaps once or twice daily. Should a system error occur, the last back-up copy is restored. Any transactions since that copy was taken are run again. Most on-line systems, however, use more sophisticated techniques, the most common being the use of journal files or what are commonly known as *audit trails*.

Recovery systems that use audit trails record database changes on an audit file. The audit trail includes the old and new values of all items updated by the transaction. The system is known to be consistent at the start of each transaction. Should a failure occur during the transaction, all the items changed by the transaction will be restored.

The user program must usually indicate the points at the program at which the database is known to be consistent. To do this BEGIN TRANSACTION and END TRANSACTION commands are included in the program logic. On execution of a BEGIN TRANSACTION command, the system writes a BEGIN TRANSACTION checkpoint on the audit file. During any subsequent writes the DBMS writes before or after images on the audit file. The before image is the old value of a changed item. The after image is the item's new value. The before and after images are written to the audit trail whenever a new value is written to the database by a WRITE statement. The execution of the END TRANSACTION command creates an END TRANSACTION checkpoint on the audit file.

The creation of an audit trail is illustrated in Figure 10.13. Here new values are created for TOTAL-SALES and TOTAL-DISCOUNT from a current sale. Consistency requires that TOTAL-DISCOUNT be updated only at the same time as TOTAL-SALES is updated. Hence the creation of new TOTAL-SALES and TOTAL-DISCOUNT values is enclosed by BEGIN and END TRANSACTION commands. If a failure were to occur, at ⊗ in Figure 10.13 the database would be in an inconsistent state, because TOTAL-SALES would have been updated in the database without a corresponding update to TOTAL-DISCOUNT. However, on recovery the system would read the audit trail backwards to a BEGIN TRANSACTION checkpoint. It would restore all updated values to their old values. Hence TOTAL-SALES would be restored to its old value, which would be consistent with the old TOTAL-DISCOUNT value. The transaction would now be run again.

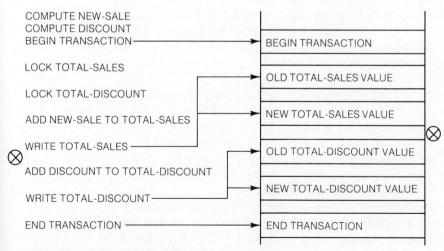

Figure 10.13 Creating an audit trail

A variety of other data can be written on the audit trail. These data can include the actual transaction or the time of the update. The transaction data would be used to determine the transactions that are to be rerun after recovery. The information written on the audit trail is determined by the database designer.

Database Privacy

The trend toward multi-user database systems requires controls to ensure that users of the database get access to only those parts of the database that they need to accomplish their tasks. Some of the data in the database may be restricted or sensitive and consequently available to only some of the system users.

DBMSs control access to the database in various ways. Control of access through user views is one possibility. A user is given access abilities to a user view that contains only the data needed. All access to the database by that user must be through the user view.

Passwords and locks can also be used to control access to databases. A lock is associated with each record type. A command that wishes to access a particular record type must provide the appropriate password to gain access to it.

Database Distribution

Most enterprises collect and use data in a variety of locations. Some of the data collected at a particular location may be of interest just at that location. Other data may be of interest to more than one location. There is therefore some advantage to keeping some of the enterprise data close to their location of use, whereas other data might be centrally located. A database that is maintained at more than one location is called a *distributed database*. Distributed databases can be either partitioned or replicated.

As shown in Figure 10.14, a partitioned database is divided into parts, and each part is stored at just one location. Thus part A is stored only at location X, part B only at location Y, and so on. This kind of distribution is useful when most of the data are of local interest only. For example, locations X, Y, and Z may be branches of a bank whose transactions take place mostly at local branches. So there is some advantage in storing accounts locally, for the transmission of data between locations is then minimized.

Replicated databases, on the other hand, become useful if data are used at more than one location. In a replicated database the same parts of a database may be stored at more than one location. Thus in Figure 10.15, database part B is stored at locations X and Y, whereas E is stored at Y and Z. Some parts in a

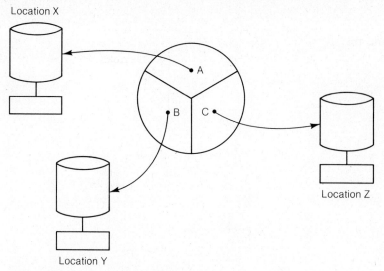

Location X

Location Z

Location Y

Figure 10.14   A partitioned database

replicated database may, however, be stored at one location only—for example, parts A and D in Figure 10.15.

It is up to the designer to choose the way the database is to be distributed. This choice is determined by the database usage patterns and the costs of transmitting data between locations. Detailed consideration of this choice is outside the scope of this text.

Technical Considerations in Distributed Databases

Distributed databases introduce new database control problems. Ideally, the location of a given database part should be transparent to a program. A program should refer to a database component only by its name, and the DBMS should determine the location of the component, given the component name. If this is achieved, the program is not affected if the component is moved from one location to another.

To realize transparency, a DBMS would need to include the functions shown in Figure 10.16. Here there are software components to communicate to distant locations as well as controls for local and global database access. A typical program request for a database component would pass through interfaces 6 and 5 to database control. Database control would determine whether the request can be satisfied locally or whether it must refer to databases at other locations. Local requests would be passed through interface 3. Requests that need access to data at other locations would pass through interfaces 4 and 1 and then be transmitted to distant sites. Conversely, requests from other sites for local data would come through transmission control and then interfaces 1 and 2.

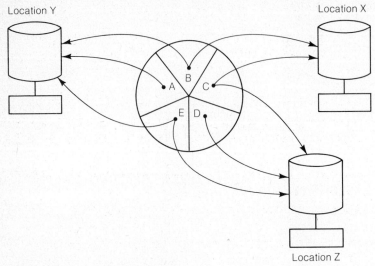

Location Y

Location X

Location Z

Figure 10.15 A replicated database

A major problem in this environment is to provide control protocols to

- converse between database management software at different locations
- provide control algorithms for global concurrency to ensure that integrity is maintained in the database at all locations

Such control protocols can generate considerable traffic between sites to secure global locks or maintain time stamps. Research is in progress to develop such protocols while ensuring that protocol control traffic does not unduly impair system performance. Most commercially available systems do not provide distributed databases that are transparent to programs. Most still require user programs to control the distribution; in this case distribution usually involves wholesale transfer of database files to make them available for local programs.

Data Dictionaries

Management of a database is usually a complex process. It requires the database administrator to keep track of all the database and user view definitions as well as their use.

Data dictionaries have been developed to aid the database administrator in this task. They are repositories of all data about a database; in fact, one view of them is as a database about a database. The most general structure of a data dictionary (Figure 10.17) contains descriptions of the database structure and

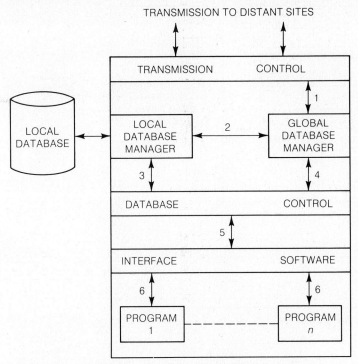

Figure 10.16 Software components for distributed systems

database use. The data in the data dictionary are maintained by a variety of programs and produce diverse reports on demand.

Most data dictionary systems are stand-alone systems, and their database is maintained independently of the DBMS. So inconsistencies can arise between the database and the data dictionary. To prevent these inconsistencies, current developments aim at integrating the data dictionary with the DBMSs. In an integrated system the schema and user view definitions would be controlled through the data dictionary and would be made available to the DBMS software.

A Typical Software Structure

In summary it is perhaps worthwhile to consider the combination of software that realizes the fundamental and operational properties of DBMSs. A typical structure is illustrated in Figure 10.18. It includes compilers to compile database definitions; these definitions are stored internally. Often the compilers also

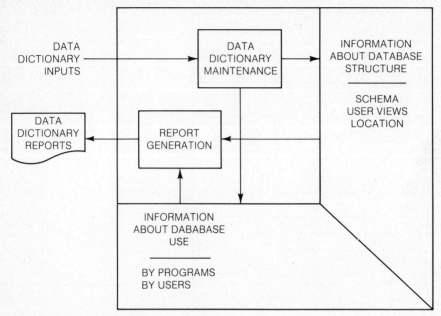

Figure 10.17   Data dictionary structure

generate an access object code. This code is later used by the program object code to reference the database.

Another set of compilers is used to generate a program object code from DML-embedded commands or inquiry languages. The object code generated by these compilers calls database control, which contains components to

- maintain database integrity
- check users' ability to access database components
- generate calls to access methods
- obtain data from distant locations (where distributed controls are supported)

The access methods are usually integrated with recovery software components to maintain audit trails. The system also includes restructuring utilities to facilitate changes in the database structure.

SUMMARY

The characteristics that distinguish DBMSs from file systems are

- the natural interface supported by DBMS
- the ability to support different user views

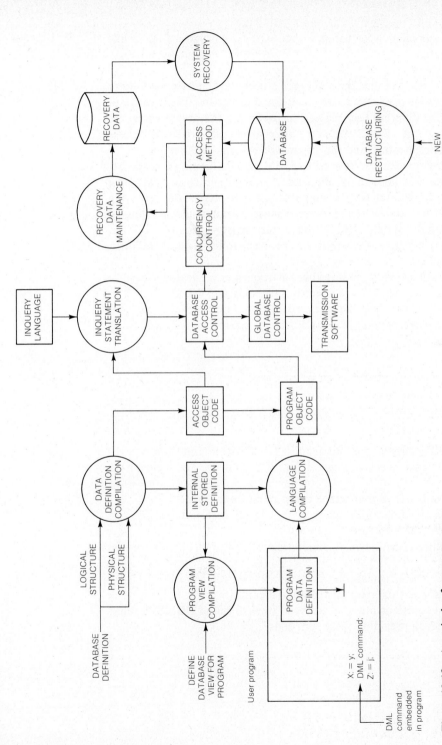

Figure 10.18 A typical software structure

- the ability to support database change without affecting programs that make no use of the change

The software structures to realize these characteristics must contain facilities to define databases and languages to access the defined databases. The access languages must cater to different user classes, in particular the programmer, the nonprogrammer, and the casual user. Two alternative software architectures are the three-level architecture and the schema-subschema architecture.

In operational environments supported by DBMSs, a distinction is made between environments that allow only one user at a time and those that allow multi-user access to the database. To support multi-user access the operating system together with a transaction processor must permit multithreading of transactions through the system. The DBMS in turn must provide the facilities to preserve database integrity, allow database recovery following system faults, and maintain privacy.

Distributed databases, which can be either partitioned or replicated, often are not transparent to programs. This problem is now being tackled.

Data dictionaries contain all the data about a database. Since they are usually maintained independently of the DBMS, an integrated system is being developed.

PROBLEMS

1. Describe the characteristics that distinguish DBMS from a file system.
2. What is the difference between physical data independence and logical data independence?
3. What are the main software interface components on a DBMS?
4. What are the main differences between three-level architectures and the subschema-schema architecture?
5. Describe the difference between single-thread and multithread on-line processing.
6. Outline the functions of transaction processor software.
7. What does transparent database distribution mean?
8. What additional functions must be provided by distributed DBMSs? What are the difficulties in providing these functions?

chapter eleven
Relational Database
Management Systems

INTRODUCTION

The relational model appears in two contexts in this book. Chapters 2 and 3 introduced the relational model in the first context—as the theoretical basis for structuring data. An important aspect of the theory is normal relations. Normal relations possess many desirable structural properties. In particular, they prevent anomalies after update, insert, or delete operations because each fact is stored once only in the database. The criteria of normal relations are subsequently applied in data analysis to realize logical structures that satisfy normal relational properties. Such logical structures can then be implemented on an available nonrelational data model.

This chapter describes the relational model in a second context—as an implementation model that is supported by a DBMS. Any relations produced during data analysis can be implemented directly on this DBMS.

Because of its tabular interface, the relational model makes an attractive implementation model. It is receptive to two types of environment:

- the traditional data processing environment, where databases are set up by professional computer programmers on behalf of database users
- environments in which nonprogrammer users set up their own databases

The relational model provides the same advantage in both types of environment. Its natural interface simplifies the design and use of the database. This is particularly so if a language with powerful selective capabilities can be provided by the DBMS. Such languages can reduce program development time and hence are attractive in commercial data-processing environments. They are also attractive to nonprogrammer users, allowing them to use the database without resorting to computer-oriented procedural languages.

There are, however, problems in relational model implementations. A powerful language such as relational algebra or SQL is necessary to realize the full potential of a relational DBMS. These languages can be expensive to implement and use. Queries in a relational language such as SQL can use any attribute as a key, and so a powerful indexing capability must be provided. Further, because of nested mappings, such queries can span a number of relations. These spans are executed as join operations. But a join operation, which compares each row in one relation to all the rows of another, can be prohibitively expensive. In a commercial environment it can render system development unfeasible.

For this reason there was considerable early skepticism about the relational model as an implementation model. The model, it was claimed, was conceptually sound but too expensive to use. Two major attempts were launched about 1974 to built experimental prototypes to illustrate the feasibility of relational implementations for commercial use. These were System R, developed at the IBM Research Laboratory in San Jose, and INGRES, developed at the University of California at Berkeley. The twofold goal of both systems was to

- develop a relational interface
- ensure that this interface can be operational in environments found in practice

In retrospect it is perhaps reasonable to claim that both System R and INGRES realized systems that satisfy the traditional data processing need—a large database is maintained for many users. Here efficient resource use and reduced programming cost to develop an application are of paramount importance. Recently, however, there has been considerable growth in an alternate environment. In this environment the database is set up by a user without using a data processing professional as an intermediary. Programmer productivity and efficient resource use can take second place to providing an easy-to-use interface. The user time saved in problem formulation can outweigh any overhead processing costs.

Systems with such interfaces have been becoming prominent in the past few years. One important development is a graphical interface supported by IBM's Query-by-Example. Easy-to-use interfaces are also an important feature of personal computers based on the microprocessor. Many personal computer systems now include some facility for database management. Although many of the DBMSs on microprocessors are predominantly file systems, the trend is to increasingly use the relational tabular form for the user interface. Most such systems, however, concentrate on the tabular interface and do not support query languages that have the selective power of SQL. The times to process a nested SQL query could be prohibitive on a personal computer system. Usually commands in query languages on personal computers are restricted to operations on one or at most two relations.

This chapter will outline developments in relational DBMSs. It will describe System R, Query-by-Example, and DBMS development on personal computer systems. The descriptions are not necessarily complete, covering only those implementation aspects that are considered important and the most interesting. They also adopt terminology consistent with the text rather than with a particular system and represent each system's state of development as described in the literature. Therefore they should not be used as a substitute for any manuals for these systems.

SYSTEM R

The structure of System R, IBM's prototype DBMS, closely follows the levels shown in Figure 9.4. Figure 11.1 illustrates the levels, together with the terminology used by System R. The relational storage system (RSS) is a System R access method specially developed for relational databases. Fundamentally, the RSS maintains relations as stored files; relation tuples are the file records. In fact, System R's standard terminology refers to relations in the database (called conceptual schema) as tables and to their stored form (internal schema) as stored files; and it then refers to the relations provided to users (external schema) as user views. To maintain consistency with the rest of the text, we will not follow System R's terminology and will use the terms *relations* (for conceptual schema), *stored relations* (for internal schema), and *user views* (for external schema).

The RSS can store the relations tuples in some specified sequence. It can also support an arbitrary number of indices to each stored relation as well as links between tuples in the stored relations. The RSS is accessible through the research storage interface (RSI). It is not directly accessible to users but is used by code generated by the Relational Data System (RDS). This code includes calls to the RSS through the RSI.

The RDS provides the System R user facilities. The user interface is based on the language SQL. SQL is in effect the outcome of development of System R. The RDS supports access to the database either by *ad hoc* SQL executed online or by SQL embedded in either PL/1 or COBOL. The RDS also provides facilities to support multiple views on a database and control facilities to maintain privacy.

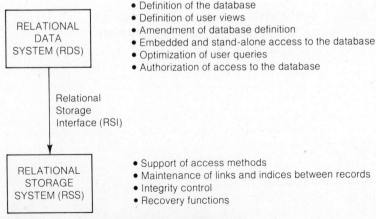

RELATIONAL DATA SYSTEM (RDS)
- Definition of the database
- Definition of user views
- Amendment of database definition
- Embedded and stand-alone access to the database
- Optimization of user queries
- Authorization of access to the database

Relational Storage Interface (RSI)

RELATIONAL STORAGE SYSTEM (RSS)
- Support of access methods
- Maintenance of links and indices between records
- Integrity control
- Recovery functions

Figure 11.1   The general structure of System R

The SQL Interface

The on-line interface of System R uses SQL. The elements of this language were defined in Chapter 2. These are based on the mapping

SELECT ⟨variable⟩ FROM ⟨relation⟩ WHERE ⟨condition⟩

This mapping enables sets of values to be selected from relation tuples; such tuples satisfy a specified condition. Chapter 2 introduced SQL as a relationally complete language and showed how the SELECT/FROM/WHERE mapping can be used to formulate user queries. The implementation of SQL on System R includes facilities to define databases, change database contents, and provide the capabilities to control access to the database.

Defining the Database

SQL provides a CREATE TABLE statement to define databases. Figure 11.2 illustrates the use of this statement. Here relations STORES and HOLD are defined. Relation STORES is defined to consist of four attributes: STORE-ID, PHONE, NO-BINS, and LOCATED-IN-CITY. The type and size of each attribute are defined as part of the CREATE TABLE statement. Here CHAR specifies a character string, INTEGER a full-word binary integer, and SMALLINT a half-word binary integer. In addition, an attribute can be defined to be NONULL. If it is defined as NONULL, it must always take a value in each relation tuple. Attributes that are not so defined may have blank values in some tuples. The attributes that make up the relation key should normally be defined as NONULL. Thus in relation STORES in Figure 11.2, STORE-ID must always take a value. PHONE, however, may initially be blank and be assigned a value later.

After the execution of a CREATE TABLE statement, a new stored relation is created. This relation is initially empty. It must then be populated by update transactions.

```
CREATE TABLE STORES    (STORE-ID (CHAR (6), NONULL),
                        PHONE (INTEGER),
                        NO-BINS (SMALLINT),
                        LOCATED-IN-CITY (CHAR (20))
CREATE TABLE HOLD      (STORE-ID (CHAR (6), NONULL),
                        ITEM-ID (CHAR (6), NONULL)),
                        QTY-HELD (INTEGER))
```

Figure 11.2 Defining relations in System R

Populating and Updating the Database

Chapter 2 described only SQL retrieval operations. SQL also contains operations to insert, delete, or change tuples in a relation.

Tuple Insertion

Now tuples are inserted into relations by the INSERT command. For example,

    INSERT INTO CUSTOMERS
      (CUST-NAME, FIRST-ORDER-DATE, LIVE-IN-CITY)
    ('MARY', '101281', 'BOSTON')

will add a new tuple to relation CUSTOMERS. The values to be added correspond to the left-to-right order of attributes enclosed by parentheses. If such an order is not specified, the values to be added correspond to the order of attributes in the relation definition.

Tuple Deletion

An existing tuple can be deleted by a DELETE statement. This statement takes a form similar to the SELECT statement. The WHERE condition in the DELETE statement selects the tuple to be deleted. For example, a CUSTOMER can be deleted by the statement

    DELETE CUSTOMERS
      WHERE CUST-NAME = 'MARY'

The DELETE statement can also cause a number of tuples to be deleted. For example, all the customers in Boston could be deleted by

    DELETE CUSTOMERS
      WHERE LIVE-IN-CITY = 'BOSTON'

Tuple Update

An UPDATE command can be used to change the value of an attribute in a tuple. The WHERE clause is used to select the tuple to be updated. A SET clause is used to nominate the attribute whose value is to be changed and to specify the new value. For example, the LIVE-IN-CITY of a customer is changed as follows:

    UPDATE CUSTOMERS
      SET LIVE-IN-CITY = 'NEW YORK'
      WHERE   CUST-NAME = 'MARY'

The value of LIVE-IN-CITY for the customer whose CUST-NAME is MARY has now been changed to NEW YORK.

Amending the Database Definition

System R enables users to change the database definition as user requirements change. It is possible to add new relations, delete relations, or add new attributes to relations. A brief description of commands available for this purpose follows.

Removing a Relation

The operation DROP TABLE is used to remove a relation. Thus, if the user no longer wished to maintain the customer file, it could be removed by the command

   DROP TABLE CUSTOMERS

Expanding a Relation

A new attribute can be added to an existing relation by the EXPAND TABLE command. For instance, suppose a user wishes to keep information about dates by which an order is to be filled. To do this, the attribute DATE-REQUIRED must be added to relation ORDERS. This attribute can be added by the command

   EXPAND TABLE ORDERS
      ADD FIELD DATE-REQUIRED (INTEGER)

Defining User Views

The syntax to define user views is illustrated in Figure 11.3. Two users views are defined. One defines the city source of all orders. The order source is the

```
DEFINE VIEW ORDER-ORIGIN (ORDER, CITY)
    AS SELECT   ORDERS.ORDER-NO, CUSTOMERS.LIVE-IN-CITY
        FROM    ORDERS, CUSTOMERS
        WHERE   ORDERS.ORDER-NO = CUSTOMERS.ORDER-NO
```
                  Origin of Orders

```
DEFINE VIEW ITEM-TOTALS (ITEM, QTY-NEEDED)
    AS SELECT   ITEM-ID, SUM (QTY-NEEDED)
        FROM    ITEMS-ORDERED
        GROUP   BY ITEM-ID
```
                  Total of Items Ordered

Figure 11.3   User views

city of the customer that made the order. The second view is the total quantity of each item ordered by all customers.

The first line of a user view definition defines the name of the relation in the user view (ORDER-ORIGIN) and its two attributes (ORDER and CITY). The relation ORDER-ORIGIN contains the attributes ORDER and the CITY of the order's originating customer. The ORDER-ORIGIN attributes correspond to the attributes in the SELECT clause. Thus ORDER corresponds to ORDERS.ORDER-NO and CITY to CUSTOMERS.LIVE-IN-CITY in the joined relation. The remainder of the SELECT clause defines the condition for joining the stored relations to obtain the user view.

The second view uses the function SUM to total the QTY-ORDERED of each item. This total appears as the attribute QTY-NEEDED in the view relation ITEM-TOTALS.

The view relations are not physically stored in the database. Any statements that refer to a view must be translated into operations on the stored relations used to derive the view.

Users are restricted in the operations they can perform on a user view. Only operations that can be uniquely translated into operations on the stored relations can be supported. Thus, for example, an operation such as

    INSERT INTO ORDER-ORIGIN (ORDER, CITY)
        ('ORD7', 'NEWYORK')

could not be translated into operations on the stored relations ORDERS or CUSTOMERS, because the customer who placed the order is not known. Similarly,

    UPDATE ITEM-TOTALS
        SET   QTY-NEEDED = QTY-NEEDED + 10
        WHERE ITEM-ID = 'I1'

could not be translated, because it implies a change to one or more tuples in ITEMS-ORDERED for I1. The command does not specify which of the ITEMS-ORDERED tuples are to be updated since it does not include an ORDER-NO. Thus most user views are used to retrieve data. INSERT, DELETE, and UPDATE operations are usually restricted to stored relations.

Embedded SQL

SQL statements can be embedded in either PL/1 or COBOL. The host language contains special features to do the following:

- Embed SQL statements in the host language. To do this each such statement is preceded by the symbol $.

- Bind variables in the SQL statements to variables in the host language. Such variables are declared as $-variables in the host language. They are referenced as $-variables in SQL statements and as variables not preceded by $ in the host language.

- Allow sets of records retrieved in one SQL statement to be accessed one by one. To do this, a cursor is associated with a SELECT SQL statement. Successive FETCHes of the cursor deliver successive records to the host-language working storage.

- Indicate the outcome of each SQL statement to the host language. To do this, a status indicator is returned in a system variable called SYR. Although the variable SYR has a more complex structure, for the purposes of this text only one component SYR-CODE of SYR will be considered. The component SYR-CODE will take the value zero if a SQL statement completes successfully. It will take a nonzero value if the statement fails. Provision exists in the SYR structure to include a message that describes the reason for the failures.

An example of the use of these features is shown in Figure 11.4. Here SQL is embedded in a COBOL program. This program includes one embedded SQL SELECT statement as well as an embedded UPDATE statement. The embedded SELECT statement refers to the relation HOLD and retrieves all the stores that hold a particular item. The binding of SQL variables with COBOL variables is illustrated by this SELECT statement. Here ITEM-ID, STORE-ID, and QTY-HELD are database variables as defined in Figure 11.2. They are not prefixed by $ in the SQL statement. The variables STORE, QTY, and ITEM-NEEDED, on the other hand, are COBOL variables. They are prefixed by $ in the SQL statement. The correspondence between the database variables and the COBOL variables is specified by their relative appearance in the INTO clause or the equality conditions. Thus STORE-ID in the database corresponds to the COBOL variable STORE, and QTY-HELD in the database corresponds to the COBOL variable QTY. Likewise, database variable ITEM-ID corresponds to COBOL variable ITEM-NEEDED. Further, COBOL variables that are used in a SQL statement are declared as $77 variables. They are not preceded by $ in COBOL statements.

The logic of the program is as follows. The user nominates a needed item (ACCEPT ITEM-NEEDED statement). A search is then made of the HOLD relation, and all the stores that hold the item are displayed. The user then chooses one of these stores (CHOSEN-STORE) and withdraws the needed items from that store. The logic is implemented as follows.

1. Read the value of ITEM-NEEDED.
2. Execute a SQL statement to find all the stores that hold ITEM-NEEDED and display the stores one by one. To do this, a cursor C1 is associated with the SQL statement. To execute the SQL statement, the cursor is first opened by a $OPEN statement. The $FETCH cursor statement is then executed. The $FETCH statement returns successive values of STORE-ID, QTY-

```
DATA DIVISION.
WORKING-STORAGE SECTION.
$77 STORE PIC IS 9(10).
$77 ITEM-NEEDED PIC IS 9(6).
$77 QTY PIC IS 9(6).
$77 CHOSEN-STORE PIC IS 9(10).
$77 AMOUNT-NEEDED PIC IS 9(4).
$SYR.
77 END-INDICATOR PIC IS 99.
$LET C1 BE SELECT STORE-ID, QTY-HELD INTO $STORE, $QTY
          FROM HOLD WHERE ITEM-ID = $ITEM-NEEDED.
PROCEDURE DIVISION.
      ACCEPT ITEM-NEEDED.
      $BEGIN TRANSACTION.
      $OPEN C1.
      MOVE 0 TO END-INDICATOR.
      PERFORM GET-STORE UNTIL END-INDICATOR=1.
      $CLOSE C1.
      ACCEPT CHOSEN-STORE, AMOUNT-NEEDED.
      $UPDATE HOLD
          SET QTY-HELD = QTY-HELD − $AMOUNT-NEEDED
              WHERE(STORE-ID = $CHOSEN-STORE AND
                  ITEM-ID = $ITEM-NEEDED)
      $END TRANSACTION.
      STOP RUN.
GET-STORE
      $FETCH C1.
      IF SYR-CODE = 0 DISPLAY STORE, QTY.
      IF SYR-CODE IS NOT EQUAL TO 0 MOVE 1 TO END-INDICATOR.
```

Figure 11.4 Embedded SQL

HELD. These values are returned in COBOL variables STORE and QTY. The value of SYR-CODE is 0 when a value is found; it is set to nonzero after all the tuples retrieved by the SQL statement have been accessed by the FETCH statement. The cursor is then closed by the $CLOSE statement.

3. The tuple for the selected store is updated by the $UPDATE statement.

4. The execution of the SQL statements are enclosed by $BEGIN TRANSACTION and $END TRANSACTION.

Any SQL statements can be embedded in COBOL or PL/1, including those used to populate or update the database. For example,

$INSERT INTO ITEMS (ITEM-ID, DESCR, SIZE, WEIGHT):
⟨$ITEM, $ITEM-DESCR, $SIZE, $WGT⟩

would add a new tuple to ITEMS. The values of the tuple attributes would need to have been entered into the COBOL variables ITEM, ITEM-DESCR, SIZE, and WGT before the execution of this statement.

Similarly, tuples can be deleted from the relations by the DELETE command. For example,

$DELETE ITEMS
    WHERE ITEM-ID = 'I3'

would delete the tuple for item I3 from relation ITEMS.

A host-language program may also contain statements to create or amend the database definition. Thus a CREATE TABLE, DROP TABLE, or EXPAND TABLE command could be included in a host language. The use of such commands enables temporary relations to be created, used, and dropped during the execution of a host-language program.

Implementation

In the general structure of System R illustrated in Figure 11.1, the fundamental objective of the Relational Data System (RDS) is to translate user commands into operations on the stored relations. An important translation function is to optimize the execution of the user commands. To do this, the RDS must contain components that accept SQL commands and then select those access paths in RSS that retrieve any tuples with minimal disk transfers.

The components of the RDS are shown in Figure 11.5. The RDS is made up of two main components:

- the PRECOMPILER (XPREP)
- the EXECUTION-TIME-SYSTEM (XRDI)

The precompiler is used to translate embedded SQL statements to call statements in the host language. The precompiler accepts a host-language problem together with embedded SQL commands. Precompilation produces two components:

- A new version of the host language with embedded SQL statements replaced by calls to XRDI. This version is subsequently compiled by the host-language compiler into object code.
- An access module is machine code specially built for the SQL commands in the host language. This module includes the code for access paths chosen by the RDS optimizer for the particular SQL statements in the host-language problem. Routines in the access module are called during the execution of XRDI.

The RDS also contains a component known as the *user friendly interface*. This interface supports *ad hoc* SQL commands. It controls dialogue with the user and terminal displays. The system treats the user friendly interface as another program and maintains an access module for it. The access module in this case, however, is not complete but contains provision for new code that may

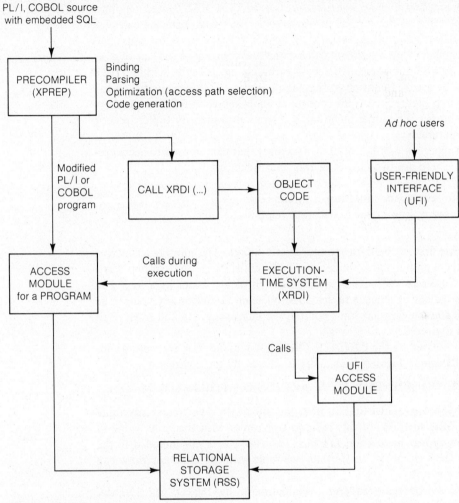

Figure 11.5   An elaboration of RDS

be generated from an *ad hoc* SQL statement. Thus on receipt of an *ad hoc* SQL command, the UFI first prepares the access code for the command and enters it into the space provided in the UFI access module. The command is then executed by using the access module code.

Access Paths

System R allows the designer to choose the most appropriate access paths for the expected usage pattern. Given an SQL command, the RDS optimizer selects one of these paths to execute the command.

To understand how access paths can be used to access individual tuples, it is necessary to understand how relations are stored. The RSS stores relations in pages, which in turn are formed into segments. Segments form the basis for storage allocation. All the pages used to store a relation must be contained within one segment. Thus a segment can expand and contract as the size of a relation, together with any associated access paths, changes. Tuples within a page are identified by a concatenation of the page address and offset number in the manner shown in Figure 9.12. This concatenation is known in RSS terminology as a *tuple identifier*. The tuple identifier is then used to identify tuples in various index structures.

The RSS supports a number of data structures that can be used to access relation tuples. There are two classes of this data structure:

• structures to access individual tuples in one relation
• structures used to link tuples in different relations

Indices   The first of the data structures are indices. The number of indices to one relation is unlimited. An index can be established on any relation attribute and can use one attribute or a combination of attributes as a key. The RDS can use indices to retrieve tuples directly, given the index key value. The RDS can also start retrieval at some point of the index sequence and retrieve all tuples within a given key value range.

An index is created by the CREATE INDEX command. For example, an index to ITEMS using ITEM-NO as a key is started by the command

CREATE UNIQUE INDEX ITEM-ACCESS ON ITEMS (ITEM-ID)

The term UNIQUE requires that at most one tuple with a particular key value can appear in the relation. In this case no two tuples with the same value of ITEM-ID can appear in relation ITEMS. If UNIQUE is not included in the CREATE-INDEX command, more than one tuple with the same key value can appear in the relation.

An index may be removed from the database by the DROP INDEX command.

Links   Links are established to provide access paths between tuples in different relations. They are useful in implementing join operations. A tuple in one relation, say, CUSTOMERS, can be linked to tuples in another relation, say, ORDERS. The link is between tuples that have the same value of CUST-NAME. Any command that uses a join operation on CUST-NAME will use these links to improve performance.

Some Operational Features

Transaction processing and recovery in System R are supported by the RSS. The calls from the RDS identify the start and end points of a transaction. The

RSS uses locking techniques to maintain database consistency. The locking system is quite elaborate and supports three levels of consistency:

1. Level 3 consistency is the highest level. It ensures integrity by restricting access to one lockable item to only one level 3 transaction and not allowing other transactions access to data locked by a level 3 transaction.

2. Level 2 consistency ensures that all data items read are consistent. It allows data items to be changed between reads by the same level 2 transaction. Hence two consecutive reads of the same data items by the same transaction may be different (although the value of the data items will still be consistent).

3. Level 1 consistency does not guarantee that data read by the program are consistent. It is useful only in applications where exact results are not needed (e.g., for gathering statistical information).

System R can maintain locks on tuples, entire relations, or entire segments. The chosen lock granularity depends on the transaction. A transaction that updates a single tuple would gain a lock to a single tuple only. Transactions that operate on sets of tuples (e.g., multiple SQL updates) may be granted locks to entire relations.

The RSS also provides functions to recover the database. It keeps a "shadow page" for each data page. Any existing page that is updated is written to its shadow page location. Thus at any instant all the pages of a segment that have not been changed are in their original (or old) location. All changed pages appear in a new location. A pointer is maintained to both the old and the new locations for each page. If there is a system failure, the new locations are removed and the pages at the old locations become the consistent state. When a checkpoint is reached, the pointers are exchanged and the new pages become the new consistent state.

QUERY-BY-EXAMPLE

Query-by-Example (QBE) is a relational system designed for nonprogrammer users. It has about the same selective power as SQL but uses a graphical interface. It is therefore suitable only for terminal use and cannot be embedded in a host language. Although QBE is provided as a stand-alone system, there is no fundamental reason why it could not be developed as a front end to any other relational system. For example, there is no reason why a QBE interface could not be one of the languages available for use with System R.

The basic notion of QBE is that the user provides the system with an example of the output expected from the system. This example takes the form of a table skeleton that specifies values to be taken by table columns in the output; it also

STORES	STORE-ID	PHONE	NO-BINS	LOCATED-IN-CITY
	P.X			

Figure 11.6   Simple retrieval

nominates columns that the system must fill in (or print). The system responds to the user's request by filling in the nominated tables with any rows that satisfy the values in any specified columns. For example, for the QBE query illustrated in Figure 11.6, the user first enters STORES, and the system returns a skeleton table with the column headings showing all the STORES attributes. The user now selects the column STORE-ID as the column whose values are to be output. This is done by entering P.X in column STORE-ID. Here P stands for "print," and X is an example element of a value to be output. The example element must be underlined. It can be an actual STORE-ID value that is expected on output, or it can be any of the STORE-IDs or for that matter anything at all. It is also possible to leave the example value out altogether and simply enter P in column STORE-ID. The output to the query in Figure 11.6 will be the set of all the STORE-IDs.

Figure 11.7 shows how a condition can be attached to a query. Now an additional entry, BOSTON, is made in column LOCATED-IN-CITY. This condition requires any selected tuple to have BOSTON as its LOCATED-IN-CITY value. The P.X in column STORE-ID indicates that values of STORE-ID of the selected tuples are to be output. Thus, in response to the query in Figure 11.7, all the BOSTON stores will be output.

Conditional Retrieval

Figure 11.7 illustrates a retrieval that specifies one condition, namely, that LOCATED-IN-CITY must take the value "BOSTON." It is also possible to specify "AND" and "OR" conditions on two or more different fields or on the same field.

Figure 11.8 illustrates retrieval with an AND condition on two fields. The

STORES	STORE-ID	PHONE	NO-BINS	LOCATED-IN-CITY
	P.X			BOSTON

Figure 11.7   Simple qualified retrieval

HOLD	STORE-ID	ITEM-ID	QTY-HELD
	P.X	I1	> 150

Figure 11.8 An AND condition on different fields

example requires ITEM-ID to be I1 and QTY-HELD > 150 in order to print
a value of STORE-ID. Hence only those stores that contain more than 150 of
item I1 will be printed out.

Figure 11.9 is a slight variation of the AND condition. Now the AND condition is on the same field, namely, ITEM-ID. The sample value $\underline{X}$ must appear
in HOLD with both I1 and I2 in ITEM-ID. Hence only those stores that hold
both I1 and I2 will be printed out (ST-A and ST-B in Figure Prob-3 in the
appendix).

HOLD	STORE-ID	ITEM-ID	QTY-HELD
	P.X	I1	
	P.X	I2	

Figure 11.9 An AND condition on the same field

Specification of OR conditions is illustrated in Figures 11.10 and 11.11. In
Figure 11.10 all the items that are either SMALL or weigh less than 10 lb are
to be output. The distinction from the AND condition is that now there are two
example output values $\underline{X}$ or $\underline{Y}$. The $\underline{X}$ example value has size SMALL and the
$\underline{Y}$ example value weighs less than 10 lb. In Figure 11.10 the OR condition is
applied on two attributes, whereas in Figure 11.11 it is applied on the same

ITEMS	ITEM-NO	DESCR	SIZE	WEIGHT
	P.X		SMALL	
	P.Y			< 10

Figure 11.10 An OR condition on different fields

CUSTOMERS	CUST-NAME	FIRST-ORDER-DATE	LIVE-IN-CITY
	P.X		BOSTON
	P.Y		NEW YORK

Figure 11.11 An OR condition on the same field

ITEMS	ITEM-ID	DESCR	SIZE	WEIGHT
	P.X̲			J

CONDITION
5 < J < 12

Figure 11.12   Using a condition box

attribute. Thus in Figure 11.11 the CUST-NAME for BOSTON or NEW YORK customers is output.

Complex conditions can be specified by using a condition box. Figure 11.12 shows an example of one such condition. Here ITEM-IDs of items whose weight is between 5 and 12 are to be printed out.

Some Options

So far all the queries specified have been such that each value in the output is unique. This may not always be the case. For example, suppose a query requests the output of all ITEM-IDs in HOLD where QTY-HELD > 250. In this case (Figure App. 3 in the appendix), I3 could appear twice in the output because its holding in stores ST-A and ST-C exceeds 250. The user can choose to either allow or suppress duplicate appearances of the same value. To allow such appearances, the word ALL follows P in the query. Thus for the query in Figure 11.13 the value I3 would appear twice in the output. If ALL were omitted, I3 would appear only once in the output.

The user can also specify that output values be ordered in ascending or descending order of some output attribute. Thus in Figure 11.14 the STORE-IDs of stores holding item I4 are to be printed out, together with the QTY-HELD of I4. The AO indicates that the output is to be in ascending sequence of STORE-ID. If DO were used in lieu of AO, the output would be in descending sequence of STORE-ID.

HOLD	STORE-ID	ITEM-ID	QTY-HELD
		P.ALL.X̲	> 250

Figure 11.13   Nonsuppression of duplicates

HOLD	STORE-ID	ITEM-ID	QTY-HELD
	P.AO.X	I4	P.Y

Figure 11.14 Ordering

Retrieval from More Than One Relation

Often it is necessary to refer to data in more than one relation. To do this, it is necessary to have the ability to link tuples in different relations. In QBE the link is made by using the same example variable in both tables. For example, Figure 11.15 is a request to print out the ORDER-NOs of orders made by customers who live in BOSTON. The link example element V1 is used to do this. A value of ORDER-NO in a tuple is printed out only if its CUST-NAME attribute value equals a value of CUST-NAME in a CUSTOMERS tuple that has BOSTON as its LIVE-IN-CITY value. This equality is implied by having V1 in both CUST-NAME columns.

ORDERS	ORDER-NO	ORDER-DATE	CUST-NAME
	P.X		V1

CUSTOMERS	CUST-NAME	FIRST-ORDER-DATE	LIVE-IN-CITY
	V1		BOSTON

Figure 11.15 Retrieval from more than relation

Linking variables can also be used to link tuples in the same relations. For example, in Figure 11.16 the linking variable is WT. The output is to be the DESCR and SIZE of items whose weight is greater than the weight of LARGE LAMP.

ITEM-ID	DESCR	SIZE	WEIGHT
	LAMP P.X	LARGE P.Y	WT. > WT.

Figure 11.16 Linking in the same relation

ITEMS-ORDERED	ITEM-ID	ORDER-NO	QTY-ORDERED
¬	I1	P.X	

Figure 11.17   Negation over a tuple

Negation

QBE allows users to select tuples that do not include certain values. Two kinds of negation are illustrated in Figures 11.17 and 11.18. In Figure 11.17 the negation is over the entire relation. The negation states that an ORDER-NO value is printed out only if there is no tuple with that ORDER-NO and I1 as the ITEM-ID value. In other words, only orders that do not include I1 are to be printed out. In this case only ORD2 would be output (Figure App. 3 in the appendix).

ITEMS-ORDERED	ITEM-ID	ORDER-NO	QTY-ORDERED
	¬I1	P.X	

Figure 11.18   Negation over a value

Figure 11.18 is a negation on a value. Now an ORDER-NO is to be output if it appears in a tuple that has a value other than I1 in ITEM-ID. Thus only those orders that include items other than I1 are to be output. In this case ORD1 and ORD2 would be output.

It is possible to combine negation with links to other relations. For example, Figure 11.19 links ORDER-NO over ORDERS and ITEMS-ORDERED. It

ORDERS	ORDER-NO	ORDER-DATE	CUST-NAME
	VAR		P.X

ITEMS-ORDERED	ITEM-ID	ORDER-NO	QTY-ORDERED
¬	I1	VAR	

Figure 11.19   Linking and negation

ORDERS	ORDER-NO	ORDER-DATE	CUST-NAME
	P.CNT.ALL.X		VICKI

Figure 11.20   Functions

requires the output of CUST-NAME of those customers that made orders that do not include I1. In Figure App. 3 in the appendix, the response to this query would be JACK.

Functions

Functions can be included in a query statement. The function name becomes part of the P column. For example, Figure 11.20 includes the function CNT. It requires the count of all orders made by VICKI. Other functions provided by QBE include sum, average, maximum, minimum, and unique.

Set Comparison

QBE allows comparisons to be made between sets of values in different relations. Set comparisons can use the subset, superset, or set equality condition. Examples of these three kinds of comparisons are illustrated in Figures 11.21, 11.22, and 11.23. Figure 11.21 illustrates tests of set equality. In this figure ALL.VAR in the ITEM-ID column of ITEMS specifies all the values of ITEM-ID that satisfy the condition, namely, DESCR is WINDOW. Thus

HOLD	STORE-ID	ITEM-ID	QTY-HELD
	P.X	ALL.VAR	

ITEMS	ITEM-ID	DESCR	SIZE	WEIGHT
	ALL.VAR	WINDOW		

Figure 11.21   Set equality condition

HOLD	STORE-ID	ITEM-ID	QTY-HELD
	P.X	[ALL.VAR]	

ITEMS	ITEM-ID	DESCR	SIZE	WEIGHT
	ALL.VAR	WINDOW		

Figure 11.22   Superset condition

HOLD	STORE-ID	ITEM-ID	QTY-HELD
	P.X	ALL.VAR	

ITEMS	ITEM-ID	DESCR	SIZE	WEIGHT
	[ALL.VAR]	WINDOW		

Figure 11.23 Subset condition

ALL.VAR will be all WINDOW items (I3 and I4 in Figure App. 3 in the appendix). The entry P.X in column STORE-ID requests the output of all STORE-ID that hold the same items (because ALL.VAR in HOLD must be the same as ALL.VAR in ITEMS). Hence the STORE-IDs of those stores that hold all the WINDOW items and only the WINDOW items are output (ST-D in Figure App. 3).

Figure 11.22 extends Figure 11.21 by allowing the output variable X to be associated with all the values in ALL.VAR, together with additional values. Thus now the STORE-IDs that store all the WINDOW items and may also hold other items are output (ST-A and ST-D in Figure App. 3).

In Figure 11.23 the condition is the inverse of that in Figure 11.22. Now all the WINDOW items must be a superset of items held in a store. Thus the response to the query will be all stores that hold only WINDOW items or some subset of them (ST-C and ST-D in Figure App. 3).

Insertion, Deletion, and Update

Insertions, deletions, and updates use the same graphical interface as retrievals, the letter I, D, or U, respectively, being placed in the column whose heading is the relation name. Insertion, for example, is illustrated in Figure 11.24. Here I in column ITEMS specifies an insertion in relation ITEMS. A new tuple for item whose ITEM-ID = I5 is inserted.

ITEMS	ITEM-ID	DESCR	SIZE	WEIGHT
I	I5	DESK	SMALL	25

Figure 11.24 Insertion

Deletion is illustrated in Figure 11.25. The D in column ITEMS-ORDERED indicates deletion, and sufficient attribute values are specified to uniquely identify a relation tuple. The user need not specify a value for QTY-ORDERED but may do so.

ITEMS-ORDERED	ITEM-ID	ORDER-NO	QTY-ORDERED
D	I1	ORD1	

Figure 11.25   Deletion

Update is illustrated in Figure 11.26. Here the value of QTY-HELD of item I2 in store ST-A is changed from 300 to 250.

HOLD	STORE-ID	ITEM-ID	QTY-HELD
U	ST-A	I2	250

Figure 11.26   Update

An insertion, deletion, or update may also affect more than one tuple in a relation. It is possible to specify a set of tuples in the same way as is done in retrieval. Each selected tuple can then be affected by the specified operation. For example, Figure 11.27 illustrates the deletion of all items ordered in ORD1.

ITEMS-ORDERED	ITEM-ID	ORDER-NO	QTY-ORDER-NO
D		ORD1	

Figure 11.27   Deletion of a set of tuples

Creation and Changes of Database Definitions

New relations are added to the database by specifying an insertion in the row used to define table and column names. For example, in Figure 11.28 the first I indicates the name of the table, in this case, ITEMS-ORDERED. The second I indicates the insertion of column names. The user is also required to insert certain details about each column.

The data provided for each column include the type and size of each column as well as its underlying domain. The user must also specify those columns that are key (K) or nonkey (NK). The system provides an index to each table column. This index can be suppressed by entering N for inversion.

I. ITEMS-ORDERED.I.	ITEM-ID	ORDER-NO	QTY-ORDERED
TYPE	CHAR	CHAR	FIXED
LENGTH	6	10	6
KEY	K	K	NK
DOMAIN	ITEMS	ORDERS	INTEGER
INVERSION	Y	N	N

Figure 11.28   Creating a new relation

Columns can also be added to existing relations, as shown in Figure 11.29. The I is now specified for only one table column.

ORDERS	ORDER-NO	ORDER-DATE	QTY-ORDERED	I. DATE-REQUIRED
				I. INTEGER
				I. 6
				I. NK

Figure 11.29   Adding an attribute to an existing relation

It is also possible to remove or drop a table from the database. In this case the letter D precedes the column name, as shown in Figure 11.30. Here the relation CITIES is deleted.

D. CITIES	CITY	HDQ-ADDRESS	STATE

Figure 11.30   Deleting a relation

PERSONAL COMPUTER SYSTEMS

DBMSs on personal computer systems based on microprocessors are generally intended for the nonprogrammer user. They differ from DBMSs supported by larger computer configurations in two significant aspects:

- the selective power of database access languages
- the interface provided to the user

Query languages in personal systems are usually restricted; each query must address only one file. There seems to be little point in allowing users to specify queries that may span a large number of relations. Such queries involve joins and may take a long time to execute, because personal computer systems are limited in their memory capacity and in the access time to storage devices. Hence the preference is to give users simple commands and require them to formulate complex queries as sequences of such commands. The more important emphasis of these systems is to provide an interactive interface that enables nonprogrammer users to easily define and populate databases.

The User Interface

There is a significant difference in the philosophy behind the interfaces for the personal computer user and those intended for the professional programmer. Many systems for the professional programmer require commands to be issued with their associated parameters to the DBMS. The DBMS in turn responds to each command by making a database change or by returning and displaying data. Hence the user in this case is expected to know the sequence of commands needed to accomplish a task and the parameters associated with each command.

Most DBMSs on personal computer systems tend to provide considerable guidance to the user. To do this, they enter into a dialogue with the user. This dialogue suggests steps that the user may take. One such typical interaction, shown in Figure 11.31, is based on the dBASE-II database system. Here the user commences by entering the word *create,* which indicates the wish to create a new relation (or file). The DBMS responds by requesting the file name. When this is given to the computer system, the DBMS requests the user to enter the record structure. It shows the attributes to be provided for each field. In Figure 11.31 these attributes are NAME, TYPE, WIDTH, and DECIMAL PLACES. After the user enters a set of attributes for one field, the DBMS requests the attributes for the next field. This procedure continues until all the file fields have been defined. dBASE-II is a trademark of Ashton-Tate of California.

The user can then, if desired, enter records. The DBMS displays the names of the record fields, and the user enters a value for each field. Hence, both when entering a new file and when creating a new record, the system displays the parameters associated with each command and shows the user how to enter values for these parameters.

Using the Personal Database

Most personal computer DBMSs include facilities for accessing the database and generating reports. Such facilities are oriented toward the nonprogrammer user. Hence they do not expect the user to have a comprehensive computing background. They enable a relatively inexperienced user to begin by employing

CREATE:_____User

ENTER FILE NAME: B:STORES

Computer response   User

ENTER RECORD STRUCTURE AS FOLLOWS: } Computer
                                              system
    FIELD   NAME, TYPE, WIDTH, DECIMAL PLACES
    001   STORE-ID, C, 6
    002   PHONE, N, 8
    003   NO-BINS, N, 4
    004   CITY, C, 20
    005

    Computer   User
    system

INPUT DATA NOW (Y/N) ? Y

RECORD #0001
STORE-ID   : ST-A
PHONE   : 667932
NO-BINS   : 200
CITY   : ALBANY

    Computer   User
    system

Figure 11.31   Defining a database and adding a new tuple

an elementary subset of database access commands and then, with experience, to proceed to the more sophisticated features. Hence access languages do not, for example, require variable declarations, because these can confuse an experienced user. Thus the system dBASE-II contains three major components to allow database access (Figure 11.32):

- a query processor to support on-line *ad hoc* queries
- a simple procedural language to store preprogrammed queries
- a report generator

Query Processor

The query processor supports a SQL-like language but restricts its application to one file or relation; hence nested queries are not supported. The usual approach is to first identify the file to be queried. Then the queries are input.

Some examples of such queries follow. They refer to the relations in Figure App. 3 in the appendix. The simplest queries are those that select particular tuples. For example, a command to retrieve all the BOSTON stores with more than 100 BINS would be

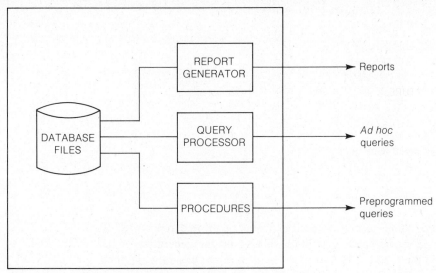

Figure 11.32   Using the personal database

USE STORES
DISPLAY STORE-ID FOR LOCATED-IN-CITY =
                          'BOSTON'.AND.NO-BINS > 100

Some arithmetic functions are also provided. For example,

USE ORDERS
COUNT FOR CUST-NAME = 'JILL'

would display the number of orders made by JILL. Similarly,

USE HOLD
SUM QTY-HELD FOR ITEM-ID = 'I3'

would display the total holding of item I3.

Procedural Language

dBASE-II provides a procedural language to enable preprogrammed queries to
be specified. The preprogrammed query shown in Figure 11.33 computes the
number of stores (STORENO) that hold more than 150 of I3 (Figure App. 3 in
the appendix). It also outputs the total holding of I3 in those stores. Thus the
output from this program, given the data in Figure App. 3, would be

NUMBER OF STORES   2
TOTAL HOLDING   800

The procedural language includes the ability to create loops (by the DO
statement) and to make conditional jumps (by the IF statement). Users can
create files that hold such procedures and then execute them as required.

```
USE HOLD
STORE 0 TO TOTALS, STORENO
DO WHILE.NOT.EOF
    IF QTY-HELD > 150 AND ITEM-ID = I3
        STORENO + 1 TO STORENO
        TOTALS + QTY-HELD TO TOTALS
    ENDIF
SKIP
ENDDO
? 'NUMBER OF STORES', STORENO
? 'TOTAL HOLDING', TOTALS
```

Figure 11.33   A preprogrammed query

Report Generator

The report generator allows users to specify layouts of printed reports. Such specifications include report heading, column width, and the generation of totals and subtotals in the report. The user must create a report program and then execute it as required. The program is created in an interactive node with guidance provided by the report generator software.

Some Advanced Facilities

Some of the more advanced personal DBMSs include facilities to

• create indices to files
• join existing files

Creating an Index

In dBASE-II an index is defined by first selecting a file and then nominating the index. For example,

    USE STORES
    INDEX ON STORE-ID TO ACCESS

would create an index named ACCESS to file STORES, using STORE-ID as the key. There can be more than one index in the same file. The index can be used to directly access file records. For example, the commands to find details about store ST-A (Figure App. 3 in the appendix) are

    USE STORES INDEX ACCESS   specifies use of an index
    LOCATE FOR STORE-ID = ST-A   positions the file
    DISPLAY   displays found record

Joining Two Files

To obtain information from two files, a user must first join the two files. A new file is created during the join. For example, consider the relations in Figure App. 3 in the appendix. If the user wishes to know the items ordered by a particular customer, relations ORDERS and ITEMS-ORDERED must first be joined across ORDER-NO. The joined relation need contain only fields CUST-NAME and ITEM-ID. The commands to create the joined file are

USE ORDERS   nominates the first file to be joined
SELECT SECONDARY }
USE ITEMS-ORDERED }   nominates the second file to be joined
JOIN TO TERM FOR ORDER-NO = S.ORDER-NO; } joins the
      FIELD CUST-NAME, ITEM-ID } files

The user could now make ad-hoc inquiries from the newly created file TERM.

SUMMARY

In the development of relational DBMSs, significant differences have evolved among DBMSs that support the same data model. The three DBMSs described in this chapter support different access languages, data definition facilities, and operational environments.

System R, one of the first relational DBMS systems, includes all the facilities normally expected of a DBMS, together with support for a multi-user operational environment. Its interface is based on the language SQL and is able either to access databases on-line by using SQL or to embed SQL in a host language.

Query-by-Example provides a totally different interface, one that is graphical and predominantly aimed at a nonprogrammer user. This interface allows the user to specify a query by using an example table. The system then responds by returning values of attributes. Because the interface is graphical, it cannot be embedded in a host language. The selective power of languages used on System R and QBE is about the same.

Finally, the kinds of DBMSs provided on personal systems usually contain a narrower set of facilities, including less powerful access languages and minimum user view support. Such restrictions are necessary because of the less powerful computer systems that support personal DBMSs. Usually personal DBMSs are supported by microprocessor systems, which in turn possess less processing capabilities as well as longer disk-device access times.

PROBLEMS

Problem 1

Given the data in Figure App. 3 in the appendix, develop a program with embedded SQL to determine the items held in stores located in the same city as the city in which a given customer lives.

Problem 2

Given the data in the appendix, assume that each relation in Figure App. 3 has been defined as a System R relation. Define user views for the following relations:

(a) VIEW 1 (CUST-NAME, ITEM-ID), showing the items ordered by each customer
(b) VIEW 2 (CITY, NO-BINS), showing the total number of storage bins in each city

Problem 3

Refer to Figure App. 3 in the appendix and formulate the following queries, using Query-by-Example:

(a) the STORE-ID of BOSTON stores
(b) the ITEM-IDs of all WINDOW items that weigh more than 14
(c) the ITEM-IDs ordered by JILL
(d) the HDQ-ADDRESS of stores that hold SMALL WINDOWs
(e) the total quantity of I1 held in BOSTON stores (from relation STORES and HOLD)
(f) the stores that hold all the items heavier than 10
(g) any store that holds all the items in order ORD1

chapter twelve
Network Data Model

INTRODUCTION

This chapter will describe the network data model and its implementation. The implementation is significant in that it was the first attempt made at a database standard. This standard was proposed in 1971 by the DBTG (Data Base Task Group) of the CODASYL Committee. Since 1970, there have been some network implementations that have adhered to the standard (although loosely in some cases). Proposals have been made to change the detailed syntax, although not the basic structure, of the DBTG standard. This text will use the syntax proposed in the 1971 DBTG report but outline some of the recommended changes.

THE NETWORK MODEL

The network model is based on the set construct. The term *set* in the network model differs from its meaning in the mathematical sense. The mathematical set is usually made of objects from one well-defined object class. The network set construct, on the other hand, is made up of objects from two object classes: the owner and the member object class. Further, each set consists of only one object from the owner object class and any number of objects from a member object class. For this reason the term *owner-coupled set* is often used to distinguish the network set from the mathematical set. Moreover, in network model literature it is also common to use the term *set occurrence* rather than set. A set occurrence consists of one object from the owner object class and any number of objects (including none) from the member object class. Set occurrences can be grouped into set classes. All set occurrences of the same set class have

- an owner from the same owner object set
- members from the same member object set

Figure 12.1 illustrates some set occurrences of set class ASSIGNED-TO. In these set occurrences, PERSON objects are grouped by the DEPT where these

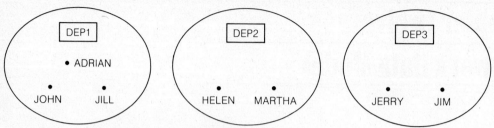

Figure 12.1 Occurrence of set class ASSIGNED-TO

persons work. Thus there are three DEPT objects: DEP1, DEP2, and DEP3. There are also seven PERSON objects. Each DEPT object is an owner of an ASSIGNED-TO set occurrence. The members of that occurrence are persons who work in the department. Thus ADRIAN, JOHN, and JILL work in DEP1, whereas HELEN and MARTHA work in DEP2.

The network model of a system is diagrammatically represented by a data structure diagram, which was first introduced by C. W. Bachman (1969). In this diagram the owner and member classes entities in the network model are represented by rectangular boxes. The owner-member relationship is represented by a line from the owner to member. Thus the data structure diagram in Figure 12.2 represents the set class ASSIGNED-TO of Figure 12.1. Here DEPT is the owner object class, and PERSON is the member object class. The link from owner to member represents the set relationship, which is given the name ASSIGNED-TO. Each occurrence of ASSIGNED-TO consists of one DEPT object and any number of PERSON objects.

The network model does not place any restrictions on the number of object classes and set classes. Neither does it place any restrictions on the participation of object classes as owners or members of different set classes. It is, for example, possible to have a hierarchy of object sets, as shown in Figure 12.3. Here there are three object classes: DEPTS, PROJECTS, and PERSONS. DEPTS manage PROJECTS, which in turn have PERSONS working in them. There are two set classes: MANAGE and WORK. Each MANAGE set occurrence is

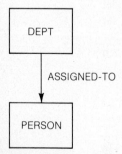

Figure 12.2 A network structure

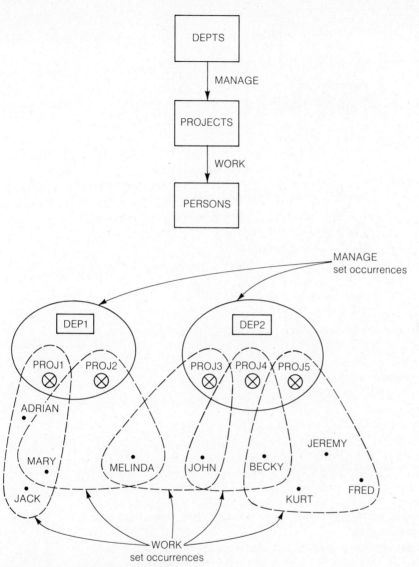

Figure 12.3 A hierarchy of object sets

owned by one DEPT and contains as members all **PROJECTS** managed by that DEPT. Thus DEP1 manages PROJ1 and PROJ2.

The next level of the hierarchy is **PROJECTS** hiring **PERSONS**. Now **PROJECTS** objects are owners of WORK set occurrences. They own **PERSONS** hired for a project. Note that in this figure some persons work on more than one project (e.g., MARY works on PROJ1 and PROJ2). Hence they appear in more than one WORK set occurrence. Later it will be seen that some

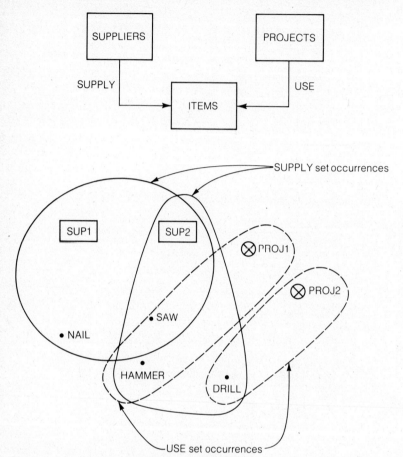

Figure 12.4 Objects with more than one owner

implementations prevent an object appearing as a member of more than one occurrence of the same set class.

Another common set structure is an object that appears in set occurrences from different classes. In this case the object has more than one owner, and each such owner can be in a different set class. For example, in Figure 12.4 there are two set classes: SUPPLY and USE. Set occurrences of both classes contain ITEMS as members. Set occurrences of SUPPLY are owned by SUPPLIERS objects and include all ITEMS supplied by the SUPPLIERS objects.

Set occurrences of USE are owned by PROJECTS and include all ITEMS used by a project. The object SAW has both SUPPLIERS and PROJECTS owners. It is owned by SUP1 and SUP2 in SUPPLY set occurrences, because it is supplied by SUP1 and SUP2. It is also owned by PROJ1 in a USE set occurrence, because it is used by PROJ1.

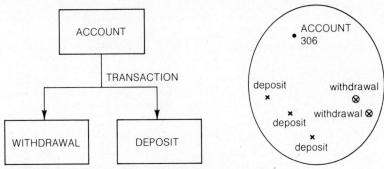

Figure 12.5   Members from more than one entity class

More Elaborate Network Model Constructs

The network model set construct can be extended to more elaborate structures. The most obvious extensions are as follows:

- To allow member objects in a given set occurrence class to come from more than one object class. Thus in Figure 12.5, set occurrences of the set class **TRANSACTION** are owned by one ACCOUNT object. They can include as members DEPOSITs and WITHDRAWALs made for this account.

- To allow an owner object in a set class to come from alternate object classes. Thus in Figure 12.6 the owner of OWN set occurrences can be either an IN-DIVIDUAL object or a COMPANY object (but not both). Each such object can own any number of VEHICLE objects.

- To allow a combination of the two preceding extensions. Now set occurrence owners can come from alternate object classes, and set occurrence members

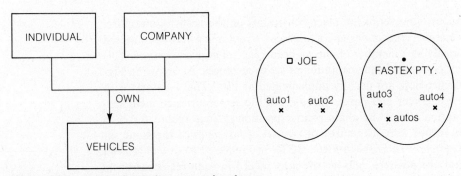

Figure 12.6   Owners from alternate entity classes

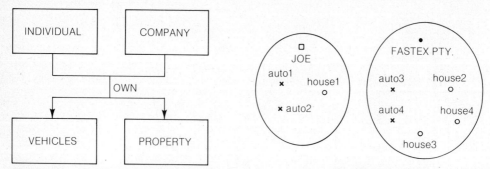

Figure 12.7 Owners from alternate entity classes, members from more than one entity class

can come from more than one object class. Thus in Figure 12.7 the owner of each OWN set occurrence can be either an INDIVIDUAL object or a COMPANY object. Its members can be VEHICLE or PROPERTY objects.

Implementations of the network model usually place restrictions on the kind of network construct that they support.

NETWORK MODEL IMPLEMENTATIONS

Implementations of the network model are record-based. Each object is implemented as a record, and a set occurrence is implemented by linking all the records in the set occurrence. Record-based network model implementations refer to object classes as record types and to set classes as set types. Thus the data structure diagrams of Figures 12.2, 12.3, and 12.4 equally represent a network model as well as a network implementation. In an implementation each rectangular box is called a *record type,* and each link between boxes is known as a *set type.*

Implementations, however, often place constraints on the network structure. Most implementations restrict designers to choose structures where each record occurrence can only be a member of one set occurrence of a given set type. This is a requirement of the list implementation of set occurrences. As shown in Figure 12.8, set occurrences are usually implemented as lists. The list starts with the set occurrence owner and passes through all the set occurrence members. The implementation allows one chain pointer position in each record for each set type. If the record were a member of two set occurrences of the same set type (as, for example, PERSON in PROJECTS in Figure 12.3), it would need to accommodate two pointers, one for the next record in each set occurrence. This cannot be done, however, because only one pointer field is provided for each set type in the record.

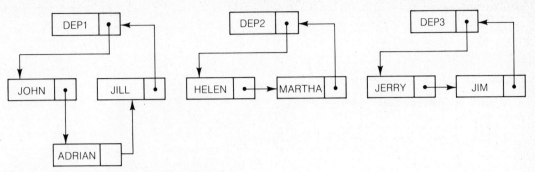

Figure 12.8   A list implementation of set types

How, then, can we implement such *N:M* relationships? In a network model we can do so by representing an *N:M* relationship by two set types. For example, take the case where a PERSON can work on any number of PROJECTs and a PROJECT can have any number of PERSONs working on it. Neither of the two structures shown in Figure 12.9 can be used to represent this enterprise. If the representation with PROJECTS as owner were chosen, a PERSONS record would appear in more than one occurrence of WORKERS, because a person can work on more than one project.

If the representation with PERSONS as owner were chosen, then a PROJ-ECTS record would appear in more than one occurrence of WORKED-ON, since a project has more than one person working on it.

A network representation that resolves this problem is shown in Figure 12.10. Now there is one record occurrence of WORK for each person-project combination. The term *intersection record* is often used to refer to records that represent relationships between two other records. It contains intersection data common to these records. For example, TIME-SPENT by a person on a project would appear in the intersection record WORK. Each WORK record occurrence will appear in one WORKERS set occurrence and one WORKED-ON set occurrence.

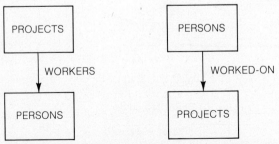

Figure 12.9   Invalid representation of *N:M* relationships

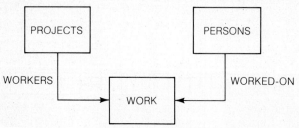

Figure 12.10   A valid representation of an *N:M* relationship

An example of such set occurrences is given in Figure 12.11. Here there are two WORKERS set type occurrences and three WORKED-ON set type occurrences. Each WORKERS occurrence is owned by one PROJECTS record; its members are the activities on that project. Thus the WORKERS set occurrence owned by PROJ1 has two members, w1 and w2. Record w1 represents JACK's activity on PROJ1, and record w2 represents MARY's activity on PROJ1. Each WORKED-ON occurrence is owned by a PERSONS record; its members are the activities of that person. Thus the WORKED-ON occurrence owned by MARY has two members, w2 and w3. Record w2 represents MARY's activity on PROJ1, and record w3 represents MARY's activity on PROJ2. Note that each WORK record participates in only one WORKERS set occurrence and only one WORKED-ON set occurrence.

A list implementation of Figure 12.11 is shown in Figure 12.12. Here each work record has provision for two pointers, one for the WORKERS set type and the other for the WORKED-ON set type. There is a list that starts at a set occurrence owner and links all set occurrence members. Thus the WORKERS

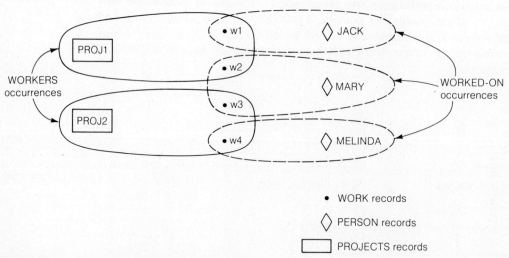

Figure 12.11   Set occurrences in *N:M* relationships

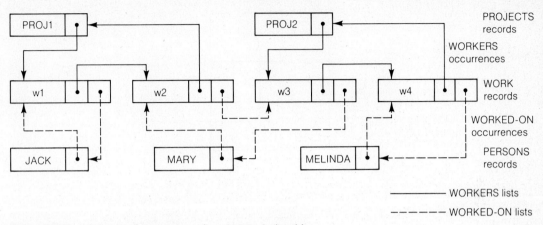

Figure 12.12 A list implementation of an *N:M* relationship

set occurrence owned by PROJ1 starts at PROJ1 and links PROJ1 to w1 and w2 and back to PROJ1. The WORKED-ON set occurrence owned by MARY commences a list with record MARY and links it to w2, then w3, and back to MARY.

Another implementation constraint prevents records of the same type from being both members and owners of the same set type. Set types of this kind would be used to model parts explosions. In Figure 12.13, for example, all objects are PARTS; each part can be an assembly made of any quantity of other parts. This quantity appears on the label between the assembly and the component. Thus an AUTO is an assembly made up of two components: one

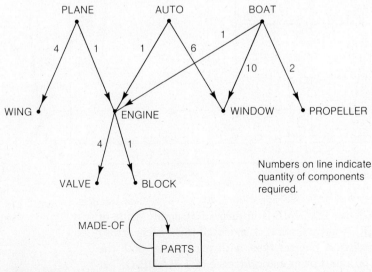

Figure 12.13 A parts explosion

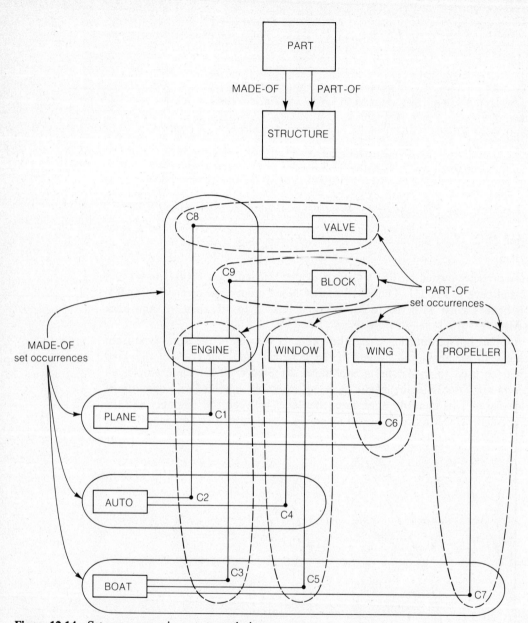

Figure 12.14   Set occurrences in a parts explosion

ENGINE and six WINDOWS. An ENGINE is in turn an assembly made of
four VALVEs and one BLOCK. A natural network model of this system is also
shown in Figure 12.13. It consists of one set type, with parts being both the
owner and the member. That is, a part owns an occurrence of a MADE-OF set
type; the members of that set occurrence are the components of that part.

The usual way to model this structure in implementations is by the network model in Figure 12.14. A new record type, STRUCTURE, is introduced. There is one STRUCTURE record for each component-assembly combination (or for each line joining two parts in Figure 12.13). It would contain intersection data such as the QTY of each component in the assembly.

Figure 12.14 also illustrates MADE-OF and PART-OF set occurrences. Each MADE-OF set occurrence is owned by one part and contains all the assembly-component combinations with that part as an assembly. Thus ENGINE owns the members C8 and C9 in a MADE-OF set occurrence. The PART-OF owners of C8 and C9 are VALVE and BLOCK, which are components of ENGINE. Each PART-OF set occurrence is owned by one part and contains all the assembly-component combinations with that part as a component. Now engine owns C1, C2, and C3 in a PART-OF set. The MADE-OF owners of C1, C2, and C3 are PLANE, AUTO, and BOAT, which have ENGINE as one of their components.

The list implementation of this structure is shown in Figure 12.15. The intersection records, WORK, contain the QTY of each component in the assembly.

Accessing Records in a Network Database

The term *navigation* is often used to describe accessing methods in the network model. The idea behind navigation is that access can begin at any object in the network and travel along the sets to other objects. Thus, to find all the projects on which a person worked in Figure 12.10 or 12.12, we would proceed as follows:

- Start at the person record.
- Follow the list of all WORKED-ON members for that record.
- Find the WORKERS owner for each WORKED-ON member (by following the WORKERS list).

Implementations provide commands that enable a program to navigate between record types by traversing set types. Thus a possible program structure to find the projects on which a person worked would be

```
FIND PERSON WITH NAME = 'x'
REPEAT FOR ALL WORK RECORDS OWNED BY PERSON
   BEGIN
      FIND NEXT WORK RECORD
      FIND WORKERS OWNER OF WORK RECORD
      OUTPUT PROJECT
   END
```

In this way a program can start at any point on the network and find any related objects by the use of owner and members of set type relationships.

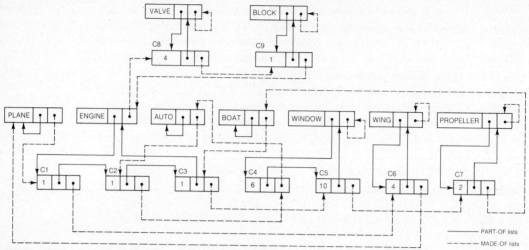

Figure 12.15 List implementation of a parts explosion

Thus the preceding program starts at a PERSON record with a given name. Each time that FIND NEXT WORK RECORD is executed, the program proceeds to the next record in the WORK list. When FIND WORKERS OWNER OF WORK RECORD is executed, the program finds the PROJECT owner of the current WORK record. This project owner is output by the program.

THE DBTG IMPLEMENTATION

The early ideas on data structuring revolved around list processing and were not amenable to the practical environment of the 1960s. The Data Base Task Group was set up in 1967, under the sponsorship of the CODASYL Committee, to develop a database capability for the COBOL language. Its goal was to incorporate some of the early ideas on data structuring into a form suitable for data processing.

In 1971 the DBTG produced what is now called the DBTG report. This report proposed the architecture shown in Figure 12.16 and already discussed to some extent in Chapter 10. This architecture includes

- A Data Definition Language (DDL) to define the entire database. This data definition is called the *schema*.

- A definition language to define a program view of the database. This view is called the *subschema*. A different subschema can be defined for each application program.

- A DML (Data Manipulation Language) to be embedded in COBOL. It provides commands to access the database.

The orientation of this report was predominantly COBOL. It proposed an environment where a database administrator is responsible for the database. The database administrator (or database administration group) defines the entire database. Subsequently, the database administrator defines the subschema for particular applications. Application groups then develop programs. The programs use the DML commands to access the database parts defined in the program subschema.

The DBTG disbanded in 1971 and its work was allocated to the following two groups:

1. The DDLC (Data Description Language Committee), which was to take responsibility for the schema definition language.
2. The DBLTG (Data Base Language Task Group) of the PLC (Programming Language Committee of CODASYL) which was to take responsibility for the Data Manipulation Language. Its goal was to develop the DML for inclusion in the *CODASYL COBOL Journal of Development (JOD)*.

The DDLC produced its first report in 1973. This report was very similar to the 1971 DBTG report. It was subsequently used (albeit in an adapted form) by the DBLTG to define a new specification for the subschema and DDL facilities in COBOL. Some of these recommendations were included in the *CODASYL COBOL Journal of Development* in 1976. During this time the ANSI report recommending the three-level architecture became widely publicized. Its rec-

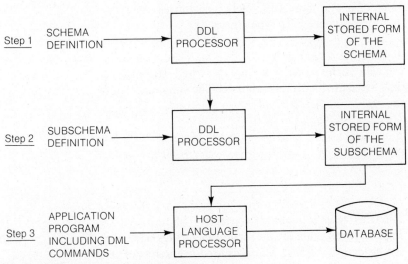

Figure 12.16 Schema and subschema

ommendation that the logical and the physical definitions of the database be separated renewed criticism of the single-schema approach used by the DBTG and carried on by the DDLC in 1973. In 1978 a new report was produced both by the DDLC and by DBLTG. A major contribution of the DDLC was to separate the database definition into two parts: the DDL to define the logical structure of the database and the Data Storage Definition Language (DSDL) to define its physical structure. The goal of this change was to improve data independence by separating the physical storage definition from the logical structure.

The DDLC report produced in 1978 was sent to ANSI to be considered as a standard. Some parts of it were considered unsatisfactory, and further changes can no doubt be expected before a standard is adopted.

The remainder of this chapter will concentrate on the 1971 DBTG report since it is adhered to in many implementations. However, the chapter will also describe some of the changes suggested in the later proposals, so that you will get some idea of the general trend in network model implementation.

The DBTG Schema

An example of a DBTG schema definition is given in Figure 12.17. It defines the network data structure shown in Figure 12.18. The schema consists of four major sections:

1. an introductory clause
2. an area section made up of one or more AREA entries
3. a record section made up of one or more RECORD type entries
4. a set section made up of one or more SET type entries

The sections appear in the schema in that order.

The introductory clause defines the name of the database and various security and privacy constraints associated with the database. The simplest form of this clause takes the form

SCHEMA NAME IS PROJECT-DATA

AREAS or REALMS

The terms AREA and REALM refer to identical concepts. The term AREA was used in the initial DBTG report; subsequent modification suggested that the term REALM be used instead of AREA. AREA is used in the rest of this text since this is the term that is still prevalent in most implementations.

```
SCHEMA NAME IS PROJECT-DATA. ──────Introductory clause
AREA NAME IS AREA1, AREA2. ─────────Area entry
RECORD NAME IS PROJECTS
      WITHIN AREA1
      LOCATION MODE IS CALC USING PROJ-ID.
      02 PROJ-ID PIC IS 9(6).
      02 PROJ-DETAILS PIC IS X(20).

RECORD NAME IS PERSONS
      WITHIN AREA1
      LOCATION MODE IS CALC USING PERSON-ID.
      02 PERSON-ID PIC IS 9(8).
      02 PERSON-DETAILS PIC IS X(30).

RECORD NAME IS WORK
      WITHIN AREA1
      LOCATION MODE IS VIA WORKERS SET.              Record
      02 PROJ-ID PIC IS 9(6).                        type
      02 PERSON-ID PIC IS 9(8).                      entries
      02 TIME-SPENT PIC IS 9(6).

RECORD NAME IS TASKS
      WITHIN AREA2
      LOCATION MODE IS VIA PROJ-DETAILS SET.
      02 TASK-NO PIC IS 9(8).
      02 TASK-START-DATE PIC IS 9(6).

RECORD NAME IS EXPENSES
      WITHIN AREA2
      LOCATION MODE IS VIA PROJ-DETAILS SET.
      02 EXPENSE-NO PIC IS 9(8).
      02 DATE-INCURRED PIC IS 9(6).

SET NAME IS WORKERS
      MODE IS CHAIN LINKED TO PRIOR
      ORDER IS SORTED INDEXED BY DEFINED KEY
      OWNER IS PROJECTS
      MEMBER IS WORK AUTOMATIC MANDATORY
      ASCENDING KEY IS PERSON-ID
      SET OCCURRENCE SELECTION IS LOCATION MODE OF OWNER.

SET NAME IS WORKED-ON
      MODE IS CHAIN
      ORDER IS FIRST
      OWNER IS PERSONS                                       Set
      MEMBER IS WORK LINKED TO OWNER MANUAL OPTIONAL         type
      SEARCH KEY IS PROJ-ID USING CALC                       entries
      SET OCCURRENCE SELECTION IS THRU CURRENT OF SET.

SET NAME IS PROJ-DETAILS
      MODE IS CHAIN
      ORDER IS SORTED BY RECORD NAME
      OWNER IS PROJECTS
      MEMBER IS TASKS MANUAL MANDATORY
      ASCENDING KEY IS TASK-START-DATE
      MEMBER IS EXPENSES MANUAL OPTIONAL
      ASCENDING KEY IS EXPENSE-NO
      SET OCCURRENCE SELECTION IS THRU CURRENT OF SET.
```

Figure 12.17   A DBTG network database definition

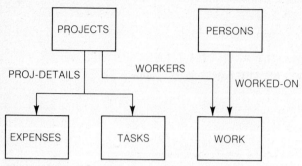

Figure 12.18 Data structure diagram of the database defined in Figure 12.17

Areas allow designers to control the placement of records or sets on physical devices. A record type, for example, can be assigned to a particular AREA; this area is then assigned to particular physical devices using the JCL (Job Control Language), as shown in Figure 12.19.

It is possible to assign records of a given type to more than one area. Programs are free to store a record occurrence in one of these areas.

There is one area entry in the schema for each area. The simplest form of an area entry is

AREA NAME IS area-name

The 1971 DBTG report recommended other clauses to be part of the AREA definition. Security and integrity constraints or specific recovery techniques for each area are specified by some implementations. Another clause was to allow areas to be defined as TEMPORARY. Some implementations also include specification of pages sizes and blocking in the area clause.

It has been suggested that AREA and REALM not appear in the DDL because they define physical structure. The storage mappings defined by the AREA clause could therefore be relegated to the DSDL. The DSDL proposes STORAGE AREA entries for this purpose.

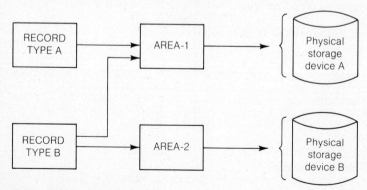

Figure 12.19 Area allocation

Record Entries

There is a record entry for each record type in the database. All record entries precede the first set entry. The record and set entry definition syntax is described in Figure 12.20.

The record entry for a record type contains

1. a description of record occurrences
2. the areas in which the record occurrences are to be placed
3. the method to be used to place and retrieve record occurrences

Description of Record Occurrences

The record occurrence is described by the items in each record occurrence. Item descriptions are the same as those used in COBOL; each item is defined at a given level (02 in Figure 12.17) and is given a name; a picture clause defines the size and type of item.

Areas of Record Placement

The area in which a record is placed is specified by the WITHIN clause in the record entry. This takes the form

WITHIN area-name-1, {area-name-2, ...}

Any number of areas may be specified for the same record type.

Control of Record Placement

The method used to place records is given by the LOCATION MODE clause. Two kinds of placement are possible:

1. CALC, where the record position is located by calculation or hashing. The procedure used for the calculation or hashing is database-procedure-name, and the keys are database-identifier-1, database-identifier-2, and so on. The DUPLICATES clause specifies whether duplicates are to be allowed.
2. VIA set-name SET, whereby the record occurrence is located as closely as possible to its owner occurrence in set-name.

Proposed Development

The 1978 DDL recommendation is to move the specification of control of record placement (in areas and within areas) to the DSDL. A KEY phrase would then be used in the DDL to nominate the logical keys used to access records. Thus the LOCATION MODE phrase is replaced by

RECORD NAME IS record-name

LOCATION MODE IS
$$\begin{Bmatrix} \text{CALC [data-base-procedure-name} \\ \text{IN data-base-data-name]} \\ \text{USING data-base-identifier-1} \\ \text{[, data-base-identifier-2]} \\ \text{DUPLICATES ARE [NOT] ALLOWED} \\ \text{VIA set-name SET} \end{Bmatrix}$$

WITHIN area-name

item-description [;item-description]

SET NAME IS set-name

MODE IS $\begin{Bmatrix} \text{CHAIN [LINKED TO PRIOR]} \\ \text{POINTER-ARRAY [DYNAMIC]} \end{Bmatrix}$

Format 1
ORDER IS $\begin{Bmatrix} \text{FIRST} \\ \text{LAST} \\ \text{NEXT} \\ \text{PRIOR} \\ \text{IMMATERIAL} \end{Bmatrix}$

Format 2
ORDER IS SORTED [INDEXED [NAME IS index-name-1]]

$$\begin{bmatrix} \text{WITHIN RECORD NAME} \\ \text{BY DATA-BASE-KEY} \\ \text{BY RECORD-NAME} \\ \text{BY DEFINED KEYS} \\ \text{DUPLICATES ARE} \\ \qquad \begin{Bmatrix} \text{FIRST} \\ \text{LAST} \\ \text{NOW ALLOWED} \end{Bmatrix} \end{bmatrix}$$

OWNER IS record-name

MEMBER IS record-name $\begin{Bmatrix} \text{MANDATORY} \\ \text{OPTIONAL} \end{Bmatrix}$ $\begin{Bmatrix} \text{AUTOMATIC} \\ \text{MANUAL} \end{Bmatrix}$ [LINKED TO OWNER]

$\begin{bmatrix} \begin{Bmatrix} \text{ASCENDING} \\ \text{DESCENDING} \end{Bmatrix} \text{ KEY IS data-base-identifier-3 [,data-base-identifier-10]} \end{bmatrix}$

DUPLICATES ARE $\begin{Bmatrix} \text{FIRST} \\ \text{LAST} \\ \text{NOT ALLOWED} \end{Bmatrix}$

[SEARCH KEY IS data-base-identified-5[,data-base-identifier-6]...

USING $\begin{bmatrix} \begin{Bmatrix} \text{CALC} \\ \text{INDEX[NAME IS index-name-1]} \end{Bmatrix} \end{bmatrix}$

DUPLICATES ARE [NOT] ALLOWED]

Format 1:
SET OCCURRENCE SELECTION IS THRU

$\begin{Bmatrix} \text{CURRENT OF SET} \\ \text{LOCATION MODE OF OWNER} \begin{Bmatrix} \text{USING data-base-identifier 4 ,} \\ \text{[,data-base-identifier-5]} \end{Bmatrix} \end{Bmatrix}$

Format 2:
SET OCCURRENCE SELECTION IS THRU set-name-2 USING

$\begin{Bmatrix} \text{CURRENT OF SET} \\ \text{LOCATION MODE OF OWNER} \begin{Bmatrix} \text{USING data-base-identifier-6} \\ \text{[,data-base-identifier-7]} \end{Bmatrix} \end{Bmatrix}$

$\begin{Bmatrix} \text{set-name-3} \begin{Bmatrix} \text{USING data-base-identifier-8} \\ \text{[,data-base-identifier-9]} \end{Bmatrix} \end{Bmatrix}$

Figure 12.20   Record and set entries

KEY GETPROJ IS ASCENDING PROJ-ID
   DUPLICATES ARE NOT ALLOWED
   FREQUENCY OF DIRECT RETRIEVAL IS HIGH

This phrase defines a key named GETPROJ. This key uses field PROJ-ID to directly access records. It also prohibits the occurrence of two records with the same PROJ-ID value, because DUPLICATES are not allowed. Any number of key fields can be defined for the one record type.

Set Entries

The database definition contains one set entry for each set type. The set entry for a set type specifies the following:

1. The owner record type of the set type
2. The member record types of the set type
3. The physical MODE used to link record occurrences within the same set occurrence
4. The ORDER in which member record occurrences are to be stored in a set occurrence
5. Classes of membership
6. The method used to select member record occurrence within a set occurrence. This method is defined by the set occurrence selection phrase.

Owner and Member Record Types

Each set type may have only one owner record type, but it can have any number of member record types. The most common set type includes only one member record type, each set occurrence being made up of

- one owner record occurrence of the owner record type
- any number of occurrences of the member record type

Record member and owner types of a set type are defined by the OWNER and MEMBER clauses. Thus

OWNER IS PROJECTS
MEMBER IS WORK

is part of the definition of set type WORKERS. This clause defines that PROJ-ECTS records own occurrences of set type WORKERS; WORK records are members of these set occurrences.

Singular Sets

A singular set type is a set type whose OWNER is SYSTEM. There can be only one occurrence of such a set type because it has a unique owner, the SYSTEM. The singular set can be used to order all records of a particular type for sequential access.

Multimember Set Types

Multimember set types have more than one record type as a member of the same set type. Occurrences of this set type may include member records from more than one record type.

   PROJ-DETAILS in Figure 12.17 is a multimember set type. Its definition includes

> **OWNER IS PROJECTS**
> **MEMBER IS TASKS**
> **MEMBER IS EXPENSES**

An occurrence of this set type can include both TASK and EXPENSE records, as in Figure 12.21.

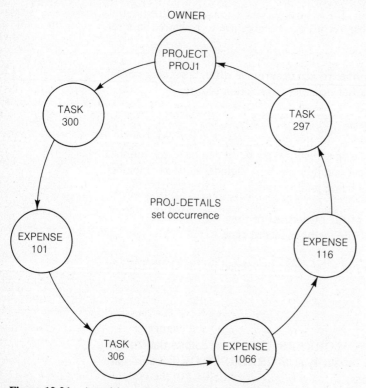

Figure 12.21   A multimember record set occurrence

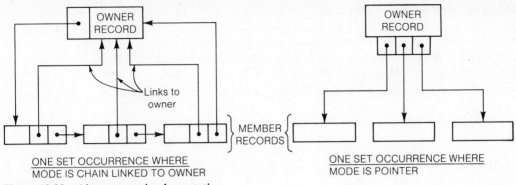

ONE SET OCCURRENCE WHERE
MODE IS CHAIN LINKED TO OWNER

ONE SET OCCURRENCE WHERE
MODE IS POINTER

Figure 12.22   Alternate set implementations

Physical Storage Mode

The DBTG recommended that sets be implemented either as CHAINs or as POINTER ARRAYs. The difference in these two methods is illustrated in Figure 12.22. When the CHAIN mode is used, all member records in a set occurrence are stored as a linked list that commences with the owner record. The POINTER mode requires all pointers to member record occurrences to be stored in the owner record. Thus in the CHAIN mode the pointers are distributed among the record types, whereas in the POINTER mode all the pointers are in the one record. Owner records in the POINTER mode can be of variable size since set occurrences can contain a variable number of members. Most implementations use chains to implement sets.

Some additional physical options are recommended by the DBTG, in particular,

1. a LINK TO OWNER clause, which establishes a physical link from each member record to its owner in the set occurrence (as illustrated in Figure 12.22)

2. a LINK TO PRIOR clause (in the CHAIN mode), which establishes pointers in two directions of the list for each set occurrence

Database access commands do not explicitly use the physical storage options. Hence the commands to access particular records need not change if new pointer options are added. But the performance, in terms of time taken to execute the commands, may depend on the chosen physical structure. For this reason the 1978 DDLC report proposes that these options be defined in the DSDL. A DSDL change should not affect logical processing.

Order of Member Records within a Set Occurrence

The order of member records in set occurrences is defined by the ORDER clause. Two formats of ORDER clause, chronological order (format 1) and SORTED order (format 2), were proposed by DBTG.

Set members in chronological sets can be ordered in one of the following ways:

1. **FIRST**   A new record is always inserted following the owner record.
2. **LAST**   A new record is always inserted following the last member record currently in the set occurrence.
3. **NEXT**   A new record is always inserted after the last member record retrieved or stored by the system.
4. **PRIOR**   A new record is always inserted before the last member record retrieved or stored by the system.
5. **IMMATERIAL**   A new record may be stored in the order most convenient to the DBMS.

SORTED Orders for Single-member Set Types   Sorting is specified as BY DEFINED KEY, and the sort key must be specified by database-identifier-3. Member records can be stored in descending or ascending order of key. The DUPLICATES clause specifies whether more than one record with the same value of the sort key can exist in the same set occurrence. For example, the sort order in WORKERS is specified as

ORDER IS SORTED BY DEFINED KEY
ASCENDING KEY IS PERSON-ID

WORK member records in WORKERS set occurrences will be stored in the order of PERSON-ID. An example is given in Figure 12.23.

SORTED Orders for Multimember Set Types   Three additional options are available for sorting multimember record type sets:

1. SORTED BY RECORD NAME
   Here the record name itself is used as the major sort key. The designer can also specify minor keys for any of the record types. Thus PROJ-DETAIL set type in Figure 12.17 is defined as

   ORDER IS SORTED BY RECORD NAME

Now EXPENSES record types will precede TASKS record types in set occurrences. If TASK-START-DATE is chosen as a minor key by

   ASCENDING KEY IS TASK-START-DATE

then all the TASKS records will be stored in TASK-START-DATE order. Similarly, if EXPENSE-NO is chosen as the sort key for EXPENSES, then

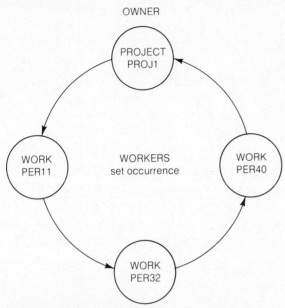

Figure 12.23 A single-member set occurrence

EXPENSES records are stored in EXPENSE-NO sequence. Figure 12.24 is an example.

2. **SORTED BY DEFINED KEYS**

Here items that can be sensibly compared in all member record types are chosen as sort keys; for example, TASK-START-DATE for TASKS records and DATE-INCURRED for EXPENSES records. Record of different types will now be intermingled in set occurrences and stored in order of the chosen keys. For an example, examine Figure 12.25. Here all member records are in date order.

3. **WITHIN RECORD NAME**

Here each member record has its own sort key. The sort keys, however, are not minor to the record type. The result is that records occurrences within a particular type are stored in the order of their key. But records of different types are intermingled within set occurrences. Thus in Figure 12.26 all EXPENSES records are in date order, and so are all TASKS records. However, both of these types of records are randomly intermingled.

Set Membership Class

The membership of records in a set can be specified as being MANDATORY or OPTIONAL and AUTOMATIC or MANUAL. If the member record has

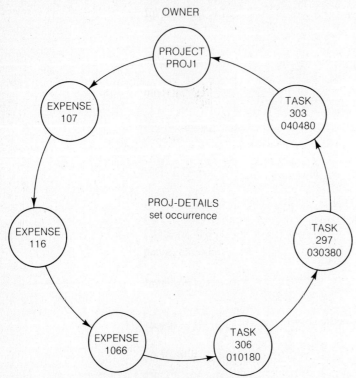

Figure 12.24 SORTED BY RECORD NAME

AUTOMATIC membership in a set, that record is inserted into a set occurrence at the time it is stored. MANUAL membership requires a record to be INSERTED into the set after it is stored. An example of MANUAL membership is that of the TASKS record in PROJ-DETAILS: a TASKS record is allowed to be stored without insertion into any occurrence of set PROJ-DETAILS. MANUAL membership models the fact that a task may be started without initially being assigned to a project. As soon as the assignment is made, the TASKS record is inserted into the appropriate PROJ-DETAILS occurrences by using the INSERT statement.

MANDATORY set membership requires that a record once placed in a set occurrence cannot be REMOVED from the set occurrence. It can, however, be moved to another occurrence of the same set type. OPTIONAL membership, on the other hand, allows us to REMOVE records from set occurrences and still retain them in the database. Thus EXPENSES in PROJ-DETAILS are OPTIONAL. An EXPENSES record can be removed from all occurrences of PROJ-DETAILS. An expense can therefore exist without being credited to any project.

The DDLC proposal includes another and stronger membership class, FIXED. This is stronger than MANDATORY because now a member can neither be

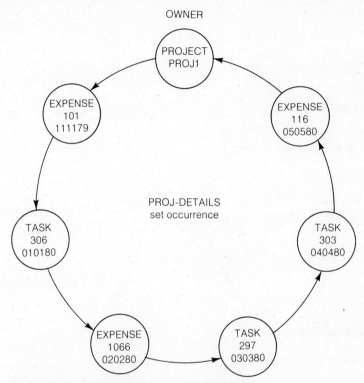

Figure 12.25 SORTED BY DEFINED KEYS

removed from a set occurrence nor be moved to another set occurrence of the same type.

A general rule is to use AUTOMATIC membership for intersection records. For example, consider Figure 12.27. Here the WORK record contains one field only, TIME-SPENT. Storing a record with only this one field value would be meaningless unless it is associated with a PERSON or PROJECT. Hence intersection records like WORK in Figure 12.27 should be AUTOMATIC MANDATORY records in SET-1 and SET-2.

The DDLC added the terms RETENTION and CONNECTION to this clause for clarity. Thus CONNECTION can be AUTOMATIC or MANUAL; RETENTION can be MANDATORY, OPTIONAL, or FIXED.

Structural Constraint

The DDLC introduced the idea of a *structural constraint* in set definitions. This structural constraint requires a member record field to equal an owner record field. For example, the WORKERS set entry could contain

STRUCTURAL CONSTRAINT IS
    PROJ-ID EQUAL TO PROJ-ID

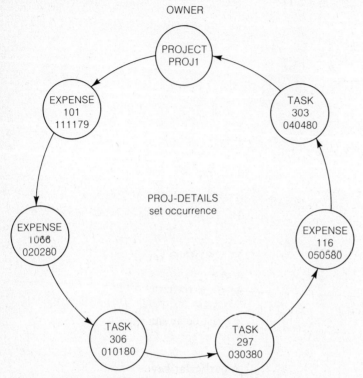

OWNER

PROJ-DETAILS
set occurrence

Figure 12.26   SORTED WITHIN RECORD NAME

The PROJ-ID value of each **WORK** record in a **WORKERS** set occurrence must now be the same as the PROJ-ID value of the owner of that set occurrence.

The structural constraint is used to prevent inconsistencies in the database. A **WORK** record applies to one project. The structural constraint ensures that the **WORK** record is inserted into a set occurrence owned by that project.

Additional Physical Structures

Two physical structures associated with sets are search keys and indices. An index can be created by the INDEXED option of the SORTED order format. The INDEXED option establishes an index to set occurrence records; the index key is the items specified by the ASCENDING or DESCENDING KEY clause. An index can improve performance because it allows a member record in a set occurrence to be retrieved directly, using the sort key. Thus records in **WORKERS** set occurrences in Figure 12.17 are indexed, and hence a member record with a given value of PERSON-ID can be retrieved directly. If records were not indexed and there were a large number of records in each chain, a lengthy search of this chain would be needed to retrieve a record with a given

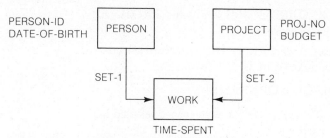

Figure 12.27 A data structure diagram

PERSON-ID value. Thus indexing the set occurrences improves performance, since there is the requirement to access a member record with a given value of sort key.

Search keys can be associated with sets to allow retrieval by using key items other than those specified in the ASCENDING or DESCENDING key clause. Thus in Figure 12.17 a SEARCH-KEY clause is included for WORKED-ON. This will improve performance, given the access requirement to retrieve WORK records within a particular PERSON, using PROJ-ID as a key. The item used as the database-identifier in the SEARCH-KEY clause must be an item in the set member record. The search key may be implemented either as CALC or as INDEX.

If CALC is chosen as a search key, the record with a particular key value is found by using a randomizing procedure. Note that CALC cannot be used with a search key if the LOCATION MODE of the indexed member record is also CALC. In this case the two CALC procedures (one in SEARCH-KEY and one in LOCATION-MODE) may hash to different locations, thus creating a system error.

The 1978 recommendations of the DDLC are to remove both the INDEXED and SEARCH-KEY options from the DDL and place them in the DSDL. The goal of this change is to achieve independence between the logical and the physical structure. Indices and search keys can be added to the DSDL without affecting the logical structure of programs.

Accessing a DBTG Network Database

The DBTG proposed DML commands for COBOL to allow COBOL programs to access the database. Primarily the goal of DML commands is to allow programmers to "navigate" a path through the database structure by successively selecting member and owner records. As an initial illustration, consider the data structure in Figure 12.10.

The persons who work on a particular project, 'PROJ1,' can be found by the following procedure:

1. Directly select a record of type PROJECTS with key value PROJ1. A FIND command is available for this purpose.
2. Select all WORK members of the set WORKERS, using the record selected in step 1 as owner. The form of command here is

      FIND NEXT WORK RECORD OF WORKERS SET

3. Find in set occurrence WORKED-ON the owner for each record selected in step 2. The form of the command here is

      FIND OWNER WORKED-ON SET

Languages that allow navigation may include additional and more complex commands. Such commands may

- allow more than one set to be traversed, using one command,
- maintain currency information, or
- allow alternate sequences of retrieval of records within the same set.

The major DML statements recommended by the DBTG are as follows:

FIND   Locates an existing record occurrence.
GET   Places the record located by a FIND statement into the program's working storage.
MODIFY   Modifies a record.
INSERT   Inserts a record into a set occurrence.
REMOVE   Removes a record from a set occurrence.
DELETE   Deletes a record from the database.
STORE   Stores a new record in the database.

The syntax for some of these statements is given in Figure 12.28, which fundamentally follows the original DBTG recommendations.

The concept of navigating the network makes considerable use of the current position of "travel." Each command defines the next record to be traversed, given the current position.

Currency

The notion of *currency* is used to define the current position. While a program is executing, the system maintains a set of currency indicators (or pointers). There can be any number of indicators associated with a typical program (sometimes called *run-unit*). The most important of these are the following three:

1. The *current of run unit*, which is the last record accessed by a program.
2. The *current of record*. There is one current of record for each record type

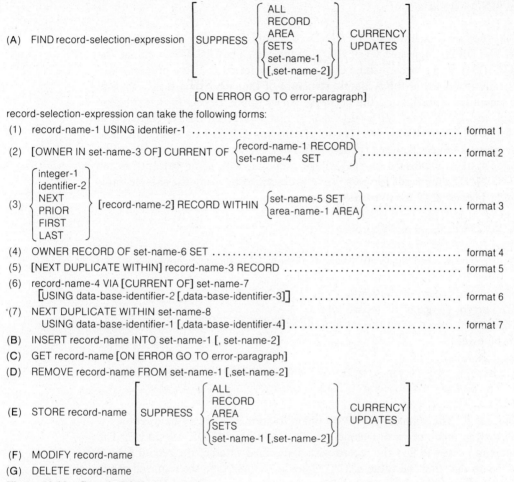

(A)   FIND record-selection-expression ⎡ SUPPRESS ⎧ ALL / RECORD / AREA / ⎰SETS / set-name-1 / [,set-name-2]⎱ ⎫ CURRENCY UPDATES ⎤

[ON ERROR GO TO error-paragraph]

record-selection-expression can take the following forms:

(1)   record-name-1 USING identifier-1 .... format 1

(2)   [OWNER IN set-name-3 OF] CURRENT OF ⎰record-name-1 RECORD / set-name-4   SET⎱ .... format 2

(3)   ⎧integer-1 / identifier-2 / NEXT / PRIOR / FIRST / LAST⎫ [record-name-2] RECORD WITHIN ⎰set-name-5 SET / area-name-1 AREA⎱ .... format 3

(4)   OWNER RECORD OF set-name-6 SET .... format 4

(5)   [NEXT DUPLICATE WITHIN] record-name-3 RECORD .... format 5

(6)   record-name-4 VIA [CURRENT OF] set-name-7
      [USING data-base-identifier-2 [,data-base-identifier-3]] .... format 6

'(7) NEXT DUPLICATE WITHIN set-name-8
      USING data-base-identifier-1 [,data-base-identifier-4] .... format 7

(B)   INSERT record-name INTO set-name-1 [, set-name-2]

(C)   GET record-name [ON ERROR GO TO error-paragraph]

(D)   REMOVE record-name FROM set-name-1 [,set-name-2]

(E)   STORE record-name ⎡ SUPPRESS ⎧ ALL / RECORD / AREA / ⎰SETS / set-name-1 [,set-name-2]⎱ ⎫ CURRENCY UPDATES ⎤

(F)   MODIFY record-name

(G)   DELETE record-name

Figure 12.28   Sample DML commands

defined in a program. The current record of a particular record type is the last record of that type accessed by the program.

3. The *current of set*. There is one current of set for each set type defined in a program. The current record of a particular set type is the last record (member or owner) of that set type accessed by the program.

Currency indicators are changed after the execution of each DML command. Changes to currency indicators can be suppressed by following a DML command with a SUPPRESS CURRENCY clause. This clause nominates the currency indicators that are to remain unchanged after the execution of the commands.

The FIND Command

Of all the DML commands, the FIND command is possibly the most extensive. The DBTG suggested seven alternate formats. The DBLTG examined the DBTG DML and proposed some changes in their formats. These proposals are generally in regard to the syntactic structure of the commands rather than to the semantics of navigating the network. For example, DBTG format 5 corresponds to 1976 *Journal of Development* format 2 (JOD2), DBTG Format 6 to JOD7, DBTG3 to JOD4, DBTG4 to JOD6, and DBTG7 to JOD3. In most cases the differences between the semantics of these formats are not great; most vendor systems are based on the DBTG proposal, with some variants. Some DBTG FIND commands formats are now described by using the sample database in Figure 12.17 for illustrative purposes.

The FIND Command and Currency

If a FIND command successfully finds a record, this record becomes

- the current record of run-unit
- the current record of its record type
- the current record of all the set types of which the record is either a member or an owner

The changing of a currency indicator from one record to another is called a *currency update*.

Format 5 The simplest FIND command is format 5. It can be used only if the location mode of record-name-3 is LOCATION MODE IS CALC. The command is used to find the record with a specified value of the record CALC key. To do this, first the value of CALC key is initialized to the required value, and then the command is executed. Thus the project whose PROJ-ID is PROJ1 is found by

MOVE 'PROJ1' TO PROJ-ID
FIND PROJECTS RECORDS

If duplicates are allowed, they can be retrieved by including

FIND NEXT DUPLICATE WITHIN PROJECTS RECORD

in a program loop. In this case all the currency indicators for the record are updated at the time that the FIND command completes.

Finding Members of a Set Occurrence Before set members can be found, it is necessary to establish the current record of set occurrences. The record of a current set occurrence can be established either by finding the set owner or by finding any set member (through some other set or by using its CALC key).

The most common way to establish the currency of a set is to find its owner. If the LOCATION MODE of the owner is CALC, the owner is found by using format 5 of the FIND statement. The successive member records of the set occurrence are then found using format 3 of the FIND statement.

Format 3   Format 3 of the FIND statements can be used in one of two ways:

- to find the FIRST or LAST member record in the current set occurrence, or
- to find a record relative to the current record of the set occurrence.

For example, consider the set occurrence in Figure 12.23. This set occurrence contains

- one owner record of type PROJECT with "PROJ1" as its key value
- three member records of type WORK representing persons who worked on the project

Suppose now the commands

```
MOVE 'PROJ1' TO PROJ-ID
FIND PROJECTS RECORD
```

are executed. Following this execution, the PROJECTS record whose key value is 'PROJ1' is found and becomes the current record of WORKERS. It also becomes the current record of PROJECTS.

Now suppose the command

```
FIND NEXT RECORD WITHIN WORKERS SET
```

is executed. It will find the next record that follows the current of WORKERS record, that is, PROJ1. This next record is the WORK record PER11. Record PER11 now becomes the current of WORKERS. Executing the FIND NEXT command again finds the NEXT record that follows PER11, namely, the PER32 record. To list all persons that worked on a PROJECT, the FIND NEXT command is included in a loop, as shown in the following program:

```
MOVE 'PROJ1' TO PROJ-NO
FIND PROJECTS RECORDS
        .
        .
        .

REPEAT UNTIL END OF WORKERS SET
BEGIN
    FIND NEXT RECORD WITHIN WORKERS SET
    GET WORK
    PRINT PERSON-ID
END
```

The employees will be printed out in ascending order of PERSON-ID because PERSON-ID is the WORKERS sort key. Appropriate status flags are set at the time that the last member record of the set has been retrieved.

Other forms of format 3 FIND locate specific records in set occurrences. Suppose the command

FIND FIRST WORK RECORD WITHIN WORKERS

is executed at the time that PROJ1 is the current of WORKERS. The record PER11 is found. It will also be found even if PER32 or PER40 is the current of set WORKERS. Suppose now the command

FIND LAST WORK RECORD WITHIN WORKERS

is executed at the time that PROJ1, PER11, or PER32 is current of the WORKER set type. Then record PER40 is found.

Format 6 and Format 7   To find a particular member record of a set by using format 3 requires the program to go through two steps:

1. Find an owner of the set occurrence.
2. Search through the set occurrence to find the member record with some required value.

Format 6 may be used to find such a record directly without searching through a set occurrence. Format 6 of the FIND command uses the SET OCCURRENCE SELECTION (SOS) phrase of the SET definition to establish a current record of set.

Set Occurrence Selection

The DBTG proposed two forms of the SOS phrase:

• format 1 to establish a current of set for member record retrieval
• format 2 for hierarchical path retrieval

Format 1 can be illustrated by considering the WORKERS set in Figure 12.17. The SOS clause for WORKERS is defined to be LOCATION MODE OF OWNER. Given this SOS, the current of set occurrence can be established by moving the CALC key value of its owner to the CALC key field. Hence a particular member record can be found by a format 6 FIND as follows:

MOVE 'PROJ1' TO PROJ-ID   (establishes current for
                                                        execution of format 6 FIND)
MOVE 'PER11' TO PERSON-ID
FIND WORK VIA WORKERS USING PERSON-ID

This statement will find record PER11. It is not necessary to explicitly FIND the projects record before finding some particular member of the set occurrence. The value of PROJ-ID is sufficient to identify the owner.

As an alternative of format 1 of SOS, the SET OCCURRENCE SELECTION is specified as CURRENT OF SET. This differs from the case in which SOS is LOCATION MODE OF OWNER in that now the set currency must be established through an explicit FIND command before the format 6 FIND is executed. Thus if the SET OCCURRENCE SELECTION for WORKERS is CURRENT OF SET, a specific employee is found by

```
MOVE 'PROJ1' TO PROJ-ID
MOVE 'PER11' TO PERSON-ID
FIND PROJECTS RECORD      (establishes current of set
                             for format 6 FIND)
FIND WORK VIA WORKERS USING PERSON-ID
```

Now the PROJECTS owner of the set occurrence must be found explicitly.

The DDL Committee substantially modified the SET OCCURRENCE SELECTION clause. In fact, it has been renamed the SET SELECTION clause. The two alternatives are now defined as

```
SET SELECTION IS THRU set-name OWNER
    IDENTIFIED BY KEY key-name
(in lieu of THRU LOCATION MODE OF OWNER)
```

and

```
SET SELECTION IS THRU set-name OWNER
    IDENTIFIED BY APPLICATION
(in lieu of CURRENT of SET)
```

Hierarchical Path Retrieval

Hierarchical path retrieval using formats 6 and 7 is illustrated in Figure 12.29, which shows six record types and five set types. The location mode of each record type is given after the letters LM, and the set occurrence selection for each set is given after the letters SOS. The two set types SET-D and SET-F both use format 2 of the SET OCCURRENCE SELECTION clause. The set type SET-D defines a path that commences with SET-B and proceeds to SET-D through SET-C. To find a member of a set occurrence of SET-D, the programmer must follow the following steps:

- *Step 1:* Select a particular set occurrence of SET-B by finding its owner record A.
- *Step 2:* Select a particular set occurrence of SET-C by finding its owner

record B. To do this, a particular member record B of the SET-B occurrence found in step 1 must be selected.
- *Step 3:* Select a particular set occurrence of SET-D by finding its owner record C. To do this, a particular member record C of the SET-C occurrence found in step 2 must be selected.
- *Step 4:* Select a particular member record D of the SET-D set occurrence found in step 3.

The following program is used to achieve this retrieval:

1. MOVE 'A-VAL' TO A-1.
2. FIND A RECORD.
3. MOVE 'B-VAL' TO B-1.
4. MOVE 'C-VAL' TO C-3.
5. MOVE 'D-VAL' TO D-1.
6. FIND D RECORD VIA SET-D USING B-1, C-3, D-1.

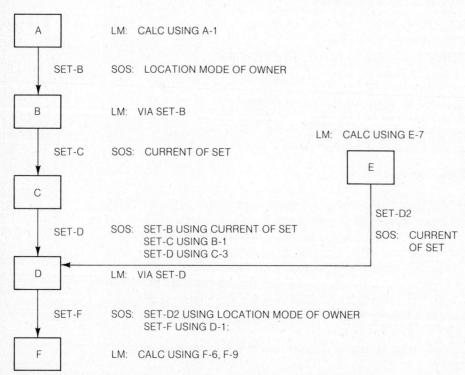

Figure 12.29 A data structure diagram including set occurrence selections

Here A-1 is a field in record type A; B-1 is a field in record type B; C-3 is a field in record type C; and D-1 is a field in record type D.

Six commands are needed here:

1. Commands 1 and 2 establish a current of record type A and of set type SET-B. This record has 'A-VAL' for its value of A-1.
2. Commands 3, 4, and 5 specify the value of specific fields of type B, C, and D records.
3. Command 6 uses the set occurrence selection for SET-D to find the required record.

Note that command 2 is used to establish a current of set B because SET-B USING CURRENT OF SET has been specified in SOS for SET-D. Had this clause instead been SET-B USING LOCATION MODE OF OWNER, statement 2 would be unnecessary.

The path specified by SOS for SET-F includes set types SET-D2 and SET-F. To find a record along this path, the program must first set the values that can be used to select particular occurrence of set types SET-D2 and SET-F. It must also specify a particular member record of the SET-F occurrence. Then a format 6 FIND command is executed. The following code is used to do this:

```
MOVE 'E-VAL' TO E-7.
FIND E RECORD.
MOVE 'D-VAL' TO D-1.
MOVE 'F-VAL' TO F-1.
FIND F RECORD VIA SET-F USING E-7, D-1, F-1.
```

Here E-7 is a field in record type E, and F-1 is a field in record type F. You may note that an F record occurrence can be found directly as LM for record type F is specified as CALC. Thus the statements

```
MOVE 'F1-VAL' TO F-6
MOVE 'F2-VAL' TO F-9
FIND F RECORD
```

also find an F record that has F1-VAL and F2-VAL values for fields F-6 and F-9.

Format 4—Finding an Owner   The formats discussed so far proceeded by finding an owner of a set and then locating its members. It is also possible to traverse the network from a member to its owner. To do this, we use format 4 of the FIND statement. Suppose a D record is found following the path SET-B, SET-C, and SET-D. To find the owner of this D record in SET-D2, we use the statement

```
FIND OWNER RECORD OF SET-D2 SET
```

The Subschema

The DBTG report proposes that a number of subschemas be generated from a schema. One subschema is available for each application program. A subschema will select those parts of a database that are to be made available to a particular application program. A subschema differs from a schema in the following ways:

1. It may not include some of the areas, records, and sets that are part of the schema.
2. Areas, records, or sets may be renamed.
3. Data items may have different attributes.
4. The order of items in a record may be changed.
5. Data items in a schema record may be omitted in the subschema.

Defining the Subschema

The simplest way of generating a subschema is through the use of the COPY verb. Suppose we wish to generate a subschema from the schema defined in Figure 12.17. The subschema is to be named WORK-DETAILS and is to include information on employee assignments in stores. The definition of this subschema is given in Figure 12.30a. A privacy lock "store assignment" is associated with the subschema, and the record type PERSONS is renamed.

Invoking the Subschema

The subschema is invoked by the COBOL program by using the INVOKE statement. The general structure of a COBOL PROGRAM that makes use of a subschema is shown in Figure 12.30b. Procedures have been included for error processing in the program in Figure 12.30b. Thus the procedure in ERROR-TYPE-1 SECTION in DECLARATIVES is invoked whenever error type "1201" occurs. Note that areas are opened independently of other areas.

SUMMARY

The network model was first introduced as a data modeling abstraction. The network model is founded on the owner-coupled set in which an owner object from one object class is associated with any number of member objects from another object class. Such associations can be used to form complex modeling structures.

Most implementations of the network modeling abstraction use lists to link all records that represent a network set occurrence. But such implementations

```
SUBSCHEMA NAME IS WORK-DETAILS
    PRIVACY LOCK IS 'store assignment'.
RENAMING SECTION.
RECORD NAME PERSONS IN SCHEMA IS CHANGED TO PEOPLE.
AREA SECTION.
COPY AREA1.
RECORD SECTION.
COPY PROJECTS, PERSONS, WORK.
SET SECTION.
COPY WORKERS, WORKED-ON.
```
(a) Defining the subschema

```
DATA DIVISION.
SCHEMA SECTION.
INVOKE SUB-SCHEMA WORK-DETAILS OF SCHEMA PROJECT-DATA.
        .
        .
PROCEDURE DIVISION.
DECLARATIVES.
ERROR-TYPE-1 SECTION.
    USE OF DATABASE-EXCEPTION "1201".
ERROR-TYPE-2 SECTION.
    USE OF DATABASE-EXCEPTION "0513".
        .
        .
        .
END DECLARATIVES.
PROCESSING SECTION.
INITIALIZE-PART.
    OPEN AREA1 USAGE IS UPDATE.
PROCESSING-PARAGRAPHS.
        DML and COBOL statements.
CLOSE-PART.
    CLOSE AREA1.
```
(b) Invoking the subschema

Figure 12.30   A DBTG subschema

place restrictions on network constructs. One important restriction is that a record cannot appear as a member in more than one occurrence of the same set type. Another is that records of the same type cannot be both owner and member records in the same set type.

In the DBTG recommendations for a standard network model implementation, several options are available to designers both for placing records with set types and for the data manipulation commands that can be used to access the records. Developments in the network standard show a decided trend to separate the definition of the database logical from the database physical structure.

PROBLEMS

Problem 1

Refer to the data structure diagram and schema for database SUPPLIES shown in Figure 12.31. (*Note:* A supplier can supply the same ITEM-NO more than once.)

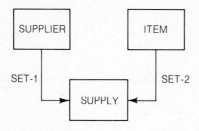

```
RECORD NAME IS SUPPLIER
      LOCATION MODE IS CALC USING SUPPLIER-NAME.
      02 SUPPLIER-NAME
      02 ADDRESS

RECORD NAME IS ITEM
      LOCATION MODE IS CALC USING ITEM-NO.
      02 ITEM-NO
      02 DESCRIPTION

RECORD NAME IS SUPPLY
      LOCATION MODE IS VIA SET-1 SET.
      02 ITEM-NO
      02 SUPPLIER-NAME
      02 QTY-SUPPLIED
      02 DATE-SUPPLIED

SET-NAME IS SET-1
      MODE IS CHAIN
      ORDER IS SORTED BY DEFINED KEY
      OWNER IS SUPPLIER
      MEMBER IS SUPPLY OPTIONAL MANUAL
          ASCENDING KEY IS DATE-SUPPLIED DUPLICATES ARE FIRST
      SET SELECTION IS THRU CURRENT OF SET.

SET NAME IS SET-2
      MODE IS CHAIN
      ORDER IS FIRST
      OWNER IS ITEM
      MEMBER IS SUPPLY MANDATORY AUTOMATIC
      SET SELECT IS THRU LOCATION MODE OF OWNER.
```

Figure 12.31 Data structure diagram and schema for Problem 1

SUPPLIER			ITEMS	
SUPPLIER-NAME	ADDRESS		ITEM-NO	DESCRIPTION
JILL	A1		I-1	PAINT
JOE	A2		I-2	BRUSH
MELINDA	A3			

SUPPLY

ITEM-NO	SUPPLIER-NAME	QTY-SUPPLIED	DATE-OF-SUPPLY
I-1	JILL	17	020380
I-1	MELINDA	23	050780
I-2	JILL	16	070980
I-1	JOE	35	030480
I-1	JILL	40	101080
I-2	JILL	37	111180
I-2	MELINDA	25	040480

Figure 12.32   Data for Problem 1(a)

In the following questions, wherever necessary assume that records are input into the database in chronological order.

(a) Draw a physical structure of the database, given the contents in Figure 12.32.

(b) What change to the physical structure would result if ASCENDING KEY in SET-1 became the following?

        ASCENDING KEY IS ITEM-NO DUPLICATES ARE FIRST

(c) What would be the result if record type SUPPLY became LOCATION MODE IS VIA SET-2 SET?

(d) What change would you make to the schema if you wished to retrieve ITEMS in the sequence of suppliers in alphanumeric order?

(e) What change would you make to the schema if you wished to retrieve the suppliers at a given address?

(f) Is it necessary to have SUPPLIER-NAME as an item in record type SUPPLY? Would the physical arrangement of records in the set occurrence be changed if SUPPLIER-NAME were not included in SUPPLY?

Problem 2

Refer to the data structure diagram and schema of database JOBS shown in Figure 12.33.

(a) Draw a physical structure of the database, given the contents of Figure 12.34.

(b) Suppose now SET-1 is changed so that

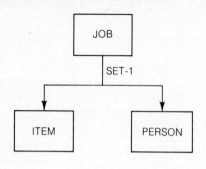

```
RECORD NAME IS JOB
      LOCATION MODE IS CALC USING JOB-NO
      02 JOB-NO
      02 DESCRIPTION
      02 MANAGER

RECORD NAME IS ITEM
      LOCATION MODE IS CALC USING ITEM
      02 ITEM-NO
      02 DATE-USED
      02 QTY-USED
      02 JOB-NO

RECORD NAME IS PERSON
      LOCATION MODE IS CALC USING NAME
      02 NAME
      02 DATE-WORKED
      02 TIME-SPENT
      02 JOB-NO

SET NAME IS SET-1
      MODE IS CHAIN
      ORDER IS SORTED BY RECORD-NAME
      OWNER IS JOB
      MEMBER IS ITEM ASCENDING KEY IS DATE-USED
           DUPLICATES ARE LAST
      MEMBER IS PERSON ASCENDING KEY IS TIME-SPENT
           DUPLICATES ARE LAST
      SET SELECTION IS THRU LOCATION MODE OF OWNER
```

Figure 12.33 Data structure diagram and schema for Problem 2

ORDER IS SORTED BY DEFINED KEYS
MEMBER IS ITEM ASCENDING KEY IS DATE-USED
     DUPLICATES ARE LAST
MEMBER IS PERSON ASCENDING KEY IS DATE-WORKED
     DUPLICATES ARE LAST

How does this change the physical structure?

JOB records

JOB-NO	DESCRIPTION	MANAGER
J-1	BUILD	M-1
J-2	DIG	M-2
J-3	MOVE	M-3

ITEM records

ITEM-NO	DATE-USED	QTY-USED	JOB-NO
I-1	020280	10	J-1
I-2	040480	20	J-2
I-1	060680	30	J-2
I-2	080880	40	J-1

PERSON records

NAME	DATE-WORKED	TIME-SPENT	JOB-NO
JOE	030380	5	J-1
JILL	050580	3	J-1
NELLY	070780	2	J-2

Figure 12.34   Data for Problem 2(a)

Problem 3

Suppose the following set of commands is executed, given the schema in Problem 1.

```
MOVE "MELINDA" TO SUPPLIER-NAME
FIND SUPPLIER RECORD
FIND FIRST SUPPLY RECORD WITHIN SET-1 SET ............ A
FIND OWNER OF SET-2
FIND FIRST SUPPLY RECORD WITHIN SET-2 SET ............ B
FIND NEXT SUPPLY RECORD WITHIN SET-2 SET ............ C
FIND NEXT SUPPLY RECORD WITHIN SET-1 SET ............ D
FIND NEXT SUPPLY RECORD WITHIN SET-2 SET ............ E
```

(a) Nominate the current of RUN-UNIT, SET-1, SET-2, ITEM, SUPPLY, and SUPPLIER at the completion of commands A, B, D, C, and E.

(b) Suppose command D becomes

    FIND NEXT SUPPLY RECORD WITHIN SET-1 SET
       SUPPRESS SET-2 CURRENCY UPDATES

What are the currents of RUN-UNIT, SET-1, SET-2, ITEM, SUPPLY, and SUPPLIER at the completion of commands D and E?

(c) Suppose commands B and C now include

    SUPPRESS SET-1 CURRENCY UPDATES

What are the currents of RUN-UNIT, SET-1, SET-2, ITEM, SUPPLY, and SUPPLIER at the completion of commands B, C, D, and E?

(d) Suppose only command C includes

    SUPPRESS SET-1 CURRENCY UPDATES

What are the currency indicators at the completion of commands C, D, and E?

Problem 4

Suppose the following set of commands is executed, given the schema in Problem 1.

    MOVE 'JILL' TO NAME
    FIND SUPPLIER RECORD

    FIND NEXT SUPPLY RECORD WITHIN SET-1 SET   } loop repeated for
    FIND OWNER OF SET-2 SET   } each SET-1 member
    OUTPUT QTY-SUPPLIED, DATE-OF-SUPPLY, DESCRIPTION } record occurrence

What is the output of this sequence?

Suppose the change in (b) of Problem 1 is made. What is the output now?

Problem 5

Suppose the following sequence of commands is executed, given the schema in Problem 2.

    MOVE 'J-1' TO JOB-NO
    FIND JOB RECORD
    FIND NEXT PERSON RECORD WITHIN SET-1 SET

What are the currency indicators at the completion of these commands? Does this change if the change in (b) of Problem 2 is made? Suppose the sequence of commands now becomes

MOVE 'J-1' TO JOB-NO
FIND JOB RECORD
FIND NEXT RECORD WITHIN SET-1 SET

What are the currency indicators after the completion of these commands?

___

Problem 6

___

Write a set of commands to list the suppliers of item I-1 in the order in which the items were supplied, given the schema in Problem 1, starting with the last supplied amount first.

___

Problem 7

___

Write a set of commands to list the quantities of I-1 that JILL supplied, given the schema in Problem 1.

___

Problem 8

___

Write a set of commands to find the time spent by JOE on job J-1, given the schema in Problem 2.

___

Problem 9

___

Would the commands in Problems 7 and 8 change if JOB-NO were not part of record types ITEM and PERSON?

___

Problem 10

___

Suppose now ITEM-NO and SUPPLIER-NAME in Problem 1 are removed from SUPPLY. Would the commands in Problems 6 and 7 change?

Problem 11

Suppose the following commands are executed:

MOVE 'I-1' TO ITEM-NO
MOVE 'JILL' TO SUPPLIER-NAME
MOVE '102' TO QTY-SUPPLIED
MOVE '121280' TO DATE-OF-SUPPLY
STORE SUPPLY

Will the newly created record appear in any set occurrences of SET-1 and SET-2, given the schema of Problem 1? If not, what would need to be done to insert them into set occurrences?

Problem 12

Define the schema for the data structure diagram shown in Figure 12.35. In your schema

(a) members of SET2 are ordered by TIME-STARTED
(b) members of SET1 are ordered by PROJECT-NO
(c) SET2 must have pointers to owner
(d) ACTIVITY records should be grouped as closely as possible to the PROJECT owner

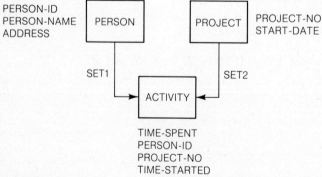

Figure 12.35   Data structure diagram for Problem 12

Problem 13

Draw a network structure diagram for the following. A COMPANY can own any number of VEHICLES, each registered in any CITY among several. Each VEHICLE can be serviced by any MECHANIC, each of whom is employed in a SERVICE-STATION in a CITY. Your network structure must include record types for COMPANY, VEHICLE, CITY, MECHANIC, and SERVICE-STATION, together with any associated records linked by sets.

Problem 14

A family tree (on the paternal side only) can be modeled by the data structure diagram shown in Figure 12.36. In this network structure, LINK records associate persons with their parents. The members of the FATHER set are LINK records that associate children to the owner of the FATHER set. The children can be found as owners of the LINK records in the FAMILY set. Draw the links between records for the following data

FATHER	CHILD
P1	P2
P1	P3
P1	P4
P2	P5
P2	P6
P6	P7
P6	P8

Write pseudocode to find all ancestors of a PERSON.

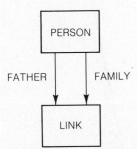

Figure 12.36 Data structure diagram for Problem 14

chapter thirteen
Hierarchical Database
Management Systems

INTRODUCTION

As was the case with network DBMSs, this chapter on hierarchical DBMSs will commence by outlining the hierarchical data model and will then cover some implementations of this model.

The discussion of implementations is of necessity less complete for hierarchical than for network DBMSs. The DBTG report has set implementation guidelines for the network model that are widely followed. There are no such guidelines for the hierarchical model, and so a large variety of hierarchical implementations exist. It is common to distinguish two classes of hierarchical model implementation: the tree traversal and the general-selection implementation. This chapter will outline one example of each. Again, bear in mind that the descriptions of the DBMSs in this text are not complete but cover only what are here considered as the major features. Hence the text should not be used as a manual.

THE HIERARCHICAL MODEL

Like the network data model, the hierarchical model delineates object classes and the relationships among them. The hierarchical model, however, differs from the network model in one important respect: it restricts each object class to having at most one parent object class. A parent object class may, however, have more than one child object class.

Records are viewed as "nodes" in a tree in the hierarchical model. The objects are organized in a parent-child relationship. In this relationship one object can have child objects that "belong" to it. Thus in Figure 13.1, department records own project records if those projects fall within the department. Similarly, projects own the records of persons assigned to the project. A comparison of Figure 13.1 with Figure 12.3 shows one important distinction between the hierarchical and the network representations of the same data. There is now a restriction that each record has at most one parent. Figure 13.1 illustrates an

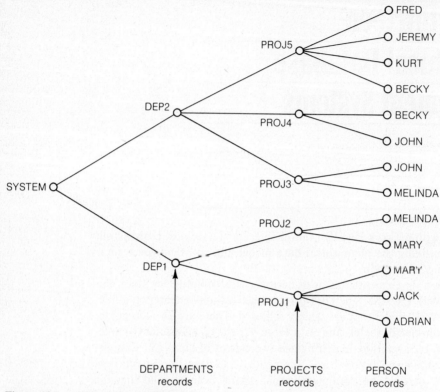

Figure 13.1   A hierarchy of objects

important consequence from the restriction of each object having at most one parent object. Now objects that belong to more than one parent must appear more than once in the database. Thus MARY works on PROJ1 and PROJ2. Hence MARY appears twice in the database. In the network model the object MARY need appear only once (see Figures 12.11 and 12.12). Only the intersection data appear in more than one set occurrence. For this reason the hierarchical model can cause problems when modeling $N{:}M$ relationships, because it often becomes necessary to duplicate data in the database.

The Hierarchical Data Structure

The hierarchical database can be represented by a structure diagram that is similar to the network data structure diagram. Object classes are represented by rectangular boxes and parent-child relationships are represented by links from the parent to the child. A data structure representation of the hierarchy of objects in Figure 13.1 is shown in Figure 13.2.

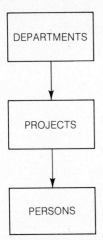

Figure 13.2   A hierarchical data structure

Parents with More Than One Child Object Class

Figure 13.3 is a hierarchical data structure in which the parent has more than one child object class. Now a project's children include both the persons who work on the project and the items used by a project. All objects of these child classes appear as children of the parent at the same level. Thus in Figure 13.4, JACK, MARY, ADRIAN, SAW, and HAMMER are all directly subordinate to PROJ1. In some implementations the order of child classes is significant, and records are retrieved in the order of their classes.

Accessing the Hierarchical Data Structure

Two alternate methods are used to access objects in a hierarchical database: tree traversal and general selection.

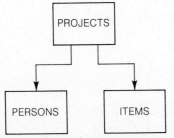

Figure 13.3   More than one child object class

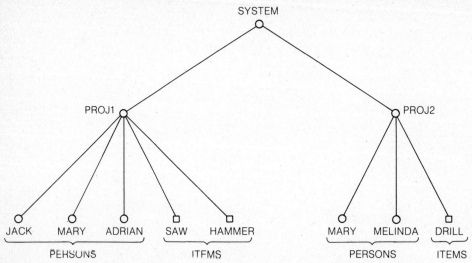

Figure 13.4 A hierarchy of objects with two object classes at the child level

Tree Traversal In tree traversal, objects are retrieved in some tree-order sequence. Usually preorder is used with the parent found before its children. Thus the preorder retrieval in objects in Figure 13.1 would result in

DEP1
PROJ1
ADRIAN
JACK
MARY
PROJ2
MARY
MELINDA
DEP2
PROJ3
MELINDA
JOHN
PROJ4
JOHN
BECKY
PROJ5
BECKY
KURT
JEREMY
FRED

A preorder tree traversal in which a parent has children of more than one class retrieves all the children from all object class for a parent before it begins with the next parent. Thus a tree traversal of Figure 13.4 results in

PROJ1
JACK   ⎫
MARY   ⎬ persons
ADRIAN ⎭
SAW   ⎫
HAMMER ⎭ items
PROJ2
MARY   ⎫
MELINDA ⎭ persons
DRILL   } item

The significance of the order of children now becomes obvious. In tree-order traversal the objects are output in the order of child records. Thus, since PERSONS comes before ITEMS in the data structure diagram in Figure 13.3 (PERSONS being the leftmost child), all the person child objects of a project are traversed before the objects item children.

General Selection   General selection does not rely on the tree sequence of objects. It selects particular objects in the structure, given some selection condition. The selection language depends on a particular system. For example,

PRINT ITEMS WHERE PROJECT = PROJ1

would output the items used by a project, PROJ1 (i.e., SAW and HAMMER), whereas

PRINT PROJECTS WHERE ITEM = SAW

would output the projects that use item SAW (i.e., PROJ1).

The logical retrieval conditions can be more complex. They can include a Boolean condition on object properties, compare properties of different objects, and compare sets of objects.

INFORMATION MANAGEMENT SYSTEM (IMS)

IMS is a hierarchical DBMS supported by IBM. It uses primarily tree traversal to access databases.

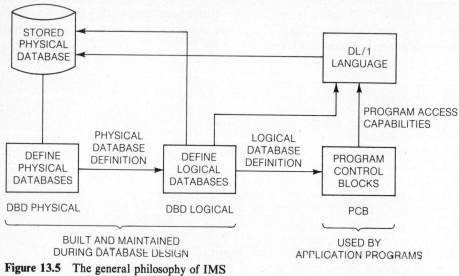

Figure 13.5 The general philosophy of IMS

The IMS Structure

The IMS structure is illustrated in Figure 13.5. An IMS database is made up of four major components:

1. The physical database, which is the database as stored by IMS.
2. The logical databases, which are the logical views. They are derived from the physical databases and are subsequently made available to the application program to refer to the database.
3. The PCB (program communication block) to select a particular logical database and make it available to an application program. The PCB defines any access restrictions on a program. For example, a program may be restricted to read but not to update access to some segments.
4. The DL/1 language to access the database. DL/1 commands are embedded in COBOL or PL/1 and refer to the database through the PCB.

Both physical and logical databases in IMS must be hierarchical. Application programs in an IMS environment can access only logical databases.

The Physical Database

An IMS database is made up of any number of physical databases. Each physical database is composed of any number of *segments,* structured as a hierarchy. Each segment can be either

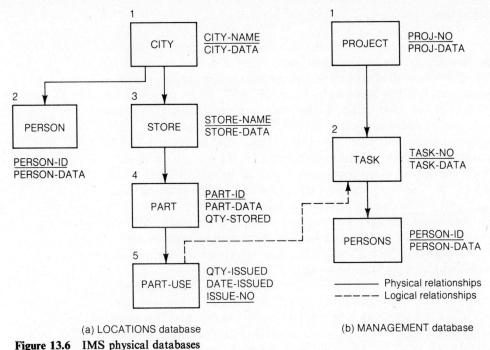

(a) LOCATIONS database   (b) MANAGEMENT database

Figure 13.6   IMS physical databases

- a root segment, in which case it has no parent segment, or
- a dependent segment, in which case it has another segment as its parent segment.

Each physical database has only one root segment.

The first step in setting up an IMS database is to divide the data into a number of physical databases. One such subdivision is illustrated in Figure 13.6. Here the database consists of two physical databases, LOCATIONS and MANAGEMENT. LOCATIONS (Figure 13.6a) stores information on the cities, together with the stores and persons in each city and the parts issued by each store. Each issue is identified by a unique ISSUE-NO. Each issue is for one part kind for one task only. The physical database MANAGEMENT (Figure 13.6b) stores information on projects, the tasks that make up each project, and the PERSONS assigned to each task.

The terms *parent* and *child* are used to describe the relationships between records. A segment may have a physical parent segment and zero, one, or more physical child segments in a physical database. Thus STORE is a physical child of CITY, and STORE is a physical parent of PART. Segment CITY has two child segments (PERSON and STORE), segment STORE has one child segment, and segment PART-USE has no child segments.

Logical Databases

There is one disadvantage in dividing the database into a number of physical databases. Sometimes information about some entity is needed in two databases. This information often appears in both databases. For example, suppose that for each issue, it is also necessary to know the TASK-DATA together with the TASK-NO of the task to which the issue is made. TASK-DATA and TASK-NO could be added to segment PART-USE, as shown in Figure 13.7a. But redundancy is now introduced into the database: TASK-NO and TASK-DATA appear in two segments. This situation does not occur in a network database because PART-USE is an intersection record between TASK and PART (see Figure 13.7b). You may note that Figure 13.6 also contains another duplication. Each part can be carried by more than one store. It will be owned by each store that carries that part. Hence PART-DATA for the same PART-ID may be stored more than once. Similarly, data about persons is also stored in two databases. Segment PERSON shows the cities where persons live, and segment PERSONS shows the tasks to which persons are assigned.

IMS allows the designer to establish logical relationships to eliminate such redundancies. Logical relationships can be defined between two segments, where each of the two segments is in a different physical database. For example, in Figure 13.6 a logical relationship is established between the TASK segment in the MANAGEMENT physical database and the PART-USE segment in the LOCATIONS physical database. Segment PART-USE now becomes the logical child of TASK, and TASK is the logical parent of PART-USE. (Note that the relationship is drawn from the logical child to the logical parent.) These logical relationships can eliminate redundancies because records logically related in a physical database can be accessed through the same logical database.

Logical databases can be derived from the physical databases and from the logical relationships between the physical databases. Such logical databases are shown in Figure 13.8. Here the CITIES logical database (Figure 13.8a) is derived from the LOCATIONS and MANAGEMENT physical database. The PROJECT-DATA logical database (Figure 13.8b), on the other hand, contains segments from one physical database (MANAGEMENT). The logical databases are themselves hierarchical according to the following rules:

1. Segment A can be the logical child of another segment B if A and B are in the same physical database and A is a physical child of B in that physical database.

2. Segment C in one physical database can be concatenated with its logical parent segment D, where D is a segment in another physical database. All physical child segments of segments C and D become logical child segments of the new concatenated segment.

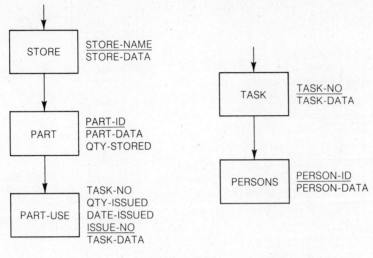

(a) Hierarchical

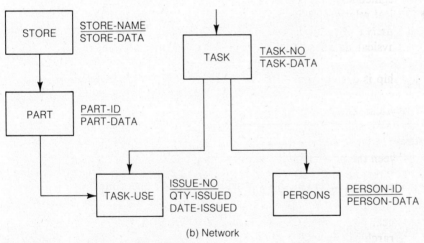

(b) Network

Figure 13.7 Adding a USE record

Thus in logical database CITIES, segment TASK is concatenated with segment PART-USE to make up the concatenated segment USES. This concatenation is logical, and TASK records are still stored once only physically. Values of TASK-NO and TASK-DATA can now be hierarchically accessed from segment PART by using logical database CITIES.

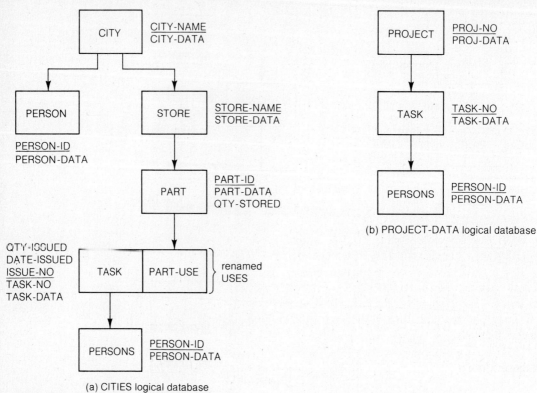

(a) CITIES logical database

(b) PROJECT-DATA logical database

Figure 13.8 IMS logical databases

IMS Physical Structures

The IMS DBMS makes use of the access methods provided by IBM's operating system, OS. These are

- SAM, a sequential access method
- ISAM, an indexed sequential access method
- VSAM, a keyed indexed sequential method

SAM and ISAM were developed before VSAM. The designers of IMS then added a special access method called OSAM (Overflow Sequential Access Method). OSAM allows records to be directly retrieved by record address. IMS provides four additional access methods of its own:

- HSAM, a hierarchical sequential access method
- HISAM, a hierarchical indexed sequential access method

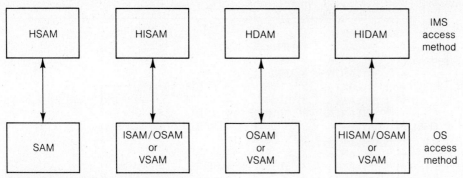

Figure 13.9   IMS access methods

- HDAM, a hierarchical direct access method
- HIDAM, a hierarchical indexed direct access method

These four methods use the OS access methods together with OSAM, as shown in Figure 13.9. Thus HSAM uses SAM, HISAM uses ISAM + OSAM, and so on. Each physical database is stored as a file by using one of the hierarchical access methods.

Record Storage

The location of a particular segment in an IMS file is determined by the hierarchical sequence key. This key is developed by concatenating the key fields of the segment and the key fields of all its ancestor segments. In addition, IMS allocates to each segment a unique number that becomes part of the hierarchical sequence key. Segment numbers are allocated in preorder sequence. In Figure 13.6, segment CITY is allocated segment number 1, segment PERSON is allocated segment number 2, and so on. Given these segment numbers, the hierarchical sequence key for a PART-USE segment occurrence will take the form shown in Figure 13.10. The first part of this key is the hierarchical sequence key of the root node of the database that contains PART-USE. The subsequent parts of the key are the concatenation of segment number and key field of all the segments from the root node to the PART-USE segment, including the PART-USE segment.

The hierarchical sequence key determines the location of a segment on a physical device. HSAM or HISAM segments are logically stored sequentially

1	Key of CITY parent	3	Key of STORE parent	4	Key of PART	5	Key of PART-USE

Figure 13.10   A hierarchical sequence key

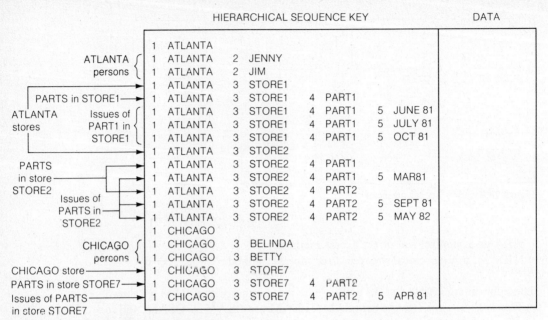

Figure 13.11 Sequential order of segments

in ascending order of their hierarchical sequence key. An example is given in Figure 13.11. Here it is assumed that the key of the CITY segment is CITY-NAME, of PERSON is PERSON-ID, of STORE is STORE-NAME, of PART is PART-ID, and of PART-USE is DATE-ISSUED. All segments for ATLANTA and its children are stored first. The SUPPLIERS segments are stored before the STORE segments for a particular city because the segment number of segment STORE is higher than the segment number of segment SUPPLIERS. The segments are therefore stored in a preorder tree traversal system.

A HSAM or HISAM database is physically stored as a set of records. Each record consists of one root segment, together with all its children segments. Each such record is indexed on the key of the root node and stored in an ISAM data set. Ideally, one record should contain a root segment together with all its descendants. If the record size for this ideal exceeds the block size of the ISAM data set, the remaining children of the root are stored in a physical block of an OSAM data set. Links are maintained from the ISAM root to its OSAM segments. In Figure 13.12, for example, there are two records with keys AT-LANTA and CHICAGO (as there are two physical root segments in physical database LOCATIONS). The records are broken up into physical blocks. The first physical block of each record is stored in the ISAM data set, and the remaining blocks are stored in the OSAM data set. All the physical blocks that contain one record are linked.

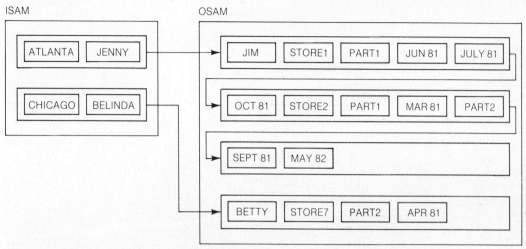

Figure 13.12   HISAM organization using ISAM/OSAM

Alternatively, a VSAM data set can be used to store a HISAM file. In a VSAM data set both the main area and the overflow area are on the same data set. A VSAM data set has one important advantage: New root segments will be inserted in the main area, using a VSAM organization. By contrast, in the ISAM + OSAM organization, new root segments will always be placed in the overflow area (OSAM), and so additional steps are necessary to retrieve the inserted records.

HDAM and HIDAM differ from HISAM in that segments need not be stored contiguously in their hierarchical key sequence. Each segment can be stored in any location on an OSAM or VSAM data set. Further, it need not be moved from the location. Preorder sequence is maintained by HDAM or HIDAM through the use of *pointers*. Segments are linked in preorder sequence. Two methods of pointer linkage are allowed in HDAM and HIDAM:

- HIER, where segments are linked in their hierarchical key sequence; here one chain is started at each root segment (Figure 13.13a).
- TWIN, where a separate chain is started for each different child segment (Figure 13.13b).

HIDAM differs from HDAM in that it uses a special index file (HISAM) for the root segments of a HIDAM database, whereas HDAM uses a hash algorithm to locate the root segment.

Logical Pointers

IMS uses logical pointers to implement logical relationships. There is usually

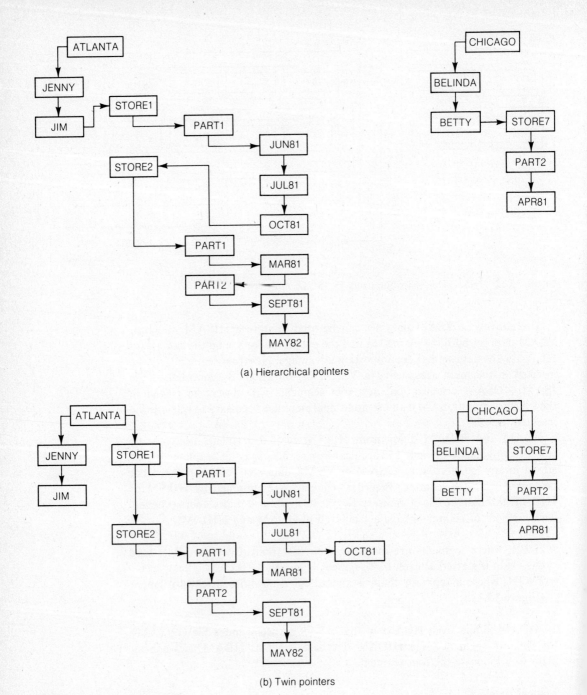

(a) Hierarchical pointers

(b) Twin pointers

Figure 13.13   Use of pointers

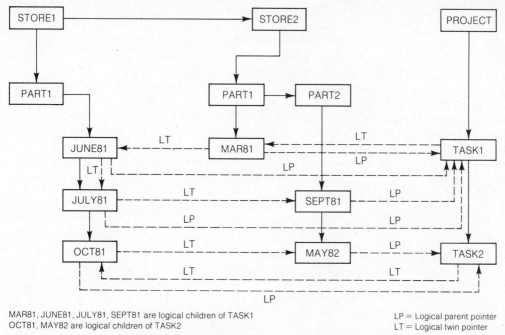

Figure 13.14   Pointers for logical relationships

MAR81, JUNE81, JULY81, SEPT81 are logical children of TASK1
OCT81, MAY82 are logical children of TASK2

LP = Logical parent pointer
LT = Logical twin pointer

• a pointer from the logical child to its logical parent
• a pointer from the logical parent that commences a chain from the parent to its logical children.

An example of the physical implementation of logical relationships is given in Figure 13.14, which is the IMS database for Figure 13.6. Here PART-USE segments are logical children of TASK segments. There is a logical parent (LP) pointer from each logical child to its logical parent (for example, from OCT81 and MAY82 to TASK2). Similarly, all logical children of the same logical parent are linked by logical twin (LT) pointers. Thus MAY82 and OCT81 are linked in a chain commencing at TASK2 by LT pointers. The logical parent pointers are the implementation of the logical concatenation of logically related segments in a logical database.

Defining the IMS Database

The IMS database definition (DBD) includes

• the physical database definition
• the logical database definitions

```
 1  DBD        NAME = LOCATIONS, ACCESS = HDAM
 2  DATASET    ...
 3  SEGM       NAME = CITY, BYTES = 50, FREQ = 20, POINTER = TWIN
 4  FIELD      NAME = (CITY-NAME, SEQ, U), BYTES = 20, START = 1, TYPE = C
 5  FIELD      NAME = CITY-DATA, BYTES = 30, START = 21, TYPE = C
 6  SEGM       NAME = PERSON, BYTES = 36, FREQ = 20000, POINTER = TWIN,
               PARENT = CITY
 7  FIELD      NAME = (PERSON-ID, SEQ, U), BYTES = 6, START = 1, TYPE = C
 8  FIELD      NAME = PERSON-DATA, BYTES = 30, START = 7, TYPE = C
 9  SEGM       NAME = STORE, BYTES = 50, FREQ = 80, PARENT = CITY, POINTER = TWIN
10  FIELD      NAME = (STORE-NAME, SEQ, U), BYTES = 20, START = 1, TYPE = C
11  FIELD      NAME = STORE-DATA, BYTES = 30, START = 21, TYPE = C
12  SEGM       NAME = PART, BYTES = 29, FREQ = 8000, POINTER = TWIN,
               PARENT = STORE
13  FIELD      NAME = (PART-ID, SEQ, U), BYTES = 8
14  FIELD      NAME = PART-DATA, BYTES = 15, TYPE = C
15  FIELD      NAME = QTY-STORED, BYTES = 6, TYPE = C
16  SEGM       NAME = PART-USE, BYTES = 18, FREQ = 3000,
               POINTER = (TWIN, LTWIN, LPARENT),
               PARENT = (PART, (TASK, MANAGEMENT))
17  FIELD      NAME = (DATE-ISSUED, SEQ, M), BYTES = 6, START = 1, TYPE = I
18  FIELD      NAME = QTY-ISSUED, BYTES = 6, START = 7, TYPE = I
19  FIELD      NAME = ISSUE-NO, BYTES = 6, START = 13, TYPE = I
20  DBD        NAME = MANAGEMENT, ACCESS = HDAM
21  DATASET    ...
22  SEGM       NAME = PROJECT, BYTES = 35, FREQ = 200, POINTER = HIER
23  FIELD      NAME = (PROJ-NO, SEQ, U), BYTES = 10, START = 1, TYPE = C
24  FIELD      NAME = PROJ-DATA, BYTES = 25, START = 11, TYPE = C
25  SEGM       NAME = TASK, BYTES = 45, FREQ = 2500, PARENT = PROJECT,
               POINTER = HIER
26  LCHILD     NAME = (PART-USE, LOCATIONS), POINTER = SNGL, RULES = FIRST
27  FIELD      NAME = (TASK-NO, SEQ, U), BYTES = 15, START = 1, TYPE = C
28  FIELD      NAME = TASK-DATA, BYTES = 30, START = 16, TYPE = C
29  SEGM       NAME = PERSONS, BYTES = 40, FREQ = 5000, PARENT = TASK,
               POINTER = HIER
30  FIELD      NAME = (PERSON-ID, SEQ, U), BYTES = 10, START = 1, TYPE = C
31  FIELD      NAME = PERSON-DATA, BYTES = 30, START = 11, TYPE = C
```

Figure 13.15 An IMS physical database definition

Defining Physical Databases

The physical databases LOCATIONS and MANAGEMENT of Figure 13.6
are defined in Figure 13.15. The definition of each physical database commences with a DBD statement. This statement includes a NAME clause to
define the database name. The ACCESS clause in the DBD statement defines

the IMS access method used to store the database. Thus database LOCA-TIONS will be stored as a HDAM database. The DBD statement is followed by the DATASET statement. The DATASET statement specifies the physical device used to store the database. The DATASET statement is not discussed in detail in this text.

The remaining statements in the physical database definition define

- the physical segments and their fields
- the logical relationships between physical segments

Figure 13.16 shows the syntax of statements used to define segments and fields in a physical database. The SEGM statement defines the segment, whereas the FIELD statement defines individual fields within the segment.

Each SEGM statement includes the name, size, and the expected number of occurrences, FREQ, of the segment. It also includes the name of its parent segment. Thus statement 1 in Figure 13.15 defines the physical database LOCA-TIONS. Statement 3 defines CITY to be segment of the database LOCA-TIONS; it has no parent. Statement 12 defines PART to be a segment in database LOCATIONS, with STORE as its physical parent.

The fields in a segment follow the segment definition. Each field is defined by a FIELD statement and includes the field NAME, SIZE, its START position in the segment, and its TYPE. One field is always chosen as the key field. The key field is specified by using SEQ phrase as part of the field NAME (for example, see statement 4). This field becomes part of the segment hierarchical sequence key and hence determines the sequence of segments in the database. A key field can be either

- U, in which case it uniquely identifies one segment within a parent, or
- M, in which case more than one segment within the same parent may have the same key value.

Defining Logical Relationships

Logical relationships also are defined by using the statements in Figure 13.16. An example is the definition of segment PART-USE of Figure 13.15. Segment PART-USE has both a physical and a logical parent. In statement 16 the PARENT clause for PART-USE contains two components:

1. PART, which defines its physical parent
2. (TASK, MANAGEMENT), which defines the logical parent TASK of physical database MANAGEMENT

Each segment can have at most one logical parent, but it can have any number of logical children. Logical children of a segment are defined by the LCHILD statement. The LCHILD statement must follow the logical parent

```
SEGM      NAME = seg-name-1
          [,PARENT = 0] or
                             ⎡SNGL⎤
              ,PARENT = ((seg-name-2 ⎣DBLE⎦)

          [,(1pseg-name ⎡VIRTUAL ⎤[,db-name 1])])
                        ⎣PHYSICAL⎦

          [,BYTES = bytes],[,FREQ = frequency]

          ⎡           ⎧HIER,HIERBWD,TWIN,TWINBWD⎫⎤
          ⎢           ⎪LTWIN,LTWINBWD           ⎪⎥
          ⎢,POINTER = ⎨LPARENT                  ⎬⎥
          ⎣           ⎩PAIRED                   ⎭⎦

          ⎡         ⎛⎡,FIRST⎤⎞⎤
          ⎢,RULES = ⎜⎢,LAST ⎥⎟⎥
          ⎣         ⎝⎣,HERE ⎦⎠⎦

          ⎡                        ⎡KEY ⎤            ⎤
          ⎢,SOURCE = ((seg-name-3 ⎣,DATA⎦[db-name 2]),..)⎥
          ⎣                                          ⎦


LCHILD    NAME = (seg-name-1[
          ⎡          ⎧SNGL⎫⎤
          ⎢          ⎪DBLE⎪⎥
          ⎢,POINTER = ⎨NONE⎬⎥
          ⎣          ⎩INDX⎭⎦

          [,PAIR = sig-name-2]
          [.INDEX = fld-name]
          ⎡        ⎧FIRST⎫⎤
          ⎢,RULES = ⎨LAST ⎬⎥
          ⎣        ⎩HERE ⎭⎦


FIELD     NAME = (fld-name[,SEQ,[U]])
                                [M]
              ,BYTES = bytes, START = start-position
          ⎡       ⎧X⎫⎤
          ⎢,TYPE = ⎨P⎬⎥
          ⎣       ⎩C⎭⎦
```

Figure 13.16   SEGM, LCHILD, and FIELD statements

SEGM statement. The segment (seg-name-1) and database (db-name) of the logical child segment are included in the LCHILD statement. Thus statement 26 in Figure 13.15 defines the logical child of the physical segment TASK; the NAME = (PART-USE, LOCATIONS) clause states that the logical child is the segment PART-USE in physical database LOCATIONS. The remaining parts of the SEGM and LCHILD statements deal with the physical linkages between segments.

Defining the Physical Structure

The physical structure is defined by the DBD and SEGM statements. The access method is defined by the ACCESS clause. In Figure 13.15, for example, statement 1 defines LOCATIONS to be a HDAM database.

The POINTER clause in the SEGM statement is used to define the pointer structure to be employed for HDAM and HIDAM databases. The pointer clause can be seen as reserving locations in the segment for pointers. Thus

- POINTERS = HIER reserves location for HIER pointers
- POINTERS = TWIN reserves location for TWIN pointers

In addition, HIERBWD or TWINBWD can be specified. In this case the pointers are bidirectional (similar to the PRIOR pointers in DBTG sets). As an example, statements 22 and 25 reserve positions for hierarchical pointers in segments TASK and PROJECT.

Logical pointer positions can also be reserved by the POINTER clause by using the keyword LPARENT or LTWIN. Statement 16 in Figure 13.15 reserves both a logical parent pointer and a logical twin pointer for the segment PART-USE. This is done to realize the physical structure shown in Figure 13.14.

Two additional options are also available with IMS:

1. The keywords SNGL and DBLE with the PARENT clause in the SEGM statement. SNGL specifies that there is to be a pointer to the first occurrence of a child segment; DBLE specifies that there is to be an additional pointer to the last occurrence of a child segment.
2. A similar keyword in the LCHILD statement. This keyword specifies whether there is to be a pointer to the last occurrence of a logical child.

Defining Logical Databases

Logical databases are derived from physical databases and are used by application programs. A DBD statement is used to define each logical database; ACCESS is specified as LOGICAL for the logical database. Similarly, a DATASET statement must be included in a logical database definition; the DATASET statement is specified to be LOGICAL. The SEGM statements specify the logical database segments. Each of these segments defines a logical segment in the logical database. The logical segments are derived from a source segment in a physical database. The source segment is specified by the SOURCE clause, which in turn specifies the physical segment name and physical database name. The name of the segment in the logical database may not be the same as the name of the segment from which it is derived.

Figure 13.17 shows a definition of the logical databases illustrated in Figure 13.8. Here CITIES is one logical database. The segments CITY, PERSON, PART, and STORE are derived from segments in the LOCATIONS physical

```
DBD       NAME = CITIES, ACCESS = LOGICAL
DATASET   LOGICAL
SEGM      NAME = CITY, SOURCE = (CITY, LOCATIONS)
SEGM      NAME = PERSON, SOURCE = (PERSON, LOCATIONS) PARENT = CITY
SEGM      NAME = STORE, SOURCE = (STORE, LOCATIONS) PARENT = CITY
SEGM      NAME = PART, SOURCE = (PART, LOCATIONS) PARENT = STORE
SEGM      NAME = USES, SOURCE = ((PART-USE, LOCATIONS), (TASK, MANAGEMENT)), PARENT = PART
SEGM      NAME = PERSONS, SOURCE = (PERSONS, MANAGEMENT), PARENT = USES
```

Figure 13.17   Logical databases

database. The segment USES in logical database CITIES is derived from segments PART-USE in database LOCATIONS and TASK in database management. It is the child of logical segment PART and the PARENT of the segment PERSONS. This corresponds to a logical relationship in the physical database.

When a logical database record that contains two concatenated physical records is read, the logical parent is presented to the program. Thus suppose logical record USES is read by a program. The data presented to the program are shown in Figure 13.18. They include

- the segment PART-USE that includes QTY-ISSUED, DATE-ISSUED, and ISSUE-NO
- the key of the PART-USE logical parent, together with the data in the logical parent

Hence the TASK-DATA is made available to the program as required without duplicating it in the database.

It is also possible to extend the database definition so that PART-DATA of parts used by a TASK can be accessed from the PROJECT segment (Figure 13.19). To do this a USE-OF-PART segment can be added to the database. Segment USE-OF-PART can now be concatenated in a logical database with PART as its parent. When USE-OF-PART is read by a program that uses this logical database, it will present to the program details of its logical parent, that is, PART.

There is only one problem with the definition in Figure 13.19. Both PART-

KEY field of TASK segment	PART-USE segment exclusive of its logical parent key	TASK segment (TASK-NO, TASK-DATA)

Figure 13.18   Logical child details presented to a program

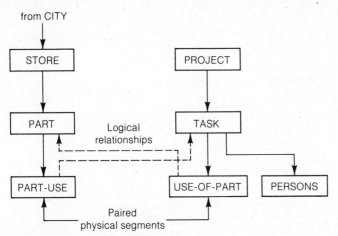

Figure 13.19   Pairing of segments

USE and USE-OF-PART store the same data. Hence, when an update is made, it must be made to both PART-USE and USE-OF-PART segments. Otherwise inconsistent data will be held in the segment. To avoid such inconsistencies, IMS allows the segments to be defined as PAIRED. If this is done, an update to one segment will be made automatically to the other (by IMS and not by the application program).

Finally, the structure in Figure 13.19 results in another undesirable property. The intersection data are stored twice in the database. To avoid this, it is possible to define one of the segments as VIRTUAL. If this is done, only one copy of the intersection data will be stored, although to the user it looks as though both segments exist in the database. Details of methods for defining PAIRED and VIRTUAL segments can be found in the literature.

Program Communication Blocks

Subsets of logical databases are made available to the application programs through the use of program communication blocks (PCBs). The DBNAME in the PCB defines the source logical database. The SENSEG statements define the segments of the source database. These segments are to be made available to the application program. All logical database segments need not be made available. The PROCOPT clause specifies the program's accessibility to the segment, which may be G (get), I (insert), R (replace), D (delete), L (load), or a combination of these. An example is given in Figure 13.20. Here the first PCB specifies that the program may insert and get any city segments from logical database CITIES. The second PCB allows a program not only to get any information about projects but also to insert, delete, or replace project TASK segments.

```
PCB       TYPE = DB, DBNAME = CITIES
SENSEG    NAME = CITY, PARENT = 0, PROCOPT = (G, I)
PCB       TYPE = DB, DBNAME = PROJECT-DATA
SENSEG    NAME = PROJECT, PARENT = 0, PROCOPT = G
SENSEG    NAME = TASK, PARENT = PROJECT, PROCOPT = (G, I, R, D)
```
Figure 13.20   Application program control blocks

Secondary Indexing

IMS also provides secondary indices to improve performance. These indices are designed to overcome problems that are inherent in logical hierarchical data structures. For example, the fact that a STORE is a child of CITY in Figure 13.6 means that information about a STORE can be found only by first accessing a CITY and then sequentially searching all the city stores for the required store. Similarly, because STORE-NAME is the STORE sequence key, a sequential search is necessary to find a store segment using a key field other than STORE-NAME.

Such problems can be overcome through the use of indices. IMS allows the following four items to be indexed:

• a root segment on a field other than the sequence field
• the root on a field in a dependent
• a dependent segment on a field in that dependent
• a dependent on a field in a lower-level dependent

The use of such indices is illustrated in Figure 13.21. An index using CITY-DATA as a key is added to segment CITY. The item CITY-DATA can be used

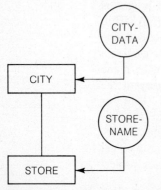

Figure 13.21   Secondary indices

as a key to CITY segments. Similarly, STORE can be accessed directly by using a field, STORE-NAME, without first accessing a CITY segment.

Indices are defined by the LCHILD statement. For example, consider an index on a field other than the sequence field of a root segment—say, an index to segment CITY, using field CITY-DATA. To define the index, the following statements would be included after the CITY SEGM statement:

LCHILD NAME = (TX1, TXDBD), POINTER = INDEX
XDFLD NAME = XTITLE, SEARCH = CITY-DATA

These statements define an index for the segment in a special physical database TXDBD. Database TXDBD had been specially created to store the index. This database is in turn defined by the database description

DBD NAME = TXDBD, ACCESS = INDEX
SEGM NAME = TX1
FIELD NAME = (CITY-DATA, SEQ)
LCHILD NAME = (STORE, LOCATIONS), INDEX = XTITLE

Here the ACCESS = INDEX clause defines the database index that has only one segment and one field; the field corresponds to the field of the indexed segment, which in turn is defined by the LCHILD statement.

See the literature for the database descriptions used to define indices on other than nonsequence field-to-root segments.

Accessing an IMS Database

Databases maintained by IMS are accessed by using a language called DL/1 (Data Language 1). Procedure calls to DL/1 can be made from application programs written in PL/1, COBOL, or Assembler Language. The calls to DL/1 require several parameters. The parameters identify various communication and I/O buffers as well as the type of call and a segment selection argument (SSA). The latter two parameters specify the segment or segments in the database to which the call refers and the kind of operation. Following are some of the commands supported by DL/1.

1. GET UNIQUE (GU): retrieves a segment that satisfies a given SSA.
2. GET NEXT (GN): retrieves the next segment in the database, using pre-order traversal.
3. GET NEXT WITHIN PARENT (GNP): is like GN but within the current parent segment.
4. GET HOLD (GHU, GHN, GHNP): is the same as GU, GN, and GNP but allows subsequent DLET and REPL.
5. INSERT (ISRT): inserts a new segment.

6. DELETE (DLET): deletes an existing segment.
7. REPLACE (REPL): replaces an existing segment.

Each call to DL/1 takes the form

CALL DL/1 (operation-type, parameters)

where parameters include the SSA; a special code is constructed to represent the parameters.

In this text a simplified (rather than the coded) form is used to describe DL/1 calls; it includes only the SSA parameter. As usual it is most convenient to commence with retrieval operations. Both direct and sequential retrievals are possible when using DL/1 calls.

Direct Retrieval

The GU call is used for direct retrieval. The SSA defines the hierarchical path used to retrieve a segment. This path can include any number of different segments. The simplest case is where the hierarchical path contains only the root segment of a physical database. The SSA argument in this case includes only the root segment name and the conditions to be satisfied by the retrieved segment. For example, given the logical database in Figure 13.8, we can retrieve a CITY segment by

GU CITY (CITY-NAME = 'ATLANTA')

It is also possible to directly retrieve segments other than the root segment. In this case the SSA argument must specify the hierarchical path to the required segment. For example, a PART-USE segment is retrieved by

```
GU  CITY      (CITY-NAME = 'ATLANTA')
    STORE     (STORE-NAME = 'STORE1')
    PART      (PART-ID = 'PART1')
    PART-USE  (DATE-ISSUED = 'JUN81')
```

This command specifies a path to a PART-USE segment through a given CITY, STORE, and PART segments. Hence it retrieves the PART-USE segment for an issue of PART1 made on JUN81 in ATLANTA store STORE1. If there were more than one issue of that part in the store for that month, the first such issue would be retrieved. Subsequent issues on that date would be retrieved by sequential retrieval commands.

Sequential Retrieval

The GN and GNP calls are used to retrieve segments in preorder sequence. A GU command establishes a current (or start) segment. The GN and GNP commands are then used to retrieve segments that follow this current segment and satisfy the conditions specified in the GN or GNP commands. There is one difference between the GN and GNP commands. The GN command calls continue the sequential search until the end of the database, setting a status indicator when the end is reached. A GNP command sets a status indicator when the end of the current parent is reached, and this indicator can then be used to terminate the search.

The GN and GNP calls include conditions that must be satisfied by the retrieved records. They retrieve only those records that satisfy these conditions. Segments are retrieved in their preorder traversal sequence in the hierarchy. For example, consider the retrieval of all stores in a city. This takes the form

```
GU CITY (CITY-NAME = 'ATLANTA')
REPEAT UNTIL end of ATLANTA stores
    GNP STORE
```

The GNP commands mean that retrieval continues within a parent, that is, the city ATLANTA. The end of ATLANTA stores is indicated by a status value returned after each DL/1 command.

If only stores that satisfy some STORE-DATA condition are to be output, STORE-DATA becomes a condition. The calls now are

```
GU CITIES (NAME = 'ATLANTA')
REPEAT UNTIL end of ATLANTA stores
    GNP STORES (STORE-DATA = '050777')
```

It is of course possible to make sequential retrievals without nominating conditions; in this case all segments will be retrieved. Thus

```
REPEAT UNTIL ALL CITY FOUND
    BEGIN
        GN CITY
        REPEAT UNTIL end of the CITY stores
            GNP STORES
    END
```

will output all cities and stores. Here all CITY records are retrieved in the outer loop. The inner loop retrieves all the store records within the current city.

Updating the Database

To delete or replace a segment a GET HOLD command must be executed first. The SSA for the GET HOLD command is the same as for the GU command.

Record deletion usually results in all the record's physical successors being deleted from the physical database. Its logical successors, on the other hand, may remain in the database, depending on the parameters associated with the delete statement.

To delete a store, the statements executed would take the form

```
GHU CITY (CITY-NAME = 'ATLANTA')
    STORE (STORE-NAME = 'XYZ')
DLET
```

This procedure would delete store XYZ from ATLANTA.

A replace (REPL) command is executed in a similar fashion. A segment is first found and held. A value in the segment is changed and the REPL command issued to replace the segment. An example is

```
GHU CITY (CITY-NAME = 'ATLANTA')
    STORE (STORE-NAME = 'STORE1')
        {change the value of STORE-DATA}
    REPL
```

This set of commands will change the value of STORE-DATA for ATLANTA store STORE1.

In the case of insertion (a segment inserted in the database), a hold command need not be executed first (as the segment does not exist). An example is

```
ISRT (CITY-NAME = 'ATLANTA'
    STORE-NAME = 'ABC')
```

This command adds a new store to ATLANTA.

Some Operational Features

IMS can be used in both batch and on-line modes. In the batch mode it is possible for more than one program to use IMS. The programs run independently of one another. Each uses a separate copy of those parts of IMS needed for program execution. There can be no loss of integrity if concurrent programs use different databases. However, database integrity can be lost if two programs update the same database (as there is no coordination between different programs). Hence each program in a batch environment usually gets exclusive use of a database to ensure integrity.

IMS can also run with a number of teleprocessing systems. When this is done, one copy of IMS can control more than one program and hence allow multithreading while maintaining system integrity. The most common monitors used with IMS are DB/DC and CICS, both IBM products. A detailed description of these systems is out of the scope of this text. The main difference between them is that CICS supports multitasking (see Figure 10.11), whereas in DB/DC there are separate activations for each executing program. Multithreading is supported by the transaction processors, and programs gain exclusive use to database components by executing the GET HOLD operations described earlier.

IMS supports database recovery by maintaining a log tape of before-and-after images of updated database segments. It includes recovery utilities to roll back the database to a previous state or to recover it to the last correct state.

GENERAL SELECTION

General-selection systems differ from traversal systems in one significant way. Tree traversal commands select one record at a time. Having selected one record, they then select the next record in a hierarchical path. Any required data are output in successive traversal steps. By contrast, general-selection systems specify the selection of all required data in one statement. For example, a general-selection statement to print the STORE-DATA of all stores in Atlanta would take a form such as

PRINT STORE-DATA WHERE CITY-NAME = 'ATLANTA'

Given this command, the hierarchical database management would itself determine the traversal path to retrieve the required records.

General-selection systems require that physical links exist between any logically related records. Any fields in these related records can then appear in one general-selection statement, and the system can find a traversal path between them, using the physical links. For this reason general-selection systems do not permit database partitioning. Or at least if the database is partitioned, each general-selection command refers to records in one partition only. If related records were in different partitions, there would be no hierarchical traversal path between them. General-selection statements, which include fields from these records, could then not be satisfied. A typical general-selection system is System 2000.

SYSTEM 2000

System 2000 (S2000) was one of the earliest general-selection systems. An S2000 database is not partitioned, and all the database is one hierarchy. The record types that make up the database are arranged into one hierarchical tree structure.

The System 2000 Data Structure

An example of a data structure that can be stored as an S2000 database is shown in Figure 13.22. It has only one root node, and each record type has only one parent. It describes the departments, the projects controlled by the depart-

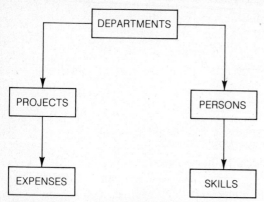

Figure 13.22   A System 2000 data structure

ments, and the persons assigned to the departments. Persons' skills and the expenses incurred by the projects are also stored in the database.

Each of the record types of the hierarchical structure in Figure 13.22 is defined as an S2000 *repeating group* (RG) (although now the term *schema record* is frequently used instead). Thus DEPARTMENTS, PROJECTS, and so on in the figure become RGs in an S2000 database. Each of these RGs is made up of any number of fields. Record occurrences of a particular RG take field values for the fields in that RG.

Populated Database

There may be any number of RG occurrences in a populated database. Each RG occurrence is made up of the fields defined for the RG and is a child of only one parent RG. One such populated database is illustrated in Figure 13.23, in which the following appear:

- two occurrences of the RG DEPARTMENT, one named ELECTRONICS and the other RESEARCH
- two occurrences of the RG PROJECT within ELECTRONICS and two within RESEARCH
- one occurrence of the RG PERSON within ELECTRONICS and none within RESEARCH
- a number of EXPENSEs for each PROJECT and SKILLs for PERSON

Defining the System 2000 Database

An S2000 schema definition defines each RG, together with the fields included in the RG. An example of a schema definition is given in Figure 13.24, which defines the data structure shown in Figure 13.22.

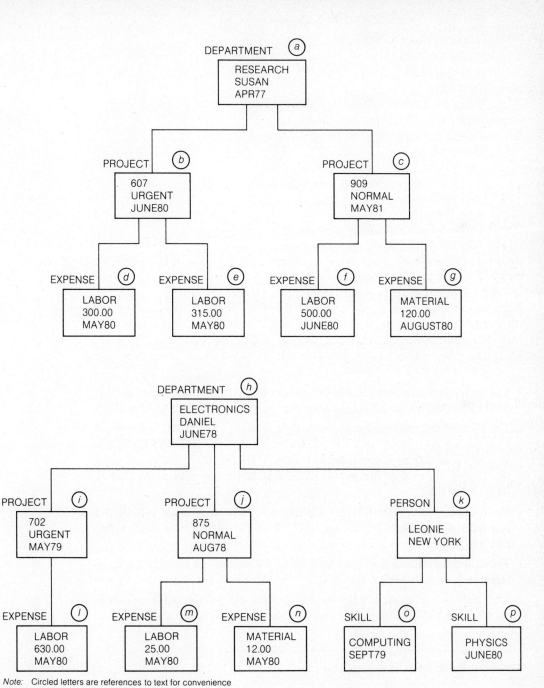

Note: Circled letters are references to text for convenience

Figure 13.23 A populated database

```
 1*  DEPARTMENT (NAME X(15))
 2*  MANAGER (NAME X(20))
 3*  DATE-ESTABLISHED (NON-KEY DATE)
 4*  PROJECTS (RG)
      5*  PROJECT-NUMBER (INTEGER NUMBER 9(6) IN 4)
      6*  PROJECT-STATUS (NAME X(10) IN 4)
      7*  DATE-STARTED (DATE IN 4)
      8*  EXPENSES (RG IN 4)
           9*  EXPENSE-TYPE (NAME X(6) IN 8)
          10*  AMOUNT (NON-KEY DECIMAL NUMBER 9(5).99 IN 8)
          11*  EXPENSE-DATE (DATE IN 8)
12*  PERSONS (RG)
     13*  PERSON-NAME (NAME X(20) IN 12)
     14*  PERSON-ADDRESS (NON-KEY NAME X(30) IN 12)
     15*  SKILL (RG)
          16*  SKILL-NAME (NAME X(10) IN 15)
          17*  DATE-ACQUIRED (DATE IN 15)
```

Figure 13.24 A schema definition

Each database component is given a number in the S2000 schema as in the following:

- The component numbers precede the names; thus 4 is the component number of RG PROJECTS, and 2 is the component number of the field MANAGER.

- The hierarchical relationship between RGs is defined in the RG description. Thus (RG IN 4) following EXPENSES states that the RG EXPENSES is an RG whose parent is component 4, that is, PROJECTS; (RG) following PERSONS states that the parent of PERSONS is the root node, that is, DEPARTMENT.

- Field names follow the RG of which they are a part; thus AMOUNT is a field within EXPENSES and PROJECT-NUMBER is a field within PROJECTS.

- The field description follows the field name. Fields may be alphanumeric, integer, real, or date fields.

- Each field is by default a KEY field unless the word NON-KEY is part of the field description (the significance of this will be discussed shortly).

Accessing the System 2000 Database

S2000 allows databases to be accessed both through commands embedded in host languages and by a stand-alone language. It allows database access commands to be embedded in COBOL, PL/1, Assembler, and FORTRAN. The stand-alone interface is known as Natural Language. This language includes options for both batch operations (Queue Access) and on-line access (Immediate Access). Some commands available for on-line access are described here to illustrate the methods used in general-selection retrieval.

Hierarchical Access Commands

One way to describe hierarchical selection commands is to make a distinction between selected database components and qualified database components. A selection command takes the general form

PRINT ⟨qualified component⟩ WHERE ⟨condition⟩

Here ⟨condition⟩ includes the selected components. For example, in the statement

PRINT DEPARTMENT WHERE PROJECT-NUMBER = 909

DEPARTMENT is the qualified component (or the component to be output), and PROJECT-NUMBER is the selected component (or the component that must satisfy the selection condition).

The qualified and selected components need not be on the same record type or RG. The usual method is to select RGs. Once this is done, the qualified components may be

- fields within the selected RG
- RGs that are hierarchical ancestors or descendants of the selected RG
- fields within qualified RGs

Hierarchical commands thus differ from those used in the network model. In the network model one record is selected. Then a series of commands are used to "navigate" from the selected record to the required (or qualified) record. Thus the relationship between the qualified and selected records is explicitly specified by a sequence of navigational commands. In hierarchical access, by contrast, the access command must both include the selection conditions and define the path between the selected and qualified records. The path between the selected and qualified records in the hierarchical model is unique (because each record type has at most one parent). This, of course, is not the case in the network model. Hence it is not necessary to specify the path from the qualified to the selected records in hierarchical access as is the case in network access. However, there are still ambiguities that can arise in hierarchical commands where qualified and selected fields are not in the same record type. These ambiguities are described in the context of S2000 Immediate Access.

System 2000 Immediate Access

The main statement used in Immediate Access retrieval is the PRINT statement. A part of the definition of the PRINT statement is given in Figure 13.25. The PRINT statement can be used with or without selection conditions.

PRINT <print clause>, <ordering clause> WHERE <condition clause>
<print clause> ::= /option list/<object list>

object list is the key, nonkey fields, and repeating groups,
referenced by name or C number. The object list also includes
system functions. Fields and functions in the object list are
outputs following the PRINT statement.

OPTIONS include (with default underlined)
SINGLE SPACE or DOUBLE-SPACE
NUMBER or NAME
REPEAT or REPEAT SUPPRESS
INDENT or BLOCK

<ordering clause> ::= ORDERED BY <ordering list>
<condition clause> ::= (any of the following clauses (a) to (e))

(a) <condition> ::=
<field name> <binary operator> <specific value>
NOTE: The field name must be defined as a KEY item
<binary operator> ::= EQ/NE/LT/GT/LE/GE

(b) <repeating group> ⌐EXISTS————————┐
                        └DOES NOT EXIST ↑

(c) <Boolean expression> ::= <condition> AND <condition>
                              <condition> OR <condition>
                              NOT <condition>

(d) <HAS clause> ::=
<repeating group> HAS <condition clause>

(e) (<condition clause>)

Figure 13.25 The PRINT statement

Output without Conditions The simplest form of the PRINT statement does not use the condition clause; in this case all components referenced in the object list are output. For example,

PRINT DEPARTMENT

will output all customer names; the resultant output is

1 * RESEARCH
1 * ELECTRONICS

If the NAME option is used, field names rather than component numbers appear in the output. Thus PRINT/NAME/DEPARTMENT results in

DEPARTMENT * RESEARCH
DEPARTMENT * ELECTRONICS

The ordering clause can be used to specify the ordering of the output. Thus PRINT DEPARTMENT ORDERED BY DEPARTMENT results in

1 * ELECTRONICS
1 * RESEARCH

Note that ELECTRONICS now precedes RESEARCH.

In an extension of the unconditional PRINT statement, items in the object list appear in different RGs. For example,

PRINT DEPARTMENT, PROJECT-STATUS, PROJECT-NUMBER

Here the project status and number for each department are to be output. The result is

```
1 * RESEARCH
    5 * URGENT
    6 * 607
1 * RESEARCH
    5 * NORMAL
    6 * 909
1 * ELECTRONICS
    5 * URGENT
    6 * 702
1 * ELECTRONICS
    5 * NORMAL
    6 * 875
```

Here the components of parent RGs are repeated for each occurrence of the child RG. Such repetition can be suppressed by using the REPEAT SUP-PRESS option. Thus

PRINT/REPEAT SUPPRESS/DEPARTMENT, PROJECT-STATUS, PROJECT-NUMBER

results in

```
1 * RESEARCH
    6 * URGENT
    5 * 607
    6 * NORMAL
    5 * 909
1 * ELECTRONICS
    6 * URGENT
    5 * 702
    6 * NORMAL
    5 * 875
```

Output with Conditions In an output with conditions, the condition clause is used to select specific RG occurrences. Two distinct classes of conditional print request can then be identified:

- The fields in the object list (i.e., the qualified fields) are either in the selected RGs or in RGs that are the descendants of the selected RG.
- The fields in the object list are in the ancestors of the selected RG.

Qualified Fields in Descendant Nodes

The first of the two classes just cited is the simplest. With qualified fields in descendant nodes it is always clear which descendants are to be qualified. For example, for Figure 13.23 the statement PRINT PROJECT-NUMBER WHERE DEPARTMENT = RESEARCH will

- select RG a
- qualify all RG descendants of RG a
- output PROJECT-NUMBER from these qualified RGs, namely,

5 * 607
5 * 909

Qualified Fields in Ancestor Nodes

In the case of qualified fields in ancestor nodes, it is not always clear which RGs qualify for output. For example, again working with Figure 13.23, suppose we wish to find "the PROJECT-NUMBER of projects that had both a LABOR and a MATERIAL expense during MAY80." As a first attempt we would propose the statement shown in Figure 13.26 for the query. However, this statement will not work because it implies an expense that is both a LABOR and a MATERIAL expense. What is needed is a statement where the clauses EXPENSE-TYPE = MATERIAL and EXPENSE-TYPE = LABOR refer to different EXPENSE records.

To resolve this problem, the HAS condition is included in the PRINT statement SYNTAX to define the RG at which qualification is to take place. Figure 13.27 uses this clause for the previous query.

The first condition in Figure 13.27 selects records d, e, l, and m (as these are LABOR expenses in MAY80). These records in turn qualify PROJECTS records b, i, and j. Similarly, the second condition in Figure 13.27 selects n because this is the only MATERIAL expense in MAY80. Record n in turn qualifies PROJECTS record j. The logical AND then requires that a PROJECTS record be qualified only if it is qualified by both conditions in Figure 13.27. Since only PROJECTS record j qualifies, the output is PROJECT-NUMBER 875.

Updating the Database Several commands are available for updating the database. These include the following:

```
PRINT  PROJECT-NUMBER
          WHERE (EXPENSE-DATE = MAY80
                 AND EXPENSE-TYPE = LABOR)
          AND (EXPENSE-DATE = MAY80
                 AND EXPENSE-TYPE = MATERIAL)
```

Figure 13.26 An incorrect query specification

```
PRINT   PROJECT-NUMBER
        WHERE (PROJECTS HAS EXPENSE
               WHERE EXPENSE-DATE = MAY80
                 AND EXPENSE-TYPE = LABOR)
        AND (PROJECTS HAS EXPENSE
               WHERE EXPENSE-DATE = MAY 80
                 AND EXPENSE-TYPE = MATERIAL)
```

Figure 13.27 Using the HAS clause

1. CHANGE ⟨field-name⟩ EQ ⟨value⟩ WHERE ⟨condition⟩
   The value of the field is changed in the qualified RG.
2. REMOVE ⎡ ⟨field⟩ ──────── ⎤ WHERE ⟨condition⟩
          ⎣ ⟨repeating group⟩ ⎦
   The qualified field or RG is removed from the database.
3. REMOVE TREE ⟨repeating group⟩ WHERE ⟨condition⟩
   The qualified RG and all its descendants are removed from the database.
4. ASSIGN TREE ⟨repeating group⟩ EQ ⟨value string⟩ WHERE ⟨condition⟩
   This command replaces RGs qualified by the condition by the tree described by the value string.
5. INSERT TREE ⟨repeating group⟩ EQ ⟨value string⟩
   ⎧ BEFORE ⎫ ⟨condition⟩
   ⎩ AFTER ⎭
   This command inserts a new RG, which is described by the value string into the database. The condition determines the position in which the new tree is inserted.

The value string is a string of values preceded by component numbers that specify a tree in preorder traversal. For example,

    * 4 * 5 * 607 * 6 * URGENT * 8 * 9 * LABOR * 10 * 300.00 *
    11 * MAY 80 * 8 * 9 * LABOR * 10 * 315.00 * 11 * MAY 80

is the value string that describes the tree made up of RGs *b*, *d*, and *e* in Figure 13.23.

A new expense can be added to the database by the command

    INSERT TREE EXPENSES EQ 9 * LABOR * 10 * 150.00 * 11 AUG 80
        AFTER C5 EQ 607 AND (C9 EQ LABOR and C11 EQ MAY 80
        and C10 EQ 315.00)

This transaction is added to PROJECT 607. It is inserted after record *e*.

Embedded Language Facilities

The S2000 embedded language allows programs to navigate the database in a manner similar to that used with the network model. It includes a LOCATE command to locate an RG that satisfies a specified condition. GET commands can then be used to retrieve the RGs found by the LOCATE command. Navigation is permitted to other RGs by the GETA and GETD statements. The GETA statement retrieves the direct ancestor of the current retrieved record. The GETD statement can be used to retrieve an RG's descendants.

Physical Database Structure

The physical structure of databases maintained by S2000 is designed to enhance performance. Two structures achieve this:

1. An inverted list that allows direct access to RGs, given some item value. One such inverted list is set up for each field, which is defined as a KEY field.
2. Internal links from each repeating group to its parent and to the next sibling within the parent.

There are three kinds of internal links:

- the PARENT (P) link to the parent of the RG
- the FIRST CHILD (FC) link to the first child of an RG
- the NEXT SIBLING (NS) link to the next RG owned by the same parent

Figure 13.28 shows this pointer structure for the database of Figure 13.23.

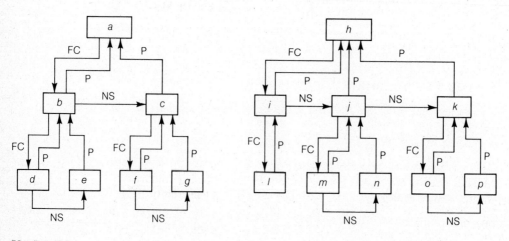

FC = first child
NS = next sibling
P = parent

Figure 13.28   Pointer structure for the database in Figure 13.23

Here, for example, the direct successors of DEPARTMENTs RG h are the PROJECT RGs i and j and the PERSON RG k. The FC pointer from h points to i, which is the first child of h; in this chain, each successor has a parent pointer to its parent—that is, there is a P pointer from each i, j, and k to h.

Note that direct paths are available from any RG to RGs that are either the ancestors or the descendants of the RG. Such paths are followed when qualifying RGs from a selected RG. Thus efficiency of processing is enhanced for two reasons:

1. An RG is selected by using an inverted list.
2. The qualifying RGs are found by following qualifying paths.

The pointer structure is maintained by internal system tables. These are illustrated in Figure 13.29 for the database in Figure 13.23 and can be described as follows:

1. The values of fields in RGs are stored in a DATA STORE.
2. The *hierarchical table* includes one entry for each RG. This table contains a pointer to the RG in the *data store* and the FC, NS, and P pointers; the last three pointers are to hierarchical table entries that correspond to the RGs.
3. The inverted lists are maintained in a *unique value* together with a *multiple occurrence table* (MOT). The MOT is used only when there are a number of RGs with the same item value.

Thus the data are stored separately from the pointer structure. All manipulations to obtain qualified RGs can be done with the hierarchical table without accessing DATA records, thus improving processing efficiency.

Some System 2000 Operational Features

System 2000 supports concurrent access and provides for recovery and privacy controls. Concurrent access is provided through a multi-user and multithread feature. These features enable RGs to be held on behalf of concurrently executing programs. In Queued Access the hold is global. A program obtains a hold when it issues an update command. No other program can modify the database until the hold is released (other programs can of course modify other databases). Other programs can, however, read a locked database. In Immediate Access, holds are local. Only the object RG is held by one program; other programs can modify other RGs in the database.

1	2	3	4	5	6	7	8	9	10	11	12	13	14	15	16
a	k	d	b	p	c	e	n	j	g	o	i	m	l	f	h

DATA STORE

HIERARCHIAL

	RG TYPE	DATA TABLE	FIRST CHILD	NEXT SIBLING	PARENT
1	C0	1	2	4	
2	C4	4	3	5	1
3	C8	3	Null	6	2
4	C0	16	8	Null	
5	C4	6	7	Null	1
6	C8	7	Null	Null	2
7	C8	15	Null	9	5
8	C4	12	13	11	4
9	C8	10	Null	Null	5
10	C8	13	Null	15	11
11	C4	9	10	12	4
12	C12	2	14	Null	4
13	C8	14	Null	Null	8
14	C15	11	Null	16	12
15	C8	8	Null	Null	11
16	C15	5	Null	Null	12

HIERARCHICAL TABLE

MULTIPLE OCCURRENCE TABLE (MOT)

1	2	8
2	5	11

UNIQUE VALUE

LAST NAME		*	ACCT TYPE		*	
RESEARCH	1	0	URGENT	1	1	Other inverted
ELECTRONICS	4	0	NORMAL	2	1	lists

INVERTED LIST made up of a UNIQUE VALUE TABLE and a MULTIPLE OCCURRENCE TABLE

*0 if POINTER to HIERARCHIAL TABLE, 1 if POINTER to MOT

Figure 13.29 Pointer maintenance in systems tables

SUMMARY

The hierarchical data model, like the network model, delineates object classes and the relationships among them. But the hierarchical model restricts each object class to having only one parent object class, though that class can have more than one child object class.

The hierarchical data model has two kinds of implementation: the tree traversal and the general-selection implementation. In tree traversal, records are arranged in a hierarchy, and each record can have at most one parent in this hierarchy. Records can be accessed by traversing the tree in some order to get the record—hence tree traversal implementation. Alternatively, records or nodes in the hierarchy can be selected by a general-selection statement; records related to the selected record by hierarchical paths are then output. Ambiguities can arise when qualified and selected records are specified in the same command.

IMS, a DBMS supported by IBM, is based on tree traversal. It can be used in both batch and on-line modes and can be run with several teleprocessing systems. System 2000, a DBMS based on general selection, supports concurrent access and provides for recovery and privacy controls.

PROBLEMS

Problem 1

Suppose a hierarchical database contains two record types, PERSON and PROJECT. The relationship between projects and persons is $N:M$, and on an average there are 40 persons assigned to a project, each person being assigned to 3 projects.

Consider the two structures in Figure 13.30.

(a) Compute the amount of data storage required to store this database for the two schema. Ignore pointer storage and assume there are 30 projects and 400 persons. Also assume the following:
- The intersection data is 10 characters.
- The person and project identifiers are 10 characters.
- Person attributes other than identifier are 30 characters.
- Project attributes other than identifier are 40 characters.

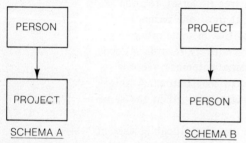

Figure 13.30   Data structures for Problem 1

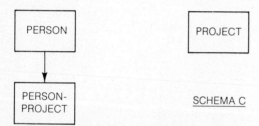

Figure 13.31   Partitioned structure for Problem 1

(b) Now the database has been partitioned and only intersection data together with the project identifier are stored in **PERSON-PROJECT**, as shown in Figure 13.31. Compute the amount of data storage used now. Would there be any difference in the data storage used if
(i) PERSON-PROJECT became subordinate to PROJECT?
(ii) the sizes of the PERSON and PROJECT identifiers were the same?

Problem 2

Suppose we have the IMS schema shown in Figure 13.32.

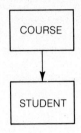

1. DBD   NAME = STUDIES, ACCESS = HSAM
2. SEGM   NAME = COURSE, BYTES = 49
3. FIELD   NAME = (COURSE-NAME, SEQ, U), BYTES = 40, START = 1
4. FIELD   NAME = FACULTY, BYTES = 6, START = 41
5. FIELD   NAME = DATE-FIRST-OFFERED, BYTES = 3, START = 47
6. SEGM   NAME = STUDENT, BYTES = 50, ACCESS = HSAM, PARENT = UNIT
7. FIELD   NAME = (STUDENT-ID, SEQ, M), BYTES = 6, START = 1
8. FIELD   NAME = STUDENT-NAME, BYTES = 40, START = 7
9. FIELD   NAME = SEMESTER-TAKEN, BYTES = 3, START = 47
10. FIELD NAME = GRADE, BYTES = 1, START = 50

Figure 13.32   IMS schema for Problem 2

(a) Illustrate the physical organization of the database, given the database population in Figure 13.33.

COURSE				STUDENT			
COURSE-NAME	FACULTY	DATE-FIRST-OFFERED	PARENT	STUDENT-ID	STUDENT-NAME	SEMESTER-TAKEN	GRADE
DATABASE SYSTEMS (DBS)	SCIENCE	280	(DBS)	769001	JOE	280	A
			(IS1)	769001	JOE	179	D
			(IS1)	769003	JILL	180	F
INFORMATION SYSTEMS 1 (IS1)	SCIENCE	170	(DBS)	769005	BETTY	281	A
			(IS1)	769006	BILL	279	C
			(IS1)	769003	JILL	280	C

Note: The STUDENT record does not contain COURSE-NAME because COURSE is the parent.
The parent for each STUDENT record is shown in parentheses.

Figure 13.33   Database population for Problem 2

(b) Write retrieval requests, using pseudocode, to find
   (i) the grade of all students in course DBS
   (ii) the grade of all students in course DBS in a semester 280
   (iii) the grade of JILL in the course IS1
Comment on the efficiency of processing these three requests.

(c) Suppose now the following change is made to the schema:

    1 ACCESS becomes ACCESS = HDAM
    6 ACCESS becomes ACCESS = HDAM, POINTER = TWIN

Illustrate the physical structure of the database given this new definition.
   Will the same code as used in (b) still be effective, given the new structure?

Problem 3

The IMS database in Figure 13.32 is now expanded to include a MAJORS
record. The new schema is given in Figure 13.34. In the new schema there are
two physical databases, together with a logical parent link from STUDENT to
MAJOR.

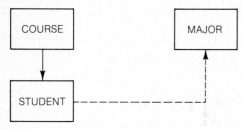

There are two physical data bases, together with a logical link from COURSE to STUDENT.

1. DBA NAME = STUDIES, ACCESS = HDAM
2. SEGM NAME = UNIT, BYTES = 49
3.
4. same as in Problem 1
5.
6. SEGM NAME = STUDENT, BYTES = 50, ACCESS
     PARENT = (UNIT, (MAJOR, MAJORS)), POINTER = TWINBWD, LPARENT, LTWIN)
7.
8.
9. same as in Problem 1
10.
11. DBD NAME = MAJORS, ACCESS = HDAM
12. SEGM NAME = MAJOR, BYTES = 16
13. LCHILD NAME = (STUDIES, STUDENT), POINTER = SNGL, RULES = FIRST
14. FIELD NAME = (MAJOR-NAME, SEQ, U), BYTES = 6
15. FIELD NAME = MANAGED-BY-FACULTY, BYTES = 6, START = 7
16. FIELD NAME = DATE-APPROVED, BYTES = 4, START = 13

Figure 13.34 IMS schema for Problem 3

(a) Illustrate the physical organization of the database, given the following:

MAJOR MAJOR-NAME	MANAGED-BY- FACULTY	DATE-APPROVED
COMPSCI	SCIENCE	1972
MATHS	SCIENCE	1961
LIBR	LIBSTU	1972

Also assume that
- JOE and JILL are enrolled in COMPSCI
- BILL and BETTY are enrolled in LIBR

(b) Define a logical database that can be used to list the majors of all students in a given course. Write the skeleton code to list the majors of all students in DBS given this logical database.

(c) Would you need to redesign the schema to answer the query to list all students taking major LIBR who are also taking courses offered by SCIENCE? (Commence by considering whether this query can be answered from one logical database.)

Problem 4

The database in Problem 2 is now defined in Figure 13.35, using System 2000. Note that only the student's current course is stored in the database.

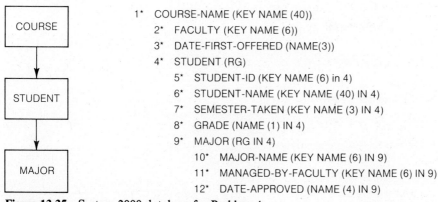

```
1*  COURSE-NAME (KEY NAME (40))
   2*  FACULTY (KEY NAME (6))
   3*  DATE-FIRST-OFFERED (NAME(3))
   4*  STUDENT (RG)
      5*  STUDENT-ID (KEY NAME (6) in 4)
      6*  STUDENT-NAME (KEY NAME (40) IN 4)
      7*  SEMESTER-TAKEN (KEY NAME (3) IN 4)
      8*  GRADE (NAME (1) IN 4)
      9*  MAJOR (RG IN 4)
         10*  MAJOR-NAME (KEY NAME (6) IN 9)
         11*  MANAGED-BY-FACULTY (KEY NAME (6) IN 9)
         12*  DATE-APPROVED (NAME (4) IN 9)
```

Figure 13.35 System 2000 database for Problem 4

Write retrieval requests to find

(a) the grade of all students in course DBS
(b) the grade of all students in course DBS in semester 280
(c) the grade of JILL in the course IS1
(d) all students in major LIBR taking courses in SCIENCE
(e) all courses that have been taken both by students currently enrolled in major LIBR and by students currently enrolled in major COMPSCI

chapter fourteen
The Design Process

INTRODUCTION

Many methodologies are used in database design. A design methodology is characterized by the design techniques it uses and the sequence in which it applies them. Most design processes are iterative. As shown in Figure 14.1, an iterative process commences with a database specification. The first step is initial design. In this first step the designer uses sets of rules to convert enterprise object sets or logical record structures to data model structures. The initial database structure is then analyzed by design analysis techniques. Design analysis techniques are generally quantitative in nature. They make quantitative

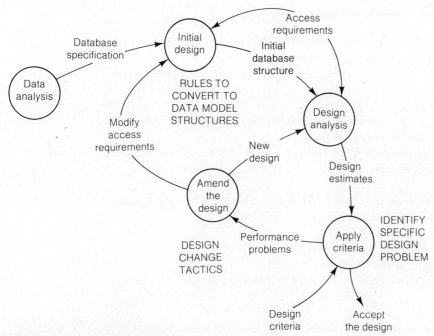

Figure 14.1 The design process

estimates of important design factors such as storage requirements or transaction response times. Criteria determined by the design environment are then applied to these estimates. Storage requirements would be an important criterion if the designer's installation has limited secondary storage. Transaction response is important in interactive systems. If the essential criteria are not met by the design, it is amended. Alternatively, if the design amendments necessary to meet some access requirement are deemed unreasonable and expensive, users may be asked to modify that requirement. Design analysis and amendments are often repeated before a satisfactory design is found.

Iterative design poses one problem: it requires tedious design computations to be repeated at each iteration. Without these repetitions, objective design trade-offs are not made and poor designs may result. For this reason database design methodologies must control the iterative process. The goal of such control is to minimize the amount of repetition while ensuring that all trade-offs are brought to light. To do this, specific design problems must be identified in an orderly way and appropriate design changes applied for each problem. Iterations can be controlled by dealing with specific problems in successive iterations.

This chapter will describe procedures used by various design methodologies and the kinds of techniques involved. Later chapters will describe these techniques in detail.

DESIGN OBJECTIVES

Database design must satisfy a number of criteria. These criteria can be divided into two major classes: structure and performance criteria.

Structure criteria concern the preservation of the data properties, specifically,

- the preservation of correspondence to normal relations to avoid anomalies and data duplication (storage criteria)
- the preservation of integrity links between object sets to prevent database inconsistencies (link criteria)

Performance criteria, on the other hand, concern resource use and database access. Important performance criteria are as follows:

- Transaction response requirements must be met.
- A minimum amount of storage should be used.
- The number of transfers between memory and storage devices must be minimized.

Database design methodologies must include all the design techniques needed to design databases that satisfy all these criteria.

DESIGN TECHNIQUES

Most database design methodologies distinguish between logical and physical design techniques. Designers usually define logical design techniques as

- the choice and naming of file or database records
- the arrangement of items into files or database records
- the choice of links between records in the same and in different files
- the choice of record keys
- physical access paths superimposed on the file or database records to provide access paths for on-line requirements

Physical design techniques, on the other hand, include

- the selection of physical file organization for files or database records
- consideration of alternative implementations of physical access
- the physical block size and the arrangement of records on physical devices
- the handling of overflow
- the arrangement of file indices

Logical and physical design takes place through the entire design process. There is some logical and physical design in the initial design stages, when the initial data structure is chosen and major physical decisions are made. Such major physical decisions may include the selection of location modes or of set orders in a DBTG database. The type of IMS hierarchical access method may also be selected for each IMS physical database during initial design. The details of each physical data structure, such as block size or overflow areas, are chosen in later iterations.

Of the various logical and physical design techniques, most take the form of rules that either

- convert a structure based on one model to a structure based on another model, given some criteria, or
- amend a structure, given a design problem.

The rules will vary depending on the models, the criteria, and the design problem.

Combining Techniques into a Design Methodology

Ideally, it would be desirable to split the design into steps so that each successive step dealt with a subset of criteria. The ideal method would use two steps:

- logical design to convert the enterprise model to a data model, using structure criteria
- physical design to amend the logical design to meet performance criteria while maintaining structure criteria

This ideal process, however, cannot always be achieved. Implementation model limitations introduce complex relationships between the criteria. These relationships are such that one set of criteria can be satisfied only at the expense of another set. One general trade-off is between storage (and normal form correspondence) and transaction response. Often duplicating data (and hence violating normal form correspondence) will improve transaction response. For this reason designs are iterative and designers make trade-offs between criteria in successive iterations.

The kind of trade-off is often influenced by the implementation model. More trade-offs are necessary if the implementation model offers few design options than if it offers a wide range of facilities. As a general rule, most record-based implementation models maintain relatively simple relationships between record types and do not directly support richer semantic abstractions such as roles or types. Such abstractions must then be mapped into "unnatural" representations by record structures. This mapping often results in some nonhomogeneity and in the loss of integrity-preserving links. In such cases designers can frequently choose to sacrifice link criteria for storage criteria, or vice versa.

A number of alternative design methods are available. The chosen method often depends on the implementation model and the importance placed on the various design criteria. Most design methods distinguish the initial design from the subsequent iterations.

INITIAL DESIGN

The goal of initial design is to produce a feasible design structure, one that will not be optimized but will satisfy all access requirements. The two most common initial design methods are illustrated in Figure 14.2. The methods differ in the sequence in which the designer considers structure and performance criteria.

The databased methods (Figure 14.2a) first convert the enterprise model to a data model structure. This first step does not consider access requirements but only structure criteria. Logical access paths are then plotted on this initial design. These access paths are similar to those plotted on the logical record structure in Chapter 8, but may differ in notation. The notation may be chosen to suit a particular data model. The access paths show the

- records required by the access requirement
- the sequence in which these records are accessed

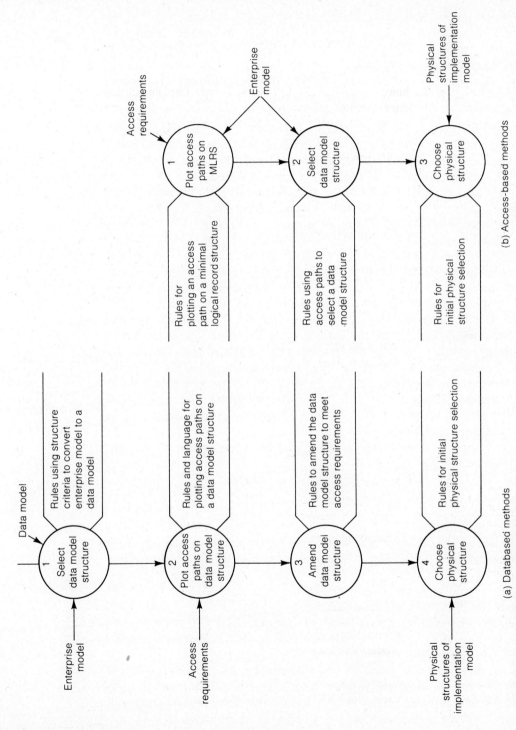

Figure 14.2 Alternative initial design methods

Design rules use these access paths to amend the data storage chosen in step 1 and to select physical access paths. That permits all records required by transactions to be directly retrieved.

The access-based methods (Figure 14.2b) emphasize performance criteria. Here access paths are first plotted on the logical record structure. These paths are used to select the data model structure as well as the initial physical structure.

The choice of method often depends on the DBMS. For example, some systems, especially the hierarchical ones, require designers to choose the root nodes as a first step. The access requirements serve to identify these root nodes, and so access-based methods are more appropriate for such systems.

A common variation of initial design is to present several alternative initial designs. One design is selected for further consideration after gross, rather than detailed, initial evaluation. For example, alternate root nodes can be tried on a hierarchical database to select the one that uses least storage.

Which method is better? It is difficult to say. An access-based approach will ensure an alternative that closely satisfies today's access requirements. The data-based approach may introduce some access inefficiencies because it includes special links to preserve structure criteria. So we would expect the access-based approach to be better tuned to today's needs. But what if these needs change? How easy will it be to adapt the existing design to these new needs? Some designers claim that databased designs are better in this respect. Here access paths are superimposed on the logical structure to satisfy access needs. It now becomes a matter of removing the access paths superimposed for the first requirements and adding access paths for new requirements. The basic logical structure remains the same. In access-based design, the logical structure itself is chosen to meet access requirements. So the logical structure will need to be changed to meet new requirements. This is always a more difficult proposition.

Choosing the Initial Physical Structure

The choice of physical structure is the same for both access-based and data-based methods. It follows the choice of logical structure. Initial physical design includes

- the choice of the physical file organization
- the arrangement of records on the chosen file organization
- the selection of physical organization for indices and links between records

In the practical sense, physical design commences by choosing the initial physical structure, using the manufacturer's recommendations and a gross knowledge of transaction traffic. The initial design can be amended during subsequent iterations by using more detailed performance estimates.

Initial physical design assumes that any indices or primary keys have already been chosen during logical design. It is now necessary to take each structure in the logical database and select a physical structure for it. The range of physical structures available for this choice vary with the DBMS. Usually the DBMS manufacturer provides recommendations for the selection of physical structure. Designers use these recommendations, or their earlier experience, to make the initial choice. Usually when manufacturers provide alternate physical organizations, then each such organization is intended for a different transaction processing profile. For example, take IBM's IMS. It provides a number of access methods. Of these, HISAM is recommended for data access requirements that include few insertions and deletions and where retrievals usually refer to clusters of records within the same parent. Direct access methods (HDAM or HIDAM), on the other hand, are preferable if there is high file volatility. The initial choice is usually made by using gross criteria of this kind. This choice can of course be modified in iterations subsequent to design analysis.

As a second step, designers must organize the arrangement of records within the chosen access method. Common decisions here are to

- choose the physical record size
- choose the blocking factor
- make provision for overflow

These decisions are in turn governed by transaction characteristics such as

- the relative frequency of insertions, deletions, and retrievals
- the file size
- the number of records accessed by each transaction

The goals of the decisions here are

- to fully utilize storage by minimizing free space in physical blocks
- to minimize effects of records in overflow areas on response times
- to allow multiple buffers for systems to allow concurrent processing of buffers

The choice of record arrangement and file space utilization introduces a number of conflicts. For example, full storage utilization with no free space in data blocks implies that newly inserted records are always placed in overflow areas. In some access method organizations both insertion and retrieval of such records may take longer because appropriate chains must be set up and traversed during file access. Hence designers must reach a satisfactory balance that leaves enough free space to minimize overflow record processing while still maintaining a high storage utilization. File size can be an important criterion here because a small increase in free space ratio means a large amount of actual storage.

A possible procedure for the arrangement of records is as follows:

1. Examine transactions to find those that select more than one logically related record.
2. Attempt to choose a blocking factor and method of blocking that blocks such records into single physical records or pages.
3. Add the suggested provision for overflow.
4. Modify the overflow provision as necessary by buffer space limitations or physical device characteristics.

The chosen structure now forms a basis for further analysis. This analysis proceeds in an iterative way.

DESIGN ITERATIONS

Once the initial design is accepted, the designer attempts to improve it. Various design trade-offs are made to reach an optimum design. Usually there are a large number of closely related trade-offs, and it becomes necessary to introduce some system and control to the design process at this stage. This is done by selecting limited objectives for each successive iteration in the manner shown in Figure 14.3. The first step here is to analyze the design and produce performance estimates. These estimates are then compared with design criteria to identify performance problems.

Performance Problems

Design analysis produces performance estimates that may indicate any of the following *performance problems:*

- The response time is too slow for some on-line transaction requirements.
- There is excessive storage use.
- The I/O channels are overloaded.

The designers then examine the design to determine any logical structures that cause these performance problems. If any such structures are found, they become *design problems* to be removed during any design amendments. Designers apply different *design tactics* to remove the problems.

Design Problems

There are many kinds of design problems: some apply to particular file organizations or database structures; others are more general. General problems include

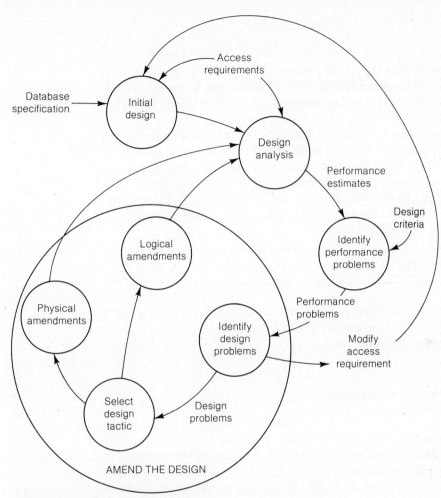

Figure 14.3   Design iterations

- PR0 too many logical records accessed in an access step
- PR1 too many access steps for an access requirement
- PR2 excessive use of intermediate files and sorting
- PR3 too many physical records accessed in access step
- PR4 excessive storage use; may be caused by unused space or use of long names as identifiers
- PR5 excessive overheads caused by the DBMS or by operating system functions

Once the design problems are identified, the designer can select various design tactics to overcome them. Ideally, a set of design tactics are provided for each problem. The designer selects one of the tactics and amends the design. Some local computations are often made to choose the most appropriate tactic.

Design Tactics

Design tactics identify both the possible changes to overcome a particular problem and the effect of these changes on design criteria. Designers can accordingly make a decision on whether they are prepared to accept the change within their environment.

The design tactics cannot, of course, be absolute in the sense that they specify a given action. They can identify only trade-offs, which can be quantitative. A typical quantitative trade-off is storage versus response time. Usually data duplication uses more storage but improves response to certain on-line requirements. The designer can therefore consider the limitations of available equipment and the importance of the response to make the necessary trade-off.

LOGICAL DESIGN TACTICS

Logical design tactics are generally directed toward problems PR0, PR1, and PR2. These problems can be overcome by rearranging data items in records or adding new data items to record types.

Reducing the Number of Access Steps

In reference to problems PR0, PR1, and PR2, the number of logical records retrieved can be reduced by changing the logical arrangement of data items in record types or by creating new record types. Usually this reduction presents a trade-off between structure and performance criteria. The new arrangement or record type is created by placing the same data items or associations between data items in more than one record type. This placement improves performance but means either that normal correspondence is lost or that the same facts are stored more than once. An evaluation must then be made to determine whether the additional storage space and update times can be accepted for any retrieval improvement.

Three major logical design tactics here are

- creation of derived relationships
- duplication of files
- the combining or joining of files

These tactics apply equally to files supported by access methods and to DBMSs. Any new record types created will become part of the database supported by the DBMS.

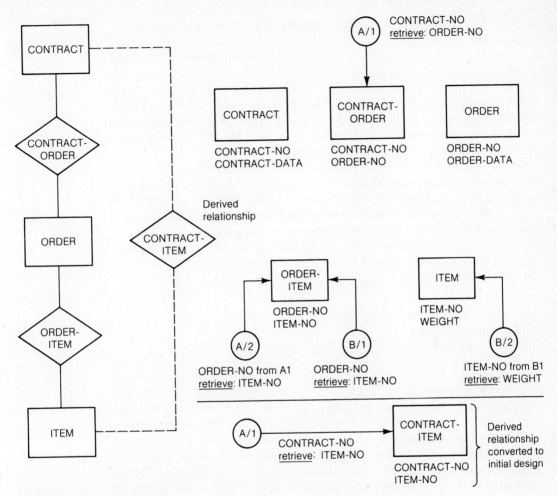

Figure 14.4 Derived relationship

Derived Relationships

A new record type is created for a derived relationship. It describes a relationship between two or more data items. This relationship does not appear in the initial design but can be derived from it.

Example

Figure 14.4, a simple example, shows the following:

1. Orders are placed against contracts, leading to a relationship between contracts and orders.

2. Orders are made up of items, leading to a relationship between orders and items.

The access path diagram for the *ad hoc* access request A, "Find all items ordered under a given contract," is also shown in Figure 14.4. Two access steps are needed to satisfy the request. One step, A/1, finds the orders in a contract; the other, A/2, finds the items in each such order.

The two access steps derive a relationship between contracts and items; this relationship describes the items ordered within each contract. It is also possible to store the relationship directly by creating a new file, CONTRACT-ITEM in Figure 14.4. Its contents are records, which contain the items ordered under a given contract. If such a file exists, the access requirement can be satisfied in one access step. Note, however, that the access request, which inserts new orders, will now need an additional access step to insert records in the file CONTRACT-ITEM.

Duplication of Data Items

Data duplication has the same effect as derived relationships: the number of access steps for retrievals can be reduced. The cost is that data are duplicated; hence storage use is increased and additional steps will be necessary for database updates. In contrast to derived relationships, no new files are created.

Consider again Figure 14.4. Access request B determines whether a particular order number contains any items whose weight exceeds some value. Two access steps are required to do this. Access step B1 is to file ORDER-ITEM to retrieve all items in an order; access step B2 is to file ITEM to check whether each such item exceeds the given weight. Access step B2 could be eliminated by storing the item WEIGHT in file ORDER-ITEM as well as file ITEM. Performance of access B is improved, but now there is data redundancy because values of WEIGHT appear in two files. Further, file ORDER-ITEM no longer corresponds to a BCNF relation.

Combining Files

Combining files is equivalent to the JOIN operation in relational algebra. The number of files in the design is reduced, often at the expense of losing BCNF equivalence. The number of access steps is invariably reduced.

To combine files, matching data items must first be chosen in both files.

File PERSONS		
PERSON-ID	PERSON-NAME	ADDRESS
101	JONES	PAGE
107	SMITH	HOLT
109	PETERS	HAWKER

File WORK		
PERSON-ID	PROJECT	HRS-WORKED
101	3	15
101	2	17
107	1	6
107	3	5
109	3	23

File DATA				
PERSON-ID	PERSON-NAME	ADDRESS	PROJECT	HRS-WORKED
101	JONES	PAGE	3	15
101	JONES	PAGE	2	17
107	SMITH	HOLT	1	6
107	SMITH	HOLT	3	5
109	PETERS	HAWKER	3	23

Figure 14.5   Combining files

Records in each file with the same value of a matching item are combined into a single record.

For example, consider Figure 14.5. Here there are two files, PERSONS and WORK. File PERSONS contains names of persons, and file WORK contains the relationship between persons, projects, and hours spent by each person on a project. Both these files correspond to relations in BCNF. The two files are now combined into file DATA.

An access request such as "Find the projects on which JONES worked" now needs one access step with file DATA. Two access steps are required when the information is stored in the two files, PERSONS and WORK. File DATA, however, no longer corresponds to a relation in BCNF; PERSON-NAME is functionally dependent on a subset, PERSON-ID, of the relation key, which in this case is PERSON-ID, PROJECT.

Another problem with file DATA occurs in the case of a person who has not been assigned to a project. In file DATA there will be a record whose relation key is not complete. This situation will add complexity to the logic of the program that updates this file; special action is necessary with persons not assigned to projects. If the files have not been joined, an unassigned person results in a record in the file PERSON but not in file WORK.

Combining into Nonhomogenous Files

Some advantage can be gained by combining files that represent roles or types of entities into one file. Such combinations were discussed in Chapter 8.

Fewer access steps here may suggest shorter programs to implement the processing requests; but such programs may be more complex because they must deal with nonhomogeneity. Hence the recommendation to combine roles and type files must be treated with care.

PHYSICAL DESIGN TACTICS

Physical design tactics are concerned principally with design problems PR3 and PR4. Problem PR3 is often the result of excessive physical storage manipulations during insertions and deletions. Problem PR4 often occurs when long names are used as entity identifiers.

Problem PR3—Pointer Manipulations

Problem PR3 is usually caused by one of the following three design problems:

- Complex pointer manipulations to update all chains or inverted file pointers that refer to a record. Each pointer update in turn requires an access to a record that contains the pointer.
- Rearrangement of physical or logical blocks during insertions or deletions.
- Excessive activity in overflow areas caused by a larger number of newly inserted records being placed in overflow areas.

Various design tactics can be used to overcome these problems. Both logical and physical tactics can be used.

Tactics to overcome complex pointer manipulations in retrieval operations include logical data duplication or derived relationships. The pointer links are often made to facilitate queries that require data from more than one record. Such data can be combined into the one record by using one of the logical tactics discussed earlier. Retrieval performance will be improved at the cost of storage and update times. The trade-off decision is up to the designer.

Tactics for the overflow problem revolve around trade-offs between additional free space storage use and block-factor changes. Increasing the blocking factor and free space reduces the number of records in overflow, again at the cost of storage. So again, it is up to the designer to make the appropriate trade-off.

Problems caused by storage rearrangement are usually resolved by choosing smaller block sizes. In this event the amount of rearrangement will always be small because the smaller blocks hold fewer records. However, smaller block sizes mean that any advantages gained by blocking records for retrieval of record clusters is now lost. The smaller sizes usually result in more unused secondary storage space. The trade-off decision is again the designer's.

Problem PR4—Excessive Storage Requirements

One tactic that can be used to reduce storage requirements is to substitute codes for long names. In many cases entity identifiers have long names—for example, part description, company name, material description, fault description, or equipment name. Where such entities appear in a number of relationships, considerable storage space may be necessary to store the relationships. It is then convenient to internally replace the entity description by shorter codes and to use these codes to identify relationships in storage. Externally, however, the actual names have meanings to the user and hence are used in query statements. Access requirements that use the long name as an access key will result in an additional access step to look up the internal code. The use of codes therefore reduces storage required for relationships at the cost of an additional query step and the necessity to keep a code file.

Problem PR5—System Overheads

Problem PR5 is caused by system overheads such as

- the opening and closing of database files
- the maintenance of recovery data

The opening and closing of database files is a particular problem in *ad hoc* queries when the database is not continually open. An access path that includes many access steps requires the operating system to open files that contain data needed by the access steps. To open such files, the operating system will use additional disk transfers to bring in various file tables. The disk accesses to get such tables will add to the query response time. Hence the goal in such DBMSs is to minimize the numbers of files accessed. To do this the designer should take either of the following steps:

- Reduce the number of access steps, using the techniques discussed earlier.
- Attempt to store record types that are selected by one query in the one file. (Some DBMSs allow more than one record type to be stored in one file.)

Care must also be exercised in specifying the generation of recovery data. Audit trials use disk accesses and add to response time. Hence only a minimal amount of recovery data should be created.

SUMMARY

Numerous methodologies are employed in data design. Either databased or access-based methods can be used for the initial design. Design iterations are then used to improve the initial design. Control of these iterations requires designers first to identify system performance problems and then to identify the design problem that caused the performance problems. Once a design problem is pinpointed, one of a number of design tactics is selected to overcome it. The combination of all these design activities usually leads to the kind of process illustrated by Figure 14.6. This process is intended for COBOL files and commences with file key selection, followed in turn by amendments for access paths, initial physical design, and design iterations. There will, of course, be some variations to this process for a DBMS. In a DBMS, for example, it is not necessary to choose master keys separately because this choice can be integrated with access path analysis.

PROBLEMS

---

1. Consider the database in the appendix. How would you introduce redundancy to reduce the number of access steps for access requirement S? Consider using
   (a) derived relationships
   (b) data duplication
2. Would it be possible to reduce access requirement G in the appendix to one access step? How could this be done? What effect would this change have on the access requirement that creates a new order?

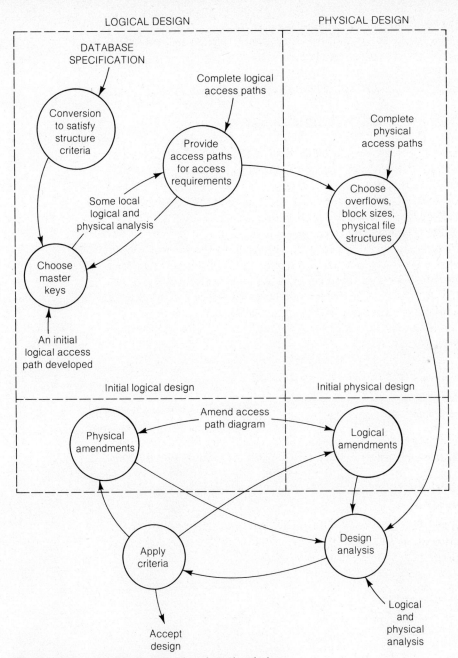

Figure 14.6 A practical approach to iterative design

chapter fifteen
Initial Design

INTRODUCTION

The initial design goal is to propose a feasible database structure. This structure must meet all the user's access requirements and ensure that records needed by on-line transactions can be accessed directly.

In the previous chapter we described alternate initial design procedures and made a distinction between databased and accessed-based methods. Two major classes of design criteria were also defined: structure criteria are concerned with the preservation of data properties, whereas performance criteria concern the use of computer resources. Design methods use a variety of logical and physical design techniques and apply them to realize designs that satisfy the design criteria. These techniques are applied in sequences that depend on the DBMS and on the relative importance placed on the two classes of criteria.

This chapter will describe some database design methods used to produce an initial design. It will deal with design methods for the three major data models, first describing the general problems associated with each model and then discussing particular implementations. Finally, some design hints will be given to the COBOL programmer.

RELATIONAL DATABASE DESIGN

Relational design by its nature is primarily databased. Normal relations already satisfy structure criteria. Hence conversion to a logical structure is trivial. Each relation, or record in the logical record structure, becomes a relation in the database schema.

The next design step is to add indices to meet access requirements. A diagram of the logical record access paths can be used for this purpose. Each access step includes names of items with known values at execution time. Hence these items become the key items of indices so that the records can be directly retrieved.

Consider the problem presented in Figure App-5 in the appendix. This figure

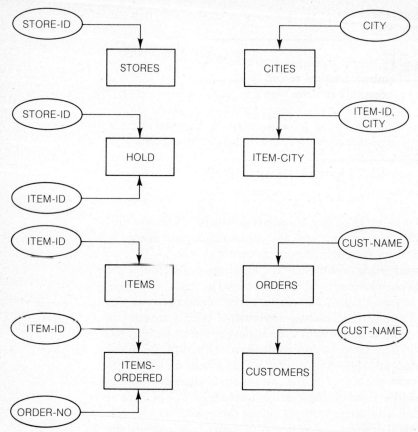

Figure 15.1 Indices for a relational database, given the access requirements in Prob-5

illustrates the logical record access paths. In the relational schema there would be one relation for each record type in App-5. If the relational DBMS architecture permits indices to be added in the database, the access step labels in Figure App-5 become keys of the indices. Thus, if App-5 were to be implemented on System R, relation STORES would have one index using STORE-ID. Relation HOLD, on the other hand, would have two indices. One would use ITEM-ID as key, and the other STORE-ID as key. Relation ITEM-CITY would have an index with the composite key ITEM-ID, CITY. Other indices used in the relational design for the problem in the appendix are illustrated in Figure 15.1.

CONVERSION TO A NETWORK MODEL

Network design can use both databased and access-based design methods. Databased methods are the simpler of the two. They commence with a minimal logical record structure (MLRS). This structure already satisfies structure criteria for the following reasons:

- The logical records satisfy normal correspondence.
- There are a minimum number of logical record types.
- Items do not appear unnecessarily in more than one record type.

The conversion from the MLRS to a network model representation is straightforward. It uses the following two network structure design rules:

1. Each record type in the MLRS becomes a network model record type.

2. Each link between record types becomes a set type in the network model. The link direction is from set owner to set member record type.

Properties of Conversion Rules

It is interesting to examine the effect of the combination of MLRS conversion and network structure rules on $1:N$ and $M:N$ relationships. This effect is illustrated in Figures 15.2 and 15.3. In Figure 15.2 a $1:N$ relationship between entity sets **STORES** and **PROJECTS** is converted to two record types and one

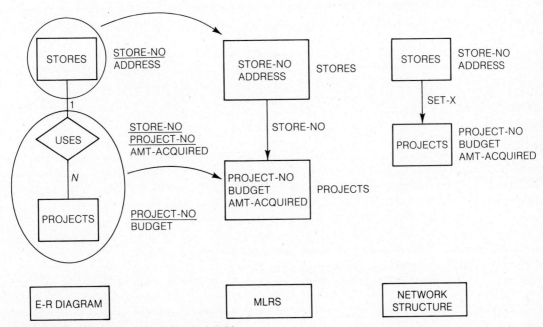

Figure 15.2 Conversion of a $1:N$ relationship

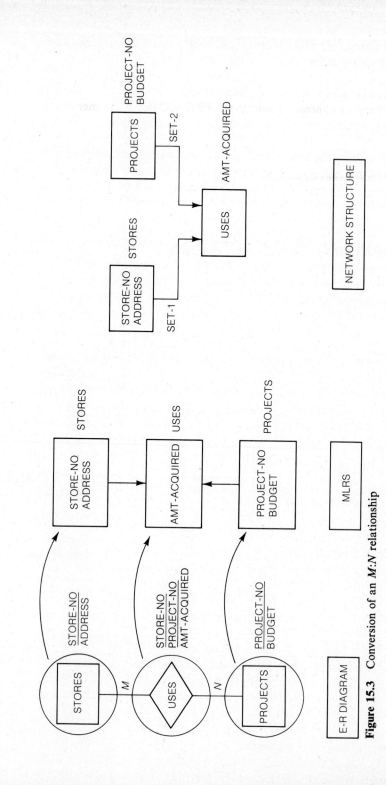

Figure 15.3 Conversion of an *M:N* relationship

set type. One record type represents entity set STORES and the other entity set PROJECTS. The set type is chosen so that

- The record type that represents entity set STORES is the owner of SET-X
- the record type that represents entity set PROJECTS is the member of SET-X

A record for a project appears in one set occurrence of SET-X because each project uses only one store. $M:N$ relationships are converted differently, as illustrated in Figure 15.3. Now a single set type no longer satisfies storage criteria. If a project were to use more than one store, a record for the same project would appear in more than one SET-X occurrence. The result would be unnecessary duplication. The combination of conversion to MLRS and network structure rules avoids this and results in the network structure shown in Figure 15.3, in which we see the following:

- Each relationship set is represented by an intersection record type, USES.
- The intersection record type is a member of set types owned by the entities in the relationship.

Each project record, as well as each store record, appears once only.

A more elaborate conversion example uses the MLRS in the appendix. When the network structure design rules are applied to this MLRS, the network shown in Figure 15.4 is generated. Figure 15.4 includes illustrations of both $1:N$ and $M:N$ relationships. One example of a $1:N$ relationship is that between CUSTOMERS and ORDERS, which is represented by two record types and the set type SET-8. The set member record type is ORDERS and the owner record type is CUSTOMERS. An example of an $M:N$ relationship is that between STORES and ITEMS. It is converted to the intersection record type HOLD, owned by record types STORES and ITEMS.

Another property of the network structure conversion rules is that intersection records do not include their entity identifiers. For example, the record HOLD does not contain the data items STORE-ID and ITEM-ID. It is possible to find these values from the record's SET-4 and SET-5 owners. It is, of course, also possible to add ITEM-ID and STORE-ID to HOLD. This would be done if dictated by the access requirements. For example, if there is a frequent requirement "to find all items for a given STORE-ID," performance can be improved by storing ITEM-ID but not STORE-ID in HOLD. The difference is illustrated in Figure 15.5. This figure shows the programs that retrieve the ITEM-NOs of items held in a given STORE-NO for the two alternatives. A FIND OWNER command is no longer required once the entity identifier is stored in the relationship record. Hence performance is better when ITEM-ID appears in HOLD. More storage space, however, is needed. So the designer must make a storage-to-performance trade-off.

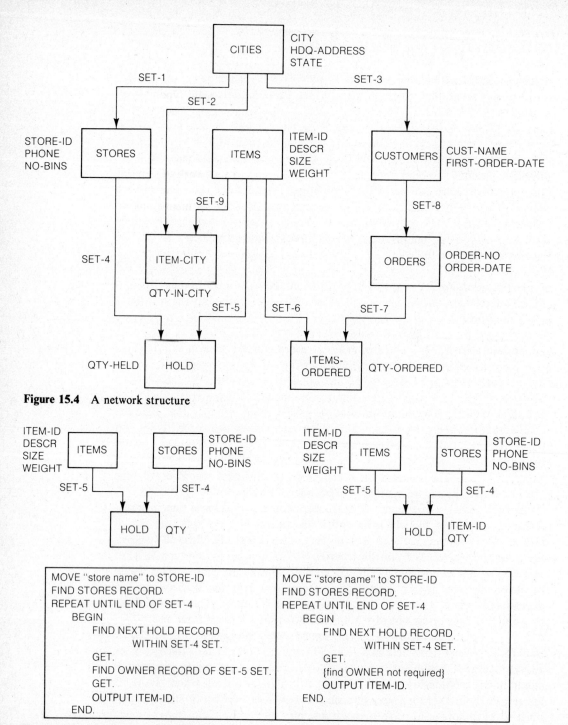

Figure 15.4 A network structure

Figure 15.5 Moving the entity identifier to the relationship record

Conversion of Roles and Types

Roles and types are represented by logical records on the MLRS. Hence the network structure design rules can be extended to include role and type object sets and their sources. This extension provides an additional option: records that represent roles or types of the same source can be combined in one multimember set type owned by the source record.

The application of this option is illustrated in Figure 15.6. Here the PATIENT and DOCTOR roles of Figure 8-6 are converted to a network structure. The standard conversion includes two set types, DOCTOR and PATIENT. DOCTOR set members are DOCTORS roles, and PATIENT set members are PATIENTS roles. The set occurrences of these set types are trivial. Each set occurrence has one member because each PERSON can take only one doctor or one patient role. The second conversion in Figure 15.6 illustrates the application of the new rule. Rather than having one set type for each role, we now have one set type, ROLE, for all roles. This choice also affects the code used to access role records. The difference is illustrated in Figure 15.6 for three cases. One case is to retrieve a specific role; the second, to retrieve all the source roles; and the third, to use a specific role in a relationship. There is no difference in case 3, and the only difference in case 1 is in the name of the set. The significant difference between the standard and optional conversions arises in the second case. In the optional conversion all source roles can be retrieved in one loop, but a test must then be made to determine what role record was last found. In the standard conversion a separate statement is used to retrieve each role.

Which Conversion to Use

The multimember set is useful if the implementation indicates the type of record retrieved in a FIND. For example, a parameter should be set at the completion of statement X in Figure 15.6 to indicate the role retrieved. Otherwise a search must be made through all the role storage areas to determine the roles found. This search, shown in Figure 15.6, is not necessary in the standard conversion because a separate FIND is issued for each role and the status returned will indicate whether that role was found. However, if there are many roles, there will be many FIND statements. Hence an implementation limitation prevents the full realization of the multimember set model of uniform roles.

There is another and more serious implementation restriction that inhibits complete flexibility for modeling roles or types. This restriction becomes apparent with nonuniform role or type sets. As an illustration, an MLRS for the E-R diagram in Figure 8.8, together and its conversion to a network structure, is shown in Figure 15.7. The conversion creates two multimember network set types owned by entity record types PROJECTS and DEPARTMENTS; these

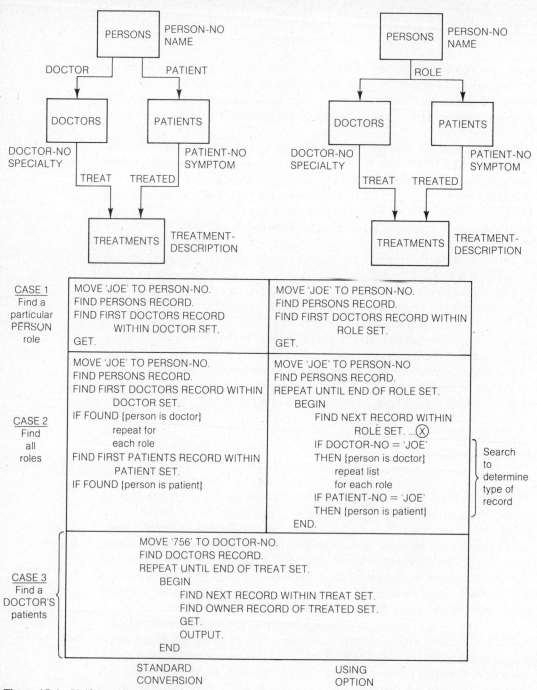

Figure 15.6 Uniform role conversion

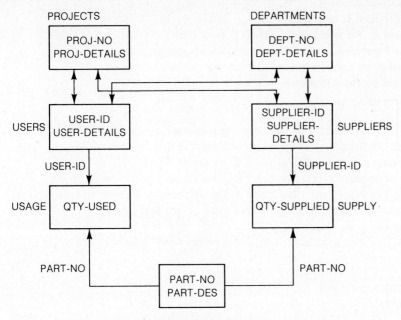

(a) Minimal logical record structure

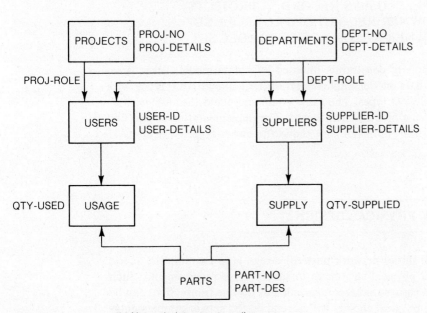

(b) Network data structure diagram

Figure 15.7 Optional role conversion

set types are named PROJ-ROLE and DEPT-ROLE in Figure 15.7b. Roles taken by the entities appear as members of PROJ-ROLE or DEPT-ROLE.

The logical structure in Figure 15.7 has, however, one disadvantage: it is not easy to find the role source given the role record. The owner in the uniform set in Figure 15.6 can be found by the command

FIND OWNER RECORD OF ROLE SET

The same FIND OWNER command can be used for any role since all sources are in the same record type. In the nonuniform set a particular SUPPLIERS or USERS record can be owned either by PROJECTS or by DEPARTMENTS. Different commands are necessary to retrieve the PROJECTS source or the DEPARTMENTS source. The command will depend on the source type. Hence the program logic would need to determine the source type before applying a FIND OWNER command. To do this, a SOURCE-TYPE field can be included in the role records. The code used to retrieve a role owner would take the form

```
MOVE 'x' TO USER-ID
FIND USERS RECORD
GET
IF SOURCE-TYPE OF USERS RECORD = 'PROJECTS'
    THEN FIND OWNER RECORD OF PROJ-ROLE SET
    ELSE FIND OWNER RECORD OF DEPT-ROLE SET
```

This is another example of constraints imposed by a data model. What is required is a network data model implementation that allows SET types with alternate owner RECORD types. The same command could then conceivably be used to find the owner of a USERS record. The implementation should find the owner and set a status indicator that shows the owner type.

INITIAL NETWORK PHYSICAL DESIGN

The main objective of initial network physical design is to examine the access requirements and add physical structures to satisfy these requirements. Such added structures must ensure that records needed by on-line transactions can be accessed directly. The physical choices will depend on the network implementation. For a DBTG implementation initial physical design should choose

- the LOCATION MODEs of record types
- the set type ORDERINGS and SEARCH KEYS to be used to access set member records

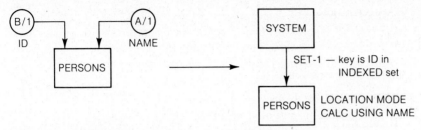

Figure 15.8   Resolving key conflicts at a record type

To make these choices, it is necessary to consider access paths. The MLRS logical access paths (carried over to the network data structure diagram) can be used to make physical design choices. The following guidelines are suggested:

1. An initial access step at a record type suggests that the access key of the step become the CALC key of the record type. When there are more than two initial access steps at a record type, one of the access keys becomes the CALC KEY. To allow direct access for the other access step, create a singular set owned by the SYSTEM with the record type as owner. The access key of the access requirement becomes a key of an ASCENDING KEY clause (see Figure 15.8). Of course, a simpler solution is possible if an implementation uses the 1978 DDLC. Each initial access step with a different access key would then become a record KEY.

2. Two successive steps from an owner to a member record type suggest that the access key at the member record type becomes the SORT key of the set type. It will be necessary to include the sort key as an item in the member record. A conflict with two sets of successive steps with two different keys is resolved by a SEARCH KEY clause, as shown in Figure 15.9. One key becomes the ASCENDING KEY of the SORT clause, whereas the other becomes the SEARCH KEY.

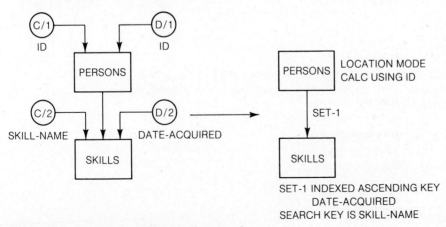

Figure 15.9   Resolving conflicts on set key order

3. Two successive steps from a member to an owner suggest either a LINK TO OWNER for the member record type to the owner or the inclusion of the owner record identifier in the member record. The latter option is favored if the access step is made to check the owner record identifier rather than to retrieve it.

4. Use SET OCCURRENCE SELECTION IS THRU CURRENT OF SET if the data in owner are to be used in output; otherwise SOS THRU LOCATION MODE OF OWNER may be preferable.

5. Two successive steps between two record types unconnected by sets suggest the inclusion of a new set type. This set type would be redundant and necessary only for performance reasons. Otherwise the second step requires a LOCATION MODE CALC key, using the access key as the CALC key.

After the above steps, the choices are as follows:

1. If a set type has no ORDER, use ORDER IS FIRST (as this uses least time on update).

2. If a record type has no CALC KEY, two choices are possible:
   (a) If the record type is not a member of any set type, choose LOCATION MODE CALC, using the record's logical identifier as key.
   (b) If the record type is a member of a set-type, define LOCATION MODE to be VIA (set-type). If it is a member of more than one set type, choose the set type with the highest owner-to-member logical record traffic.

These choices may later have to be modified in light of the block-sizes of the chosen records.

Example

Consider the problem (and the MLRS access paths for it) in the appendix.
   Guideline 1 suggests that the following record types are defined to have LOCATION MODE CALC:

- STORES with CALC key STORE-ID
- ITEMS with CALC key ITEM-ID
- ORDERS with CALC key ORDER-NO
- CUSTOMERS with CALC key CUST-NAME

   Guideline 3 suggests that LINK TO OWNER be included in the following set types:

SET-4 (A/2 → A/3, S/4 → S/5, G/5 → G/6)
SET-7 (D/4 → D/5)
SET-6 (G/3 → G/4, S/2 → S/3)
SET-5 (D/2 → D/3)
SET-1 (S/5 → S/6)
SET-2 (Z/2 → Z/3)
SET-3 (X/1 → X/2)

All set-type orders will be defined FIRST since no orders are specified. It now remains to choose the LOCATION MODEs of the remaining record types. The LOCATION MODE of CITIES becomes CALC, using CITY because CITIES is not a member of any set type. The other record types are defined to be VIA set types as follows:

HOLD   VIA SET-5
ITEMS-ORDERED   VIA SET-6
ITEM-CITY   VIA SET-9

To understand the reason for this choice, consider record type HOLD. The number of HOLD records accessed by following SET-4 from STORES to HOLD is

100,000 by D/2

The number of HOLD records accessed by following SET-5 from ITEMS to HOLD is

40,000 by G/5
40,000 by S/4
60,000 by A/2

for a total of 140,000. Hence HOLD is VIA SET-5 because it carries more traffic.

HIERARCHICAL DESIGN

Hierarchical database design is more difficult than network design because it introduces additional conflicts in early design steps. In network design it is possible to separate the design into two steps. The first step deals with structure criteria only and produces an initial design, which satisfies structure criteria. The procedure involved in this set is as follows:

1. Package the E-R model into a logical record structure.
2. Directly convert the logical record structure into a network structure diagram. In this conversion logical records become record types, and links between records become set types.

The initial design is later modified to meet performance criteria. To do this, access paths are developed and used to choose physical access structures.

Hierarchical design cannot make a clear distinction between the steps used to satisfy structure criteria and those used to satisfy performance criteria. The reason for this is that new trade-offs between structure and performance criteria are imposed by hierarchical DBMSs.

Hierarchical systems require each record to have at most one parent; two terminating logical links in a logical record structure imply two logical parents in a hierarchical model and hence cannot be implemented. In the appendix, for example, record type HOLD in the logical structure has two parents, ITEMS and STORES. Direct conversion is now not possible because HOLD cannot have two parents in the hierarchical structure. Thus the logical record structure must be decomposed in some way into a hierarchical structure. Three alternative decompositions can be used (Figure 15.10):

- *Decomposition 1:* Decompose the logical structure into a number of hierarchies (this decomposition is often called *partitioning*). Now record HOLD appears as a child in two hierarchies.

- *Decomposition 2:* Convert a logical parent to a logical child. Now either STORES or ITEMS becomes a child of HOLD, but the database is still one hierarchy rather than a number of hierarchies.

- *Decomposition 3:* Combine a number of logical record types into a single record type. Now either record type ITEMS or STORES is combined with record type HOLD. The database is still one hierarchy.

These decompositions do not satisfy structure storage criteria. Duplication occurs in each case. In fact, there are two kinds of duplication, which are here called *occurrence duplication* and *data duplication*. Occurrence duplication is illustrated in Figure 15.11. The hierarchical structure in the figure was obtained by combining the ITEMS logical record with the HOLD logical record (decomposition 3). Now suppose an item is held by more than one store. For example, both stores ST-A and ST-B hold item I1. In this event the details of I1 appear in the ST-A and ST-B hierarchies. Hence there is occurrence duplication. This duplication cannot be avoided by making ITEMS the parent of a STORES/HOLD record. In that case details of stores would be duplicated.

Data duplication is illustrated in Figure 15.12. The hierarchical structure in this figure was obtained by partitioning the database (decomposition 1). Now the QTY-HELD of items held by a particular store appears twice in the database: once in the store hierarchy and once in the item hierarchy. Thus ST-A holds 300 of I1; this fact is stored in both the ST-A and the I1 hierarchies.

In data duplication, unlike the case in occurrence duplication, a particular fact is duplicated only twice. For example, a particular QTY-HELD value for a

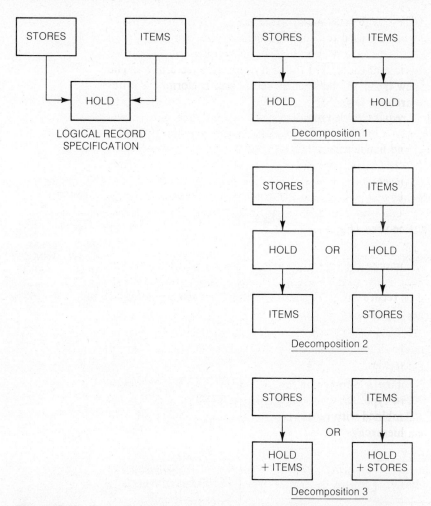

Figure 15.10   Converting logical record networks into hierarchical structures

store/item combination will occur twice: once owned by the store and once owned by the item. In occurrence duplication, on the other hand, a particular fact may occur any number of times. For example, WEIGHT of an item in Figure 15.11 will occur as many times as there are stores that hold that item. Obviously occurrence duplication is the more serious of the two types of duplication. It is avoided only in the first of the three decompositions in Figure 15.10.

Choosing a Hierarchical Design Method

The ability to partition databases allows designers to attempt to reduce occurrence duplication. Hence a variety of design methods can be found in hierarchi-

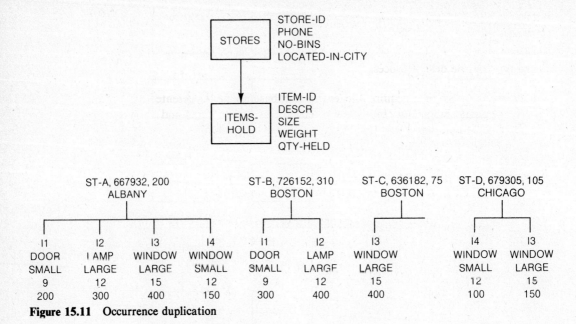

Figure 15.11   Occurrence duplication

Figure 15.12   Data duplication

cal design. The chosen method depends on the constraints imposed by the available DBMS.

Three broad classes of DBMSs can be identified, each imposing its own constraints on the design process:

- *Class 1:* DBMSs that require the entire database to be represented by a single hierarchy (but allow direct access, using items and various levels in the hierarchy).
- *Class 2:* DBMSs that allow partitioning and direct access only through the root node of a partition.
- *Class 3:* DBMSs that allow partitioning and direct entry (using physical indices) through the root node as well as other nodes.

Different design methods are appropriate for each DBMS class. In this text they are called Class 1, Class 2, and Class 3 design methods.

Class 1 Design Methods

The objective of Class 1 design methods is to create a single hierarchical database. The method commences with a minimal logical record structure (MLRS) and proceeds as follows:

1. Select one logical record as the database root node. It is preferred that the selected node should not have a logical link terminating on it.
2. Follow all the links from the selected root node. Each link must be traversed once and once only. On the traversal of a link from record A to B, two possibilities arise:
   - If the traversal is in the same direction as the logical link, B becomes a child of A in the hierarchy.
   - If the traversal is in the opposite direction to the logical link, record B (or its key if B already appears elsewhere in the structure) may be combined with A or it may become a child of A in the hierarchy.

Note that traversal in the direction opposite to the link direction implies occurrence duplication. Hence it is important to have the minimum number of link reversals on each path from the root node. Thus, in Figure 15.13, record PROJECTS was chosen as the conversion root node. There are two link reversals in the conversion, but each is on a different path from PROJECTS. The reversals cause occurrence duplication. COLOR of an item is repeated for all projects that use that item. ADDRESS of a person is repeated for all projects to which the person is assigned. If either PERSONS or ITEMS were chosen as the root node, there would still be two reversals, but both would be on the same path from the root node. Another example is Figure 15.14. Here the database

458 Database Design

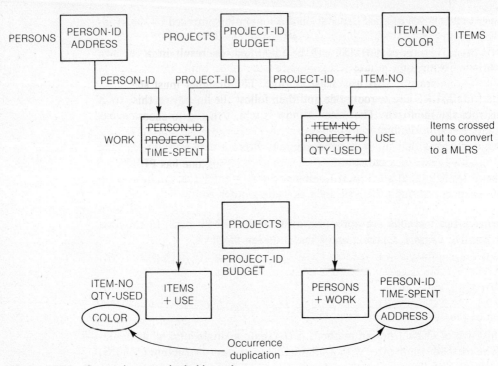

Figure 15.13 Conversion to a single hierarchy

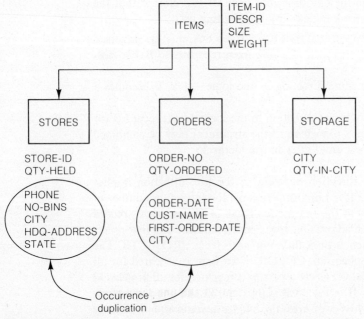

Figure 15.14 Class 1 rules applied to the database specification in the appendix

specification in the appendix is converted to one hierarchy, using ITEMS as the root node. There is some occurrence duplication in this conversion.

Conversion to a single hierarchy will, in most cases, result in occurrence duplication. So an appropriate design tactic here is to minimize storage by choosing that hierarchy that uses least storage. The designer must select one record of the MLRS as the root node and then follow the links from this record to construct the hierarchy. The question now is which record to choose as the root node. Usually some computation is necessary to choose the alternative that uses least storage. One such computation is illustrated in Figure 15.15. Here two alternatives exist to convert the MLRS to hierarchies; one has PERSONS and the other has PROJECTS as the parent node. A storage estimate is made as follows:

- The record size of each record type is computed by adding all its item sizes.
- The number of occurrences of each record is found.
- The two are multiplied to give the space used by records in each record type.

There are 100 PROJECTS records in alternative 1 (each of the 50 persons works on 2 projects). Similarly, there are 100 PERSONS records in alternative 2 (each of the 10 projects has 10 persons working on it).

Alternative 1 in Figure 15.15 uses less storage and would therefore be accepted. It is difficult to choose an alternative without such computations because the amount of storage used depends on the record occurrences and sizes. There is no simple rule for choosing the minimal storage alternative without actual computations.

Partitioned Design

Partitioned design is a variation on Class 1 design methods. Now the MLRS is partitioned into a number of parts, and each part is reduced to a hierarchical database. There are thus two steps in this design:

- *Step 1:* Partition the MLRS into parts by "breaking" logical links. If a logical link is broken, the logical link label is entered into the record on which the link terminates.
- *Step 2:* Choose one logical record in each partition to be the root node. Develop the hierarchical database from the root node, using the Class 1 reduction.

In Figure 15.16, an example of partitioned design, the logical link between records PROJECTS and WORK is broken. The item on the link label is entered into record WORK. Hence PROJECT-ID appears in record WORK in the hierarchical database.

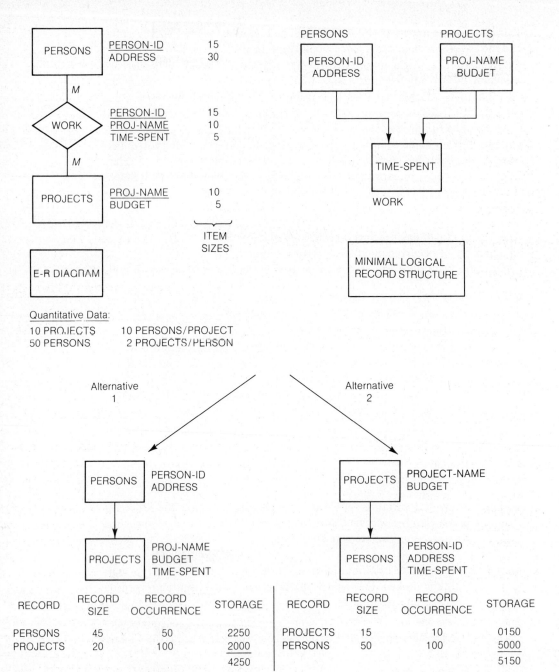

Figure 15.15 Storage estimates

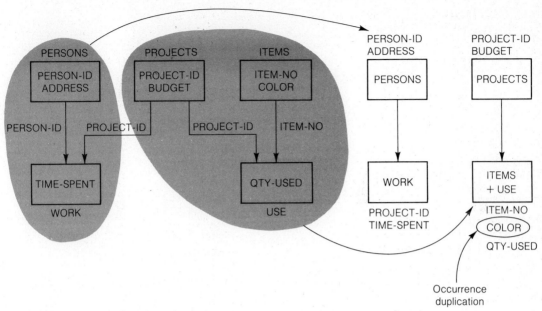

Figure 15.16   Hierarchical conversion by partitioning

Partitioning

Once the break is made, one logical record in each partition is chosen as the root node. The hierarchies are developed from each root node, using Class 1 design rules. Records with no incoming logical links should be chosen as root nodes. In Figure 15.16, records PERSONS and PROJECTS are selected as the root nodes of each hierarchy.

Figure 15.17 is also a partitioned design. It differs from Figure 15.16 in that partitioning is now controlled; no link reversal takes place during the reduction of any partition to a hierarchy.

The question now is how to partition root nodes in the MLRS. The choice depends on the importance placed on structure and performance criteria. Typical rules using structure criteria are as follows:

- No link reversal should occur in any partition and hence no occurrence duplication.
- No record type should appear in more than one partition.

Most hierarchical design methods, however, use access requirements to determine partitioning. These methods ensure that hierarchical root nodes are entry points for access requirements, and hence performance is improved. Class 2 and Class 3 design methods are access-based.

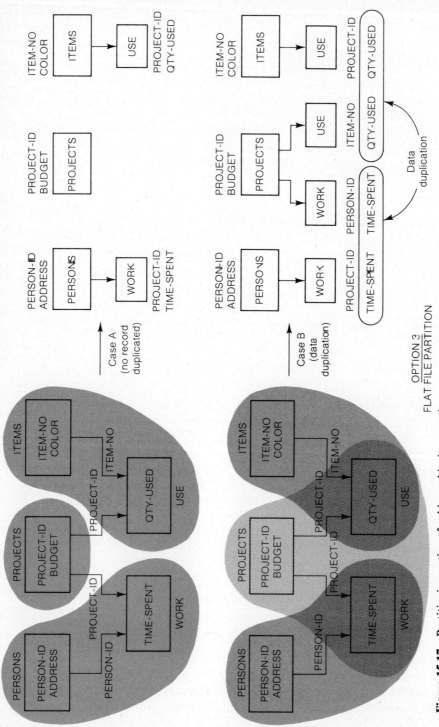

Figure 15.17   Partitioning options for hierarchical conversion

Class 2 Design Methods

Class 2 design methods are intended for DBMSs that allow partitioning but allow entry only at the root node of each partition. To partition the database, it is necessary to determine entry points for each user requirement. So access paths must be plotted *before* partitioning. The first step of each access determines the entry point and hence identifies candidate root records for each partition. Therefore the first step in logical design is to plot an access path on the MLRS. An example of such access paths is given in Figure 15.18.

Once the access paths are developed, the following rules can be used to partition the structure:

- *Rule 1:* Each logical record with an entry point (i.e., step 1 of an access requirement) becomes the root node of a hierarchy. In Figure 15.18, records PERSONS, PROJECTS, and ITEMS become root nodes.

- *Rule 2:* If two successive access steps s1 and s2 are plotted against records J and K, respectively, and there is a logical link from J to K in the MLRS, a new K record is constructed. This record becomes a child of J in a hierarchical database. If two copies of J exist at the time of rule application and one of them is the root node, K becomes a child of the root node. Thus, in Figure 15.18, logical record WORK becomes a child of record PERSONS because steps X/1 and X/2 traverse from PERSONS to WORK. Similarly, WORK becomes a child of PROJECTS and USE becomes a child of ITEMS. If a copy of K exists at the time of rule application and that copy is a root node, then the new record constructed need only contain those items that are the root node identifiers.

- *Rule 3:* If two successive access steps s1 and s2 are plotted against records J and K, respectively, and there is a link from K to J, the link between J and K is broken and K becomes a root node in another partition (if it is not one already). The item label on the logical link is added to record J. For this reason PROJECT-ID is added to record WORK in one partition because $X/2 \rightarrow X/3$ traverses the link labeled PROJECT-ID in the direction opposite to the link. Similarly, PERSON-ID is added to record WORK in another partition.

- *Rule 4A:* Any logical record not placed in a hierarchy following the application of rules 1, 2, and 3 to all access paths are placed as follows:
  - If it has no parent in the MLRS, the record becomes a root node.
  - If it has one parent in the MLRS, the record becomes a child of that parent in the hierarchical structure.
  - If it has more than one parent in the MLRS, all but one link is broken and the record becomes a parent of the unbroken link.

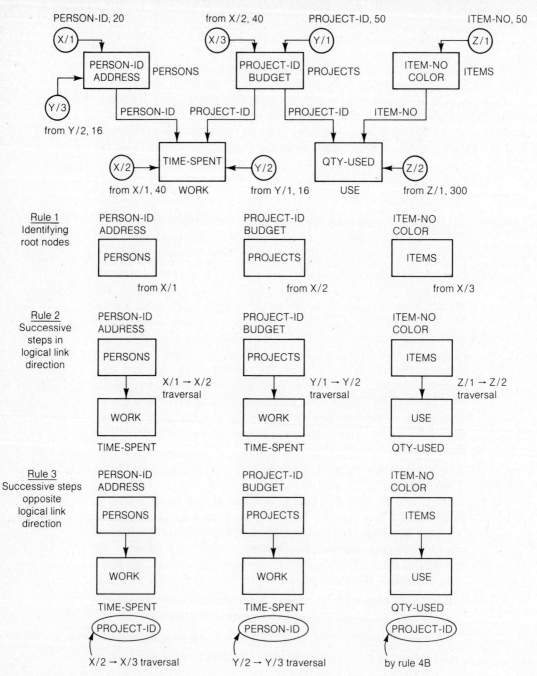

X: Find the time spent on projects by a given person.
Y: Find the time spent by persons on a given project.
Z: Find the color of a given item number.

Figure 15.18 Reduction to hierarchical structure

- *Rule 4B:* Any logical links not traversed by the access requirements has rule 2 or 3 applied to it (with an imaginary access step across the link).

Obviously, if these rules are used, if an access requirement has two access steps to separate records, then the chosen sequence of access steps will affect the final hierarchical design. Reversing the two steps will change the design. Hence for this particular design method it is important not to impose unnecessary sequencing. Should a sequence not be important (as in most insertions), then the steps should not be sequenced. The best way to apply the rules is to first apply rule 1 to all access requirements and construct the root nodes. Then in turn take each access requirement with sequence steps and apply the rules as you follow the access steps. Then take access requirements with unsequenced steps and apply the steps in a sequence that takes advantage of existing root nodes and hierarchical paths.

Some other examples of the effect of Class 2 design rules are shown in Figure 15.19. The effect of two access paths traversing the same link in opposite directions is of particular interest. If this situation occurs, one of the access paths must be in a direction opposite to the link, whereas the other is in the same direction as the link. The result is shown in Figure 15.19a. Record WORK is now duplicated and appears in two partitions. It appears in partition A because of the application of rule 2 to steps $X/2$ and $X/1$. It appears also in partition B because of the application of rule 2 to steps $Y/1$ and $Y/2$. The contents of records derived from WORK are different in each partition since a different logical link is broken in each case. Record WORK1 in partition A includes PERSON-ID; this is added to USE because the link between PERSONS and WORK is broken by steps $X/2$ to $X/3$. Similarly, record WORK2 in partition B includes PROJ-NO because the link between PROJECTS and WORK is broken by steps $Y/2$ to $Y/3$. Such duplication is repeated in the other examples in Figure 15.19. Note, however, that this is data duplication rather than occurrence duplication.

There is a reason for this data duplication. It arises from the intended effect of Class 2 design rules. That is, these rules aim not only to avoid occurrence duplication (although not necessarily data duplication) but also to allow an access to traverse more than one database partition in such a way that a path terminating on one partition begins again at the root node of the next. For example, access X in Figure 15.19c would start at CITIES and then go to SUPPLIERS2 in the first partition. It would then use the value of SUPPLIER in SUPPLIERS2 to enter record SUPPLIER at the second partition and then go on to record EMPLOYEES.

Figure 15.20 is a partitioned design for the database specification in the appendix. It was developed using Class 2 design rules, given the access requirements in the appendix. Note the following points:

- The HOLD record appears twice—that is, on access paths traversals from both STORES ($D/1$ to $D/2$) and ITEMS ($S/3$ to $S/4$).

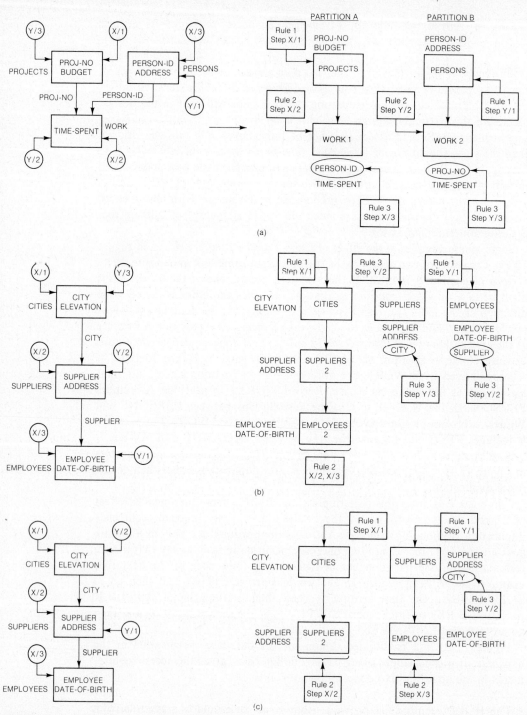

Figure 15.19 Application of Class 2 design rules

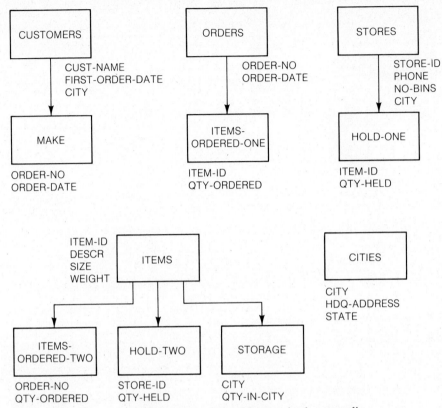

Figure 15.20   Class 2 rules applied to the problem set in the appendix

- The ITEMS-ORDERED record appears twice—that is, on access paths traversals from both ITEMS (D/3 to D/4) and ORDERS (G/2 to G/3).
- CITIES appears as a separate partition by the application of rule 4A.

Class 3 Design Methods

When Class 3 design is used, designers are no longer constrained to enter all hierarchies at the root node. Hence it becomes possible to minimize the number of root nodes (and often, as a consequence, to minimize data duplication). Hence the objectives of Class 3 design are

- to avoid occurrence duplication
- to minimize the number of partitions

To achieve these aims, the minimal logical record structure is partitioned so that the results are as follows:

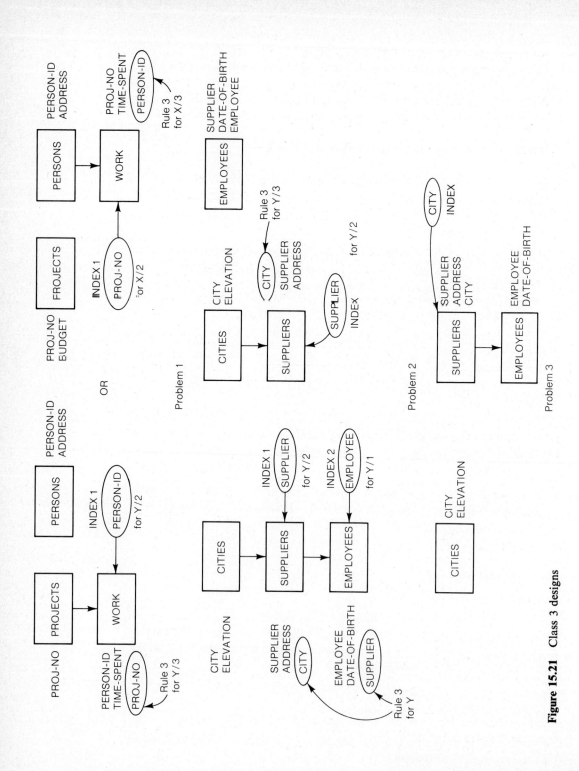

Figure 15.21 Class 3 designs

- No record appears in more than one partition.
- There is at least one record in each partition from which there is a directed path to each other record in the partition.
- Whenever a logical link is broken by partitioning, the label on the logical link becomes an item in the record on which this logical link terminates.

Here is a set of steps that can be followed in Class 3 design:

- *Step 1:* Choose a subset of records with entry points as partition root nodes.

- *Step 2:* Develop the partitions from the root nodes, applying the rules for breaking links. That is, add the link label to the record on which the link terminates.

- *Step 3:* Whenever two successive access steps s1 and s2 traverse a hierarchy from a child to parent (in the hierarchical partition), include the parent identifier in the child record and add an index to the parent. The index uses the parent identifier. Note that this step implements the equivalent of a DBTG find-owner command.

- *Step 4:* Resolve any key conflicts introduced at root nodes by using indices.

- *Step 5:* Where necessary, use the access step key. An access step entering a partition at a record other than the root record creates an index to that record. The index key becomes the access step key.

Normally, in Class 3 design, access requirements are not considered until step 3. Sometimes, however, access requirements can be used to select root nodes for the partitions.

Some examples of the application of Class 3 design rules are shown in Figure 15.21. The three problems in this figure are the same as those used in Figure 15.19. Indices are used in Figure 15.21. For example, the first alternative for Problem 1 has an index with PERSON-ID as key. This index is used by step Y/2 to directly access WORK records. PROJ-NO is added to WORK records; it is used by step Y/3 to access the PROJECTS parent of WORK records.

Conversion of Roles and Types

The hierarchical design rules can be applied to MLRSs that contain role or type logical records. However, optional roles can lead to some complications. It is preferable that optional roles or types

- do not become root nodes
- are not combined with other records unless the designer is prepared to tolerate nonhomogeneity

Some examples of hierarchical reductions are shown in Figures 15.22 and 15.23. These reduce option 1 of Figures 8.6 and 8.7 to a single hierarchy. In Figure 15.22 the reduction uses PERSONS as a root. In Figure 15.23 the reduction uses USERS as the root record. Figure 15.24 shows two alternate reductions for nonuniform optional roles. Each uses PARTS as the root record. However, in the first alternative department and project details are combined with their usage or supply details (Figure 15.24a), as required by Class 1 reduction. There is nonhomogeneity in both USERS and SUPPLIERS records. The second alternative (Figure 15.24b) does not combine records, and, as a result, there is no nonhomogeneity. This alternative corresponds to the logical record structure in Figure 8.9.

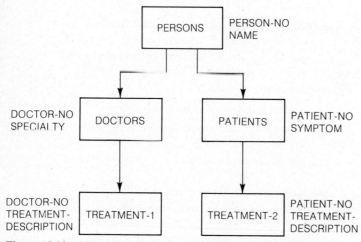

Figure 15.22 Hierarchical structure for uniform roles in Figure 8.6

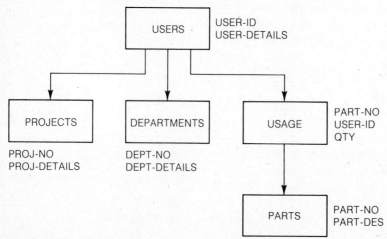

Figure 15.23 Hierarchical structure for nonuniform mandatory roles in Figure 8.7

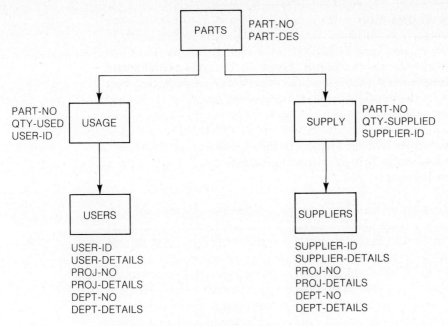

(a) A single hierarchy with sources in roles

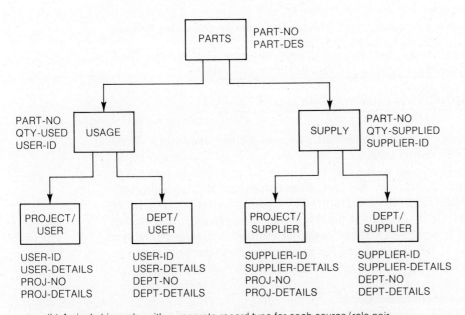

(b) A single hierarchy with a separate record type for each source/role pair

Figure 15.24 Hierarchical structure for nonuniform optional roles in Figure 8.8

INITIAL PHYSICAL DESIGN

The precise activity in physical design will depend on the specific DBMS used and its physical options. Most DBMS manufacturers usually include guidelines for choosing alternative physical structures. For example, consider IMS. Here the options include

- selection of a particular storage structure (HISAM, HDAM, or HIDAM)
- use of logical relationships between physical databases
- use of secondary indexing

The designer can start with a Class 2 design and not use either logical relationships or secondary indexing. The choice is between HISAM or a direct access method to implement the databases. It is suggested that HISAM be used unless file volatility is high. HISAM rearranges physical records during insertion and requires reorganization to physically remove logically deleted records or more newly inserted segments from overflow to main data areas. Hence if volatility is high, HDAM or HIDAM should be preferred in the initial design.

Logical relationships can be added later, after a more detailed analysis. These relationships can be used to eliminate some of the data redundancy inherent in Class 2 designs.

Another possibility is to commence with a Class 3 design and direct files and then replace some indices by logical relationships.

COBOL FILE DESIGN

COBOL file design is greatly influenced by access method constraints. These constraints usually restrict each file to one access key. Ideally, a databased approach that produces a set of flat files is attractive. It is shown in option 1 in Figure 15.25, which illustrates that part of the database in the appendix made up of the STORES, ITEMS, and HOLD file. Each object set is converted to one file in a flat file design. A flat file design has the advantage that normal correspondence is preserved and the design is symmetric. Symmetric access allows any item to be chosen as the file master key. Now the next step is to choose the file keys. This choice depends on whether the access method

- allows only one index to the file, or
- allows the file to have secondary keys.

The latter case simplifies the design. The key of access steps at the file now becomes a secondary index. A problem arises if there are more access keys than allowed secondary indices. In this case there are key conflicts, and they must be resolved.

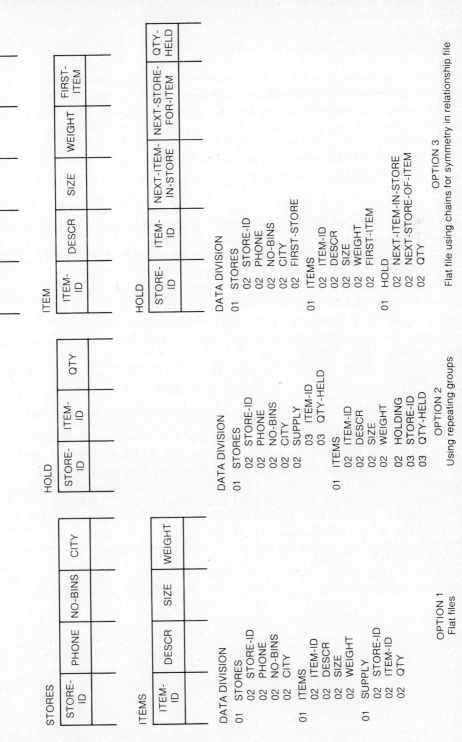

Figure 15.25 Options for conversion of entities and relationships to COBOL files

Key Conflicts

Key conflicts occur when it is not possible to allow each on-line access requirement direct access to a file. If this occurs, the access key of the most frequent requirement becomes the primary key. Secondary keys, if available, then become the access keys of the next highest occurring requirements. Other methods must be used to meet the needs of those access requirements that cannot access files directly. One of a number of tactics can be employed to resolve key conflicts while maintaining structure criteria. The following are the most common:

- *List structures:* A data item that is an access key but not a master key is chosen. Records with the same value of access key are linked; data access procedures can access records with a given access key value by following the chain. As a result, only selected records are retrieved.
- *Inverted structures:* A new index file or an existing file is used as an index. The index file is accessed by using a data item that is an access key but not a master key to the main file; this data item, however, is the master key to the index file. The index file contains the master key value of the records in the main file with a given value of access key.
- *Use of RGs:* An RG is added to a file so that the access uses the master key of the file and retrieves the items in the repeating group.

One example of a key conflict is illustrated in Figure 15.26. Here the key used by Y/1 differs from the master key of file HOLD; hence a sequential search is necessary. Changing the master key from STORE-ID to ITEM-ID does not eliminate design problems. Now X/1 will become a sequential search.

Figure 15.25 shows the resolution of this conflict. Option 2 uses RGs, whereas option 3 uses a list. In option 2, RGs are added to the STORES and ITEMS files. The RG in STORES shows the QTY-HELD of each item held by each store. The RG in ITEMS shows the QTY-HELD of the item used by each store. Direct access can now be used by both access requirements X and Y.

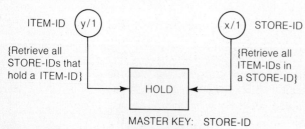

Figure 15.26   Key conflict in file HOLD

Access requirement X would access STORES directly, whereas access requirement Y would access ITEMS directly.

Option 3 resolves the conflict by using lists. There are now two lists (using symbolic pointers) through HOLD. All STORES holdings are linked by commencing at the store record in file STORES. All the holdings of ITEMS are linked by commencing at the items record in file ITEMS.

Access requirements X and Y now commence with a direct read and then follow the symbolic pointers. For example, the pseudocode for access requirement X now becomes

```
READ STORES DIRECTLY
MOVE FIRST-ITEM TO KEY-PART-1
MOVE STORE-ID TO KEY-PART-2
REPEAT UNTIL KEY-PART-1 = 0
BEGIN
   READ HOLD RECORD DIRECTLY
   OUTPUT ITEM-ID, QTY
   MOVE NEXT-ITEM-IN-STORE TO KEY-PART-1
END
```

Conversion of Roles and Types

A number of alternative conversions are possible here. For uniform roles, any of the alternative logical record options described in Figure 8.6 can be chosen. Thus suppose option 1 is chosen. In this option each entity set and each role is converted into a record type with no explicit links between them. Such conversion has two disadvantages:

1. There can be large number of files; the management of these files can increase the amount of code in programs and add to the complexity of the system.

2. Addition of a new role or type requires a new file; program stability is reduced and existing programs will need to be rewritten to include this new file.

Hence most designers prefer option 3 or 4 to reduce the number of logical record types. However, these options often lead to nonhomogeneity. For example, consider option 3 as shown in Figure 15.27. This figure defines the PERSONS record, which represents a multirole entity. There is one group for each role that PERSON can take. Where PERSON at most takes one role, there will always be one unused group in each record occurrence. Hence a compromise has been made. The designer is prepared to tolerate some nonhomogeneity to reduce the number of files. Where a source takes at most one role, waste

```
01   PERSONS.
     02   PERSON-NO   PIC IS 9(6).
     02   NAME        PIC IS A(30).
     02   DOCTOR-ROLE.
          03   SPECIALTY   PIC IS A(20).
     02   PATIENT-ROLE.
          03   SYMPTOM   PIC IS A(20).
```

Figure 15.27   A multirole entity

space can be minimized. Thus if PERSON can at most take one role, such wasted space can be eliminated by overlaying, as illustrated in Figure 15.28.

Conversion of Nonuniform Roles and Types

It is interesting to note that nonhomogeneity does not cause problems with nonuniform mandatory roles. Designers can choose option 1 or option 3 in Figure 8.7 to preserve storage criteria and avoid nonhomogeneity. One further advantage of option 3 is that it does not require special role records. The role is included in the entity record, as shown in Figure 15.29.

As the role is mandatory, the USER-ID and USER-DETAILS fields will take values. However, in option 3 the details of USER are spread across the PROJECTS and DEPARTMENTS record types. No duplication, however, results because user roles are taken either by projects or by departments, and therefore the same USER-ID would not appear in both the PROJECTS and the DEPARTMENTS record types.

Option 2 for nonuniform mandatory roles, on the other hand, causes problems. The USERS record would now be defined as shown in Figure 15.30. There is considerable nonhomogeneity in Figure 15.30 because a user can be either a project or a department but not both. Hence option 2 for nonuniform mandatory roles is generally not recommended to designers.

```
01   PERSONS.
     02   PERSON-NO   PIC IS 9(6).
     02   NAME        PIC IS A(30).
     02   ROLE        PIC IS A(6).
     02   PERSON-ROLE PIC IS A(20).
     02   DOCTOR-ROLE REDEFINES PERSON-ROLE.
          03   SPECIALTY PIC IS A(20).
     02   PATIENT-ROLE REDEFINES PERSON-ROLE.
          03   SYMPTOM PIC IS A(20).
```

Figure 15.28   Overlaying roles

```
01   PROJECT.
     02   PROJECT-NO      PIC IS 9(8).
     02   PROJ-DETAILS    PIC IS A(20).
     02   USER-ID         PIC IS 9(10).
     02   USER-DETAILS    PIC IS A(30).
```
Figure 15.29   Source combined with nonuniform roles

Optional Nonuniform Roles and Types

In general, storage criteria can be satisfied for nonuniform mandatory roles if option 3 is used. The same, however, cannot be said for the case where the nonuniform roles are optional and designers wish to reduce the number of record types. In this case option 3 in Figure 8.8 can be chosen. The records PROJECTS and DEPARTMENTS are now multirole and include provision for all the roles, some of which may be optional, as shown in Figure 15.31. The case is now the same as in Figure 15.27 because each entity takes only a subset of its possible roles.

The choice of options has one other effect. If option 3 is used and nonuniform roles are removed into their source, any other records in which these roles participated are nonuniform. For example, take the SUPPLY and USAGE records in option 3 of Figure 8.8. The SUPPLY or USAGE records can be linked to either a project or a department record (but not both). To maintain a symbolic link, the record type of the record at the other end of the link must be stored in both USAGE and SUPPLY. The way this is done is shown in SUPPLY record in Figure 15.32. Now SOURCE-TYPE indicates whether the SUPPLIER-ID belongs to a project or to a department. A similar structure would be used for the USAGE record type.

```
01   USERS.
     02   USER-ID         PIC IS 9(10).
     02   SOURCE-TYPE     PIC IS A(6).
     02   SOURCE          PIC IS X(48).
     02   PROJECT-SOURCE REDEFINES SOURCE.
          03   PROJ-NO         PIC IS 9(8).
          03   PROJ-DETAILS  PIC IS A(40).
     02   DEPT-SOURCE REDEFINES SOURCE.
          03   DEPT-NO         PIC IS 9(8).
          03   DEPT-DETAILS  PIC IS 9(40).
```
Figure 15.30   Source combined into nonuniform roles

```
01  PROJECTS.
    02  PROJ-NO        PIC IS 9(8).
    02  PROJ-DETAILS   PIC IS A(40).
    02  USER.
        03  USER-ID        PIC IS 9(10).
        03  USER-DETAILS   PIC IS A(30).
    02  SUPPLIER.
        03  SUPPLIER-ID        PIC IS 9(10).
        03  SUPPLIER-DETAILS   PIC IS A(50).
```

Figure 15.31 Nonuniform optional roles

Links with Roles

Symbolic links can be readily maintained in all of the implementations of the previous section. The way that this is done depends on the implementation. For example:

- Multirole entity implementations store the role identifier in the entity record (Figures 15.27, 15.29, and 15.31).
- Nonuniform role implementations combine the role identifier with the target object source (Figures 15.30 and 15.32).

In all these cases the symbolic links could be replaced by physical pointers. It is, however, a fair comment that in most cases both physical pointers and symbolic links result in nonhomogeneity. The only two cases in which this does not happen are those in which one of the following situations occurs:

- The roles are mandatory.
- The source takes at most one of its optional roles. In this case the REDEFINES clause is used to eliminate waste space.

Conflicts with Performance Criteria

Many of the design choices for implementing role structures will also affect performance. Where roles or types are included as groups within their sources,

```
01  SUPPLY.
    02  PART-NO        PIC IS 9(8).
    02  SOURCE-TYPE    PIC IS A(6).
    02  SUPPLIER-ID    PIC IS 9(10).
    02  QTY-SUPPLIED   PIC IS 9(6).
```

Figure 15.32 Indicating the type

access must always be through the target structure. Where sources are included in the role or type records, sources must be accessed through their role or type. Thus, in Figure 15.29, particular projects or departments could be accessed only through their USER-ID. This again is another reason why this option is not recommended. Users would more likely prefer to use PROJ-NO or DEPT-NO to access particular projects or departments.

SUMMARY

The conversion used in the initial design steps depends on the kind of enterprise model and the kind of implementation model. In the simplest conversion both of these are the same, and the enterprise model is directly converted to the implementation model. Thus the enterprise model that uses relations can be directly converted to a relational database schema. Indices are then added to the relations to meet access requirements.

Conversion from an E-R model to a network model can also be deterministic and straightforward. This conversion (like the conversion from the relational enterprise model to a relational database schema) places initial emphasis on structure criteria. It commences by first converting the E-R model to a logical record structure. Then each logical record type becomes a network record type and each logical link becomes a set type. Access paths can be added to satisfy access requirements.

The most difficult conversions are to a hierarchical implementation model or to COBOL files. Here there are implementation model constraints that determine the kind of partitioning allowed and the direct access points to each partition. Three types of hierarchical model restrictions are as follows:

- DBMSs that require the entire database to be represented by a single hierarchy. Direct access is, however, possible at any record in the hierarchy.
- DBMSs that allow partitioning but in which direct access is possible only through the root node of each partition.
- DBMSs that allow partitioning and direct access through any node in each partition.

Different design conversions can be used to deal with these classes of hierarchical DBMSs. Each conversion is access-based and uses access requirements to choose the hierarchical arrangement of record types.

COBOL file design introduces its own restrictions. The most important restriction is the number of secondary indices allowed for each record type. Key conflicts can arise if the number of access keys is greater than the number of indices. The designer must then use list structures or inverted lists or duplicate the data to permit direct access for all the access requirements. Additional problems arise when role or type structures are converted to COBOL files.

Each role or type must be converted to one file if nonhomogeneity is to be avoided. Several options are available to reduce the number of files for different role structures.

PROBLEMS

You are now in a position to convert the database specification to an initial design. It is suggested that you produce initial designs for at least Design Projects A and B (at the end of the text). Logical record structures should have been developed for these projects at the conclusion of Chapter 8.

It is suggested that in the first instance an initial design be proposed for the network data model, assuming a DBTG implementation. Subsequently, you should apply hierarchical conversion algorithms. In particular, a Class 1 design should be attempted for a System 2000 DBMS. Then a Class 2 design should be proposed for IMS, using HISAM only. Finally, Class 3 designs, assuming use of indices, should be attempted.

chapter sixteen
Evaluating Designs

INTRODUCTION

Database evaluations are made at all the system development steps. However, the types of evaluations at each step differ. The first step is an evaluation used to select a DBMS. Most installations can now support more than one DBMS. The designer should attempt to select the DBMS that best meets the enterprise requirements.

Having selected a DBMS, the designer begins database design. The design must be chosen to make best use of the DBMS facilities. It must perform user tasks with minimum resource use and meet transaction response requirements. Some design computations are usually necessary at this stage to yield estimates about expected system performance of a proposed design. As discussed in Chapter 14, performance estimates are part of an iterative process. Successive steps use the performance estimates to indicate design problems. Design tactics are then used to overcome the performance problems. Once a design with satisfactory estimated performance is found, that design is implemented on the DBMS.

After implementation, the system is continually monitored to verify that it is performing according to design estimates. The DBMS provides regular statistics to show the system transaction traffic and the number of accesses made to the database record types. Any variation from design estimates can be used to amend (or tune) the design.

This chapter is concerned primarily with the second of these evaluations, namely, making performance estimates, given a proposed design. Computations to make such estimates will be presented. But first we will give a brief summary of the other two kinds of DBMS evaluation.

SELECTING A DBMS

DBMS selection is a complex task. It can be done properly only if there is a well-defined set of user operational and functional needs. Thus before DBMS selection can begin, the organization should define its critical DBMS require-ments. These requirements can include

- the type of database end-user and consequently the access language requirements
- the privacy control requirements
- the type of restructuring to be supported by the DBMS
- the volume of data to be supported by the DBMS
- recovery and concurrency control requirements
- performance monitoring requirements
- the general access methods supported by the DBMS

Selection proceeds by evaluating the technical, economic, and operational feasibility of each candidate DBMS. A DBMS meets the technical criteria if it can satisfy all the critical needs. Any DBMS that does not meet the critical needs is not usually considered further. If, say, privacy is an important issue and a particular DBMS does not possess adequate privacy control, that DBMS will be out of the running.

Benchmarks are frequently used to evaluate and compare the technical per-formance of different DBMSs. The idea of the benchmark is to write the same test programs for all candidate DBMSs to test some critical feature. For exam-ple, benchmarks are often used to make performance measures. A subset of a database may be set up and the most frequent transactions run against this sub-set. The same critical transactions run on different DBMSs provide perform-ance data that can be used to compare the systems.

It is important to ensure that benchmarks use realistic data. For example, representative record sizes and file sizes should be used. The traffic against the test database should also have a representative mix of transactions. This mix should include an expected proportion of delete, insert, update, and retrieve transactions to ensure typical use of overflow areas.

DBMSs with proven technical feasibility can then be chosen on economic and operational grounds. The least cost is always a criterion, but the chosen DBMS should also be easily integrated into the operational environment. The DBMS should be readily integrated with other system software and should not present undue training problems to familiarize existing staff with its use.

MONITORING THE DATABASE

Monitoring comes into force after a design is implemented. It is used to mea-sure actual transaction traffic during real-life system operation. Many DBMSs provide monitoring software to measure activities such as

- number of records of each type accessed
- the number of times a link is traversed
- the use of various indices

These data can be used to detect changes in usage patterns or to compare actual resource use against estimated use. The database administrator can employ such variations to add or delete indices to the database or to change the database physical structures.

PERFORMANCE ESTIMATES

The two major performance estimates are

- estimates of storage use
- estimates of records transferred across the physical record interface

Storage estimates indicate the amount of secondary storage needed to store the database. Estimates of records transferred serve as a measure of on-line transaction performance. The number of records transferred is closely proportional to transaction response times and can serve to compare alternate designs, using transaction performance as a criterion. The goal is to minimize the number of record transfers.

Another important estimate, especially in larger systems, is disk channel utilization. There are a number of channels supported by hardware, and each channel has a limited capacity for record transfers. Designers must ensure that they do not exceed this capacity.

The estimates use access paths developed from access requirements. Each access step of an access path is used to estimate the number of logical records accessed (LRA) at the access step. This estimate is then used to determine the number of physical record transfers. These two steps are called *logical analysis* and *physical analysis* in this text.

Logical and Physical Design Analysis

Logical and physical on-line design analysis is an organized process for estimating storage use, transaction response, and input-output channel utilization. The input to the analysis is a design proposal and a set of on-line and batch requirements. The output comprises specific estimates of storage use and I/O transfers. The analysis considers the following:

1. The type of hardware devices on which files or databases are stored.
2. The proposed file organizations.
3. The physical structures, such as blocking, queueing, and buffering.
4. The access requirements.
5. The procedure logic used to meet access requirements; the procedures that access databases are called *data access procedures* in this text.

Accuracy of Estimates

What is the level of computational detail necessary to make useful design estimates? In answering this question, we must note that design estimates are used to compare alternative designs, not to provide absolute performance factors. To provide absolute factors, the design computations would also need to take into account all those processes that are executed concurrently with the data access procedures. In particular, they would have to consider those additional disk I/O's that are made by the operating system to service database accesses but that are independent of the type of access. For comparative purposes, disk accesses made by the operating system can be considered to be proportional to the data accesses made by access requirements. Logical and physical analysis methods compute only the resource usage to update and retrieve data from files by the access requirements. This contribution is computed in terms of disk I/O's and channel time.

Generality of Analysis

Analysis methods should be general; they should be applicable to both elementary files and DBMSs. The analysis techniques described here are based on access diagrams that use *record structures;* each record structure is represented by one rectangular box. Examples of a record structure are

- COBOL files that include one record type
- a database segment in IMS
- a record type in CODASYL systems

Access requests access and select occurrences of record structures; each occurrence of a record structure is here called a *record*. This occurrence may be one record in a basic file, one record in an IMS segment, or an occurrence of a CODASYL record type.

Record Access

Design computations differentiate between *selected records* and *accessed records*. Selected records include

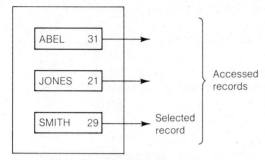

Figure 16.1   Record selection

- existing records that are deleted from the database
- existing database records that are modified
- new records that are inserted into the database
- existing database records that are needed to produce outputs for the access requirement

Accessed records are all records transferred between peripheral storage devices and main memory by the data access procedures. Each access request must specify the data records that are to be deleted, modified, inserted, or used to produce output for that access request. An *access key* is often used to do this. It is a set of data items whose values are known at the time of the access request. Records that satisfy the access key item values must be transferred between secondary storage devices and main memory. Often files or database designs are such that data access procedures must also access additional records; these additional records are not deleted, inserted, modified, or needed to produce outputs.

Figure 16.1, for example, is a sequential file of three records. Each record has two fields, NAME and AGE. Now take the access request, "Find the age of SMITH"; NAME is the access key. The data access procedures must read the entire file; three logical records are accessed as a result. Only one record is needed by the access request, namely, that where NAME = "SMITH." Hence three records are accessed while one record is selected. The term *hit ratio* is often used to specify the ratio of records selected to those accessed. In our example the hit ratio is 1:3.

Ideally, the number of selected and accessed records should be equal (the hit ratio equals 1). This ideal can be achieved when two conditions are met: the access key and the master key of the file are the same, and direct access can be made to the file. The access in our request in Figure 16.1 matches the master key. However, direct access is not possible in sequential files, so a serial search is made. A serial search is also necessary in sequential files even if the access key and master key are different; all records are then accessed and only those that satisfy the access key value are selected.

Analysis Procedures

The design analysis described here consists of four parts:

1. *Storage requirements analysis.* The specification of record contents and data item sizes is used to compute the amount of secondary storage that is needed to support the design.

2. *Access path analysis.* Each access requirement is analyzed to determine the record types needed to satisfy that requirement. To do this, the designer either plots an access path or uses pseudocode. Either of these techniques must show the actual database access commands applied to each record type. These access commands are then analyzed in the next two steps to derive the number of logical and physical records accessed and selected at the particular step.

3. *Logical analysis.* The access diagram or pseudocode is used to estimate the number of accessed and selected logical records. To do this, the commands applied at each logical record are examined. Knowledge of the access method is then used to estimate the logical records accessed and selected by each command.

4. *Physical analysis.* The number of physical data transfers between memory and peripheral devices for each access requirement is computed. This computation uses the output from logical analysis. The accessed logical records are converted into transfers between memory and peripheral devices. Some knowledge of peripheral characteristics or access method operation is necessary in this conversion.

These four parts combine to form the analysis process. The designer uses either the access diagrams or the pseudocode together with logical and physical analysis, initially to estimate the number of peripheral transfers and then to estimate channel usage. Physical analysis produces the estimate of peripheral data transfers; channel usage estimates can be found by multiplying the number of transfers by the channel time used by each transfer. Estimates of channel times per transfer are found from manufacturer's specifications.

These analysis techniques will first be illustrated by using indexed sequential files and direct access methods. Later, extensions to DBMs will be discussed.

The database specification in the appendix is used to illustrate the analysis techniques. It is initially assumed that all object sets in the specification are implemented as indexed sequential files. The fields in each file are shown in the file design table in Figure App. 7 of the appendix. This table also shows the file master keys. It is assumed that the file system does not support secondary access keys.

Our example commences with an analysis of storage requirements. This analysis is illustrated in Figure 16.2. Logical and physical analysis for access requirements S and V of the appendix are illustrated in Figure 16.3.

File Name / Design Factor	Unit	STORES	CITIES	ITEMS	ORDERS	CUSTOMERS	HOLD	ITEM-CITY	ITEMS-ORDERED			Total
Data record size		50	60	59	36	46	18	34	22			
Record occurences		100	50	1,000	100	70	20,000	15,000	10,000			
Data storage		5,000	3,000	59,000	3,600	3,220	360,000	510,000	220,000			1,163,820
Block-factor		3	3	3	5	3	10	5	8			
Hardware block size		180	180	180	180	180	180	180	180			
Data hardware blocks		34	17	334	20	24	2,000	3,000	1,250			
Overflow blocks		4	2	34	2	3	200	300	125			
Index hardware blocks		4	2	34	2	3	200	300	125			
Total hardware blocks		42	21	402	24	30	2,400	3,600	1,500			8,019
Total physical storage												1,443,420

Figure 16.2 Storage requirements table

Storage Requirements

Estimates of storage requirements use the table of storage requirements (Figure 16.2). Each column in this table is used to estimate the size of one file. Following is a description of the rows of the table:

1. *Data record size.* The amount of storage to store each record of a file; the sum of all the data item sizes and any pointers in the record.
2. *Record occurrences.* The number of record occurrences in the file.
3. *Data storage.* The number of occurrences multiplied by data record size.
4. *Hardware block size.* The size in terms of some storage units of a hardware block; disk sector, track, and segment are examples. Where the size is variable, a range is indicated. It is assumed that the contents of one block are transferred as one physical record.
5. *Block-factor.* The number of logical records stored in a hardware block or transferred as one physical record. A variable range is indicated if this is supported by the file organization software.
6. *Data hardware blocks.* The number of hardware blocks required to store the data in the file. It is the number of record occurrences divided by the block-factor.
7. *Overflow blocks.* The number of hardware blocks allocated to the overflow area for a file.
8. *Index hardware blocks.* The number of hardware blocks required to store the index for a file.
9. *Total hardware blocks.* The data hardware blocks plus index hardware blocks plus overflow buckets for a file.
10. *Total physical storage.* The total hardware blocks multiplied by hardware block size for a file.

The data record size in Figure 16.2 is computed from the file design shown in the file design table in Figure App. 7 in the appendix. This table shows the design file structures, the items in the records in each file structure, and the size of each item. The item sizes are added to give the record size in Figure 16.2. The record occurrences given in Figure 16.2 were obtained as part of the quantitative data in the database specification (see Figure App. 9).

1. Each store holds an average of 200 item kinds.
2. Each order is for an average of 100 different item kinds.

A block size of 180 is also assumed. Thus three STORES records ($3 \times 50 = 150$) can be stored in one block; four records would overflow the block). Computations in Figure 16.2 add 10% of the data storage for overflow and another 10% for the index storage associated with each file.

Figure 16.2 is equally applicable to DBMSs and elementary files. In database estimates each column represents files that store a defined record structure. Thus there would be a column for each record type in a network database. Data record sizes also include pointers associated with set types. Hardware block sizes, block structures, and the placement of logical records into blocks depend on the implementation, and designers would need to use the manufacturer's specifications to make proper estimates.

Logical Analysis

The logical and physical analysis in Figure 16.3 uses access requirements S and V. The pseudocode for these access requirements is given in Figures 16.4 and 16.5, respectively. The pseudocode uses commands appropriate to the chosen file structure. Following is an explanation of the commands in Figure 16.4:

- READ NEXT filename RECORD denotes a sequential read (steps S/1 and S/3).
- READ filename AT condition denotes a direct read (steps S/2, S/4, and S/5).
- START filename AT condition (step S/3) denotes a positioning of an indexed sequential file.

You may note that requirement S reads file ITEMS-ORDERED sequentially (step S/1). The ITEMS-ORDERED file master key is ITEM-ID, but the known value (access key) at the beginning of the access requirement is ORDER-NO; hence a sequential search is necessary. If in the sequential search an ITEMS-ORDERED record with a required value of ORDER-NO is found (it is assumed that the required ORDER-NO is in KEY1), a check is made to see whether the item is "LAMP" (step S/2). If it is "LAMP," the HOLD file is then searched (step S/3), using a selective sequential search to find all the stores that hold that item. Note that ITEM-ID is the key of file HOLD. So all the HOLD records for the same ITEM-ID are stored sequentially, thus making a selective sequential search possible. For all those HOLD records where QTY-HELD is greater than 150, the store's city is found (steps S/4), and then a direct read of a CITIES record is made to find the city's HDQ-ADDRESS (step S/5).

Requirement V differs from requirement S in that it is executed in batch mode. Two files (ORDERS and ITEMS-ORDERED) are sorted before record selection begins. File ORDERS has been sorted in CUST-NAME order, whereas file ITEMS-ORDERED has been sorted into ORDER-NO order. The sorted ORDERS file is now read sequentially (step V/3). For each ORDERS

Problem: HOLDINGS

alternative 1 Page: 1

Access	Access Rate Per week	Access Step	Access Key	File	File Master Key	LOGICAL DESIGN ANALYSIS — Data records for one access step: Accessed	Selected	TOTAL for one access occurrence: Selected (accessed)	TOTAL: Selected (accessed)	Block Size Logical records	PHYSICAL — Data records for one access step	Index records for one access step	TOTAL records for one access step	TOTAL for one access occurrence	TOTAL
S	100														
		S/1	ORDER-NO	ITEMS-ORDERED	ITEM-ID	10,000	100			8	$\frac{10,000}{8}$	0	1,250		
		S/2	ITEM-ID	ITEMS	ITEM-ID	100 × 1	100 × 1			3	100 × 1	100 × 1	200		
		S/3	ITEM-ID	HOLD	ITEM-ID	5 × 20	5 × 20	500 (10,400)	50,000 (1,040,000)	10	$5 \times \frac{20}{10}$	5 × 1	15	1,865	186,500
		S/4	STORE-ID	STORES	STORE-ID	100	100			3	100 × 1	100 × 1	200		
		S/5	CITY	CITIES	CITY	100	100			3	100 × 1	100 × 1	200		
V	1														
		V/1		ORDERS		100				5	$\frac{100}{5} \times 3$	0	60		
		V/2		ITEMS-ORDERED		10,000				8	$\frac{10,000}{8} \times 3$	0	3,750		
		V/3		ORDERS-SORT		100				5	$\frac{100}{5}$	0	20		
		V/4		ITEMS-ORDERED SORT		100 × 100		420,200 (420,200)	420,200 (420,200)	8	$100 \times \frac{100}{8}$	100	1,350	235,180	235,180
		V/5		HOLD		10,000×20				10	$10,000 \times \frac{20}{10}$	10,000	30,000		
		V/6		OUTPUT		200,000				1	200,000	0	200,000		
								Totals						Totals	421,680

Figure 16.3 Design analysis

```
MOVE INPUT-ORDER-VALUE TO KEY1
REPEAT FOR ALL ITEMS-ORDERED RECORDS
   BEGIN
      READ NEXT ITEMS-ORDERED RECORD ─────────────────────── (S/1)
      IF ORDER-NO IN ITEMS-ORDERED = KEY1 THEN
         BEGIN
            MOVE ITEM-ID IN ITEMS-ORDERED TO KEY2
            READ ITEMS AT ITEM-ID IN ITEMS = KEY2 ──────────── (S/2)
            IF DESCR IN ITEMS = 'LAMP' THEN
               BEGIN
                  START HOLD AT ITEM-ID = KEY2 ─────────────── (S/3)
                  REPEAT FOR ALL HOLD RECORDS WITH ITEM-ID = KEY2
                     BEGIN
                        READ NEXT HOLD RECORD ────────────────┘
                        IF QTY-HELD > 150 THEN
                           BEGIN
                              MOVE STORE-ID IN HOLD TO KEY3
                              READ STORES RECORD ───────────── (S/4)
                                 AT STORE-ID = KEY3
                              MOVE LOCATED-IN-CITY
                                 IN STORES TO KEY4
                              READ CITIES RECORD ───────────── (S/5)
                                 AT CITY =KEY4
                              OUTPUT HDQ-ADDRESS
                           END
                     END
               END
         END
   END
END
```

Figure 16.4   Pseudocode for requirement S

record read, a selective sequential search (step V/4) of the sorted ITEMS-ORDERED file is made to find all the items in that order. The selective sequential search is possible because the sorted ITEMS-ORDERED file is in ORDER-NO sequence. Each item in the order is used as a key in a selective sequential search of the HOLD file (which is in ITEM-ID order) to find all the stores that hold that item (step V/5). All the retrieved information is then written to an output file.

Logical analysis commences by examining the pseudocode to determine the accesses made to the file. The number of records accessed by the access commands is computed. One row in Figure 16.3 is used for each access step. The computation uses information on record occurrences from Figure 16.2 as well as information about the access key and the file master key. If the access key and the file master key are the same, direct access or selective sequen-

Requirement V assumes the file keys are given in the file design table in the appendix. It also assumed that no alternate keys are allowed. Requirement V is a computation equivalent to

$R1$ = JOIN ORDERS, ITEMS-ORDERED OVER ORDER-NO

$R2$ = JOIN $R1$, HOLD OVER ITEM-ID

OUTPUT = PROJECT $R2$ OVER CUST-NAME, ORDER-NO, ITEM-ID, STORE-NO

The files are first sorted to ensure that a file can be accessed directly on the items used in a join. The sort order is also that required by the output file.

```
SORT ORDERS FILE IN CUST-NAME ORDER INTO ORDERS-SORTED-FILE ──────────── V/1
SORT ITEMS-ORDERED FILE IN ORDER-NO ORDER INTO ITEMS-ORDERED-
                                              SORTED-FILE ──────────── V/2

FOR EACH RECORD IN ORDERS-SORTED-FILE
  BEGIN
    READ NEXT ORDERS-SORTED-FILE RECORD ──────────────────────────── V/3
    MOVE ORDER-NO IN ORDERS-SORTED-FILE TO KEY1
    START ITEMS-ORDERED-SORTED-FILE AT ORDER-NO = KEY1 ──────────┐
    REPEAT FOR ALL ITEMS-ORDERED-SORTED-FILE RECORDS WITH ORDER-NO = KEY1
      BEGIN
        READ NEXT ITEMS-ORDERED-SORTED-FILE RECORD ──────────────┴─── V/4
        MOVE ITEM-ID IN ITEMS-ORDERED-SORTED-FILE TO KEY2
        START HOLD FILE AT ITEM-ID = KEY2 ──────────────────────┐
        REPEAT FOR ALL HOLD RECORDS WITH ITEM-ID = KEY2
          BEGIN
            READ NEXT HOLD RECORD ──────────────────────────────┴─── V/5
            WRITE CUST-NAME, ORDER-NO, ITEM-ID, STORE-ID
                                   TO OUTPUT FILE ──────────────────── V/6
          END
      END
  END
```

Figure 16.5 Pseudocode for indexed sequential file for requirement V

tial searches are used. If the two keys are different, a sequential file search is necessary.

The number of logical records accessed and selected by each access step is entered in the column "Data records for one access step" in Figure 16.3. Similarly, the number of these access records that are selected for later processing is also included in this column. The sums of the accessed records and the sums of the selected records for all steps in one execution of an access request are entered in the column "TOTAL for one access occurrence"; the number of accessed records is given in brackets. The column "TOTAL" contains the number of file accesses over a given period; it equals the values in the column "TOTAL for one access occurrence" multiplied by the column "Access rate." The "Access rate" column contains the number of executions of an access request in a given interval. The "Total" column contains the number of records accessed and selected in that interval. Again, the number of accessed records is given in brackets in the "Total" column.

The computations in Figure 16.3 are for the access requests S and V. An explanation of the computations follows.

Logical Analysis—Access Requirement S

Here are the steps taken to compute access request S:

- *Step S/1:* The whole file is read sequentially because the access key and file master key are not the same. Hence each of the 10,000 records is accessed. Only records with a given value of the order identifier ORDER-NO are selected for further processing. On the average there are 100 such records selected because an average order is for 100 item kinds.
- *Step S/2:* The READ ITEMS command is executed once for each selected record in step S/1. Each execution of command READ ITEMS is direct and accesses one record only. This record is also selected. The entry of 100×1 in Figure 16.3 signifies 100 executions of step S/2.
- *Step S/3:* The START command in this step is executed only if the item retrieved in step S/2 is LAMP. It is assumed that 1 out of 20 item kinds is a lamp. Hence the START command in step S/3 is executed (100/20), that is, five times for each execution of access request S. Each START is followed by the retrieval of 20 records because each item kind is, on the average, held by 20 stores (20,000 in HOLD/1000 in PARTS). Thus the START command in Figure 16.3 is executed five times and there are an average of 20 READ NEXT HOLD RECORD executions for each START COMMAND execution.
- *Step S/4:* The READ STORES command is executed once for each selected record in step S/3 with QTY greater than 150. It is assumed that all records have QTY greater than 150. Each READ STORES command accesses one record because access is direct. There are 100 executions of step S/4 for each execution of access request S.
- *Step S/5:* Same as step S/4.

Analysis of Batch Processing

Batch processing adds a further level of complexity to the analysis since it is necessary to estimate

- the number of records accessed and selected during sorting
- the number of records in any intermediate files

In Figure 16.3 it is assumed that all records in the sort file are both accessed and selected. The number of records in intermediate files depends on the source file. For example:

- If the source file is rearranged in a new order, the number of records in the intermediate file is the same as in the source file.

- If two source files are combined into an intermediate file, the number of records in the collection file is usually the higher of the number of records in the source file.

Batch processing is exemplified by access requirement V.

Logical Analysis—Access Requirement V

Access requirement V uses two sort files and an output file. The steps in logical analysis for access request V are as follows:

- *Step V/1:* Each record in file ORDERS is accessed and selected during sorting, and a sort file created. The sort file will contain 100 records.

- *Step V/2:* Each record in file ITEMS-ORDERED is accessed and selected during sorting, and a sort file created. The sort file will contain 10,000 records.

- *Step V/3:* The whole file comprising 100 records is read sequentially; hence each record is accessed and selected.

- *Step V/4:* The START command is executed once for each record selected in step V/3. So since 100 records are selected in step V/3, the start command is executed 100 times. After each START, all the item kinds in an order are accessed—an average of 100. These records are accessed by the READ NEXT command in step V/4. Hence a total of 100×100 records are accessed by V/4 for each execution of access request V.

- *Step V/5:* The START command is executed once for each record selected in step V/4. Since 10,000 records are selected in step V/4, the START command is executed 10,000 times. After each START, there is an access of all the stores that hold an item kind (an average of 20). Hence a total of $10,000 \times 20$ records are accessed for each execution of access request V.

- *Step V/6:* One record is written to the output file for each selected record in step V/4. All records accessed in step V/4 are also selected.

Physical Analysis

Peripheral transfer estimates are made in physical analysis. Estimates of accessed logical records in logical analysis are examined and used to estimate the number of peripheral transfers needed to transfer these logical records between memory and storage devices. The physical analysis computations for access requests S and V are illustrated in Figure 16.3.

Estimating Data Record Transfers

In Figure 16.3 the estimate of physical data records transferred is entered in the column "Data records for one access step." The number of data records transferred will depend on the type of activity and the file organization. Hence any estimate must use the manufacturer's specifications to determine the number of physical record transfers required to transfer logical records. Some typical estimating procedures are shown in Figure 16.6 for COBOL file organizations. Such a figure is sometimes called a *costing table*.

Estimating Index Transfers

Physical analysis of indexed sequential files must also include an estimate of index record transfers. The number of these transfers depends on a particular implementation and must be found from the manufacturer's specifications. The following is assumed in subsequent computations:

File Org.	Access	Kind of Activity			
		Retrieving	Deleting	Inserting	Modifying
Sequential	Sequential	Records assumed to be stored sequentially; Z/N physical transfers made	Must rewrite file; 2Z/N transfers made	Must rewrite file; 2Z/N transfers made	Must rewrite file; 2Z/N transfers made
"	In-situ	"	Z/N to read file	Z/N to read plus one additional transfer for inserted record	Z/N to read plus one additional transfer for modified record
I-S	Sequential	"	"	"	"
"	Direct	One physical record transfer for each logical record	One physical record transfer for each logical record deleted	One physical record transfer for each logical record inserted	Two physical transfers: one I/O to read the record and one to write its modified form
"	Selective sequential	K/N transfers, where K is the number of logical records accessed	As for retrieve	As for retrieve, with one extra transfer to insert the new record	As for retrieve, with one extra transfer to rewrite the modified record
Relative	Direct	One physical record transfer for each logical record accessed	One physical record transfer for each logical record deleted	One physical record transfer for each logical record inserted	Two physical transfers: one to read the record and one to write its modified form

N = blocking factor
Z = number of logical records in file

Figure 16.6 Estimating data transfer for COBOL files

1. For direct data retrieval or modification, one index read per data record modified or retrieved.
2. For direct data insertion or deletion, one index read and one index write per data record is inserted or deleted.
3. For all sequential processing there is no read of the index.
4. One index read is assumed each time a START command is executed.

No index records are transferred with relative or sequential files.

The number of index records transferred is entered into the column "Index records for one access step" in Figure 16.3.

Estimating Total Transfers

The remaining columns of Figure 16.3 contain the following totals:

- "TOTAL records for one access step" is the total transfers for an access step (data + index transfers).
- "TOTAL for one access occurrence" is the sum of the totals of all access steps for one access request.
- TOTAL is "TOTAL for one access occurrence" multiplied by the access rate.

The estimate of total physical transfers for a proposed design is given in the bottom line of the figure.

Physical Analysis—Access Requirement S

The procedure for the physical analysis for access request S is as follows:

- *Step S/1:* The 10,000 records in Figure 16.3 are read serially; to do this (10,000/8) = 1250 physical records are transferred. The logical records are divided by the blocking factor because the records are read sequentially.
- *Step S/2:* Each execution of this step is a direct read; one index record and one data record are transferred for each execution.
- *Step S/3:* Each of the five executions of this step results in one index transfer for the START command. Twenty records are then read, resulting in (20/10) physical data transfers. The blocking factor is used because the records that are read are sequentially contiguous.
- *Step S/4:* Each of the 100 executions of this step accesses one record directly. For this procedure, one index and one data record must be transferred.
- *Step S/5:* Same as step S/4.

Physical Analysis—Access Requirement V

Some further information is required to do physical analysis for batch accesses; in particular, it is necessary to know

- the number of physical transfers made during sorting
- the size of records and hence block size for the intermediate files

The number of physical transfers made during sorting depends on the kind of sort algorithm used; designers will need to ascertain this number from the specification of the particular sort algorithm that is to be used. In the computation in Figure 16.3 it is assumed that, on the average, the following apply:

- Each data record is transferred three times during sorting (it is assumed that this is the costing factor of the particular SORT package used in this step).
- Sort files use the same blocking factor as the source file.

For example, step V/2 sorts a file of 10,000 records whose block size is 8; hence 10,000/8 physical records are read with every scan of the file. We assume three scans of the file for each sort; hence $3 \times (10,000/8) = 3750$ physical records are transferred during the sort.

The blocking factors for sort files and intermediate files can be different from those in the source file. This is particularly the case in intermediate files that contain records made up from two or more source files. For example, records in the output file contain the items ORDER-NO, CUST-NAME, FIRST-ORDER-DATE, ITEM-ID, DESCR, STORE-ID, and PHONE—a total size of 98 characters. The blocking factor of the output file then becomes 1.

Variations

Obviously, estimates of physical data transfers will depend on the physical organization of records on physical devices. Following are examples of variations:

- In indexed sequential file organizations that do not store records in order of master key, blocking factors cannot be used to reduce physical transfers during selective sequential searches.
- Methods and overheads of maintaining variable length records vary significantly between systems.

It is strongly suggested that designers consult the specifications of their elementary COBOL files and produce an estimating (or costing) guide similar to that shown in Figure 16.6 for their particular installation. Once this table is constructed, it can be used in physical analysis.

Estimates for DBMSs

Logical analysis for implementations that use DBMSs can proceed in the same way as for elementary COBOL file implementations. The differences are in the

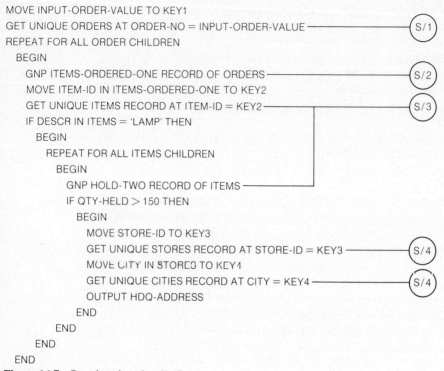

```
MOVE INPUT-ORDER-VALUE TO KEY1
GET UNIQUE ORDERS AT ORDER-NO = INPUT-ORDER-VALUE ——————————— S/1
REPEAT FOR ALL ORDER CHILDREN
  BEGIN
    GNP ITEMS-ORDERED-ONE RECORD OF ORDERS ——————————— S/2
    MOVE ITEM-ID IN ITEMS-ORDERED-ONE TO KEY2
    GET UNIQUE ITEMS RECORD AT ITEM-ID = KEY2 ——————————— S/3
    IF DESCR IN ITEMS = 'LAMP' THEN
      BEGIN
        REPEAT FOR ALL ITEMS CHILDREN
          BEGIN
            GNP HOLD-TWO RECORD OF ITEMS —————
            IF QTY-HELD > 150 THEN
              BEGIN
                MOVE STORE-ID TO KEY3
                GET UNIQUE STORES RECORD AT STORE-ID = KEY3 ——————— S/4
                MOVE CITY IN STORES TO KEY4
                GET UNIQUE CITIES RECORD AT CITY = KEY4 ——————— S/4
                OUTPUT HDQ-ADDRESS
              END
          END
      END
  END
END
```

Figure 16.7 Pseudocode using IMS

pseudocode and the costing of access steps. The pseudocode (or access path diagram) now includes commands used by the DBMS. Thus the pseudocode shown in Figure 16.4 is appropriate for COBOL files. The pseudocode used in, say, an IMS evaluation would use pseudocode appropriate to IMS. For example, Figure 16.7 is pseudocode for requirement S, assuming the logical design shown in Figure 15.20.

Logical record analysis now proceeds much as it does in COBOL file analysis, the steps in the pseudocode being used to estimate the number of logical and physical record transfers for each access requirement. Given the chosen physical file organization or access method, this estimate is usually done in two stages:

1. Each DL/1 command is used to estimate the number of records accessed.
2. The number of physical transfers made is estimated. To do this, a costing table is used to derive the physical data transfers, given the estimate of logical records accessed in step 1.

For example, a GU read command to a HDAM or HIDAM physical database results in one OSAM or VSAM read. Hence one logical record read is recorded for logical analysis against a GU command. The number of physical record transfers are estimated by considering performance figures for the VSAM or OSAM data set. Thus a read in VSAM will usually retrieve a number of B-tree index records to get to the data record. The execution of a GNP command will also depend on the access method. For example, in a HISAM structure all the records are blocked, and so the GN sequential search can proceed by taking advantage of blocking factors. With direct access methods, estimates will differ. Now each record owned by the same parent can appear in different physical records. The worst-case estimate of the number of physical records accessed here will be the same as the estimate of the number of logical records accessed.

What is required to make this analysis successful is a cost table similar to that in Figure 16.6 for DL/1 commands. This table would then be used in conjunction with the pseudocode for logical and physical analysis. Tables of this kind can usually be found in manufacturers' manuals. Many manufacturers also provide automatic design aids to assist in design computations.

ANALYTICAL MODELING METHODS

Logical and physical record analysis is suggested in this text for comparing alternate designs. Other methods are used to evaluate absolute database performance or to improve the estimates obtained by logical and physical record analysis. These methods are

- benchmarks for critical transactions
- analytical or simulation models

Benchmarks were discussed earlier in this chapter. A brief description of analytical models is given in the next section. It should be noted that designers of databases do not often resort to analytical modeling, for it requires designers to develop a mathematical, or probabilistic, model for transaction processing.

Computations in analytical modeling produce

- probabilistic estimates of logical and physical records accessed
- estimates of absolute transaction response times

Some Probabilistic Estimates

One important estimate is the probability of a record being in the main or the overflow area. An important parameter used in the computation of this probability is the amount of free space initially available in a file. This free space is measured by the number of free spaces left for logical records in a physical rec-

F1 \ F2	.2	.6	1.0	2.0	5.0
1	9.4	24.8	36.8	56.8	80.1
2	.6	4.5	10.4	27.1	60.9
3	—	.6	2.3	10.9	43.4
5	—	—	.1	1.1	17.5

$F1$ = number of free
record spaces in
each physical record

$F2$ = ratio of $\dfrac{\text{new records added}}{\text{physical records in the file}}$

Figure 16.8 Percentage of records in overflow

ord after initial loading. Thus if a blocking factor is five and initially only three records are stored in each physical record, two spaces are free. The other parameter is the number of new logical records inserted in the file. The number of records in overflow increases with the number of records added and decreases as the amount of initial free space increases. The percentage of records in overflow can be computed by using statistical techniques. Some representative figures are shown in Figure 16.8.

For those interested in statistics the table in Figure 16.8 is derived as follows. The probability of the number of new logical records hitting a given physical record is given by the Poisson distribution. Hence if the number of physical records is N and the number of new logical records is A, the probability of a new logical record hitting a given physical record is A/N ($= F2$). Then the probability of there being i hits to one physical record is $e^{-\lambda}\lambda^i/i!$ where $\lambda = F2$. Alternatively, $N(e^{-\lambda}\lambda^i/i!)$ physical records have i logical record hits. Now if each physical record has $F1$ empty spaces, the number of records not in overflow will be

R_D = number of records inserted into physical records with less than $F1$ hits + number of records inserted into physical records with $F1$ or more hits

$$\left\{ \sum_{i=0}^{F1} \frac{e^{-\lambda}\lambda^i}{i!} i + \left(1 - \sum_{i=0}^{F1} \frac{e^{-\lambda}\lambda^i}{i!} \right) F1 \right\} N$$

$$= XN$$

The fraction of records in the overflow area will then be

$$\frac{A - R_D}{A} = 1 - \frac{R_D}{A} = 1 - \frac{X}{F2}$$

The table in Figure 16.8 can be used to amend estimates in logical record analysis. For example, suppose a file with a blocking factor of 5 and 2500 physical records is used to store 10,000 logical records, and that subsequently 500 new records are added to the file. The amount of free space in each block is initially 1 ($F1 = 1$). The total file space is 12,500 (2500 × 5) logical records and only 10,000 are used. Hence 2500 logical records are initially free and

$F1 = 1$, because there are 2500 physical records. The parameter $F2$ becomes $500/2500 = .2$.

Figure 16.8 shows that 9.4% of the newly added records will be in overflow. Hence logical and physical analysis estimates could take this factor into account in computing the number of physical record transfers.

There are many other performance calculations that need statistical estimates, and such estimates are not easily derived. One example is the estimation of physical records hit by a set of transactions. Each transaction needs to access a distinct logical record. In a worst-case analysis, we would expect these logical records to be in different physical records. Hence the number of disk transfers would equal the number of logical records. Statistically, however, some of these logical records may be stored in the same physical record. The number of physical records accessed would then be less than the number of logical records accessed.

A good summary of the statistical estimates made for this situation is given by Pezarro (1976), who quotes a number of suitable estimating methods. In one method, proposed by Walters (1975), the expected number of physical records hit is given as

$$p\left[1 - \left(1 - \frac{t}{l}\right)^b\right]$$

where b = number of logical records stored in each physical record (the blocking factor)

t = number of transactions

l = total number of logical records

p = total number of physical records

A useful table that uses this result is given in Figure 16.9. It shows the fraction of physical records accessed, given the blocking factor and the ratio $B = t/p$. The previous formula reduces to

$$\text{fraction of physical records accessed} = \left[1 - \left(1 - \frac{B}{b}\right)^b\right]$$

Some representative values of this fraction are given in Figure 16.9.

As an example, suppose a file consists of 20,000 records and a blocking factor of 10 ($b = 10$). The file is to be updated with 40 transactions, each of which selects 20 logical records. In this case B is computed as:

$$\frac{\text{number of logical records selected}}{\text{number of physical records}} = \frac{800}{2000} = .4$$

From Figure 16.9, the number of physical records accessed is

$.34 \times 2000 = 680$

Figure 16.9 assumes that the logical records accessed by each transaction are

B \ b	2	10	20
.1	.1	.1	.1
.2	.19	.18	.18
.4	.36	.34	.33
1.0	.75	.65	.64
4.0	1.0	1.0	.99

b = number of logical records in a physical record

B = ratio of $\dfrac{\text{logical records selected}}{\text{total number of physical records}}$

Figure 16.9　Physical records accessed

randomly distributed. If this is not the case, a statistical model that considers record clustering must be developed.

Estimating Response Times

A common use of analytical models is to estimate transaction response time. To do this, the analytical model delineates the flow of a transaction through the system and determines the time spent by the transaction at each system component. The computation requires statistical estimates of time spent waiting in system resource queues.

A simple model of transaction flow is shown in Figure 16.10. The transaction commences at a user terminal, passes through a communication network, and is processed at the processor system. The processor system uses data stored on peripheral devices. The result of the computation at the processor is then sent back to the user. The response time will be the time spent by the transaction at all the components shown in Figure 16.10. The time spent at each component is modeled by a more detailed model. For example, Figure 16.11 models the transaction at the processor and the peripheral device. Times spent at these components include

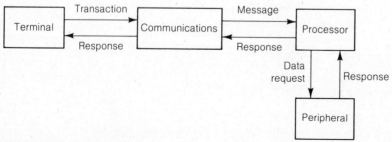

Figure 16.10　Transaction flow

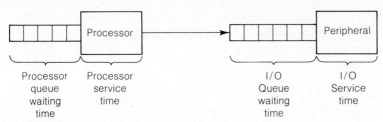

Figure 16.11   Queuing for resources

- service time, which is the time actually spent using each component
- waiting time to obtain access to the component

Estimates of resource service time require the detailed examination of activities at each resource. Thus processor service time would consider the instructions used by program modules in their tasks and the time required to process these instructions.

Input/output service time includes the estimate of the number of I/O requests and of the disk operations needed to satisfy each request. The estimates of the number of I/O requests can be obtained by logical and physical record analysis modified by statistical factors. The estimate of disk device service times uses disk drive characteristics. Thus each access to the disk device is made up of

- seek time for the reading head to reach the required track
- rotation time to find the required record on the track
- transfer time to transfer a record from disk to memory

Actual times for these operations are obtained from manufacturers' manuals.

The waiting time is out of the control of the database designer. It depends on other processes within the computer. These other processes may be competing with database transactions for resource time. Waiting times are statistically determined and depend on

- the utilization of system components
- the distribution of transaction arrival times

The utilization of each component is computed as

$$U_c = \frac{\text{time the component is used}}{\text{time the component is available}}$$

Utilization increases with the use of the component.

The simplest estimate of waiting time assumes a situation in which transactions arrive randomly. This kind of arrival pattern is known as an *exponential arrival rate;* here the time of arrival of one transaction is independent of previous transaction arrivals. Given an exponential arrival rate, we can compute T, the expected time spent by a transaction at a component, as

$$T = \frac{t}{1 - U}$$

where t = service time for the transaction, and U = component utilization. To compute the actual waiting time, you should recall that expected time spent (T) = waiting time plus service time (t). The actual waiting time can therefore be computed as

$$T - t = \frac{tU}{1 - U}$$

Some examples follow. In these examples it is assumed that a system is dedicated to one application and that the application programs are continuously resident in memory. In that case, only data (and no program code) is transferred between memory and the peripheral device.

Example 1

Suppose a system transaction rate is 10 transactions per second. Logical and physical analysis has determined that each transaction transfers two 2000-character physical records from disk. It also uses 60-msec processor time. Disk characteristics are such that

average arm motion time = 25 msec
rotation time = 16.7 msec (60 revolutions/sec)
disk transfer time = 1200 kilobytes/sec

The service time for each disk transfer

$$= \text{average arm motion time} + \text{average time to find record or track} \\ + \text{time to transfer record}$$

$$= 25 + \frac{16.7}{2} + \frac{2000}{1200} \text{ msec} = 35 \text{ msec}$$

To compute waiting time, the processor and disk utilization is needed.

$$\text{Processor utilization} = \frac{\text{time utilized/sec}}{1 \text{ sec}} = \frac{60 \text{ msec} \times 10 \text{ trans}}{1 \text{ sec}}$$
$$= .6$$

$$\text{Disk utilization} = \frac{\text{time utilized/sec}}{1 \text{ sec}} = \frac{35 \text{ msec} \times 2 \times 10}{1 \text{ sec}}$$
$$= .7$$

The time spent by a transaction at the processing site

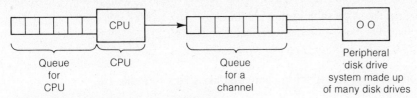

Figure 16.12 Two channels to disk drives

$$= \text{time spent at the processor} + \text{time spent at the disk}$$

$$= \frac{60 \text{ msec}}{1 - .6} + \frac{70 \text{ msec}}{1 - .7}$$

$$= 150 \text{ msec} + 233 \text{ msec}$$

$$= 383 \text{ msec}$$

To compute the total response time for the transaction, it is also necessary to estimate the time taken to transmit the transaction through the communication systems and to display it at the user's terminal. This estimated time would be added to the time spent at the processor and the disk channels.

The model just discussed is relatively simple. It models transactions of the same kind with one queue at each resource. Many systems are more complicated and may include

- locking out of transactions simultaneously trying to access the same record
- disks sharing the same channel
- different types of transactions

Analytical models based on statistical techniques have been formulated to cater to such systems. A brief outline of some variations follows.

If the number of channels connected to a set of disk drives is k, as shown in Figure 16.12, the channel time spent is given by

$$\begin{array}{l} \text{Channel time spent} \\ \text{per disk I/O request} \end{array} = \frac{\mu(\lambda/\mu)^k}{(k-1)!\,(k\mu - \lambda)^2}\,po + \frac{1}{\mu} \dots \dots (6)$$

$$\text{where} \quad po = \frac{1}{\displaystyle\sum_{n=0}^{k-1}(1/n!)(\lambda/\mu)^n + (1/k!)(\lambda/\mu)^k(k\mu/(k\mu - \lambda))}$$

$\dfrac{1}{\mu} = $ average service time in seconds (t) for one channel

$\dfrac{1}{\lambda} = $ average time between disk I/O requests in seconds

If $k = 2$, the channel time spent by each request reduces to

$$\frac{1/\mu}{1 - (\lambda/2\mu)^2}$$

We note that utilization need not be explicitly computed using this formula. In fact, utilization here is $\lambda/k\mu$.

Example 2

Here we extend the previous example so that there are now two channels between the processor and the disk drives. The processor time spent is still the same because adding a new channel does not change processor utilization.

We now have

$$\frac{1}{\mu} = \text{average service time in seconds for one channel}$$

$$= 35 \text{ msec}$$

$$\frac{1}{\lambda} = \text{average time between disk I/O requests in seconds}$$

$$= \frac{1}{20}$$

where $20 = \text{(number of disk accesses/transaction)} \times \text{(transactions/second)}$.

We note that $\lambda/k\mu = .35$, which is half the utilization obtained earlier. This result is expected because we now have twice as many channels to handle the same load.

Channel time spent per disk I/O will now be

$$\frac{35}{1 - (.35)^2} = 39.9 \text{ msec}$$

compared to 117 msec with one channel.

It may be noted that in this case, if the processor or the I/O capacity drops by, say, 50% owing to some fault occurring, the response time will more than double. The following example illustrates this effect.

Example 3

Suppose

$$U1 = U2 = \tfrac{9}{20} \quad \text{and} \quad t = 5 \text{ sec}$$

Then

$$\text{response time} = \frac{5}{1 - (9/20)} = 9.1 \text{ sec}$$

If capacity drops by $\frac{1}{2}$ so that $U1 = U2 = \frac{9}{10}$, then

$$\text{response time} = \frac{5}{1 - (9/10)} = 50 \text{ sec}$$

This explains why there is very significant degradation if only a small part of some processor fails. The change in performance is more noticeable as the initial utilization approaches 1.

Variations in Distribution

If we assume that the distribution of the service time, t, required to process each request is constant rather than exponential, the channel time spent by the request is

$$\frac{t(2 - U)}{2(1 - U)}$$

where U = device utilization. The formulas become complex once there is more than a single channel here.

Extensions to Analytic Modeling

The methods described in the previous section were relatively simple. They all assumed that the database transactions are the only users of the system. They also assumed a simple hardware configuration with one processor and direct channels from the processor and the disk drives. This kind of modeling and analysis is applicable only to dedicated systems in which the transaction programs are continually resident in memory.

Analytical modeling of necessity becomes more complex in the following cases:

- There are procedures other than the transaction processing procedures and these must be swapped with the transaction processing procedures.
- The operating system contributes to system utilization, and this contribution depends on the mix of procedures using the system.
- The hardware configuration is more complex and includes multiprocessor systems, buffering, and alternate paths to disk devices (or alternative secondary storage devices).

The analytical models for such systems will of necessity be more complex than those shown in Figures 16.10, 16.11, and 16.12, as will the statistical models used to analyze them. The coverage of such analytical models is out of the scope of this text.

SUMMARY

In evaluating database performance, we can identify three kinds of evaluation:

- evaluating to select a DBMS for a proposed database
- estimating performance of a proposed design on a given DBMS
- monitoring database performance after a database is implemented

This chapter has concentrated on the second of these evaluations, describing an organized way to make storage estimates and to estimate record transfers for each access requirement. Using the suggested estimates, the designer can compare alternate designs and select the most satisfactory from among them.

Storage estimates are made by computing the size of each record, given the size of its items, and then multiplying this record size by the estimated number of record occurrences. The estimate is then modified by the expected index and overflow requirements.

Estimates of record transfers center on access path analysis. First the number of accessed records for each access step is estimated. Then these estimates are converted to estimates of physical record transfers by using knowledge of the physical file organization. The estimates of physical record transfers serve to compare relative transaction response times for alternative database designs.

Analytical models are commonly used to compute actual response times. In selecting a modeling method for this computation, the designer must take into account the total system utilization and the interaction of database management software with other computer system components.

PROBLEMS

Problem 1

Consider the pseudocode in Figure 16.13. It defines two access requirements applied to files USE and SUPPLY.

Access requirement A is to find all suppliers of a given ITEM-NO. Access requirement B is to find all the projects that use items supplied by a given supplier.

Carry out the logical and physical analysis for these access requirements, given the following:

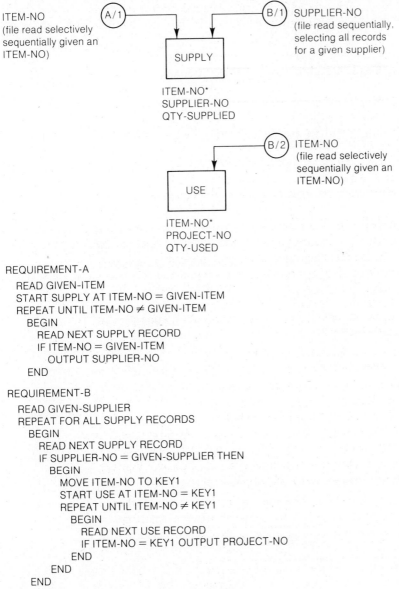

ITEM-NO
(file read selectively
sequentially given an
ITEM-NO)

A/1

B/1

SUPPLIER-NO
(file read sequentially,
selecting all records
for a given supplier)

SUPPLY

ITEM-NO*
SUPPLIER-NO
QTY-SUPPLIED

B/2

ITEM-NO
(file read selectively
sequentially given an
ITEM-NO)

USE

ITEM-NO*
PROJECT-NO
QTY-USED

REQUIREMENT-A
  READ GIVEN-ITEM
  START SUPPLY AT ITEM-NO = GIVEN-ITEM
  REPEAT UNTIL ITEM-NO ≠ GIVEN-ITEM
    BEGIN
      READ NEXT SUPPLY RECORD
      IF ITEM-NO = GIVEN-ITEM
        OUTPUT SUPPLIER-NO
    END

REQUIREMENT-B
  READ GIVEN-SUPPLIER
  REPEAT FOR ALL SUPPLY RECORDS
    BEGIN
      READ NEXT SUPPLY RECORD
      IF SUPPLIER-NO = GIVEN-SUPPLIER THEN
        BEGIN
          MOVE ITEM-NO TO KEY1
          START USE AT ITEM-NO = KEY1
          REPEAT UNTIL ITEM-NO ≠ KEY1
            BEGIN
              READ NEXT USE RECORD
              IF ITEM-NO = KEY1 OUTPUT PROJECT-NO
            END
        END
    END

Figure 16.13   Access requirements for Problem 1

1. Both files are indexed sequential.
2. Block-factors are 5 for SUPPLY and 10 for USE.
3. The master keys for both files are ITEM-NO.
4. On an average, each SUPPLIER-NO supplies 15 ITEM-NOs; an ITEM-NO is used by 30 PROJECTS; and an ITEM-NO is supplied by 20 SUPPLIERS.
5. File sizes are 10,000 records for SUPPLY and 5000 records for USE.

Problem 2

You are required to carry out the logical and physical design analysis for the access requirements defined in Figure 16.14. The access requirements are as follows:

- Requirement A: List all departments.
- Requirement B: Output the PROJECT-START-DATE for all projects assigned to a department.
- Requirement C: Output all projects to which a particular person is assigned.

Here are the file design characteristics and statistics:

1. All files are indexed sequential.
2. The master keys for the files are marked with an asterisk (*). All files except WORK have a single item as their master key. File WORK has a composite key with PROJECT-NO as the major item.
3. The blocking factors are shown in Figure 16.14.
4. There is a list structure in WORK; it links all records for the same person. The start for each list is given in PERSONS for each person.
5. The sizes of the files are

   - FILE DEPTS: 100 records (number of departments)
   - FILE WORK: 40,000 records
   - FILE PERSONS: 4000 records (number of persons)
   - FILE PROJECTS: 600 records (number of projects)
   - FILE ASSIGN: 5000 records

6. FILE ASSIGN stores the assignment of projects to departments.
7. FILE WORK stores the assignment of persons to projects. Assume an even distribution of persons between projects and of projects between departments. Files A, C, and D store the information about departments, persons, and projects, respectively.

Problem 3

Figure 16.15 illustrates three files. File PERSONS contains the details of persons in an organization and includes the SECTION to which a person is assigned. Persons make orders for items. The orders made by persons are stored in file ORDERS. The items that make up an order are stored in file CONTENTS.

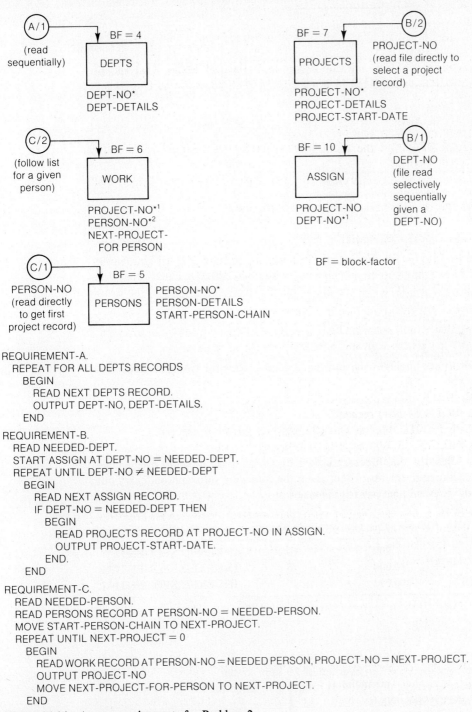

REQUIREMENT-A.
  REPEAT FOR ALL DEPTS RECORDS
    BEGIN
      READ NEXT DEPTS RECORD.
      OUTPUT DEPT-NO, DEPT-DETAILS.
    END

REQUIREMENT-B.
  READ NEEDED-DEPT.
  START ASSIGN AT DEPT-NO = NEEDED-DEPT.
  REPEAT UNTIL DEPT-NO ≠ NEEDED-DEPT
    BEGIN
      READ NEXT ASSIGN RECORD.
      IF DEPT-NO = NEEDED-DEPT THEN
        BEGIN
          READ PROJECTS RECORD AT PROJECT-NO IN ASSIGN.
          OUTPUT PROJECT-START-DATE.
        END.
    END

REQUIREMENT-C.
  READ NEEDED-PERSON.
  READ PERSONS RECORD AT PERSON-NO = NEEDED-PERSON.
  MOVE START-PERSON-CHAIN TO NEXT-PROJECT.
  REPEAT UNTIL NEXT-PROJECT = 0
    BEGIN
      READ WORK RECORD AT PERSON-NO = NEEDED PERSON, PROJECT-NO = NEXT-PROJECT.
      OUTPUT PROJECT-NO
      MOVE NEXT-PROJECT-FOR-PERSON TO NEXT-PROJECT.
    END

Figure 16.14 Access requirements for Problem 2

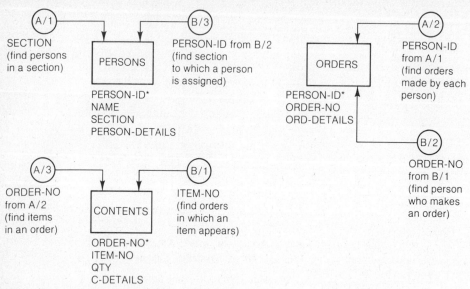

Figure 16.15 Access path diagram for Problem 3

Figure 16.15 also includes the shortened access paths for two access requirements: namely

- **A** Find the ITEM-NOs ordered for a given SECTION.
- **B** Find the SECTIONs for which ITEM-NO has been ordered.

The master keys for each file are marked by an asterisk. Develop pseudocode for these access requirements. Then, given the following information, carry out a logical and physical analysis for the queries.

File	Number of records	Block-factor	Organization
PERSONS	200	10	INDEXED SEQUENTIAL
ORDERS	10,000	5	INDEXED SEQUENTIAL
CONTENTS	200,000	10	INDEXED SEQUENTIAL

Assume the following:

1. A person on an average places 50 orders.
2. An order is made up on an average of 20 item kinds.
3. There are an average of 5 persons ordering in a section.
4. There are 4000 item kinds.

Problem 4

(a) Suppose an on-line system is to process transactions at the rate of 2 transactions-sec. The message flow of transactions at the central processing site is as shown in the following table.

	Processing (msec)	I/O number of disk I/Os
Security check	50	1
Message handling	100	3
Application processing	200	5

Compute the contribution to response time at the processor, assuming there is one disk channel and each disk I/O uses 50 msec of disk channel time.

(b) What would be the response time if a second disk channel that can be used to access all disk drives is added?

Problem 5

(a) An on-line system is required to process transactions at a maximum rate of 1 transaction/sec. The programs that will carry out the necessary processing require

- 7 disk accesses to the application files for each transaction
- 5 disk accesses to the system files for each transaction
- 400-msec processor time

Application and system files are distributed among a number of disk drives, and there is one channel only between the processor and the disk drives, with each disk drive connected to that channel. The disk subsystem hardware is such that an average of 50 msec is used to transfer each physical record between disk and memory.

Compute the contribution to response time by the processor and by the disk system.

(b) What maximum throughput could be handled by the system, given that a response time of 5 sec from the processor subsystem is tolerable?

(c) A number of possibilities of improving response time are to be considered. Which of these would you choose if they are equally expensive?

  1. Two separate channels with half of the disk drives attached to one channel and the other half to the other channel. One set of disks would be for application data, the other for the operating system files.

2. Two channels with each channel connected to each disk drive.

(d) Is the response time improved if we can reduce the number of disk transfers by 3 while increasing processing time from 400 msec to 500 msec?

Problem 6

(a) A dedicated computer system is being planned. The system will consist of a processor, a disk channel, a number of disk packs, and a telecommunication channel to support a large number of terminals.

The characteristics of the disk system are that the average time to access a record = 50 msec, and the disk channel can be used concurrently with the processor.

Two programs continuously execute on the system. Each program handles a different transaction class. The resources required by the two transaction classes are as follows:

	Processor time	*Disk I/O's*
Class A	400 msec	8
Class B	1200 msec	16

The transaction rates are one every 2 sec for Class A and one every 4 sec for Class B.

Compute the time spent by Class A transactions at the computer system.

(b) Suppose now a third class of transaction (Class C) is to be added to the system. This will be a short enquiry transaction that requires 100 msec of processor time and five disk I/O's. There will be two such transactions arriving each second. What effect will these new transactions have on Class A and Class B transactions (in terms of time spent)?

(c) Suppose it is unacceptable for the expected time spent at the computer system of any transaction to exceed 6 sec. To avoid the overtime, would you find it necessary to

- double the processor capacity?
- add another disk channel?
- do both?

chapter seventeen
Choosing Design
Methodologies

INTRODUCTION

The last three chapters discussed a variety of techniques used in database design. It is now fitting to conclude by showing how these techniques can be combined into integrated design methodologies. The goal of integration is to create a top-down design process in which user database requirements are reduced through a number of stages to a computer database structure. To do this, design methodologies structure the database design problem into a sequence of problem steps so that each step solves one well-defined design problem. The methodologies include

- the techniques to solve the design problems at each step, using semantics appropriate to the step
- the techniques to combine all the steps into an integrated design methodology

Usually the design methodologies include a formal documentation that is to be produced at the completion of each step so as to serve as the input to the next step.

A database designer must first select (or design) a database design methodology. A number of choices are possible.

CONSTRUCTING A DESIGN METHODOLOGY

Design methodologies are constructed by

- identifying the design stages
- selecting the techniques and documentation methods appropriate to each stage
- selecting the conversion techniques between stages to ensure continuity between stages

The design stages must follow the natural design process. They must commence by collecting and analyzing the data about the enterprise. The database specification is then prepared and technical design follows. Correspondingly, the designer must make the following major choices when selecting a methodology.

- *Choice 1:* Choose the method for collecting information about the enterprise.
- *Choice 2:* Choose the methods for analyzing the collected information.
- *Choice 3:* Choose the packaging for the database specifications.
- *Choice 4:* Choose the method used to convert the enterprise model to logical designs.
- *Choice 5:* Choose the design analysis method.

Each choice includes the selection of design techniques and a documentation method for documenting the output from the design stages.

Selecting Design Techniques

Design techniques must be chosen to solve the problems at each stage, using terms natural to that stage. The chosen techniques should also allow the designer to satisfy all the design criteria at a particular stage. Further, the techniques must be chosen so that the output of one stage can be used directly as input for the next stage.

The choice of design techniques should be based on a computer system design theory that provides the principles for making design choices. The development of such theory is still in its embryonic phases and covers only parts of the design process. This is not to say that such theory is not slowly evolving. This text has suggested a number of formal theoretical foundations for design. Relational theory is the most obvious and is a widely accepted basis for structuring data. Conversion to implementation models is also now becoming formalized. Many formal conversions to implementation models have now appeared, and it is expected that a formal conversion theory will gradually evolve. There are also a large number of formal techniques that can be used to evaluate database designs. Database designers must select the most appropriate technique for their purpose.

Selecting Documentation Methods

Documentation serves two purposes in a design methodology:

1. It is the medium that presents the decisions made at each stage.

2. It provides administrative controls for the management of the design process.

Up to now, this text has not concentrated on formal documentation methods but has stressed design techniques. It has, however, illustrated diagrammatic representations of the database at various design stages. Documentation concerns the packaging of these representations into a form that can be used to formally document design commitments for managerial purposes. This documentation of decisions and recommendations is the formal output of each design stage. It is a control that ensures that all work allocated to a stage has been adequately completed. Documentation at one stage must be approved before subsequent stages proceed. The exact form of the documentation depends on the design techniques and stages chosen. There are no standards set for documentation, although most methodologies now include some form of data flow chart, data dictionaries, program structure charts, or data structure diagrams. Usually the database documentation methods are chosen so that they fit in with the existing system documentation.

CHOICE 1: COLLECTING DATA

The goal of data collection is to produce a formal document of user requirements. This document must include the data needed by users as well as the use made of the data. Various sources of such information are available, and there are also diverse techniques to collect and document the requirements.

Sources of Information

Sources of information about enterprise data are as follows:

1. *Documents* in the enterprise; for example, invoices, orders.
2. *Transactions* in the enterprise; for example, update account, hire person.
3. *Functional descriptions* of business functions; for example, "widgets are constructed from parts by production employees."
4. *Scenario analysis,* a detailed examination of the enterprise activities. This analysis differs from functional descriptions in that the latter define principally the inputs and outputs of enterprise functions. Scenario analysis is a deeper examination of the relationships that exist between objects in the function. It searches mainly for the activities in the enterprise and builds from them.

5. *Data item definitions*, which define known items in the enterprise.

6. *Object property definitions*, which define the properties of enterprise objects.

Definitions of data items and object properties are usually obtained as detailed elaborations of the other kinds of sources.

Many design methodologies use one or more of these sources. Often the same information is collected in more than one way. The information obtained from alternate sources is usually cross-correlated to validate the specification. Any differences are resolved by consultations with users.

Goals of Data Collection

Although the techniques and especially the documentation differ markedly for different data collection methods, many of the methods have three important common goals:

1. A hierarchical reduction of specifications. Top-level functions or objects are reduced into detailed objects and activities in a series of reductions.

2. Assurance that the analysis and user requirements concentrate on what the logical processes are and not on how they are accomplished.

3. Documentation of both the data and the access requirements, plus their integration.

These goals have evolved over time with a specific purpose in mind. In regard to the first goal, data collection involves considerable system analysis to determine the goals and objectives of the user system. Such analysis usually proceeds in a top-down way by first identifying the topmost system processes and then elaborating them in greater detail.

It is also important that, as the second goal, the initial analysis concentrates on what the system is doing—not on how it is doing it, for that often places constraints on current system operations. Duplicating these constraints in a new system may prevent advantages inherent in different implementations from being incorporated in the new design. Hence the methods used in the initial stages must ensure that user requirements are not too unduly influenced by implementation constraints. The goal of the initial stages is to precisely specify what is being done or what is to be done. How it is done is left to the later stages.

Finally, as the third goal, the initial stages must define both the data and the processing needs of the enterprise. The data needs eventually become the database, whereas the processing needs become the user programs. Subsequent stages must integrate these two needs.

Chapter 14 discussed two fundamental alternatives in database design: databased and access-based methods. The methods differ not only in the techniques used in database design but also in the way they integrate with data collection techniques that match the initial database design stages. Hence it is possible to distinguish between two kinds of data collection methods:

1. *Data flow methods*. The database requirements are gathered as a by-product of defining data flows in the system. These methods can be integrated with access-based database design.
2. *Data-oriented methods*. The database requirements are gathered independently of any data flow or access requirements. These techniques are more suitable for databased database design.

It can be argued that these two kinds of methods will use different information sources. That is, data flow methods should concentrate on sources that describe processing, whereas data-oriented methods should concentrate on sources that describe data. It would, however, be an oversimplification to say that each kind of method uses a different kind of information source. All the methodologies use information from all kinds of sources. Perhaps it would be best to say that data flow methods concentrate on document structures transaction flows, whereas data-oriented methods concentrate on business functions or scenario analysis.

Further, the distinction between data flow and data-oriented methods gradually diminishes as we proceed toward the later design stages, and all methods become the same when physical database design and programming begin.

It is out of the scope of this text to discuss all the available data collection methods, and so only a sample will be described to indicate the kinds of analysis techniques used and to illustrate the difference between the two kinds of methods.

Data Flow Methods

A well-known data flow method is structured systems analysis (DeMarco, 1978, Gane and Sarson, 1979). Here the analyzer's primary objective is to determine the information flows in an enterprise. These are graphically documented in data flow diagrams. Data structures and elements that appear in the information flows are documented in a data dictionary.

An example of the kind of system description produced by structured systems analysis is shown in Figure 17.1. It consists of several components:

- A *data flow diagram* made up of a number of *processes*. These processes may be leveled down into more detailed data flow diagrams—for example, process 2 in the figure. Hence the method satisfies the goal of hierarchical reduction.
- *Data stores* that store information in the system; there are two data stores, D1 and D2.

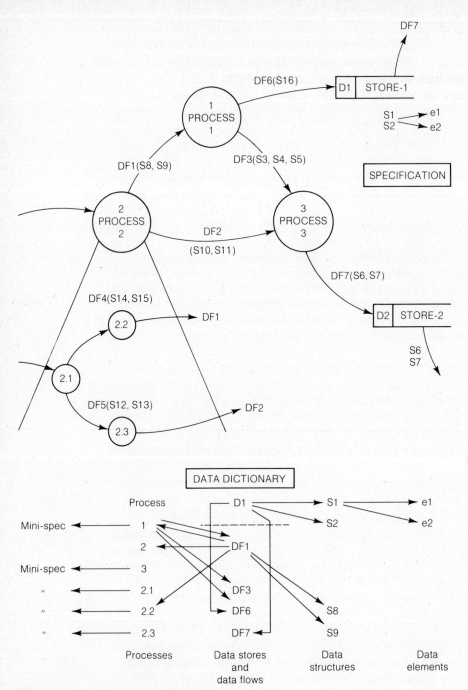

Figure 17.1 Specifications to data dictionary

- *Data flows* that carry the information between processes or between processes and data stores. There are six data flows, DF1 through to DF6.
- The information in the data stores or data flows, which is made up of *data structures;* the data structures are in turn made up of *data elements.* The data structures are labeled S1 to S16. Only two data elements are shown: e1 and e2.
- *Mini-specs* that describe the process computations. The mini-specs often use either structured or tight English and decision tables or decision trees.

These components are connected. Thus there is a connection between a process and those data flows in and out of the process. Similarly, there is a connection between a data store and the data flows in and out of it. The data structures are connected to the data flows and data stores that contain them; the data elements are connected to the data structures that contain them.

Usually the results of structured systems analysis are documented in a data dictionary. The data dictionary stores the components of the specification as well as the connections between them. Thus the data dictionary contains a description of

- data elements
- data structures
- data flows
- data stores
- processes
- mini-specs

The details stored about each component will vary, particularly in automated systems.

An example of a data dictionary entry for data elements is given in Figure 17.2. It contains the data element name together with its characteristics, such as size, type, and range of values. The connections between the elements are shown by the data dictionary arrows in Figure 17.1.

Data Structure in Data Flow Methods   Data in data flow methods are usually stored on hierarchical data structures. An example of a data structure is shown in Figure 17.3. Here the data structure consists of three levels:

1. ORDER, a top level. It contains the document identifier, ORDER-NO, together with the DATE-OF-ORDER and TOTAL-VALUE of the order.
2. ORDERLINE, which can occur any number of times within each ORDER. It contains the orderline identifier, ORDERLINE-NO, together with the orderline ORDERLINE-DATE.

Data element	Size	Type	Range of Values	Comments
Project number	6	X	Letter followed by 5 digits	Assigned by project manager
Termination date	6	D		
Commencement date	6	D		
Person's name	20	X		Initials followed by surname
ID-number	6	X	Letter followed by 5 digits	
Home-address	20	X		
Current job title		X		
Status	1	9	1 = assigned; 2 = terminated	
Number of hours	3	9		

Figure 17.2 A data element table

3. ARTICLE, which can occur any number of times within each ORDER-LINE. It contains the article identifier, ARTICLE-NO, together with its ARTICLE-NAME and ORDER-PRICE.

All the descriptions of data structures in data flows and data stores use the hierarchical description format shown in Figure 17.3.

Access Requirements in Data Flow Methods In data flow methods, the access requirements are a natural by-product of analysis. The information flows identify the access requirements and the data that they use. In data-oriented methods such access requirements are analyzed independently of the data. Usually designers first identify the major enterprise functions. Then they determine the activities in these functions and the data used in these activities. These data in turn define the user access requirements.

Most methodologies now include a structured rather than an informal description of user access requirements. Data flow methods introduced techniques such as structured English, tight English, and pseudocode to specify processes; and these techniques are now increasingly used to specify processes and the database access requirements that they generate. The goal of these methods is to structure natural language statements of user requirements into some well-defined logical form. Thus a pseudocode specification to output articles in a particular order takes the form

```
REPEAT-UNTIL no-more orders
    obtain and output order-details of next order
        REPEAT-UNTIL no-more-orderlines-in-order
            obtain and output orderline-details of next orderline
                REPEAT-UNTIL no-more-articles-in-orderline
                    obtain and output article-details of next article
```

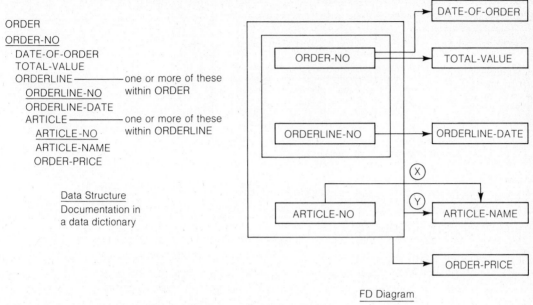

```
ORDER
ORDER-NO
  DATE-OF-ORDER
  TOTAL-VALUE
  ORDERLINE———————one or more of these
    ORDERLINE-NO      within ORDER
    ORDERLINE-DATE
    ARTICLE——————one or more of these
      ARTICLE-NO     within ORDERLINE
      ARTICLE-NAME
      ORDER-PRICE
```

Data Structure
Documentation in
a data dictionary

FD Diagram

Figure 17.3   Deriving FD diagrams for hierarchical data structures

A key phrase such as **REPEAT-UNTIL** or **REPEAT** is used to structure the specification.

Integration between the data structures and access requirements at the user requirement level is achieved by using the same data names in the data structures and in the access requirements.

Data-Oriented Methods

Data-oriented methods concentrate on the role of data in an organization. Many of these methods commence by first identifying the business functions and activities and the objects that participate in them. Following is a typical set of steps here:

- *Step 1:* Identify the activities in the enterprise.
- *Step 2:* Identify the object types that participate in each activity.
- *Step 3:* Describe the participating object types in terms of their properties or components.
- *Step 4:* Identify the interactions between the participating object types or between their components and the properties of the interactions.

An example of this process is shown in Figure 17.4, which describes a **PROJECT-ASSIGNMENT** activity. The object types in the activity are identified by circling them (step 2) and their attributes are identified by under-

Persons in organizations are assigned to projects Each
project is identified by a project number, and the
commencement and termination dates of the project are stored.
Persons are each identified by an id-number, and information is
kept about their name, home-address, the date on which
they commenced work in the organization, and their current job
title. Each person's status with a project is also stored, and
it may show that the person is currently assigned or has
terminated on a project. The number of hours that a person
has spent on the project is stored as well.

Figure 17.4 Selecting objects in an activity description

lining. Usually the object types are the nouns in the activity description. The
analyzer looks for the interactions, which are usually verbs in the activity description. These data elements are usually described in a data dictionary of the
kind shown in Figure 17.2. They are also used by the designer to construct an
initial E-R diagram of the enterprise. Such E-R diagrams are verified with the
users to ensure their correctness. Alternatively, documentation from this stage
can be a tabular description of the E-R model. An example is given in Figure
17.5; it is called an *attribute table*.

In the attribute table, object sets appear as columns; data elements appear as
rows. Object set names are placed at the top of the column that represents the
object set. Attribute names also appear in this column. Each attribute name is
placed in the row of the data element that corresponds to that attribute. Attributes are assigned unique names within each object set. One data element can,
however, have different names in the different rows in which that data element
appears. For example, ARTICLE-NO is called NUMBER in the ARTICLES
object set and ARTICLE in the ORDERED object set. Later these names will
become field names within database records.

ATTRIBUTE TABLE

Data Element \ Abstraction / Name / Type	ORDERS	ORDERLINES	ORDERED	ARTICLES
	Entity	Dependent entity	Relationship	Entity
ORDER-NO	ORDER-NO	ORDER-NO	ORDER-NO	
ORDERLINE-NO		ORDERLINE	ORDERLINE	
ARTICLE-NO		ARTICLE	ARTICLE	NUMBER
ARTICLE-NAME				NAME
DATE-OF-ORDER	DATE			
TOTAL-VALUE	TOTAL-VALUE			
ORDERLINE-DATA		DATE		
LINE-PRICE			PRICE	

Figure 17.5 Documenting semantic abstractions

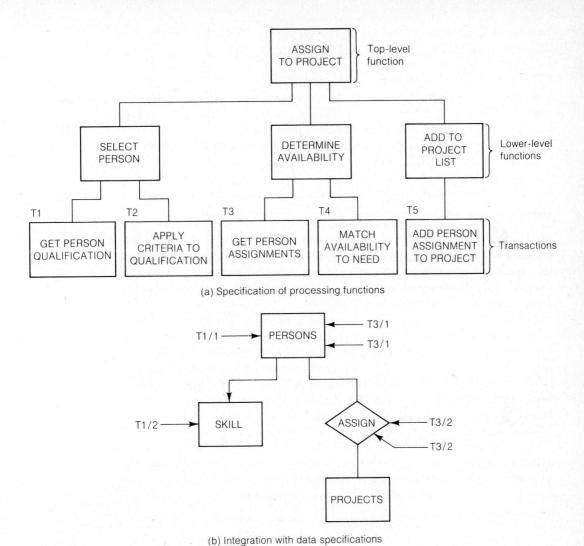

(a) Specification of processing functions

(b) Integration with data specifications

Figure 17.6 Integrating processes and data structure

Access Requirements in Data-Oriented Methods Data-oriented methods usually define access requirements by a decomposition of system functions. Figure 17.6a shows the kind of structure that is often created during functional analysis. The top level is the major system function, which may be decomposed through any number of levels to lower-level functions. The final decomposition is into transactions that operate on the system data.

Integration between the processing function and the data structure usually employs the idea of access steps discussed in Chapter 8. The function transactions are plotted onto the E-R diagram to show the data objects needed by the transactions. A typical example is shown in Figure 17.6b.

CHOICE 2: ANALYZING ENTERPRISE DATA

Once the user system is documented, the next step is to analyze it and identify any system problems and propose new system objectives. A new user system to meet these objectives is then proposed. The documentation of the proposed system uses the same techniques as those used to describe the existing system. The proposed system is then reduced to a technical specification. The reduction depends on the method used to describe the system.

Data Flow Analysis

Reduction in data flow analysis often commences by normalizing the hierarchical logical structures in the data dictionary, using the methods described in Chapter 2. A prescriptive series of steps for such normalization is shown in Figure 4.1. Another is given in Figure 17.3.

In Figure 17.3 an FD diagram is developed from a data structure description. Since DATE-OF-ORDER and TOTAL-VALUE are unique to the whole order, they are functionally dependent on the order identifier, ORDER-NO. The data value ORDERLINE-DATE, on the other hand, is dependent on ORDER-LINE-NO within an order; hence it is functionally dependent on the combined values of ORDER-NO and ORDERLINE-NO. Similarly, ARTICLE-NAME and ORDER-PRICE are functionally dependent on the combined values of ORDER-NO, ORDERLINE-NO, and ARTICLE-NO.

This process can result in a number of redundant FDs. For example, it is probably obvious to you that ARTICLE-NO → ARTICLE-NAME, although this is not obvious from the description of ORDER. However, this FD will be found from a description of another document called "Add new article," which may take the form

    ARTICLE-ADD
    ARTICLE-NO
    ARTICLE-NAME

Analysis of this document indicates that ARTICLE-NAME is functionally dependent on ARTICLE-NO. This dependency is added to the FD diagram in Figure 17.3; it is marked by Ⓧ.

It is possible that, after analysis of a large number of documents, the FD diagram will contain many redundant FDs. So analysts will have to remove these redundancies before proceeding to logical design. The FD marked Ⓨ, for example, is redundant and would be removed. The final output of such an analysis is usually a set of relations.

Analyzing Access Requirements

The most frequent activity in data flow methods at this stage is to elaborate in detail each access, including the man–machine interface and the determination of error conditions and their treatment. The same documentation techniques are used here as in the early analysis, namely, mini-specs and data flow diagrams.

Data-Oriented Analysis

Detailed elaboration in databased analysis methods usually begins with the E-R model. Many methodologies have a prescriptive set of formal steps here. For example:

1. Choose entities and their attributes.
2. Choose the relationships.
3. Refine the entities and relationships.

The first two steps are part of the initial analysis. Refinement begins later. Refinement can mean the kind of reduction to a "normalized" E-R model that was described in Chapter 8. Often refinement involves introducing into the model the role and type concepts that were described in Chapter 6.

Analyzing Access Requirements

Access requirements and functions are elaborated in the same way as they are in the flow methods. It is usually at this stage that transactions are developed in detail and plotted on the data structure diagram.

CHOICE 3: PACKAGING THE DATABASE SPECIFICATION

The next choice is to select the packaging for the database specification. The choice depends on the data analysis methods used. Data flow methods will usually produce documents that are like a data dictionary. This data dictionary specification includes a set of FDs (Figure 17.3). A set of relations is produced from the data structures in the data dictionary. These relations can be packaged into a logical record specification, using the methods described in Chapter 8. The access requirements are often reduced to pseudocode at this stage. The pseudocode then becomes the basis for program development.

The result of the databased procedures is usually the same as that from the flow-based methods. A logical data structure is produced and access requirements are reduced to pseudocode.

CHOICE 4: CONVERTING TO LOGICAL DESIGN

The choice of method for conversion to a logical design was described in Chapter 14. Usually the choice is between databased and access-based database design methods; it often depends on the implementation model. Part of this choice is to select the logical design conversion roles and the methods to be used in database evaluation.

Distinctions are usually made between the initial design and subsequent iterations. Initial design methods were described in Chapter 15, where a distinction was made between logical and physical designs. Designers approach the initial choice of logical structure in the way described in Chapter 15, using a method appropriate to the implementation model. Some initial physical decisions are also made before any logical and physical analysis is carried out.

Often organizations develop their own database conversion standards or guidelines. The standards are usually adaptations of the technique described in Chapters 15 and 16 to a particular DBMS.

Access requirements should be converted to logical program structures in parallel with the development of the logical data structure. Once the logical data structure is chosen, the process specification can be converted to a pseudocode that uses the DML commands of the DBMS.

The link between the program and the database conversion is not usually very strong after this stage. The access specifications have served their basic purpose in database design. They have shown the database designer how the data are to be used in terms of access steps. The database designer can use this information in logical and physical analysis. Similarly, once the logical data structure is chosen, program development can proceed independently of database design because the programmers can use the pseudocode to develop their programs.

Documenting the Logical Design

The output of logical design is usually in two parts:

- a set of program structure charts, together with a pseudocode for each structure chart module
- a data structure diagram, together with a description of the contents of each record type and the definition of links between the record types

The form of the data structure diagram depends on the file or DBMS to be used in the implementation. Various logical data structure diagrams have been described in the text. The contents of each record type can be also listed in a table, such as the file design table for COBOL files that appears in the appendix (Figure App. 7).

CHOICE 5: SELECTING A DESIGN ANALYSIS MODEL

Alternate design analysis methods were described in Chapter 16. In most cases designers resort to logical record analysis and do not use mathematical modeling techniques. Logical record analysis is considered to be sufficient to compare alternate designs. It provides enough criteria to choose the most satisfactory design. To choose the physical structure, most designers use costing tables and the guidelines for physical structure selection that are provided by vendors of database management software. The system performance is then monitored during system operation, and physical structures are changed as necessary.

SUMMARY

Database design proceeds through a number of stages, and it is important that the chosen techniques be able both to solve the design problems at each design stage and to be integrated into an effective design methodology.

The choices open to designers can be grouped into five categories:

1. Data collection method
2. Enterprise data analysis
3. Packaging of the database specification
4. Conversion to a logical design
5. Design analysis method

A distinction is made between data flow methods and data-oriented methods. In data flow methods, database requirements are gathered as a by-product of defining data flows in the system. Data-oriented methods, on the other hand, collect data about the database independently of data flows and access requirements.

To achieve the integration between design stages, it is important to match techniques in the early stages. This matching is achieved more easily if early design stages use either data-oriented or data flow methods but not a mixture of both.

Database Design Projects

This section contains four database design projects. The projects support the technical design chapters of the text. Each project assumes that data analysis has been completed and presents to the designer a specification composed of

- FD and E-R diagrams
- access requirements
- quantitative data

Technical design can use any of the implementation models described in the text. It is suggested that one or two of the design projects be chosen and followed through as you proceed through Chapters 8 to 16. The following procedure is suggested.

After Chapter 8, convert the enterprise model of the design project specification to a logical record structure. The conversion should use the packaging methods outlined in that chapter. The question that often arises in this conversion is what option to choose when converting roles or types. It is recommended that you experiment with all these options to get a feel of the alternatives they provide. The chosen option will usually depend on the implementation model used in the design.

During a study of Chapter 15 the logical record structure can be converted to an initial design by using any of the implementation models described in Chapters 9–12. Again it is suggested that the logical record structure derived in Chapter 8 be converted to each of

- a set of COBOL files
- a relational model implementation
- a DBTG implementation
- both a partitioned and a nonpartitioned hierarchical implementation

Once the initial design is obtained, the analysis techniques described in Chapter 16 should be applied to it. Because of time limitations, you will probably have to carry out logical and physical analysis for only one or two of the implementation models. Perhaps the logical and physical analysis techniques should

531

first be applied to a COBOL file design. This design is probably the most straightforward and can serve to illustrate the principles of logical and physical analysis. Then an analysis on one of the DBMS designs could be attempted.

Analysis of a DBMS design will in most cases stop at the logical analysis stage unless you have cost tables available for a particular DBMS. Once an initial DBMS design is made, it is a good idea to write a pseudocode, using DML statements appropriate to the DBMS. The DML statements can then be used to make estimates of the logical records accessed. If a set of cost tables are available, the analysis can be extended to physical analysis.

DESIGN PROJECT A:
CONTRACT-SUPPLIES SYSTEM

Figures A.1 and A.2 are the FD and E-R diagrams for a CONTRACT-SUPPLIES system. This system works as follows:

1. The company for which the system is designed negotiates contracts with several suppliers for the supply of various amounts of selected item kinds at a price that forms part of the contract.

2. Orders are placed against any of the negotiated contracts for the supply of items at the price quoted in the contract. An order can consist of any amount of those items that are in that contract. Any number of orders can be made against a contract. However, the sum of any given item kind in all orders against one contract cannot exceed the amount of that item kind quoted in that contract. An inquiry would be made to establish if a sufficient quantity of an item is available before an order for that item is placed. All the items in an order must be supplied as part of the same contract.

3. Each order is placed only against one contract and is made on behalf of one project. An order is made for one or more item kinds (in that contract).

The access requirements for this system are given in Figure A.3. The volume data are given in Figure A.4, and the data item sizes in Figure A.5.

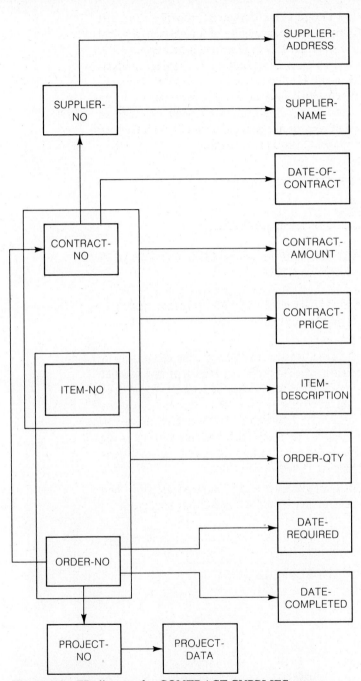

Figure A.1   FD diagram for **CONTRACT-SUPPLIES** system

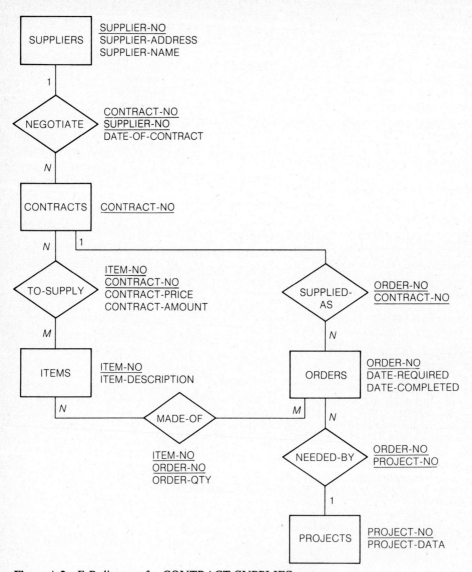

Figure A.2 E-R diagram for **CONTRACT-SUPPLIES** system

On-line Transactions

A. Enter a new SUPPLIER-NO with SUPPLIER-ADDRESS and SUPPLIER-NAME (infrequent).

B. Enter a new ITEM-NO with ITEM-DESCRIPTION (infrequent).

C. Enter a new PROJECT-NO with PROJECT-DATA (infrequent).

D. Enter a new CONTRACT-NO with DATE-OF-CONTRACT together with the ITEM-NO, CONTRACT-PRICE, and CONTRACT-AMOUNT for all items in the contract (infrequent).

E. Enter a new order (100/day):

    enter ORDER-NO, DATE-REQUIRED, PROJECT-NO, CONTRACT-NO
    <u>for</u> each ordered item
       <u>begin</u>
         enter ITEM-NO, ORDER-NO, ORDER-QTY
       <u>end</u>

F. Find the items in an order (30/day).

G. Find the price of an item in an order. The price of the item is the price negotiated for the order's contract (5/day).

H. Find the orders in which a particular item appears (20/day).

I. Find the price for a given item in a contract (150/day).

J. Find a particular contract together with its supplier (20/day).

K. Find the quantity of a given item still available under a given contract (100/day). Detailed pseudocode of the access requirement is

    find the CONTRACT-AMOUNT for the ITEM-NO in the CONTRACT-NO
    amount available = CONTRACT-AMOUNT
    <u>for</u> all orders in the contract
       <u>begin</u>
         if the order contains the given ITEM-NO
           <u>then</u> amount-available = amount available − ORDER-QTY.
       <u>end</u>
    output amount available

Batch Requirement

L. Summarize the purchases by CONTRACT-NO of all items ordered in ITEM-NO order. Produce the summary with ITEM-NO listed within CONTRACT-NO (weekly).

    For each CONTRACT-NO
      for each ORDER-NO in CONTRACT
        for each ITEM-NO in order
          create <CONTRACT-NO, ITEM-NO, ORDER-QTY> temporary record.
    Sort in <CONTRACT-NO, ITEM-NO> sequence
    Sum all ORDER-QTY for same CONTRACT-NO and ITEM-NO and output.

Figure A.3   Access requirements for CONTRACT-SUPPLIES system

Number of contracts	50
Average no. of items/contract	100
Max. no of items/contract	500
Av. no. of orders/contract	1200
Max. no of orders/contract	6000
Av. no. of contracts/supplier	1
Max. no. of contracts/supplier	2
Av. no. of items/order	10
Max. no. of items/order	100
Av. no of orders/month	5000
Number of items	2000
(Assume 20 days per month)	
Number of projects	50

Figure A.4   Data volumes for CONTRACT-SUPPLIES system

SUPPLIER-NO	6	CONTRACT-PRICE	8
SUPPLIER-ADDRESS	30	CONTRACT-AMT	6
SUPPLIER-NAME	20	ORDER-NO	6
CONTRACT-NO	6	DATE-REQUIRED	6
CONTRACT-DATE	6	DATE-COMPLETED	6
ITEM-NO	8	ORDER-QTY	6
ITEM-DESCRIPTION	20	PROJECT-NO	4
		PROJECT-DATA	20

Figure A.5   Item sizes for CONTRACT-SUPPLIES system

DESIGN PROJECT B: REQUISITION SYSTEM

The results of data analysis of an enterprise are given by the FD diagram in Figure B.1 and the E-R diagram in Figure B.2. Details are as follows:

1. Projects are broken up into tasks, and the tasks are assigned to departments. Each task is given a unique TASK-NO identifier. A task is created for one project and is assigned to one department.

2. Requisitions are made for projects. Each requisition can be for any QTY of one or more ITEM-NOs.

3. Each requisition is for one project and is made to one SUPPLIER-NO.

4. Each ITEM-NO identifies an item-kind. Items can be either equipment items or material items. The material and equipment type sets that model these types of items are uniform. Hence their identifiers, EQUIPMENT-CODE and MATERIAL-CODE, come from the same domain as ITEM-NO.

5. Suppliers send regular price notices to advise the enterprise of any changes in the price of items. Each price advice is identified by a unique PRICE-ADVICE-NO.

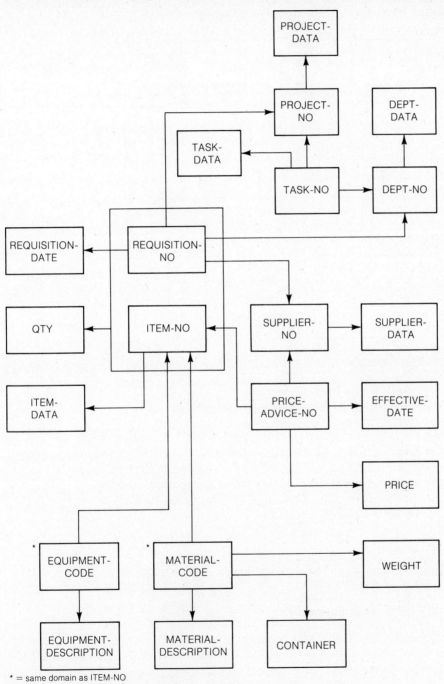

* = same domain as ITEM-NO

Figure B.1 FD diagram for requisition system

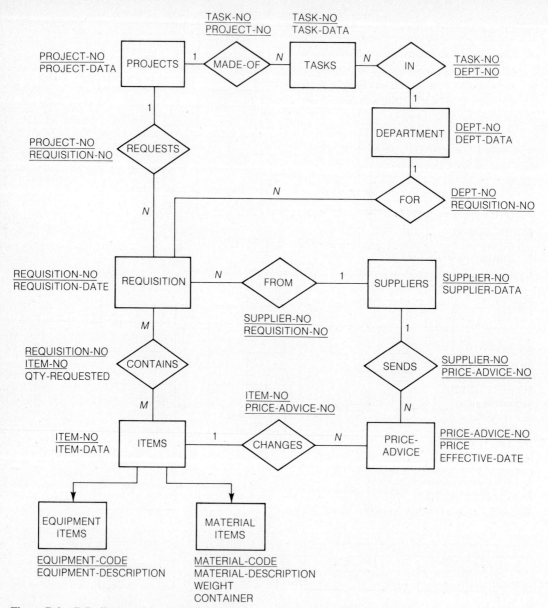

Figure B.2   E-R diagram for requisition system

The enterprise access requirements are given in Figure B.3, and the quantitative data in Figures B.4 and B.5. Figure B.5 specifies the item sizes, and Figure B.4 specifies the object volumes.

Update of Transactions

A. Add price advice with all its attributes (50/day).

B. Create requisition with all its attributes (20/day).

C. Add new ITEM and its attributes (infrequent).

D. Add new MATERIAL-CODE with its attributes (infrequent).

E. Add new EQUIPMENT-CODE with its attributes (infrequent).

F. Create a new task (2/day).

G. Create a new project (infrequent).

H. Create a new department (infrequent).

I. Create a new supplier (infrequent)

Enquiry

J. Who is the supplier to whom REQUISITON-NO = "x" is allocated (30/day)?

K. What is the latest price of ITEM-NO = "x" quoted by SUPPLIER = "y" (50/day)?

Batch Processing

L. A weekly summary of all requisitions in the database sorted by project and by department within project.

M. A weekly summary of all requisitions in the database sorted by supplier, giving total price for each requisition.

Figure B.3 Processing requirements for requisition system

Database Size

Number of equipment items	50
Number of material items	250
Number of projects	100
Number of tasks	2,000
Number of items	300
Number of suppliers	20
Number of departments	10
Number of requisitions	5,000
Number of price advices	20,000
Average items/supplier	30
Average items/requisition	10

Figure B.4 Database statistics for requisition system

PROJECT-NO	6	REQUISITION-NO	12
PROJECT-DATA	20	REQUISITION-DATE	6
TASK-NO	10	QTY	6
TASK-DATA	25	PRICE-ADVICE-NO	10
DEPT-NO	6	EFFECTIVE-DATE	6
DEPT-DATA	30	PRICE	6
SUPPLIER-NO	20	EQUIPMENT-DESCRIPTION	20
SUPPLIER-DATA	40	MATERIAL-DESCRIPTION	20
ITEM-NO	8	CONTAINER	20
ITEM-DATA	15	WEIGHT	8
QTY-REQUESTED			6

Figure B.5 Data sizes for requisition system

DESIGN PROJECT C:
JOB-SHOP ACCOUNTING SYSTEM

Figure C.1 is an FD diagram of FDs between data elements in a job-shop accounting system. Figure C.2 is the E-R diagram of this enterprise.

This system is part of an organization that manufactures special-purpose assemblies for customers. Each assembly is identified by a unique ASSEMBLY-ID, and the CUSTOMER for the assembly and DATE-ORDERED are stored in the database. To manufacture assemblies, the organization contains a number of processes, each identified by a unique PROCESS-ID and each supervised by one department.

Processes are classified into three types: PAINT, FIT, and CUT. The type sets that represent these processes are uniform and hence use the same identifier as the process. The following information is kept about each type of process:

- PAINT: PAINT-TYPE, PAINTING-METHOD
- FIT: FIT-TYPE
- CUT: CUTTING-TYPE, MACHINE-TYPE

During manufacture an assembly can pass through any sequence of processes in any order; it may pass through the same process more than once.

A unique JOB-NO is assigned every time a process begins on an assembly. Information recorded about a JOB-NO includes the COST, DATE-COMMENCED, and DATE-COMPLETED at the process as well as additional information that depends on the type of JOB process. JOBs are classified into job type sets. These type sets are uniform and hence use the same identifier as JOB-NO. Information stored about particular job types is

- CUT-JOB: MACHINE-TYPE-USED, MACHINE-TIME-USED, MATERIAL-USED, LABOR-TIME (only one machine and machine type and only one type of material is used with each CUT process)
- PAINT-JOB: COLOR, VOLUME, and LABOR-TIME, with only one COLOR used by each PAINT process
- FIT-JOB: LABOR-TIME

An accounting system is maintained by the organization to maintain expenditure for

- each PROCESS-ID
- each ASSEMBLY
- each DEPT

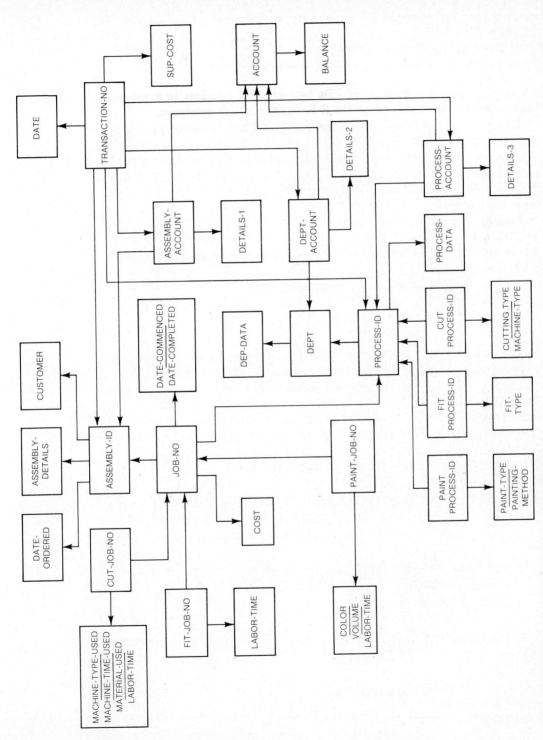

Figure C.1 FD diagram for job-shop accounting system

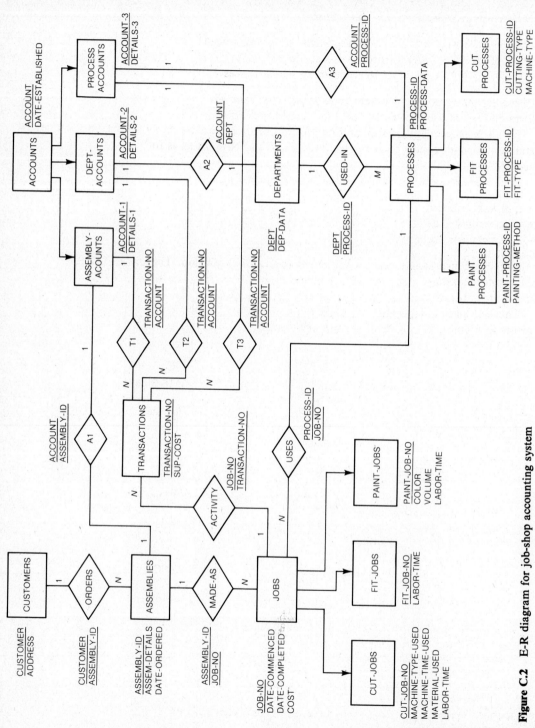

Figure C.2 E-R diagram for job-shop accounting system

Three types of account are maintained:

- ASSEMBLY-ACCOUNTS to record costs for assemblies
- DEPT-ACCOUNTS to record costs for departments
- PROCESS-ACCOUNTS to record costs for processes

These account types can be kept in different type sets. The type sets are uniform and hence use a common identifier, ACCOUNT.

As a job proceeds, cost transactions can be recorded against it. Each such transaction is identified by a unique TRANSACTION-NO and is for a given cost, SUP-COST.

Each transaction of necessity updates three accounts:

- a process account
- an assembly account
- a department account

The updated process account is for the process used by a job. The updated department account is for the department that manages that process. The updated assembly account is for the assembly that requires the job.

The item sizes for this enterprise are given in Figure C.6, the access requirements in Figures C.3 and C.4, and the database volumes in Figure C.5.

Update Transactions

A. Enter a new assembly with its CUSTOMER, ASSEMBLY-DETAILS, and DATE-ORDERED
(40/day)

B. Enter a new PROCESS-ID and its department together with its type and information relevant to the type (infrequent).

C. Create a new account and associate it with the PROCESS, ASSEMBLY, or DEPT to which it is applicable. (40/day)

D. Enter a new JOB-NO, its ASSEMBLY-ID, PROCESS-ID, and DATE-COMMENCED.
(2000/day)

E. At the completion of a job enter the DATE-COMPLETED together with COST and the information relevant to the type of job. (2000/day)

F. Enter the TRANSACTION-NO and its SUP-COST and update all the DETAILs of the affected accounts. (2000/day)

Enquiry Transactions

G. Retrieve cost incurred on an ASSEMBLY-ID to date (by retrieving the BALANCE in the ACCOUNT for the ASSEMBLY-ID). (100/day)

H. Retrieve the LABOR-TIME recorded to date on an ASSEMBLY-ID (sum the LABOR-TIME for all jobs on the ASSEMBLY-ID). (30/day)

I. Retrieve the total LABOR-TIME within a DEPT for jobs completed in the DEPT during a given month. (20/day)

J. Retrieve the PROCESSes through which a given ASSEMBLY-ID has passed so far (in date-commenced order) and the DEPT responsible for each process. (100/day)

K. Retrieve the JOBs (together with their type information and ASSEMBLY-ID) completed during a given month in a given DEPT. (20/day)

Figure C.3 On-line access requirements for job-shop accounting system

Batch Reports (All Weekly)
1. Account listing
    for each account in ACCOUNT order
        begin
            output ASSEMBLY-ID, PROCESS-ID or DEPT of the account
            output BALANCE
        end

2. Assembly summary
    for each assembly in ASSEMBLY-ID order
        begin
            output ASSEMBLY-ID, CUSTOMER, DATE-ORDERED, ASSEMBLY-DETAILS
            for each job on the assembly in DATE-COMMENCED order
                begin
                    output JOB-NO, PROCESS-ID of job and DEPT supervising PROCESS-ID
                end
        end

3. Jobs in departments
    for each dept in DEPT order
        begin
            for all jobs using processes in the dept
                begin
                    output JOB-NO, ASSEMBLY-ID of the jobs assembly
                end
        end

Figure C.4 **Batch access requirements for job-shop accounting system**

1.	Number of Assemblies	10,000
2.	Number of Processes	1,500
3.	Number of Departments	50
4.	Number of Jobs/Assembly	50
5.	Number of Processes/Job	45
6.	Average time to complete an assembly	5 months
7.	Jobs completed for month	20,000

Assume even distribution whenever necessary

Figure C.5 **Database volumes for job-shop accounting system**

	Type	Size
TRANSACTION-NO	NUMBER	12
DATE	"	6
SUP-COST	REAL	10
ACCOUNT	NUMBER	15
AMOUNT	REAL	10
PROCESS-ACCOUNT	NUMBER	15
ASSEMBLY-ACCOUNT	"	15
DEPT-ACCOUNT	"	15
PROCESS-ID	"	8
DEPT	"	4
PAINT-PROCESS-ID	"	8
FIT-PROCESS-ID	"	8
CUT-PROCESS-ID	"	8
PAINT-TYPE	ALPHA	20
PAINTING-METHOD	"	20
FIT-TYPE	"	30
CUTTING-TYPE	"	15
MACHINE-TYPE	"	25
ASSEMBLY-ID	NUMBER	20
DATE-ORDERED	"	6
CUSTOMER	"	20
DATE-COMMENCED	"	6
DATE-COMPLETED	"	6
JOB-NO	"	20
COST	REAL	6
CUT-JOB-NO	NUMBER	20
FIT-JOB-NO	"	20
PAINT-JOB-NO	"	20
COLOR	ALPHA	15
VOLUME	REAL	6
LABOR-TIME	"	6
MACHINE-TYPE-USED	ALPHA	25
MACHINE-TIME-USED	REAL	6
MATERIAL-USED	ALPHA	15
DEP-DATA	ALPHA	50
PROCESS-DATA	"	50
DETAILS-1	"	50
DETAILS-2	"	50
DETAILS-3	"	50
ASSEMBLY-DETAILS	"	70
BALANCE	REAL	8

Figure C.6 Item sizes for job-shop accounting system

DESIGN PROJECT D: COURSE SYSTEM

A private educational institution provides courses on subject areas related to computing. You have ascertained the following facts from initial discussions with the institution's personnel:

1. Each course in the institution is identified by a given COURSE-NO. It also has a DESCRIPTIVE-TITLE (for example, DATA ANALYSIS FOR USERS) together with an originator and an approved COMMENCE-MENT-DATE. Each course has a certain LENGTH (measured in days) and is of a given CLASS (for example, "DATABASE").

2. Each course may be offered any number of times. Each course presentation commences on a given START-DATE at a given location. The (COURSE-NO, LOCATION-OFFERED, START-DATE) is the composite identifier of each offering.

3. The course may be presented either to the general public (GENERAL-OFFERING) or, as a special presentation (SPECIAL-OFFERING), to a specific organization.

4. There can be any number of attendees at each course presentation. Each attendee has a name and is associated with some organization.

5. A fee structure is associated with each course. There is a standard FEE for each attendee at a general offering. There is also a separate SPECIAL-FEE if the course is a SPECIAL-OFFERING on an organization's premises. In that case only a fixed fee is charged for the whole course to the organization and there is no extra fee for each attendee.

6. Employees of the organization can be authorized to be LECTURERs or ORIGINATORs. The sets that represent these nodes are uniform and use the same identifier as the source entity, EMPLOYEE.

7. Each lecturer may spend any number of days on one presentation of a given course (provided that such an assignment does not exceed the length of the course). The DAYS-SPENT by a lecturer on a course offering are recorded.

The E-R diagram for this problem is shown in Figure D.1, and the access requirements are given in Figures D.2 and D.3. The quantitative data are shown in two parts. The volume data are included in Figure D.1, the data item sizes in Figure D.4. A method of packaging the object sets is suggested by the lines encircling the object sets in Figure D.1.

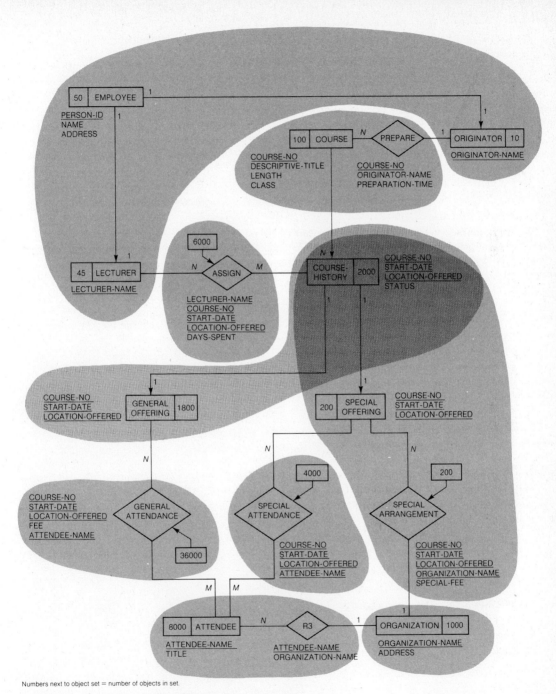

Numbers next to object set = number of objects in set.

Figure D.1 "Normalized" E-R diagram for course system

F. Add a new employee (infrequent). Insert a new employee with given values of PERSON-ID, NAME, and ADDRESS.

G. Authorize an employee to lecture (infrequent). Find an employee with a given PERSON-ID value and allow that employee to take a LECTURER role.

H. Authorize an employee to originate courses (infrequent). Find an employee with a given PERSON-ID value and allow that employee to take an ORIGINATOR role.

I. Enter a new course with its originator (infrequent). Find an originator with a given ORIGINATOR-NAME. Create a course with given values of COURSE-NO, DESCRIPTIVE-TITLE, LENGTH, and CLASS. The course will be developed by the given originator. A course falls into a class such as "database," "operating system," or "compiler."

J. Enter a special course offer (2/week). Find an organization with a given ORGANIZATION-NAME. Find a course with a given COURSE-NO. Create a COURSE-HISTORY for a special offering with given values for COURSE-NO, START-DATE, LOCATION-OFFERED, and SPECIAL-FEE, and a STATUS value of "PLAN."

K. Enter a general course offering (18/week). Find a course with a given COURSE-NO. Create a COURSE-HISTORY for a general offering with given values for COURSE-NO, START-DATE, and LOCATION-OFFERED, and a STATUS value of "PLAN."

L. Assign a lecturer to a course (60/week). Find a lecturer with a given LECTURER-NAME. Find a COURSE-HISTORY with a given START-DATE and LOCATION-OFFERED. Assign the lecturer to that course with a given value of DAYS-SPENT.

M. Enter a new general attendance (360/week). Assume that a prior check has been made for the existence of an attendee (retrieval request 1). Find a given course offering, identified by COURSE-NO, START-DATE, and LOCATION-OFFERED. If the course is found, enter the attendee into that course offering with a given value of FEE.

N. Enter a new special attendance (40/week). This request is similar to request 8 except that no FEE is stored.

Figure D.2 Update of access requirements for course system

A. Check for an attendee (400/week). Find an attendee with a given value of ATTENDEE-NAME. If this is not found, enter the attendee into the database with a given TITLE and ATTENDEE-NAME. If the attendee organization is not in the database, also enter the organization into the database with a given ORGANIZATION-NAME and ADDRESS. (Assume that, on an average, 50% of the time an employee is found and 75% of the time the employee's organization is in the database.)

B. Find a lecturer who has previously taught a course of class "x" and who is available at the time of a given course offering (600/week). Find all COURSES whose class is 'x' and find the lecturers who have lectured any of the course offerings of these courses. Determine whether each such lecturer is assigned to an offering in a given START-TIME. If not, output that lecturer name. In any estimates assume that on an average 15 lecturers satisfy the CLASS criteria. Also assume that there are 10 different classes, and that an average of 10 lecturers have lectured in a particular COURSE-NO.

    for all courses where CLASS = 'x'
      begin
        for all offerings (COURSE-HISTORY) of the course
          begin
            if the lecturer is not assigned to any other course offering or START-DATE
              then output LECTURER-NAME
          end
      end
    end

C. List all the courses to which a given lecturer has been assigned. Include COURSE-NO, CLASS, START-DATE, LOCATION-OFFERED, and DAYS-SPENT.

D. List all the COURSE-NOs attended (either in general or in special offerings) by a given attendee.

E. Retrieve the amount spent by a given organization for courses in a given year. This amount will include the sum of all the FEEs and SPECIAL-FEEs paid by the organization.

Figure D.3 Retrieval requests for course system

Data Element Name	Size
PERSON-ID	4
ADDRESS	30
NAME (also ORIGINATOR-NAME	
LECTURER-NAME)	20
COURSE-NO	6
PREPARATION-TIME	4
DESCRIPTIVE-TITLE	20
LENGTH	2
CLASS	2
START-DATE	6
LOCATION-OFFERED	20
STATUS	5
DAY-SPENT	2
ATTENDEE-NAME	20
ORGANIZATION-NAME	20
ORG-ADDRESS	20
TITLE	10
FEE	8
SPECIAL-FEE	8

Figure D.4   Data element dictionary for course system

Appendix A:
A Sample Database

The text has several examples that use the database presented in this appendix. The database describes an enterprise that consists of a number of stores. The stores hold a variety of items. The quantity of items (QTY-HELD) held by each store appears in relation HOLD. The stores themselves are described in relation STORES. In addition, the database stores information about the enterprise customers. The city location of the customer, together with the data of the customer's first order, is stored in the database. Each customer lives in one city only. The customers order items from the enterprise. Each such order can be for any quantity (QTY-ORDERED) of any number of items, and the items ordered are stored in ITEMS-ORDERED. Each order is uniquely identified by its value of ORDER-NO.

The location of stores is also kept in the database. Each store is located in one city. There may be many stores in that city. Each city has a main coordination center known as HDQ-ADDRESS for all its stores, and there is one HDQ-ADDRESS for each city. The goal, then, will be to meet all of a customer's order requirements from stores located in the customer's city.

The database also contains some derived data. The data in ITEM-CITY are derived from STORES and HOLD. Thus each item is taken, and the quantities of that item (QTY-HELD) in all the stores in a city are totaled into QTY-IN-CITY and stored in ITEM-CITY. The information in ITEM-CITY is thus redundant and would not normallly be stored in a database. It is simply included here as an example of redundant data.

The text uses the following access requirements:

- *Requirement A:* Find all the stores that hold item I1.
- *Requirement D:* Find the orders for items that are held in a given store. This requirement is met by first finding all the items held in the given store. All orders for those items are then output. To be output, an order must require at least one item held in the store.
- *Requirement G:* Find the stores that hold items ordered by a given customer. All the customer's orders must first be found. Then the items ordered in each order are found. Finally, the stores that hold the required items are output. To be output, the store must hold at least one item in the order.

- *Requirement S:* Find the HDQ-ADDRESS of all stores that hold more than 150 of any item with DESCR "LAMP" contained in order ORD1.
- *Requirement V:* List by order within CUSTOMER the item ordered in the order and the stores that contain that item.
- *Requirement X:* Find the city in which a given CUSTOMER lives.
- *Requirement Z:* Find the QTY-HELD of item X in city Y (without using ITEMS-CITY).

The following diagrams are presented in this appendix:

1. The E-R diagram for the enterprise (Figure App. 1).
2. The FDs between attributes in the enterprise (Figure App. 2).
3. A set of relations with sample contents (Figure App. 3).
4. A logical record structure that is derived from the E-R diagram (Figure App. 4).
5. Access paths on a logical record structure for the on-line access requirements (Figure App. 5).
6. Access paths on a minimal logical record structure (MLRS) for the on-line access requirements (Figure App. 6).
7. A file design table (Figure App. 7) that shows how the enterprise model has been converted to a set of indexed sequential files. Note that each logical record type in Figure App. 4 becomes an indexed sequential file in the file design table. Each column in an indexed sequential file and entries in the column are fields in this file.
8. The frequency of access requirements (Figure App. 8).
9. Data volumes (Figure App. 9). (Item sizes can be found in the file design table in Figure App. 7.) Note that the following information can be derived, on the average, from the volume data:

   - There are 200 items per store.
   - There are 100 items in each order.
   - Each item appears in 10 orders.
   - Each item is held in 20 stores.

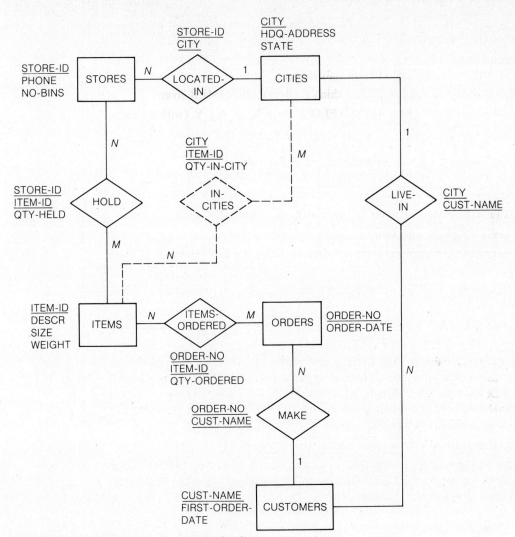

Figure App. 1 E-R diagram for sample database

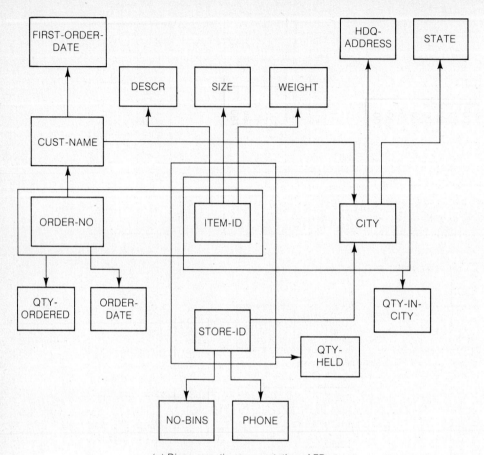

(a) Diagrammatic representation of FDs

CUST-NAME → FIRST-ORDER-DATE, CITY
ORDER-NO → CUST-NAME, ORDER-DATE
STORE-ID → PHONE, NO-BINS, CITY
CITY → HDQ-ADDRESS, STATE
ITEM-ID → DESCR, SIZE, WEIGHT
STORE-ID, ITEM-ID → QTY-HELD
ORDER-NO, ITEM-ID → QTY-ORDERED
ITEM-ID, CITY → QTY-IN-CITY

(b) Mathematical representation of FDs

Figure App. 2   FDs for sample database

STORES

STORE-ID	PHONE	NO-BINS	LOCATED-IN-CITY
ST-A	667932	200	ALBANY
ST-B	725172	310	BOSTON
ST-C	636182	75	BOSTON
ST-D	679305	105	CHICAGO

CITIES

CITY	HDQ-ADDRESS	STATE
ALBANY	ADD1	NY
BOSTON	ADD2	MASS
CHICAGO	ADD3	ILL

HOLD

STORE-ID	ITEM-ID	QTY-HELD
ST-A	I2	300
ST-A	I1	200
ST-A	I3	400
ST-D	I3	150
ST-B	I1	300
ST-B	I2	400
ST-A	I4	150
ST-C	I3	400
ST-D	I4	100

ITEMS

ITEM-ID	DESCR	SIZE	WEIGHT
I1	DOOR	SMALL	9
I2	LAMP	LARGE	12
I3	WINDOW	LARGE	15
I4	WINDOW	SMALL	12

ITEM-CITY

ITEM-ID	IN-CITY	QTY-IN-CITY
I1	ALBANY	200
I1	BOSTON	300
I2	BOSTON	400
I2	ALBANY	300
I3	CHICAGO	150
I3	ALBANY	400
I4	ALBANY	150
I4	CHICAGO	100
I3	BOSTON	400

ORDERS

ORDER-NO	ORDER-DATE	CUST-NAME
ORD1	10980	JILL
ORD2	10680	JACK
ORD3	150380	VICKI
ORD4	220780	VICKI

ITEMS-ORDERED

ITEM-ID	ORDER-NO	QTY-ORDERED
I1	ORD1	11
I2	ORD2	3
I3	ORD1	11
I1	ORD3	7
I4	ORD2	9
I1	ORD4	22

CUSTOMERS

CUST-NAME	FIRST-ORDER-DATE	LIVE-IN-CITY
JILL	140972	BOSTON
JACK	120276	ALBANY
VICKI	90777	BOSTON

Figure App. 3 Sample relations

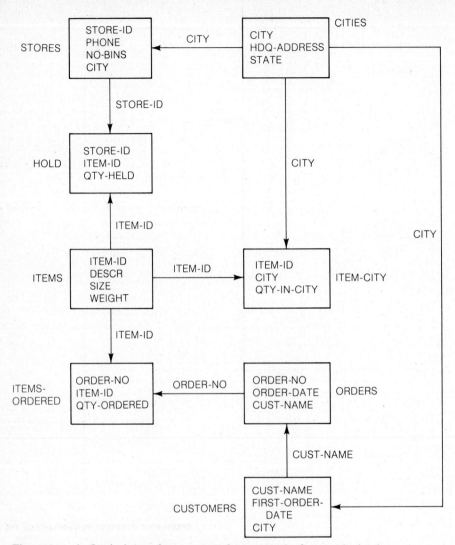

Figure App. 4   Logical record structure and access paths for sample database

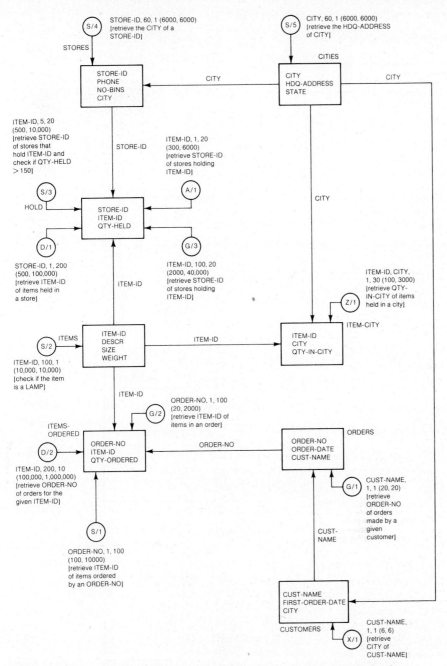

Figure App. 5   Minimal logical structure and access paths for sample database

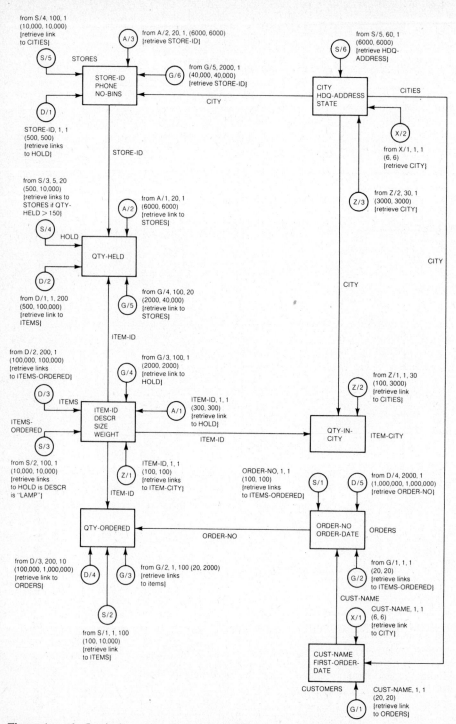

Figure App. 6   Logical access paths on the MLRS for sample database

Field	Type	Size	STORES	CITIES	ITEMS	ORDERS	CUSTOMERS	HOLD	ITEM-CITY	ITEMS-ORDERED
(Name / Org / Range)			I-S	I-S	I-S	I-S	I-S	I-S	I-S	I-S
STORE-ID		6	STORE-ID *1					STORE		
PHONE		20	PHONE							
NO-BINS		4	NO-BINS							
CITY		20	LOCATED-IN-CITY	CITY *1			LIVE-IN-CITY		CITY	
HDQ-ADDRESS		30		HDQ-ADDRESS						
STATE		10		STATE						
ITEM-ID		6			ITEM-ID *1			ITEM *1	ITEM *1	ITEM *1
DESCR		30			DESCR					
SIZE		15			SIZE					
WEIGHT		8			WEIGHT					
ORDER-NO		10				ORDER-NO *1				ORDER
ORDER-DATE		6				ORDER-DATE				
CUST-NAME		20				CUSTOMER	CUST-NAME *1			
FIRST-ORDER-DATE		6					FIRST-DATE			
QTY-HELD		6						QTY		
QTY-IN-CITY		8							QTY	
QTY-ORDERED		6								USED

The symbol '*i' indicates the field is the *i*th component of MASTER-KEY.

Figure App. 7   File design table for sample database

Access Requirement	Frequency
A	300/day
D	500/day
G	20/day
S	100/day
V	Irregular batch need
X	6/day
Z	100/day

Figure App. 8   Frequency of access requirements for sample database

Record Type	Number of Occurrences
STORES	100
CITIES	50
ITEMS	1000
ORDERS	100
CUSTOMERS	70
HOLD	20000
ITEM-CITY	15000
ITEMS-ORDERED	10000

Figure App. 9   Data volumes for sample database

Bibliography

Each author entry ends with one or two letters from the following code to indicate the major topic(s) of the reference.

- A   Multilevel architectures
- C   Database distribution
- D   Data dictionaries
- I   Database recovery and integrity
- L   Database query languages
- M   Design methodologies
- N   Database restructuring
- P   Performance calculations
- R   Relational theory
- S   Database modeling concepts, including semantic models
- T   Database technology, including database management systems and the implementation of data models
- U   Data collection and system analysis methods

Aho, A. V., et al. 1979. "The Theory of Joins in Relational Databases." *ACM Transactions on Database Systems* 4(3): 297–314. (R)

Allen, F. W., Loomis, M. E., and Mannino, M. V. 1982. "The Integrated Dictionary/Directory System." *ACM Computing Surveys* 14(2): 245–286. (D)

Armstrong, W. W. 1974. "Dependency Structures of Data Base Relationships." *Proceedings of the IFIP Congress, 1974,* pp. 580–583. Amsterdam: North-Holland. (R)

Armstrong, W. W., and Delobel, C. 1980. "Decompositions and Functional Dependencies in Relations." *ACM Transactions on Database Systems* 5(4): 404–430. (R)

Atkinson, M., ed. 1980. "Data Design." *Infotech State of the Art Report,* Series 8, no. 4. Maidenhead, Berkshire, England: Infotech. (M)

Atkinson, M., ed. 1981. *Database.* Infotech State of the Art Report, Series 9, no. 8. Maidenhead, Berkshire, England: Infotech. (T)

Astrahan, M. M., et al. 1976. "System R: Relational Approach to Database Management." *ACM Transactions on Database Systems* 1(2): 97–137. (T, R)

Atre, S. 1980. *Data Base: Structured Techniques for Design, Performance and Management.* New York: Wiley. (M)

Atzeni, P., et al. 1982. "A Computer Aided Tool for Conceptual Data Base Design." In *Automated Tools for Information Systems Design,* edited by H. Schneider and A. I. Wasserman, pp. 85–106. Amsterdam: North-Holland. (M)

Aurdal, E., and Solvberg, A. 1977. "A Multi-level Procedure for Design of File Organizations." *Proceedings of the National Computer Conference*, pp. 509–521. (M)

Bachman, C. W. 1969. "Data Structure Diagrams." *Data Base Journal, ACM SIGBDP* 1(2): 4–10. (S)

Bachman, C. W. 1977. "The Role Concept in Data Models." *Proceedings of the Third International Conference on Very Large Data Bases*, Tokyo, pp. 464–476. (S)

Barley, K. S., and Driscoll, J. R. 1981. "A Survey of Data-Base Management Systems for Microprocessors." *BYTE* (November): 208–234. (T)

Baroody, A. J., and DeWitt, D. J. 1981. "An Object-oriented Approach to Database System Implementation." *ACM Transactions on Database Systems* 6(4): 576–601. (S)

Batini, C., Lenzerini, M., and Santucci, G. 1982. "A Computer-aided Methodology for Conceptual Database Design." *Information Systems* 7(3): 265–280. (M)

Bayer, R., Heller, M., and Reiser, A. 1980. "Parallelism and Recovery in Database Systems." *ACM Transactions of Database Systems* 5(2): 139–156. (I)

Becker, H. B. 1978. "Let's Put Information Networks into Perspective." *Datamation* (March): 81–86. (C)

Beeri, C. 1980. "On the Membership Problem for Functional and Multivalued Dependencies in Relational Databases." *ACM Transactions on Database Systems* 5(3): 241–259. (R)

Beeri, C., Bernstein, P. A., and Goodman, N. 1978. "A Sophisticate's Introduction to Database Normalization Theory." *Proceedings of the Fourth International Conference on Very Large Data Bases*, West Berlin, pp. 113–124. (R)

Beeri, C., Fagin, R., and Howard, J. 1977. "A Complete Axiomatization for Functional and Multivalued Dependencies in Database Relations." *Proceedings of the ACM SIGMOD International Conference on the Management of Data*, Toronto, pp. 47–62. (C)

Berild, S., and Machmens, S. 1977. "CS4—A Tool for Database Design by Infological Simulation." *Proceedings of the Third International Conference on Very Large Data Bases*, Tokyo, pp. 85–94. (M)

Bernstein, P. A. 1976. "Synthesizing Third Normal Form Relations from Functional Dependencies." *ACM Transactions on Database Systems* 1(4): 277–298. (R)

Bernstein, P. A., and Goodman, N. 1981. "Concurrency Control in Distributed Database Systems." *ACM Computing Surveys* 13(2): 185–223. (C)

Bernstein, P. A., Rothnie, J. B., and Shipman, D. W., eds. 1980. *TUTORIAL: Distributed Data Base Management*. Cat. no. EHO-141-2. Long Beach, Calif.: IEEE Computer Society. (C)

Biller, H., and Neuhold, E. J. 1978. "Semantics of Data Bases: The Semantics of Data Models." *Information Systems* 3(1): 11–30. (S)

Biskup, J., Dayal, U., and Bernstein, P. A. 1979. "Synthesizing Independent

Database Schemas." *Proceedings of the ACM SIGMOD International Conference on the Management of Data,* Boston, pp. 143–151. (R)

Borkin, S. A. 1980. *Data Models: A Semantic Approach for Database Systems.* Cambridge, Mass.: MIT Press. (S)

Bracchi, G., and Nijssen, G. M., eds. 1979. *Data Base Architecture.* Amsterdam: North-Holland. (S)

Bradley, J. 1983. *Introduction to Data Base Management in Business.* New York: Holt, Rinehart and Winston. (T)

Bubenko, J. A. 1980. "Information Modelling in the Context of System Development." *Proceedings of the IFIP Congress, 1980,* Melbourne, pp. 395–411. Amsterdam: North-Holland. (M)

Bubenko, J. A., et al. 1976. "From Information Requirements to DBTG-Data Structures." Special issue on the Proceedings of the Conference on Data: Abstraction, Definition and Structure. *ACM SIGPLAN Notices* 8(2). (M)

Buchman, A. P., and Dale, A. G. 1979. "Evaluating Criteria for Logical Database Design Methodologies." *Computer Aided Design* 11(3): 121–126. (M)

Canning, R. G. 1981a. "DBMS for Mini-computers." *EDP Analyzer* (March): 1–12. (T)

Canning, R. G. 1981b. "A New View of Data Dictionaries." *EDP Analyzer* (July): 1–12. (D)

Carlson, C. R., and Arora, A. K. 1982. "The Application of Functional Dependency Theory to Relational Databases." *Computer Journal* 25(1): 68–71. (R)

Ceri, S., Pelagatti, G., and Bracchi, G. 1980. "Integrated Specifications of Static and Dynamic Requirements of Database Applications: The Transaction Definition Language." *Proceedings of the IFIP Congress, 1980,* Melbourne, pp. 449–504. Amsterdam: North-Holland. (M)

Chamberlin, D. D. 1976. "Relational Data-Base Management Systems." *ACM Computing Surveys* 8(1): 43–66. (R, T)

Chamberlin, D. D., et al. 1976. "SEQUEL 2: A Unified Approach to Data Definition, Manipulation and Control." *IBM Journal of Research and Development* (November): 560–575. (R, L)

Chamberlin, D. D., et al. 1981a. "A History and Evaluation of System R." *Communications of the ACM* 24(10): 632–646. (T, R)

Chamberlin, D. D., et al. 1981b. "Support for Repetitive Transactions and Ad Hoc Queries in System R." *ACM Transactions on Database Systems* 6(1): 70–94. (T, R)

Champine, G. A. 1977. "Six Approaches to Distributed Data Bases." *Datamation* (May): 69–72. (C)

Champine, G. S. 1980. *Distributed Computer Systems.* Amsterdam: North-Holland. (C)

Chen, P. P. 1976. "The Entity-Relationship Model—Toward a Unified View of Data." *ACM Transactions on Database Systems* 1(1): 9–36. (S)

Chen, P. P., ed. 1980. *Entity-Relationship Approach to Systems Analysis and Design.* Amsterdam: North-Holland. (S, M)

Chen, P. P., and Yao, S. B. 1977. "Design and Performance Tools for Data Base Systems." *Proceedings of the Third International Conference on Very Large Data Bases,* Tokyo, pp. 3–15. (M)

Childs, D. L. 1968. "Description of a Set-Theoretic Data Structure." *Proceedings of the Fall Joint Computer Conference,* pp. 557–564. (S)

Chu, W. W., and Chen, P. P. 1979. *TUTORIAL: Centralized and Distributed Data Base Systems.* Cat. no. EHO-154-5. Long Beach, Calif.: IEEE Computer Society. (C)

CODASYL Systems Committee. 1971a. *Feature Analysis of Generalized Data Base Management Systems.* New York: ACM. (T)

CODASYL Systems Committee. 1971b. *CODASYL Data Base Task Group Report.* New York: ACM. (T)

Codd, E. F. 1970. "A Relational Model of Data for Large Shared Data Banks." *Communications of the ACM* 13(6): 377–387. (R)

Codd, E. F. 1971. "A Data Base Sublanguage Founded on the Relational Calculus." *Proceedings of the 1971 ACM SIGFIDET Conference on Data Description, Access and Control,* San Diego, pp. 35–68. (L, R)

Codd, E. F. 1972. "Further Normalization of the Data Base Relational Model." In *Data Base Systems,* edited by R. Rustin, pp. 33–64. Englewood Cliffs, N.J.: Prentice-Hall. (R)

Codd, E. F. 1979. "Extending the Database Relational Model to Capture More Meaning." *ACM Transactions on Database Systems* 4(4): 397–434. (R, S)

Curtice, R. M. 1976. "The Outlook for Data Base Management." *Datamation* (April): 46–49. (T)

Date, C. J. 1981. *An Introduction to Database Systems.* 3rd ed. Reading, Mass.: Addison-Wesley. (T)

Davenport, R. A. 1978a. "Data Analysis for Database Design." *Australian Computer Journal* 10(4): 122–137. (M)

Davenport, R.A. 1978b. "Distributed Data Base Technology—A Survey." *Computer Networks* 2(3): 155–167. (C)

Davenport, R. A. 1979. "Logical Database Design—From Entity Model to DBMS Structure." *Australian Computer Journal* 11(3): 82–97. (M)

Dayal, U., and Bernstein, P. A. 1978. "On the Updatability of Relational Views." *Proceedings of the Fourth International Conference on Very Large Data Bases,* West Berlin, pp. 113–124. (A)

De, P., Haseman, W. D., and Yuk Ho So. 1981. "Four-Schema Approach: An Extended Model for Database Architecture." *Information Systems* 6(2): 177–224. (A)

Deen, S. M. 1977. *Fundamentals of Data Base Systems.* London: Macmillan Press. (T)

Delobel, C. 1978. "Normalization and Hierarchical Dependencies in the Relational Data Model." *ACM Transactions on Database Systems* 3(3): 201–222. (R)

Delobel, C. 1980. "An Overview of Relational Theory." *Proceedings of the IFIP Congress, 1980,* Melbourne, pp. 413–426. (R)

Delobel, C., and Casey, R. G. 1973. "Decomposition of a Data Base and the Theory of Boolean Switching Functions." *IBM Journal of Research and Development* 17(5): 374–386. (R)

De Marco, T. 1980. *Structured Analysis and System Specification.* New York: Yourdon Press. (U)

Dieckmann, E. M. 1981. "Three Relational DBMS." *Datamation* (September): 137–148. (T)

Fagin, R. 1977. "Multivalued Dependencies and a New Normal Form for Relational Databases." *ACM Transactions on Database Systems* 2(3): 262–278. (R)

Fagin, R. 1981. "A Normal Form for Relational Databases That Is Based on Domains and Keys." *ACM Transactions on Database Systems* 6(3): 387–415. (R)

Falkenberg, E. 1976. "Significations: The Key to Unify Data Base Management." *Information Systems* 2(1): 19–28. (A, S)

Finnerman, T. R., and Henry, J. S. 1977. "Structured Analysis for Data Base Design." *Datamation* (November): 99–113. (M)

Flavin, M. 1981. *Fundamental Concepts of Information Modelling.* New York: Yourdon Press. (S)

Flores, I. 1981. *Data Base Architecture.* New York: Van Nostrand Reinhold. (T)

Fredericksen, D. H. 1973. "Describing Data in Computer Networks." *IBM Systems Journal,* no. 3: 257–282. (C)

Gambino, T. J., and Gerritsen, R. 1977. "A Data Base Design Decision Support System." *Proceedings of the Third International Conference on Very Large Data Bases,* Tokyo, pp. 534–544. (M)

Gane, G., and Sarson, T. 1979. *Structured Systems Analysis: Tools and Techniques.* Englewood Cliffs, N.J.: Prentice-Hall. (U)

Gerritsen, R. 1975. "A Preliminary System for the Design of DBTG Data Structures." *Communications of the ACM* (October): 551–557. (M)

Grabowsky, H., and Eigner, M. 1979. "Semantic Data Model Requirements and Realization with a Relational Data Structure." *Computer Aided Design* 11(3): 159–168. (M)

Gray, J., et al. 1981. "The Recovery Manager of the System R Database Manager." *ACM Computing Surveys* 13(2): 223–242. (I)

Greenblatt, D., and Waxman, J. 1978. "A Study of Three Database Query Languages." In *Databases: Improving Usability and Responsiveness,* edited by B. Schneiderman, pp. 77–97. New York: Academic Press. (L)

Griffiths, R. L. 1982. "Three Principles of Representation for Semantic Networks." *ACM Transactions on Database Systems* 7(3): 417–442. (S)

Guez, J. C. 1980. "Data Base Experience with IMS in Data Design." *Infotech State of the Art Report,* Series 8, no. 4: 215–254. Maidenhead, Berkshire, England: Infotech. (M)

Hammer, M., and McLeod, D. 1981. "Database Description with SDM: A Semantic Database Model." *ACM Transactions on Database Systems* 6(3): 351–386. (S)

Hardgrave, W. T. 1978. "Distributed Data Base Technology: An Assessment." *Information and Management* 1(4): 157–167. (C)

Hardgrave, W. T. 1980. "Ambiguity in Processing Boolean Queries on TDMS Tree Structures: A Study of Four Different Philosophies." *IEEE Transactions on Software Engineering* (July): 357–372. (L)

Hawryszkiewycz, I. T. 1980a. "Alternate Implementations of the Conceptual Schema." *Information Systems* 5(3): 203–217. (A)

Hawryszkiewycz, I. T. 1980b. "Data Analysis—What Are the Necessary Concepts?" *Australian Computer Journal* 12(1): 2–14. (S)

Heath, I. J. "Unacceptable File Operations in a Relational Data Base." *Proceedings of the 1971 ACM-SIGFIDET Workshop on Data Description, Access and Control,* San Diego, pp. 19–33. (R)

Housel, B. C., et al. 1979. "The Functional Dependency Model for Logical Data Base Design." *Proceedings of the Fifth International Conference on Very Large Data Bases,* Rio de Janeiro, pp. 1–15. (M)

Hubbard, G. H. 1979. "Computer Assisted Logical Database Design." *Computer-aided Design* 11(3): 169–179. (M)

Hunter, J. J. 1976. "Distributing a Data Base." Computer Decisions (June): 36–40. (C)

Hutt, A. T. F. 1979. *A Relational Data Base Management System.* New York: Wiley. (T, R)

Infotech State of the Art Report. 1979. *Distributed Data Bases,* vol. 1: *Analysis and Bibliography;* vol. 2: *Invited Papers.* Maidenhead, Berkshire, England: Infotech International. (C)

Inmon, W. H. 1981. *Effective Data Base Design.* Englewood Cliffs, N.J.: Prentice-Hall. (M)

Jardine, D. A. 1977. The ANSI/SPARC DBMS Model. Amsterdam: North-Holland. (A, T)

Katz, R. H., and Wong, E. 1980. "An Access Path Model for Physical Database Design." *Proceedings of the ACM SIGMOD International Conference on the Management of Data,* Santa Monica, pp. 22–29. (M)

Katz, R. H., and Wong, E. 1982. "Decompiling CODASYL DML into Relational Queries." *ACM Transactions on Database Systems* 7(1): 1–23. (A)

Kaunitz, J., and Van Ekert, L. 1981. "Data Base Backup—The Problem of Very Large Data Bases." *Australian Computer Journal* 13(4): 143–159. (I)

Kay, M. H. 1975. "An Assessment of the CODASYL DDL for Use with a Relational Subschema." In *Data Base Description,* edited by B. C. M. Douque and G. M. Nijssen, pp. 109–214. Amsterdam: North-Holland. (A)

Kent, W. 1978. *Data and Reality.* Amsterdam: North-Holland. (S)

Kent, W. 1979. "Limitations of Record-Based Information Models." *ACM Transactions on Database Systems* 4(1): 107–131. (S)

Kent, W. 1980. "Splitting the Conceptual Schema." *Proceedings of the Sixth International Conference on Very Large Data Bases,* Montreal, pp. 10–14. (A)

Kent, W. 1981. "Consequences of Assuming a Universal Relation." *ACM Transactions on Database Systems* 6(4): 539–557. (R)

Kerschberg, L., Klug, A., and Tsichritzis, D. 1976. "A Taxonomy of Data Models." In *Systems for Large Data Bases,* edited by P. C. Lockeman and E. J. Neuhold, pp. 43–64. Amsterdam: North-Holland. (S)

Kim, W. 1979. "Relational Data Base Systems." *ACM Computing Surveys* 11(3): 185–211. (T, R)

Klimbie, J. W., and Koffeman, K. L., eds. 1974. *Concepts for Data Base Management.* Amsterdam: North-Holland. (S)

Klug, A., and Tsichritzis, D. 1978. "Multiple View Support within the ANSI/ SPARC Framework." *Proceedings of the Third International Conference on Very Large Data Bases,* Tokyo, pp. 477–488. (A)

Kohler, W. H. 1981. "A Survey of Techniques for Synchronization and Recovery in Decentralized Computer Systems." *ACM Computing Surveys* 13(2): 149–184. (C)

Krass, P., and Wiener, M. 1981. "The DBMS Market is Booming." *Datamation* (September): 153–170. (T)

Kroenke, D. 1983. *Database Processing: Fundamentals, Modeling, Implementation.* 2nd ed. Palo Alto, Calif.: Science Research Associates. (T)

Langefors, B., and Samuelson, K. 1976. *Information and Data in Systems.* New York: Petrocelli-Charter. (S)

Lefkowitz, H. C. 1977. *Data Dictionary Systems.* Woolesley, Mass.: Q.E.D. Information Sciences. (D)

Loomis, M. E. S. 1981. "The Changing Nature of DBMS." *Infosystems* 28(9): 66–72. (T)

Lorin, H. 1980. *Aspects of Distributed Computer Systems.* New York: Wiley. (C)

Lusk, E. L., et al. 1980. "A Practical Design Methodology for the Implementation of IMS Databases, Using the Entity-Relationship Model." *Proceedings of the ACM SIGMOD International Conference on the Management of Data,* Santa Monica, pp. 9–21. (M)

McGee, W. C. 1977. "The Information Management System IMS/VS." *IBM Systems Journal,* no. 2: 84–168. (T)

Maryanski, F. J. 1976. "A Survey of Developments in Distributed Database Management Systems." *Computer* (February): 28–38. (C)

Martin, J. 1975. *Computer Data-Base Organization.* Englewood Cliffs, N.J.: Prentice-Hall. (T)

Martin, J. 1976. *Principles of Data-Base Management.* Englewood Cliffs, N.J.: Prentice-Hall. (T)

Methlie, L. B. 1978. "Schema Design Using a Data Structure Matrix." *Information Systems* 3(2): 81–91. (M)

Mitoma, M. F., and Irani, K. B. 1975. "Automatic Data Base Schema Design and Optimization." *Proceedings of the First International Conference on Very Large Data Bases,* Boston, pp. 286–320. (M)

Molina, F. W. 1979. "A Practical Data Base Design Method." *DATABASE* (Summer): 3–11. (M)

Mommens, J. H., and Smith, S. E. 1975. "Automatic Generation of Physical

Data Base Structure." *Proceedings of the ACM SIGMOD International Conference on the Management of Data,* San Jose, Calif., pp. 157–165. (M)

Navathe, S. B. 1976. "Restructuring for Large Data Bases: Three Levels of Abstraction." *ACM Transactions on Database Systems* 1(2): 138–158. (N)

Navathe, S. B. 1980. "Schema Analysis for Database Restructuring." *ACM Transactions on Database Systems* 5(2): 157–184. (N)

Nijssen, G. M. 1976a. "A Gross Architecture for the Next Generation Database Management Systems." In *Modelling in Data Base Management Systems,* edited by G. M. Nijssen, pp. 1–24. Amsterdam: North-Holland. (S)

Nijssen, G. M., ed. 1976b. *Modelling in Data Base Management Systems.* Amsterdam: North-Holland. (S)

Nijssen, G. M., ed. 1977. *Architecture and Models in Data Base Management Systems.* Amsterdam: North-Holland. (S)

Ng, P. A. 1981. "Further Analysis of the Entity-Relationship Approach to Database Design." *IEEE Transactions on Software Engineering,* SE-7(1): 85–99. (S)

Olle, T. W. 1978. *The Codasyl Approach to Data Base Management.* New York: Wiley. (T)

Parkin, A. 1982. "Data Analysis and System Design by Entity-Relationship Modelling." *Computer Journal* 25(4): 401–409. (M)

Patel, H. 1981. "How to Upgrade a DBMS." *Datamation* (September): 127–132. (T)

Peat, L. R. 1982. *Practical Guide to DBMS Selection.* Berlin: Walter de Gruyter. (T)

Peebles, R., and Manning, E. 1978. "System Architecture for Distributed Data Management." *Computer* (January): 40–47.

Pelagatti, G., Paolini, P., and Bracchi, G. 1978. "Mapping External Views to a Common Data Model." *Information Systems* 3(2): 141–151. (A)

Pezarro, M. T. 1976. "A Note on Estimating Hit Ratios for Direct-Access Storage Devices." *Computer Journal* 19(3): 271–272. (P)

Raver, N., and Hubbard, G. U. 1977. "Automated Logical Data Base Design: Concepts and Applications." *IBM Systems Journal,* no. 3: 287–312. (M)

Reisner, P. 1981. "Human Factors Studies of Database Query Languages: A Survey Assessment." *ACM Computing Surveys* 13(1): 13–32. (L)

Reisner, P., Boyce, R. F., and Chamberlin, D. D. 1975. "Human Factors Evaluation of Two Data Base Query Languages—Square and Sequel." *Proceedings of the National Computer Conference,* pp. 447–452. (L)

Rissasen, J. 1977. "Independent Components of Relations." *ACM Transactions on Database Systems* 2(4): 317–325. (R)

Robinson, M. A. 1981. "A Review of Data Base Query Languages." *Australian Computer Journal* 13(4): 143–159. (L)

Rosenkrantz, D. J., et al. 1978. "System Level Concurrency Control for Distributed Database Systems." *ACM Transactions on Data Base Systems* 3(2): 178–198. (C)

Roussopoulus, N., and Mylopoulus, J. 1975. "Using Semantic Networks for Data Base Management." *Proceedings of the First International Conference on Very Large Data Bases,* Boston, pp. 144–172. (M)

Sakai, H. 1980. "Entity-Relationship Approach to the Conceptual Schema Design." *Proceedings of the ACM SIGMOD International Conference on Management of Data,* Santa Monica, pp. 1–8. (S)

Samet, P. A., ed. 1981. *Query Languages: A Unified Approach.* London: Heydon. (L)

Schkolnick, M. 1978. "A Survey of Physical Database Design Methodology and Techniques." *Proceedings of the Fourth International Conference on Very Large Data Bases,* West Berlin, pp. 474–487. (M)

Schmid, H. A., and Swenson, J. R. 1975. "On the Semantics of the Relational Data Model." *Proceedings of the ACM SIGMOD International Conference on Management of Data,* San Jose, Calif., pp. 211–223. (R)

Schneider, L. S., and Spath, C. R. 1975. "Quantitative Data Description." *Proceedings of the ACM SIGMOD International Conference on the Management of Data,* San Jose, Calif., pp. 167–185. (M)

Senko, M. E. 1976. "DIAM as a Detailed Example of the ANSI SPARC Architecture." In *Modelling in Data Base Management Systems,* edited by G. M. Nijssen, pp. 73–95. Amsterdam: North-Holland. (A, S)

Senko, M. E., Altman, E. B., Astrahan, M. M., and Fehder, P. L. 1973. "Data Structures and Accessing in Data-Base Systems." *IBM Systems Journal,* no. 1: 30–44. (S)

Sheuermann, P. 1978. "On the Design and Evaluation of Data Bases." *Computer* (February): 46–55. (M)

Shipman, D. W. 1981. "The Functional Data Model and the Data Language DAPLEX." *ACM Transactions on Database Systems* 6(1): 140–173. (S)

Shneiderman, B., and Thomas, G. 1980. "Path Expressions for Complex Queries and Automatic Database Program Conversion." *Proceedings of the Sixth International Conference on Very Large Data Bases,* Montreal, pp. 33–44. (M)

Sibley, E. M., ed. 1976. "Data Base Management Systems." Special issue of *ACM Computing Surveys* 8(1). [Papers describing the relational, hierarchical, and network models and the database management systems that support these models.] (T)

Sibley, E. H., and Kerschberg, L. 1977. "Data Architecture and Data Model Considerations." *Proceedings of the National Computer Conference,* pp. 85–96. (S)

Smith, J. M., and Smith, D. C. P. 1977. "Database Abstractions: Aggregation and Generalization." *ACM Transactions on Database Systems* 2(2): 105–133. (S)

Sockut, G. M., et al. 1979. "Data Base Reorganization—Principles and Practice." *ACM Computing Surveys* 11(4): 371–398. (N)

Sprowls, R. C. 1976. *Management Data Bases.* New York: Wiley. (T)

Stamper, R. K. 1979. "Towards a Semantic Normal Form." In *Data Base Architecture,* edited by G. Bracchi and G. M. Nijssen, pp. 317–339. Amsterdam: North-Holland. (S)

Stonebraker, M. R., Wong, E., and Kreps, P. 1976. "The Design and Implementation of INGRES." *ACM Transactions on Database Systems* 1(3): 189–222. (T, R)

Sundgren, B. 1975. *Theory of Data Bases.* New York: Petrocelli-Charter. (S)

Sy, S. Y. W., Lam, H., and Der Hu Lo. 1981. "Transformation of Data Traversals and Operations in Application Programs to Account for Semantic Changes of Databases." *ACM Transactions on Database Systems* 6(2): 255–294. (N)

Symons, C. R., and Tijsma, P. 1982. "A Systematic and Practical Approach to the Definition of Data." *Computer Journal* 25(4): 401–409. (M)

Teorey, T. J., and Fry, J. P. 1978. "Logical Data Base Design: A Pragmatic Approach." In *Infotech State of the Art Report: Data Base Technology,* vol. 2, pp. 357–383. Maidenhead, Berkshire, England: Infotech International. (M)

Teorey, T. J., and Fry, J. P. 1980. "The Logical Record Access Approach to Database Design." *ACM Computing Surveys* 12(2): 179–212. (M)

Teorey, T. J., and Fry, J. P. 1982. *Design of Database Structures.* Englewood Cliffs, N.J.: Prentice-Hall. (M)

Tsichritzis, D. C., and Klug, A. 1978. "The ANSI/X3/SPARC DBMS Framework Report of the Study Group on Database Management Systems." *Information Systems* 3(3): 175–191. (A)

Tsichritzis, D. C., and Lochovsky, F. H. 1977. *Data Base Management Systems.* New York: Academic Press. (T)

Tsichritzis, D. C., and Lochovsky, F. H. 1982. *Data Models.* Englewood Cliffs, N.J.: Prentice-Hall. (S)

Ullman, J. D. 1982. *Principles of Database Systems.* 2d ed. London: Pitman. (T)

Vandijck, E. 1977. "Towards a More Familiar Relational Retrieval Language." *Information Systems* 2(4): 159–169. (R, L)

Verhofstad, J. S. M. 1978. "Recovery Techniques for Database Systems." *ACM Computing Surveys* 10(2): 167–196. (I)

Verrijn-Stuart, A. A. 1975. "Information Algebras and Their Uses." *Management Datamatics* 4(5): 187–196. (S)

Vetter, M. 1977. "Data Base Design by Applied Data Synthesis." *Proceedings of the Third International Conference on Very Large Data Bases,* Tokyo, pp. 428–440. (M)

Vetter, M., and Maddison, R. N. 1981. *Database Design Methodology.* London: Prentice-Hall International. (M)

Walters, S. J. 1975. "Estimating Magnetic Disk Seeks." *Computer Journal* 18(1): 12–19. (P)

Weldon, J. 1980. "Using Data Base Abstractions for Logical Design." *Computer Journal* 23(1): 41–45. (M)

Wiederhold, G. 1977. *Database Design.* New York: McGraw-Hill. (M)

Wood, C., Summers, R. C., and Fernandez, E. B. 1979. "Authorization in Multilevel Database Models." *Information Systems* 4(2): 155–161. (A)

Yao, S. B. 1976. "Modelling and Performance Evaluation of Physical Data Base Structures." *Proceedings of the ACM National Conference,* pp. 303–309. (M)

Yao, S. B., and Merton, A. G. 1975. "Selection of File Organization Using an Analytical Model." *Proceedings of the First International Conference on Very Large Data Bases,* Boston, pp. 255–267. (M)

Yao, S. B., et al., eds. 1982. *Data Base Design Techniques.* Berlin: Springer-Verlag. (M)

Young, J. W., and Kent, H. K. 1968. "Abstract Formatulation of Data Processing Problems." *Journal of Industrial Engineering* (November–December): 471–479. (S)

Zaniolo, C. 1979. "Design of Relational Views over Network Schemas." *Proceedings of the ACM-SIGMOD International Conference on Management of Data,* Boston, pp. 179–190. (A)

Zaniolo, C., and Melkanoff, M. A. 1981. "On the Design of Relational Database Schemata." *ACM Transactions on Database Systems* 6(1): 1–47. (R)

Zaniolo, C., and Melkanoff, M. A. 1982. "A Formal Approach to the Definition and the Design of Conceptual Schemata for Database Systems." *ACM Transactions on Database Systems* 7(1): 24–58. (R)

Zloof, M. M. 1977. "Query-by-Example: A Data Base Sublanguage." *IBM Systems Journal* 16(4): 324–343. (R, L)

Index